The Gender Reader

Second Edition

EVELYN ASHTON-JONES
University of Southern Mississippi

GARY A. OLSON
University of South Florida

MERRY G. PERRY
University of South Florida

ALLYN AND BACON
BOSTON   LONDON   TORONTO   SYDNEY   TOKYO   SINGAPORE

Vice President, Humanities: Joseph Opiela
Editorial Assistant: Mary Beth Varney
Marketing Manager: Lisa Kimball
Production Administrator: Rowena Dores
Editorial-Production Service: Lauren Green Shafer
Cover Administrator: Jenny Hart
Composition Buyer: Linda Cox
Manufacturing Buyer: Suzanne Lareau
Electronic Composition: Omegatype Typography, Inc.

Library of Congress Cataloging-in-Publication Data
The gender reader / Evelyn Ashton-Jones, Gary A. Olson, Merry G.
  Perry. – 2nd ed.
     p.   cm.
  ISBN 0-205-28530-9
    1. Sex role.   2. Sex discrimination against women.   3. Sexism.
  I. Ashton-Jones, Evelyn.   II. Olson, Gary A.
  III. Perry, Merry G.
  HQ1075.G465   1999
  305.3–dc21   99–26099
                                                        CIP

Credits
Pages 4–11: Virginia Adams, "Male and Female: Differences Between Them," *Time,*
March 3, 1972. © 1972 Time Inc. Reprinted by permission.
Pages 12–21: Pamela Weintraub, "The Brain: His and Hers," *Discover,* April 1981. © 1981
Pamela Weintraub. Reprinted with permission of Discover Magazine.
Pages 23–29: Dorothy L. Sayers, "Are Women Human?" from *Unpopular Opinions,* pub-
lished by Gollancz. Reprinted by permission of David Higham Associates.
Pages 31–34: Alan Alda, "What Every Woman Should Know About Men," *Ms. Magazine,* Oc-
tober 1975. © 1975, Alan Alda. All rights reserved. Reprinted by permission of Alan Alda.
Credits continued on page 497, which constitutes an extension of the copyright page.

Printed in the United States of America
10 9 8 7 6 5 4 3 2 1   02 01 00 99

Contents

Foreword

When my father came to my forty-eighth birthday party, he put a damper on the occasion by solemnly declaring, "My mother died when she was your age." Then he added wistfully, "And she was an old woman." And, indeed, she probably was. She had given birth to ten children, had never lived in a home with running water, and, during the winter months when her schoolteaching husband was away in any small town that would give him a job, she had been a single parent who ran the family farm, who kept her children fed, clothed, and in school, and who served as a nurse and midwife in the small isolated community where she lived in northern Arizona. She died from pneumonia that developed after she walked through a snowstorm to care for a sick neighbor.

There at my birthday party was a seventy-eight-year-old man standing Januslike between two generations—his mother and his daughter—and pondering the differences. I had given birth to only three children, the last when I was twenty-six years old. When my grandmother died at forty-eight, her youngest child was only eight years old; on my forty-eighth birthday, my youngest child was twenty-two years old and away at college. My house not only had running water but also an automatic washing machine and dryer, a dishwasher, a vacuum cleaner, and a microwave oven. But more important, I had a good chance of living a productive and useful life for another *thirty* years, according to statisticians.

The differences between my grandmother's life and my own are fairly typical, and they underlie and motivate today's feminist movement. We've probably all heard some variation of this statement: If women would just quit complaining, then this whole feminist movement would go away and we could settle down and concentrate on more important issues. But my birthday-party story suggests that the feminist movement is not bringing the changes. Rather, they have come from outside, and they are forcing people to react in new ways and to choose from options never before available.

Technological advances have brought many of these changes. Better medical care for women means that they live longer and healthier lives. This same improved medical care means that their children also have a better chance for survival; consequently, women no longer feel they need to have ten children in hopes of raising five or six. Nor do families feel they need five or six children to work the family farm. And better methods of birth control allow women to decide how many children they will have.

Technology also helps protect us from the elements and makes our daily work easier. When my father was a child, most men in his community were engaged in hard physical labor; although a schoolteacher, his own father couldn't provide food for a large family without a farm. Ranching, farming, and building all require physical strength, and these men's wives would have been at a disadvantage had they been doing the same jobs their husbands did. But today in my community, most men are engaged in jobs based on intellectual work; they are teachers, lawyers, sales representatives, computer programmers, doctors, business people, bankers, and engineers. My women friends and I have the physical strength to do the jobs our husbands do; in fact, today many husbands and wives are in similar professions, as the phrase "dual-career couple" suggests.

In industrialized nations, power machinery and conveyor belts do much of the lifting and hauling that used to require "manpower." Even war has changed: as it has moved away from hand-to-hand combat, women have become involved. This change results at least partly from the difference in women's and men's physical strength, which dissipate when the strength of a human being—male or female—is combined to the power of an airplane or a tank.

Technology changes in the last sixty years have changed women's lives more than men's. Both men's and women's life expectancies have increased over the last three generations, but the increase for women has been almost twice as great, primarily because women are the ones who give birth to children, a health-related area that has improved tremendously. Women's lives have also changed more because of technology's "push-pull" effect: women are pushed from their homes by electricity and modern appliances that make housework for today's smaller families less than a full-time job; and they are pulled into the work force because today's economy requires more workers and because most jobs—including those requiring physical labor—are jobs that women can do.

Echoing earlier times when physical strength was a primary value, many jobs today are still sorted into "male" and "female" categories—but on the basis of prestige rather than physical labor. For example, the male pilot of a large passenger plane exerts less physical energy than does a female stewardess who serves drinks and dinner to 150 passengers during a three-hour flight. Nor does a male grocery-store manager expend as much physical energy as does a female cashier who every day lifts thousands of pounds of groceries from shopping carts, passes them in front of the register as she rings up the prices, and bags them on the other side. In a similar way, a male school principal does not exert the same physical effort as do teachers, especially those teaching very young or handicapped children who often must be lifted and carried.

Because the most profound changes have come to women's lives, women were the ones who first noticed and began talking about "consciousness raising" and then about "women's liberation," "the women's movement," and "feminism." But people soon realized that men, too, were being affected by the same kinds of changes and by what was happening to the women in their lives. These changes influence every aspect of modern living so intimately that all of us—whether male or female—are being forced to think about their effects. This change explains why this book is titled *The Gender Reader* and why it was written for male as well as female students.

Social systems are complex sets of agreements—some so subtle that we aren't aware of having bought into them. Nevertheless, these agreements determine our attitudes, values, and behavior. When a society is stable, most of its members have little trouble "fitting in" because they model their own behavior after their parents' and friends' behavior. But changes bring new pieces to an old puzzle, and as we try to make these new pieces fit in, we inevitably have some bumping and shoving. Sometimes this bumping is literal. When a man and a woman both approach a door at the same time, the old system required that the woman always stand back and wait for the man to open the door, but today either or both may reach out to open it.

The way in which we address business letters provides another example. We used to automatically begin such letters with "Dear Sir" or "Gentlemen," but now we're forced to stop and think about the matter. On eighty letters of application for a professor's job at the university where I work, most writers avoided the old masculine greetings, but they weren't sure what else to use. As a result, they relied on twenty forms, including "Good Morning," "Dear Reader," "Dear Selection Committee," "Dear Sir/Madam,"

"Dear Colleagues," "Gentlepeople," and "To Whom It May Concern." Ten years from now we will probably settle down to one or two nonsexist options, but for now we're confused.

At the grocery store the other night, I had an experience that illustrates how clever people can take advantage of a social system in change. When the bagger, a petite young woman, took one of my shopping carts to the car, I asked her if it had been difficult to get a job as a "carry-out boy." She laughingly explained, "Oh, no. The manager looks for carry-outs like me because when I offer to take people's groceries out, most say they'll do it themselves. That way I can take care of all the lines. But if we have athletic-looking boys, everyone says yes, and it takes three or four of them to keep the customers happy."

Although these examples are taken from the simplest levels, they illustrate the extent to which changes have upset the system, and that people are groping for solutions to what used to be non-problems. To understand how we are being affected and what we need to do to benefit our lives and society, we must undergo many such experiences. But it isn't enough just to have these experiences. We need to ponder and discuss and see how our reactions fit with other people's reactions. Before laws can be made, we have to arrive at group decisions through consensus. And because many of the attitudes and behaviors involved are too subtle to be controlled by laws, they will always be subject to informal group consensus.

I might end this foreword with the cliché, "Happy reading!" But that would be less than honest. Change makes people insecure and uncomfortable, and this is a book about change. Therefore, it isn't likely to provide you with the kind of happy feeling you can get from reading a wish-fulfilling romance or a sports story. Nevertheless, I'm confident that you will enjoy the book because it's exciting to study cultural change and to participate in determining how change will occur. That's what *The Gender Reader* is about. As you read, ponder, think, write, discuss, and even argue, remember that you are playing a role in shaping society for the year 2000 and beyond.

Alleen Pace Nilsen
Arizona State University

Preface

According to a Pakistani proverb, "Woman's place is in the home or the grave." A similar North American saying decrees that a woman should be kept "barefoot, pregnant, and in the kitchen." These popular expressions reveal an attitude that we have come to call "sexist." But, like many frequently repeated words and phrases, the word *sexist* has almost become a cliché; it has lost the power of its meaning. As many authors of the selections in this text suggest, sexism is the counterpart of racism. Just as *racism* refers to the doctrine that inherent differences among races make the people of one race superior to those of another and thereby justify the mistreatment and even abuse of the "inferior" race, *sexism* refers to the doctrine that perceived inherent differences between men and women make one sex (almost always men) superior to the other and thereby justify discrimination toward and abuse of the "inferior" sex. Like racism, sexism—as the proverbs cited above suggest—is a kind of hatred, a degrading of an entire group of people based solely on their sex or, in the case of racism, skin color. In both cases, the "inferior" group is treated as an underclass.

Just as the second half of the twentieth century has witnessed a growing consciousness of and sensitivity toward racial prejudice, so too have we become more conscious of the effects of sexual discrimination. The women's movement has led the struggle to educate society to reexamine attitudes about gender. Consequently, the roles of men and women—indeed, our very notions of gender—are in transition. What is "woman's place"—her role? What is man's role in society? *The Gender Reader* explores these complex and fascinating questions as well as numerous other issues related to gender relations.

This text is appropriate for students taking courses in composition or women's studies or anyone else who is thinking and writing about questions of gender. The fifty-one essays in the collection represent a wide range of perspectives on numerous important issues.

Although most of the selections were published in the last few decades, several are historical pieces that provide a sense of continuity with the past.

We like to think of these selections as voices in an age-old "conversation" about the nature of men and women and their social roles. Like any conversation among multiple participants, it is characterized by agreement and disagreement, consensus and dissension, bickering and debate, reasoned argument and emotional pleading. As a whole, however, the conversation itself is enlightening because it awakens consciousness, stirs dormant emotions, forces people to become involved, to take issue, and, we hope, to enter the conversation themselves.

The metaphor of voices in a conversation is especially apt, we believe, because not only does it frame the subject as an organic, ever-changing, human activity (rather than as a dualistic right-or-wrong search for truth), but it also alludes to a key feminist theme: that throughout the ages male-dominated social and legal institutions have conspired to "silence" women, to prevent them from participating in society's largest, most important "conversations." Most germane to our present purposes, however, is that seeing this subject as a continuing discussion may help students discover that they too have voices, that they too can participate in this conversation, that they need not be intimidated by the essays in this collection simply because they were written by "published authors" and "great thinkers." We invite you to join the discussion.

The conversation begins in Part I, "Gender Roles: Difference and Change," with an exploration of differences between men and women and a debate over the source of these differences. The participants also discuss changing notions of femininity, masculinity, and sexual identity. Part II, "Women's Role: Historical Perspectives," presents voices from and about the past, examining previous views of women as well as their role and status in society. The authors represented in Part III, "Language and Sexism," analyze the nature and effects of sexist language, and those in Part IV, "Gender and Social Institutions," talk about gender relations in the educational system, the family, and the workplace. Part V, "Sexism and the Status of Women," presents several passionate discussions about psychological and physical violence against women in specific cultural and global settings.

Together, these fifty-one voices provide but a sampling of the larger conversation, but they illustrate, we trust, several crucial gender issues and suggest the range of perspectives on them. The writings provide ample background for rich classroom discussion and thoughtful student essays on the intricacies of gender relations.

Each selection is followed by two sets of questions: "Reflecting on Meaning" and "Exploring Rhetorical Strategies." We call the first set "Reflecting on Meaning" because these are challenging discussion questions that often transcend the text itself, asking students not only to analyze the text but also to make connections beyond the text with their own experience. The questions in this section are demanding, and they are not meant to be "answered" as, for example, "homework" questions. Rather, they are intended to stimulate critical thinking and classroom discussion, and, of course, they may suggest topics and themes that can be explored in an extended way in formal essays. The questions called "Exploring Rhetorical Strategies" will help students examine the essays *as pieces of writing*. We avoid strictly formalistic questions, though, asking students instead to examine how the authors use rhetorical devices to further meaning. Again, the focus is on critical thinking and discussion.

Following each of the five main parts of the book is a section called "Taking a Stand: Questions for Consideration." These critical thinking questions are "intertextual," asking students to make connections and compare assumptions and evidence among several essays in each part of the book. Through analyzing and synthesizing essays from various sections, students can begin to formulate their own reasoned opinions and assumptions about the subject—a necessary step in preparing to make their own voices heard, both in and out of writing.

As you and your students listen to the voices recorded in *The Gender Reader,* we hope that you become angry and pleased, outraged and optimistic, disturbed and comforted—so much so that you become impatient to add your own voices to this age-old conversation.

We'd like to recognize Joseph Opiela at Allyn and Bacon for his enthusiasm in producing both editions of this text. Thanks are due also to several readers who examined and commented on the manuscript for the second edition: Nancy Burns-McCoy, University of Idaho; Krista L. May, Texas A&M University; Peggy Muldoon, Forest Park Community College; Elizabeth Renfro, California State University, Chico; and Mary White Stewart, University of Nevada, Reno.

In addition, we wish to thank those readers whose comments contributed to the success of the first edition of *The Gender Reader:* Rebecca E. Burnett, Carnegie-Mellon University; Kathleen Shine Cain, Merrimack College; Cyndia Clegg, Pepperdine University; Susan Gabriel, Southern Illinois University at Edwardsville; C. Jeriel Howard, Northeastern Illinois University; Mary Lay, Clarkson University; Susan Miller, University of Utah; Louise Z. Smith,

University of Massachusetts-Boston; and Judith Stanford, Rivier College. Finally, we'd like to thank Warren Perry, Jonathan Perry, Jeffrey Perry, Marlyne S. Olson, Colleen Connolly, and Christian Weisser for their assistance in this project.

Evelyn Ashton-Jones
Gary A. Olson
Merry G. Perry

Part I

Gender Roles: Difference and Change

Are the qualities we most commonly associate with gender—with femininity and masculinity—a function of our biological makeup, or are they the product of social forces? That is, is our "femaleness" or "maleness" inherent within each of us—a product of our genes—or are these roles *constructed* by the assumptions, values, and prejudices of our culture? These two perspectives frame the debate among scholars, researchers, and commentators interested in gender studies, a debate that became especially active (and heated) during the 1970s and 1980s as our traditional notions of femininity and masculinity began to change. The essays in Part I address these issues from a number of perspectives.

In the first group of essays, "Gender Differences: Sociology or Biology?" the authors explore the differences between men and women. In doing so they enter, consciously or not, the sociology-biology debate. Virginia Adams begins the section by reviewing scientific research that attempts to establish exactly what are the differences between men and women. Similarly, Pamela Weintraub surveys research into the physical differences between the male and female brains. Finally, Dorothy L. Sayers argues that any attempt to place human beings into two classes—women and men—is unjust.

Perhaps any discussion of the differences between women and men is difficult because our very definitions of femininity

1

and masculinity continue to change radically. In the next section, "Masculinity in Transition," Alan Alda parodies the traditional "macho" male and, in doing so, implies that the emerging male role is quite different. Herb Goldberg argues that, contrary to popular opinion, the male condition is not one of privilege—that men, too, are oppressed by society's expectations of their gender roles. In fact, writes Harold Rosenberg, the "masculine ideal" has almost vanished. Finally, Mary Kay Blakely humorously argues that while contemporary men have changed some of their sexist behaviors toward women, most men still do not really empathize with women's position in our sexist society. The four essays in this chapter provide perspectives not only on masculinity in transition, but also on the changing idea of gender itself.

The third group of essays, "Femininity and Culture," probes the concept of "femininity" and the bonds that unite women and the forces that separate them in a common cause. Simone de Beauvoir suggests that what leads to women's oppression is that women are defined as "other"—that is, not as individuals equal to men but in contradistinction to men; men represent the norm, women the variance from the norm. Naomi Weisstein shows how the field of psychology has helped to "construct" what it means to be female. Susan Brownmiller, also interested in psychology, explores the kinds of emotions "appropriate" for each sex, and concludes that society looks negatively on so-called feminine expressions of emotion. Finally, Gloria Steinem describes the shared experiences and feelings that unite all women regardless of age, class, or race.

Any contemporary discussion of gender would be incomplete without a consideration of how sexual identity is formed and culturally reinscribed. In the fourth group of essays, "Gender and Sexual Identity," the authors expose the interrelationships between gender identity and sexual orientation by considering homosexuality. Mary McIntosh considers how traditional theorists have primarily concerned themselves with defining homosexuality as a condition—which segregates "deviants" from "normal" heterosexuals—rather than as a role. Edmund White makes us closely examine our preconceived assumptions about gender and sexuality when he defines "gay" and "straight" culture. Using historical data and research studies, Rose Weitz argues that lesbians and other women are stigmatized for their independence and deviance from submission to male social authority. After analyzing how the masculine role/identity is a cultural construct, Patrick D. Hopkins posits that homophobia will only be eliminated when identity construction ceases to be based on anatomy.

All of the essays in Part I explore in one way or another the question of gender roles, but together they provide only a glimpse of the complexity of this central issue. In their struggles to understand gender, these authors present many views for us to consider.

Chapter 1 _____

GENDER DIFFERENCES: SOCIOLOGY OR BIOLOGY?

Male and Female: Differences Between Them

VIRGINIA ADAMS

"Are women immutably different from men?" In the following selection, essayist Virginia Adams poses and attempts to answer this question by surveying research in the natural and social sciences. She suggests that differences do indeed exist—some a result of social conditioning, but others fundamentally biological in origin and thus "immutable." Nevertheless, she concludes, "most women are capable of doing whatever they want."

T he Book of Genesis had it wrong. In the beginning God created Eve," says Johns Hopkins Medical Psychologist John Money. What he means is that the basic tendency of the human fetus is to develop as a female. If the genes order the gonads to become testicles and put out the male hormone androgen, the embryo will turn into a boy; otherwise it becomes a girl: "You have to add something to get a male," Money notes. "Nature's first intention is to create a female."

Nature may prefer women, but virtually every culture has been partial to men. That contradiction raises an increasingly pertinent question (as well as the hackles of militant feminists): Are women immutably different from men? Women's Liberationists believe that any differences—other than anatomical—are a result of conditioning by society. The opposing view is that all of the differences are fixed in the genes. To scientists, however, the nature-nurture controversy is oversimplified. To them, what human beings are results from a complex interaction between both forces. Says Oxford Biologist Christopher Ounsted: "It is a false dichotomy to say that this difference is acquired and that one genetic. To try and differentiate is like asking a penny whether it is really a heads penny or a tails penny." As Berkeley Psychologist Frank Beach suggests, "Predispositions may be genetic; complex behavior patterns are probably not."

The idea that genetic predispositions exist is based on three kinds of evidence. First, there are the "cultural universals" cited by Margaret Mead. Almost everywhere, the mother is the principal caretaker of the child, and male dominance and aggression are the rule. Some anthropologists believe there has been an occasional female-dominated society; others insist that none have existed.

Sex Typing

Then there is the fact that among most ground-dwelling primates, males are dominant and have as a major function the protection of females and offspring. Some research suggests that this is true even when the young are raised apart from adults, which seems to mean that they do not learn their roles from their society.

Finally, behavioral sex differences show up long before any baby could possibly perceive subtle differences between his parents or know which parent he is expected to imitate. "A useful strategy," says Harvard Psychologist Jerome Kagan, "is to assume that the earlier a particular difference appears, the more likely it is to be influenced by biological factors."

Physical differences appear even before birth. The heart of the female fetus often beats faster, and girls develop more rapidly. "Physiologically," says Sociologist Barbette Blackington, "women are better-made animals." Males do have more strength and endurance—though that hardly matters in a technological society.

Recent research hints that there may even be sex differences in the brain. According to some experimenters, the presence of the male hormone testosterone in the fetus may "masculinize" the brain, organizing the fetal nerve centers in characteristic ways. This possible "sex typing" of the central nervous system before birth may make men and women respond differently to incoming stimuli, Sociologist John Gagnon believes.

In fact, newborn girls do show different responses in some situations. They react more strongly to the removal of a blanket and more quickly to touch and pain. Moreover, experiments demonstrate that twelve-week-old girls gaze longer at photographs of faces than at geometric figures. Boys show no preference then, though eventually they pay more attention to figures. Kagan acknowledges the effect of environment, but he has found that it exerts a greater influence on girls than on boys. The female infants who experienced the most "face-to-face interaction" with their mothers were more attentive to faces than girls whose mothers did not exchange looks with them so much. Among boys, there was no consistent relationship.

Internal Organs

As some psychologists see it, this very early female attention to the human face suggests that women may have a greater and even partly innate sensitivity to other human beings. Perhaps this explains why girls seem to get more satisfaction from relationships with people.

Even after infancy, the sexes show differential interests that do not seem to grow solely out of experience. Psychoanalyst Erik Erikson has found that boys and girls aged ten to twelve use space differently when asked to construct a scene with toys. Girls often build a low wall, sometimes with an elaborate doorway, surrounding a quiet interior scene. Boys are likely to construct towers, façades with cannons, and lively exterior scenes. Erikson acknowledges that cultural influences are at work, but he is convinced that they do not fully explain the nature of children's play. The differences, he says, "seem to parallel the morphology [shape and form] of genital differentiation itself: in a male, an external organ, erectible and intrusive; internal organs in the female, with vestibular access, leading to statically expectant ova."

In aptitude as well as in interest, sex differences become apparent early in life. Though girls are generally less adept than boys at mathematical and spatial reasoning, they learn to count sooner and to talk earlier and better. Some scientists think this female verbal superiority may be caused by sex-linked differences in the brain. Others believe it may exist because, as observation proves, mothers talk to infant girls more than to baby boys. But does the mother's talking cause the child to do likewise, or could it be the other way round? Psychologist Michael Lewis suggests the possibility that girls are talked to more because, for biological reasons, they respond more than boys to words and thus stimulate their mothers to keep talking.

Evidence that parental behavior does affect speech comes from tests made by Kagan among poor Guatemalan children.

There, boys are more highly valued than girls, are talked to more and become more verbal. In the U.S., Psychiatrist David Levy has found that boys who are atypically good with words and inept with figures have been overprotected by their mothers. Psychologist Elizabeth Bing has observed that girls who excel at math and spatial problems have often been left to work alone by their mothers, while highly verbal girls have mothers who offer frequent suggestions, praise and criticism.

While girls outdo boys verbally, they often lag behind in solving analytical problems, those that require attention to detail. Girls seem to think "globally," responding to situations as a whole instead of abstracting single elements. In the "rod and frame test," for instance, a subject sits in a dark room before a luminous rod inside a slightly tilted frame, and is asked to move the rod to an upright position. Boys can separate the rod visually from the frame and make it stand straight; girls, misled by the tipped frame, usually adjust the rod not to the true vertical but to a position parallel with the sides of the frame.

In another experiment, children are asked to group related pictures. Boys again pay attention to details, perhaps putting together pictures that show people with an arm raised; girls make functional groups of, for example, a doctor, a nurse and a wheelchair.

In all such differences, environmental influence is suggested by the fact that children who think analytically most often prove to have mothers who have encouraged initiative and exploration, while youngsters who think globally have generally been tied to their mothers' apron strings. In Western society, of course, it is usually boys who are urged toward adventure. Herein, perhaps—there is no proof—lies an explanation for the apparent male capacity to think analytically.

In IQ tests, males and females score pretty much alike. Since this is true, why do women seem less creative? Many social scientists are convinced that the reasons are cultural. Women, they say, learn early in life that female accomplishment brings few rewards. In some cases, women cannot be creative because they are discriminated against. In other instances, a woman's creativity may well be blunted by fear of nonconformity, failure or even success itself. Unlike men, Kagan says, women are trained to have strong anxiety about being wrong.

To many psychoanalysts, however, the explanation lies in the fact that women possess the greatest creative power of all: bringing new life into being; thus they need not compensate by producing works of art. Men, it is theorized, are driven to make up for what seems to them a deficiency. That they feel keenly, though unconsciously, their inability to bear children is shown in dreams reported on the analyst's couch, in the behavior of small boys who play with dolls and walk around with their stomachs thrust forward in imitation of their pregnant mothers and in primitive rites and ancient myths. According to these myths, presumably conceived by males, Adam delivered Eve from his rib cage, Zeus gave birth to Athena out of his head, and when Semele was burned to death, Zeus seized Dionysus from her womb and sewed him up in his thigh until the infant had developed.

There are personality differences between the sexes too. Although no trait is confined to one sex—there are women who exceed the male average even in supposedly masculine characteristics—some distinctions turn up remarkably early. At New York University, for example, researchers have found that a female infant stops sucking a bottle and looks up when someone comes into the room; a male pays no attention to the visitor.

Another Kagan experiment shows that girls of twelve months who become frightened in a strange room drift toward their mothers, while boys look for something interesting to do. At four months, twice as many girls as boys cry when frightened in a strange laboratory. What is more, Kagan says, similar differences can be seen in monkeys and baboons, which "forces us to consider the possibility that some of the psychological differences between men and women may not be the product of experience alone but of subtle biological differences."

Female Passivity

Many researchers have found greater dependence and docility in very young girls, greater autonomy and activity in boys. When a barrier is set up to separate youngsters from their mothers, boys try to knock it down; girls cry helplessly. There is little doubt that maternal encouragement—or discouragement—of such behavior plays a major role in determining adult personality. For example, a mother often stimulates male autonomy by throwing a toy far away from her young son, thus tacitly suggesting to him that he leave her to get it.

Animal studies suggest that there may be a biological factor in maternal behavior: mothers of rhesus monkeys punish their male babies earlier and more often than their female offspring; they also touch their female babies more often and act more protective toward them.

As for the controversial question of female "passivity," Psychoanalyst Helen Deutsch believes that the concept has been misunderstood. "There is no contradiction between being feminine and working. The ego can be active in both men and women," she says. It is only in love and in sex that passivity is particularly appropriate for women. As she sees it, passivity is no more than a kind of openness and warmth; it does not mean "inactivity, emptiness or immobility."

Another controversy rages over the effect of hormones. Militant women, who discount hormonal influence, disagree violently with scientific researchers, who almost unanimously agree that hormones help determine how people feel and act. So far, there have been few studies of male hormones, but scientists think they may eventually discover hormonal cycles in men that produce cyclic changes in mood and behavior. As for females, studies have indicated that 49% of female medical and surgical hospital admissions, most psychiatric hospital admissions and 62% of violent crimes among women prisoners occur on premenstrual and menstrual days. At Worcester State Hospital in Massachusetts, Psychologists Donald and Inge Broverman have found that estrogen sharpens sensory perception. They believe that this heightened sensitivity may lead more women than men to shy away from situations of stress.

Fierce Bulls

One trait thought to be affected by hormones is aggressiveness. In all cultures, investigators report, male infants tend to play more aggressively than females. While scientists think a genetic factor may be involved, they also observe that society fosters the difference by permitting male aggression and encouraging female adaptability. Some suggest that females may be as aggressive as men—but with words instead of deeds.

The definitive research on hormones and aggression is still to be done. However, it has been established that the female hormone estrogen inhibits aggression in both animal and human males. It has also been proved that the male hormone androgen influences aggression in animals. For example, castration produces tractable steers rather than fierce bulls.

The influence of androgen begins even before birth. Administered to pregnant primates, the hormone makes newborn females play more aggressively than ordinary females. Moreover, such masculinized animals are usually aggressive as long as they live, even if they are never again exposed to androgen.

According to some experts, this long-lasting effect of hormones administered or secreted before birth may help explain why boys are more aggressive than girls even during their early years when both sexes appear to produce equal amounts of male and female hormones. Other observers have suggested that the spurt in male-hormone production at puberty could be one of the causes of delinquency in adolescent boys, but there is no proof that this is so.

Will there some day be a "unisex" society with no differences between men and women, except anatomical ones? It seems unlikely. Anatomy, parturition and gender, observes Psychologist Joseph Adelson, cannot be wished away "in a spasm of the distended will, as though the will, in pursuit of total human possibility, can amplify itself to overcome the given." Or, as Psychoanalyst Therese Benedek sees it, "biology precedes personality."

"Nature has been the oppressor," observes Michael Lewis. Women's role as caretaker "was the evolutionary result of their biological role in birth and feeding." The baby bottle has freed women from some of the tasks of that role, but, says University of Michigan Psychologist Judith Bardwick, "the major responsibility for child rearing is the woman's, even in the Soviet Union, the Israeli kibbutz, Scandinavia and mainland China." Furthermore, though mothering skills are mostly learned, it is a fact that if animals are raised in isolation and then put in a room with the young of the species, it is the females who go to the infants and take care of them.

"Perhaps the known biological differences can be totally overcome, and society can approach a state in which a person's sex is of no consequence for any significant activity except childbearing," admits Jerome Kagan. "But we must ask if such a society will be satisfying to its members." As he sees it, "complementarity" is what makes relationships stable and pleasurable.

Psychoanalyst Martin Symonds agrees. "The basic reason why unisex must fail is that in the sexual act itself, the man has to be assertive, if tenderly, and the woman has to be receptive. What gives trouble is when men see assertiveness as aggression and women see receptiveness as submission." Unisex, he sums up, would be "a disaster," because children need roles to identify with and rebel against. "You can't identify with a blur. A unisex world would be a frictionless environment in which nobody would be able to grow up."

The crucial point is that a difference is not a deficiency. As Biologist Ounsted puts it, "We are all human beings and in this sense equal. We are not, however, the same." In the opinion of John Money, "You can play fair only if you recognize and respect authentic differences."

Though scientists disagree about the precise nature and causes of these differences, there is no argument about two points:

society plays a tremendous part in shaping the differences, and most women are capable of doing whatever they want. Only in the top ranges of ability, says Kagan, are innate differences significant; for typical men and women, "the biological differences are totally irrelevant." Psychiatrist Donald Lunde agrees. "There is no evidence," he asserts, "that men are any more or less qualified by biological sex differences alone to perform the tasks generally reserved for them in today's societies."

REFLECTING ON MEANING

1. Adams surveys numerous research studies that examine differences between men and women. What have these studies concluded? What specific differences have they identified? Do these studies attribute differences to biology, psychology, or sociology? What differences have they *not* been able to verify?

2. Adams cites several scientists about the likelihood of a "unisex" society in the future. How does Adams define this society? Do the scientists think that such a society will come about? Why or why not? How do they feel about such a society? How do their feelings about the differences between men and women influence their feelings about a unisex society? Do you agree with Kagan and Symonds on the value of gender differences? Why or why not?

3. What "answer" to the question of difference can you derive from the information Adams provides? Are gender differences innate? Are they a result of socialization? What does her concluding paragraph suggest about differences and their origins? Do you agree that "most women are capable of doing whatever they want"?

EXPLORING RHETORICAL STRATEGIES

1. Adams's essay appeared in *Time* magazine in 1972 as part of a special issue dedicated to women's issues and the achievements of the women's movement. Is it possible that *Time*'s editorial policies influenced Adams as she planned and composed her essay? In what ways? What concerns might her audience—*Time*'s readership—have presented for her?

2. Adams's second paragraph places her essay in the context of the debate over gender differences. What three voices in the debate does she distinguish? Which voice does she encourage her audience to

identify with? How does she accomplish this goal? Is this rhetorical tactic a fair one? Why doesn't she identify with the other
voices?

3.   Adams twice uses the adjective *militant* to describe women with
     feminist viewpoints, and she claims that these militants "disagree
     violently with scientific researchers." Why does she characterize
     feminists in this way? Is her characterization valid? Are men who
     "disagree violently" considered militant, or have the women she
     is describing violated a social model of behavior? Which model?
     What does Adams's word choice tell you about her concerns as
     a writer and as a woman?

The Brain: His and Hers

PAMELA WEINTRAUB

*Journalist and publisher Pamela Weintraub surveys re-
search on the brain in order to offer a firm answer to the question of difference: "Yes," she states, "male and female brains do
differ." Drawing on diverse scientific disciplines to support her
assertion, Weintraub suggests that physical differences in the
brain may account for differences in women's and men's thinking and behavior. She concludes that scientific research to establish biological explanations for difference will not undermine
women's efforts to achieve social equality; rather, it can prove
beneficial for men and women alike.*

Are the brains of men and women different? If so, do men
and women differ in abilities, talents, and deficiencies? A
scientific answer to these questions could affect society
and culture, and variously shock, intrigue, delight, depress, and reassure people of both sexes. Now an answer is coming into sight:
Yes, male and female brains do differ.

That men and women think and behave differently is a widely
held assumption. Generations of writers have lavished their atten-

tion on these differences, proclaiming, for example, that aggressiveness and promiscuity are natural to the male, that domesticity is the legacy of the female. Today's feminists acknowledge some differences, but hotly dispute the notion that they are innate. They stress that it is society, not nature, that gives men the drive to dominate and keeps women from achieving careers and power. But proof that behavioral and intellectual differences between the sexes are partly rooted in the structure of the brain, that women are inherently superior in some areas of endeavor and men in others would in no way undermine legitimate demands for social equality. Instead the result could be a better, more realistic relationship between the sexes.

The evidence suggesting differences between male and female brains comes from research in behavior, biochemistry, anatomy, and neuropsychology. The most recent study deals with the long-established fact that skill in mathematics is far more common among men than women. Feminists—and many scientists—blame sexual stereotyping. But psychologists Camilla Benbow and Julian Stanley, at Johns Hopkins University, challenged that interpretation after testing 9,927 seventh and eighth graders with high IQs. As Benbow told *Discover* reporter John Bucher, of the students who scored 500 or better on the math part of the Scholastic Aptitude Test, boys outnumbered girls by more than two to one. In other words, the psychologists argue, male superiority in math is so pronounced that, to some extent, it must be inborn.

This finding follows several recent studies proving that male and female brains, at least in animals, are physically different. From the hypothalamus, the center for sexual drive, to the cerebral cortex, the seat of thought, scientists have found consistent variations between the sexes. The causes of these differences, they say, are the sex hormones—the male androgens and female estrogens and progesterones that are secreted by the sex glands and carried through the blood stream to distant parts of the body, where they control everything from menstruation to the growth of facial hair.

Basic to all the studies of gender and the brain are the facts of sex determination. When a child is conceived, each parent contributes a sex chromosome, either an X or a Y (so-called for their shapes). When two X's combine, the fetus develops ovaries and becomes a girl. An X and a Y produce a boy; the Y chromosome makes a protein that coats the cells programmed to become ovaries, directing them to become testicles instead. The testicles then pump out two androgens, one that absorbs what would have become a uterus, and another, testosterone, that causes a penis to develop.

Though scientists have not yet been able to pinpoint any physiological differences between the brains of men and women, they think that the development of the brain parallels that of the genitals. If the fetus is a boy, they say, the testosterone that produces the penis also masculinizes tissue in the hypothalamus and other nearby structures deep within the brain. New data suggest that if the fetus is a girl, estrogen secreted by the ovaries feminizes brain tissue in the surrounding cerebral cortex. Scientists cannot dissect living human brains, but they have found ingenious ways to test their theories. The major approaches:

Human Behavior

To shed light on the sexuality of the brain, endocrinologist Julianne Imperato-McGinley of Cornell Medical College in New York City studied 38 men in an isolated part of the Dominican Republic who, because of a genetic disorder, started life as girls. They stayed indoors playing with dolls and learning to cook while boys fought and shouted outside. At the age of eleven, when the breasts of normal girls began to enlarge, the children studied by Imperato-McGinley showed no change. But at twelve, most of them began to feel stirrings of sexual desire for girls. At puberty, their voices deepened, their testicles descended, and their clitorises enlarged to become penises.

These children came from a group of families carrying a rare mutant gene that deprived them of an enzyme needed to make testosterone work in the skin of their genitals. For this reason, their external genitals looked female at birth. But at puberty their bodies were able to use testosterone without the enzyme, and it became obvious that they were males—as chromosome tests confirmed. All but two are now living with women. They have male musculature and, although they cannot sire children, they can have sexual intercourse. They have assumed masculine roles in their society. "To the world," says Imperato-McGinley, "they looked like girls when they were younger. But their bodies were actually flooded with testosterone." She concludes that they were able to adjust easily because hidden in the girl's body was a male brain, virilized by testosterone before birth and activated by another rush of testosterone during adolescence.

Although Imperato-McGinley suggests that brain structure determines behavior, another scientist thinks that the reverse may also be true: Anne Petersen, director of the Adolescent Laboratory at the Michael Reese Hospital and Medical Center in Chicago, says that cultural experiences can masculinize or feminize the brain. In a recent study, Petersen found that boys who excel in athletics also excel in spatial reasoning—a skill controlled by the right hemisphere of the cerebral cortex, and defined as the ability to understand maps and mazes or objects rotating in space. Says Petersen, "An athlete must be constantly aware of his own body and a whole constellation of other bodies in space." A daily game of basketball might, through some still mysterious mechanism, stimulate the secretion of hormones that prime a player's brain for success in basketball. The same brain structures would be used to deal with spatial problems. "Women are far less athletic than men," says Petersen, "and also less adept at spatial reasoning. Part of the problem may be their lack of involvement in sports. Perhaps some women just never develop the area of the brain specialized for spatial control."

Like Petersen, endocrinologist Anke Ehrhardt thinks that society plays an important part in shaping gender behavior. Nevertheless, she says, "certain types of sexual behavior are influenced by the sex hormones." Leafing through the clutter of papers and books that cover her desk at New York City's Columbia Presbyterian Medical Center, Ehrhardt cites cases of girls whose adrenal glands, because of an enzyme defect, produced abnormally large amounts of androgens while they were still in the womb. "We find that they are extremely tomboyish," she says. "They are career oriented, and spend little time with dolls. And we've just learned that boys exposed before birth to drugs that contain high doses of feminizing hormones engage in less roughhousing than other boys."

Animal Behavior

Ehrhardt admits that labeling the pursuit of a career masculine and playing with dolls feminine seems like stereotyping. To substantiate her evidence, she has compared her results with those obtained from studies of animals, whose gender behavior is rigid and easily defined.

Animal physiologists first made the connection between hormones and behavior in 1849, when the German scientist Arnold Berthold castrated roosters and found that they stopped fighting with other roosters and lost interest in attracting hens. When he transplanted the testicles into the abdominal cavities of the castrated birds, the roosters became aggressive again. Observing that the transplanted testicles did not develop connections with the rooster's nervous system but did develop connections with its circulatory system, he speculated that their influence on behavior came from a blood-borne substance, which was later identified as a hormone.

In 1916, Frank Lillie, a Canadian physiologist, noticed that the freemartin, a genetically female (X-X) cow that looks and acts like a male, always had a male twin. He speculated that the freemartin's gonads were masculinized in the womb by hormones secreted by the testicles of the twin.

Fascinated by this finding, scientists began using testosterone to make "freemartin" guinea pigs, rats, monkeys, and dogs. This set the stage for the landmark experiment conducted at the University of Kansas in 1959 by physiologists William Young and Robert Goy.

"We injected pregnant guinea pigs with huge amounts of testosterone," explains Goy. "This produced a brood of offspring in which those that were genetically female had male genitalia as well as ovaries." When the females were 90 days old, the researchers removed their ovaries and injected some of them with still more testosterone. The injected females began to act like males, mounting other females and trying to dominate the group. Says Goy, "We realized that we had changed the sex of the guinea pig's brain."

The researchers concluded that hormones affect behavior in two ways. Before birth, hormones imprint a code on the brain, "just as light can stamp an image on film," Goy says. "Later, throughout life, other hormones activate the code, much as a developer brings out an image on film. Whether the animal behaves like a male or a female depends on the code."

Goy has spent the past two decades proving that theory for a whole range of species, including the rhesus monkey. Now at the Primate Research Center at the University of Wisconsin in Madison, he has found that masculinized monkeys display sexual behavior that ranges from female to male in direct proportion to the amount of testosterone they are given while in the womb and throughout life. "It doesn't much matter whether it's rough-and-tumble play, mounting peers, or attempting to dominate the group," he says. "It's all related to the duration of treatment."

Perhaps more important, Goy has found that by varying the treatment he can produce monkeys that are physically female but behave like males. This is proof, he says, "that these animals behave like boys because of masculinizing hormones, not because of a male appearance that causes the other animals to treat them like boys."

Like the human brain, the brain of the rhesus monkey has a highly elaborate and convoluted cortex. But Goy believes that monkeys can be compared with people only up to a point. For while primitive drives may be similar, he says, human beings are guided by their culture to a greater degree than monkeys. "Nevertheless," he adds, "there are instances when people seem to be less bound by culture. Then they begin to look very much like our monkeys."

Biochemistry

Other scientists have substantiated this evidence with hard biochemical data. To learn where sex hormones operate, neurobiologist Donald Pfaff of New York City's Rockefeller University injected various animals with radioactive hormones and removed their brains. He cut each brain into paper-thin sections, then placed each section on film sensitive to radioactivity. He thus made maps showing that the hormones collected at specific places, now called receptor sites, are similarly located in the brains of species ranging from fish to rats to the rhesus monkey.

The primary site for hormone action, Pfaff saw, was the hypothalamus, a primitive structure at the base of the brain stem. That made sense, because the hypothalamus is the center for sex drive and copulatory behavior. "But the most intriguing thing," says Pfaff, "may be the receptors found in the amygdala [a part of the brain above each ear]. During the 1960s, surgeons found that when they destroyed the amygdala, patients with fits of aggression became completely passive. So we now suspect that sex hormones may control aggression, even fear." Neurologist Bruce McEwen, also of Rockefeller, recently found estrogen receptors in the cerebral cortex of the rat—receptors that disappear three weeks after birth. The cortex controls thought and cognition, but McEwen does not know the significance of these receptors.

The receptors are located at the same sites in both sexes, but because each sex has its own characteristic mix of hormones, male and female brains function differently. To unravel the secret of hormone operation, McEwen has been analyzing the chemistry of the rat brain. He has discovered that receptor sites are hormone-specific; a testosterone site, for example, is insensitive to estrogen. Perhaps more important, he has learned that once hormones pair up with receptors, they mold the structure of the brain by directing nerve cells to manufacture proteins. Early in life, the proteins build nerve cells, creating permanent structures that may exist in the brain of one sex but not the other. Later in life, the proteins produce the chemicals that enable one nerve cell to communicate with another, and precipitate various kinds of sexual behavior.

McEwen and Pfaff have not dissected human brains, but they feel justified in applying some of their findings to people. For, as Pfaff explains, evolution is a conservationist. "As new species evolved, nature didn't throw away old parts of the brain," he says. "Rather, new systems were added. Everyone has a fish brain deep inside. Outside the fish brain there is a reptilian brain, depressingly similar to the way it would look in a lizard. Wrapped around the reptilian brain there is a mammalian brain, and then, finally, the cerebral cortex in such animals as monkeys and human beings." McEwen thinks that the receptors in the hypothalamus probably have similar effects in people and rats. "The difference," he says, "is that human beings can override their primitive drives with nerve impulses from the powerful cerebral cortex."

Anatomy

Anatomical evidence that sex hormones change the structure of the brain came recently from Roger Gorski, a neuroendocrinologist at the University of California at Los Angeles. Examining the hypothalamus in rats, he found a large cluster of nerve cells in the males and a small cluster in females. By giving a female testosterone shortly after birth, he created a large cluster of cells in her hypothalamus that resembled that in the male. If he castrated a male after birth, its cell cluster shrank. Gorski has no idea what the cell structure signifies, but he does know that it varies with changes in sexual behavior.

The anatomical differences do not stop there. Fernando Nottebohm, of Rockefeller, has discovered a large brain-cell cluster in the male canary and a small one in the female. These cells are not in the spinal cord or the hypothalamus but in the forebrain—the songbird equivalent of the cerebral cortex, the part that controls thought and cognition.

The function that Nottebohm studied was song. Only the male songbird can sing, and the more intricate the song the more females he attracts. That takes brainwork, says Nottebohm. "The canary puts songs together just as the artist creates. A large collection of syllables can be combined in infinite ways to form a repertoire in which each song is unique."

Until Nottebohm discovered the large cluster of male brain cells that control the muscles of the syrinx, the singing organ, he had assumed that male and female brains were anatomically identical. He found that if he gave female canaries testosterone before they hatched and again during adulthood, they could learn to sing. When he studied the brains of the singing females, he found that their cell clusters had grown. Says Nottebohm, "The intriguing thing is that the size of the repertoire was more or less proportional to the size of the cell clusters."

Scientists studying mammals have also discovered anatomical differences between the sexes in the thinking part of the brain—in this case, the cerebral cortex of the rat. Marian Diamond, of the University of California at Berkeley, discovered that in the male rat the right hemisphere of the cortex was thicker than the left—and that in the female the left was thicker than the right. But if she castrated the male rat at birth or removed the ovaries from the female, she could alter the pattern. Administering female hormones to males and male hormones to females also affected the width of the cortex. Says Diamond, "Hormones present during pregnancy, hormones present in the birth-control pill, all affect the dimensions of the cortex."

Jerre Levy, a neuropsychologist at the University of Chicago, is encouraged by Diamond's findings because they provide strong anatomical evidence for her theory: the cortex is different in men and women, largely because of hormones that early in life alter the organization of the two hemispheres.

Levy is responsible for much of what is known about the human brain's laterality—the separation of the roles performed by the right and left hemispheres. Levy began her work in this field in the 1960s, when she was studying "split brain" patients, epileptics whose hemispheres had been surgically separated as a means of controlling violent seizures. The researchers found that the hemispheres could operate independently of each other, somewhat like two minds in a single head. The right hemisphere specialized in the perception of spatial relationships, like those in mazes and solid geometry, and the left controlled language and rote memory.

Levy has found that these abilities vary with gender. In test after test, men excelled in spatial reasoning and women did better with language. Fascinated by the discrepancy, she decided to test laterality in normal people and based her experiments on a well known fact: light and sound perceived by the eye and ear on one side of the head travel to the hemisphere on the other side for processing.

She discovered that the right ear and eye are more sensitive in women, the left in men. She concluded that the right hemisphere dominates the masculine brain, and the left the feminine.

Levy points to the work of neuropsychologist Deborah Waber, of Harvard Medical School, who found that children reaching puberty earlier than normal have brains that are less lateralized—that is, their left and right hemispheres seem to share more tasks. Because girls generally reach puberty two years before boys, these findings have caused speculation that the bundle of nerve connections, the corpus callosum, between the two hemispheres of the female brain have less time to lateralize, or draw apart, during puberty. If that is true, says Levy, it could help to explain female intuition, as well as male superiority in mechanics and math. The two intimately connected hemispheres of the female brain would communicate more rapidly—an advantage in integrating all the detail and nuance in an intricate situation, but according to Levy a disadvantage "when it comes to homing in on just a few relevant details." With less interference from the left hemisphere, Levy says, a man could "use his right hemisphere more precisely in deciphering a map or finding a three-dimensional object in a two-dimensional representation."

All this brings Levy back to hormones. She thinks that the estrogen that changes the size of the cortex in Marian Diamond's rats may also change the size and organization of the human cortex. Her new tests are designed to study the organization of the cerebral cortex in people with hormonal abnormalities—girls who produce an excess of androgen and boys who are exposed to large amounts of estrogen before birth.

Levy has ambitious plans for future research, including scans of living brains and tests of babies whose mothers have undergone stress during pregnancy. Much remains to be done, for though the existence of physical differences between male and female brains now seems beyond dispute, the consequences are unclear. Talent in math, for example, is obviously not confined to men, nor talent in languages to women; the subtleties seem infinite. Already the new findings promise to color the modern view of the world. But the implications can easily be misconstrued.

Gunther Dörner, an East German hormone researcher, has claimed that he can put an end to male homosexuality by injecting pregnant women with testosterone. Dörner bases his theory on studies done by two American researchers, who subjected pregnant rats to stress by confining them in small cages under bright lights. They found that the rats' male offspring had low levels of testosterone during certain critical periods, and exhibited homosexual behavior. Dörner concluded that stress on pregnant females alters sexual preference patterns in the brains of their male offspring, and that this finding applies to human beings as well. His suggested antidote: testosterone.

His conclusions appall the American researchers, who agree that mothers under stress produce male offspring with abnormal behavior, but argue that Dörner has gone too far. Dörner's work is supported by the East German government, which is notorious in its aversion to homosexuality, and American scientists fear that he may get a chance to put his ideas into practice on human beings.

Another example of misinterpretation is the article that appeared in *Commentary* magazine in December [1980], citing the "latest" in brain research as an argument against equal rights for women. This angers Anne Petersen. "A lot of people have been making a lot of political hoopla about our work," she says. "They've used it to say that the women's movement will fail, that women are inherently unequal. Our research shows nothing of this sort, of course. There are things that men do better, and things that women do better. It's very important to differentiate between the inferences and the scientific findings."

These findings could influence fields ranging from philosophy, psychiatry, and the arts to education, law, and medicine. If women are indeed at a disadvantage in mastering math, there could be different methods of teaching, or acceptance of the fact that math is not important for certain jobs. For example, tests of mathematical competence have been used as criteria for admission to law school, where math is barely used; tests of spatial ability have been used to screen people for all types of nontechnical pursuits. If scientists can prove that such tests discriminate unnecessarily against women, hiring policies could be changed. Eventually, psychiatrists and lawyers may have to assess their male and female clients in a new light. And brain surgeons may have to consider the sex of a patient before operating. For if the two hemispheres of the brain are more intimately connected in women than in men, then women may be able to control a function like speech with either hemisphere. Surgeons could feel confident that a woman would recover the ability to talk, even if her normal speech center were destroyed; they might proceed with an operation that they would hesitate to perform on a man.

Investigators have made amazing progress in their work on the sexes and the brain, but they have really just begun. They will have to link hundreds of findings from widely diverse areas of brain science before they can provide a complete explanation for the shared, but different, humanity of men and women.

REFLECTING ON MEANING

1. Weintraub summarizes studies from a number of disciplines to support her assertion that male and female brains differ. Does this research establish proof that human brains are masculinized or feminized? What empirical evidence exists for this hypothesis? Can the various theories Weintraub summarizes be considered scientific evidence? Which of these theories are based on proven data? Which seem most reasonable to you? Why?

2. Anne Petersen's research reverses the cause-effect pattern of the majority of the studies Weintraub summarizes. Whereas these

studies hypothesize that the brain produces gender-specific behaviors, Petersen conversely suggests that "cultural experiences
can masculinize or feminize the brain." What evidence does she
offer to support this interpretation of her data? Do you find her
claim convincing? Why or why not?

3. Jerre Levy's research focuses on the human brain's "laterality."
   What is this physical phenomenon? What does it suggest about
   men's and women's reasoning processes? To what might Petersen
   attribute the differences that Levy observes in the brains of men
   and women? What else might cause these differences?

EXPLORING RHETORICAL STRATEGIES

1. Weintraub's introduction reveals that she is concerned with the
   way her audience will respond to her essay. In fact, she seems to
   be addressing at least two different audiences with possibly conflicting interests. Who are these audiences? What evidence can
   you find of their interests?

2. What in Weintraub's introduction tells you that she is aware that
   her topic is controversial and that her discussion may further fuel
   the controversy? Which public group does she clearly wish to
   disassociate herself from? Why does she want to do this? How
   does she accomplish her goal?

3. Why does Weintraub make extensive use of animal studies in an
   essay about humans? Do these studies advance her viewpoint in
   a constructive way? Is it reasonable to use these studies to theorize about the biological origins of gender-specific thinking patterns and behaviors in humans?

Are Women Human?

DOROTHY L. SAYERS

Are women and men of different species? Is human *a word exclusively reserved for men? Mystery writer and cultural critic Dorothy L. Sayers claims that women have for too long suffered the indignities of "classification." She argues that the time has come to admit women to the human race—but not as a class or a group. They are individuals, she argues, entitled as such to the same consideration that men receive as individuals in our society.*

I t is the mark of all movements, however well-intentioned, that their pioneers tend, by much lashing of themselves into excitement, to lose sight of the obvious. In reaction against the age-old slogan, "woman is the weaker vessel," or the still more offensive, "woman is a divine creature," we have, I think, allowed ourselves to drift into asserting that "a woman is as good as a man," without always pausing to think what exactly we mean by that. What, I feel, we ought to mean is something so obvious that it is apt to escape attention altogether, viz.: not that every woman is, in virtue of her sex, as strong, clever, artistic, levelheaded, industrious and so forth as any man that can be mentioned; but, that a woman is just as much an ordinary human being as a man, with the same individual preferences, and with just as much right to the tastes and preferences of an individual. What is repugnant to every human being is to be reckoned always as a member of a class and not as an individual person. A certain amount of classification is, of course, necessary for practical purposes: there is no harm in saying that women, as a class, have smaller bones than men, wear lighter clothing, have more hair on their heads and less on their faces, go more pertinaciously to church or the cinema, or have more patience with small and noisy babies. In the same way, we may say that stout people of both sexes are commonly better-tempered than thin ones, or that university dons of both sexes are more pedantic in their speech than agricultural labourers, or that Communists of both sexes are more ferocious than Fascists—or the other way round. What is unreasonable and irritating is to assume that *all* one's tastes and preferences have to be conditioned by the class to which one belongs. That has been the very common error into which men have frequently fallen about women—and it is the error into which feminist women are, perhaps, a little inclined to fall into about themselves.

Take, for example, the very usual reproach that women nowadays always want to "copy what men do." In that reproach there is a great deal of truth and a great deal of sheer, unmitigated and indeed quite wicked nonsense. There are a number of jobs and pleasures which men have in times past cornered for themselves. At one time, for instance, men had a monopoly of classical education. When the pioneers of university training for women demanded that women should be admitted to the universities, the cry went up at once: "Why should women want to know about Aristotle?" The answer is NOT that *all* women would be the better for knowing about Aristotle—still less, as Lord Tennyson seemed to think, that they would be more companionable wives for their husbands if they did know about Aristotle—but simply: "What women want as a class is irrelevant. *I* want to know about Aristotle. It is true that most women care nothing about him, and a great many male undergraduates turn pale and faint at the thought of him—but I, eccentric individual that I am, do want to know about Aristotle, and I submit that there is nothing in my shape or bodily functions which need prevent my knowing about him." . . .

So that when we hear that women have once more laid hands upon something which was previously a man's sole privilege, I think we have to ask ourselves: is this trousers or is it braces? Is it something useful, convenient and suitable to a human being as such? Or is it merely something unnecessary to us, ugly, and adopted merely for the sake of collaring the other fellow's property? These jobs and professions, now. It is ridiculous to take on a man's job just in order to be able to say that "a woman has done it—yah!" The only decent reason for tackling any job is that it is *your* job and *you* want to do it.

At this point, somebody is likely to say: "Yes, that is all very well. But it *is* the woman who is always trying to ape the man. She is the inferior being. You don't as a rule find the men trying to take the women's jobs away from them. They don't force their way into the household and turn women out of their rightful occupations."

Of course they do not. They have done it already.

Let us accept the idea that women should stick to their own jobs—the jobs they did so well in the good old days before they started talking about votes and women's rights. Let us return to the Middle Ages and ask what we should get then in return for certain political and educational privileges which we should have to abandon.

It is a formidable list of jobs: the whole of the spinning industry, the whole of the dyeing industry, the whole of the weaving industry. The whole catering industry and—which would not please
Lady Astor, perhaps—the whole of the nation's brewing and dis-
tilling. All the preserving, pickling and bottling industry, all the
bacon-curing. And (since in those days a man was often absent
from home for months together on war or business) a very large
share in the management of landed estates. Here are the women's
jobs—and what has become of them? They are all being handled by
men. It is all very well to say that woman's place is the home—but
modern civilization has taken all these pleasant and profitable activities out of the home, where the women looked after them, and
handed them over to big industry, to be directed and organized by
men at the head of large factories. Even the dairy-maid in her simple bonnet has gone, to be replaced by a male mechanic in charge
of a mechanical milking plant.

Now, it is very likely that men in big industries do these jobs
better than the women did them at home. The fact remains that the
home contains much less of interesting activity than it used to contain. What is more, the home has so shrunk to the size of a small
flat that—even if we restrict woman's job to the bearing and rearing
of families—there is no room for her to do even that. It is useless to
urge the modern woman to have twelve children, like her grandmother. Where is she to put them when she has got them? And
what modern man wants to be bothered with them? It is perfectly
idiotic to take away woman's traditional occupations and then
complain because she looks for new ones. Every woman is a human being—one cannot repeat that too often—and a human being
must have occupation, if he or she is not to become a nuisance to
the world.

I am not complaining that the brewing and baking were taken
over by the men. If they can brew and bake as well as women or
better, then by all means let them do it. But they cannot have it both
ways. If they are going to adopt the very sound principle that the
job should be done by the person who does it best, then that rule
must be applied universally. If the women make better office workers than men, they must have the office work. If any individual
woman is able to make a first-class lawyer, doctor, architect or en-
gineer, then she must be allowed to try her hand at it. Once lay
down the rule that the job comes first and you throw that job open
to every individual, man or woman, fat or thin, tall or short, ugly or
beautiful, who is able to do that job better than the rest of the world.

Now, it is frequently asserted that, with women, the job does
not come first. What (people cry) are women doing with this liberty

of theirs? What woman really prefers a job to a home and family? Very few, I admit. It is unfortunate that they should so often have to make the choice. A man does not, as a rule, have to choose. He gets both. In fact, if he wants the home and family, he usually has to take the job as well, if he can get it. Nevertheless, there have been women, such as Queen Elizabeth and Florence Nightingale, who had the choice, and chose the job and made a success of it. And there have been and are many men who have sacrificed their careers for women—sometimes, like Antony or Parnell, very disastrously. When it comes to a *choice,* then every man or woman has to choose as an individual human being, and, like a human being, take the consequences.

As human beings! I am always entertained—and also irritated—by the newsmongers who inform us, with a bright air of discovery, that they have questioned a number of female workers and been told by one and all that they are "sick of the office and would love to get out of it." In the name of God, what human being is *not,* from time to time, heartily sick of the office and would *not* love to get out of it? The time of female office-workers is daily wasted in sympathizing with disgruntled male colleagues who yearn to get out of the office. No human being likes work—not day in and day out. Work is notoriously a curse—and if women *liked* everlasting work they would not be human beings at all. *Being* human beings, they like work just as much and just as little as anybody else. They dislike perpetual washing and cooking just as much as perpetual typing and standing behind shop counters. Some of them prefer typing to scrubbing—but that does not mean that they are not, as human beings, entitled to damn and blast the typewriter when they feel that way. The number of men who daily damn and blast typewriters is incalculable; but that does not mean that they would be happier doing a little plain sewing. Nor would the women.

I have admitted that there are very few women who would put their job before every earthly consideration. I will go further and assert that there are very few men who would do it either. In fact, there is perhaps only one human being in a thousand who is passionately interested in his job for the job's sake. The difference is that if that one person in a thousand is a man, we say, simply, that he is passionately keen on his job; if she is a woman, we say she is a freak. It is extraordinarily entertaining to watch the historians of the past, for instance, entangling themselves in what they were pleased to call the "problem" of Queen Elizabeth. They invented the most complicated and astonishing reasons both for her success as a sovereign and for her tortuous matrimonial policy. She was the tool of Burleigh, she was the tool of Leicester, she was the fool of Essex; she was diseased, she was deformed, she was a man in disguise. She was a mystery, and must have some extraordinary solution. Only recently has it occurred to a few enlightened people that the solution might be quite simple after all. She might be one of the rare people who were born into the right job and put that job first. Whereupon a whole series of riddles cleared themselves up by magic. She was in love with Leicester—why didn't she marry him? Well, for the very same reason that numberless kings have not married their lovers—because it would have thrown a spanner into the wheels of the State machine. Why was she so bloodthirsty and unfeminine as to sign the death-warrant of Mary Queen of Scots? For much the same reasons that induced King George V to say that if the House of Lords did not pass the Parliament Bill he would create enough new peers to force it through—because she was, in the measure of her time, a constitutional sovereign, and knew that there was a point beyond which a sovereign could not defy Parliament. Being a rare human being with her eye to the job, she did what was necessary; being an ordinary human being, she hesitated a good deal before embarking on unsavory measures—but as to feminine mystery, there is no such thing about it, and nobody, had she been a man, would have thought either her statesmanship or her humanity in any way mysterious. Remarkable they were—but she was a very remarkable person. Among her most remarkable achievements was that of showing that sovereignty was one of the jobs for which the right kind of woman was particularly well fitted.

Which brings us back to this question of what jobs, if any, are women's jobs. Few people would go so far as to say that all women are well fitted for all men's jobs. When people do say this, it is particularly exasperating. It is stupid to insist that there are as many female musicians and mathematicians as male—the facts are otherwise, and the most we can ask is that if a Dame Ethel Smyth or a Mary Somerville turns up, she shall be allowed to do her work without having aspersions cast either on her sex or her ability. What we ask is to be human individuals, however peculiar and unexpected. It is no good saying: "You are a little girl and therefore you ought to like dolls"; if the answer is, "But I don't," there is no more to be said. Few women happen to be natural born mechanics; but if there is one, it is useless to try and argue her into being something different. What we must *not* do is to argue that the occasional appearance of a female mechanical genius proves that all women would be mechanical geniuses if they were educated. They would not.

Where, I think, a great deal of confusion has arisen is in a failure to distinguish between special *knowledge* and special *ability*.

There are certain questions on which what is called "the woman's point of view" is valuable, because they involve special *knowledge.* Women should be consulted about such things as housing and domestic architecture because, under present circumstances, they have still to wrestle a good deal with houses and kitchen sinks and can bring special knowledge to the problem. Similarly, some of them (though not all) know more about children than the majority of men, and their opinion, *as women,* is of value. In the same way, the opinion of colliers is of value about coal-mining, and the opinion of doctors is valuable about disease. But there are other questions—as for example, about literature or finance—on which the "woman's point of view" has no value at all. In fact, it does not exist. No special knowledge is involved, and a woman's opinion on literature or finance is valuable only as the judgment of an individual. I am occasionally desired by congenital imbeciles and the editors of magazines to say something about the writing of detective fiction "from the woman's point of view." To such demands, one can only say, "Go away and don't be silly. You might as well ask what is the female angle on an equilateral triangle." . . .

A man once asked me—it is true that it was at the end of a very good dinner, and the compliment conveyed may have been due to that circumstance—how I managed in my books to write such natural conversation between men when they were by themselves. Was I, by any chance, a member of a large, mixed family with a lot of male friends? I replied that, on the contrary, I was an only child and had practically never seen or spoken to men of my own age till I was about twenty-five. "Well," said the man, "I shouldn't have expected a woman [meaning me] to have been able to make it so convincing." I replied that I had coped with this difficult problem by making my men talk, as far as possible, like ordinary human beings. This aspect of the matter seemed to surprise the other speaker; he said no more, but took it away to chew it over. One of these days it may quite likely occur to him that women, as well as men, when left to themselves, talk very much like human beings also.

Indeed, it is my experience that both men and women are fundamentally human, and that there is very little mystery about either sex, except the exasperating mysteriousness of human beings in general. And though for certain purposes it may still be necessary, as it undoubtedly was in the immediate past, for women to band themselves together, as women, to secure recognition of their requirements as a sex, I am sure that the time has now come to insist more strongly on each woman's—and indeed each man's—requirements as an individual person. It used to be said that women had no *esprit de corps;* we have proved that we have—do not let us run into the opposite error of insisting that there is an aggressively feminist "point of view" about everything. To oppose one class perpetually to another—young against old, manual labor against brain-worker, rich against poor, woman against man—is to split the foundations of the State; and if the cleavage runs too deep, there remains no remedy but force and dictatorship. If you wish to preserve a free democracy, you must base it—not on classes and categories, for this will land you in the totalitarian State, where no one may act or think except as the member of a category. You must base it upon the individual Tom, Dick and Harry, on the individual Jack and Jill—in fact, upon you and me.

REFLECTING ON MEANING

1. In her opening paragraph, Sayers confronts head-on the issue of classification: "What is repugnant to every human being is to be reckoned always as a member of a class and not as an individual person." What is classification? Why does Sayers find it repugnant? Isn't classifying a useful activity for making sense of the world? Does classifying differ from stereotyping? In what ways are they similar? How are they different?

2. With increasing conviction, Sayers repeatedly asserts that a woman is "just as much an ordinary human being as a man." What does she mean? Why does she feel compelled to emphasize this point? Is she stating and restating the obvious? Do you think there's a need to make this point at all? What specific situation or situations do you think she might be reacting to?

3. What point is Sayers making when she states that a man who likes his job is considered "passionately keen" on it while a woman with the same enthusiasm is considered a "freak"? What social phenomenon does she believe causes such a disparity in perception? Do you think her point is valid? What evidence can you offer to support it? What other examples of this phenomenon can you give?

EXPLORING RHETORICAL STRATEGIES

1. Sayers's essay is shaped in a way that suggests she is responding to an argument about women. If you were to conceive of her

piece as one voice in a conversation among many, how might you describe this conversation? What are the topics being debated? What viewpoints are being expressed? What is Sayers's part in this conversation? If you were to enter this conversation, what might you contribute to it?

2. How would you describe the tone of this essay? For example, is Sayers playful, serious, hostile, conciliatory, exasperated, sarcastic, or sincere? How do her many italicized words contribute to her tone? How is the exclamation "As human beings!" typical of her tone? What image of Sayers does her tone suggest? In what ways does her tone contribute to the persona she adopts in this essay?

3. Sayers integrates the opposition viewpoint throughout her essay. Where and how does she do this? How does this strategy contribute to the structure of the essay? How does the way she introduces various factions of the opposition encourage you to see them in a negative light? For example, what is the effect of referring to one such faction as "newsmongers"?

Chapter 2 ⎯⎯⎯⎯⎯⎯⎯⎯⎯⎯

MASCULINITY IN TRANSITION

What Every Woman Should Know About Men

ALAN ALDA

With tongue in cheek, actor Alan Alda portrays stereotypical masculine behavior as a disease. He provides a test for self-diagnosis, several remedies, and some suggestions for those who must cope with a "sufferer" of this gender-specific ailment.

Everyone knows that testosterone, the so-called male hormone, is found in both men and women. What is not so well known is that men have an overdose.

Until now it has been thought that the level of testosterone in men is normal simply because they have it. But if you consider how abnormal their *behavior* is, then you are led to the hypothesis that almost all men are suffering from *testosterone poisoning*.

The symptoms are easy to spot. Sufferers are reported to show an early preference (while still in the crib) for geometric shapes. Later, they become obsessed with machinery and objects to the exclusion of human values. They have an intense need to rank everything, and are obsessed with size. (At some point in his life, nearly every male measures his penis.)

It is well known that men don't look like other people. They have chicken legs. This is symptomatic of the disease, as is the fact that those men with the most aviary underpinnings will rank women according to the shapeliness of *their* legs.

The pathological violence of most men hardly needs to be mentioned. They are responsible for more wars than any other leading sex.

Testosterone poisoning is particularly cruel because its sufferers usually don't know they have it. In fact, when they are most under its sway they believe that they are at their healthiest and most attractive. They even give each other medals for exhibiting the most advanced symptoms of the illness.

But there is hope.

Sufferers can change (even though it is harder than learning to walk again). They must first realize, however, that they are sick. The fact that this condition is inherited in the same way that dimples are does not make it cute.

Eventually, of course, telethons and articles in the *Reader's Digest* will dramatize the tragedy of testosterone poisoning. In the meantime, it is imperative for your friends and loved ones to become familiar with the danger signs.

Have the men you know take this simple test for—

The Seven Warning Signs of Testosterone Poisoning

1. *Do you have an intense need to win?* When having sex, do you take pride in always finishing before your partner? Do you always ask if this time was "the best"—and gnaw on the bedpost if you get an ambiguous answer?
2. *Does violence play a big part in your life?* Before you answer, count up how many hours you watched football, ice hockey, and children's cartoons this year on television. When someone crosses you, do you wish you could stuff his face full of your fist? Do you ever poke people in your fantasies or throw them to and fro at all? When someone cuts you off in traffic, do violent, angry curses come bubbling out of your mouth before you know it? If so, you're in big trouble, fella, and this is only question number two.
3. *Are you "thing" oriented?* Do you value the parts of a woman's body more than the woman herself? Are you turned on by things that even *remind* you of those parts? Have you ever fallen in love with a really great doorknob?
4. *Do you have an intense need to reduce every difficult situation to charts and figures?* If you were present at a riot, would you tend to count the crowd? If your wife is despondent over a deeply felt setback that has left her feeling helpless, do you take her temperature?
5. *Do you tend to measure things that are really qualitative?* Are you more impressed with how high a male ballet dancer can leap than with what he does while he's up there? Are you more con-

cerned with how long you can spend in bed, and with how many orgasms you can have, than you are with how you or your partner feels while you're there?

6. *Are you a little too mechanically minded?* Would you like to watch a sunset with a friend and feel at one with nature and each other, or would you rather take apart a clock?

7. *Are you easily triggered into competition?* When someone tries to pass you on the highway, do you speed up a little? Do you find yourself getting into contests of crushing beer cans—with the beer still in them?

If you've answered yes to three or fewer of the above questions, you may be learning to deal with your condition. A man answering yes to more than three is considered sick and not someone you'd want to have around in a crisis—such as raising children or growing old together. Anyone answering yes to all seven of the questions should seek help immediately before he kills himself in a high-wire act.

What to Do If You Suffer from Testosterone Poisoning

1. *Don't panic.* Your first reaction may be that you are sicker than anyone else—or that you are the one man in the world able to fight it off—or, knowing that you are a sufferer, that you are the one man ordained to lead others to health (such as by writing articles about it). These are all symptoms of the disease. Just relax. First, sit back and enjoy yourself. Then find out how to enjoy somebody else.

2. *Try to feel something.* (Not with your hands, you oaf.) Look at a baby and see if you can appreciate it. (Not how *big* it's getting, just how nice she or he is.) See if you can get yourself to cry by some means other than getting hit in the eye or losing a lot of money.

3. *See if you can listen while someone is talking.* Were you the one talking? Perhaps you haven't got the idea yet.

4. *Practice this sentence:* "You know, I think you're right and I'm wrong." (Hint: it is useful to know what the other person thinks before you say this.)

For Women Only: What to Do If You Are Living with a Sufferer

1. Remember that a little sympathy is a dangerous thing. The sufferer will be inclined to interpret any concern for him as appropriate submissiveness.

2.   Let him know that you expect him to fight his way back to health and behave like a normal person—for his own sake, not for yours.

3.   Only after he begins to get his condition under control and has actually begun to enjoy life should you let him know that there is no such thing as testosterone poisoning.

REFLECTING ON MEANING

1.   What are the symptoms of "testosterone poisoning"? Have you encountered any cases of it in your own experience?

2.   According to Alda, what is the "cure" for testosterone poisoning? Do his remedies seem effective?

3.   Why does Alda end his essay by claiming that "there is no such thing as testosterone poisoning"? Whom is he talking to? Why does he recommend keeping this "fact" a secret?

EXPLORING RHETORICAL STRATEGIES

1.   How would you describe Alda's tone? Why do you think he chose to adopt this tone? How does it help him make his point?

2.   Who is Alda's intended audience? How do you know?

3.   What kind of popular article format is Alda spoofing? In what kind of magazine do these articles appear? What are the issues these articles tend to address? What persona do the authors of these articles typically adopt? How does Alda satirize these articles? What effect does he create?

In Harness:
The Male Condition

HERB GOLDBERG

---

*Are women the only victims of gender stereotyping and so-
cial oppression? Writer Herb Goldberg offers an emphatic no
to this question. It is time, he argues, for men to "remove the
disguises of privilege and reveal the male condition for what it
really is."*

Most men live in harness. Richard was one of them. Typically he had no awareness of how his male harness was
choking him until his personal and professional life and
his body had nearly fallen apart.

Up to that time he had experienced only occasional short
bouts of depression that a drink would bring him out of. For Richard it all crashed at an early age, when he was thirty-three. He
came for psychotherapy with resistance, but at the instruction of
his physician. He had a bad ulcer, was losing weight, and, in spite
of repeated warnings that it could kill him, he was drinking heavily.

His personal life was also in serious trouble. He had recently
lost his job as a disc jockey on a major radio station because he'd
been arrested for drunk driving. He had totaled his car against a
tree and the newspapers had a picture of it on the front page.
Shortly thereafter his wife moved out, taking with her their eight-
year-old daughter. She left at the advice of friends who knew that
he had become violent twice that year while drunk.

As he began to talk about himself it became clear that he had
been securely fitted into his male harness early in his teens. In high
school he was already quite tall and stronger than most. He was
therefore urged to go out for basketball, which he did, and he got
lots of attention for it.

He had a deep, resonant voice that he had carefully cultivated. He was told that he should go into radio announcing and
dramatics, so he got into all the high school plays. In college he ma-
jored in theater arts.

In his senior year in college he dated one of the most beautiful
and sought-after girls in the junior class. His peer group envied

him, which reassured Richard that he had a good thing going. So he married Joanna a year after graduating and took a job with a small radio station in Fresno, California. During the next ten years he played out the male role; he fathered a child and fought his way up in a very competitive profession.

It wasn't until things had fallen apart that he even let himself know that he had any feelings of his own, and in therapy he began to see why it had been so necessary to keep his feelings buried. They were confusing and frightening.

More than anything else, there was a hypersensitive concern over what others thought about him as a "man." As other suppressed feelings began to surface they surprised him. He realized how he had hated the pressures of being a college basketball player. The preoccupation with being good and winning had distorted his life in college.

Though he had been to bed with many girls before marriage and even a few afterward, he acknowledged that rarely was it a genuine turn-on for him. He liked the feeling of being able to seduce a girl but the experience itself was rarely satisfying, so he would begin the hunt for another as soon as he succeeded with one. "Some of those girls were a nightmare," he said. "I would have been much happier without them. But I was caught in the bag of proving myself and I couldn't seem to control it."

The obsessive preoccupation in high school and college with cultivating a deep, resonant "masculine" voice he realized was similar to the obsession some women have with their figures. Though he thought he had enjoyed the attention he got being on stage, he acknowledged that he had really disliked being an entertainer, or "court jester," as he put it.

When he thought about how he had gotten married he became particularly uncomfortable. "I was really bored with Joanna after the first month of dating but I couldn't admit it to myself because I thought I had a great thing going. I married her because I figured if I didn't one of the other guys would. I couldn't let that happen."

Richard had to get sick in his harness and nearly be destroyed by role-playing masculinity before he could allow himself to be a person with his own feelings, rather than just a hollow male image. Had it not been for a bleeding ulcer he might have postponed looking at himself for many years more.

Like many men, Richard had been a zombie, a daytime sleepwalker. Worse still, he had been a highly "successful" zombie, which made it so difficult for him to risk change. Our culture is saturated with successful male zombies, businessman zombies, golf zombies, sports car zombies, playboy zombies, etc. They are playing by the rules of the male game plan. They have lost touch with, or are running away from, their feelings and awareness of themselves as people. They have confused their social masks for their essence and they are destroying themselves while fulfilling the traditional definitions of masculine-appropriate behavior. They set their life sails by these role definitions. They are the heroes, the studs, the providers, the warriors, the empire builders, the fearless ones. Their reality is always approached through these veils of gender expectations.

When something goes seriously wrong, they discover that they are shadows to themselves as well as to others. They are unknown because they have been so busy manipulating and masking themselves in order to maintain and garner more status that a genuine encounter with another person would threaten them, causing them to flee or to react with extreme defensiveness.

Men evaluate each other and are evaluated by many women largely by the degree to which they approximate the ideal masculine model. Women have rightfully lashed out against being placed into a mold and being related to as a sex object. Many women have described their roles in marriage as a form of socially approved prostitution. They assert that they are selling themselves out for an unfulfilling portion of supposed security. For psychologically defensive reasons the male has not yet come to see himself as a prostitute, day in and day out, both in and out of the marriage relationship.

The male's inherent survival instincts have been stunted by the seemingly more powerful drive to maintain his masculine image. He would, for example, rather die in the battle than risk living in a different way and being called a "coward" or "not a man." He would rather die at his desk prematurely than free himself from his compulsive patterns and pursuits. As a recently published study concluded, "A surprising number of men approaching senior citizenship say they would rather die than be buried in retirement."

The male in our culture is at a growth impasse. He won't move—not because he is protecting his cherished central place in the sun, but because he *can't* move. He is a cardboard Goliath precariously balanced and on the verge of toppling over if he is pushed even ever so slightly out of his well-worn path. He lacks the fluidity of the female who can readily move between the traditional definitions of male or female behavior and roles. She can be wife and mother or a business executive. She can dress in typically feminine fashion or adopt the male styles. She will be loved for having "feminine" interests such as needlework or cooking, or she will be admired for sharing with the male in his "masculine" interests. That will make her a "man's woman." She can be sexually assertive or sexually passive. Meanwhile, the male is rigidly caught in his masculine pose and, in many subtle and direct ways, he is severely punished when he steps out of it.

Unlike some of the problems of women, the problems of men are not readily changed through legislation. The male has no apparent and clearly defined targets against which he can vent his rage. Yet he is oppressed by the cultural pressures that have denied him his feelings, by the mythology of the woman and the distorted and self-destructive way he sees and relates to her, by the urgency for him to "act like a man" which blocks his ability to respond to his inner promptings both emotionally and physiologically, and by a generalized self-hate that causes him to feel comfortable only when he is functioning well in harness, or when he lives for joy and for personal growth.

The prevalent "enlightened" male's reaction to the women's liberation movement bears testimony to his inability to mobilize himself on his own behalf. He has responded to feminist assertions by donning sack cloth, sprinkling himself with ashes, and flagellating himself—accusing himself of the very things she is accusing him of. An article entitled, "You've Come a Long Way, Buddy," perhaps best illustrates the male self-hating attitude. In it, the writer said,

> The members of the men's liberation movement are…a kind of embarrassing vanguard, the first men anywhere on record to take a political stand based on the idea that what the women are saying is right—men are a bunch of lazy, selfish, horny, unhappy oppressors.

Many other undoubtedly well-intentioned writers on the male condition have also taken a basically guilt- and shame-oriented approach to the male, alternately scolding him, warning him, and preaching to him that he better change and not be a male chauvinist pig anymore. During many years of practice as a psychotherapist, I have never seen a person grow or change in a self-constructive, meaningful way when he was motivated by guilt, shame, or self-hate. That manner of approach smacks of old-time religion and degrades the male by ignoring the complexity of the binds and repressions that are his emotional heritage.

Precisely because the tenor and mood of the male liberation efforts so far have been one of self-accusation, self-hate, and a repetition of feminist assertions, I believe it is doomed to failure in its present form. It is buying the myth that the male is culturally favored—a notion that is clung to despite the fact that every critical statistic in the area of longevity, disease, suicide, crime, accidents, childhood emotional disorders, alcoholism, and drug addiction shows a disproportionately higher male rate.

Many men who join male liberation groups do so to please or impress their women or to learn how to deal with and hold on to their recently liberated wives or girlfriends. Once in a male liberation group they intellectualize their feelings and reactions into lifelessness. In addition, the men tend to put each other down for thinking like "typical male chauvinists" or using words like "broad," "chick," "dike," etc. They have introjected the voices of their feminist accusers and the result is an atmosphere that is joyless, self-righteous, cautious, and lacking in a vitalizing energy. A new, more subtle kind of competitiveness pervades the atmosphere: the competition to be the least competitive and most free of the stereotyped version of male chauvinism.

The women's liberation movement did not effect its astounding impact via self-hate, guilt, or the desire to placate the male. Instead it has been energized by anger and outrage. Neither will the male change in any meaningful way until he experiences his underlying rage toward the endless, impossible binds under which he lives, the rigid definitions of his role, the endless pressure to be all things to all people, and the guilt-oriented, self-denying way he has traditionally related to women, to his feelings, and to his needs.

Because it is so heavily repressed, male rage only manifests itself indirectly and in hidden ways. Presently it is taking the form of emotional detachment, interpersonal withdrawal, and passivity in relationship to women. The male has pulled himself inward in order to deny his anger and to protect himself and others from his buried cascade of resentment and fury. Pathetic, intellectualized attempts not to be a male chauvinist pig will *never* do the job.

There is also a commonly expressed notion that men will somehow be freed as a by-product of the feminist movement. This is a comforting fantasy for the male but I see no basis for it becoming a reality. It simply disguises the fear of actively determining his own change. Indeed, by responding inertly and passively, the male will be moved, but not in a meaningful and productive direction. If there is to be a constructive change for the male he will have to chart his own way, develop his own style, and experience his own anxieties, fear, and rage because *this time mommy won't do it!*

Recently, I asked a number of men to write to me about how they see their condition and what liberation would mean to them. A sense of suffocation and confusion was almost always present.

A forty-six-year-old businessman wrote: "From what do I need to be liberated? I'm too old and tired to worry about myself. I know that I'm only a high-grade mediocrity. I've come to accept a life where the dreams are now all revealed as unreality. I don't know how my role or my son's role should change. If I knew I suppose it would be in any way that would make my wife happier and less of a shrew."

A thirty-nine-year-old carpenter discussing the "joys" of working responded: "I contend that the times in which it is fun and rewarding in a healthy way have been fairly limited. Most of the time it has been a question of running in fear of failure." Referring to his relationships, he continued, "There is another aspect of women's and men's lib that I haven't experienced extensively. This is the creation of close friendships outside of the marriage. My past experiences have been stressful to the point where I am very careful to limit any such contact. What's the fear? I didn't like the sense of insecurity developed by my wife and the internal stresses that I felt. It created guilt feelings."

A fifty-seven-year-old college professor expressed it this way: "Yes, there's a need for male lib and hardly anyone writes about it the way it really is, though a few make jokes. My gut reaction, which is what you asked for, is that men—the famous male chauvinist pigs who neglect their wives, underpay their women employees, and rule the world—are literally slaves. They're out there picking that cotton, sweating, swearing, taking lashes from the boss, working fifty hours a week to support themselves and the plantation, only then to come back to the house to do another twenty hours a week rinsing dishes, toting trash bags, writing checks, and acting as butlers at the parties. It's true of young husbands and middle-aged husbands. Young bachelors may have a nice deal for a couple of years after graduating, but I've forgotten, and I'll never again be young! Old men. Some have it sweet, some have it sour.

"Man's role—how has it affected my life? At thirty-five, I chose to emphasize family togetherness and income and neglect my profession if necessary. At fifty-seven, I see no reward for time spent with and for the family, in terms of love or appreciation. I see a thousand punishments for neglecting my profession. I'm just tired and have come close to just walking away from it and starting over; just research, publish, teach, administer, play tennis, and travel. Why haven't I? Guilt. And love. And fear of loneliness. How should the man's role in my family change? I really don't know how it can, but I'd like a lot more time to do my thing."

The most remarkable and significant aspect of the feminist movement to date has been woman's daring willingness to own up to her resistances and resentment toward her time-honored, sanctified roles of wife and even mother. The male, however, has yet to fully realize, acknowledge, and rebel against the distress and stifling aspects of many of the roles he plays–from good husband, to good daddy, to good provider, to good lover, etc. Because of the inner pressure to constantly affirm his dominance and masculinity, he continues to act as if he can stand up under, fulfill, and even enjoy all the expectations placed on him no matter how contradictory and devitalizing they are.

It's time to remove the disguises of privilege and reveal the male condition for what it really is.

REFLECTING ON MEANING

1. Goldberg emphasizes that men's roles are more constraining than women's are; in fact, he argues that men are "severely punished" for stepping out of their roles, whereas women can adopt "masculine" behavior without penalty. What evidence does he offer to support these points? Is this evidence convincing? Why or why not? Do you agree or disagree that men are more trapped by gender expectations than women are? Can you think of any instances when men are allowed the freedom not to be "men," or when women are not allowed to shift roles? What are they?

2. Goldberg clearly views "enlightened" males with scorn. Why? Aren't these men attempting to move beyond the masculine roles that Goldberg finds so stifling? How does Goldberg depict these men? How can you reconcile his attitudes toward them with his vision of freedom from the male stereotype? Is Goldberg arguing for gender-neutral roles or for something else? Does he want men to be able to move freely between masculine and feminine roles, or does he want men to reassert their masculinity? How do you know?

3. Goldberg's attitude toward the women's movement is perhaps best described as ambivalent. In several instances he appears to envy it; in others he displays open hostility toward it. What

evidence of both attitudes can you identify in the essay? What might account for his envy? At the same time, why might he display hostility? How can you reconcile these disparate reactions to the women's movement? Are his attitudes reasonable or unreasonable? Why?

EXPLORING RHETORICAL STRATEGIES

1. What metaphor does Goldberg use to describe the oppression of men? What does it suggest to you about the nature of this oppression? How appropriate is the metaphor? What is Goldberg's thesis? In what ways does the metaphor advance his thesis?

2. Goldberg says that Richard had become a "hollow male image," a man almost "destroyed by role-playing masculinity." What do these descriptions suggest about the nature of Richard's "condition"? How does Goldberg's summary of Richard's life help illustrate his point? How effective is this illustration?

3. What rhetorical strategies has Goldberg borrowed from feminist rhetoric? What kind of persona does he adopt? What is the tone of his essay? How do these strategies work in arguing the case for men's liberation?

Masculinity: Style and Cult

HAROLD ROSENBERG

The masculine ideal has played a vital role in the cultural mythology of past societies. But according to literary critic Harold Rosenberg, the American version of this ideal has lost any usefulness it may have once had, and attempts to revitalize it are doing more harm than good. In this essay, Rosenberg describes the American masculine ideal, explains what has happened to it, and recommends that it be put aside in favor of a yet-to-emerge "maleness."

Societies of the past have admired different personifications of the manly virtues: the warrior, the patriarch, the sage; the lover, the seducer; Zeus the Thunderer, Jehovah the Lawgiver.

In America, masculinity is associated primarily with the outdoors, and with such outdoor trades as cattledriving, railroading, whaling, and trucking. The outdoor type is presumed to possess masculine character traits: toughness, resourcefulness, love of being alone, fraternity with animals, and attractiveness to women and the urge to abandon them. To the man of the open spaces is also attributed the ultimate mark of manliness, the readiness to die.

From the outdoors America derives the boots, lumber jackets and shirts, sailor's caps, pipes, and guns that are its paraphernalia of masculinity. Oddly enough, in the United States, military and police uniforms do not confer masculinity, as they do among Cossacks and Hussars. One can as readily imagine women in our army uniform as men. To prove that he was all man, General Patton had to augment his battle costume with a pearl-handled revolver. (It is true, however, that he wrote poetry and may have felt the need to overcome this handicap.)

As to hair, masculinity is ambivalent. Long hair belongs to the style of frontier scouts and trappers, the most male of men. Yet "longhairs" is the name applied to intellectuals, a breed always suspected of sexual inauthenticity. Beards used to be a material evidence of maleness; today they are as frequently an appurtenance of masquerade.

In the last century the outdoors represented genuine hazards. It took self-reliance, identifiable with masculinity (though the pioneer mother had it, too), to venture very far from the farm or town.

Today there are still risky occupations–piloting spaceships, handling nuclear substances–but these trades have become increasingly technical and depersonalized. As for the rugged outdoors, it is used chiefly for sports; and a vacation at a ranch or ski lodge, or shooting lions in Kenya, is about as hazardous as a trip to the Riviera.

The outdoors, representing once-hostile nature, has been transformed into a stage set. Masculinity in the American sense has thus lost its locale and, perhaps, its reason for being. On the neon-lighted lonesome prairie, masculinity is a matter of certain traditional costume details: the cowboy hat, jeans, and guitar. It has become clear that the traditional traits of the man's man (and the ladies' man) can be put on, too. One *plays* manliness, with or without dark goggles.

Big-game hunters, mountain climbers, horsemen, and other representative male types are actors in a charade of nostalgia. Old masculine pursuits, like baseball or wrestling, when carried on at night under the glare of fluorescent tubes, come to resemble spectacles on television and wind up in the living room. In the epoch of the picture window, outdoors and indoors have lost their separateness.

In modern mass societies the uniforms of all kinds of cults compete with one another. Masculinity is one of these cults, and to create an impression the practitioner of maleness must stand out in a crowd. Persons with other interests are not disposed to make an issue of their sex. Only psychiatrists and sociologists complain that boys and girls today look alike and are often mistaken for each other. Even tough adolescents, like members of big-city gangs, don't mind if their girls wear the same shirts and jeans as the men. All are more concerned with identifying themselves as outsiders than as males and females.

Masculinity today is a myth that has turned into a comedy. A ten-gallon hat still seems to bestow upon its wearer the old male attributes of taciturnity, resourcefulness, courage, and love of solitude. At the same time, the virility of the cowboy and the truck driver, like that of the iceman of yesterday, is a joke that everyone sees through.

A person uncertain of his sexual identity dresses up in boots, bandanna, and riding breeches not so much to fool the public as to parade his ambiguity. Those who have gone over the line may advertise their desires for male company by wearing a beard in addition to sheepskins. Women can be masculine too, of course, in the degree necessary to make them irresistible to feminine men.

Hemingway, who constantly kept the issue of masculinity alive in his writings, flaunted both the look of the outdoor man and his presumed character qualities of daring, self-detachment, contempt for the overcivilized, and eagerness to court death.

Hemingway's he-man performance was, among other things, a means of combatting the American stereotype of the writer as a sissy. In the United States, the artist and man of ideas have always lived under the threat of having their masculinity impugned. Richard Hofstadter, in his *Anti-Intellectualism in American Life,* lists a dozen instances in which the "stigma of effeminacy" was branded upon intellectuals by political bullies, ranging from Tammany Hall leaders in the nineteenth century, who attacked reformers as "political hermaphrodites," to Communist Party hacks in the 1930s, who denounced independent writers as "scented whores." Evidently, it has always been possible to convince the common man that his intellectual superiors fall short of him in manliness.

To the overhanging charge of being contaminated by a lady-like occupation, Hemingway responded by injecting the romance of masculinity into the making of literature. At least as far as he was concerned, the sexual legitimacy of the male writer was to be put beyond question. Besides lining up with traditional outdoor types, such as bullfighters and deep-sea fishermen, Hemingway's strategy included identification with the new activist male image of the Depression decade: the leather-jacketed revolutionist allied with the peasant and factory worker. One might say that each of his novels originated in a new choice of male makeup.

Unfortunately, demonstrating his manhood was not enough for Hemingway. He found it necessary to challenge the masculinity of other writers. Like Theodore Roosevelt earlier in the century, he became an instance of the intellectual who slanders intellectuals generally, in the hope of putting himself right with the regular guys. During the Spanish Civil War he forgot himself to the extent of sneering publicly at Leon Trotsky for remaining at his typewriter in Mexico, implying that the former chief of the Red Army lacked the manliness to go to Spain and fight. He, himself, of course, went to Spain to write. In *For Whom the Bell Tolls* he identified himself with the dynamiter Jordan who also shook the earth by his love feats in a sleeping bag.

Thirty years ago not all of Hemingway's contemporaries were convinced that he had established his masculinity through displaying an appetite for violence, sex, and death. In *no thanks,* e. e. cummings translated Hemingway's romance of maleness back into the daydreams of boyhood:

> what does little Ernest croon
> in his death at afternoon?
> (kow dow r 2 bul retoinis
> wus de woids uf lil Oinis)

To cummings, Hemingway's heroics were not only childish ("lil Oi-nis") but feminine ("kow dow r").

The post-Hemingway he-man has labored under the handi-cap of a masculinity that is generally recognized to be a masquer-ade. The adventurer living dangerously has disintegrated into the tongue-in-cheek élan of James Bond. Neither at work nor at home is maleness any longer endowed with glamour or privilege. The cosmonaut is less a birdman than a specialist minding his signals and dials. The father who has entered into a diapering partnership with his wife has nothing in common with the patriarch. To the public of Norman Mailer (more male?), the outdoor rig (Mailer in sea captain's cap on the jacket of *Advertisements for Myself*) and chronicles of supersex are suspect, both psychologically and as playing to the gallery. It is no secret that a Bogartean toughness with women may represent the opposite of male self-confidence.

The mass media exploit the ambiguity of the male role and the sexual sophistication that goes with the increasing awareness of it. In male comedy teams, one of the partners almost invariably plays the "wife," confident that the audience will know when to smirk. Analysts of mass culture speak of the decline of the Ameri-can male and of the "masculinity crisis" as topics capable of arous-ing libidinous responses. The public is given the image of luscious females starving in vain for the attention of men, and of men who, egged on and deprived by frigid seductresses, end by falling into each other's arms.

Masculinity-building is urged, a theme which the media are not slow to adapt for their own purposes. Masculinity is the alfalfa peddled in Marlboro Country. It is the essence of worn leather laced with campfire smoke that provides the aroma of the man of distinction. It also comes in powder form, none genuine without the Shaggy Dog on the wrapping.

To those who resent the fact that their pretension to masculin-ity is not taken seriously, one means is available for gaining re-spect: violence. The victim of rape is not inclined to question the virility of her assailant.

The relation between masculinity that has been put into doubt and violence reveals itself most clearly in the recent history of the Civil Rights movement. The black has derived from white America the lesson that physical force is the mark of manhood. White society is "the Man," whose insignia of power are the club, the whip, the bloodhounds. The presence of the Man impeaches the masculinity of the young black and demands that he prove himself. He becomes full grown when he resolves to fight the Man. To confront the Man, the black militant has resurrected the figure of the radical activist of the thirties, the model of Hemingway's he-man, honor-bound to risk his life in physical combat.

An article in the *New York Times Magazine* on the Black Panthers is illustrated by photographs of its two leaders. Both wear the traditional leather jackets and berets of the Left fighters of thirty years ago—these could be photographs of two Lincoln Brigade volunteers. A statement by one of the Panthers touches the philosophical essence of the romantic conception of masculinity: to be a man one must dare to die. "The ghetto black," said Bobby Seale, "isn't afraid to stand up to the cops, because he already lives with violence. He expects to die any day."

In our culture all human attributes tend to be over-defined and become a basis of self-consciousness. The behavioral sciences collaborate with the mass media in making a man anxious about his sex status; both then provide him with models of aggressiveness by which to correct his deficiencies. Yet the present uneasiness about masculinity, coupled with theatrical devices for attaining it, may be more harmful than any actual curtailment of manliness discovered by researchers and editorialists. The real damage may lie in the remedy rather than the ailment, since the desire to have one's masculinity acknowledged may lead, as we have seen, to absurd postures and acts of force. It is hard to believe that Americans would be worse off by becoming more gentle. Nor that mildness in manners and social relations would make them less manly. In the real world nothing is altogether what it is. True maleness is never without its vein of femininity. The Greeks understood this and made it the theme of their tales of sexual metamorphosis, the remarkable account of Hercules, of all men, taking on temporarily the character of a woman and wearing women's clothes. Total masculinity is an ideal of the frustrated, not a fact of biology. With the cult of masculinity put aside, maleness might have a better chance to develop in the United States.

REFLECTING ON MEANING

1. Rosenberg notes the prominent role of the masculine "ideal" in past societies and describes the unique American version of this ideal. This masculine ideal, Rosenberg claims, has "lost its locale and, perhaps, its reason for being." What does he mean? According to Rosenberg, what has happened to masculinity in America?

To what extent does the masculine ideal still play a significant role? To whom is it important?

2. What does Rosenberg mean when he describes masculinity as "a myth that has turned into a comedy" and as "a joke that everyone sees through"? Is he suggesting that the "real men" of the past have become the "wimps" of today? Or that real men never existed? Or that the masculine ideal is a fantasy? What exactly, in Rosenberg's view, has changed? How do you know? Why is masculinity a joke? What is comic about it?

3. The solution to the problem of masculine identity, as Rosenberg sees it, is contained in the statement, "Total masculinity is an ideal of the frustrated, not a fact of biology." What does he mean? Why does he urge that "the cult of masculinity be put aside"? What is the difference between masculinity and maleness? Why does Rosenberg prefer maleness to masculinity? Do you agree with his solution? Why or why not?

EXPLORING RHETORICAL STRATEGIES

1. What is the extended metaphor that Rosenberg uses to depict the current state of masculinity in America? How many instances of this metaphor can you identify in his essay? In what ways does this metaphor help Rosenberg convey his point? How does it help unify the essay?

2. How is the title of the essay significant? Did you grasp its significance before reading the essay? What did it lead you to expect in the ensuing discussion? What does the word *style* suggest to you? What about the word *cult*? How do these words transform the word *masculinity* in the title?

3. This essay originally appeared in *Vogue* in 1967. Knowing what you do of the sixties and of *Vogue,* can you speculate on the characteristics of Rosenberg's audience? How would you describe it? How is this discussion of masculinity appropriate for its audience?

He's a Feminist, But...

MARY KAY BLAKELY

In this humorous essay from the October 1982 Ms. *magazine, Mary Kay Blakely discusses how "Fred, the Feminist Man" represents numerous men who have changed some of their sexist behaviors toward women, yet who still do not possess true empathy for the female experience. She suggests that equality between the sexes cannot be realized until men develop a true appreciation for how women feel.*

I was shocked to learn that the first stage of this wave of feminism is over. Men are rumored to have changed. Everywhere I look—newspaper headlines, conference reports, coffee-break gossip—evidence piles up: a Bell Telephone employee not only asked for paternity leave last year, but he actually used it; the chair of a men's conference on the East Coast enthusiastically announced that women don't need to be angry any more—men are allies now—and declared the beginning of "no-fault liberation"; on the West Coast, groups of men are attending classes with their toddlers and are learning to speak in little tongues; and a friend wrote recently that her physician/husband has even "learned to pick up some of his things."

But here I am, still standing on the sidelines at halftime, still holding my unopened bag of confetti in my hand. My mind is preoccupied with the problem of Fred, the Feminist Man. While Fred has made considerable progress on issues like violence against women and equal pay and child care, I cannot see that he has yet developed any real empathy. I dread what the next 10 years might mean for women if men continue to labor under this handicap.

"Hit the ball and drag Fred," my friend sighed, summarizing our discussion of a "nice guy" who didn't quite "get it." She was referring to the punch line about the golfer who returned home two hours late from his game and explained to his wife that his companion, Fred, had a case of sunstroke and collapsed on the ninth hole.

"It was awful," he shook his head sadly. "For the next nine holes, it was 'hit the ball and drag Fred, hit the ball and drag Fred.'"

Fred is the generous, likable man who genuinely wants the approval of the women he admires and takes pride in the label "feminist." Much of his behavior has changed, it's true. He no longer calls the women he works with "honey" or "toots." He makes his own coffee. Pampers do not frighten him. But when these changes spring solely from his desire to please, there's no guarantee that actual comprehension has happened. Fred understands feminism only as a set of rules: Don't call women "girls." Let them open their own doors (sometimes). Let them have their own names and credit cards. Don't beat them. Don't rape them.

But where Fred has managed to grasp some of the particulars of the Women's Movement, the whole picture still eludes him. In other words, he has learned something, but still understands very little. It's a failure of empathy.

As a result, every new issue comes as a surprise. ("I can understand equal pay, but why do you need your own checking account? Don't you trust me?") Every time the allied front moves forward an inch, Fred has apoplexy and expires from the game. A "time out" must be called to revive him and explain.

This Fredness is a serious drain on energy. I remember once, after a long public discussion of rape (What *is* rape, really, and do women like it at all, and aren't women ever responsible for it?), there was a strong feeling of mutuality among the women and men who worked so hard to understand one another. Shortly afterward, I published a column that destroyed the equanimity. It was on sexual harassment. Friends reported that confusion broke out in private conversations with the significant men in their lives. These men, some of whom were in consciousness-raising groups, or belonged to organizations with names like Men Against Violence Against Women, took serious exception to my objections to men's commonplace behavior.

The discussions, as it turned out, proved to be fruitful. The women reported that lights had dawned, comprehensions were reached. It was another good "learning experience."

At first, I readied my bag of confetti. Here, five good men had traveled through surprise and affront and hurt and moved, bumpily, and unsteadily, toward recognition. Another victory, another hurdle surmounted, another issue set to rest. Yes, harassment offended women. Yes, it was a male power play.

But why did it take five separate women five separate hours to convince these men of the same truth they had argued the year before? The truth was cast in a different environment—from the devastating landscape of rape to the common fields of harassment—but the truth was the same.

The whole experience left me in despair, wishing to move on to new truths—pressing, urgent truths we need to discover about war and the earth and our places in it. Instead, we are still wallowing around arguing the same truths over and over and over. These men are naming the cost of liberation: few men can learn and accept equality without exhausting some woman in the process. These are the terms of change.

So I'm keeping my confetti bagged until I see that sign of self-learning, that glimmer of independent thought. Rather than teaching men "things"—details, items, facts—one simple clue should suffice: "Imagine that you are me." Let all assumptions about women be filtered through that phrase. Think of your masculinity, your sexuality, your livelihood, your education, your relationships, through the light of that idea. Imagine yourself as your wife/mother/daughter/sister/lover/secretary/waitress. This is the method that women have used to survive for centuries, the uncanny ability to divine and imagine and recognize men's needs—from protecting their egos to memorizing their underwear size.

I'd like to think that men might learn to think like a woman. My "liberation" depends on it.

Imagine what life would be like if men developed that ability. Suppose the visible, external changes were to evolve into an invisible, internal consciousness. Fred would be able to see how every detail contributes to the whole: how harassment is a dangerous tentacle of rape, how language is an expression of the oppression we bear; how the way he thinks of his mother has everything to do with the way he thinks of me; how unquestioned manhood and fatherland loyalties will lead inevitably to war.

In the meantime, Fredness threatens to overwhelm us.

A friend of mine has been changing diapers for years without applause, but she was recently complimented on her husband's ability to do the same. Yes, it was wonderful, she agreed. "And next week," she said, in a voice tellingly drained of enthusiasm, "we're going to learn how to call the baby-sitter." Hit the ball and drag Fred.

REFLECTION ON MEANING

1. According to Blakely, "Men are rumored to have changed." In what ways have men changed their behaviors? Who is "Fred, the Feminist Man," and what is "Fredness"? Fred labors under what "handicap"? What is Fred's understanding of feminism? Why has Fred changed his behavior toward women?

2. Blakely expresses her frustration that "we are still wallowing around arguing the same truths over and over and over." What are these "same truths," and what "new truths" do we need to seek? Rather than teaching men "things" or rules for nonsexist behavior, what does Blakely suggest that men need to imagine?

3. Can men ever learn to "think like a woman"? Is this question re-inscribing an essentialist view of male and female thinking? What would life be like if men developed empathy for female experience? Is this even possible? How could empathy for a female's position change male behavior? According to Blakely, why isn't a change in behavior enough?

EXPLORING RHETORICAL STRATEGIES

1. What rhetorical effect does Blakely's use of the joke "hit the ball and drag Fred" have on her essay? How does her use of the term *Fredness* advance her argument? Does her humorous and satiric tone contribute to the essay's overall effectiveness? What game metaphor does she use to frame her essay? What words and phrases contribute to this metaphor?

2. Blakely begins her essay with several examples of how men have changed their behavior toward women. She then problematizes her discussion by questioning the reasons for these behavior changes. Do the examples that she provides advance her argument? Why does she end her essay with the narrative about the husband who has learned to change diapers but doesn't know how to call the babysitter?

3. "He's a Feminist, But..." was first published in *Ms.* magazine in 1982. How might Blakely's argument be particularly appropriate for this essay's original audience? How might a contemporary audience's response be different? How might it be the same?

Chapter 3 _____

FEMININITY AND CULTURE

Woman as Other

SIMONE DE BEAUVOIR

*In this selection, philosopher Simone de Beauvoir explores
the historical oppression of women. She examines the concepts
of* woman *and* man *in relation to the larger concept of*
humanity *and concludes that women's status is not simply a
matter of definition but a fundamental way of thinking that
has political consequences.*

What is a woman?
To state the question is, to me, to suggest, at once,
a preliminary answer. The fact that I ask it is in itself significant. A man would never get the notion of writing a book on the
peculiar situation of the human male. But if I wish to define myself,
I must first of all say: "I am a woman"; on this truth must be based
all further discussion. A man never begins by presenting himself as
an individual of a certain sex; it goes without saying that he is a
man. The terms *masculine* and *feminine* are used symmetrically only
as a matter of form, as on legal papers. In actuality the relation of
the two sexes is not quite like that of two electrical poles, for man
represents both the positive and the neutral, as is indicated by the
common use of *man* to designate human beings in general; whereas
woman represents only the negative, defined by limiting criteria,
without reciprocity. In the midst of an abstract discussion it is vex-
ing to hear a man say: "You think thus and so because you are a
woman"; but I know that my only defense is to reply: "I think thus
and so because it is true," thereby removing my subjective self

from the argument. It would be out of the question to reply: "And you think the contrary because you are a man," for it is understood that the fact of being a man is no peculiarity. A man is in the right in being a man; it is the woman who is in the wrong. It amounts to this: just as for the ancients there was an absolute vertical with reference to which the oblique was defined, so there is an absolute human type, the masculine. Woman has ovaries, a uterus; these peculiarities imprison her in her subjectivity, circumscribe her within the limits of her own nature. It is often said that she thinks with her glands. Man superbly ignores the fact that his anatomy also includes glands, such as the testicles, and that they secrete hormones. He thinks of his body as a direct and normal connection with the world, which he believes he apprehends objectively, whereas he regards the body of woman as a hindrance, a prison, weighed down by everything peculiar to it. "The female is a female by virtue of a certain *lack* of qualities," said Aristotle; "we should regard the female nature as afflicted with a natural defectiveness." And St. Thomas for his part pronounced woman to be an "imperfect man," an "incidental" being. This is symbolized in Genesis where Eve is depicted as made from what Bossuet called "a supernumerary bone" of Adam.

Thus humanity is male and man defines woman not in herself but as relative to him; she is not regarded as an autonomous being. Michelet writes: "Woman, the relative being...." And Benda is most positive in his *Rapport d'Uriel:* "The body of man makes sense in itself quite apart from that of woman, whereas the latter seems wanting in significance by itself.... Man can think of himself without woman. She cannot think of herself without man." And she is simply what man decrees; thus she is called "the sex," by which is meant that she appears essentially to the male as a sexual being. For him she is sex—absolute sex, no less. She is defined and differentiated with reference to man and not he with reference to her; she is the incidental, the inessential as opposed to the essential. He is the Subject, he is the Absolute—she is the Other.

The category of the *Other* is as primordial as consciousness itself. In the most primitive societies, in the most ancient mythologies, one finds the expression of a duality—that of the Self and the Other. This duality was not originally attached to the division of the sexes; it was not dependent upon any empirical facts. It is revealed in such works as that of Granet on Chinese thought and those of Dumézil on the East Indies and Rome. The feminine element was at first no more involved in such pairs as Varuna-Mitra, Uranus-Zeus, Sun-Moon, and Day-Night than it was in the contrasts between Good and Evil, lucky and unlucky auspices, right and left, God and Lucifer. Otherness is a fundamental category of human thought.

Thus it is that no group ever sets itself up as the One without at once setting up the Other over against itself. If three travelers chance to occupy the same compartment, that is enough to make vaguely hostile "others" out of all the rest of the passengers on the train. In small-town eyes all persons not belonging to the village are "strangers" and suspect; to the native of a country all who inhabit other countries are "foreigners"; Jews are "different" for the anti-Semite, Negroes are "inferior" for American racists, aborigines are "natives" for colonists, proletarians are the "lower class" for the privileged.

Lévi-Strauss, at the end of a profound work on the various forms of primitive societies, reaches the following conclusion: "Passage from the state of Nature to the state of Culture is marked by man's ability to view biological relations as a series of contrasts; duality, alternation, opposition, and symmetry, whether under definite or vague forms, constitute not so much phenomena to be explained as fundamental and immediately given data of social reality." These phenomena would be incomprehensible if in fact human society were simply a *Mitsein* or fellowship based on solidarity and friendliness. Things become clear, on the contrary, if, following Hegel, we find in consciousness itself a fundamental hostility toward every other consciousness; the subject can be posed only in being opposed—he sets himself up as the essential, as opposed to the other, the inessential, the object.

But the other consciousness, the other ego, sets up a reciprocal claim. The native traveling abroad is shocked to find himself in turn regarded as a "stranger" by the natives of neighboring countries. As a matter of fact, wars, festivals, trading, treaties, and contests among tribes, nations, and classes tend to deprive the concept *Other* of its absolute sense and to make manifest its relativity; willynilly, individuals and groups are forced to realize the reciprocity of their relations. How is it, then, that this reciprocity has not been recognized between the sexes, that one of the contrasting terms is set up as the sole essential, denying any relativity in regard to its correlative and defining the latter as pure otherness? Why is it that women do not dispute male sovereignty? No subject will readily volunteer to become the object, the inessential; it is not the Other who, in defining himself as the Other, establishes the One. The Other is posed as such by the One in defining himself as the One. But if the Other is not to regain the status of being the One, he must be submissive enough to accept this alien point of view. Whence comes this submission in the case of woman?

There are, to be sure, other cases in which a certain category has been able to dominate another completely for a time. Very often this privilege depends upon inequality of numbers—the majority imposes its rule upon the minority or persecutes it. But women are not a minority, like the American Negroes or the Jews; there are as many women as men on earth. Again, the two groups concerned have often been originally independent; they may have been formerly unaware of each other's existence, or perhaps they recognized each other's autonomy. But a historical event has resulted in the subjugation of the weaker by the stronger. The scattering of the Jews, the introduction of slavery into America, the conquests of imperialism are examples in point. In these cases the oppressed retained at least the memory of former days; they possessed in common a past, a tradition, sometimes a religion or a culture.

The parallel drawn by Bebel between women and the proletariat is valid in that neither ever formed a minority nor a separate collective unit of mankind. And instead of a single historical event it is in both cases a historical development that explains their status as a class and accounts for the membership of *particular individuals* in that class. But proletarians have not always existed, whereas there have always been women. They are women in virtue of their anatomy and physiology. Throughout history they have always been subordinated to men, and hence their dependency is not the result of a historical event or a social change—it was not something that *occurred*. The reason why otherness in this case seems to be an absolute is in part that it lacks the contingent or incidental nature of historical facts. A condition brought about at a certain time can be abolished at some other time, as the Negroes of Haiti and others have proved; but it might seem that a natural condition is beyond the possibility of change. In truth, however, the nature of things is no more immutably given, once for all, than is historical reality. If woman seems to be the inessential which never becomes the essential, it is because she herself fails to bring about this change. Proletarians say "We"; Negroes also. Regarding themselves as subjects, they transform the bourgeois, the whites, into "others." But women do not say "We," except at some congress of feminists of similar formal demonstration; men say "women," and women use the same word in referring to themselves. They do not authentically assume a subjective attitude. The proletarians have accomplished the revolution in Russia, the Negroes in Haiti, the Indochinese are battling for it in Indochina; but the women's effort has never been anything more than a symbolic agitation. They have gained only what men have been willing to grant; they have taken nothing, they have only received.

The reason for this is that women lack concrete means for organizing themselves into a unit which can stand face to face with the correlative unit. They have no past, no history, no religion of their own; and they have no such solidarity of work and interest as that of the proletariat. They are not even promiscuously herded together in the way that creates community feeling among the American Negroes, the ghetto Jews, the workers of Saint-Denis, or the factory hands of Renault. They live dispersed among the males, attached through residence, housework, economic condition, and social standing to certain men—fathers or husbands—more firmly than they are to other women. If they belong to the bourgeoisie, they feel solidarity with men of that class, not with proletarian women; if they are white, their allegiance is to white men, not to Negro women. The proletariat can propose to massacre the ruling class, and a sufficiently fanatical Jew or Negro might dream of getting sole possession of the atomic bomb and making humanity wholly Jewish or black; but woman cannot even dream of exterminating the males. The bond that unites her to her oppressors is not comparable to any other. The division of the sexes is a biological fact, not an event in human history. Male and female stand opposed within a primordial *Mitsein,* and woman has not broken it. The couple is a fundamental unity with its two halves riveted together, and the cleavage of society along the line of sex is impossible. Here is to be found the basic trait of woman: she is the Other in a totality of which the two components are necessary to one another.

One could suppose that this reciprocity might have facilitated the liberation of woman. When Hercules sat at the feet of Omphale and helped with her spinning, his desire for her held him captive; but why did she fail to gain a lasting power? To revenge herself on Jason, Medea killed their children; and this grim legend would seem to suggest that she might have obtained a formidable influence over him through his love for his offspring. In *Lysistrata* Aristophanes gaily depicts a band of women who joined forces to gain social ends through the sexual needs of their men; but this is only a play. In the legend of the Sabine women, the latter soon abandoned their plan of remaining sterile to punish their ravishers. In truth woman has not been socially emancipated through man's need—sexual desire and the desire for offspring—which makes the male dependent for satisfaction upon the female.

Master and slave, also, are united by a reciprocal need, in this case economic, which does not liberate the slave. In the relation of master to slave the master does not make a point of the need that he has for the other; he has in his grasp the power of satisfying this need through his own action; whereas the slave, in his dependent condition, his hope and fear, is quite conscious of the need he has for his master. Even if the need is at bottom equally urgent for both, it always works in favor of the oppressor and against the oppressed. That is why the liberation of the working class, for example, has been slow.

Now, woman has always been man's dependent, if not his slave; the two sexes have never shared the world in equality. And even today woman is heavily handicapped, though her situation is beginning to change. Almost nowhere is her legal status the same as man's, and frequently it is much to her disadvantage. Even when her rights are legally recognized in the abstract, long-standing custom prevents their full expression in the mores. In the economic sphere men and women can almost be said to make up two castes; other things being equal, the former hold the better jobs, get higher wages, and have more opportunity for success than their new competitors. In industry and politics men have a great many more positions and they monopolize the most important posts. In addition to all this, they enjoy a traditional prestige that the education of children tends in every way to support, for the present enshrines the past—and in the past all history has been made by men. At the present time, when women are beginning to take part in the affairs of the world, it is still a world that belongs to men—they have no doubt of it at all and women have scarcely any. To decline to be the Other, to refuse to be a party to the deal—this would be for women to renounce all the advantages conferred upon them by their alliance with the superior caste. Man-the-sovereign will provide woman-the-liege with material protection and will undertake the moral justification of her existence; thus she can evade at once both economic risk and the metaphysical risk of a liberty in which ends and aims must be contrived without assistance. Indeed, along with the ethical urge of each individual to affirm his subjective existence, there is also the temptation to forgo liberty and become a thing. This is an inauspicious road, for he who takes it—passive, lost, ruined—becomes henceforth the creature of another's will, frustrated in his transcendence and deprived of every value. But it is an easy road; on it one avoids the strain involved in undertaking an authentic existence. When man makes of woman the *Other,* he may, then, expect her to manifest deep-seated tendencies toward complicity. Thus, woman may fail to lay claim to the status of subject because she lacks definite resources, because she feels the necessary bond that ties her to man regardless of reciprocity, and because she is often very well pleased with her role as the *Other.*

REFLECTING ON MEANING

1. De Beauvoir argues that the act of defining oneself is different for women and men. What is the difference? Where must a woman's definition start? Why? Why doesn't a man have to begin defining himself in this way?

2. What does it mean to define man as the "subject" and woman as the "other"? What is de Beauvoir suggesting about the relationship of men and women to each other and to humanity in general? What is the definition of *human* and *humanity* according to this system?

3. As a social group defined as "other," what do women have in common with ethnic minorities and the working class? What are the differences? What has caused the oppression of each of these groups? What allows some of them to unite to resist oppression? What makes women's oppression a "natural condition" rather than the result of a historical event? Does this suggest that women cannot hope or seek to overcome their oppression? Why or why not?

EXPLORING RHETORICAL STRATEGIES

1. "Woman as Other" was published in 1949 as a chapter in de Beauvoir's *The Second Sex*. What does the title of the book suggest about the status of women? How does the chapter reprinted here connect to this idea? What other topics might you expect de Beauvoir to discuss in the remaining chapters of her book? Why?

2. Who is de Beauvoir's intended audience? How do you know? Do you think she expected her audience to resist or to accept her observations on women's status? How do you know? Would readers today respond in the same way? Why or why not?

3. What kind of persona does de Beauvoir adopt? What does the type of evidence she uses tell you about her persona? Why doesn't she use personal experiences, anecdotes, and interviews to make her case? How is her persona appropriate for her intended audience?

Psychology Constructs
the Female

NAOMI WEISSTEIN

Although scientific research may seem to offer irrefutable proof of natural differences in men's and women's behavior, Guggenheim-winning philosopher of psychology Naomi Weisstein suggests otherwise. In a carefully crafted refutation of the "evidence," Weisstein argues that the most basic assumptions of psychological research are misinformed. Furthermore, she contends, research in biology and anthropology has been selectively applied in order to support misleading conceptions of the behavior considered natural to women and men.

It is an implicit assumption that the area of psychology which concerns itself with personality has the onerous but necessary task of describing the limits of human possibility. Thus when we are about to consider the liberation of women, we naturally look to psychology to tell us what "true" liberation would mean: what would give women the freedom to fulfill their own intrinsic natures. Psychologists have set about describing the true natures of women with a certainty and a sense of their own infallibility rarely found in the secular world. Bruno Bettelheim, of the University of Chicago, tells us that

> We must start with the realization that, as much as women want to be good scientists or engineers, they want first and foremost to be womanly companions of men and to be mothers.

Erik Erikson of Harvard University, upon noting that young women often ask whether they can "have an identity before they know whom they will marry, and for whom they will make a home," explains somewhat elegiacally that

> Much of a young woman's identity is already defined in her kind of attractiveness and in the selectivity of her search for the man (or men) by whom she wishes to be sought. . . .

Mature womanly fulfillment, for Erikson, rests on the fact that a woman's

... somatic design harbors an "inner space" destined to bear the offspring of chosen men, and with it, a biological, psychological, and ethical commitment to take care of human infancy.

Some psychiatrists even see the acceptance of woman's role by women as a solution to social problems "Woman is nurturance...," writes Joseph Rheingold (1964), a psychiatrist at the Harvard Medical School, "... anatomy decrees the life of a woman ... when women grow up without dread of their biological functions and without subversion by feminist doctrine, and therefore enter upon motherhood with a sense of fulfillment and altruistic sentiment, we shall attain the goal of a good life and a secure world in which to live it."

These views from men who are assumed to be experts reflect, in a surprisingly transparent way, the cultural consensus. They not only assert that a woman is defined by her ability to attract men, they see no alternative definitions. They think that the definition of a woman in terms of a man is the way it should be; and they back it up with psychosexual incantation and biological ritual curses. A woman has an identity if she is attractive enough to obtain a man, and thus, a home; for this will allow her to set about her life's task of "joyful altruism and nurturance."

Business certainly does not disagree. If views such as Bettelheim's and Erikson's do indeed have something to do with real liberation for women, then seldom in human history has so much money and effort been spent on helping a group of people realize their true potential. Clothing, cosmetics, home furnishings, are multi-million dollar businesses: if you don't like investing in firms that make weaponry and flaming gasoline, then there's a lot of hard cash in "inner space." Sheet and pillowcase manufacturers are concerned to fill this inner space:

Mother, for a while this morning, I thought I wasn't cut out for married life. Hank was late for work and forgot his apricot juice and walked out without kissing me, and when I was all alone I started crying. But then the postman came with the sheets and towels you sent, that look like big bandana handkerchiefs, and you know what I thought? That those big red and blue handkerchiefs are for girls like me to dry their tears on so they can get busy and do what a housewife has to do. Throw open the windows and start getting the house ready, and the dinner, maybe clean the silver and put new geraniums in the box. *Everything to be ready for him when he walks through that door.*[1]

Of course, it is not only the sheet and pillowcase manufacturers, the cosmetics industry, the home furnishings salesmen who profit from and make use of the cultural definitions of man and woman. The example above is blatantly and overtly pitched to a particular kind of sexist stereotype: the child nymph. But almost all aspects of the media are normative, that is, they have to do with the ways in which beautiful people, or just folks, or ordinary Americans, should live their lives. They define the possible; and the possibilities are usually in terms of what is male and what is female. Men and women alike are waiting for Hank, the Silva Thins man, to walk back through that door.

It is an interesting but limited exercise to show that psychologists and psychiatrists embrace these sexist norms of our culture, that they do not see beyond the most superficial and stultifying media conceptions of female nature, and that their ideas of female nature serve industry and commerce so well. Just because it's good for business doesn't mean it's wrong. What I will show is that it *is wrong;* that there isn't the tiniest shred of evidence that these fantasies of servitude and childish dependence have anything to do with women's true potential; that the idea of the nature of human possibility which rests on the accidents of individual development of genitalia, on what is possible today because of what happened yesterday, on the fundamentalist myth of sex organ causality, has strangled and deflected psychology so that it is relatively useless in describing, explaining, or predicting humans and their behavior.

It then goes without saying that present psychology is less than worthless in contributing to a vision which could truly liberate—men as well as women.

The central argument of my paper, then, is this. Psychology has nothing to say about what women are really like, what they need and what they want, essentially because psychology does not know. I want to stress that this failure is not limited to women; rather, the kind of psychology which has addressed itself to how people act and who they are has failed to understand, in the first place, why people act the way they do, and certainly failed to understand what might make them act differently.

The kind of psychology which has addressed itself to these questions divides into two professional areas: academic personality research, and clinical psychology and psychiatry. The basic reason for failure is the same in both these areas: the central assumption for most psychologists of human personality has been that human behavior rests on an individual and inner dynamic, perhaps fixed in infancy, perhaps fixed by genitalia, perhaps simply arranged in a rather immovable cognitive network. But this assumption is rapidly losing ground as personality psychologists fail again and again to get consistency in the assumed personalities of their subjects. Meanwhile, the evidence is collecting that what a person does and who she believes herself to be, will in general be a function of what people around her expect her to be, and what the overall situation in which she is acting implies that she is. Compared to the influence of the social context within which a person lives, his or her history and "traits," as well as biological makeup, may simply be random variations, "noise" superimposed on the true signal which can predict behavior.

Some academic personality psychologists are at least looking at the counter evidence and questioning their theories; no such corrective is occurring in clinical psychology and psychiatry: Freudians and neo-Freudians, nudie-marathonists and touchy-feelies, classicists and swingers, clinicians and psychiatrists, simply refuse to look at the evidence against their theory and practice. And they support their theory and practice with stuff so transparently biased as to have absolutely no standing as empirical evidence.

To summarize: the first reason for psychology's failure to understand what people are and how they act is that psychology has looked for inner traits when it should have been looking for social context; the second reason for psychology's failure is that the theoreticians of personality have generally been clinicians and psychiatrists, and they have never considered it necessary to have evidence in support of their theories.

Theory Without Evidence

Let us turn to this latter cause of failure first: the acceptance by psychiatrists and clinical psychologists of theory without evidence. If we inspect the literature of personality, it is immediately obvious that the bulk of it is written by clinicians and psychiatrists, and that the major support for their theories is "years of intensive clinical experience." This is a tradition started by Freud. His "insights" occurred during the course of his work with his patients. Now there is nothing wrong with such an approach to theory *formulation;* a person is free to make up theories with any inspiration that works: divine revelation, intensive clinical practice, a random numbers table. But he/she is not free to claim any validity for his/her theory until it has been tested and confirmed. But theories are treated in no such tentative way in ordinary clinical practice. Consider Freud. What he thought constituted evidence violated the most minimal conditions of scientific rigor. In *The Sexual Enlightenment of Children,* the classic document which is supposed to demonstrate empirically the existence of a castration complex and its connection to a phobia, Freud based his analysis on the reports of the father of the little boy, himself in therapy, and a devotee of Freudian theory. I really don't have to comment further on the contamination in this kind of evidence. It is remarkable that only recently has Freud's classic theory on the sexuality of women—the notion of the double orgasm—been actually tested physiologically and found just plain wrong. Now those who claim that fifty years of psychoanalytic experience constitute evidence enough of the essential truths of Freud's theory should ponder the robust health of the double orgasm. Did women, until Masters and Johnson,[2] believe they were having two different kinds of orgasm? Did their psychiatrists badger them into reporting something that was not true? If so, were there other things they reported that were also not true? Did psychiatrists ever learn anything different than their theories had led them to believe? If clinical experience means anything at all, surely we should have been done with the double orgasm myth long before the Masters and Johnson studies.

But certainly, you may object, "years of intensive clinical experience" is the only reliable measure in a discipline which relies for its findings on insight, sensitivity, and intuition. The problem with insight, sensitivity, and intuition, is that they can confirm for all time the biases that one started with. People used to be absolutely convinced of their ability to tell which of their number were engaging in witchcraft. All it required was some sensitivity to the workings of the devil.

Years of intensive clinical experience is not the same thing as empirical evidence. The first thing an experimenter learns in any kind of experiment which involves humans is the concept of the "double blind." The term is taken from medical experiments, where one group is given a drug which is presumably supposed to change behavior in a certain way, and a control group is given a placebo. If the observers or the subjects know which group took which drug, the result invariably comes out on the positive side for the new drug. Only when it is not known which subject took which pill is validity remotely approximated. In addition, with judgments of human behavior, it is so difficult to precisely tie down just what behavior is going on, let alone what behavior should be expected, that one must test again and again the reliability of judgments. How many judges, blind, will agree in their observations? Can they replicate their own judgments at some later time? When, in actual practice, these judgment criteria are tested for clinical judgments, then we find that the judges cannot judge reliably, nor can they judge consistently: they do no better than chance in identifying which of a certain set of stories were written by men and which by women; which of a whole battery of clinical test results are the products of homosexuals and which are the products of heterosexuals, and which, of a battery of clinical test results *and* interviews (where questions are asked such as "Do you have delusions?") are products of psychotics, neurotics, psychosomatics, or normals. Lest this summary escape your notice, let me stress the implications of these findings. The ability of judges, chosen for their clinical expertise, to distinguish male heterosexuals from male homosexuals on the basis of three widely used clinical projective tests—the Rorschach, the TAT, and the MAP—was *no better than chance*. The reason this is such devastating news, of course, is that sexuality is supposed to be of fundamental importance in the deep dynamic of personality; if what is considered gross sexual deviance cannot be caught, then what are psychologists talking about when they, for example, claim that at the basis of paranoid psychosis is "latent homosexual panic"? They can't even identify what homosexual anything is, let alone "latent homosexual panic."[3] More frightening, expert clinicians cannot be consistent on what diagnostic category to assign to a person, again on the basis of both tests and interviews; a number of normals in the Little and Schneidman study were described as psychotic, in such categories as "schizophrenic with homosexual tendencies" or "schizoid character with depressive trends." But most disheartening, when the judges were asked to rejudge the test protocols some weeks later, their diagnoses of the same subjects on the basis of the same protocol differed markedly from their initial judgments. It is obvious that even simple descriptive conventions in clinical psychology cannot be consistently applied; if clinicians were as faulty in recognizing food from nonfood, they'd poison themselves and starve to death. That their descriptive conventions have any explanatory significance is therefore, of course, out of the question.

As a graduate student at Harvard some years ago, I was a member of a seminar which was asked to identify which of two piles of a clinical test, the TAT, had been written by males and which by females. Only four students out of twenty identified the piles correctly, and this was after one and a half months of intensively studying the differences between men and women. Since this result is below chance—that is, the result would occur by chance about four out of a thousand times—we may conclude that there is finally a consistency here; students are judging knowledgeably within the context of psychological teaching about the differences between men and women; the teachings themselves are simply erroneous.

You may argue that the theory may be scientifically "unsound" but at least it cures people. There is no evidence that it does. In 1952, Eysenck reported the results of what is called an "outcome of therapy" study of neurotics which showed that, of the patients who received psychoanalysis the improvement rate was 44 percent; of the patients who received psychotherapy the improvement rate was 64 percent; and of the patients who received no treatment at all the improvement rate was 72 percent. These findings have never been refuted; subsequently, later studies have confirmed the negative results of the Eysenck study. How can clinicians and psychiatrists, then, in all good conscience, continue to practice? Largely by ignoring these results and being careful not to do outcome-of-therapy studies. The attitude is nicely summarized by Rotter: "Research studies in psychotherapy tend to be concerned more with psychotherapeutic procedure and less with outcome.... To some extent, it reflects an interest in the psychotherapy situation as a kind of personality laboratory." Some laboratory.

The Social Context

Thus, since we can conclude that because clinical experience and tools can be shown to be worse than useless when tested for consistency, efficacy, agreement, and reliability, we can safely conclude that theories of a clinical nature advanced about women are also worse than useless. I want to turn now to the second major point in my paper, which is that, even when psychological theory is constructed so that it may be tested, and rigorous standards of evidence are used, it has become increasingly clear that in order to understand why people do what they do, and certainly in order to change what people do, psychologists must turn away from the theory of the causal nature of the inner dynamic and look to the social context within which individuals live.

Before examining the relevance of this approach to the question of women, let me first sketch the groundwork for this assertion.

In the first place, it is clear that personality tests never yield consistent predictions; a rigid authoritarian on one measure will be an unauthoritarian on the next. But the reason for this inconsistency is only now becoming clear, and it seems overwhelmingly to have much more to do with the social situation in which the subject finds him/herself than with the subject him/herself.

In a series of brilliant experiments, Rosenthal and his co-workers have shown that if one group of experimenters has one hypothesis about what they expect to find, and another group of experimenters has the opposite hypothesis, both groups will obtain results in accord with their hypotheses. The results obtained are not due to mishandling of data by biased experimenters; rather, somehow, the bias of the experimenter creates a changed environment in which subjects actually act differently. For instance, in one experiment, subjects were to assign numbers to pictures of men's faces, with high numbers representing the subject's judgment that the man in the picture was a successful person, and low numbers representing the subject's judgment that the man in the picture was an unsuccessful person. Prior to running the subjects, one group of experimenters was told that the subjects tended to rate the faces high; another group of experimenters was told that the subjects tended to rate the faces low. Each group of experimenters was instructed to follow precisely the same procedure: they were required to read to subjects a set of instructions, and to say *nothing else.* For the 375 subjects run, the results showed clearly that those subjects who performed the task with experimenters who expected high ratings gave high ratings, and those subjects who performed the task with experimenters who expected low ratings gave low ratings. How did this happen? The experimenters all used the same words; it was something in their conduct which made one group of subjects do one thing, and another group of subjects do another thing.[4]

The concreteness of the changed conditions produced by expectation is a fact, a reality: even with animal subjects, in two separate studies, those experimenters who were told that rats learning mazes had been especially bred for brightness obtained better learning from their rats than did experimenters believing their rats to have been bred for dullness. In a very recent study, Rosenthal and Jacobson (1968) extended their analysis to the natural classroom situation. Here, they tested a group of students and reported to the teachers that some among the students tested "showed great promise." Actually, the students so named had been selected on a random basis. Some time later, the experimenters retested the group of students: those students whose teachers had been told that they were "promising" showed real and dramatic increments in their IQs as compared to the rest of the students. Something in the conduct of the teachers towards those who the teachers believed to be the "bright" students, made those students brighter.

Thus, even in carefully controlled experiments, and with no outward or conscious difference in behavior, the hypotheses we start with will influence enormously the behavior of another organism. These studies are extremely important when assessing the validity of psychological studies of women. Since it is beyond doubt that most of us start with notions as to the nature of men and women, the validity of a number of observations of sex differences is questionable, even when these observations have been made under carefully controlled conditions. Second, and more important, the Rosenthal experiments point quite clearly to the influence of social expectation. In some extremely important ways, people are what you expect them to be, or at least they behave as you expect them to behave. Thus, if women, according to Bettelheim, want first and foremost to be good wives and mothers, it is extremely likely that this is what Bruno Bettelheim, and the rest of society, want them to be.

There is another series of brilliant social psychological experiments which point to the overwhelming effect of social context. These are the obedience experiments of Stanley Milgram in which subjects are asked to obey the orders of unknown experimenters, orders which carry with them the distinct possibility that the subject is killing somebody.

In Milgram's experiments, a subject is told that he/she is administering a learning experiment, and that he/she is to deal out shocks each time the other "subject" (in reality, a confederate of the experimenter) answers incorrectly. The equipment appears to provide graduated shocks ranging upwards from 15 volts through 450 volts; for each of four consecutive voltages there are verbal descriptions such as "mild shock," "danger, severe shock," and, finally, for the 435- and 450-volt switches, a red XXX marked over the switches. Each time the stooge answers incorrectly, the subject is supposed to increase the voltage. As the voltage increases, the stooge begins to cry in pain; he/she demands that the experiment stop; finally, he/she refuses to answer at all. When he/she stops responding, the experimenter instructs the subject to continue increasing the voltage; for each shock administered the stooge shrieks in agony. Under these conditions, about 62½ percent of the subjects administered shocks that they believed to be possibly lethal.

No tested individual differences between subjects predicted how many would continue to obey, and which would break off the experiment. When forty psychiatrists predicted how many of a group of 100 subjects would go on to give the lethal shock, their predictions were orders of magnitude below the actual percentages; most expected only one-tenth of one percent of the subjects to obey to the end.

But even though *psychiatrists* have no idea how people will behave in this situation, and even though individual differences do not predict which subjects will obey and which will not, it is easy to predict when subjects will be obedient and when they will be defiant. All the experimenter has to do is change the social situation. In a variant of Milgram's experiment, two stooges were present in addition to the "victim"; these worked along with the subject in administering electric shocks. When these two stooges refused to go on with the experiment, only 10 percent of the subjects continued to the maximum voltage. This is critical for personality theory. It says that behavior is predicted from the social situation, not from the individual history.

Finally, an ingenious experiment by Schachter and Singer showed that subjects injected with adrenaline which produces a state of physiological arousal in all but minor respects identical to that which occurs when subjects are extremely afraid, became euphoric when they were in a room with a stooge who was acting euphoric, and became extremely angry when they were placed in a room with a stooge who was acting extremely angry.

To summarize: If subjects under quite innocuous and noncoercive social conditions can be made to kill other subjects and under other types of social conditions will positively refuse to do so; if subjects can react to a state of physiological fear by becoming euphoric because there is somebody else around who is euphoric, or angry because there is somebody else around who is angry; if students become intelligent because teachers expect them to be intelligent, and rats run mazes better because experimenters are told the rats are bright, then it is obvious that a study of human behavior requires, first and foremost, a study of the social contexts within which people move, the expectations as to how they will behave, and the authority which tells them who they are and what they are supposed to do.

Biologically Based Theories

Biologists also have at times assumed they could describe the limits of human potential from their observations not of human, but of animal behavior. Here, as in psychology, there has been no end of theorizing about the sexes, again with a sense of absolute certainly surprising in "science." These theories fall into two major categories.

One category of theory argues that since females and males differ in their sex hormones, and sex hormones enter the brain, there must be innate behavioral differences. But the only thing this argument tells us is that there are differences in physiological state. The problem is whether these differences are at all relevant to behavior.

Consider, for example, differences in levels of the sex hormone testosterone. A man who calls himself Tiger[5] has recently argued that the greater quantities of testosterone found in human males as compared with human females (of a certain age group) determine innate differences in aggressiveness, competitiveness, dominance, ability to hunt, ability to hold public office, and so forth. But Tiger demonstrates in this argument the same manly and courageous refusal to be intimidated by evidence which we have already seen in our consideration of the clinical and psychiatric tradition. The evidence does not support his argument, and in most cases, directly contradicts it. Testosterone level does not seem to be related to hunting ability, dominance, or aggression, or competitiveness. As Storch has pointed out, all normal *male mammals* in the reproductive age group produce much greater quantities of testosterone than females; yet many of these males are neither hunters nor are they aggressive (e.g. rabbits). And, among some hunting mammals, such as the large cats, it turns out that more hunting is done by the female than the male. And there exist primate species where the female is clearly more aggressive, competitive, and dominant than the male. Thus, for some species, being female, and therefore, having less testosterone than the male of that species means hunting more, or being more aggressive, or being more dominant. Nor does having *more* testosterone preclude behavior commonly thought of as "female"; there exist primate species where females do not touch infants except to feed them; the males care for the infants at all times. So it is not clear what testosterone or any other sex-hormonal difference means for differences in nature, or sex-role behavior.

In other words, one can observe identical types of behavior which have been associated with sex (e.g. "mothering") in males and females, despite known differences in physiological state, i.e. sex hormones, genitalia, etc. What about the converse to this? That is, can one obtain differences in behavior given a single physiological state? The answer is overwhelmingly yes, not only as regards non-sex-specific hormones (as in the Schachter and Singer experiment cited above), but also as regards gender itself. Studies of hermaphrodites with the same diagnosis (the genetic, gonadal, hormonal sex, the internal reproductive organs, and the ambiguous appearances of the external genitalia were identical) have shown that one will consider oneself male or female depending simply on whether one was defined and raised as male or female:

> There is no more convincing evidence of the power of social interaction on gender-identity differentiation than in the case of congenital hermaphrodites who are of the same diagnosis and similar degree of hermaphroditism but are differently assigned and with a different postnatal medical and life history. (Money, 1970, p. 743)

Thus, for example, if out of two individuals diagnosed as having the adrenogenital syndrome of female hermaphroditism, one is raised as a girl and one as a boy, each will act and identify her/himself accordingly. The one raised as a girl will consider herself a girl; the one raised as a boy will consider himself a boy; and each will conduct her/himself successfully in accord with that self-definition.

So, identical behavior occurs given different physiological states; and different behavior occurs given an identical physiological starting point. So it is not clear that differences in sex hormones are at all relevant to behavior.

The other category of theory based on biology, a reductionist theory, goes like this. Sex-role behavior in some primate species is described, and it is concluded that this is the "natural" behavior for humans. Putting aside the not insignificant problem of observer bias (for instance, Harlow, of the University of Wisconsin, after observing differences between male and female rhesus monkeys, quotes Laurence Sterne to the effect that women are silly and trivial, and concludes that "men and women have differed in the past and they will differ in the future"), there are a number of problems with this approach.

The most general and serious problem is that there are no grounds to assume that anything primates do is necessarily natural, or desirable in humans, for the simple reason that humans are not non-humans. For instance, it is found that male chimpanzees placed alone with infants will not "mother" them. Jumping from hard data to ideological speculation, researchers conclude from this information that *human* females are necessary for the safe growth of human infants. It would be reasonable to conclude, following this logic, that it is quite useless to teach human infants to speak, since it has been tried with chimpanzees and it does not work.

One strategy that has been used is to extrapolate from primate behavior to "innate" human preference by noticing certain trends in primate behavior as one moves phylogenetically closer to humans. But there are great difficulties with this approach. When behaviors from lower primates are directly opposite to those of higher primates, or to those one expects of humans, they can be dismissed on evolutionary grounds—higher primates and/or humans grew out of that kid stuff. On the other hand, if the behavior of higher primates is counter to the behavior considered natural for humans, while the behavior of some lower primate is considered the natural one for humans, the higher primate behavior can be dismissed also, on the grounds that it has diverged from an older, prototypical pattern. So either way, one can select those behaviors one wants to prove innate for humans. In addition, one does not know whether the sex-role behavior exhibited is dependent on the phylogenetic rank, or on the environmental conditions (both physical and social) under which different species live.

Is there then any value at all in primate observations as they relate to human females and males? There is a value but it is limited: its function can be no more than to show some extant examples of diverse sex-role behavior. It must be stressed, however, that this is an extremely limited function. The extant behavior does not begin to suggest all the possibilities, either for non-human primates or for humans. Bearing these caveats in mind, it is nonetheless interesting that if one inspects the limited set of observations of existing non-human primate sex-role behaviors, one finds, in fact, a much larger range of sex-role behavior than is commonly believed to exist. "Biology" appears to limit very little; the fact that a female gives birth does not mean, even in non-humans, that she necessarily cares for the infant (in marmosets, for instance, the male carries the infant at all times except when the infant is feeding); "natural" female and male behavior varies all the way from females who are much more aggressive and competitive than males (e.g. Tamarins) and male "mothers" (e.g. Titi monkeys, night monkeys, and marmosets[6]) to submissive and passive females and male antagonists (e.g. rhesus monkeys).

But even for the limited function that primate arguments serve, the evidence has been misused. Invariably, those primates have been cited which exhibit exactly the kind of behavior that the proponents of the biological fixedness of human female behavior wish were true for humans. Thus, baboons and rhesus monkeys are generally cited: males in these groups exhibit some of the most irritable and aggressive behavior found in primates, and if one wishes to argue that females are naturally passive and submissive, these groups provide vivid examples. There are abundant counter examples, such as those mentioned above; in fact, in general, a counter example can be found for every sex-role behavior cited, including, as mentioned in the case of marmosets, male "mothers."

But the presence of counter examples has not stopped florid and overarching theories of the natural or biological basis of male privilege from proliferating. For instance, there have been a number of theories dealing with the innate incapacity in human males for monogamy. Here, as in most of this type of theorizing, baboons are a favorite example, probably because of their fantasy value: the family unit of the hamadryas baboon, for instance, consists of a highly constant pattern of one male and a number of females and their young. And again, the counter examples, such as the invariably monogamous gibbon, are ignored.

An extreme example of this maiming and selective truncation of the evidence in the service of a plea for the maintenance of male privilege is a recent book, *Men in Groups* by Tiger. The central claim of this book is that females are incapable of "bonding" as in "male bonding." What is "male bonding"? Its surface definition is simple: "...a particular relationship between two or more males such that they react differently to members of their bonding units as compared to individuals outside of it." If one deletes the word male, the definition, on its face, would seem to include all organisms that have any kind of social organization. But this is not what Tiger means. For instance, Tiger asserts that females are incapable of bonding; and this alleged incapacity indicates to Tiger that females should be restricted from public life. Why is bonding an exclusively male behavior? Because, says Tiger, it is seen in male primates. All male primates? No, very few male primates. Tiger cites two examples where male bonding is seen: rhesus monkeys and baboons. Surprise, surprise. But not even all baboons: as mentioned above, the hamadryas social organization consists of one-male units; so does that of the gelada baboon. And the great apes do not go in for male bonding much either. The "male bond" is hardly a serious contribution to scholarship; one reviewer for *Science* has observed that the book "...shows basically more resemblance to a partisan political tract than to a work of objective social science," with male bonding being "...some kind of behavioral phlogiston."

In short, primate arguments have generally misused the evidence; primate studies themselves have, in any case, only the very limited function of describing some possible sex-role behavior; and at present, primate observations have been sufficiently limited so that even the range of possible sex-role behavior for non-human primates is not known. This range is not known since there is only minimal observation of what happens to behavior if the physical or social environment is changed. In one study, different troops of Japanese macaques were observed. Here, there appeared to be cultural differences: males in 3 out of the 18 troops observed differed in the amount of their aggressiveness and infant-caring behavior. There could be no possibility of differential evolution here; the differences seemed largely transmitted by infant socialization. Thus, the very limited evidence points to some plasticity in the sex-role behavior of non-human primates; if we can figure out experiments which massively change the social organization of primate groups, it is possible that we might observe great changes in behavior. At present, however, we must conclude that given a constant physical environment, non-human primates do not change their social conditions by themselves very much and thus the "innateness" and fixedness of their behavior is simply not known. Thus, even if there were some way, which there isn't, to settle on the behavior of a particular primate species as being the "natural" way for humans, we would not know whether or not this were simply some function of the present social organization of that species. And finally, once again it must be stressed that even if non-human primate behavior turned out to be relatively fixed, this would say little about our behavior. More immediate and relevant evidence, e.g. the evidence from social psychology, points to the enormous plasticity in human behavior, not only from one culture to the next, but from one experimental group to the next. One of the most salient features of human social organization is its variety; there are a number of cultures where there is at least a rough equality between men and women. In summary, primate arguments can tell us very little about our "innate" sex-role behavior; if they tell us anything at all, they tell us that there is no one biologically "natural" female or male behavior, and that sex-role behavior in non-human primates is much more varied than has previously been thought.

Conclusion

In brief, the uselessness of present psychology (and biology) with regard to women is simply a special case of the general conclusion: one must understand the social conditions under which humans live if one is going to attempt to explain their behavior. And, to understand the social conditions under which women live, one must understand the social expectations about women. How are women characterized in our culture, and in psychology? They are inconsistent, emotionally unstable, lacking in a strong conscience or superego, weaker, "nurturant" rather than productive, "intuitive" rather than intelligent, and, if they are at all "normal," suited to the home and the family. In short, the list adds up to a typical minority group stereotype of inferiority: if they know their place, which is in the home, they are really quite lovable, happy, childlike, loving creatures. In a review of the intellectual differences between little boys and little girls, Eleanor Maccoby has shown that there are no intellectual differences until about high school, or, if there are, girls are slightly ahead of boys. At high school, girls begin to do worse on a few intellectual tasks, such as arithmetic reasoning, and beyond high school, the achievement of women now measured in terms of productivity and accomplishment drops off even more rapidly. There are a number of other, non-intellectual tests which show sex differences; I choose the intellectual differences since it is seen clearly that women start becoming inferior. It is no use to talk about women being different but equal; all of the tests I can think of have a "good" outcome and a "bad" outcome. Women usually end up at the "bad" outcome. In light of social expectations about women, what is surprising is that little girls don't get the message that they are supposed to be stupid until high school; and what is more remarkable is that some women resist this message even after high school, college, and graduate school.

My paper began with remarks on the task of the discovery of the limits of human potential. Psychologists must realize that it is they who are limiting discovery of human potential. They refuse to accept evidence, if they are clinical psychologists, or, if they are rigorous, they assume that people move in a context-free ether, with only their innate dispositions and their individual traits determining what they will do. Until psychologists begin to respect evidence, and until they begin looking at the social context within which people move, psychology will have nothing of substance to offer in this task of discovery. I don't know what immutable differences exist between men and women apart from differences in their genitals; perhaps there are some other unchangeable differences; probably there are a number of irrelevant differences. But it is clear that until social expectations for men and women are equal, until we provide equal respect for both men and women, our answers to this question will simply reflect our prejudices.

NOTES

1. Fieldcrest advertisement in *The New Yorker,* 1965. My italics.
2. W. H. Masters and V. E. Johnson, *Human Sexual Response* (Boston: Little, Brown, 1966).
3. It should be noted that psychologists have been as quick to assert absolute truths about the nature of homosexuality as they have about the nature of women. The arguments presented in this paper apply equally to the nature of homosexuality: psychologists know nothing about it; there is no more evidence for the "naturalness" of heterosexuality. Psychology has functioned as a pseudoscientific buttress for patriarchal ideology and patriarchal social organization: women's liberation and gay liberation fight against a common victimization.
4. I am indebted to Jesse Lemisch for his valuable suggestions in the interpretation of these studies.
5. H. N. G. Schwarz-Belkin claims that the name was originally Mouse, but this may be a reference to an earlier L. Tiger (putative).
6. All these are lower-order primates, which makes their behavior with reference to humans unnatural, or more natural; take your choice.

REFLECTING ON MEANING

1. According to Weisstein, what is the mission of the field of psychology? What issues do psychologists address in their practice and research? What is their "central assumption" about why human beings behave as they do? Why does Weisstein find this assumption erroneous? To what extent do you find this assumption valid or invalid?

2. Weisstein argues that psychologists' views are merely reflections of a "cultural consensus" on human behavior. What does she mean by cultural consensus? What is the cultural consensus on the behavior of women and men? What role do business and the media play in establishing and reinforcing a consensus on gender-typed behavior? How does business "make use of the cultural definitions of man and woman"? According to Weisstein, how does psychology both draw on and reinforce these cultural definitions? To what extent do you agree that this poses a problem in society?

3. Weisstein claims that theorists in psychology do not have evidence for their theories about women, and therefore their theories are "worse than useless." Do they offer any evidence at all? What kind? Why doesn't Weisstein consider this "evidence"? What do you think Weisstein's definition of evidence is? To what extent do you agree that these theories require the kind of evidence Weisstein demands? For Weisstein, why does lack of such evidence make these theories potentially harmful?

EXPLORING RHETORICAL STRATEGIES

1. Weisstein is particularly careful in constructing her argument, outlining assertions in advance, providing detailed evidence, and presenting summaries at appropriate intervals. Why is her argument constructed in this way? What might this pattern have to do with her purpose? What does the pattern illuminate about the arguments she criticizes? How does the essay's pattern contribute to her point?

2. Weisstein's tone might be described as skeptical or, perhaps, wry. To conclude her discussion of the failure of psychological theory to "cure" people, for example, she cites Rotter's commentary on the preoccupation of research studies with "the psychotherapy situation as a kind of personality laboratory" and responds with a simple two-word observation: "Some laboratory." What is the effect of this statement? How does it encourage you to view psy-

chological research? In what ways is this an appropriate conclusion to the first part of her argument? What are some other examples of Weisstein's wry tone?

3. The full title of Weisstein's essay is "Psychology Constructs the Female, or, The Fantasy Life of the Male Psychologist (with Some Attention to the Fantasies of His Friends, the Male Biologist and the Male Anthropologist)." What does this title lead readers to expect in the essay? What does the word *construct* suggest about the nature and origins of women's gender identity? What does Weisstein imply by attributing a gender to researchers and theorists working in psychology, biology, and anthropology? What do *fantasy life* and *fantasy* suggest about the vested interest these male professionals may have in theories about women? To what extent does the title forecast and summarize Weisstein's main point?

Emotion

SUSAN BROWNMILLER

Do men and women differ in temperament? Writer Susan Brownmiller explores answers to this question by examining emotions considered "appropriate" for each gender, as well as the ways in which society perceives and evaluates these emotions. Women, she concludes, are caught in a double bind: They are not only forced to express their emotions in "feminine ways," but society itself defines these ways in negative terms.

A 1970 landmark study, known in the field as Broverman and Broverman, reported that "Cries very easily" was rated by a group of professional psychologists as a highly feminine trait. "Very emotional," "Very excitable in a minor crisis" and "Feelings easily hurt" were additional characteristics on the femininity scale. So were "Very easily influenced," "Very subjective," "Unable to separate feelings from ideas," "Very illogical" and "Very sneaky." As might be expected, masculinity was defined by opposing, sturdier values: "Very direct," "Very logical," "Can make decisions easily," "Never cries." The importance of Broverman and Broverman was not in nailing down a set of popular assumptions and conventional perceptions—masculine-feminine scales were well established in the literature of psychology as a means of ascertaining normality and social adjustment—but in the authors' observation that stereotypic femininity was a grossly negative assessment of the female sex and, furthermore, that many so-called feminine traits ran counter to clinical descriptions of maturity and mental health.

Emotional femininity is a tough nut to crack, impossible to quantify yet hard to ignore. As the task of conforming to a specified physical design is a gender mission that few women care to resist, conforming to a prepackaged emotional design is another imperative task of gender. To satisfy a societal need for sexual clarification, and to justify second-class status, an emblematic constellation of inner traits, as well as their outward manifestations, has been put forward historically by some of the world's great thinkers as proof of the "different" feminine nature.

"Woman," wrote Aristotle, "is more compassionate than man, more easily moved to tears. At the same time, she is more jealous, more querulous, more apt to scold and to strike. She is, furthermore, more prone to despondency and less hopeful than man, more void of shame or self-respect, more false of speech, more deceptive and of more retentive memory. She is also more wakeful, more shrinking, more difficult to rouse to action, and she requires a smaller amount of nutriment."

Addressing a suffrage convention in 1855, Ralph Waldo Emerson had kindlier words on the nature of woman, explicating the nineteenth-century view that her difference was one of superior virtue. "Women," he extolled, "are the civilizers of mankind. What is civilization? I answer, the power of good women. . . . The starry crown of woman is in the power of her affection and sentiment, and the infinite enlargements to which they lead." (In less elevated language, the Emersonian view was perhaps what President Reagan had in mind when he cheerfully stated, "Why, if it wasn't for women, we men would still be walking around in skin suits carrying clubs.")

A clarification is in order. Are women believed to possess a wider or deeper emotional range, a greater sensitivity, say, to the beauties of nature or to the infinite complexities of feeling? Any male poet, artist, actor, marine biologist or backpacker would strenuously object. Rather, it is commonly agreed that women are tossed and buffeted on the high seas of emotion, while men have the tough mental fiber, the intellectual muscle, to stay in control. As for the civilizing influence, surely something more is meant than sophistication, culture and taste, using the correct fork or not belching after dinner. The idealization of emotional femininity, as women prefer to see themselves affirmed, is more exquisitely romantic: a finer temperament in a more fragile vessel; a gentler nature ruled by a twin need to love and to be protected; one who appreciates—without urgency to create—good art, music, literature and other public expressions of the private soul; a flamebearer of spiritual values by whose shining example the men of the world are inspired to redemption and to accomplish great things.

Two thousands years ago *Dominus flevit,* Jesus wept as he beheld Jerusalem. "Men ceased weeping," proposed Simone de Beauvoir, "when it became unfashionable." Now it is Mary, *Mater Dolorosa,* who weeps with compassion for mankind. In mystical visions, in the reliquaries of obscure churches and miraculous shrines, the figure of the Virgin, the world's most feminine woman, has been seen to shed tears. There are still extant cultures in which men are positively lachrymose (and kissy-kissy) with no seeming detriment to their masculine image, but the Anglo-Saxon tradition, in particular, requires keeping a stiff upper lip. Weeping, keening women shrouded in black are an established fixture in mourning rites in many nations. Inconsolable grief is a feminine role, at least in its unquiet representations. In what has become a stock photograph in the national news magazines, women weep for the multitudes when national tragedy (a terrorist bombing, an air crash, an assassination) strikes.

The catharsis of tears is encouraged in women—"There, there, now, let it all out"—while a man may be told to get a grip on himself, or to gulp down a double Scotch. Having "a good cry" in order to feel better afterward is not usually recommended as a means of raising the spirits of men, for the cathartic relief of succumbing to tears would be tempered by the uncomfortable knowledge that the loss of control was hardly manly. In the 1972 New Hampshire Presidential primary, Senator Edmund Muskie, then the Democratic front-runner, committed political suicide when he publicly cried during a campaign speech. Muskie had been talking about some harsh press comments directed at his wife when the tears filled his eyes. In retrospect it was his watershed moment: Could a man who became tearful when the going got rough in a political campaign be expected to face the Russians? To a nation that had delighted in the hatless, overcoatless macho posturing of John F. Kennedy, the military successes of General Ike and the irascible outbursts of "Give 'em hell" Harry Truman, the answer was No. Media accounts of Muskie's all-too-human tears were merciless. In the summer of 1983 the obvious and unshakable grief displayed by Israeli prime minister Menachem Begin after the death of his wife was seized upon by the Israeli and American press as evidence that a tough old warrior had lost his grip. Sharing this perception of his own emotional state, perhaps, Begin shortly afterward resigned.

Expressions of anger and rage are not a disqualifying factor in the masculine disposition. Anger in men is often understood, or excused, as reasonable or just. Anger in men may even be cast in a heroic mold—a righteous response to an insult against honor that will preclude a manly, aggressive act. Because competitive acts of personal assertion, not to mention acts of outright physical aggression, are known to flow from angry feelings, anger becomes the most unfeminine emotion a woman can show.

Anger in a woman isn't "nice." A woman who seethes with anger is "unattractive." An angry woman is hard, mean and nasty; she is unreliably, unprettily out of control. Her face contorts into unpleasant lines: the jaw juts, the eyes are narrowed, the teeth are bared. Anger is a violent snarl and a hostile threat, a declaration of war. The endless forbearance demanded of women, described as the feminine virtue of patience, prohibits an angry response. Picture a charming old-fashioned scene: The mistress of the house bends low over her needlework, cross-stitching her sampler: "Patience is a virtue, possess it if you can / Seldom seen in women, never seen in man." Does the needle jab through the cloth in uncommon fury? Does she prick her thumb in frustration?

Festering without a permissible release, women's undissolved anger has been known to seep out in petty, mean-spirited ways—fits of jealousy, fantasies of retaliation, unholy plots of revenge. Perhaps, after all, it is safer to cry. "Woman's aptitude for facile tears," wrote Beauvoir, "comes largely from the fact that her life is built upon a foundation of impotent revolt."[1]

Beauvoir hedged her bet, for her next words were these: "It is also doubtless true that physiologically she has less nervous control than a man." Is this "doubtless true," or is it more to the point, as Beauvoir continues, that "her education has taught her to let herself go more readily"?

Infants and children cry out of fear, frustration, discomfort, hunger, anxiety at separation from a parent, and rage. Surveying all available studies of crying newborns and little children, psychologists Eleanor Maccoby and Carol Jacklin found no appreciable sexual difference. If teenage girls and adult women are known to cry more than men—and there is no reason to question the pop-

ular wisdom in this regard—should the endocrine changes of adolescence be held to account? What of those weepy "blue days" of
premenstrual tension that genuinely afflict so many women? What
about mid-life depression, known in some circles as "the feminine
malady"? Are these conditions, as some men propose, a sign of
"raging hormonal imbalance" that incapacitates the cool, logical
functioning of the human brain? Or does feminine depression result, as psychiatrist Willard Gaylin suggests, when confidence in
one's coping mechanism is lost?

Belief in a biological basis for the instability of female emotions has a notorious history in the development of medical science. Hippocrates the physician held that hysteria was caused by a
wandering uterus that remained unfulfilled. Discovery in the seventeenth century that the thyroid gland was larger in women inspired the proposition that the thyroid's function was to give added
grace to the feminine neck, but other beliefs maintained that the
gland served to flush impurities from the blood before it reached
the brain. A larger thyroid "was necessary to guard the female system from the influence of the more numerous causes of irritation
and vexation" to which the sex was unfortunately disposed.
Nineteenth-century doctors averred that womb-related disorders
were the cause of such female complaints as "nervous prostration."
For those without money to seek out a physician's care, Lydia E.
Pinkham's Vegetable Compound and other patent medicines were
available to give relief. In the 1940s and '50s, prefrontal lobotomy
was briefly and tragically in vogue for a variety of psychiatric disorders, particularly among women, since the surgical procedure
had a flattening effect on raging emotions. Nowadays Valium appears to suffice.

Beginning in earnest in the 1960s, one line of research has attempted to isolate premenstrual tension as a contributing cause of
accidents, suicide, admittance to mental hospitals and the commission of violent crimes. Mood swings, irritability and minor emotional upsets probably do lead to more "acting out" by females at
a cyclical time in the month, but what does this prove beyond the
increasingly accepted fact that the endocrine system has a critical
influence on the human emotional threshold? Suicide, violent
crime and dangerous psychiatric disorders are statistically four to
nine times more prevalent in men. Should we theorize, then, that
"raging hormonal imbalance" is a chronic, year-round condition in
males? A disqualifying factor? By any method of calculation and
for whatever reason—hormonal effects, the social inhibitions of
femininity, the social pleasure of the masculine role, or all of
these—the female gender is indisputably less prone to irrational,

antisocial behavior. The price of inhibited anger and a nonviolent temperament may well be a bucketful of tears.

Like the emotion of anger, exulting in personal victory is a harshly unfeminine response. Of course, good winners of either sex are supposed to display some degree of sportsmanlike humility, but the merest hint of gloating triumph—"Me, me, me, I did it!"—is completely at odds with the modesty and deference expected of women and girls. Arm raised in a winner's salute, the ritualized climax of a prizefight, wrestling match or tennis championship, is unladylike, to say the least. The powerful feeling that victory engenders, the satisfaction of climbing to the top of the heap or clinching a deal, remains an inappropriate emotion. More appropriate to femininity are the predictable tears of the new Miss America as she accepts her crown and scepter. Trembling lip and brimming eyes suggest a Cinderella who has stumbled upon good fortune through unbelievable, undeserved luck. At her moment of victory the winner of America's favorite pageant appears over come, rather than superior in any way. A Miss America who raised her scepter high like a trophy would not be in keeping with the feminine ideal.

The maidenly blush, that staple of the nineteenth-century lady's novel, was an excellent indicator of innocent virginal shyness in contrast to the worldliness and sophistication of men. In an age when a variety of remarks, largely sexual, were considered uncouth and not for the ears of virtuous women, the feminine blush was an expected response. On the other side of the ballroom, men never blushed, at least not in romantic fiction, since presumably they were knowledgeable and sexually practiced. Lowered eyes, heightened color, breathlessness and occasional swooning were further proofs of a fragile and innocent feminine nature that required protection in the rough, indelicate masculine world. (In the best-selling Harlequin and Silhouette books devoured by romance addicts who need the quick fix, the maidenly blush is alive and well.)

In a new age of relative sexual freedom, or permissiveness, at any rate, squeals and moans replace the blush and the downcast eye. Screaming bobbysoxers who fainted in the aisle at the Paramount Theater when a skinny young Frank Sinatra crooned his love ballads during the 1940s (reportedly, the first wave of fainting girls was staged by promoters) presaged the whimpering orgasmic ecstasy at rock concerts in huge arenas today. By contrast, young men in the audience automatically rise to their feet and whistle and shout when the band starts to play, but they seldom appear overcome.

Most emphatically, feminine emotion has gotten louder. The ribald squeal of the stereotypic serving wench in Elizabethan times, a supposed indicator of loose, easy ways, seems to have lost its lower-class stigma. One byproduct of our media-obsessed society, in which privacy is considered a quaint and rather old-fashioned human need, has been the reproduction of the unmistakable sounds of female orgasm on a record (Donna Summer's "Love to Love You Baby," among other hits). More than commercialization of sex is operative here. Would the sounds of male orgasm suffice for a recording, and would they be unmistakable? Although I have seen no studies on this interesting sex difference, I believe it can be said that most women do vocalize more loudly and uncontrollably than men in the throes of sexual passion. Is this response physiological, compensatory or merely symptomatic of the feminine mission to display one's feelings (and the corresponding masculine mission to keep their feelings under control)?

Feminine emotion specializes in sentimentality, empathy and admissions of vulnerability—three characteristics that most men try to avoid. Linking these traits to female anatomy became an article of faith in the Freudian school. Erik Erikson, for one, spoke of an "inner space" (he meant the womb) that yearns for fulfillment through maternal love. Helene Deutsch, the grande dame of Freudian feminine psychology, spoke of psychic acceptance of hurt and pain; menstrual cramps, defloration and the agonies of childbirth called for a masochistic nature she believed was innate.

Love of babies, any baby and all babies, not only one's own, is a celebrated and anticipated feminine emotion, and a woman who fails to ooh and ahh at the snapshot of a baby or cuddle a proffered infant in her arms is instantly suspect. Evidence of a maternal nature, of a certain innate competence when handling a baby or at least some indication of maternal longing, becomes a requirement of gender. Women with no particular feeling for babies are extremely reluctant to admit their private truth, for the entire weight of woman's place in the biological division of labor, not to mention the glorification of motherhood as woman's greatest and only truly satisfactory role, has kept alive the belief that all women yearn to fulfill their biological destiny out of a deep emotional need. That a sizable number of mothers have no genuine aptitude for the job is verified by the records of hospitals, family courts and social agencies where cases of battery and neglect are duly entered—and perhaps also by the characteristic upper-class custom of leaving the little ones to the care of the nanny. But despite this evidence that day-to-day motherhood is not a suitable or a stimulating occupation for all, the myth persists that a woman who prefers to remain childless must be heartless or selfish or less than complete.

Books have been written on maternal guilt and its exploitation, on the endemic feeling that whatever a mother does, her loving care may be inadequate or wrong, with consequences that can damage a child for life. Trends in child care (bottle feeding, demand feeding, not picking up the crying baby, delaying the toilet training or giving up an outside job to devote one's entire time to the family) illuminate the fear of maternal inadequacy as well as the variability or "expert" opinion in each generation. Advertising copywriters successfully manipulate this feminine fear when they pitch their clients' products. A certain cereal, one particular brand of packaged white bread, must be bought for the breakfast table or else you have failed to love your child sufficiently and denied him the chance to "build a strong body twelve ways." Until the gay liberation movement began to speak for itself, it was a commonplace of psychiatric wisdom that a mother had it within her power to destroy her son's heterosexual adjustment by failing to cut his baby curls, keep him away from dance class or encourage his interest in sports.

A requirement of femininity is that a woman devote her life to love—to mother love, to romantic love, to religious love, to amorphous, undifferentiated caring. The territory of the heart is admittedly a province that is open to all, but women alone are expected to make an obsessional career of its exploration, to find whatever adventure, power, fulfillment or tragedy that life has to offer within its bounds. There is no question that a woman is apt to feel most feminine, most confident of her interior gender makeup, when she is reliably within some stage of love—even the girlish crush or the stage of unrequited love or a broken heart. Men have suffered for love, and men have accomplished great feats in the name of love, but what man has ever felt at the top of his masculine form when he is lovesick or suffering from heartache?

Gloria Steinem once observed that the heart is a sex-distinctive symbol of feminine vulnerability in the marketing of fashion. Heartshaped rings and heart-shaped gold pendants and heart-shaped frames on red plastic sunglasses announce an addiction to love that is beyond the pale of appropriate design for masculine ornamentation. (A man does not wear his heart on his sleeve.) The same observation applies a little less stringently to flowers.

Rare is the famous girl singer, whatever her age, of popular music (blues, country, Top Forty, disco or rock) who is not chiefly identified with some expression of love, usually its downside. Torchy bittersweet ballads and sad, suffering laments mixed with vows of eternal fidelity to the rotten bastard who done her wrong communicate the feminine message of love at any cost. Almost unique to the female singer, I think, is the poignant anthem of battered survival, from Fanny Brice's "My Man" to Gloria Gaynor's "I

Will Survive," that does not quite shut the door on further emotional abuse if her man should return.

But the point is not emotional abuse (except in extreme, aberrant cases); the point is feeling. Women are instructed from childhood to be keepers of the heart, keepers of the sentimental memory. In diaries, packets of old love letters and family albums, in slender books of poetry in which a flower is pressed, a woman's emotional history is preserved. Remembrance of things past—the birthday, the anniversary, the death—is a feminine province. In the social division of labor, the wife is charged with maintaining the emotional connection, even with the husband's side of the family. Her thoughtful task is to make the long-distance call, select the present and write the thank-you note (chores that secretaries are asked to do by their bosses). Men are busy; they move forward. A woman looks back. It is significant that in the Biblical parable it was Lot's wife who looked back for one last precious glimpse of their city, their home, their past (and was turned into a pillar of salt).

Love confirms the feminine psyche. A celebrated difference between men and women (either women's weakness or women's strength, depending on one's values) is the obstinate reluctance, the emotional inability of women to separate sex from love. Understandably. Love makes the world go round, and women are supposed to get dizzy—to rise, to fall, to feel alive in every pore, to be undone. In place of a suitable attachment, an unlikely or inaccessible one may have to do. But more important, sex for a woman, even in an age of accessible contraception, has reproductive consequences that render the act a serious affair. Casual sex can have a most uncasual resolution. If a young girl thinks of love and marriage while a boy thinks of getting laid, her emotional commitment is rooted not only in her different upbringing but in her reproductive biology as well. Love, then, can become an alibi for thoughtless behavior, as it may also become an identity, or a distraction, à la Emma Bovary or Anna Karenina, from the frustrations of a limited life.[2]

Christian houses of worship, especially in poor neighborhoods, are filled disproportionately by women. This phenomenon may not be entirely attributable to the historic role of the Catholic and Protestant religions in encouraging the public devotions of women (which Judaism and Islam did not), or because women have more time for prayer, or because in the Western world they are believed to be more religious by nature. Another contributing factor may be that the central article of Christian faith, "Jesus loves you," has particular appeal for the gender that defines itself through loving emotions.

Women's special interest in the field of compassion is catered to and promoted. Hollywood "weepies," otherwise known as four-handkerchief movies, were big-studio productions that were tailored to bring in female box-office receipts. Columns of advice to the lovelorn, such as the redoubtable "Dear Dorothy Dix" and the current "Dear Abby," were by tradition a woman's slot on daily newspapers, along with the coverage of society births and weddings, in the days when females were as rare in a newsroom as they were in a coal mine. In the heyday of the competitive tabloids, sob-sister journalism, that newsroom term for a human-interest story told with heart-wrenching pathos (usually by a tough male reporter who had the formula down pat), was held in contempt by those on the paper who covered the "hard stuff" of politics, crime and war. (Nathanael West's famous antihero labored under the byline of Miss Lonelyhearts.) Despite its obvious audience appeal, "soft stuff" was, and is, on the lower rungs of journalism—trivial, weak and unmanly.

In Government circles during the Vietnam war, it was considered a sign of emotional softness, of lily-livered liberals and nervous nellies, to suggest that Napalmed babies, fire-bombed villages and defoliated crops were reason enough to pull out American forces. The peace movement, went the charge, was composed of cowards and fuzzy thinkers. Suspicion of an unmanly lack of hard practical logic always haunts those men who espouse peace and nonviolence, but women, the weaker sex, are permitted a certain amount of emotional leeway. Feminine logic, after all, is reputedly governed by the heartstrings. Compassion and sentiment are the basis for its notorious "subjectivity" compared to the "objectivity" of men who use themselves as the objective standard.

As long as the social division of labor ordains that women should bear the chief emotional burden of caring for human life from the cradle to the grave while men may demonstrate their dimorphic difference through competitive acts of physical aggression, emblematic compassion and fear of violence are compelling reasons for an aversion to war and other environmental hazards. When law and custom deny the full range of public expression and economic opportunity that men claim for themselves, a woman must place much of her hopes, her dreams, her feminine identity and her social importance in the private sphere of personal relations, in the connective tissue of marriage, family, friendship and love. In a world out of balance, where men are taught to value toughness and linear vision as masculine traits that enable them to think strategically from conquest to conquest, from campaign to campaign without looking back, without getting sidetracked by vulnerable feelings, there is, and will be, an emotional difference between the sexes, a gender gap that may even appear on a Gallup poll.

If a true shape could emerge from the shadows of historic oppression, would the gender-specific experience of being female still suggest a range of perceptions and values that differ appreciably from those of men? It would be premature to offer an answer. Does a particular emotion ultimately resist separation from its historic deployment in the sexual balance of power? In the way of observation, this much can be said: The entwining of anatomy, history and culture presents such a persuasive emotional argument for a "different nature" that even the best aspects of femininity collaborate in its perpetuation.

NOTES

1. "Facile" is the English translator's match for the French *facile,* more correctly rendered as "easy." Beauvoir did not mean to ascribe a stereotype superficiality to women in her remark.
2. The overwhelming influence of feminine love is frequently offered as a mitigating explanation by women who do unfeminine things. Elizabeth Bentley, the "Red Spy Queen" of the cold war Fifties, attributed her illegal activities to her passion for the Russian master spy Jacob Golos. Judith Coplon's defense for stealing Government documents was love for another Russian, Valentin Gubichev. More recently, Jean Harris haplessly failed to convince a jury that her love for "Scarsdale diet" Doctor Herman Tarnower was so great that she could not possibly have intended to kill him.

REFLECTING ON MEANING

1. Brownmiller says that the significance of the study by Broverman and Broverman is *not* its confirmation of gender stereotyping in society. Rather, she claims, the study is important because it showed (a) that "stereotypic femininity was a grossly negative assessment of the female sex," and (b) that "many so-called feminine traits ran counter to clinical descriptions of mental health." What distinction is Brownmiller making? Is it important? Why or why not? Does the study suggest that women are emotionally unhealthy, or does it imply something else? How do you know?

2. Brownmiller asserts that "a requirement of femininity is that a woman devote her life to love"; in fact, she says, women are required to make an "obsessional career" of love. What is her evidence for

this assertion? Do you agree with it? What are some of your own experiences and observations that support or refute her point? Why aren't men expected to devote their lives to love? Or are they?

3. Consider the essay's concluding statement: "The entwining of anatomy, history and culture presents such a persuasive emotional argument for a 'different nature' that even the best aspects of femininity collaborate in its perpetuation." What are the "best aspects" of femininity? In what ways and for what reasons might femininity cooperate in maintaining the idea that women and men have different temperaments? What is Brownmiller ultimately suggesting about the origins of this idea? To what extent do you agree or disagree with her? Why?

EXPLORING RHETORICAL STRATEGIES

1. Brownmiller hints at her thesis early in the essay by stating that femininity is a socially constructed myth. She doesn't explicitly state her thesis, however, until she reaches her next-to-last paragraph. What is her thesis? Why do you think she delayed stating it until the end of the essay? What are the advantages she gained in doing this?

2. Throughout the essay, Brownmiller employs an interesting device, a kind of reverse image: Miss America raising "her scepter high like a trophy"; a man overcome with tears, or "lovesick or suffering from heartache"; a woman sewing in "fury" and "frustration"; the sounds of male orgasm on a top-forty recording. What is your reaction to these images? What is the effect of this device? How do these reversals help Brownmiller make her point?

3. The nature of Brownmiller's voice in this essay is, as she says of feminine emotions, "a tough nut to crack." Her diction ranges from the formal to the colloquial; she even uses clichés. What overall tone does her varied use of language create? What kind of persona has it helped her create? What is your image of Brownmiller? What are your reactions to this image?

Sisterhood

GLORIA STEINEM

In this essay, activist Gloria Steinem describes the changes that "sisterhood" brought about in her own life and the lives of other women. She describes sisterhood as a process that brings together women of different ages, races, and economic standing through discovery of their shared experiences as women.

A very, very long time ago (about three or four years), I took a certain secure and righteous pleasure in saying the things that women are supposed to say. I remember with pain—

"My work won't interfere with marriage. After all, I can always keep my typewriter at home." Or:

"I don't want to write about women's stuff. I want to write about foreign policy." Or:

"Black families were forced into matriarchy, so I see why black women have to step back and let their men get ahead." Or:

"I know we're helping Chicano groups that are tough on women, but *that's their culture.*" Or:

"Who would want to join a women's group? I've never been a joiner, have you?" Or (when bragging):

"He says I write like a man."

I suppose it's obvious from the kinds of statements I chose that I was secretly nonconforming. I wasn't married. I was earning a living at a profession I cared about. I had basically—if quietly—opted out of the "feminine" role. But that made it all the more necessary to repeat the conventional wisdom, even to look as conventional as I could manage, if I was to avoid some of the punishments reserved by society for women who don't do as society says. I therefore learned to Uncle Tom with subtlety, logic, and humor. Sometimes, I even believed it myself.

If it weren't for the women's movement, I might still be dissembling away. But the ideas of this great sea-change in women's view of ourselves are contagious and irresistible. They hit women like a revelation, as if we had left a dark room and walked into the sun.

At first my discoveries seemed personal. In fact, they were the same ones so many millions of women have made and are continuing to make. Greatly simplified, they go like this: Women are human beings first, with minor differences from men that apply largely to the single act of reproduction. We share the dreams, capabilities, and weaknesses of all human beings, but our occasional pregnancies and other visible differences have been used—even more pervasively, if less brutally, than racial differences have been used—to create an "inferior" group and an elaborate division of labor. The division is continued for a clear if often unconscious reason: the economic and social profit of males as a group.

Once this feminist realization dawned, I reacted in what turned out to be predictable ways. First, I was amazed at the simplicity and obviousness of a realization that made sense, at last, of my life experience. I couldn't figure out why I hadn't seen it before. Second, I realized how far that new vision of life was from the system around us, and how tough it would be to explain this feminist realization at all, much less to get people (especially, though not only, men) to accept so drastic a change.

But I tried to explain. God knows (*she* knows) that women try. We make analogies with other groups that have been marked for subservient roles in order to assist blocked imaginations. We supply endless facts and statistics of injustice, reeling them off until we feel like human information-retrieval machines. We lean heavily on the device of reversal. (If there is a male reader to whom all my *pre*realization statements seem perfectly logical, for instance, let him read each sentence with "men" substituted for "women"—or himself for me—and see how he feels: "My work won't interfere with marriage..."; "...Chicano groups that are tough on men..." You get the idea.)

We even use logic. If a woman spends a year bearing and nursing a child, for instance, she is supposed to have the primary responsibility for raising that child to adulthood. That's logic by the male definition, but it often makes women feel children are their only function, keeps them from doing any other kind of work, or discourages them from being mothers at all. Wouldn't it be just as logical to say that the child has two parents, therefore both are equally responsible for child rearing, and the father should compensate for that extra year by spending *more* than half the time caring for the child? Logic is in the eye of the logician.

Occasionally, these efforts at explaining actually succeed. More often, I get the feeling that most women are speaking Urdu and most men are speaking Pali.

Whether joyful or painful, both kinds of reaction to our discovery have a great reward. They give birth to sisterhood.

First, we share the exhilaration of growth and self-discovery, the sensation of having the scales fall from our eyes. Whether we are giving other women this new knowledge or receiving it from them, the pleasure for all concerned is enormous. And very moving.

In the second stage, when we're exhausted from dredging up facts and arguments for the men whom we had previously thought advanced and intelligent, we make another simple discovery: women understand. We may share experiences, make jokes, paint pictures, and describe humiliations that mean little to men, but *women understand.*

The odd thing about these deep and personal connections among women is that they often leap barriers of age, economics, worldly experience, race, culture—all the barriers that, in male or mixed society, seem so impossible to cross.

I remember meeting with a group of women in Missouri who, because they had come in equal numbers from the small town and from its nearby campus, seemed to be split between wives with white gloves welded to their wrists and students with boots who used words like "imperialism" and "oppression." Planning for a child-care center had brought them together, but the meeting seemed hopeless until three of the booted young women began to argue among themselves about a young male professor. The leader of the radicals on campus, he accused all women unwilling to run Mimeograph machines of not being sufficiently devoted to the cause. As for child-care centers, he felt their effect of allowing women to compete with men for jobs was part of a dreaded "feminization" of the American male and American culture.

"He sounds just like my husband," said one of the white-gloved women. "He wants me to have bake sales and collect door-to-door for his Republican party." The young women had sense enough to take it from there. What difference did boots or white gloves make if they were all getting treated like servants and children? Before they broke up, they were discussing some subjects that affected them all (like the myth of the vaginal orgasm) and planning to meet every week. "Men think we're whatever it is we do for men," explained one of the housewives. "It's only by getting together with other women that we'll ever find out who we are."

Even racial barriers become a little less formidable once we discover this mutuality of our life experiences as women. At a meeting run by black women domestics who had formed a job cooperative in Alabama, a white housewife asked me about the consciousness-raising sessions or "rap groups" that are often an organic path to feminism. I explained that while men, even minority men, usually had someplace—a neighborhood, a bar, a street corner, something—where they could get together and be themselves, women were isolated in their houses and families; isolated from other females. We had no street corners, no bars, no offices, no territory that was recognized as ours. Rap groups were an effort to create something of our own, a free place—an occasional chance for total honesty and support from our sisters.

As I talked about isolation, about the feeling that there must be something wrong with us if we aren't content to be housekeepers and mothers, tears began to stream down the cheeks of this dignified woman—clearly as much of a surprise to her as to us. For the black women, some distance was bridged by seeing this white woman cry.

"He does it to us both, honey," said the black woman next to her, putting an arm around her shoulders. "If it's your own kitchen or somebody else's, you still don't get treated like people. Women's work just doesn't count."

The meeting ended with the housewife organizing a support group of white women who would extract from their husbands a living wage for domestic workers and help them fight the local authorities who opposed any pay raises; a support group without which the domestic workers felt their small and brave cooperative could not survive.

As for the "matriarchal" argument that I swallowed in prefeminist days, I now understand why many black women resent it and feel that it's the white sociologists' way of encouraging the black community to imitate a white suburban life-style. "If I end up cooking grits for revolutionaries," explained a black woman poet from Chicago, "it isn't my revolution. Black men and women need to work together: you can't have liberation for half a race." In fact, some black women wonder if criticism of the strength they were forced to develop isn't a way to keep half the black community working at lowered capacity and lowered pay, as well as to attribute some of black men's sufferings to black women, instead of to their real source—white racism. I wonder with them.

Looking back at all those male-approved things I used to say, the basic hang-up seems clear—a lack of esteem for women, whatever our race, and for myself.

This is the most tragic punishment that society inflicts on any second-class group. Ultimately the brainwashing works, and we ourselves come to believe our group is inferior. Even if we achieve a little success in the world and think of ourselves as "different," we don't want to associate with our group. We want to identify up, not down (clearly my problem in not wanting to join women's groups). We want to be the only woman in the office, or the only black family on the block, or the only Jew in the club.

The pain of looking back at wasted, imitative years is enormous. Trying to write like men. Valuing myself and other women according to the degree of our acceptance by men—socially, in politics, and in our professions. It's as painful as it is now to hear two grown-up female human beings competing with each other on the basis of their husband's status, like servants whose identity rests on the wealth or accomplishments of their employers.

And this lack of esteem that makes us put each other down is still the major enemy of sisterhood. Women who are conforming to society's expectations view the nonconformists with justifiable alarm. *Those noisy, unfeminine women,* they say to themselves. *They will only make trouble for us all.* Women who are quietly nonconforming, hoping nobody will notice, are even more alarmed because they have more to lose. And that makes sense, too.

The status quo protects itself by punishing all challengers, especially women whose rebellion strikes at the most fundamental social organization: the sex roles that convince half the population that its identity depends on being first in work or in war, and the other half that it must serve as docile, unpaid, or underpaid labor.

In fact, there seems to be no punishment inside the white male club that quite equals the ridicule and personal viciousness reserved for women who rebel. Attractive or young women who act forcefully are assumed to be either unnatural or male controlled. If they succeed, it could only have been sexually, through men. Old women or women considered unattractive by male standards are accused of acting out of bitterness, because they could not get a man. Any woman who chooses to behave like a full human being should be warned that the armies of the status quo will treat her as something of a dirty joke. That's their natural and first weapon. She will *need* sisterhood.

All of that is meant to be a warning but not a discouragement. There are more rewards than punishments.

For myself, I can now admit anger and use it constructively, where once I would have submerged it and let it fester into guilt or collect for some destructive explosion.

I have met brave women who are exploring the outer edge of human possibility, with no history to guide them, and with a courage to make themselves vulnerable that I find moving beyond the words to express it.

I no longer think that I do not exist, which was my version of that lack of self-esteem afflicting many women. (If male standards weren't natural to me, and they were the only standards, how could I exist?) This means that I am less likely to need male values and approval and am less vulnerable to classic arguments. ("If you don't like me, you're not a real woman"—said by a man who is coming on. "If you don't like me, you can't relate to other people, you're not a real person"—said by anyone who understands black-mail as an art.)

I can sometimes deal with men as equals and therefore can afford to like them for the first time.

I have discovered politics that are not intellectual or superimposed. They are organic. I finally understand why for years I inexplicably identified with "out" groups: I belong to one, too. And I know it will take a coalition of such groups to achieve a society in which, at a minimum, no one is born into a second-class role because of visible difference, because of race or of sex.

I no longer feel strange by myself or with a group of women in public. I feel just fine.

I am continually moved to discover I have sisters.

I am beginning, just beginning, to find out who I am.

REFLECTING ON MEANING

1. Steinem describes a stage in her life when she was "secretly non-conforming." What conventions wasn't she conforming to? Given her nonconformity, why did she nevertheless find it "necessary to repeat the conventional wisdom" and to look "conventional"? What does *conventional* mean in this context? Why was she so concerned about being seen as conventional? Why does she say that she had "learned to Uncle Tom"?

2. According to Steinem, what is sisterhood? What are its origins? How, in Steinem's view, is it more a process than a state of being? What does it achieve? What kinds of people does it bring together? How? What kind of bond does it create?

3. What does Steinem mean when she says that "outsiders" such as women "want to identify up, not down"? Why do they want to do this? In what ways might "identifying up" be a positive move for an individual? In what ways might it be negative? Why?

EXPLORING RHETORICAL STRATEGIES

1. "Sisterhood" was first published in *Ms.* magazine in 1972. For what audience was Steinem writing? What evidence in the essay, if any, suggests that she expected resistance from her audience?

What assumptions do you think she expected her intended audience to share with her? How might "Sisterhood" have been different if Steinem had been writing for a magazine such as *Family Circle* or *GQ?*

2. Analogies, facts and statistics, logic, and the "device of reversal"—these are some of the strategies feminists use to support their beliefs, according to Steinem. To what extent does Steinem herself use these kinds of evidence to support her thesis? Which of these ways of supporting a point do you find especially effective? What other kinds of support does Steinem provide? To what extent does she rely on personal experience, anecdotes, and concrete examples? How do these sources of support influence the tone of her essay?

3. To illustrate how sisterhood emphasizes connections among women in disparate situations, Steinem tells the stories of three women: a young student whose male professor expected her "to run Mimeograph machines" for "the cause"; a "white-gloved" woman whose husband wanted her to hold "bake sales and collect door-to-door for his Republican party"; and a black woman who announced, "If I end up cooking grits for revolutionaries, it isn't my revolution." How does the concrete detail of each situation make these examples effective? How does the common theme running through the examples reinforce Steinem's point?

Chapter 4

GENDER AND SEXUAL IDENTITY

The Homosexual Role

MARY MCINTOSH

Feminist theorist Mary McIntosh begins this essay by differentiating between two contradictory conceptions of homosexuality: as a condition and as a role. Defining homosexuality as a condition acts as a mechanism of social control by segregating so-called "deviant" homosexuals from "normal" heterosexuals. Instead, McIntosh uses cross-cultural and historical evidence to assert that while homosexual feelings and behaviors do exist, we should view homosexuality as a social role that exists only in certain societies.

Recent advances in the sociology of deviant behavior have not yet affected the study of homosexuality, which is still commonly seen as a condition characterizing certain persons in the way that birthplace or deformity might characterize them. The limitations of this view can best be understood if we examine some of its implications. In the first place, if homosexuality is a condition, then people either have it or do nor have it. Many scientists and ordinary people assume that there are two kinds of people in the world: homosexuals and heterosexuals. Some of them recognize that homosexual feelings and behavior are not confined to the persons they would like to call "homosexuals" and that some of these persons do not actually engage in homosexual behavior. This should pose a crucial problem, but they evade the crux by retaining their assumption and puzzling over the question of how to tell whether someone is "really" homosexual or not. Lay people too will discuss whether a certain person is "queer" in much the same way as they might question whether a certain pain indicated cancer. And in much the same way they will often turn to scientists or to medical men for a surer diagnosis. The scientists, for their part, feel it incumbent on them to seek criteria for diagnosis.

Thus one psychiatrist, discussing the definition of homosexuality, has written:

> I do not diagnose patients as homosexual unless they have engaged in overt homosexual behaviour. Those who also engage in heterosexual activity are diagnosed as bisexual. An isolated experience may not warrant the diagnosis, but repetitive homosexual behaviour in adulthood, whether sporadic or continuous, designates a homosexual. (Bieber 1965:248)

Along with many other writers, he introduces the notion of a third type of person, the "bisexual," to handle the fact that behavior patterns cannot be conveniently dichotomized into heterosexual and homosexual. But this does not solve the conceptual problem, since bisexuality too is seen as a condition (unless as a passing response to unusual situations such as confinement in a one-sex prison). In any case there is no extended discussion of bisexuality; the topic is usually given a brief mention in order to clear the ground for the consideration of "true homosexuality."

To cover the cases where the symptoms of behavior or of felt attractions do not match the diagnosis, other writers have referred to an adolescent homosexual phase or have used such terms as "latent homosexual" or "pseudo homosexual." Indeed one of the earliest studies of the subject, by Krafft-Ebing (1965), was concerned with making a distinction between the "invert" who is congenitally homosexual and others who, although they behave in the same way, are not true inverts.

A second result of the conceptualization of homosexuality as a condition is that the major research task has been seen as the study of its etiology. There has been much debate as to whether the condition is innate or acquired. The first step in such research has commonly been to find a sample of "homosexuals" in the same way that a medical researcher might find a sample of diabetics if he wanted to study that disease. Yet after a long history of such studies, the results are sadly inconclusive, and the answer is still as much a matter of opinion as it was when Havelock Ellis's *Sexual Inversion* was published seventy years ago. The failure of research to answer the question has not been due to lack of scientific rigor or to any inadequacy of the available evidence; it results rather from the fact that the wrong question has been asked. One might as well try to trace the etiology of "committee chairmanship" or "Seventh Day Adventism" as of "homosexuality."

The vantage point of comparative sociology enables us to see that the conception of homosexuality as a condition is, in itself, a possible object of study. This conception and the behavior it supports operate as a form of social control in a society in which homosexuality is condemned. Furthermore the uncritical acceptance of the conception by social scientists can be traced to their concern with homosexuality as a social problem. They have tended to accept the popular definition of what the problem is, and they have been implicated in the process of social control.

The practice of the social labeling of persons as deviant operates in two ways as a mechanism of social control. In the first place it helps to provide a clear-cut, publicized, and recognizable threshold between permissible and impermissible behavior. This means that people cannot so easily drift into deviant behavior. Their first moves in a deviant direction immediately raise the question of a total move into a deviant role with all the sanctions that this is likely to elicit. Second, the labeling serves to segregate the deviants from others, and this means that their deviant practices and their self-justifications for these practices are contained within a relatively narrow group. The creation of a specialized, despised, and punished role of homosexual keeps the bulk of society pure in rather the same way that the similar treatment of some kinds of criminals helps keep the rest of society law-abiding.

However, the disadvantage of this practice as a technique of social control is that there may be a tendency for people to become fixed in their deviance once they have become labeled. This too is a process that has become well-recognized in discussion of other forms of deviant behavior, such as juvenile delinquency and drug taking, and indeed of other kinds of social labeling, such as streaming in schools and racial distinctions. One might expect social categorizations of this sort to be to some extent self-fulfilling prophecies: if the culture defines people as falling into distinct types—black and white, criminal and non-criminal, homosexual and normal—then these types will tend to become polarized, highly differentiated from each other. Later in this paper I shall discuss whether this is so in the case of homosexuals and "normals" in the United States today.

It is interesting to notice that homosexuals themselves welcome and support the notion that homosexuality is a condition.

For just as the rigid categorization deters people from drifting into deviancy, so it appears to foreclose on the possibility of drifting back into normality and thus removes the element of anxious choice. It appears to justify the deviant behavior of the homosexual as being appropriate for him as a member of the homosexual category. The deviancy can thus be seen as legitimate for him and he can continue in it without rejecting the norms of the society.

The way in which people become labeled as homosexual can now be seen as an important social process connected with mechanisms of social control. It is important therefore that sociologists should examine this process objectively and not lend themselves to participation in it, particularly since, as we have seen, psychologists and psychiatrists on the whole have not retained their objectivity but have become involved as diagnostic agents in the process of social labeling.

It is proposed that the homosexual should be seen as playing a social role rather than as having a condition. The role of "homosexual," however, does not simply describe a sexual behavior pattern. If it did, the idea of a role would be no more useful than that of a condition. For the purpose of introducing the term "role" is to enable us to handle the fact that behavior in this sphere does not match popular beliefs: that sexual behavior patterns cannot be dichotomized in the way that the social roles of homosexual and heterosexual can.

It may seem rather odd to distinguish in this way between role and behavior, but if we accept a definition of role in terms of expectations (which may or may not be fulfilled), then the distinction is both legitimate and useful. In modern societies where a separate homosexual role is recognized, the expectation, on behalf of those who play the role and of others, is that a homosexual will be exclusively or very predominantly homosexual in his feelings and behavior. In addition there are other expectations that frequently exist, especially on the part of non-homosexuals, but affecting the self-conception of anyone who sees himself as homosexual. These are the expectation that he will be effeminate in manner, personality, or preferred sexual activity, the expectation that sexuality will play a part of some kind in all his relations with other men, and the expectation that he will be attracted to boys and very young men and probably willing to seduce them. The existence of a social expectation, of course, commonly helps to produce its own fulfillment. But the question of how far it is fulfilled is a matter for empirical investigation rather than *a priori* pronouncement.

In order to clarify the nature of the role and demonstrate that it exists only in certain societies, we shall present the cross cultural and historical evidence available. This raises awkward problems of method because the material has hitherto usually been collected and analyzed in terms of culturally specific modern Western conceptions.

The Homosexual Role in Various Societies

To study homosexuality in the past or in other societies we usually have to rely on secondary evidence rather than on direct observation. The reliability and the validity of such evidence is open to question because what the original observers reported may have been distorted by their disapproval of homosexuality and by their definition of it, which may be different from the one we wish to adopt....

Allowing for such weaknesses, the Human Relations Area Files are the best single source of comparative information. Their evidence on homosexuality has been summarized by Ford and Beach (1952), who identify two broad types of accepted patterns: the institutionalized homosexual role and the liaison between men and boys who are otherwise heterosexual.

The recognition of a distinct role of *berdache* or transvestite is, they say, "the commonest form of institutionalized homosexuality." This form shows a marked similarity to that in our own society, though in some ways it is even more extreme. The Mojave Indians of California and Arizona, for example, recognized both an *alyhā*, a male transvestite who took the role of the woman in sexual intercourse, and a *hwamē*, a female homosexual who took the role of the male. People were believed to be born as *alyhā* or *hwamē*, hints of their future proclivities occurring in their mothers' dreams during pregnancy. If a young boy began to behave like a girl and take an interest in women's things instead of men's, there was an initiation ceremony in which he would become an *alyhā*. After that he would dress and act like a woman, would be referred to as "she" and could take "husbands."

But the Mojave pattern differs from ours in that although the *alyhā* was considered regretable and amusing, he was not condemned and was given public recognition. The attitude was that "he was an *alyhā*, he could not help it." But the "husband" of an *alyhā* was an ordinary man who happened to have chosen an *alyhā*, perhaps because they were good housekeepers or because they were believed to be "lucky in love," and he would be the butt of endless teasing and joking.

This radical distinction between the feminine, passive homosexual and his masculine, active partner is one which is not made very much in our own society, but which is very important in the

Middle East. There, however, neither is thought of as being a "born" homosexual, although the passive partner, who demeans himself by his feminine submission, is despised and ridiculed while the active one is not. In most of the ancient Middle East, including among the Jews until the return from the Babylonian exile, there were male temple prostitutes. Thus even cultures that recognize a separate homosexual role may not define it in the same way as our culture does.

Many other societies accept or approve of homosexual liaisons as part of a variegated sexual pattern. Usually these are confined to a particular stage in the individual's life. Among the Aranda of Central Australia, for instance, there are long-standing relationships of several years' duration between unmarried men and young boys, starting at the age of 10 to 12 years (Ford and Beach 1952: 132). This is rather similar to the well-known situation in classical Greece, but there, of course, the older man could have a wife as well. Sometimes, however, as among the Siwans of North Africa (Ford and Beach 1952: 131–2), all men and boys can and are expected to engage in homosexual activities, apparently at every stage of life. In all of these societies there may be much homosexual behaviour, but there are no "homosexuals."

The Development of the Homosexual Role in England

The problem of method is even more acute in dealing with historical material than with anthropological, for history is usually concerned with "great events" rather than with recurrent patterns. There are some records of attempts to curb sodomy among minor churchmen during the medieval period (May 1938: 65, 101), which seem to indicate that it was common. At least they suggest that laymen feared on behalf of their sons that it was common. The term "catamite," meaning "boy kept for immoral purposes," was first used in 1593, again suggesting that this practice was common then. But most of the historical references to homosexuality relate either to great men or to great scandals. However, over the last seventy years or so various scholars have tried to trace the history of sex, and it is possible to glean a good deal from what they have found and also from what they have failed to establish.

Their studies of English history before the seventeenth century consist usually of inconclusive speculation as to whether certain men, such as Edward II, Christopher Marlowe, William Shakespeare, were or were not homosexual. Yet the disputes are inconclusive not because of lack of evidence but because none of these men fits the modern stereotype of the homosexual.

It is not until the end of the seventeenth century that other kinds of information become available, and it is possible to move from speculations about individuals to descriptions of homosexual life. At this period references to homosexuals as a type and to a rudimentary homosexual subculture, mainly in London, begin to appear. But the earliest descriptions of homosexuals do not coincide exactly with the modern conception. There is much more stress on effeminacy and in particular on transvestism, to such an extent that there seems to be no distinction at first between transvestism and homosexuality. The terms emerging at this period to describe homosexuals—Molly, Nancy-boy, Madge-cull—emphasize effeminacy. In contrast the modern terms—like fag, queer, gay, bent—do not have this implication.

By the end of the seventeenth century, homosexual transvestites were a distinct enough group to be able to form their own clubs in London. Edward Ward's *History of the London Clubs,* first published in 1709, describes one called "The Mollie's Club" which met "in a certain tavern in the City" for "parties and regular gatherings." The members "adopt[ed] all the small vanities natural to the feminine sex to such an extent that they try to speak, walk, chatter, shriek and scold as women do, aping them as well in other respects." The other respects apparently included the enactment of marriages and childbirth. The club was discovered and broken up by agents of the Reform Society. There were a number of similar scandals during the course of the eighteenth century as various homosexual coteries were exposed.

A writer in 1729 describes the widespread homosexual life of the period:

> They also have their Walks and Appointments, to meet and pick up one another, and their particular Houses of Resort to go to, because they dare not trust themselves in an open Tavern. About twenty of these sort of Houses have been discovered, besides the Nocturnal Assemblies of great numbers of the like vile Persons, what they call the Markets, which are the Royal Exchange, Lincoln's Inn, Bog Houses, the south side of St. James's Park, the Piazzas in Covent Garden, St Clement's Churchyard, etc.
>
> It would be a pretty scene to behold them in their clubs and cabals, how they assume the air and affect the name of Madam or Miss, Betty or Molly, with a chuck under the chin, and "Oh you bold pullet, I'll break your eggs," and then frisk and walk away. [Taylor 1965: 142]

The notion of exclusive homosexuality became well established during this period:

two Englishmen, Leith and Drew, were accused of paederasty.... The evidence given by the plaintiffs was, as was generally the case in these trials, very imperfect. On the other hand the defendants denied the accusation, and produced witnesses to prove their predeliction for women. They were in consequence acquitted. [Bloch 1938: 334]

This could only have been an effective argument in a society that perceived homosexual behaviour as incompatible with heterosexual tastes.

During the nineteenth century there are further reports of raided clubs and homosexual brothels. However, by this time the element of transvestism had diminished in importance. Even the male prostitutes are described as being of masculine build, and there is more stress upon sexual licence and less upon dressing up and play-acting....

Conclusion

This paper has dealt with only one small aspect of the sociology of homosexuality. It is, nevertheless, a fundamental one. For it is not until he sees homosexuals as a social category, rather than a medical or psychiatric one, that the sociologist can begin to ask the right questions about the specific content of the homosexual role and about the organization and functions of homosexual groups. All that has been done here is to indicate that the role does not exist in many societies, that it only emerged in England towards the end of the seventeenth century, and that, although the existence of the role in modern America appears to have some effect on the distribution of homosexual behaviour, such behaviour is far from being monopolized by persons who play the role of homosexual.

REFERENCES
Bieber, I. 1965. *Homosexuality.* New York: Basic Books.
Bloch, I. 1938. *Sexual Life in England, Past and Present.* London: Francis Alder.
Ford, C. S. and Beach, F. 1952. *Patterns of Sexual Behavior.* London: Metheun.
Krafft-Ebing, R. Von 1965. *Psychopathic Sexualis.* New York: G. P. Putnam's & Sons.
May, G. 1938. *Social Control of Sex.* London: Allen & Unwin.

REFLECTING ON MEANING

1. How does McIntosh differentiate between homosexuality as a "condition" and as a "role"? What does she mean when she says

that the "conception of homosexuality as a condition is, in itself, a possible object of study"? Why does she want us to accept a definition of "role" in terms of expectations that may or may not be fulfilled? She argues that only when sociologists begin to view "homosexuals as a social category, rather than a medical or psychiatric one," will they be able to do what?

2. Explain the two ways that the "practice of the social labeling of persons as deviant" operates as a "mechanism of social control." How is this similar to the way in which the treatment of criminals helps to control the behavior of the rest of society? Why should sociologists examine this process "objectively"?

3. McIntosh examines the homosexual role in various societies: the Mojave Indians, the ancient Middle East, the Aranda of Central Australia, classical Greece, and the Siwans of North Africa. How is the homosexual role different in each of these societies? Describe the development of the homosexual role in England. What is the difference between the earliest descriptions of homosexuals and the modern conception of them? How are terms used to describe homosexuals in the seventeenth century different from those used today?

EXPLORING RHETORICAL STRATEGIES

1. McIntosh's essay is divided into various sections: discussion of homosexuality as a condition and a role; the homosexual role in various societies; the development of the homosexual role in England; and a conclusion. Does the evidence that she presents and its organization convince you of her thesis? Why or why not? How might she have improved her essay's organization?

2. This essay is an excerpted version of an original piece that appeared over thirty years ago. How might the original audience have responded to McIntosh's discussion of homosexuality? How might a contemporary audience's response be different?

3. McIntosh includes many terms in her essay that have been used to describe homosexuals. What rhetorical effect do McIntosh's descriptions of the *berdache, alyhā,* and *hwamē* have on her argument? What point does she make about seventeenth-century terms (*Molly, Nancy-boy,* and *Madge-cull*) in contrast to late 1960s terms (*fag, queer, gay, bent*)? Recently, the words *queer* and *gay* have been reappropriated by homosexuals, for what purpose?

Sexual Culture

EDMUND WHITE

---

*In this essay, writer Edmund White challenges social as-
sumptions about gay society. White attempts to define what it
means to be gay, and he argues that sexuality alone cannot
adequately define either "gays" or "straights." His observations
on both gay and straight culture are thought-provoking and
controversial.*

"Do gay men have friends—I mean," she said, "are they
friends with each other?" Since the woman asking was
a New Yorker, the owner of one of the city's simplest
and priciest restaurants, someone who's known gays all her life, I
found the question honest, shocking, and revealing of a narrow but
bottomless abyss between us.

Of course New York is a city of total, even absolute strangers
rubbing shoulders: the Hasidim in their yellow school bus being
conveyed back to Brooklyn from the jewelry district, beards and
black hats glimpsed through mud-splattered windows in a sun-
dimmed daguerreotype; the junkie pushing the baby carriage and
telling his wife, the prostitute, as he points to his tattooed biceps, "I
haven't partied in this vein for years"; Moonies doing calisthenics
at midnight in their Eighth Avenue center high above empty
Thirty-fourth Street. . . . But this alienation wasn't religious or ethnic. The woman and I spoke the same language, knew the same
people; we both considered Marcella Hazan fun but no substitute
for Simone Beck. How odd that she, as lower-upper-middle-class as
I, shouldn't know whether gay men befriended one another.

It was then that I saw how mysterious gay culture is—not homosexuality, which is merely an erotic tropism; but modern American gay culture, which is a special way of laughing, spending
money, ordering priorities, encoding everything from song lyrics
to mirror-shiny military shoes. None of the usual modes for a subculture will do, for gay men are brought up by heterosexuals to be
straight, they seek other men through what feels very much like a
compulsion though they enter the ghetto by choice, yet once they

make that choice it reshapes their lives, even their bodies, certainly their wardrobes. Many gay men live among straights as Marranos, those Spanish Jews who pretended during the Inquisition to convert to Christianity but continued to observe the old rites in cellars, when alone, in the greatest secrecy. Gays aren't *like* blacks or Jews since they often *are* black or Jewish, and their affectional preference isn't a color or a religion though it has spawned a culture not unlike an ethnic minority's. Few Jews have Christian siblings, but most gays have straight brothers and sisters or at least straight parents. Many American Jews have been raised to feel they belong to the Chosen People, at once superior and inferior to gentiles, but every gay discovers his sexual nature with a combination of pain and relief, regret at being excluded from the tribe but elation at discovering the solution to the puzzle.

Gays aren't a nationality. They aren't Chicanos or Italo-Americans or Irish-Americans, but they do constitute one of the most potent political forces in big cities such as New York, Philadelphia, Washington (where gays and blacks elected Marion Barry mayor), Houston, Los Angeles, and San Francisco (where gays are so numerous they've splintered into countless factions, including the lesbian S/M group Samois and the Sisters of Perpetual Indulgence, a group of drag nuns, one of whose members ran in a cowl and wimple as a candidate in the last citywide election). Not ethnic but a minority, not a polis but political, not a nationality but possessed of a costume, customs, and a patois, not a class but an economic force (not only as a market for records, films, vacations, and clothes but also as an army of worker ants who, for better or worse, have gentrified the center cities, thereby creating a better tomorrow for single young white heterosexual professionals).

Imagine a religion one enters against one's parents' will—and against one's own. Imagine a race one joins at sixteen or sixty without changing one's hue or hair texture (unless at the tanning or beauty salon). Imagine a sterile nation without descendants but with a long, misty regress of ancestors, without an articulated self-definition but with a venerable history. Imagine an exclusive club that includes a P.R. (Puerto Rican) boy of sixteen wearing ankle-high black-and-white Converse basketball shoes and a petrol green shirt sawed off to reveal a Praxitelean stomach—and also includes a P.R. (Public Relations) WASP executive of forty in his Prince of Wales plaids and Cole-Haan tasseled loafers.

If one is gay, one is always in a crucial relationship to gayness as such, a defining category that is so full it is nearly empty (Renaud Camus writes: "Homosexuality is always elsewhere because it is everywhere"). No straight man stands in rapt contemplation of his straightness unless he's an ass. To be sure, heterosexuals may wonder over the significance of their homosexual fantasies, though even that morbid exercise is less popular now than formerly; as Barbara Ehrenreich acutely observes in her new study of the heterosexual male revolt, *The Hearts of Men,* the emergence of gay liberation ended the period in which everyone suspected everyone else of being "latently" homosexual. Now there are open homosexuals, and heterosexual men are exempt from the automatic suspicion of deviance.

No homosexual can take his homosexuality for granted. He must sound it, palpate it, auscultate it as though it were the dead limb of a tree or the living but tricky limb of a body; for that reason all homosexuals are "gay philosophers" in that they must invent themselves. At a certain point one undergoes a violent conversion into a new state, the unknown, which one then sets about knowing as one will. Surely everyone experiences his or her life as an artifact, as molten glass being twirled and pinched into a shape to cool, or as a novel at once capacious and suspenseful, but no one is more a *Homo faber* (in the sense of both "fabricator" and "fabulist") than a homo. It would be vain, of course, to suggest that this creativity is praiseworthy, an ambition rather than a response.

Sometimes I try to imagine how straights—not fundamentalist know-nothings, not rural innocents, not Freudian bigots, but educated urban heterosexuals—look at gay men (do they even see lesbians?). When they see gay men, what do they see? A mustache, a pumped-up body in black jeans and a tank top, an eye-catching tattoo (braided rope around the biceps)? And what do they think ("they," in this case, *hypocrite lecteur,* being *you*)? Do you see something at once ludicrous and mildly enviable in the still youthful but overexercised body of this forty-year-old clone with the aggressive stare and soft voice? If you're a woman, do you find so much preening over appearance in a grown man...well, if not offensive, at least unappetizing; energy better spent on a career, on a family— on you? If you're a man, does it incense you that this jerk is out of harness, too loose, too free, has so lightly made a mockery of manhood? Once, on a radio call-in show a cop called in to tell me he had to admire the old-style queens back when it was rough being queer but that now, jeez, these guys swapping spit wit' a goil one week, wit' a guy the next, they're too lazy, they just don't know the fine art of being a man, it's all just too easy.

Your sentiments, perhaps?

Do you see gays as menacing satyrs, sex fiends around whom it's dangerous to drop your soap, *and* as feeble sissies, frail wood

nymphs locked within massive trunks and limbs? Or, more positively if just as narrowly, are you a sybaritic het who greets the sight
of gays with cries of glee, convinced you've stumbled on liberty
hall, where sexual license of every sort–including your sort–is
bound to reign? In fact, such sybarites often do regard gay men as
comrades in arms, fellow libertines, and fellow victims in a country
phobic to pleasure.

Or do gays just irk you? Do you regard them as a tinselly distraction in your peripheral vision? As errant, obstinate atoms that
can't be drawn into any of the usual social molecules, men who if
they insist on their gayness won't really do at any of the solemni-
ties, from dinner parties to debutante balls, all of which depend on
strict gender dimorphism for a rational seating plan? Since any
proper gathering requires the threat of adultery for excitement and
the prospect of marriage as a justification, of what earthly use are
gays? Even the few fearless straight guys who've invaded my gay
gym drift toward one another, not out of soap-dropping panic but
because otherwise their dirty jokes fall on deaf or prettily blushing
ears and their taunting, butt-slapping mix of rivalry and camaraderie provokes a weird hostility or a still weirder thrill.

And how do gays look at straights? In Andrew Holleran's su-
perb new novel, *Nights in Aruba,* the narrator wonders "what it would
be like to be the head of a family, as if with that all my problems
would drop away, when in fact they would have merely been replaced by another set. I would not have worried about the size of my
penis, the restrictions of age, the difficulty of finding love; I would
have worried about mortgages, tuition, my youngest daughter's
asthma, my competition at Shearson Loeb Rhoades." What makes
this speculation so characteristically gay is that it is so focused on the
family man, for if the nineteenth-century tart required, even invented the convent-bred virgin to contemplate, in the same way the
homosexual man today must insult and revere, mock and envy this
purely imaginary bourgeois paterfamilias, a creature extinct except
in gay fantasies. Meanwhile, of course, the family man devotes his
time to scream therapy and tai chi, ticking off Personals in the *Village
Voice* and wriggling out of visits from his kids, two punked-out teens
who live in a feminist compound with his divorced wife, now a lesbian potter of great sensitivity and verve if low energy.

So much for how the two sexes (straight and gay) regard each
other. If the camera were to pull back and frame both worlds in the
lens, how would the two systems compare?

The most obvious difference is that whereas heterosexuality
does include two sexes, since homosexuality does not it must improvise a new polarity moment by moment. Such a polarity seems

necessary to sexual desire, at least as it is constructed in our culture. No wonder that some gay men search out the most extreme opposites (someone of a distant race, a remote language, another class or age); no wonder that even that convinced heterosexual Flaubert was finally able to unbend with a boy prostitute in Egypt, an exotic who provided him with all the difference desire might demand. Other gay men seek out their twins—so that the beloved, I suppose, can stand in for oneself as one bows down to this false god and plays in turn his father, teacher, son, godfather, or god. Still others institutionalize the polarity in that next-best thing to heterosexuality: sadomasochism, the only vice that anthologizes all family and romantic relationships.

Because every gay man loves men, he comes to learn at first hand how to soothe the savage breast of the male ego. No matter how passive or girlish or shy the new beau might be in the boudoir, he will become the autocrat of the dinner table. Women's magazines are always planning articles on gay men and straight women; I'd say what they have most in common, aside from a few shared sexual techniques, is a body of folk wisdom about that hardhead, that bully, that maddeningly self-involved creature, the human male. As studies have surprisingly shown, men talk more than women, interrupt them more often, and determine the topics of conversation and object to women's assertions with more authority and frequency. When two gay men get together, especially after the first romantic urge to oblige the other wanes, a struggle for conversational dominance ensues, a conflict only symptomatic of larger arguments over every issue from where to live to how and whom to entertain.

To be sure, in this way the gay couple resembles the straight duo that includes an assertive, liberated woman. But while most of the young straight liberated women I know, at least, may protect their real long-range interests (career, mode of life, emotional needs) with vigilance, they're still willing to accommodate *him* in little social ways essential to harmony.

One benign side of straight life is that women conceive of men as "characters," as full-bodied, multifaceted beings who are first social, second familial, third amorous or amicable, and only finally physical. I'm trying politely to say that women are lousy judges of male beauty; they're easily taken in by such superficial traits as loyalty, dependability, charm, a sense of humor. Women don't, or at least didn't, judge men as so much beefcake. But men, both straight and gay, start with looks, the most obvious currency of value, worth, price. Let's say that women see men as characters in a long family novel in which the men are introduced complete with phrenology, genealogy, and one annoying and two endearing traits, whereas men see their partners (whether male or female) as cars, makes to be instantly spotted, appraised, envied, made. A woman wants to be envied for her husband's goodness, his character, whereas a man wants to be envied for his wife's beauty, rarity, status—her drivability. Straight life combines the warmth and *Gemütlichkeit* of the nineteenth-century bourgeois (the woman) with the steely corporate ethos of the twentieth-century functionary (the man). If gay male life, freed of this dialectic, has become supremely efficient (the trapdoor beside the bed) and only momentarily intimate (a whole life cycle compressed into the one-night stand), then the gain is dubious, albeit an extreme expression of one trend in our cultural economy.

But of course most morality, that is, popular morality—not real morals, which are unaffected by consensus, but mores, which are a form of fashion—is nothing but a species of nostalgia, a cover-up for pleasurable and profitable but not yet admissible innovations. If so many people condemn promiscuity, they do so at least partly because there is no available rhetoric that could condone, much less glamorize, impermanence in love. Nevertheless, it strikes me that homosexuals, masters of improvisation fully at home with the arbitrary and equipped with an internal compass that orients them instantly to any social novelty, are perhaps the most sensitive indicators of the future.

The birthrate declines, the divorce rate climbs, and popular culture (movies, television, song lyrics, advertising, fashions, journalism) is so completely and irrevocably secularized that the so-called religious revival is of no more lasting importance than the fad for Kabuki in a transistorized Japan—a temporary throwback, a slight brake on the wheel. In such a world the rate of change is so rapid that children, once they are in school, can learn little from their parents but must assimilate new forms of behavior from their peers and new information from specialized instructors. As a result, parental authority declines, and the demarcations between the generations become ever more formidable. Nor do the parents regret their loss of control, since they're devoting all their energy to cultivating the inner self in the wholesale transition of our society from an ethic of self-sacrifice to one of self-indulgence, the so-called aristocraticization of middle-class life that has dominated the peaceful parts of this century in the industrialized West.

In the contemporary world the nineteenth-century experiment of compassionate marriage, never very workable, has collapsed utterly. The exact nature of the collapse isn't very clear yet because of our distracting, probably irrelevant habit of psychologizing every crisis (thus the endless speculations in the lowbrow press on the Irresponsible Male and the Defeminized Female or

the paradoxical and cruelly impracticable advice to women readers to "go for it all–family, career, marriage, romance, *and* the rev-
eries of solitude"). We treat the failure of marriage as though it
were the failure of individuals to achieve it–a decline in grit or maturity or commitment or stamina rather than the unraveling of a
poorly tied knot. Bourgeois marriage was meant to concentrate
friendship, romance, and sex into an institution at once familial
and economic. Only the most intense surveillance could keep such
a bulky, ill-assorted load from bursting at the seams. Once the he-
donism of the '60s relaxed that tension, people began to admit that
friendship tranquilizes sexual desires (when mates become siblings, the incest taboo sets in) and that romance is by its very nature
evanescent though indefinitely renewable given an endless supply
of fresh partners. Neither sexual nor romantic attraction, so capricious, so passionate, so unstable, could ever serve as the basis for
an enduring relationship, which can be balanced only on the plinth
of esteem, that easy, undramatic, intimate kind of love one would
say resembled family love if families were more loving.

It is this love that so many gay couples know about, aim for,
and sometimes even express. If all goes well, two gay men will
meet through sex, become lovers, weather the storms of jealousy
and the diminution of lust, develop shared interests (a hobby, a
business, a house, a circle), and end up with a long-term, probably
sexless camaraderie that is not as disinterested as friendship or as
seismic as passion or as charged with contradiction as fraternity.
Younger gay couples feel that this sort of relationship, when it happens to them, is incomplete, a compromise, and they break up in
order to find total fulfillment (i.e., tireless passion) elsewhere. But
older gay couples stay together, cultivate their mild, reasonable
love, and defend it against the ever-present danger of the sexual al-
lure exercised by a newcomer. For the weak point of such marriages is the eternally recurring fantasy, first in one partner and
then the other, of "total fulfillment." Needless to say, such couples
can wreak havoc on the newcomer who fails to grasp that Bob and
Fred are not just roommates. They may have separate bedrooms
and regular extracurricular sex partners or even beaux, but Bob
monitors Fred's infatuations with an eye attuned to nuance, and at
a certain point will intervene to banish a potential rival.

I think most straight people would find these arrangements
more scandalous than the infamous sexual high jinks of gays. Because these arrangements have no name, no mythology, no public
or private acknowledgment, they're almost invisible even to the
participants. Thus if you asked Bob in a survey what he wanted, he
might say he wanted a "real" lover. He might also say Fred was

"just a roommate, my best friend, we used to be lovers." So much for explicit analysis, but over the years Bob has cannily steered his affair with Fred between the Scylla of excessive fidelity (which is finally so dull no two imaginative gay men could endure it) and the Charybdis of excessive tolerance (which could leave both men feeling so neglected they'd seek love elsewhere for sure).

There are, of course, countless variants to this pattern. The men live together or they don't. If they don't, they can maintain the civilized fiction of romance for years. They plan dates, honeymoons, take turns sleeping over at each other's house, and avoid conflicts about domestic details. They keep their extracurricular sex lives separate, they agree not to snoop—or they have threeways. Or one of the pair has an active sex life and the other has abandoned the erotic arena.

Are gay men friends with each other? the woman asked me.

The question may assume that gays are only sexual, and that a man eternally on the prowl can never pause for mere affection that a gay Don Juan is lonely. Or perhaps the question reveals a confusion about a society of one gender. Since a straight woman has other women for friends and men for lovers, my questioner might have wondered how the same sex could serve in both capacities.

The first supposition—that gay men are only sexual—is an ancient prejudice, and like all prejudices mostly untrue but in one sense occasionally accurate. If politically conscious homosexuals prefer the word *gay* to *homosexual,* they do so because they want to make the world regard attraction to members of the same gender as an affectional preference as well as a sexual orientation.

For instance, there are some gay men who prefer the feel of women's bodies to men's, who are even more comfortable sexually with women, but whose emotions crave contact with other men. Gay men have unfinished emotional business with other men—scary, promising, troubling, absorbing business—whereas their sentiments toward women (at least women not in their family) are much simpler, more stable, less fraught. Affection, passionate affection, is never simple; it is built out of equal parts of yearning, fear, and appetite. For that reason the friendship of one gay man fiercely drawn to another is as tense as any heterosexual passion, whereas a sexless, more disinterested gay friendship is as relaxed, as good-tempered as a friendship, say, between two straight men.

Gay men, then, do divide other gays into two camps—those who are potential partners (lovers) and those who are not (friends). But where gay life is more ambiguous than the world at large (and possibly for that reason more baffling to outsiders) is that the members of the two camps, lovers and friends, are always switching places or hovering somewhere in the margin between. It is these unconfessed feelings that have always intrigued me the most as a novelist—the unspoken love between two gay men, say, who pretend they are just friends, cruising buddies, merely filling in until Mr. Right comes along (mercifully, he never does).

In one sense, the public's prejudice about a gay obsession with sex is valid. The right to have sex, even to look for it, has been so stringently denied to gays for so many centuries that the drive toward sexual freedom remains a bright, throbbing banner in the fierce winds whipping over the ghetto. Laws against sex have always created the biggest problems for homosexuals; they helped to define the very category of homosexuality. For that reason, the gay community, despite its invention of a culture no more eroticized than any other, still cannot give up its origin in sexual desire and its suppression.

But what about the "excessive" promiscuity of gay men, the infamous quickies, a phenomenon only temporarily held in check by the AIDS crisis? Don't the quickies prove that gay men are essentially bizarre, fundamentally lacking in judgment—*oversexed?* Of course, gay men behave as all men would were they free of the strictures of female tastes, needs, prohibitions, and expectations. There is nothing in gay male life that cannot be attributed either to its minority status or to its all-male population. All men want quick, uncomplicated sexual adventure (as well as sustained romantic passion); in a world of all men, that desire is granted.

The very universality of sexual opportunity within the modern gay ghetto has, paradoxically, increased the importance of friendship. In a society not based on the measured denial or canalization of sexual desire, there is more energy left over for friendship. Relationships are less loaded in gay life (hence the celebrated gay irony, a levity equivalent to seeing through conventions). In so many ways gays are still prisoners of the dominant society, but in this one regard gays are freer than their jailers: because gay relationships are not disciplined by religious, legal, economic, and political ceremonies but only by the dictates of conscience and the impulses of the heart, they don't stand for anything larger. They aren't symbols but realities, not laws but entities sufficient unto themselves, not consequential but ecstatic.

REFLECTING ON MEANING

1. The question "Are gay men friends with each other?" illuminates a certain assumption about the accepted definition of gayness. What is this assumption? How does society define gayness? Why

does White make a distinction between *gay* and *homosexual?* What is gay culture? By implication, what is White suggesting about the labels *straight* and *heterosexual?* About straight culture? Do you agree that culture, rather than sexuality, provides a firmer foundation for defining both gays and straights? Why or why not?

2. White argues that the most obvious difference between homosexual and heterosexual relationships is that homosexuals "must improvise a new polarity moment by moment." How do gays achieve "polarity" in their relationships? What polarity is inherent in straight relationships? According to White, why is polarity an essential component of all sexual relationships? Do you agree that "polarity seems necessary to sexual desire"? Why or why not?

3. Consider White's observation on the similarities between gay men and straight women: "I'd say what they have most in common, aside from a few shared sexual techniques, is a body of folk wisdom about that hardhead, that bully, that maddeningly self-involved creature, the human male." What is White suggesting about the way both gays and women perceive their male partners? What is he suggesting about the ways they interact with male partners? Do you think that White's observation is valid or reasonable? Why or why not?

EXPLORING RHETORICAL STRATEGIES

1. Well into the essay, why does the "they" of White's discussion shift to a "you"? Who is the "you" that White addresses? Is this "you" gay or straight? What effect does this shift in address create? As you were reading, how did it make you feel? Why do you think White makes this shift? What is his strategy here? In what ways does it help him make his point?

2. Another of White's strategies is to highlight the role of perception in determining our realities. At one point in his essay, White clues us in to one of his strategies for making this point: "If the camera were to pull back and frame both worlds in the lens, how would the two systems compare?" What is this strategy? What was his camera focused on prior to this statement? What kind of "picture" was he presenting? How does the perspective he offers change in the discussion that follows this statement? In what ways does this strategy help him make his point about the ways perception influences reality?

3. How might you characterize the tone of White's essay? If you could hear him speaking, what tone of voice would he be using? How has White used tone to convey a certain picture of himself to his audience? How would you describe the persona he adopts in this essay?

What Price Independence?
Social Reactions to Lesbians, Spinsters, Widows, and Nuns

ROSE WEITZ

Sociologist Rose Weitz uses a wealth of historical facts and research to demonstrate how lesbians and other independent women—witches, nuns, spinsters, and widows—threaten male dominance and are thus stigmatized by the social order.

For seven days in 1981, nineteen-year-old Stephanie Rieth-miller was held captive by two men and a woman in a secluded Alabama cabin. During that time, according to Riethmiller, her captors constantly harangued her on the sinfulness of homosexuality, and one captor raped her nightly. Riethmiller's parents, who feared that their daughter was involved in a lesbian relationship with her roommate, had paid $8,000 for this "deprogramming"; her mother remained in the next room throughout her captivity. When the kidnappers were brought to trial, the jury, in the opinion of the judge, "permit[ted] their moral evaluations to enter into their legal conclusions" and failed to bring in a guilty verdict (Raskin 1982, 19).

As the Riethmiller case shows, the individual who identifies herself as a lesbian—or who is so labeled by others—may face severe social, economic, and legal sanctions. Along with communists, the diseased, and the insane, persons who openly acknowledge their homosexuality may be denied admission to the United States. In most U.S. jurisdictions, discrimination against homosexuals in housing, employment, child custody and other areas of life is legal, while homosexual behavior is illegal. Gay persons are not covered under any of the national civil rights acts, and most court decisions have held that they are not covered under the equal protection clause of the United States Constitution. (For an excellent review of the legal status of homosexuality, see Rivera 1979.)

These legal restrictions reflect generally held social attitudes. Surveys conducted during the 1970s using large national probability samples found that between 70 percent and 75 percent of the Americans interviewed believed that sexual relations between two members of the same sex were always wrong (Glenn and Weaver 1979).

Cross-Cultural and Historical Views of Lesbianism

To most Americans, stigmatization and punishment of lesbianism seem perfectly natural. Yet such has not always been the case. In fact, a study of attitudes toward homosexuality in seventy-six cultures around the world found that in 64 percent of those cultures "homosexual activities of one sort or another" are considered normal and socially acceptable for certain members of the community" (Ford and Beach 1951, 130).

In the Western world, male homosexuality, which had been an accepted part of Greek and Roman culture, was increasingly rejected by society as the power of the Christian church grew (Barrett 1979). Yet lesbianism generally remained unrecognized legally and socially until the beginning of the modern age. Instead, beginning with the Renaissance, intimate "romantic friendships" between women were a common part of life, at least among the middle and upper classes (Faderman 1981).[1]

> Women who were romantic friends were everything to each other. They lived to be together. They thought of each other constantly. They made each other deliriously happy or horribly miserable by the increase or abatement of their proffered love. They were jealous of other female friends (and certainly of male friends) who impinged on their beloved's time or threatened to carry away a portion of her affections. They vowed that if it were at all possible they would someday live together, or at least die together, and they declared that both eventualities would be their greatest happiness. They embraced and kissed and walked hand in hand, and some even held each other all night in sleep. But unless they were transvestites or considered "unwomanly" in some male's conception, there was little chance that their relationships would be considered lesbian [Faderman 1981, 84].

We cannot know whether most romantic friends expressed their love for women genitally, and we do know that most were married to men (at least in part for economic survival). A reading of letters and journals from this period leaves no doubt, however, of the erotic and emotional intensity of these relationships between women and little doubt that in another era the relationships would have been expressed sexually (Smith-Rosenberg 1975; Faderman 1981). Yet belief in the purity of these relationships lingered even into the twentieth century. For example, when the British Parliament attempted in 1885 to add mention of lesbianism to its criminal code, Queen Victoria refused to sign the bill, on the ground that such behavior did not exist (Ettorre 1980).

Given that lesbianism has not always elicited negative social reactions, the current intolerance of it cannot derive from some universal biological or ethical law. What, then, causes these negative social reactions? I suggest in this article that at least part of the answer lies in the threat that lesbianism presents to the power of males in society. Furthermore, I suggest that whenever men fear women's sexual or economic independence, all unmarried women face an increased risk of stigmatization and punishment. The experience of such diverse groups as lesbians, medieval nuns, and Hindu widows shows the interrelated social fates of all women not under the direct control of men.

Lesbians and the Threat to Male Power

Western culture teaches that women are the weaker sex, that they cannot flourish—or perhaps even survive—without the protection of men. Women are taught that they cannot live happy and fulfilled lives without a Prince Charming, who is superior to them in all ways. In the struggle to find and keep their men, women learn to view each other as untrustworthy competitors. They subordinate the development of their own psychological, physical, and professional strengths to the task of finding male protectors who will make up for their shortcomings. In this way, Western culture keeps women from developing bonds with each other, while it maintains their dependence on men.

Lesbians[2] throw a large wrench into the works of this cultural system. In a society that denigrates women, lesbians value women enough to spend their lives with women rather than with men. Lesbians therefore do not and cannot rely on the protection of men. Knowing that they will not have that protection, lesbians are forced to develop their own resources. The very survival of lesbians therefore suggests the potential strength of all women and their ability to transcend their traditional roles. At the same time, since lesbians do not have even the illusion of male protection that marriage provides, and since they are likely to see their fate as tied to other women rather than to individual men, lesbians may be more likely than heterosexual women to believe in the necessity of fighting for women's rights; the heavy involvement of lesbians in the feminist movement seems to support this thesis (Abbott and Love 1972).

Lesbians also threaten the dominant cultural system by presenting, or at least appearing to present, an alternative to the typical inequality of heterosexual relationships. Partners attempting to equalize power in a heterosexual relationship must first neutralize deeply ingrained traditional sex roles. Since lesbian relationships generally contain no built-in assumption of the superiority of one partner,[3] developing an egalitarian relationship may be easier. Lesbian relationships suggest both that a love between equals is possible and that an alternative way of obtaining such a love may exist. Regardless of the actual likelihood of achieving equality in a lesbian relationship, the threat to the system remains, as long as lesbian relationships are believed to be more egalitarian. This threat increases significantly when, as in the past few years, lesbians express pride in and satisfaction with their life-style.

If lesbianism incurs social wrath because of the threat it presents to existing sexist social arrangements, then we should find that lesbianism is most negatively viewed by persons who hold sexist beliefs. Evidence from various studies (summarized in Weinberger and Millham 1979) supports this hypothesis. Homophobia (i.e., fear and hatred of homosexuals) appears strongly correlated with support for traditional sex roles. Survey data suggest that support for traditional sex roles explains homophobia better than do negative or conservative attitudes toward sex in general (MacDonald et al. 1973; MacDonald and Games 1974).

Historical data on when and under what circumstances lesbianism became stigmatized also support the contention of a link between that stigma and the threat lesbianism poses to male power. As described above, romantic friendships between women were common in both Europe and America from the Renaissance through the late nineteenth century. The women involved were generally accepted or at least tolerated by society even in the few cases where their relationships were openly sexual. That acceptance ceased, however, if either of the women attempted to usurp male privilege in some way—by wearing men's clothing, using a dildo, or passing as a man. Only in these circumstances were premodern-era lesbians likely to suffer social sanctions. In looking at both historical records and fiction from the thirteenth through the nineteenth centuries, Faderman (1981) found that women were, at

most, lightly punished for lesbianism unless they wore male clothing.[4] She therefore concludes that "at the base it was not the sexual
aspects of lesbianism as much as the attempted usurpation of male
prerogative by women who behaved like men that many societies
appeared to find most disturbing" (Faderman 1981, 17).

As long as the women involved did not attempt to obtain
male privileges, romantic friends ran little risk of censure before
the late nineteenth century. The factors behind the shift in attitude
that occurred at that time again suggest the importance of the
threat that lesbianism seemed to pose to male power.

Before the twentieth century, only a small number of independently wealthy women (such as the Ladies of Llangollen [Mayor
1973]) were able to establish their own households and live out
their lives with their female companions (Faderman 1981). By the
second half of the nineteenth century, however, the combined effects of the Civil War in this country and of male migration away
from rural areas in both the United States and Europe had created
a surplus of unmarried women in many communities. At the same
time, the growth of the feminist movement had led to increased educational opportunities for women. These factors, coupled with the
growth of industrialization, opened the possibility of employment
and an independent existence to significant numbers of women.

Once female independence became a real economic possibility, it became a serious concern to those intent on maintaining
the sexual status quo. Relationships between women, which previously had seemed harmless, now took on a new and threatening
appearance. Only at this point do new theories emerge that reject
the Victorian image of the passionless woman (Cott 1978), acknowledge females as sexual beings, and define lesbianism as
pathological.

Stereotypes of lesbianism, first developed in the early twentieth century, reduce the threat to existing social arrangements by
defusing the power of lesbianism as a viable alternative life-style.
According to these stereotypes, all lesbians are either butches or
femmes,[5] and their relationships merely mimic heterosexual relationships. Lesbianism, therefore, seems to offer no advantages over
heterosexuality.

Cultural stereotypes defuse lesbian sexuality by alternately denying and exaggerating it. These stereotypes hold that women become lesbians because of either their inability to find a man or their
hatred of men. Such stereotypes deny that lesbianism may be a positive choice, while suggesting that lesbianism can be cured by the
right man. The supposed futility of lesbian sexuality was summed
up by best-selling author Dr. David Reuben in the phrase, "one

vagina plus another vagina still equals zero" (1969, 217). (Reuben further invalidated lesbianism by locating his entire discussion of the subject within his chapter on prostitution; male homosexuality was "honored" with its own chapter.) In other cultural arenas, lesbians and lesbianism are defined in purely sexual terms, stripped of all romantic, social, or political content. In this incarnation, lesbianism can be subverted into a vehicle for male sexual pleasure; in the world of pornographic films, men frequently construct lesbian scenes to play out their own sexual fantasies.

   In sum, strong evidence suggests that the negative social reactions to lesbianism reflect male fears of female independence, and the social sanctions and cultural stereotypes serve to lessen the threat that these independent women pose to male power.

   If this hypothesis is true, then it should also hold for other groups of women not under direct male control. Next, I briefly discuss how, historically, negative social reactions to such women seem most likely to develop whenever men fear women's sexual or economic independence.

Spinsters, Widows, and Women Religious

   The inquisition against witches that occurred from the fifteenth through the seventeenth centuries represents the most extreme response in the Western world to the threat posed by independent women. The vast majority of the persons executed for witchcraft were women; estimates of the number killed range from under one hundred thousand to several million (Daly 1978). Accusations of witchcraft typically involved charges that the women healed sickness, engaged in prohibited sexual practices, or controlled reproduction (Ehrenreich and English 1973). Such activities threatened the power of the church by giving individuals (especially women) greater control over their own lives, reducing their dependence on the church for divine intervention while inhibiting the natural increase of the Catholic population.

   The witchcraft trials occurred in a society undergoing the first throes of industrialization and urbanization (Nelson 1979). The weakening of the rural extended family forced many women to look for employment outside the home. These unattached women proved especially vulnerable to accusations of witchcraft (Nelson 1979; Daly 1978). As Mary Daly points out, "The targets of attack in the witchcraze were not women defined by assimilation into the patriarchal family. Rather, the witchcraze focused predominantly upon women who had rejected marriage (Spinsters) [sic] and some who had survived it (widows)" (1978, 184).

Contemporary theological beliefs regarding female sexuality magnified the perceived economic and social threat posed by unmarried women. The medieval church viewed all aspects of female sexuality with distrust; unless a woman was virginal or proven chaste, she was believed to be ruled by her sexual desires (Ehrenreich and English 1973). Catholic doctrine blamed Eve's licentiousness for the fall from grace in the Garden of Eden. According to the most popular medieval "manual" for witchhunters, the *Malleus Maleficarum,* most witches were women because "all witchcraft comes from carnal lust, which is in women insatiable" (Kramer and Sprenger 1971, 120). Given this theology, any woman not under the direct sexual control of a man would appear suspect, if not outright dangerous.

For most women living before the nineteenth century who wished to or were forced to remain unmarried, entering the religious life was the only socially acceptable option.[6] During the Middle Ages, a woman could either become a nun or join one of the "secular convents" known as *Beguines* (Nelson 1979; Boulding 1976). Beguines arose to serve the population of surplus unmarried women that had developed in the early European cities. Residents of Beguines took a vow of chastity and obedience while living there, but they could marry thereafter. They spent their days in work and prayer.

Beguines threatened the monopolies of both the guilds and the church. The guilds feared the economic competition of these organized skilled women workers, while the church feared their social and religious independence (Nelson 1979); the Beguines' uncloistered life seemed likely to lead women into sin, while the lack of perpetual vows freed them from direct church supervision. For these reasons, the church in the fourteenth century ordered the Beguine houses dissolved, although some have continued nonetheless to the present day. Residents were urged either to marry or to become nuns (Boulding 1976).

The history of convents similarly illustrates the church's distrust of independent women (Eckenstein 1963). In the early medieval period, many nuns lived with their families. Some nuns showed their religious vocation through the wearing of a veil, while others wore no distinctive dress. Convents served as centers of learning for women, providing educational opportunities not available elsewhere. During this period, many "double monasteries" flourished, in which male and female residents lived and shared decision-making authority.

Given medieval ideas regarding the spiritual weakness and inherent carnality of women, the independence of early medieval nuns could not be allowed to last long. The developing laws of feudalism increasingly restricted the right of women to own land, so that, by the Renaissance, women faced increasing difficulties in attempting to found or to endow convents, while friars began to take over the management of existing convents (Eckenstein 1963). The church gradually closed all double monasteries, pressuring nuns to enter cloisters and to wear religious habits. Education for nuns increasingly seemed unnecessary or even dangerous. For this reason, by the sixteenth century church authorities had significantly decreased the educational opportunities available in most convents, although some convents did manage to preserve their intellectual traditions. Once Latin ceased to be taught, nuns were effectively excluded from all major church decisions.

As Protestant ideas began to infiltrate Europe, the status of unmarried women declined. One of the few areas in which Catholics and early Protestants agreed was the danger presented by independent women. Responding to flagrant sexual offenses in medieval monasteries, Protestants concluded that few men—let alone women, given their basically carnal nature—could maintain a celibate life. They therefore viewed "the religious profession [as] a thing of evil and temptation in which it was not possible to keep holy" (Charitas Perckheimer, quoted in Eckenstein 1963, 467). To Protestants, "marriage was the most acceptable state before God and . . . a woman has no claim to consideration except in her capacity as wife and mother" (Eckenstein 1963, 433). These beliefs, coupled with the political aims of Protestant rulers, culminated in the forced dissolution of convents and monasteries in many parts of Europe. In Protestant Europe, women were left without a socially acceptable alternative to marriage, while, in Catholic Europe, nuns had been stripped of their autonomy.

The belief in female carnality continued until the nineteenth century. At that point, while lower-class women were still considered sexually wanton by their social betters, prescriptive literature began to paint an image of upper-class women as passionless (Cott 1978). In this situation, unmarried lower-class women continued to suffer severe social sanctions as real or suspected prostitutes. Unmarried upper-class women continued to be stigmatized as unnatural, since they were not fulfilling their allotted role as wives and mothers. These upper-class women did not seem particularly threatening, however, since they were assumed, at least in public discourse, to be asexual beings. As a result, social sanctions against them diminished sharply, not to emerge again until women's newfound economic independence significantly changed the social context of romantic friendships among women.

In this historical overview I have so far discussed only events in the Western world. In the West, widows probably evoke less of a sense of threat than do other unmarried women, since widows do not generally seem to have chosen their fate. It is instructive to compare the fate of Hindu widows, who are believed to have caused their husbands' deaths by sins they committed in this or a previous life (Daly 1978; Stein 1978).

Since a Hindu woman's status is determined by her relationship to a man, and since Hindu custom forbids remarriage, widows literally have no place in that society. A widow is a superfluous economic burden on her family. She is also viewed as a potential source of dishonor, since Hindus believe that "women are by nature sexually unreliable and incapable of leading chaste lives without a husband to control them" (Stein 1978, 255). For the benefit of her family and for her own happiness in future lives, a widow was in the past expected to commit suttee—to throw herself alive onto her husband's burning funeral pyre.[7] The horror of suttee was multiplied by the practice of polygamy and by the practice of marrying young girls to grown men, which resulted in the widowing of many young girls before they even reached puberty (Stein 1978; Daly 1978). Suttee, child marriage, and polygamy are illegal under the current government, but they do still occur.

As her only alternative to suttee, a widow was allowed to adopt a life of such poverty and austerity that she rarely survived for long. Her life was made even more miserable by the fact that only faithful wives were permitted to commit suttee. The refusal to commit suttee might therefore be regarded as an admission of infidelity. If a woman declined to immolate herself, her relatives might force her to do so, to protect both her honor and the honor of her family.

Stigmatization of Male Homosexuals

. . . this article has discussed male homosexuality only in passing. Nevertheless, it cannot be ignored that the sanctions against male homosexuality appear even stronger than those against lesbianism. Why might this be so? First, I would argue that anything women do is considered relatively trivial—be it housework, mothering, or lesbianism. Second, whereas lesbians threaten the status quo by refusing to accept their inferior position as women, gay males may threaten it even more by appearing to reject their privileged status as men. Prevailing cultural mythology holds that lesbians want to be males. In a paradoxical way, therefore, lesbians may be perceived as upholding "male" values. Male homosexuality, on the other hand, is regarded as a rejection of masculine values; gay males are regarded as feminized "sissies" and "queens." Thus male homosexuality, with its implied rejection of male privilege, may seem even more incomprehensible and threatening than lesbianism. Finally, research indicates that people in general are more fearful and intolerant of homosexuals of their own sex than of homosexuals belonging to the opposite sex (Weinberger and Millham 1979). The greater stigmatization of male than female homosexuality may therefore simply reflect the greater ability of males to enforce their prejudices.

Conclusions

The stigmatization of independent women—whether spinster, widow, nun, or lesbian—is neither automatic nor natural. Rather, it seems to derive from a particular social constellation in which men fear women's sexual and economic independence. Sociological theory explains how stigmatizing individuals as deviant may serve certain purposes for the dominant community, regardless of the accuracy of the accusations leveled (Erikson 1962). First, particularly when social norms are changing rapidly, labeling and punishing certain behaviors as deviant emphasizes the new or continued unacceptability of those behaviors. The stigmatization of "romantic friendships" in the early twentieth century, for example, forced all members of society to recognize that social norms had changed and that such relationships would no longer be tolerated. Second, stigmatizing certain groups as deviant may increase solidarity within the dominant group, as the dominant group unites against its common enemy. Third, stigmatizing as deviant the individuals who challenge traditional ideas may reduce the threat of social change, if those individuals either lose credibility or are removed from the community altogether.

These principles apply to the stigmatization of independent women, from the labeling of nontraditional women as witches in medieval society to the condemnation of lesbians in contemporary society. Medieval inquisitors used the label *witch* to reinforce the normative boundaries of their community, to unite that community against the perceived source of its problems, and to eliminate completely women who seemed to threaten the social order. Currently, the word *lesbian* is used not only to describe women who love other women but also to censure women who overstep the bounds of the traditional female role and to teach all women that such behavior will not be tolerated. Feminists, women athletes, professional women, and others risk being labeled lesbian for their actions and beliefs. Awareness of the potential social consequences of that label exerts significant pressure on all women to remain in their traditional roles.

Antifeminist forces have used the lesbian label to denigrate all feminists, incite community wrath against them, and dismiss their political claims. In 1969 and 1970, some feminists responded to this social pressure by purging lesbians from their midst and proclaiming their moral purity (Abbott and Love 1972). This tactic proved extremely self-destructive, as movement organizations collapsed in bitterness and dissension. In addition, eliminating lesbian members had little effect, since lesbian-baiting by antifeminists was equally damaging to the movement whether or not it was accurate.

By late 1970, many feminists had realized that trying to remove lesbians from their organizations was both self-destructive and ineffective. In response to this knowledge, various feminist organizations went on record acknowledging sexual preference as a feminist and a civil rights issue and supporting the rights of lesbians (Abbott and Love 1972). In a press conference held in December 1970, various women's liberation activists stated:

> Women's Liberation and Homosexual Liberation are both struggling toward a common goal: a society free from defining and categorizing people by virtue of gender and/or sexual preference. "Lesbian" is a label used as a psychic weapon to keep women locked into their male-defined "feminine role." The essence of that role is that a woman is defined in terms of her relationship to men. A woman is called a Lesbian when she functions autonomously. Women's autonomy is what Women's Liberation is all about [quoted in Abbott and Love 1972, 124).

A leaflet distributed the same month by the New York branch of the National Organization for Women acknowledged that, when charges of lesbianism are made, "it is not one woman's sexual preference that is under attack—it is the freedom of all women to openly state values that fundamentally challenge the basic structure of patriarchy" (quoted in Abbott and Love 1972, 122).

It seems, then, that the fates of feminists and lesbians are inextricably intertwined. Unless and until women's independence is accepted, lesbians will be stigmatized, and unless and until the stigma attached to lesbianism diminishes, the lesbian label will be used as a weapon against those who work for women's independence.

NOTES

1. We have little first-hand data about the intimate lives of lower-class women. Few poorer women could write, and, even if they could and did record their lives, their letters and journals were rarely preserved.

2. I am using the terms *lesbian* and *heterosexual* as nouns simply to ease the flow of the writing. This article focuses on stigmatization, not on some intrinsic quality of individuals. Hence, in this article, *lesbian* and *heterosexual* refer to persons who adopt a particular lifestyle or who are labeled as doing so by significant others. These terms reflect shared social fates, not some essential, inflexible aspect of the individual.
3. While there is no way to ascertain exactly what proportion of lesbian couples adopted butch-femme relationships in the past, recent studies suggest that such relationships have all but disappeared, especially among younger and more feminist lesbians (Wolf 1979; Tanner 1978).
4. The crime for which Joan of Arc was eventually condemned was not witchcraft but the heretical act of wearing male clothing.
5. *butches . . . femmes:* women who adopt particularly masculine or feminine appearance and behavior.
6. However, it should be realized that convent life was not always a chosen refuge. Just as a father could marry his daughter to whatever man he chose, so too could he "marry" his daughter to the church.
7. Suttee was most common among the upper castes (where a widow meant an extra mouth, but not an extra pair of hands), but it occurred throughout Hindu society (Stein 1978).

WORKS CITED

Abbott, Sidney and Barbara Love. *Sappho Was a Right-on Woman: A Liberated View of Lesbianism*. New York: Stein and Day Publishers, 1972.

Barrett, Ellen M. "Legal Homophobia and the Christian Church." *Hastings Law Journal* 30(4): 1019–27, 1979.

Boulding, Elise. *The Underside of History*. Boulder, Colo.: Westview Press, 1976.

Cott, Nancy. "Passionlessness: An Interpretation of Victorian Sexual Ideology, 1790–1850." *Signs: Journal of Women in Culture and Society* 4(2): 219–36, 1978.

Daly, Mary. *Gyn/ecology: The Metaethics of Radical Feminism*. Boston: Beacon Press, 1978.

Eckenstein, Lina. *Women under Monasticism*. New York: Russell and Russell, 1963.

Ehrenreich, Barbara, and Deirdre English. *Witches, Midwives and Nurses: A History of Women Healers*. Old Westbury, N.Y.: Feminist Press, 1973.

Erikson, Kai T. "Notes on the Sociology of Deviance." *Social Problems* 9(Spring): 307–14, 1962.

Ettorre, E. M. *Lesbians, Women and Society*. London: Routledge and Kegan Paul, 1980.

Faderman, Lillian. *Surpassing the Love of Men: Romantic Friendship and Love between Women from the Renaissance to the Present*. New York: William Morrow and Co., 1981.

Ford, Clellan S., and Frank A. Beach. *Patterns of Sexual Behavior*. New York: Harper and Row, 1951.

Glenn, Norval D., and Charles N. Weaver. "Attitudes towards Premarital, Extramarital and Homosexual Relationships in the United States in the 1970s." *Journal of Sex Research* 15(2): 108–17, 1979.

Kramer, H., and J. Sprenger. *Malleus Maleficarum*. Translated by Montague Summers. New York: Dover Publications, 1971.

MacDonald, A. P., and R. G. Games. "Some Characteristics of Those Who Hold Positive and Negative Attitudes towards Homosexuals." *Journal of Homosexuality* 1(1): 9–28, 1974.

MacDonald, A. P., J. Huggins, S. Young, and R. A. Swanson. "Attitudes towards Homosexuality: Preservation of Sex Morality or the Double Standard." *Journal of Consulting and Clinical Psychology* 40(1): 161, 1973.

Mayor, Elizabeth. *The Ladies of Llangollen: A Study of Romantic Friendship*. New York: Penguin Books, 1973.

Nelson, Mary. "Why Witches Were Women." In Jo Freeman (ed.), *Women: A Feminist Perspective*, 2d ed. Palo Alto, Calif.: Mayfield Publishing Co., 1979.

Raskin, Richard. "The 'Deprogramming' of Stephanie Riethmiller," *Ms.*, Sept. 1982, 19.

Reuben, David. *Everything You Always Wanted to Know about Sex But Were Afraid to Ask*. New York: David McKay Co., 1969.

Rivera, Rhonda R. "Our Straight-laced Judges: The Legal Position of Homosexual Persons in the United States." *Hastings Law Journal* 30(4): 799–956, 1979.

Smith-Rosenberg, Carroll. "The Female World of Love and Ritual: Relations between Women in Nineteenth Century America." *Signs: Journal of Women in Culture and Society* 1(1): 1–29, 1975.

Stein, Dorothy K. "Women to Burn: Suttee as a Normative Institution." *Signs: Journal of Women in Culture and Society* 4(2): 253–68, 1978.

Tanner, Donna M. *The Lesbian Couple*. Lexington, Mass.: D. C. Heath and Co., 1978.

Weinberger, Linda E., and Jim Millham. "Attitudinal Homophobia and Support of Traditional Sex Roles." *Journal of Homosexuality* 4(3): 237–45, 1979.

Wolf, Deborah Goleman. *The Lesbian Community*. Berkeley: University of California Press, 1979.

REFLECTING ON MEANING

1. What social, economic, and legal sanctions do lesbians face? What is the attitude of most Americans toward lesbianism? How do other cultures view homosexuality? What threat does lesbianism pose to the power of males in society? Why would lesbians be "more likely than heterosexual women to believe in the necessity of fighting for women's rights"? How might lesbian relationships differ from typically unequal heterosexual relationships? Lesbianism is most negatively viewed by people with what beliefs? Why?

2. Historically, how has lesbianism been viewed and censured? At what point in history did lesbianism become stigmatized? What are some current cultural stereotypes about lesbians? What connection does Weitz make between women's changing roles and negative social reactions to lesbians?

3. Weitz discusses lesbians and other "independent" women: witches, nuns, spinsters, and widows. What evidence does she offer about each of these groups to support her thesis? Why do "sanctions against male homosexuality appear even stronger than those against lesbianism"? How does this relate to the cultural mythology that "lesbians want to be males"? Why might male homosexuality be more threatening to the status quo?

4. How are people who deviate from traditional societal expectations stigmatized by language? Why are the words *witch* and *lesbian* particularly powerful? Why have antifeminist forces used the word *lesbian* to denigrate all feminists? Why are the fates of lesbians and feminists "inextricably intertwined"?

EXPLORING RHETORICAL STRATEGIES

1. Weitz begins her essay with a narrative about the attempted deprogramming of a lesbian. What is your emotional response to this narrative of the rape and abuse of Stephanie Riethmiller?

2. Does Weitz's use of historical facts and research findings support her argument that independent women are threatening to male powers? What is your opinion of her repeated references to the church's attempted domination and control of independent women? Do you agree or disagree with Weitz's assessment of social, economic, and legal sanctions against lesbians and other independent women?

3. Weitz argues that language acts as a powerful method of social control. How have words been used to control and modify the actions of women? Has this essay's language and thesis modified your attitude toward lesbians and other independent women? Why or why not?

Gender Treachery
Homophobia, Masculinity, and Threatened Identities[1]

PATRICK D. HOPKINS

Educator Patrick D. Hopkins explores the relationship between masculinity and homophobia by illustrating how homosexuality is often viewed as a threat to a man's sense of self—his personhood. He suggests that only by changing our traditional concepts of masculinity can we effectively challenge homophobia.

One of my first critical insights into the pervasive structure of sex and gender categories occurred to me during my senior year of high school. The seating arrangement in my American Government class was typical—the "brains" up front and at the edge, the "jocks" at the back and in the center. Every day before and after class, the male jocks bandied insults back and forth. Typically, this "good-natured" fun included name-calling. Name-calling, like most pop cultural phenomena, circulates in fads, with various names waxing and waning in popularity. During the time I was taking this class, the most popular insult/name was used over and over again, *ad nauseam*. What was the insult?

It was simply, "girl."

Suggestively, "girl" was the insult of choice among the male jocks. If a male student was annoying, they called him "girl." If he made a mistake during some athletic event, he was called "girl." Sometimes "girl" was used to challenge boys to do their masculine best ("don't let us down, girl"). Eventually, after its explicitly derogatory use, "girl" came to be used among the male jocks as merely a term of greeting ("hey, girl").

But the blatantly sexist use of the word "girl" as an insult was not the only thing that struck me as interesting in this case. There was something different about this school, which in retrospect leads to my insight. My high school was a conservative Christian institution; no profanity (of a defined type) was allowed. Using "bad" words was considered sinful, was against the rules, and was formally punished. There was, therefore, a regulated lack of access to the more commonly used insults available in secular schools. "Faggot," "queer," "homo," or "cocksucker" were not available for use unless one was willing to risk being overheard by school staff, and thus risk being punished. However, it is important to note that, for the most part, these words were not restricted because of any sense of hurtfulness to a particular group or because they expressed prejudice. They were restricted merely because they were "dirty" words, "filthy" words, gutter-language words, like "shit" or "asshole." "Girl" was not a dirty word, and so presented no risk. It was used flagrantly in the presence of staff members, and even used by staff members themselves.[2]

In a curious twist, the very restriction of discursive access to these more common profanities (in the name of morality and decency) reveals a deeper structure of all these significations. "Girl," as an allowable, non-profane substitute for "faggot," "homo," and "cocksucker," mirrors and thus reveals a common essence of these insults. It signifies "not-male," and as related to the male speaker, "not-me."

"Girl," like these other terms, signifies a failure of masculinity, a failure of living up to a gendered standard of behavior, and a gendered standard of identity. Whether it was the case that a "failure of masculinity" actually occurred (as in fumbling the football) or whether it was only the "good-natured" intimation that it would occur (challenging future masculine functioning), the use of such terms demonstrates that to levy a successful insult, it was enough for these young men to claim that their target was insufficiently male; he was inadequately masculine, inadequately gendered.[3]

This story can, of course, be subjected to countless analyses, countless interpretations. For my purposes here, however, I want to present this story as an illustration of how important gender is to the concept of one's self. For these young males, being a man was not merely another contingent feature of their personhood. They did not conceive of themselves as people who were also male. They were, or wanted to be, *Men*. "Person" could only be a less descriptive, more generic way of talking about humans in the abstract. But there are no abstract humans; there are no "persons," rigorously speaking. There are only men and women. Or so we believe.

In what follows, I use this insight into gendered identity to make a preliminary exploration of the relationships between masculinity and homophobia. I find that one way to read homophobia and heterosexism in men is in terms of homosexuality's threat to masculinity, which in light of the connection between gender and personal identity translates into a threat to what constitutes a man's sense of self. To form a genuine challenge to homophobia, there-

fore, will not result from or result in merely increased social tolerance, but will be situated in a fundamental challenge to traditional
concepts of masculinity itself.

What It Means to Be (a) Gendered Me

Categories of gender, in different ways, produce a multiplicity
of other categories in a society. They affect—if not determine—labor,
reproduction-associated responsibilities, childrearing roles, distri-
butions of political power, economic status, sexual practices, uses
of language, application of certain cognitive skills, possession of
personality traits, spirituality and religious beliefs, and more. In
fact, all members of a given society have their material and psychological statuses heavily determined by their identification as a particular gender. However, not only individuals' physical, economic,
and sexual situations are determined by gender categories, but also
their own sense of personal identity—their personhood. I use "personhood" here as a metaphor for describing individuals' beliefs
about how they fit into a society, how they fit into a world, who and
what they think they *are*.[4] Personhood is critically linked (or perhaps worse, uncritically linked) to the influence of the gender categories under which an individual develops.

Individuals' sense of personhood, their sense-of-self, is largely
a result of their construction as members of particular social groups
within society-at-large: religions, ethnicities, regional affinities, cultural heritages, classes, races, political parties, family lineages, etc.
Some of the most pervasive, powerful, and hidden of these iden-
tity-constructing "groups" are the genders; pervasive because no
individual escapes being gendered, powerful because so much else
depends on gender, and hidden because gender is uncritically presented as a natural, biological given, about which much can be discovered but little can (or should) be altered. In most cultures,
though not all, sex/gender identity and thus much of personal
identity is regulated by a binary system—man and woman.[5] Men
and women are constructed from the socially raw material of newborn human bodies—a process that masquerades as natural rather
than constructive.[6] To a very large extent, what it means to be a
member of society and thus what it means to be a person, *is* what
it means to be a girl or a boy, a man or a woman. There is no such
thing as a sexually or gender undifferentiated person.[7]

Identity is fundamentally relational. What it means to have a
particular identity depends on what it means not to have some
other identity, and by the kinds of relationships one has to other
possible and actual identities. To have personhood, sense-of-self,

regulated by a binary sex/gender system means that the one identity must be different from the other identity; a situation requiring
that there be identifiable, performative, behavioral, and psychological characteristics that allow for clear differentiation. Binary
identities demand criteria for differentiation.

For a "man" to qualify as a man, he must possess a certain (or
worse, uncertain) number of demonstrable characteristics that
make it clear that he is not a woman, and a woman must possess
characteristics demonstrating she is not a man. These characteristics are, of course, culturally relative, and even intraculturally dynamic, but in late twentieth-century U.S. culture the cluster of
behaviors and qualities that situate men in relation to women include the by now well-known litany: (hetero)sexual prowess, sexual conquest of women, heading a nuclear family, siring children,
physical and material competition with other men, independence,
behavioral autonomy, rationality, strict emotional control, aggressiveness, obsession with success and status, a certain way of walking, a certain way of talking, having buddies rather than intimate
friends, etc.[8]

Because personal identity (and all its concomitant social, political, religious, psychological, biological, and economic relations)
is so heavily gendered, any threat to sex/gender categories is de-
rivatively (though primarily non-consciously) interpreted as a
threat to personal identity—a threat to what it means to be and especially what it means to be me. A threat to manhood (masculinity)
is a threat to personhood (personal identity). Not surprisingly then,
a threat to established gender categories, like most other serious
threats, is often met with grave resistance, for challenging the reg-
ulatory operations of a gender system means to destabilize fundamental social, political, and personal categories (a profoundly
anxiety-producing state), and society is always prejudiced toward
the protection of established categories. Inertia is a force in culture
as well as in physics.

There are many different threats to gendered identity, but I
think they can all be generally grouped together under the rubric
of "gender treachery."[9] A gender traitor can be thought of as anyone who violates the "rules" of gender identity/gender performance, i.e., someone who rejects or appears to reject the criteria by
which the genders are differentiated.[10] At its most obvious, gender
treachery occurs as homosexuality, bisexuality, cross-dressing, and
feminist activism. Any of these traitorous activities may result in a
serious reaction from those individuals and groups whose concept
of personal and political identity is most deeply and thoroughly
sexed by traditional binary categories.[11] However, homosexuality

is particularly effective in producing the extreme (though not un-common) reaction of homophobia—a response that is often mani-fested in acts of physical, economic, and verbal assault against perceived gender traitors, queers.[12] Homosexuals, intentionally or not, directly challenge assumptions concerning the relational as-pects of the binary categories of sex/gender, and as such threaten individual identities. Since the homophobic reaction can be lethal and so theoretically suggestive, it deserves serious attention.

Homophobia/Heterosexism

Theorists debate the value of using the term "homophobia." For some, the "phobia" suffix codes anti-gay and anti-lesbian activ-ity as appertaining to psychiatric discourse—the realm of irration-ality, uncontrollable fear, a realm where moral responsibility of political critique seems inapplicable due to the clinical nature of the phobia.[13] We do not punish people for being claustrophobic; we do not accuse agoraphobics of ignorance or intolerance; why should we treat homophobics any differently?

Other terms have been used to describe the aggregation of prej-udices against gays and lesbians, including homoerotophobia, homo-sexism, homonegativism, anti-homosexualism, anti-homosexuality, and homohatred.[14] "Heterosexism" has become the terminology of choice for some theorists, emphasizing similarities to racism and sexism. "Heterosexism" characterizes a political situation in which heterosexuality is presented and perceived as natural, moral, practi-cal, and superior to any non-heterosexual option. As such, hetero-sexuals are *justly* accorded the privileges granted them—political power, sexual freedom, religious sanction, moral status, cultural val-idation, psychiatric and juridical non-interference, occupational and tax privilege, freedom to have or adopt children and raise families, civil rights protection, recourse against unfair hiring practices, pub-lic representation in media and entertainment industries, etc.

For many of us, however, "heterosexism," though accurate and useful, does not possess the rhetorical and emotional impact that "homophobia" does. "Heterosexism" is appropriate for de-scribing why all television couples are straight, why marriage and joint tax returns are reserved for heterosexuals, why openly lesbian or gay candidates face inordinate difficulty in being elected to of-fice, or why only heterosexuals can adopt children or be foster par-ents. But "heterosexism," though perhaps still technically accurate, does not seem strong enough to describe the scene of ten Texas teenage boys beating a gay man with nail-studded boards and stab-bing him to death.[15] The blood pooling up on the ground beneath that dying body is evidence for something more than the protection of heterosexual privilege. It is evidence for a radical kind of evil.

It is neither my goal nor my desire here to set out specific definitions of homophobia. Though I will use the term primarily with reference to physical violence and strong verbal, economic, and juridical abuse against gays, I do not claim to establish a clear boundary between homophobia and heterosexism. No stable boundary could be set, nor would it be particularly useful to try to do so—they are not discrete. "Homophobia" and "heterosexism" are political words, political tools; they are ours to use as specific situations present specific needs.

However, for my purposes here, heterosexism—loosely characterized as valorizing and privileging heterosexuality (morally, economically, religiously, politically)—can be seen as the necessary precursor to homophobia. Heterosexism is the backdrop of the binary division into heterosexual and homosexual (parasitic on the man/woman binary), with, as usual, the first term of the binary good and second term bad. Heterosexism constructs the field of concepts and behaviors so that some heterosexists' hierarchical view of this binary will be reactionary, for a variety of reasons, thus becoming homophobic (read: violent/abusive/coercive). In the same way that a person doesn't have to be a member of a white supremacist organization to be racist, a person doesn't have to be homophobic to be heterosexist. This is not to say that heterosexism is not as bad as homophobia, but rather that though heterosexism presents less of an obvious, direct, personal physical threat to gays, it nonetheless situates the political arena such that homophobia can and is bound to exist. Heterosexism is culpable for the production of homophobia. Heterosexists are politically culpable for the production of homophobics.

But even when we choose to use the term "homophobia" for cases of brutality, fanatic claims, petitions for fascistic laws, or arbitrarily firing gay employees, this does not mean that we must always characterize homophobia as an irrational, psychiatric/clinical response. Such a characterization would be grossly inadequate. "Homophobia" has evolved as primarily a political term, not as a psychiatric one, and does not parallel claustrophobia or agoraphobia, for the political field is not the same.

Religious and political rhetorics of moral turpitude and moral danger do not attach to closed-in spaces or wide-open spaces in the way they attach to same-sex eroticism. In other words, the fear and abhorrence of homosexuals is often taught as a moral and practical virtue and political oppression is massed against gays and lesbians. As a result, oppositional strategies to homophobia must be located in political discourse, not just psychiatric or pop-psychiatric discourse. Homophobia is supported and subsidized by cultural and governmental institutions in ways that demand the need for a variety of analyses. Though homophobia may often seem irrational or semi-psychotic in appearance, it must not be dismissed as simply an obsessive individual psychological aberration. Homophobia is a product of institutional heterosexism and gendered identity.

How do people explain homophobia? And especially, though not exclusively, how do people in queer communities explain homophobia? Being the victims of it, what do they see in it? Why is it that some men react so strongly and so virulently to the mere presence of gay men?

The Repression Hypothesis

One of the most common explanations of homophobia among gay men is that of repressed homosexuality. Men who constantly make anti-gay slurs, tell anti-gay jokes, use anti-gay language, obsess about the dire political and moral impact of homosexuality on the family and country, or even who are known to attack gays physically are often thought to be repressing their own sexual attraction toward men. As a result of their terror in coming to grips with their own sexuality, they overcompensate, metastasizing into toxic, hypermasculine, ultra-butch homophobes who seem to spend far more time worrying about homosexuality than openly gay men do.

This kind of repressed-homosexual explanation was aptly demonstrated by one of my straight undergraduate ethics professors. While teaching a section on sexual ethics, my professor and the entire class read a series in the college newspaper by our Young Republican student editor about how "the homosexuals" were taking over the country and converting all the children. Finally, after yet another repetition of the "but they can't have babies and they're unnatural" columns, my exasperated professor wrote a response to the paper, and after a lengthy list of counterarguments, ended by saying simply, "Methinks thou doth protest too much."

His intimation was clear. He believed that the Young Republican's arguments were more for his benefit than for his readers'. As the typical response goes among gays who hear men constantly ranting about the perils of homosexuality and the virtues of heterosexuality–"He's not trying to convince us. He's trying to convince himself."

I think for many men this theory of repression is accurate. It is not unusual for openly gay men to talk about their days in the closet and report that they were assertively heterosexist/homophobic– and that yes, they were desperately trying to convince themselves

that they were really heterosexual. Sadly enough, many of these repressed homosexuals manage to maintain their repression at great
cost to themselves and often at great cost to others. Some marry,
and live a lie, unfulfilled emotionally and sexually, deceiving their
wives and children, sometimes having furtive, sexual affairs with
other men. They manage psychologically to compartmentalize
their erotic orientation and same-sex sexual experiences so radically, that they live two separate, tortuous lives. Some repressives
become anti-gay activists and spend their lives trying to force gays
and lesbians back into the closet, working against gay civil rights
and protections.[16] Horrifyingly, some others undergo an even
worse schism in their personalities, resulting in a bizarre, malignant,
and persistent internalized war between homophobia and ho-
mophilia. This war can culminate in what John Money calls the ex-
orcist syndrome, in which the repressive picks up, seduces, or even
rapes a gay man, and then beats him or kills him in order to exor-
cise the repressive's "homosexual guilt."[17]

But while the repressive hypothesis is certainly accurate for
some men, it is not accurate for all. I have no doubt that there are
indubitably heterosexual men who hate and assault gays. To some
extent, the explanation of repressed homosexuality may be wish
fulfillment on the part of some gays. Forced by necessity of survival
to be secretive and cryptic themselves, many gay men find it emi-
nently reasonable to suspect any man of potential homosexual desire, and in fact, want such to be the case. It is reasonable, if
optimistic, to hope that there are really more of you than there
seem to be. And in light of the fact that many openly gay men report that they used to be homophobic themselves, the repression
theory seems to be both empirically sound as well as emotionally
attractive. There is also a certain sense of self-empowerment resulting from the repression hypothesis—out gays may see themselves as
morally, cognitively, and emotionally superior to the men who
continue to repress their sexuality. But homophobia is not so simple. What about those homophobes who clearly are not repressing
their own homosexuality? What explanation fits them?

The Irrationality/Ignorance Hypothesis

Another explanation, one in perfect keeping with the roots of the
word, is that homophobia is an irrational fear, based in ignorance
and resulting from social training.[18] This explanation is also popular among liberal heterosexuals as well as liberal lesbians and gays.
The stereotype of this kind of cultural/developmental homophobia
is that of a little boy who grows up in a poorly educated, very conservative family, often in a rural area, who hears his parents and

other relatives talk about the fags on TV or the homo child molester they caught in the next county, and how he ought to be "strung up and shot." As the little boy grows, he models his parents' behavior, identifying with their emotions and desiring to emulate them. Although the boy has no idea of what a "fag" or "homo" is, he nevertheless learns the appropriate cues for application of those terms to situations and individuals, and the emotions associated with that application. He begins to use them himself, often as a general-use insult (like young children calling each other "nigger" even when they do not know what it means). He learns that certain kinds of behaviors elicit being called a fag and that he can achieve a degree of peer approval when he uses those terms. So he stands on the playground at recess and calls the boy who takes piano lessons a homo; his friends laugh. He asks the girls who are jumping rope with another boy why they are playing with a faggot; his friends laugh. Simultaneously, of course, the boy is learning all the other dictums of traditional heteromasculinity— girls are weak, boys are strong, girls play stupid games, boys play real games, girls that want to play football are weird, boys that do not want to play football are faggots. Eventually the boy learns the more complete definition of "faggot," "homo," "queer." Homos aren't just sissies who act like girls; they aren't just weak. They like to "do things" with other boys. Sick things. Perverted things.

A little knowledge is a very dangerous thing and the boy becomes a full-fledged homophobe who thinks boys who play the piano and do not like football want to touch him "down there." He learns that grown-up homos like to grab young boys and "do bad things to them." He learns that just as one can become a tougher, stronger, more masculine man by killing deer and by "slaughtering" the guys on the opposing football team, one can become more masculine, or prove one's masculinity, by verbally abusing or beating up queers.

Though this scenario may seem hyperbolic, it certainly does occur. I have seen it happen myself. The lesson that gets learned is that of the recurring conflict of essence and performance.

Essence: You (the little boy) have a natural, core, normal, good, essential identity; you are a *boy,* a *young man,* male, not-a-girl. This is just what you are. You were born this way. Little girls will like you. You have buddies. You're lucky. You are our *son.* It's natural and obvious that you will grow up and get married and be a *daddy.*

Performance: But even though you just *are* a little boy, even though it's perfectly natural, you must make sure you do not act (how? why?) like a girl. You must always make sure that you exhibit the right behavior for a boy (but isn't it natural?). Don't ever act like not-a-boy! Don't betray that which you are naturally, comfortably, normally. Don't not-be what you are. Perform like a man.

The stage is set. The child knows that he is a he and that being a he is a good, normal, natural thing. Being a he requires no effort. You just are a boy. But at the same time, there is lingering on the horizon the possibility, amorphous and not always spoken, that you might do something which violates what you are. It might be quiet—"Now put those down, son. Boys don't play with dolls." It might be loud—"What the hell are you doing playing with dolls like some sissy??!!" The little boy internalizes the expectations of masculinity.

This kind of explanation of homophobia, though useful and accurate for many purposes, tends to characterize homophobia as learned but completely irrational, unfounded, arbitrary, ignorant, counterproductive, and dysfunctional. However, such a simple analysis excludes much of the experience of the homophobe. It is not actually the case that the poor mindless homophobe simply veers through life distorting reality and obsessing over nothing, frothing at the mouth and seeing faggots behind every corner and homosexual conspiracies in every liberal platform, ruining his own life as well as others. In fact, homophobia is not dysfunctional in the way that agoraphobia is. Homophobia has functional characteristics.[19]

For example, in the story given above, the boy does not simply "catch" the obsessive, dysfunctional view of the world that his parents have. He learns that certain kinds of behaviors elicit rewarding emotions not only from his parents directly, but also from within himself when away from his parents. When the little boy plays with toy soldiers and pretends to slaughter communists or Indians, his parents smile, encourage him, and even play with him sometimes. If he plays house with his little sister, he is always the daddy and she is always the mommy and he pretends to get home from work and she pretends to have supper fixed for him—a game in which roles are correctly modeled and are thus emotionally rewarding—"I'm just like my daddy."

However, the emotional (and sometimes corporal) punishments function the same way. If the boy is caught playing with dolls, or pretending to be the mommy, he may be told that he is doing something wrong, or be punished, or may simply detect a sense of worry, disapproval, or distaste from his parents. Homophobic tendencies will be carried along with all the other traits of conservative masculinity. He will be "just like his daddy" when he calls some effeminate boy a sissy—an emotionally rewarding experience. He will receive approval from his peers when he pushes the class homo around—he will be tough and formidable in their eyes. And perhaps most importantly, he will be clearly and unambiguously performing the masculine role he perceives (correctly in context) to be so valued—an advantage in power, safety, admiration, and self-esteem. It is also in no small sense that homophobia can be functional in keeping other heterosexuals in line. The potential to accuse another boy of being a faggot, to threaten ostracism or physical assault, is a significant power.[20]

Thus, it is not the case that homophobia is somehow obviously dysfunctional on an individual or group level.[21] Homophobic activity carries with it certain rewards and a certain power to influence. In the case of the repressed homosexual, it externalizes the intrapsychic conflict and reaffirms a man's appearance of heterosexuality and thus his sense of stability, safety, and self. In the case of childhood modeling, homophobic activity wins approval from peers and authority figures, protects one from becoming the target of other homophobes, and reaffirms one's place in a larger context of gender appropriate behavior—protecting one's personal identity.

The Political Response Hypothesis

The recognition that there are rational, functional aspects of homophobia (in a heteropatriarchal context) leads to a third explanation of homophobia that reverses the second. This theory says that queers are a genuine political threat to heterosexuals and really do intend to eliminate heterosexual privileges. Homophobia, therefore, is a rational political response.[22] Radical feminist lesbians and certain radical gay men directly challenge the hetero-male-dominated structure of society, rejecting patriarchal rule, conventional morality, and patriarchal modes of power distribution. All of the primary institutional sites of power that have maintained patriarchal domination—the state, the church, the family, the medical profession, the corporation—are being challenged from without by queers who do not want merely to be accepted, or tolerated, or left alone, but who want to dismantle heteropatriarchal society and build something different in its place. In response to liberal heterosexuals who promote the irrationalist theory of homophobia, supporters of this theory might say that many of the so-called "ignorant" and "false" stereotypes of queers are in fact correct, but they are not bad stereotypes; they are good and should be praised, should be revered, should replace heterosexual values. Yes, lesbians do hate men. Yes, fags do want to destroy the nuclear family. Yes, dykes do want to convert children. Yes, homos are promiscuous.

The impetus for this theory of homophobia comes from lesbians and gays who view their sexuality as primarily a political identity, having chosen to reject heterosexuality and become lesbian or gay as a political act of resistance. They have chosen this identification because they want to fight, destroy, or separate from hetero-male-dominated society. According to this theory, homophobia is a perfectly rational, reasonable reaction to the presence of queers, because queers pose a genuine threat to the status of heterosexual privilege. It is only logical that heterosexuals would fight back, because if they do not fight back, their privilege, their power, and their dominance will be stripped away all the sooner.

There are people who seem, at least partially, to confirm this theory. It has been interesting to see that over the past ten years or so, it has become common for neoconservative activist organizations to use the word "family" in their names. Among many gay, lesbian, and feminists activists, any organization with "Family" as part of its name is automatically suspected to be anti-gay, anti-lesbian, anti-feminist.[23] The frequency of the word "family" as an identification tag is seen as signifying a belief in the moral superiority of the traditional, heterosexual, nuclear family. This suggests that some "pro-family" activists trace and justify their anti-homosexual activism to the belief that lesbians and gays are threatening to destroy The Family and thus to destroy heterosexual morality.

It is also true that over the past twenty years or so, lesbian and gay thought has become radicalized in a variety of ways. Lesbians and gays have moved away from merely the hope of demedicalization and decriminalization to the hope of building cultures, ethics, practices, and politics of their own, hopes that include the destruction of heterosexist, or even heterosexual, society. There are some radical, separatist lesbians and separatist gays who view most human behavior in terms of rational, political aims, and for them homophobia is a predictable political response to their own oppositional politics. Nineteen ninety-two Republican presidential candidate Pat Buchanan was not simply being hyperbolic when he gravely predicted that the 1990's would be the decade of the radical homosexual. One of his campaign ads, featuring a film clip of near-nude, dancing, gay leathermen, formed the background for an attack on the grant policies of the National Endowment for the Arts. Such ads demonstrate that his homophobia is partially directed against queer-specific political and sexual challenges to his conservative Christian morality.

However, the political response hypothesis, like the others, accounts only for some homophobes, and I think, relatively few. This hypothesis suffers from too great a dose of modernist political rationalism. Like many traditional models of political activity, it overrationalizes the subjects involved. It assumes that members of the oppressor class interpret the world in political terms similar to that of members of an oppositional movement. Thus, the characterization of a homophobe is that of a rational individual with immoral goals who recognizes that the particular oppositional group of gays and lesbians is a genuine political threat to his or her power and privilege, and as such must take an active stand against that insurgent group. One of the best tactics for resisting the insurgents is terror—on individual levels with violence, on institutional levels with oppressive laws, and on sociocultural levels with boogeyfag propaganda.[24]

While this model has merit and may be partially accurate in accounting for some homophobia, it endows homophobes (and homosexuals) with a hyperrationality that does not seem to be in evidence. Most homophobes, even those who openly admit their involvement in physical and verbal attacks on gays and lesbians, do not consider their activity to be political. Most of them, in fact, do not perceive any obvious threat from the people they attack. Gary Comstock claims that perpetrators of anti-queer violence typically list the "recreational, adventuresome aspect of pursuing, preying upon, and scaring lesbians and gay men" as the first and foremost reason for their behavior. Only secondarily and less often do they list things like the "wrongness of homosexuality" as a reason for their activity. But even this "wrongness" is not listed as an explanation or political justification for their behavior as much as a background assumption that functions as cultural permission.[25]

A recent television news program interviewed a perpetrator of anti-gay violence and, like Comstock's interviewee, he had little or no explanation for why he was doing what he was doing except that it was fun. When asked how he could have fun hurting people, he said that he had never really thought of queers as real people. I think this suggests that interpreting all, or even most, homophobic violence as conscious political activity ignores that much of the "reasoning" behind homophobia, when there is any active reasoning at all, relies on a very abstract and loosely integrated background of heterosexist assumptions. Many homophobes view gays and lesbians as politically, morally, and economically insignificant. For those who have never had any personal interaction (positive or negative) with openly gay or lesbian folk, lesbian/gay people may be such an abstract other that they do not enter into one's political and moral consideration any more than people who kick dogs for fun consider the political and moral significance of dogs, except perhaps in terms of legal consequences.

Performing Gender and Gender Treachery

All three explanations of homophobia have one thing in common. They reside on a field of unequal, binary, sexual and gender differentiation. Behind all homophobia, regardless of its development, expression, or motivation, is the background of heterosexism. Behind all heterosexism is the background of gendered identities.

The gender category of men constructs its members around at least two conflicting characterizations of the essence of manhood. First, your masculinity (being-a-man) is natural and healthy and innate. But second, you must stay masculine—do not ever let your masculinity falter. So, although being a man is seen as a natural and automatic state of affairs for a certain anatomical makeup, masculinity is so valued, so valorized, so prized, and its loss such a terrible thing, that one must always guard against losing it. Paradoxically, then, the "naturalness" of being a man, of being masculine, is constantly guarding against the danger of losing itself. Unaware, the "naturalness," the "rightness," of masculinity exposes its own uncertainties in its incessant self-monitoring—a self-monitoring often accomplished by monitoring others. In fact, although the stable performance of masculinity is presented as an *outcome* of being a man, what arises in looking at heterosexism/homophobia is that being a man, or continuing to be a man, is the *outcome* of performing masculinity. But of course, not just anybody can make the performance. Anatomy is seen as prior even as the performance is required to validate the anatomy. Thus the performance produces the man, but the performance is also limited to and compulsory for a "man."[26]

The insults of the male high school jocks are telling. Even though one is recognized as a man (or boy) prior to evidenced masculinity, evidence must also be forthcoming in order to merit that continued "unproblematic" status. Whether performative evidence is provided with ease or with difficulty, it is nonetheless a compulsory performance, as compulsory as the initial anatomically based gender assignment. But because (proof of) masculinity has to be maintained not merely by anatomical differentiation but by performance, the possibility of failure in the performance is always there. It is enough to insult, to challenge, to question personal identity by implying that one is not being masculine enough.

The logic of masculinity is demanding—protect and maintain what you are intrinsically, or you could lose it, mutate, become something else. The insults of my student peers suggest that the "something else" is being a girl—a serious enough demotion in a patriarchal culture. But of course, this is metaphor. One does not actually become a girl; the power of prior anatomy is too spellbinding, even when the performance fails. The "something else" is a male without masculinity, a monster, a body without its essential spirit, a mutation with no specifiable identity.[27]

So one mutation, which is so offensive it becomes the template of all mutations, occurs when a man finds that his erotic orientation is toward other men.[28] If he acts on that erotic orientation, he violates a tenet of masculinity, he fails at masculinity, and most importantly, appears to reject standards by which real men are defined as selves, as subjects. In a binary gender system, however, to be unmasculine means to be feminine; that is the only other possibility. But even as a cultural transformation into the feminine is attempted, it appears to be seriously problematic; it is not without resistance that the unmasculine male is shunted off to the realm of the feminine, for though femininity is devalued as the repository of the unmasculine, its presence as a discernible nonmasculine essence/performance is required to maintain the boundary of masculinity, and "feminine essences" do not easily coincide with "male" bodies.

The male body, which is supposed to house masculine essence from the first time it is identified as male, is out of place in the realm of unmasculine. That body is a manifestation of confusion, a reminder of rejection, an arrogant affront to all that is good and true about men, real men, normal men, natural men. How could this "man" give up his natural power, his natural strength, his real self? Why is he rejecting what he should be, what I am?

If the male is neither masculine, nor feminine enough, what is he? He becomes a homosexual, a member of that relatively new species of creature, originally delineated by psychiatry, which does not simply engage in unmasculine behavior, but which has an essential, unmasculine essence; no positive essence of his own, mind you, but rather a negative essence, an absence of legitimate essence, and thus the absence of legitimate personhood.[29] But what is the response to a creature with an illegitimate essence, to a creature with the husk of a man but with the extremely present absence of masculinity? That depends entirely on the situatedness of the responder in the distribution of gender identities and personal identities.

The repressive sees and fears becoming *that,* and must distance himself from *that* by any means necessary, often overcompensating, revealing his repression through his obsession, sometimes through active malignancy—assaulting or killing or merely registering disgust at that which he hates embodied in that which he desires.[30]

The ignorant will dismiss *those* as not really human, creatures so unidentified that they do not merit the response given to genuine identities (whether positive or negative—even enemies have genuine, if hated, identities). *It* can be killed, can be beaten, can be played with, can be dismissed.

The heterosupremacist reactionary will raise the warning– *They* are dangerous! *They* are getting out of hand! *They* are here! *They* are threatening your homes, your churches, your families, your children! And in some sense the threat may be real; *they* really do reject many of the beliefs upon which the heterosupremacists' political and personal identities are maintained.

Fortunately, the logic of masculinity, like any other logic, is neither universal nor irresistibly stable. Not every individual classified as a male in this culture will be adequately represented in my sketchy characterization of masculine personhood. My characterization is not to be interpreted so much as an empirically accurate description of all men in this society as it is a description of the mythology of masculinity that informs all constructions of men, the masculine, the "self" in Western culture, and that which could threaten them. I do not claim that all heterosexual males are homophobic (although I do think that the vast majority of heterosexual males are heterosexist). While I describe three homophobic reactions to the identity threat represented by gay men (repression, abusive ignorant bigotry, political reactionism), these in no way exhaust the variety of male reactions.

Some men, though they hate and are sickened by gays, lack the bravado to do anything more about their hate than make private slurs. Others, particularly liberals, are tolerantly heterosexist; they have no "real" problem with gays provided they are discreet and replicate the model of conventional heterosexual morality and family. And then there is the rare, genuinely subversive heterosexual man, a kind of gender traitor himself, whose identity is not coextensive with his assignment as a man. Although comfortable with himself, he wouldn't mind being gay, or mind being a woman–those are not the categories by which he defines, or wants to define, his personhood.

Do not, however, take this as a disclaimer to the effect that homophobia is the exception, the out-of-nowhere, the unusual case. Heterosexism may be the father of homophobia, modeling in public what is done more blatantly in hiding, but hidden does not mean rare. Do not think that homophobes, even violent ones, are few and far between–occasional atavistics "suffering" from paleolithic conceptions of sex roles. Even though many instances of anti-gay/anti-lesbian crime go unreported due to fear of outing, lack of proof, fear of retaliation, or police hostility, evidence is accumulating that such crime is widespread and that violent attack is higher among gays and lesbians than for the population at large. In

a recent Philadelphia study, 24 percent of gay men and 10 percent
of lesbians *responding* said that they had been physically attacked–
a victimization rate twice as high for lesbians and four times as high
for gay men than for women and men in the urban population at
large.[31] Economic threat and verbal assault are, of course, even more
common.

The gender demographics of physical homophobic attack
suggest something about the correlation between masculinity and
homophobia. Consider the findings in a recent study on violence
against lesbians and gays by Gary Comstock: 1) 94 percent of all
attackers were male; 2) 99 percent of perpetrators who attacked
gay men were male, while 83 percent of those who attacked lesbians were male; 3) while 15 percent of attacks on lesbians were
made by women, only 1 percent of attacks on gay men were made
by women.[32]

Homophobic violence seems to be predominantly a male
activity. What is the relationship between homophobia and masculinity? Is the man who attacks gay men affirming or reaffirming,
consciously or subconsciously, his own masculinity/heterosexuality
and thus his own sense of self? How is masculinity implicated in
homophobia?

I have suggested in this essay that one reading of homophobia
is that queers pose a threat to (compulsory) masculinity and as such,
pose a threat to men whose personhood is coextensive with their
identity as men. Certainly, homophobia could not exist without the
background assumptions of (heterosexist) masculine identity. There
could be no fear or hatred of gays and lesbians if there were no concept of a proper gender identity and a proper sexual orientation.
Masculinity assumes, essentializes, naturalizes, and privileges heterosexuality. A violation of heterosexuality can be seen as treachery
against masculinity, which can register as an affront or threat to a
man's core sense of self, a threat to his (male) identity. In this sense,
homophobia requires masculinity (and femininity); it is necessarily
parasitic on traditional categories of sex/gender identity. Homophobia is the malignant "correction" to a destabilizing deviation.
Without gendered standards of identity there could be nothing
from which to deviate, and thus nothing to "correct."

If this reading is accurate, homophobia is not just a social
prejudice (on the xenophobic/minoritarian model) that can be
eliminated by education or tolerance training.[33] It will not be eliminated just by persuading people to be "more accepting." While
these approaches may be helpful, they do not get at the basis of
homophobia–binary gender systems and heterosexism. The only
way to ensure that heterosexism and its virulent manifestation

homophobia are genuinely eliminated is to eliminate the binary it-self–challenge the assumption that one must be sexed or gendered to be a person. Eliminate the binary and it would be impossible to have heterosexism or homophobia, because hetero and homo would have no meaning. This does not mean humans would have to be "fused" into some androgynous entity ("androgyny" has no meaning without the binary). It means simply that identities would no longer be distributed according to anatomically based "sexes."

While this hope may seem utopian and may have theoretical problems of its own, it nonetheless suggests an approach to studies of masculinity that may be incommensurable with other ap-proaches. When using the model of masculinity (and femininity) as a social construct that has no intrinsic interpretation, there seems to be little use in trying to reconstruct masculinity into more "positive" forms, at least as long as masculinity is somehow viewed as an in-trinsically appropriate feature of certain bodies. To make masculin-ity "positive" could easily devolve into retracting the boundaries of appropriate behavior without challenging the compulsory nature of that behavior. Delving into mythology and folklore (along the lines of some of the men's movement models) to "rediscover" some ar-chetypal masculine image upon which to base new male identities is not so much wrong or sexist as it is arbitrary. Discovering what it means, or should mean, to be a "real man" is an exercise in useless-ness. A "real man" is nothing. A "real man" could be anything. This is not to say that searching through mythohistory for useful meta-phors for living today is not useful. I believe that it is.[34] But such a search will never get anyone closer to being a "real man" or even to being just a "man." There is no such thing. Nor should there be.

For some of us who have been embattled our entire lives be-cause our desires/performances/identities were "immorally" or "il-legally" or "illegitimately" cross-coded with our anatomies, we fear the flight into rediscovering masculinity will be a repetition of what has gone before. Gendered epistemologies will only reproduce gendered identities. I personally do not want to be a "real man," or even an "unreal man." I want to be unmanned altogether. I want to evaluate courses of behavior and desire open to me on their prag-matic consequences, not on their appropriateness to my "sex." I want to delve into the wisdom of mythology but without the prior restrictions of anatomy.

I want to betray gender.

NOTES

1. I want to thank Larry May for his encouragement and editing sugges-tions throughout the writing of this paper. I also want to make it clear

that although I think some of this essay is applicable to hatred and vio- lence directed against lesbians (sometimes called lesbophobia), for the purposes of a volume specifically on masculinity I have deliberately (though not exclusively) focused on males and hatred and violence di- rected against gay males. Even with this focus, however, I am indebted to work on homophobia by lesbian researchers and theorists. In a fu- ture, more comprehensive project I will explore the oppression and marginalization of a wider variety of gender traitors.

2.   Although the scope of this essay prevents a lengthy discussion, it should be pointed out that many male teachers and coaches call their students and team members "girls": to be playful, to be insulting, or to shame them into playing more roughly.

3.   It should also be pointed out that gay men often use the word "girl" to refer to each other. In these cases, however, signifying a lack of mascu- linity is not registering insult. Often, it is expressing a sentiment of community—a community formed by the shared rejection of compul- sory heterosexuality and compulsory forms of masculinity.

4.   I deliberately sidestep the philosophical debate over the existence of "self" in this discussion. While I am quite skeptical of the existence of a stable, core self, I do not think the argument in this paper turns on the answer to that problem. "Self" could simply be interpreted as a meta- phor for social situatedness. In any case, I do not mean to suggest that subverting gender is a way to purify an essential human "self"

5.   For work on Native American societies that do not operate with a sim- ple gender binary, see Walter L. Williams, *The Spirit and the Flesh: Sexual Diversity in American Indian Culture* (Boston: Beacon Press, 1986) and Will Roscoe (ed.), *Living the Spirit: A Gay American Indian Anthology* (New York: St. Martin's Press, 1988).

6.   For works on the social construction of gender and sexuality see: Judith Butler, *Gender Trouble: Feminism and the Subversion of Identity* (New York: Routledge, 1990); Michel Foucault, *Herculine Barbin: Being the Recently Discovered Memoirs of a Nineteenth Century French Hermaphrodite* (New York: Pantheon, 1980); Michel Foucault, *The History of Sexuality: Volume 1. An Introduction* (New York: Vintage Books, 1980); Montique Wittig, *The Straight Mind and Other Essays* (Boston: Beacon Press, 1992).

7.   In the United States and many other countries, if a baby is born with an- atomical genital features that do not easily lend themselves to a classifica- tion within the gender/sex system in place, they are surgically and hormonally altered to fit into the categories of male or female, girl or boy.

8.   I am grateful to Bob Strikwerda for pointing out that none of these char- acteristics taken by itself is absolutely necessary to be perceived as mas- culine in contemporary U.S. culture (except perhaps heterosexuality). In fact, a man who possessed every characteristic would be seen as a parody.

9.   I borrow the insightful term "gender treachery" from Margaret Atwood. In her brilliant dystopian novel, *The Handmaids' Tale* (Boston: Houghton Mifflin, 1986), set in a post-fundamentalist Christian takeover [in] America, criminals are executed and hanged on a public wall with the name of their crime around their necks for citizens to see. Homosexuals bear the placard "gender traitor."

10. It doesn't matter if this rejection is "deliberate" or not in the sense of direct refusal. Any deviant behavior can be seen as treacherous unless perhaps the individual admits "guilt" and seeks a "cure" or "forgiveness."

11. Someone might ask: But why those people most *thoroughly* sexed rather than those most insecure in their sexuality? My point here is a broad one about the categories of gender. Even those people who are insecure in their sexuality will be laboring under the compulsory ideal of traditional binary gender identities.

12. "Queers"—the name itself bespeaks curiosity, treachery, radical unidentifiability, the uncategorized, perverse entities, infectious otherness.

13. See Gregroy M. Herek, "On Heterosexual Masculinity: Some Psychical Consequences of the Social Construction of Gender and Sexuality," *American Behavioral Scientist,* vol. 29, no. 5, May/June 1986, 563–77.

14. For all these terms except "homohatred," see Gregory M. Herek, "Stigma, Prejudice, and Violence Against Lesbians and Gay Men," pp. 60–80, in J. C. Gonsiorek and J. D. Weinrich (eds.), *Homosexuality: Research Implications for Public Policy* (London: Sage Publications, Inc., 1991). For "homohatred," see Marshall Kirk and Hunter Madsen, *After the Ball: How America Will Conquer Its Fear & Hatred of Gays in the 90's* (New York: Penguin Books, 1989).

15. See Jacob Smith Yang's article in *Gay Community News,* August 18–24, vol. 19, no. 6, 1991, p. 1. The brutal July 4 murder of Paul Broussard sparked an uproar in Houston's queer community over anti-gay violence and police indifference. To "quell the recent uproar," Houston police undertook an undercover operation in which officers posed as gay men in a well-known gay district. Although police were skeptical of gays' claims of the frequency of violence, within one hour of posing as gay men, undercover officers were sprayed with mace and attacked by punks wielding baseball bats.

16. See Kirk and Madsen, p. 127. They mention the case of Rose Mary Denman, a United Methodist minister who was a vocal opponent of the ordinations of gays and lesbians until she eventually acknowledged her own lesbianism. Upon announcing this, however, she was defrocked. Kirk and Madsen quote a *New York Times* article that states; "In retrospect, she attributed her previous vehement stand against ordaining homosexuals to the effects of denying her unacknowledged lesbian feelings."

17. See John Money, *Gay, Straight and In-Between: The Sexology of Erotic Orientation* (Oxford: Oxford University Press, 1988), pp. 109–110.

18. See Suzanne Pharr, *Homophobia: A Weapon of Sexism* (Little Rock, AR: Chardon Press, 1988) and also Kirk and Madsen, *After the Ball.* The stereotypical story is one I have elaborated on from Kirk and Madsen's book, chapter 2.

19. See Herek, "On Heterosexual Masculinity...," especially pp. 572–73.

20. One can think of the typical scene where one boy challenges another boy to do something dangerous or cruel by claiming that if he does not do so, he is afraid—a sissy. Similarly, boys who are friends/peers of homophobes may be expected to engage in cruel physical or verbal be-

havior in order to appear strong, reliable, and most importantly of all, not faggots themselves. They know what happens to faggots.

21. See Herek, *On Heterosexual Masculinity,* p. 573.
22. See Celia Kitzinger, *The Social Construction of Lesbianism* (London: Sage Publications, Inc., 1987).
23. For example, in my own area of the country we have Rev. Don Wildmon's American Family Association, headquartered in Tupelo, Mississippi—an ultraconservative media watchdog group dedicated to the elimination of any media image not in keeping with right-wing Christian morality. Also, in Memphis, Tennessee, there is FLARE (Family Life America for Responsible Education Under God, Inc.), a group lobbying for Christian prayer in public schools, the elimination of sex education programs, and the installation of a "Family Life Curriculum" in public schools that would stress sexual abstinence and teach that the only form of morally acceptable sexual activity is married, heterosexual sex.
24. I borrow the term "boogeyfag" from David C. Powell's excellent unpublished manuscript, *Deviations of a Queen: Episodic Gay Theory.* Powell deconstructs California Congressman Robert Dornan's claim that "The biggest mass murderers in history are gay."
25. Gary David Comstock, *Violence Against Lesbians and Gay Men* (New York: Columbia University Press, 1991), p. 172.
26. For this analysis of masculinity and performance, I owe much to insights garnered from Judith Butler's article "Imitation and Gender Insubordination," in Diana Fuss, *Inside/Out: Lesbian Theories, Gay Theories* (New York: Routledge, 1991).
27. I use the term "monster" here in a way similar to that of Donna Haraway in her essay "A Cyborg Manifesto: Science, Technology, and Socialist-Feminism in the Late Twentieth Century," reprinted in her book *Simians, Cyborg, and Women: The Reinvention of Nature* (New York: Routledge, 1991). Haraway says: "Monsters have always defined the limits of community in Western imaginations. The Centaurs and Amazons of ancient Greece established the limits of the centred polis of the Greek male human by their disruption of marriage and boundary pollutions of the warrior with animality and woman" (p. 180). I loosely use "monster" in referring to homosexuality in the sense that the homosexual disrupts gender boundaries and must therefore be categorized into its own species so as to prevent destabilizing those boundaries.
28. Aquinas, for example, viewed the "vice of sodomy" as the second worst "unnatural vice," worse even than rape—a view echoed in contemporary legal decisions such as Bowers v. Hardwick (106 S. Ct. 2841, 1986), which upheld the criminal status of homosexuality. See Arthur N. Gilbert, "Conceptions of Homosexuality and Sodomy in Western History," in Salvatore J. Licata and Robert P. Peterson (eds.), *The Gay Past: A Collection of Historical Essays* (New York: Harrington Park Press, 1985), pp. 57–68.
29. On the creation of homosexuality as a category, see Foucault, *The History of Sexuality.*
30. In this sense: The repressive hates the species "homosexual," but nonetheless desires the body "man." It is only an historically contingent

construction that desiring a certain kind of body "makes" you a certain kind of person, "makes" you have a certain kind of "lifestyle." Unfortunately, it is also true that being a certain "kind" of person can carry with it serious dangers, as is the case for homosexuals.

31. See Comstock, p. 55.

32. See Comstock, p. 59.

33. This is not to say that gays and lesbians are not often treated as a minority; good arguments have been made that they are. See Richard D. Mohr, "Gay Studies as Moral Vision," *Educational Theory,* vol. 39, no. 2, 1989.

34. In fact, I very much enjoy studies in applied mythology, particularly the work of Joseph Campbell. However, I am extremely skeptical about any application of mythology that characterizes itself as returning us to some primal experience of masculinity that contemporary culture has somehow marred or diminished. There is always the specter of essentialism in such moves.

REFLECTING ON MEANING

1. How does Hopkins define personhood? How is identity fundamentally relational? What are the demonstrable characteristics that a male must possess to be considered a man in our society? Why is any threat to sex/gender categories a threat to personhood? What is gender treachery? Describe the characteristics of a gender traitor. What groups of people are considered gender traitors in our society?

2. Why have theorists debated over the appropriateness of the term homophobia? Define *heterosexism.* Why might the term heterosexism be an innappropriate descriptor of violent acts against homosexuals? How is homophobia a product of institutional heterosexism and gendered identity?

3. Hopkins describes several common explanations of homophobia: the repression hypothesis, the irrationality/ignorance hypothesis, and the political response hypothesis. Explain each of those hypotheses. How are they similar? How are they different? What are some of the flaws or weaknesses in each hypothesis? How does each of these hypotheses depend on gendered identity?

4. Explain the irony in these two conflicting charaterizations of manhood: "...masculinity (being-a-man) is natural and healthy and innate"; and men "must stay masculine–do not ever let your masculinity falter." How does this conflict relate to the idea of mascu-

linity as performative? What is the monstrous "something else" that Hopkins describes? What connection does Hopkins make between homophobic violence as primarily a male activity and heterosexist masculine identity? How could eliminating the sex/gender binary eliminate both heterosexism and homophobia?

EXPLORING RHETORICAL STRATEGIES

1. Hopkins begins his essay by using personal narrative to describe his initiation into sex and gender categorization in his senior year of high school. How effective is his use of personal narrative to introduce his discussion? Why is the use of the word *girl* appropriate for his discussion of insults?

2. The last line of Hopkins's essay, "I want to betray gender," is rhetorically linked to the title of his essay, "Gender Treachery," and his discussion of gender traitors. What other words and lines of his discussion continue this trope of treachery and betrayal? Are you sympathetic to his argument or not?

3. Who is Hopkins's intended audience? How do you know? How might a heterosexual, homosexual, or bisexual audience member respond? What evidence would you use to support your opinion? How might a male's or a female's reponse to this essay differ? Do you believe that it is possible to have a society in which identity construction is no longer based on one's anatomical sex? Why or why not?

TAKING A STAND
QUESTIONS FOR CONSIDERATION

1. In this part, several authors describe differences between women and men. Pick an area of difference that interests you (for example, verbal ability, conversational style, personality, values), summarize the observations of the appropriate authors on the nature of this difference, and draw your own conclusions about its significance. How pervasive is the difference? To what extent and in what ways does it influence the lives of women and men? What "rules" does it suggest for "feminine" and "masculine" codes of conduct? In what ways does it fit into a larger system of gender differences? How does it contribute to socially accepted definitions of masculinity and femininity? In thinking about this topic, you might wish to consider the essays by Adams, Goldberg, Rosenberg, Brownmiller, and Steinem. You may also find helpful the essays by Steinem and Roiphe that appear in Part III.

2. Adams and Weintraub both review research that confirms biological origins for some of the differences between women and men. Weisstein, however, refutes such conclusions. Do Adams's and Weintraub's essays hold up under Weisstein's scrutiny of scientific research? Are their arguments still as convincing as they were when you first read them? How does Weisstein's discussion help put Adams's and Weintraub's beliefs into context?

3. Brownmiller argues that the rules of "femininity" are very much alive, despite advances in achieving women's rights. While Rosenberg argues that the idea of "masculinity" is dying, Hopkins outlines the damaging results of our cultural reification of a heterosexist masculine identity. What do you think? Are models of masculinity and femininity still operative? Do they still influence men's and women's ways of thinking and acting? Is one model perhaps changing more than the other? Are these ideas dying out, or have they simply been modified?

4. The cluster of essays on men and masculinity suggests that women aren't the only ones "trapped" by social models of gender behavior. According to Alda, Goldberg, Rosenberg, Blakely, and Hopkins, how are men expected to believe in ways appropriate to their sex? According to these authors, to what extent are men's personalities, temperaments, and life options influenced by social expectations? Do you agree that men suffer social oppression as a consequence of gender roles? What is the nature of this oppression? How is it different from that of women? To what

extent, if any, do masculine roles translate into social power and feminine roles into powerlessness? Why? How might exploring the nature of these roles help explain gender inequities in society? What insights does Brownmiller provide to help you explore these questions?

5. The relationship between gender difference and social inequality is itself a controversial issue. De Beauvoir's discussion of women suggests that the very idea of difference is at the root of women's oppression, and Hopkins describes how identity is relational—having one type of identity depends on not having another kind of identity. Weintraub suggests that the more we know about gender differences, the greater the chance that women can achieve real social equality. What is the central issue in this debate? On what point, if any, do these authors agree? Where do their viewpoints diverge? To what extent does their disagreement derive from differing assumptions about the origins of gender differences? To what extent do you find social inequity a consequence of the idea of difference? To what extent do you find it an unrelated issue?

6. Goldberg argues that women can shift roles if they choose, but men are not permitted the luxury of acting "out of role" at all. Hopkins and Weitz suggest that both men and women are severely punished for behaving in ways considered inappropriate for their sex. What do you think? Are children punished for such "inappropriate" behavior? Are adults also punished? Do both sexes have the option of acting out of role? Do either men or women have more freedom to do so? In shaping your response, you might want to draw on the essays of several other authors, especially Rosenberg and Brownmiller.

7. Aren't women considered human? Sayers and de Beauvoir examine this issue at length. Why is this a recurring issue in discussions of women's oppression? What does it suggest about the nature of women's oppression? How do McIntosh's, White's, Weitz's, Hopkins's, and de Beauvoir's explorations of identity and self-definition illustrate this issue? According to these authors, what problems do women and homosexuals share in defining themselves? Why do they encounter these difficulties? What does this issue suggest about homosexuals and women as oppressed groups in society? What other similarities exist between the two groups? What is the significance of such similarities?

8. Consider the essays by McIntosh, White, Weitz, and Hopkins. What important issues do these authors address concerning sexual

identity formation? How similar is the experience of lesbians and gay men? How is it different? Both Weitz and Hopkins offer solutions to the problem of sexual identity formation in a patriarchal heterosexist society. How are their solutions similar? How are they different? How realistic are their solutions?

9. Several of the authors represented hold assumptions about the goals and achievements of feminism. What are their assumptions? In what ways do they agree or disagree? What might account for their differing perspectives on feminism? What do you think are the goals of feminism? In establishing your own position, you may want to explore the essays by Adams, Weintraub, Goldberg, Steinem, and Weitz.

Part II
Women's Role: Historical Perspectives

    Although there has been an intense interest in gender relations over the last four decades, the subject certainly is not new. The role and status of women have been topics of discussion since the earliest writings of the Greek philosophers. Not surprisingly, many of the same themes addressed by feminist scholars in the 1990s have been addressed by writers throughout the ages. Part II contributes a historical perspective to our exploration of women's role in society.

    The first section, "Voices From and About the Past," contains five essays that reveal attitudes about women in past eras. Plato discusses the differences between men and women and the role women should play in an ideal society. Mary Daly interprets biblical history from a feminist perspective, connecting sexist assumptions in the Bible to the historical oppression of women. Pope Pius XI reaffirms the views held for centuries by the Catholic church on marriage and the role of women. Dorothy Gies McGuigan documents historical discrimination against women and the obstacles they must face in obtaining an education. Finally, Kate Millett describes patriarchal socialization and proposes a manifesto for sexual revolution.

    In "Women and Equal Rights," the second section continues our historical perspective with a look at some of the earliest truly "feminist" writings. Mary Wollstonecraft, a courageous, pioneering feminist of the late eighteenth century, writes articulately about the bitter oppression of women by an unfeeling patriarchal

society. Frederick Douglass, an important nineteenth-century abolitionist, persuasively argues that women should be entitled to
the same rights as men. Similarly, John Stuart Mill forcefully contends that our social and legal institutions have conspired to make
men tyrants over their wives, and that such tyranny is out of place
in our democratic society. Charlotte Perkins Gilman, who like
Douglass and Mill also wrote during the nineteenth century, examines the economic status of women, claiming that what little
economic power they do enjoy, they derive solely from marriage.
Finally, in two separate selections written in the first few decades
of the twentieth century, Margaret Sanger champions women's
right to control their bodies.

The third section, "Race and Femininity," considers how
the issue of race intersects with feminist concerns. In her 1851
speech to a white audience comprised of women's suffragists
and "men of the cloth," Sojourner Truth argues that all women—
regardless of their skin color—deserve equality. Meanwhile,
Ellen Willis proposes that many black feminists are so focused
on the issue of racism and its relationship to economic exploitation that they virtually ignore sexism within the black community. Mitsuye Yamada describes how Asian American women
have been rendered virtually invisible and powerless by American society. Finally, bell hooks, after discussing how America's
historical tradition of racism has effectively separated white
women and black women, calls for feminist solidarity across racial boundaries.

From Plato's *Republic,* to early feminist writing decrying the
economic oppression of women, to contemporary discussions of
racism and various feminisms, questions of gender have remained crucial issues throughout the ages. Part II illustrates that
women of the late twentieth century share many of the same
struggles with their historical counterparts.

Chapter 5 _____

VOICES FROM AND ABOUT THE PAST

The Role of Women in the Ideal Society

PLATO

In this excerpt from Plato's Republic, *Socrates and Glaucon discuss how women should fit into the ideal society. The crux of their debate remains relevant even today: If men and women are indeed different, to what extent should their differences influence their position, status, and function in society?*

I t may be right after the men have played their part that the women should come on in their turn, especially when you demand it in this way. For men who are, by nature and education, such as we have described, there is, in my opinion, no right possession or use of children and women except along the lines on which we originally started them. We tried in our argument, if you remember, to make our men like guardians of a flock."

"Yes."

"Then let us follow this up and give corresponding rules for birth and nurture, and see whether we approve the result or not."

"How?" he asked.

"In this way. Do we think that the females of watchdogs ought to watch as well as the males, ought to hunt with them, and generally share their occupations, or should they be kept indoors in the kennels, on the ground that breeding and rearing the puppies disables them for anything else, while the hard work and all the care of the flocks is reserved for the males?"

"They should share in everything," he said. "Only we treat the females as the weaker and the males as the stronger."

"Can you," I said, "use any living creature for the same work as another unless you rear and train it in the same way?"

"No," he said.

"Then if we employ women at the same tasks as men, we must give them the same instruction?"

"Yes."

"The men were given music and gymnastic."

"Yes."

"Then we must assign to the women also these two arts, and the art of war in addition, and treat them in the same way."

"That follows from what you say," he said....

"But must we not first come to an agreement as to whether these proposals are practical or not, and allow any one, whether he is a jester or a serious person, to raise the question whether female human nature is capable of sharing with the male in all his occupations, or in none of them, or whether it is capable of some and not of others, and to ask in the last case to which of these classes warfare belongs? Would not this naturally be the best beginning, and lead to the best conclusion?"

"Much the best," he said.

"Then," I said, "shall we on behalf of these other people put the question to ourselves, that the other side may not be besieged without having defenders?"

"There is nothing to hinder us," he said.

"Then shall we say on their behalf: 'Socrates and Glaucon, there is no need for others to raise an objection against you. For in the beginning of your settlement of the city, you yourselves admitted that each should, as nature provides, do his own work, one person one work.'"

"I think we did. How could we do otherwise?"

"'But is not a woman by nature very different from a man?'"

"Certainly she is different."

"'And ought not different tasks be assigned to different individuals in accordance with the nature of each?'"

"Yes."

"'Then are you not mistaken and inconsistent now in maintaining, as you do, that men and women should do the same things, seeing that they have widely different natures?' Will you be able to offer any defence to that, my wonderful friend?"

"It is certainly not easy just at the moment," he said. "But I shall have to ask you, as I do now, to interpret our argument also, whatever it is."

"This, Glaucon," I said, "with many other similar difficulties, is what I have foreseen all this time. For that was why I was afraid, and hesitated to touch on the law concerning the possession and nurture of women and children."

"I don't wonder," he said. "By Zeus, no, it is not an easy task."

"It is not," I said. "But the truth is, whether a man falls into a small swimming-bath or into the middle of the mighty ocean, he has to swim all the same."

"Certainly."

"Well, then, we must strike out and try to get safe out of the argument, in the hope of a dolphin taking us up, or of some other impossible means of salvation."

"It looks like it," he said.

"Come, then," I said, "let us see whether we can possibly find a way out. We admit that different natures ought to do different things, and that the natures of a man and of a woman are different, but now we say that these different natures should do the same things. Is that the accusation against us?"

"It is."

"A noble thing, Glaucon," I said, "is the power of the art of controversy."

"Why do you say so?"

"Because," I said, "many people seem to me to fall into it quite against their will, and to think that discussion which is really contention, because they cannot examine the subject of their argument by analyzing its various forms, but will urge their contradiction of what has been said in reliance on the mere sound of the word, dealing with one another by contention, and not by scientific argument."

"Yes," he said, "that happens with very many people. But does it touch us at this moment?"

"Most certainly it does," I said, "for we seem, quite against our will, to be dealing with controversial arguments."

"In what way?"

"When we insist that what are not the same natures ought not to have the same pursuits, we cling to the verbal point most bravely and contentiously, but we have never inquired at all of what kind were the sameness and the difference and with reference to what we were then distinguishing them, when we proposed to give different pursuits to different natures, and the same pursuits to the same natures."

"No," he said, "we did not inquire."

"In the same way," I said, "we might evidently ask ourselves whether bald and hairy men had the same or opposite natures; and, agreeing that they have opposite natures, might forbid hairy men to be shoemakers if bald men are, or forbid bald men if hairy men are."

"Well, that would be ridiculous," he said.

"But would it not be ridiculous," I said, "simply because, in that proposition, we did not mean same and different in general? Our rule was only directed against that particular form of likeness and difference which concerns those particular pursuits. We meant, for example, that the soul possessed of medical capacity and a doctor have the same nature. Do you agree with me?"

"I do."

"But a doctor and a carpenter have different natures."

"Of course."

"Then," I said, "if we find either the male or the female sex excelling the other in any art or other pursuit, then we shall say that this particular pursuit must be assigned to one and not to the other; but if we find that the difference simply consists in this, that the female conceives and the male begets, we shall not allow that that goes any way to prove that a woman differs from a man with reference to the subject of which we are speaking, and we shall still consider that our guardians and their wives ought to follow the same pursuits."

"And quite rightly," he said.

"Is not our next step to invite the supporters of the contrary opinion to show us in reference to what art or what pursuit among all those required for the service of the city, the nature of men and women is not the same, but different?"

"That is certainly just."

"Perhaps others might make the same reply as was made by you a little while ago, that it is not easy to give a satisfactory answer at the moment, but that it would not be difficult after consideration."

"They might."

"Then shall we request our objector to follow us, in the hope that we may prove to him that there is no occupation in the organization of the city which is peculiar to women?"

"Certainly."

"'Come, then,' we shall say to him, 'answer this. When you say that one man has a natural talent for anything, and another is naturally unfitted for it, do you mean that the first learns it easily, while the second learns it with difficulty? that the first, after a little study, would find out much for himself in the subject which he has studied; but the second, in spite of much study and practice, would not even keep what he had learned? that in the one the mind would be well served by the bodily powers, in the other it would be thwarted? Are not these the only signs by which you meant to determine in any case natural talent or the want of it?'"

"No one," he said, "will name any others."

"Then, do you know any human occupation in which the male sex does not in all these particulars surpass the female? Need I bore you by referring to weaving and the making of pastry and preserves, in which, indeed, the female sex is considered to excel, and where their discomfiture is most laughed at?"

"What you say is true," he said. "Speaking generally, the one sex is easily beaten by the other all round. There are indeed many cases of women being better than men in many different employments, but, as a general rule, it is as you say."

"Then, my friend, there is not one of those pursuits by which the city is ordered which belongs to women as women, or to men as men; but natural aptitudes are equally distributed in both kinds of creatures. Women naturally participate in all occupations, and so do men; but in all women are weaker than men."

"Certainly."

"Shall we, then, assign all occupations to men and none to women?"

"Of course not."

"But we shall say, I fancy, that one woman is by nature fit for medicine, and another not; one musical, and another unmusical?"

"Surely."

"And is not one woman a lover of gymnastic and of war, and another unwarlike and no lover of gymnastic?"

"I should think so."

"And one a lover and another a hater of wisdom; one spirited, another spiritless?"

"Yes."

"Then one woman will be capable of being a guardian and another not. For did we not select just this nature for our men guardians?"

"We did."

"Then for the purposes of guarding the city the nature of men and women is the same, except that women are naturally weaker, men naturally stronger?"

"Apparently."

"Then we must select women of the necessary character to share the life of men of like character and guard the city along with them, inasmuch as they are capable and of a kindred nature?"

"Certainly."

"Then must we not assign the same occupations to the same natures?"

"Yes."

"So we are come round to what we said before, and allow that there is nothing unnatural in assigning music and gymnastic to the wives of the guardians?"

"Most certainly."

"Then our legislation has not been an impracticable dream, seeing that we have made our law in accordance with nature? Present conditions which depart from this are evidently much more a departure from nature."

"Evidently."

"Now were we not inquiring whether our proposals are practicable and desirable?"

"We were."

"And we are agreed that they are practicable?"

"Yes."

"Then we must next come to an agreement on their desirability?"

"Obviously."

"Then surely if women are to become fit to be guardians, we shall not have one education to make guardians of the men and another for the women, especially when education will have the same nature to work upon?"

"No."

"What is your opinion in a question like this?".

"Like what?"

"How do you conceive to yourself one man as better and another as worse? or do you think that all are alike?"

"Certainly not."

"Then, in this city which we were founding, do you think that our guardians, who have received the education we have described, will be better men than the shoemakers who have been trained in shoemaking?"

"The question is ridiculous," he said.

"I understand," I said. "Then are not these the best of all the citizens?"

"Much the best."

"Further, will not these women be the best of the women?"

"Yes, much the best also."

"Then is anything better for a city than that it should contain the best possible men and women?"

"Nothing."

REFLECTING ON MEANING

1. One of the questions Socrates and Glaucon attempt to answer is the extent to which women's and men's differences are the result of nature or of learning. What does Socrates mean by "natural talent" and "natural aptitudes"? Is he implying that the differences are innate or socially constructed?

2. Socrates suggests that perhaps the nature of women's and men's differences, rather than the fact of difference itself, is the key. This difference, he says, is that "the female conceives and the male begets." To what extent does this difference influence the accepted division of labor in society? Should reproductive functions determine one's fitness in other avenues of life? What seems to be Socrates's answer to this question? Do you agree or disagree? Why?

3. During their discussion, Socrates and Glaucon explore the question of differences in men's and women's education and the fitness of women for combat. What are the implications of their discussion for these questions? What are your views?

EXPLORING RHETORICAL STRATEGIES

1. Socrates compares men and women to male and female watchdogs. In what ways does this analogy help him advance the discussion? How does framing the issue of difference in another context illuminate assumptions about the social roles of men and women? Is the analogy appropriate? Why or why not?

2. The Socratic dialogue differs significantly from the traditional thesis-driven argumentative essay. In what ways does it differ? What are the advantages of dialogue as a genre? What are its limitations?

3. Socrates makes a distinction between "discussion" and "contention." What is this distinction? Do you consider this dialogue a form of discussion or contention? Why?

I Thank Thee, Lord, That Thou Has Not Created Me a Woman

MARY DALY

A contemporary theologian and philosopher, Mary Daly reinterprets the Bible and Christian history to show how they "have served as powerful instruments for the reinforcement of the subjection of women in Western society."

The situation of women in Western society has always been fraught with ambiguity. The writings of innumerable authors in a variety of fields attest to the existence of the problem, although there is by no means agreement concerning the nature of the problem. Adherents of the "eternal feminine" mystique accept as normative the feminine stereotypes of our culture, according to which a "true woman" does not achieve self-actualization through intellectual creativity and participation in political, economic, and social life on a level equal to that of men. Rather, according to this view, her destiny lies in generic fulfillment through motherhood, physical or spiritual, and in being a helpmate to her husband. Opposition to this position is strong. Radically opposed to the idea that the feminine stereotype is "natural" are the findings of anthropology, which suggest that "many, if not all, of the personality traits that we have called masculine or feminine are as lightly linked to sex, as are the clothing, the manners, and the form of head-dress that a society at a given period assigns to sex." Recent research in experimental psychology also tends to refute the idea that the cluster of qualities expressed by the "eternal feminine" stereotype are innate and peculiar to women. A growing number of authors argue that the characteristics of the "eternal feminine" are opposed to those of a developing, authentic person, who must be unique, self-critical, active, and searching. Modern feminists argue that the biological burdens associated with maternity and the restrictions imposed by cultural conditioning have held women back from the attainment of full human stature. They note with irony that the compensation offered by society to women for acceptance of the restrictions which it has imposed upon them in the political, economic, social, educational, and moral spheres has been imprisonment upon a pedestal.

The oppressive situation of women in ancient times is reflected in the Bible. The authors of both the Old and the New Testaments were men of their times, and it would be naive to think that they were free of the prejudices of their epochs. Indeed, the Bible contains much to jolt the modern woman, who is accustomed to think of herself, at least to some extent, as an autonomous person. In the writings of the Old Testament, women emerge as subjugated and inferior beings. Although the wife of an Israelite was not on the level of a slave, and however much better off she was than wives in other Near-Eastern nations, it is indicative of her inferior condition that the wife addressed her husband as a slave addressed his master, or a subject his king. In the Decalogue a man's wife is listed among his possessions, along with such items as his ox and his ass (Exodus 20:17; Deuteronomy 5:21). While her husband could repudiate her, she could not claim a divorce. Misconduct on the part of the wife was severely punished among the ancient Hebrews, whereas infidelity on the part of the man was punished only if he violated the rights of another man by taking a married woman as his accomplice. A man could sell his daughter as well as his slaves. If a couple did not have children, it was assumed to be the fault of the wife. In summary, although Hebrew women were honored as parents and often treated with kindness, their social and legal status was that of subordinate beings. Hebrew males prayed: "I thank thee, Lord, that thou has not created me a woman."

Throughout the centuries, Christian authors have placed great importance upon the account of the creation of Eve in the second chapter of Genesis. Combined with the story of the Fall, this seemed to present irrefutable evidence of woman's essentially inferior intellectual and moral stature. Indeed, through the ages the anti-feminine tradition in Christian culture has justified itself to a large extent on the story of the origin and activities of the "first mother," which until recently was not understood to be androcentric myth but rather was taken as straight historical fact. A psychoanalyst who is also a student of biblical literature has summarized the situation succinctly: "The biblical story of Eve's birth is the hoax of the millennia."

Androcentric tendencies in Western culture, rooted also in the profound misogynism of the Greeks, are reflected in the New Testament as well, which in turn has served as a basis for their perpetuation throughout Christendom. The most strikingly anti-feminine passages are in the Pauline texts. Paul was greatly concerned with order in society and in Christian assemblies in particular. It seemed important to him that women should not have a predominant place in Christian assemblies, that they should not "speak" in public or unveil their heads. This could have caused scandal and ridicule of the new sect, which already had to face charges of immorality and effeminacy. Thus he repeatedly insisted upon "correct" sexual behavior, including the subjection of wives at meetings. Paul went further and looked for theological justification for the prevailing customs. Thus, for example: "For a man ought not to cover his head, since he is the image and glory of God; but woman is the glory of man. For man was not made from woman, but woman from man. Neither was man created for woman, but woman for man" (I Corinthians 11:7ff.). Paul was basing his theological assertion here upon the then commonly held interpretation of Genesis. The extent of the effect is inestimable. For nearly two thousand years sermons and pious literature have been based upon the "glory of man" theme, and this has been accepted as God's inspired word.

Another frequently quoted Pauline text (probably not written by Paul but traditionally attributed to him) based on the then current interpretation of Genesis and used ever since as authority for the subordination of women is the following:

> Let a woman learn in silence with all submissiveness. I permit no woman to teach or to have authority over men; she is to keep silent. For Adam was formed first, then Eve; and Adam was not deceived, but the woman was deceived and became a transgressor. Yet woman will be saved through bearing children, if she continues in faith and love and holiness, with modesty (I Timothy 2:11–15).

As for women's place in domestic society, the Pauline teaching was most explicit: "As the Church is subject to Christ, so let wives be subject in everything to their husbands" (Ephesians 5:24).

Such texts, understood as divinely inspired and without reference to the cultural context in which they were written, have served as powerful instruments for the reinforcement of the subjection of women in Western society. They have been used by religious authorities down through the centuries as a guarantee of divine approval for the transformation of woman's subordinate status from a contingent fact into an immutable norm of the feminine condition. They have been instrumental in withholding from women equal education, legal and economic equality, and access to the professions.

The low esteem for women in Western society during the early centuries of Christianity is reflected in the writings of the Church

Fathers. The characteristics they considered to be typically feminine include fickleness and shallowness, garrulousness and weakness, slowness of understanding, and instability of mind. There were some violent tirades, such as that of Tertullian: "Do you not know that you are Eve?... You are the devil's gateway.... How easily you destroyed man, the image of God. Because of the death which you brought upon us, even the Son of God had to die" (*De cultu feminarum,* libri duo I, 1). On the whole, the attitude was one of puzzlement over the seemingly incongruous fact of woman's existence. Augustine summed up the general idea in saying that he did not see in what way it could be said that woman was made to be a help for man, if the work of child-bearing be excluded.

The Fathers found in Genesis an "explanation" of woman's inferiority which served as a guarantee of divine approval for perpetuating the situation which made her inferior. There was uncritical acceptance of the androcentric myth of Eve's creation and refusal, in varying degrees of inflexibility, to grant that woman is the image of God—an attitude in large measure inspired by Paul's first epistle to the Corinthians. Thus Augustine wrote that only man is the image and glory of God. According to him, since the believing woman cannot lay aside her sex, she is restored to the image of God only where there is no sex, that is, in the spirit (*De Trinitate,* XII, 7).

Together with the biblical account and the teachings of Church Fathers, those living in the early centuries of the Christian era were confronted with an image of women produced by oppressive conditions which were universal. A girlhood of strict seclusion and of minimal education prepared them for the life of mindless subordinates. This was followed by an early marriage which effectively cut them off from the possibility of autonomous action for the rest of their lives. Their inferiority was a fact; it appeared to be "natural." Thus experience apparently supported the rib story just as the myth itself helped "explain" the common experience of women as incomplete and lesser humans. The vicious circle was complete.

REFLECTING ON MEANING

1. Daly implicates the story of Eve's creation and the story of the Fall in the historical oppression of women. What are these stories? Why does Daly call them examples of "androcentric myth" as opposed to "straight historical fact"? How have these biblical accounts helped shape the position of women in Western society?

2. Daly maintains that the Pauline texts include the "most strikingly anti-feminine passages" in the New Testament. What do these passages say about women? Why does Daly discuss Paul's values when she presents his writings? According to Daly, why is it naive to think that the authors of the biblical accounts and the Church Fathers were "free of the prejudices of their epochs"? Why is it important to consider the cultural context in which the books of the Bible and the texts of the Church Fathers were produced?

3. What is the "vicious circle" that Daly alludes to? What does she mean when she states that women's "inferiority was a fact"? To what extent, if any, does Christianity still perpetuate this circle? To what extent, if any, does it still perpetuate the "myth" of women's inferiority?

EXPLORING RHETORICAL STRATEGIES

1. What kinds of evidence does Daly provide to support her assertions? On what foundation is her argument based? Do you find her reinterpretation of history reasonable albeit controversial? Why or why not?

2. What is the tone of Daly's essay? How does it contribute to the persona she creates? What is your reaction to this persona? How do you think she expected readers to respond to her views? Why?

3. In her last paragraph, Daly places the words *natural* and *explain* in quotation marks. Why? How does this emphasis change the meaning of these words? How does it help Daly convey her point of view? Why, also, does she refer to the biblical account of the creation of Eve as the "rib story"? What is the effect of this strategy?

On Christian Marriage

POPE PIUS XI

Pope Pius XI issued the encyclical, or official papal letter, Casti Connubii *on the subject of marriage and the family in 1930. Defining marriage as a holy sacrament, Pope Pius reaffirms traditional Christian views on the relationship of spouses within the family.*

How great is the dignity of chaste wedlock, Venerable Brethren, may be judged best from this that Christ Our Lord, Son of the Eternal Father, having assumed the nature of fallen man, not only, with His loving desire of compassing the redemption of our race, ordained it in an especial manner as the principle and foundation of domestic society and therefore of all human intercourse, but also raised it to the rank of a truly and "great sacrament" of the New Law, restored it to the original purity of its divine institution, and accordingly entrusted all its discipline and care to His spouse the Church.

In order, however, that amongst men of every nation and every age the desired fruits may be obtained from this renewal of matrimony, it is necessary, first of all, that men's minds be illuminated with the true doctrine of Christ regarding it; and secondly, that Christian spouses, the weakness of their wills strengthened by the internal grace of God, shape all their ways of thinking and of acting in conformity with that pure law of Christ so as to obtain true peace and happiness for themselves and for their families.

Yet not only do We, looking with paternal eye on the universal world from this Apostolic See as from a watchtower, but you also, Venerable Brethren, see, and seeing deeply grieve with Us that a great number of men, forgetful of that divine work of renewal, either entirely ignore or shamelessly deny the great sanctity of Christian wedlock, or relying on the false principles of a new and utterly perverse morality, too often trample it underfoot. And since these most pernicious errors and depraved morals have begun to spread even amongst the faithful and are gradually gaining ground, in Our office as Christ's Vicar upon earth and Supreme Shepherd and Teacher We consider it Our duty to raise Our voice to keep the flock committed to Our care from poisoned pastures and, as far as in Us lies, to preserve it from harm.

We have decided therefore to speak to you, Venerable Brethren, and through you to the whole Church of Christ and indeed to the whole human race, on the nature and dignity of Christian marriage, on the advantages and benefits which accrue from it to the family and to human society itself, on the errors contrary to this most important point of the Gospel teaching, on the vices opposed to conjugal union, and lastly on the principal remedies to be applied. In so doing We follow the footsteps of Our predecessor, Leo XIII, of happy memory, whose encyclical *Arcanum,* published fifty years ago, We hereby confirm and make Our own, and while We wish to expound more fully certain points called for by the conditions and needs of our times, nevertheless We declare that, far from being obsolete, it retains its full force at the present day.

And to begin with that same encyclical, which is almost wholly concerned in vindicating the divine institution of matrimony, its sacramental dignity, and its perpetual stability, let it be repeated as an immutable and inviolable fundamental doctrine that matrimony was not instituted or restored by man but by God; not by man were the laws made to strengthen and confirm and elevate it, but by God, the Author of nature, and by Christ Our Lord by Whom nature was restored, and hence these laws cannot be subject to any human decrees or to any contrary pact even of the spouses themselves. This is the doctrine of Holy Scripture, this is the constant tradition of the Universal Church, this is the solemn definition of the sacred Council of Trent, which declares and establishes from the words of Holy Writ itself that God is the Author of the perpetual stability of the marriage bond, its unity and its firmness. . . .

[The] mutual inward moulding of husband and wife, this determined effort to perfect each other, can in a very real sense, as the Roman Catechism teaches, be said to be the chief reason and purpose of matrimony, provided matrimony be looked at not in the restricted sense as instituted for the proper conception and education of the child, but more widely as the blending of life as a whole and the mutual interchange and sharing thereof.

By this same love it is necessary that all the other rights and duties of the marriage state be regulated as the words of the Apostle: "Let the husband render the debt to the wife, and the wife also in like manner to the husband, not only a law of justice, but of charity."

Domestic society being confirmed, therefore, by this bond of love, there should flourish in it that "order of love," as St. Augustine calls it. This order includes both the primacy of the husband with regard to the wife and children, the ready subjection of the wife and her willing obedience, which the Apostle commends in these words: "Let women be subject to their husbands as to the Lord, because the husband is the head of the wife, as Christ is the head of the church."

This subjection, however, does not deny or take away the liberty which fully belongs to the woman both in view of her dignity as a human person, and in view of her most noble office as wife and mother and companion; nor does it bid her obey her husband's every request if not in harmony with right reason or with the dignity due to a wife; nor, in fine, does it imply that the wife should be put on a level with those persons who in law are called minors, to whom it is not customary to allow free exercise of their rights on account of their lack of mature judgment, or of their ignorance of human affairs. But it forbids that exaggerated liberty which cares not for the good of the family; it forbids that in this body which is the family, the heart be separated from the head to the great detriment of the whole body and the proximate danger of ruin. For if the man is the head, the woman is the heart, and as he occupies the chief place in ruling, so she may and ought to claim for herself the chief place in love.

Again, this subjection of wife to husband in its degree and manner may vary according to the different conditions of persons, place and time. In fact, if the husband neglect his duty, it falls to the wife to take his place in directing the family. But the structure of the family and its fundamental law, established and confirmed by God, must always and everywhere be maintained intact.

With great wisdom Our predecessor Leo XIII, of happy memory, in the encyclical on *Christian Marriage* which We have already mentioned, speaking of this order to be maintained between man and wife, teaches: "The man is the ruler of the family, and the head of the woman; but because she is flesh of his flesh and bone of his bone, let her be subject and obedient to the man, not as a servant but as a companion, so that nothing be lacking of honor or of dignity in the obedience which she pays. Let divine charity be the constant guide of their mutual relations, both in him who rules and in her who obeys, since each bears the image, the one of Christ, the other of the Church."...

The same false teachers who try to dim the luster of conjugal faith and purity do not scruple to do away with the honorable and trusting obedience which the woman owes to the man. Many of them even go further and assert that such a subjection of one party to the other is unworthy of human dignity, that the rights of husband and wife are equal; wherefore, they boldly proclaim, the emancipation of women has been or ought to be effected. This emancipation, in their opinion, must be threefold, in the ruling of the domestic society, in the administration of family affairs and in the rearing of the children. It must be social, economic, physiological; physiological, that is to say, the woman is to be freed at her own good pleasure from the burdensome duties properly belonging to a wife as companion and mother (We have already said that this is not an emancipation but a crime); social inasmuch as the wife being freed from the care of children and family, should, to the neglect of these, be able to follow her own bent and devote herself to business and even public affairs; finally economic, whereby the woman even without the knowledge and against the will of her husband may be at liberty to conduct and administer her own affairs, giving her attention chiefly to these rather than to children, husband and family.

This, however, is not the true emancipation of woman, nor that rational and exalted liberty which belongs to the noble office of a Christian woman and wife; it is rather the debasing of the womanly character and the dignity of motherhood, and indeed of the whole family, as a result of which the husband suffers the loss of his wife, the children of their mother and the home and the whole family of an ever watchful guardian. More than this, this false liberty and unnatural equality with the husband is to the detriment of the woman herself, for if the woman descends from her truly regal throne to which she has been raised within the walls of the home by means of the Gospel, she will soon be reduced to the old state of slavery (if not in appearance, certainly in reality) and become, as amongst the pagans, the mere instrument of man.

This equality of rights, which is so much exaggerated and distorted, must indeed be recognized in those rights which belong to the dignity of the human soul and which are proper to the marriage contract and inseparably bound up with wedlock. In such things undoubtedly both parties enjoy the same rights and are bound by the same obligations; in other things there must be a certain inequality and due accommodation, which is demanded by the good of the family and the right ordering and unity and stability of home life.

As, however, the social and economic conditions of the married woman must in some way be altered on account of the changes in social intercourse, it is part of the office of the public authority to adapt the civil rights of the wife to modern needs and requirements, keeping in view what the natural disposition and temperament of the female sex, good morality, and the welfare of the family demand, and provided always that the essential order of the domestic society remain intact, founded as it is on something higher than human authority and wisdom, namely on the authority and wisdom of God, and so not changeable by public laws or at the pleasure of private individuals.

REFLECTING ON MEANING

1. According to Pope Pius, marriage is designed and authorized by whom? What significance does this authorization hold for the views on marriage and family that he outlines?

2. What is the "order of love" in marriage that Pope Pius affirms? What is its "structure" and "fundamental law"? What earlier sources does he draw on to outline the implications of this order?

3. Pope Pius claims that the "subjection" he describes "does not deny or take away the liberty which fully belongs to the woman." Moreover, he asserts that the equality some have called for is not "emancipation but a crime," a "debasing of the womanly character and the dignity of motherhood." How does Pope Pius justify his assertions? Do you find his reasoning acceptable or not? Why?

EXPLORING RHETORICAL STRATEGIES

1. Definition is an important element of Pope Pius's argument in this letter. How does he define such concepts as marriage, subjection, obedience, and emancipation? In what ways are these definitions crucial to his reasoning?

2. Pope Pius outlines and refutes opposing viewpoints in his letter. What strategies does he use to disarm opponents? Do you find his arguments effective? Why or why not?

3. Analogy plays a key role in the argument Pope Pius presents. What instances of analogy can you find? How do they help advance his conception of gender roles in marriage?

To Be a Woman and a Scholar

DOROTHY GIES McGUIGAN

Throughout the centuries, education and the professions were closed to women. Despite seemingly insurmountable barriers, however, some women became scholars in their own right. As historian Dorothy Gies McGuigan suggests in this survey, the efforts of these women to educate themselves illuminate the historical plight that all women faced.

O n a Saturday morning in June exactly three hundred years ago this year [1978], the first woman in the world to receive a doctoral degree mounted a pulpit in the cathedral of Padua to be examined in Aristotelian dialectics.

Her name was Elena Lucrezia Cornaro Piscopia. She was thirty-two years old, single, daughter of one of the wealthiest families in Venice. Precociously brilliant, she had begun to study Aristotle at the age of seven. Her father had backed her studies and supplied the best of tutors; by the time she enrolled in the University of Padua, she knew not only Latin and Greek, French, English, and Spanish, but also Hebrew, Arabic, and Chaldaic.

News of the unique phenomenon of a woman scholar had drawn such throngs to witness her doctoral trial that it had to be moved from the hall of the University of Padua into the cathedral. Elena had first applied to take her doctorate in theology, but the Chancellor of the university's Theological Faculty, Cardinal Gregorio Barbarigo, Bishop of Padua, had refused indignantly. "Never," he replied. "Woman is made for motherhood, not for learning." He wrote later of the incident, "I talked with a French cardinal about it and he broke out in laughter." Reluctantly Barbarigo agreed that she be allowed to take the doctoral examination in philosophy. A modest, deeply religious young woman, Elena Cornaro had quailed before the prospect of the public examination; it was her proud, ambitious father who had insisted. A half hour before the solemn program began, Elena expressed such anguish and reluctance that her confessor had to speak very sternly to persuade her to go through with it. Her examiners were not lenient because of her sex, for the prestige of the university was at stake. But Elena's replies—in Latin, of course—were so brilliant that the judges declared the doctorate in philosophy was "hardly an honor for so towering an intellect." The doctoral ring was placed on Elena's finger, the ermine cape of teacher laid about her shoulders, and the laurel crown of poet placed on her dark curly head. The entire assembly rose and chanted a Te Deum.

What was it like to be a gifted woman, an Elena Cornaro, three hundred years ago? What happened to a bright woman in the past who wanted to study another culture, examine the roots of a language, master the intricacies of higher mathematics, write a book—or prevent or cure a terrible disease?

To begin with, for a woman to acquire anything that amounted to real learning, she needed four basics.

She needed to survive. In the seventeenth century women's life expectancy had risen only to thirty-two; not until 1750 did it begin to rise appreciably and reach, in the mid-nineteenth century, age forty-two. A woman ambitious for learning would do well to choose a life of celibacy, not only to avoid the hazards of childbirth but because there was no room for a scholar's life within the confines of marriage and childbearing. Elena Cornaro had taken a vow of chastity at the age of eleven, turned down proposals of marriage to become an oblate of the Benedictine Order.

Secondly, to aspire to learning a woman needed basic literacy; she had to be one of the fortunate few who learned at least to read and write. Although literacy studies in earlier centuries are still very incomplete and comparative data on men's and women's literacy are meager, it appears that before 1650 a bare 10 percent of women in the city of London could sign their names. What is most striking about this particular study is that when men are divided by occupation—with clergy and the professions at the top, 100 percent literate, and male laborers at the bottom of the scale, about 15 percent literate—women as a group fell below even unskilled male laborers in their rate of literacy. By about 1700 half the women in London could sign their names; in the provinces women's literacy remained much lower.

The third fundamental a woman needed if she aspired to learning was, of course, an economic base. It was best to be born, like Elena Cornaro, to a family of wealth who owned a well-stocked library and could afford private tutors. For girls of poor families the chance of learning the bare minimum of reading and writing was small. Even such endowed charity schools as Christ's Hospital in London were attended mostly by boys; poor girls in charity schools were apt to have their literacy skills slighted in favor of catechism, needlework, knitting, and lace-making in preparation for a life in domestic service.

The fourth fundamental a woman scholar needed was simply a very tough skin, for she was a deviant in a society where the learned woman, far from being valued, was likely to hear herself preached against in the pulpit and made fun of on the public stage. Elena Cornaro was fortunate to have been born in Italy, where an array of learned women had flourished during the Renaissance and where the woman scholar seems to have found a more hospitable ambiance than in the northern countries.

In eighteenth-century England the gifted writer Lady Mary Wortley Montagu, writing in 1753 about proposed plans for a little granddaughter's education, admonished her daughter with some bitterness "to conceal whatever Learning [the child] attains, with as much solicitude as she would hide crookedness or lameness."

In post-Renaissance Europe two overriding fears dominated thinking on women's education: the fear that learning would unfit women for their social role, defined as service to husband and children and obedience to the church; and, a corollary of the first, that open access to education would endanger women's sexual purity. For while humanist philosophy taught that education led to virtue, writers on education were at once conflicted when they applied the premise to women. Nearly all, beginning with the influential sixteenth-century Juan Luis Vives, opted for restricting women's learning. Only a few radical thinkers—some men, such as Richard Mulcaster in Tudor England and the extraordinary Poullain de la Barre in seventeenth-century France, some women, like the feisty Bathsua Makin and revolutionary Mary Wollstonecraft—spoke out for the full development of women's intellectual potential.

In any case, since institutions of higher learning were designed for young men entering the professions—the church, the law, government service—from which women were excluded, they were excluded too from the universities that prepared for them. And, just as importantly, they were excluded from the grammar or preparatory schools, whose curriculum was based on Latin, the code language of the male intellectual elite. Since most scholarly texts were written in Latin, ignorance of that language prevented women from reading scholarly literature in most fields—which only gradually and belatedly became available in translation.

Richard Hyrde, a tutor in the household of Sir Thomas More and himself a defender of learning in women, cited the common opinion:

> ... that the frail kind of women, being inclined of their own courage unto vice, and mutable at every newelty [sic], if they should have skill in many things that must be written in the

Latin and Greek tongue . . . it would of likelihood both inflame
their stomachs a great deal the more to that vice, that men say
they be too much given unto of their own nature already and
instruct them also with more subtility and conveyance, to set
forward and accomplish their forward intent and purpose.

And yet, despite all the hurdles, some bright women did manage to make a mark as scholars and writers. Sometimes girls listened
in on their brothers' tutored lessons. A fortunate few, like Elena Cornaro, had parents willing and able to educate daughters equally with
sons. The daughters of Sir Thomas More, of the Earl of Arundel, and
of Sir Anthony Cooke in Tudor England were given excellent edu-
cations. Arundel's daughter, Lady Joanna Lumley, produced the
earliest known English translation of a Greek drama.

But by far the largest number of women scholars in the past
were almost totally self-educated. Through sheer intellectual curiosity, self-discipline, often grinding hard work, they taught themselves what they wanted to know. Such self-teaching may well be
the only truly joyous form of learning. Yet it has its drawbacks: it
may also be haphazard and superficial. Without access to laboratory, lecture, and dissecting table, it was all but impossible for
women to train themselves in higher mathematics, for instance, in
science, in anatomy.

Mary Wollstonecraft wrote in 1792 that most women who
have acted like rational creatures or shown any vigor of intellect
have accidentally been allowed "to run wild," and running wild in
the family library was the usual way intellectually ambitious
women educated themselves. Such a self-taught scholar was Elizabeth Tanfield, Viscountess Cary, who as a girl in Elizabethan England taught herself French, Spanish, Italian, Latin, and added
Hebrew "with very little teaching." Her unsympathetic mother refused to allow her candles to read at night, so Elizabeth bribed the
servants, and by her wedding day—she was married at fifteen—she
had run up a candle debt of a hundred pounds. She wrote numerous translations, poetry—most of which she destroyed—and at least
one play, *Mariam, the Faire Queen of Jewry.*

Very often the critical phase of women's intellectual development took place at a different period in their lives from the normal
time of men's greatest development. Gifted women often came to
a period of intellectual crisis and of intense self-teaching during
adulthood.

When Christine de Pisane, daughter of the Italian astrologer
and physician at the court of Charles V of France, found herself
widowed at twenty-five with three children to support, she turned

to writing—certainly one of the first, if not the first, woman in Europe to support herself through a literary career. But Christine found her education wholly inadequate, and at the age of thirty-four she laid down a complete course of study for herself, teaching herself Latin, history, philosophy, literature. She used her pen later on to urge better educational opportunities for women, to defend her sex from the charges of such misogynistic writers as Jean de Meung. In her book, *The City of Ladies,* Christine imagined talented women building a town for themselves where they could lead peaceful and creative lives—an existence impossible, she considered, in fifteenth century France.

Like Christine de Pisane, the Dutch scholar Anna van Schurman of Utrecht, a contemporary of Elena Cornaro, found her early education superficial and unsatisfying. Like most upper middle class girls of the seventeenth century, Anna, precocious though she was, had been taught chiefly to sing nicely, to play musical instruments, to carve portraits in boxwood and wax, to do needlework and tapestry and cut paperwork. At the age of twenty-eight, frustrated by the lack of intellectual stimulation in her life, Anna turned her brilliant mind to serious studies, became one of the finest Latinists of her day, learned Hebrew, Syriac, Chaldaic, wrote an Ethiopian grammar that was the marvel of Dutch scholars, carried on an international correspondence—in Latin, of course—with all the leading scholars of continental Europe. When a professor of theology at Leyden wrote that women were barred from equality with men "by the sacred laws of nature," Anna wrote a Latin treatise in reply in 1641, defending the intellectual capacity of women and urging, as Christine de Pisane had, much greater educational opportunities. Her work was widely translated and made Anna van Schurman a model for women scholars all over Europe.

In France, during the lifetime of Anna van Schurman, a group of bright, intellectually malnourished women—most of them convent-educated—developed one of the most ingenious devices for women's lifelong learning. Bored with the dearth of cultivated conversation at the French court, the Marquise de Rambouillet, Mlle de Scudéry, Mme de Lafayette, and a host of others opened their town houses in Paris, invited men and women of talent and taste to hone their wits and talk of science and philosophy, literature and language, love and friendship. The salon has been described as "an informal university for women." Not only did it contribute to adult women's education, but it shaped standards of speaking and writing for generations in France and profoundly influenced French culture as a whole.

An offshoot of the salons were the special lecture courses offered by eminent scholars in chemistry, etymology, and other subjects—lectures largely attended by women. Fontenelle wrote his popular book on astronomy, *The Plurality of Worlds,* specifically for a female readership, and Descartes declared he had written his *Discourse on Method* in French rather than Latin so that women too would be able to read it.

There was, rather quickly, a backlash. Molière's satires on learned women did much to discredit the ladies who presided at salons—and who might at times be given to a bit of overelegance in speech and manner. When Abbé Fénélon wrote his influential treatise, *On the Education of Girls,* in 1686—just eight years after Elena Cornaro had won her doctorate—he mentioned neither Elena Cornaro nor Anna van Schurman nor Christine de Pisane. He inveighed against the pernicious effect of the salons. Declaring that "A woman's intellect is normally more feeble and her curiosity greater than those of men, it is undesirable to set her to studies which may turn her head. A girl," admonished that worthy French cleric, "must learn to obey without respite, to hold her peace and allow others to do the talking. Everything is lost if she obstinately tries to be clever and to get a distaste for domestic duties. The virtuous woman spins, confines herself to her home, keeps quiet, believes and obeys."

So much for the encouragement of women scholars in late seventeenth century France.

Across the Channel in England in the second half of the seventeenth century, bright ambitious women were studying not only the classics and languages but learning to use the newly perfected telescope and microscope, and to write on scientific subjects. Margaret Cavendish, Duchess of Newcastle, a remarkable woman with a wide-ranging mind and imagination, wrote not only biography, autobiography, and romance, but also popular science—she called it "natural philosophy"—directed especially to women readers. The versatile and talented writer Aphra Behn—the first woman in England to make her living by her pen—translated Fontenelle's *Plurality of Worlds* into English in 1688. In the preface she declared she would have preferred to write an original work on astronomy but had "neither health nor leisure" for such a project; it was, in fact, the year before her death and she was already ailing. But she defended the Copernican system vigorously against the recent attack by a Jesuit priest, did not hesitate to criticize the author, Fontenelle, and to correct an error in the text on the height of the earth's atmosphere.

But the learned lady in England as in France found herself criticized from the pulpit and satirized on the stage. Margaret

Cavendish was dubbed "Mad Madge of Newcastle." Jonathan Swift poked fun at Mary Astell for her proposal to found a women's college. Thomas Wright in *The Female Virtuosos,* the anonymous authors of *The Humours of Oxford* and *Female Wits,* Shadwell, Congreve, and others lampooned the would-be woman scholar. The shy poet, Anne, Countess of Winchilsea, who had only reluctantly identified herself as author of a published volume of verse, was cruelly pilloried by Pope and Gay in their play *Three Hours After Marriage.* And Aphra Behn, author of a phenomenal array of plays, poems, novels, and translations, could read this published verse about herself and her work at about the same time she was translating Fontenelle:

> Yet hackney writers, when their verse did fail
> To get 'em brandy, bread and cheese, and ale,
> Their wants by prostitution were supplied;
> Show but a tester [sixpence] you might up and ride;
> For punk and poetess agree so pat
> You cannot well be this, and not be that.

So if one asks what it was like to be a gifted woman, to aspire to learning at the time of Elena Cornaro, the answer might be that it was a difficult and demanding choice, requiring not merely intellectual gifts but extraordinary physical and mental stamina, and only a rare few women succeeded in becoming contributing scholars and writers. All the usual scholarly careers were closed to women, so that even for women who succeeded in educating themselves to the level of their male colleagues, the opportunities to support themselves were meager.

In a day when it was considered impermissible for a woman to speak in public, it was also considered inappropriate and unfeminine to draw attention to herself by publishing a work under her own name. Many—perhaps most—women scholars and writers—from Anne, Countess of Winchilsea, Lady Mary Wortley Montagu down to Fanny Burney and Jane Austen—published their works at first either anonymously or pseudonymously. Nor was Elizabeth Tanfield the only woman scholar who destroyed her own writings before they were published.

And what of Elena Cornaro's life after she won her doctorate in 1678? During the six years she lived after that event, she divided her time between scholarly pursuits and service to the poor, sick, and needy. Baroque Italy paid honor to its unique woman scholar. Certainly Elena Cornaro aroused no antagonisms, but rather filled with discretion the approved nunlike role designated for the woman in Catholic countries who chose not to marry. Scholars and statesmen from several countries made a point of visiting her in Padua, and she was invited to join fellow scholars in the Academy of Ricovrati in Padua. When she died of tuberculosis in 1684 at the age of thirty-eight—a disease that was in a measure responsible for her eminence, for she had been sent to Padua partly to escape the damp air of Venice—her funeral attracted a greater throng than her doctoral examination. A delegation of distinguished university faculty accompanied the procession through the streets of Padua, and on her coffin were heaped books in the languages she had mastered and the sciences she had studied. She was buried in the Chapel of St. Luke among the Benedictine monks, having carefully instructed her maid to sew her robe together at the hem so that even in death her modesty would be preserved.

Of her writings very little has survived. She had arranged to have her correspondence and many of her manuscripts destroyed before she died, and the remainder of her writings were disseminated as souvenirs among family and friends.

After Elena Cornaro's death a half century passed before a second woman, again Italian, Laura Maria Catherina Bassi, was awarded a doctorate at the University of Bologna. Not until 150 years later did American universities admit women for degrees, and two centuries passed before Oxford and Cambridge conferred degrees on women. Only in our own decade, in 1970, did the Catholic Church finally award the degree of Doctor of Theology that had been denied Elena Cornaro to two women: one to the sixteenth century Spanish saint, Teresa of Avila, the other to fourteenth century St. Catherine of Siena, who had in fact never learned to read and write. One hopes that in some academic elysium those two saintly ladies are proudly showing off their belated scholarly credentials.

REFLECTING ON MEANING

1. In the past, what obstacles to education have women faced? What four basics, according to McGuigan, did they need in order to overcome these obstacles? Why were these considerations so important? What were the odds that a woman would be able to meet these needs? Why didn't men encounter the same obstacles? Does McGuigan imply that all men had access to education? What limitations might some men have confronted? In what ways were these limitations compounded for women?

2. What social prejudices was a learned woman likely to encounter? Why would others have considered her deviant? Why did Lady Montagu counsel her daughter to conceal her own daughter's learning? For what reasons was education considered superfluous and even negative for women?

3. McGuigan suggests that women who did become educated had to take special care to fulfill "feminine" roles in other aspects of their lives. What specific behaviors did they adopt? In what ways did this make their scholarly pursuits more socially acceptable?

EXPLORING RHETORICAL STRATEGIES

1. McGuigan frames her survey of learned women with the story of Elena Cornaro. Why does she do this? In what ways does this story establish a foundation for the rest of the essay?

2. How does McGuigan's encapsulated history of learned women advance the main point she makes? How does it help answer the questions that she initiates the essay with?

3. The essay concludes with an ironic twist that brings her survey into the seventies. What is the irony of the Catholic church's honoring two women with the title Doctor of Theology? What point do you think McGuigan is making by ending on this note?

Sexual Politics: A Manifesto for Revolution

KATE MILLETT

Kate Millett, one of the most influential members of the early feminist movement, published this "Manifesto" in 1969 in her groundbreaking feminist book, Sexual Politics. *After listing three socialization practices that continually reinforce patriarchy, she explains the goals and positive results of a "Sexual Revolution."*

W hen one group rules another, the relationship between the two is political. When such an arrangement is carried out over a long period of time it develops an ideology (feudalism, racism, etc.). All historical civilizations are patriarchies: their ideology is male supremacy.

Oppressed groups are denied education, economic independence, the power of office, representation, an image of dignity and self-respect, equality of status, and recognition as human beings. Throughout history women have been consistently denied all of these, and their denial today, while attenuated and partial, is nevertheless consistent. The education allowed them is deliberately designed to be inferior, and they are systematically programmed out of and excluded from the knowledge where power lies today— e.g., in science and technology. They are confined to conditions of economic dependence based on the sale of their sexuality in marriage, or a variety of prostitutions. Work on a basis of economic independence allows them only a subsistence level of life—often not even that. They do not hold office, are represented in no positions of power, and authority is forbidden them. The image of woman fostered by cultural media, high and low, then and now, is a marginal and demeaning existence, and one outside the human condition—which is defined as the prerogative of man, the male.

Government is upheld by power, which is supported through consent (social opinion), or imposed by violence. Conditioning to an ideology amounts to the former. But there may be a resort to the latter at any moment when consent is withdrawn—rape, attack, sequestration, beatings, murder. Sexual politics obtains consent through the "socialization" of both sexes to patriarchal policies. They consist of the following:

1. the formation of human personality along stereotyped lines of sexual category, based on the needs and values of the master class and dictated by what he would cherish in himself and find convenient in an underclass: aggression, intellectuality, force and efficiency for the male; passivity, ignorance, docility, "virtue," and ineffectuality for the female.
2. the concept of sex role, which assigns domestic service and attendance upon infants to all females and the rest of human interest, achievement and ambition to the male; the charge of leader at all times and places to the male, and the duty of follower, with equal uniformity, to the female.
3. the imposition of male rule through institutions: patriarchal religion, the proprietary family, marriage, "The Home," masculine oriented culture, and a pervasive doctrine of male superiority.

A Sexual Revolution would bring about the following conditions, desirable upon rational, moral and humanistic grounds:

1. the end of sexual repression—freedom of expression and of sexual mores (sexual freedom has been partially attained, but it is now being subverted beyond freedom into exploitative license for patriarchal and reactionary ends).
2. Unisex, or the end of separatist character-structure, temperament and behavior, so that each individual may develop an entire—rather than a partial, limited, and conformist—personality.
3. re-examination of traits categorized into "masculine" and "feminine," with a total reassessment as to their human usefulness and advisability in both sexes. Thus if "masculine" violence is undesirable, it is so for both sexes, "feminine" dumb-cow passivity likewise. If "masculine" intelligence or efficiency is valuable, it is so for both sexes equally, and the same must be true for "feminine" tenderness or consideration.
4. the end of sex role and sex status, the patriarchy and the male supremacist ethic, attitude and ideology—in all areas of endeavor, experience, and behavior.
5. the end of the ancient oppression of the young under the patriarchal proprietary family, their chattel status, the attainment of the human rights presently denied them, the professionalization and therefore improvement of their care, and the guarantee that when they enter the world, they are desired, planned for, and provided with equal opportunities.

6. Bisex, or the end of enforced perverse heterosexuality, so that the sex act ceases to be arbitrarily polarized into male and female, to the exclusion of sexual expression between members of the same sex.
7. the end of sexuality in the forms in which it has existed historically—brutality, violence, capitalism, exploitation, and warfare—that it may cease to be hatred and become love.
8. the attainment of the female sex to freedom and full human status after millennia of deprivation and oppression, and of both sexes to a viable humanity.

REFLECTING ON MEANING

1. Millett begins by stating, "All historical civilizations are patriarchies; their ideology is male supremacy." She then discusses the treatment of oppressed groups, specifically women. What are oppressed groups denied? Why is the education of women "deliberately designed to be inferior"? How does this relate to women's economic dependence? What other privileges are women denied? How do media images also subjugate women? What other examples of the powerlessness of women does Millett discuss?

2. Millett writes, "Government is upheld by power." How is power supported? How is power imposed? What is the relationship between power and ideology? How is ideology a form of consent? When consent is withdrawn, what may occur? What are the patriarchal policies to which both sexes are socialized?

3. What is the purpose of Millett's "Sexual Revolution"? How would this revolution alter the following: relationships between males and females, gender role stereotyping, socialization and care of children, attitudes toward homosexuals, and cross-cultural relationships?

EXPLORING RHETORICAL STRATEGIES

1. Millett's rhetoric is very straightforward, orderly, and logical, with no extraneous or unnecessary adjectives. How does this style of rhetoric influence your acceptance of her position?

2. Describe the organization of her argument. How effective is her use of two lists in organizing her points of contention? Are there

any points in either list with which you disagree? Why or why not? Do you consider any of Millett's claims to be unreasonable?

3. This piece was originally published in 1969. How many of Millett's goals have yet to be accomplished? How might her original audience have responded to this "Manifesto"? What is your reaction to it?

Chapter 6 —————————

WOMEN AND EQUAL RIGHTS

From A Vindication of the Rights of Woman

MARY WOLLSTONECRAFT

In 1792 Mary Wollstonecraft published A Vindication of the Rights of Woman, *a treatise arguing that women and men must share true equality before either can be free. In the following excerpt she indicts the "false system of education" that perpetuates women's inequality, and she proposes a new system that will allow women to become independent, calling for nothing less than a "revolution in female manners."*

Introduction

I have turned over various books written on the subject of education, and patiently observed the conduct of parents . . . and the management of schools; but what has been the result?—a profound conviction that the neglected education of my fellow-creatures is the grand source of the misery I deplore; and that women, in particular, are rendered weak and wretched by a variety of concurring causes, originating from one hasty conclusion. The conduct and manners of women, in fact, evidently prove that their minds are not in a healthy state; for, like the flowers which are planted in too rich a soil, strength and usefulness are sacrificed to beauty; and the flaunting leaves, after having pleased a fastidious eye, fade, disregarded on the stalk, long before the season when they ought to have arrived at maturity. One cause of this barren blooming I attribute to a false system of education, gathered from the books written on this subject by men who, considering females rather as women than human creatures, have been more anxious to make them alluring mistresses than affectionate wives and rational mothers; and the understanding of the sex has been so bubbled by this specious homage, that the civilized women of the present century, with a few exceptions, are only anxious to inspire love, when they ought to cherish a nobler ambition, and by their abilities and virtues exact respect.

In a treatise, therefore, on female rights and manners, the works which have been particularly written for their improvement must not be overlooked; especially when it is asserted, in direct terms, that the minds of women are enfeebled by false refinement; that the books of instruction, written by men of genius, have had the same tendency as more frivolous productions; and that, in the true style of Mahometanism, they are treated as a kind of subordinate beings, and not as a part of the human species, when improveable reason is allowed to be the dignified distinction which raises men above the brute creation, and puts a natural sceptre in a feeble hand.

Yet, because I am a woman, I would not lead my readers to suppose that I mean violently to agitate the contested question respecting the quality or inferiority of the sex; but as the subject lies in my way, and I cannot pass it over without subjecting the main tendency of my reasoning to misconstruction, I shall stop a moment to deliver, in a few words, my opinion. In the government of the physical world it is observable that the female in point of strength is, in general, inferior to the male. This is the law of nature; and it does not appear to be suspended or abrogated in favour of woman. A degree of physical superiority cannot, therefore, be denied—and it is a noble prerogative! But not content with this natural pre-eminence, men endeavour to sink us still lower, merely to render us alluring objects for a moment; and women, intoxicated by the adoration which men, under the influence of their senses, pay them, do not seek to obtain a durable interest in their hearts, or to become the friends of the fellow creatures who find amusement in their society. . . .

My own sex, I hope, will excuse me, if I treat them like rational creatures, instead of flattering their *fascinating* graces, and viewing them as if they were in a state of perpetual childhood, unable to stand alone. I earnestly wish to point out in what true dignity and human happiness consists—I wish to persuade women to endeavour to acquire strength, both of mind and body, and to convince them that the soft phrases, susceptibility of heart, delicacy of sentiment, and refinement of taste, are almost synonymous with epithets of weakness, and that those beings who are only the objects of pity and that kind of love, which has been termed its sister, will soon become objects of contempt.

Dismissing, then, those pretty feminine phrases, which the men condescendingly use to soften our slavish dependence, and despising that weak elegancy of mind, exquisite sensibility, and sweet docility of manners, supposed to be the sexual characteristics of the weaker vessel, I wish to show that elegance is inferior to virtue, that the first object of laudable ambition is to obtain a character as a human being, regardless of the distinction of sex; and that secondary views should be brought to this simple touchstone. . . .

The education of women has, of late, been more attended to than formerly; yet they are still reckoned a frivolous sex, and ridiculed or pitied by the writers who endeavour by satire or instruction to improve them. It is acknowledged that they spend many of the first years of their lives in acquiring a smattering of accomplishments; meanwhile strength of body and mind are sacrificed to libertine notions of beauty, to the desire of establishing themselves,—the only way women can rise in the world,—by marriage. And this desire making mere animals of them, when they marry they act as such children may be expected to act:—they dress, they paint, and nickname God's creatures. Surely these weak beings are only fit for a seraglio!—Can they be expected to govern a family with judgment, or take care of the poor babes whom they bring into the world? . . .

Woman are, in fact, so much degraded by mistaken notions of female excellence, that I do not mean to add a paradox when I assert, that this artificial weakness produces a propensity to tyrannize, and gives birth to cunning, the natural opponent of strength, which leads them to play off those contemptible infantine airs that undermine esteem even whilst they excite desire. Let men become more chaste and modest, and if women do not grow wiser in the same ratio, it will be clear that they have weaker understandings. It seems scarcely necessary to say, that I now speak of the sex in general. Many individuals have more sense than their male relatives; and, as nothing preponderates where there is a constant struggle for an equilibrium, without it has naturally more gravity, some women govern their husbands without degrading themselves, because intellect will always govern.

The Prevailing Opinion of a Sexual Character Discussed

To account for, and excuse the tyranny of man, many ingenious arguments have been brought forward to prove, that the two sexes, in the acquirement of virtue, ought to aim at attaining a very different character: or, to speak explicitly, women are not allowed to have sufficient strength of mind to acquire what really deserves the name of virtue. Yet it should seem, allowing them to have souls, that there is but one way appointed by Providence to lead *mankind* to either virtue or happiness.

If then women are not a swarm of ephemeron triflers, why should they be kept in ignorance under the specious name of innocence? Men complain, and with reason, of the follies and caprices of our sex, when they do not keenly satirize our headstrong passions and grovelling vices. Behold, I should answer, the natural effect of ignorance! The mind will ever be unstable that has only prejudices to rest on, and the current will run with destructive fury when there are no barriers to break its force. Women are told from their infancy, and taught by the example of their mothers, that a little knowledge of human weakness, justly termed cunning, softness of temper, *outward* obedience, and a scrupulous attention to a puerile kind of propriety, will obtain for them the protection of man; and should they be beautiful, everything else is needless, for, at least, twenty years of their lives. . . .

By individual education, I mean, for the sense of the word is not precisely defined, such an attention to a child as will slowly sharpen the senses, form the temper, regulate the passions as they begin to ferment, and set the understanding to work before the body arrives at maturity; so that the man may only have to proceed, not to begin, the important task of learning to think and reason.

To prevent any misconstruction, I must add, that I do not believe that a private education can work the wonders which some sanguine writers have attributed to it. Men and women must be educated, in a great degree, by the opinions and manners of the society they live in. In every age there has been a stream of popular opinion that has carried all before it, and given a family character, as it were, to the century. It may then fairly be inferred, that, till society be differently constituted, much cannot be expected from education. It is, however, sufficient for my present purpose to assert, that, whatever effect circumstances have on the abilities, every being may become virtuous by the exercise of its own reason; for if but one being was created with vicious inclinations, that is positively bad, what can save us from atheism? or if we worship a God, is not that God a devil?

Consequently, the most perfect education, in my opinion, is such an exercise of the understanding as is best calculated to strengthen the body and form the heart. Or, in other words, to enable the individual to attain such habits of virtue as will render it independent. In fact, it is a farce to call any being virtuous whose virtues do not result from the exercise of its own reason. This was Rousseau's opinion respecting men: I extend it to women, and confidently assert that they have been drawn out of their sphere by false refinement, and not by an endeavour to acquire masculine qualities. Still the regal homage which they receive is so intoxicating, that till the manners of the times are changed, and formed on more reasonable principles, it may be impossible to convince them that the illegitimate power, which they obtain, by degrading themselves, is a curse, and that they must return to nature and equality, if they wish to secure the placid satisfaction that unsophisticated affections impart. . . .

Many are the causes that, in the present corrupt state of society, contribute to enslave women by cramping their understandings and sharpening their senses. One, perhaps, that silently does more mischief than all the rest, is their disregard of order.

To do everything in an orderly manner, is a most important precept, which women, who, generally speaking, receive only a disorderly kind of education, seldom attend to with that degree of exactness that men, who from their infancy are broken into method, observe. This negligent kind of guess-work, for what other epithet can be used to point out the random exertions of a sort of instinctive common sense, never brought to the test of reason? prevents their generalizing matters of fact—so they do to-day, what they did yesterday, merely because they did it yesterday.

This contempt of the understanding in early life has more baneful consequences than is commonly supposed; for the little knowledge which women of strong minds attain, is, from various circumstances, of a more desultory kind than the knowledge of men, and it is acquired more by sheer observations on real life, than from comparing what has been individually observed with the results of experience generalized by speculation. Led by their dependent situation and domestic employments more into society, what they learn is rather by snatches; and as learning is with them, in general, only a secondary thing, they do not pursue any one branch with that persevering ardour necessary to give vigour to the faculties, and clearness to the judgment. In the present state of society, a little learning is required to support the character of a gentleman; and boys are obliged to submit to a few years of discipline. But in the education of women, the cultivation of the understanding is always subordinate to the acquirement of some corporeal accomplishment; even while enervated by confinement and false notions of modesty, the body is prevented from attaining that grace and beauty which relaxed half-formed limbs never exhibit. Besides, in youth their faculties are not brought forward by emulation; and having no serious scientific study, if they have natural sagacity it is turned too soon on life and manners. They dwell on effects, and modifications, without tracing them back to causes;

and complicated rules to adjust behaviour are a weak substitute for simple principles.

As a proof that education gives this appearance of weakness to females, we may instance the example of military men, who are, like them, sent into the world before their minds have been stored with knowledge or fortified by principles. The consequences are similar; soldiers acquire a little superficial knowledge, snatched from the muddy current of conversation, and, from continually mixing with society, they gain, what is termed a knowledge of the world; and this acquaintance with manners and customs has frequently been confounded with a knowledge of the human heart. But can the crude fruit of casual observation, never brought to the test of judgment, formed by comparing speculation and experience, deserve such a distinction? Soldiers, as well as women, practise the minor virtues with punctilious politeness. Where is then the sexual difference, when the education has been the same? All the difference that I can discern, arises from the superior advantage of liberty, which enables the former to see more of life. . . .

Standing armies can never consist of resolute, robust men; they may be well disciplined machines, but they will seldom contain men under the influence of strong passions, or with very vigorous faculties. And as for any depth of understanding, I will venture to affirm, that it is as rarely to be found in the army as amongst women; and the cause, I maintain, is the same. It may be further observed, that officers are also particularly attentive to their persons, fond of dancing, crowded rooms, adventures, and ridicule. Like the *fair* sex, the business of their lives is gallantry. They were taught to please, and they only live to please. Yet they do not lose their rank in the distinction of sexes, for they are still reckoned superior to women, though in what their superiority consists, beyond what I have mentioned, it is difficult to discover.

The great misfortune is this, that they both acquire manners before morals, and a knowledge of life before they have, from reflection, any acquaintance with the grand ideal outline of human nature. The consequence is natural; satisfied with common nature, they become a prey to prejudices, and taking all their opinions on credit, they blindly submit to authority. So that, if they have any sense, it is a kind of instinctive glance, that catches proportions, and decides with respect to manners; but fails when arguments are to be pursued below the surface, or opinions analyzed.

May not the same remark be applied to women? Nay, the argument may be carried still further, for they are both thrown out of a useful station by the unnatural distinctions established in civilized life. Riches and hereditary honours have made cyphers of women to give consequence to the numerical figure; and idleness has produced a mixture of gallantry and despotism into society, which leads the very men who are the slaves of their mistresses to tyrannize over their sisters, wives, and daughters. This is only keeping them in rank and file, it is true. Strengthen the female mind by enlarging it, and there will be an end to blind obedience; but, as blind obedience is ever sought for by power, tyrants and sensualists are in the right when they endeavour to keep women in the dark, because the former only want slaves, and the latter a plaything. The sensualist, indeed, has been the most dangerous of tyrants, and women have been duped by their lovers as princes by their ministers, whilst dreaming that they reigned over them. . . .

Women are, therefore, to be considered either as moral beings, or so weak that they must be entirely subjected to the superior faculties of men.

Let us examine this question. Rousseau declares that a woman should never, for a moment, feel herself independent, that she should be governed by fear to exercise her natural cunning, and made a coquetish slave in order to render her a more alluring object of desire, a *sweeter* companion to man, whenever he chooses to relax himself. He carries the arguments, which he pretends to draw from the indications of nature, still further, and insinuates that truth and fortitude, the corner stones of all human virtue, should be cultivated with certain restrictions, because, with respect to the female character, obedience is the grand lesson which ought to be impressed with unrelenting rigour.

What nonsense! When will a great man arise with sufficient strength of mind to puff away the fumes which pride and sensuality have thus spread over the subject! If women are by nature inferior to men, their virtues must be the same in quality, if not in degree, or virtue is a relative idea; consequently, their conduct should be founded on the same principles, and have the same aim. . . .

Youth is the season for love in both sexes; but in those days of thoughtless enjoyment provision should be made for the more important years of life, when reflection takes place of sensation. But Rousseau, and most of the male writers who have followed his steps, have warmly inculcated that the whole tendency of female education ought to be directed to one point:—to render them pleasing.

Let me reason with the supporters of this opinion who have any knowledge of human nature, do they imagine that marriage can eradicate the habitude of life? The woman who has only been taught to please will soon find that her charms are oblique sunbeams, and that they cannot have much effect on her husband's heart when they are seen every day, when the summer is passed and gone. Will she then have sufficient native energy to look into herself for comfort, and cultivate her dormant faculties? or, is it not more rational to expect that she will try to please other men; and, in the emotions raised by the expectation of new conquests, endeavour to forget the mortification her love or pride has received? When the husband ceases to be a lover—and the time will inevitably come, her desire of pleasing will then grow languid, or become a spring of bitterness; and love, perhaps, the most evanescent of all passions, gives place to jealousy or vanity.

I now speak of women who are restrained by principle or prejudice; such women, though they would shrink from an intrigue with real abhorrence, yet, nevertheless, wish to be convinced by the homage of gallantry that they are cruelly neglected by their husbands; or, days and weeks are spent in dreaming of the happiness enjoyed by congenial souls till their health is undermined and their spirits broken by discontent. How then can the great art of pleasing be such a necessary study? it is only useful to a mistress; the chaste wife, and serious mother, should only consider her power to please as the polish of her virtues, and the affection of her husband as one of the comforts that render her task less difficult and her life happier.—But, whether she be loved or neglected, her first wish should be to make herself respectable, and not to rely for all her happiness on a being subject to like infirmities with herself. . . .

Women ought to endeavour to purify their heart; but can they do so when their uncultivated understandings make them entirely dependent on their senses for employment and amusement, when no noble pursuit sets them above the little vanities of the day, or enables them to curb the wild emotions that agitate a reed over which every passing breeze has power? To gain the affections of a virtuous man, is affectation necessary? Nature has given woman a weaker frame than man; but, to ensure her husband's affections, must a wife, who by the exercise of her mind and body whilst she was discharging the duties of a daughter, wife, and mother, has allowed her constitution to retain its natural strength, and her nerves a healthy tone, is she, I say, to condescend to use art and feign a sickly delicacy in order to secure her husband's affection? Weakness may excite tenderness, and gratify the arrogant pride of man; but the lordly caresses of a protector will not gratify a noble mind that pants for, and deserves to be respected. Fondness is a poor substitute for friendship!

In a seraglio, I grant, that all these arts are necessary; the epicure must have his palate tickled, or he will sink into apathy; but have women so little ambition as to be satisfied with such a condition? Can they supinely dream life away in the lap of pleasure, or the languor of weariness, rather than assert their claim to pursue reasonable pleasures and render themselves conspicuous by practising the virtues which dignify mankind? Surely she has not an immortal soul who can loiter life away merely employed to adorn her person, that she may amuse the languid hours, and soften the cares of a fellow-creature who is willing to be enlivened by her smiles and tricks, when the serious business of life is over.

Besides, the woman who strengthens her body and exercises her mind will, by managing her family and practising various virtues, become the friend, and not the humble dependent of her husband; and if she, by possessing such substantial qualities, merit his regard, she will not find it necessary to conceal her affection, nor to pretend to an unnatural coldness of constitution to excite her husband's passions. In fact, if we revert to history, we shall find that the women who have distinguished themselves have neither been the most beautiful nor the most gentle of their sex. . . .

The Same Subject Continued

. . . Women are every where in this deplorable state; for, in order to preserve their innocence, as ignorance is courteously termed, truth is hidden from them, and they are made to assume an artificial character before their faculties have acquired any strength. Taught from their infancy that beauty is woman's sceptre, the mind shapes itself to the body, and, roaming round its gilt cage, only seeks to adorn its prison. Men have various employments and pursuits which engage their attention, and give a character to the opening mind; but women, confined to one, and having their thoughts constantly directed to the most insignificant part of themselves, seldom extend their views beyond the triumph of the hour. But were their understanding once emancipated from the slavery to which the pride and sensuality of man and their short-sighted desire, like that of dominion in tyrants, of present sway, has subjected them, we should probably read of their weaknesses with surprise. . . .

Let not men then in the pride of power, use the same arguments that tyrannic kings and venal ministers have used, and fallaciously assert that woman ought to be subjected because she has always been so. But, when man, governed by reasonable laws, enjoys his natural freedom, let him despise woman, if she do not share it with him; and, till that glorious period arrives, in descanting on the folly of the sex, let him not overlook his own.

Women, it is true, obtaining power by unjust means, by practising or fostering vice, evidently lose the rank which reason would assign them, and they become either abject slaves or capricious tyrants. They lose all simplicity, all dignity of mind, in acquiring power, and act as men are observed to act when they have been exalted by the same means.

It is time to effect a revolution in female manners—time to restore to them their lost dignity—and make them, as a part of the human species, labour by reforming themselves to reform the world. It is time to separate unchangeable morals from local manners. If men be demi-gods—why let us serve them! And if the dignity of the female soul be as disputable as that of animals—if their reason does not afford sufficient light to direct their conduct whilst unerring instinct is denied—they are surely of all creatures the most miserable! and, bent beneath the iron hand of destiny, must submit to be a *fair defect* in Creation. But to justify the ways of Providence respecting them, by pointing out some irrefragable reason for thus making such a large portion of mankind accountable and not accountable, would puzzle the subtilest casuist. . . .

Why do men halt between two opinions, and expect impossibilities? Why do they expect virtue from a slave, from a being whom the constitution of civil society has rendered weak, if not vicious?

Still I know that it will require a considerable length of time to eradicate the firmly rooted prejudices which sensualists have planted; it will also require some time to convince women that they act contrary to their real interest on an enlarged scale, when they cherish or affect weakness under the name of delicacy, and to convince the world that the poisoned source of female vices and follies, if it be necessary, in compliance with custom, to use synonymous terms in a lax sense, has been the sensual homage paid to beauty. . . .

Besides, if women be educated for dependence; that is, to act according to the will of another fallible being, and submit, right or wrong, to power, where are we to stop? Are they to be considered as viceregents allowed to reign over a small domain, and answerable for their conduct to a higher tribunal, liable to error?

It will not be difficult to prove that such delegates will act like men subjected by fear, and make their children and servants endure their tyrannical oppression. As they submit without reason, they will, having no fixed rules to square their conduct by, be kind, or cruel, just as the whim of the moment directs; and we ought not to wonder if sometimes, galled by their heavy yoke, they take a malignant pleasure in resting it on weaker shoulders. . . .

With respect to religion, she never presumed to judge for herself; but conformed, as a dependent creature should, to the ceremonies of the church which she was brought up in, piously believing that wiser heads than her own have settled that business—and not to doubt is her point of perfection. She therefore pays her tythe of mint and cummin—and thanks her God that she is not as other women are. These are the blessed effects of a good education! These the virtues of man's help-mate! . . .

I wish to sum up what I have said in a few words, for I here throw down my gauntlet, and deny the existence of sexual virtues, not excepting modesty. For man and woman, truth, if I understand the meaning of the word, must be the same; yet to the fanciful female character, so prettily drawn by poets and novelists, demanding the sacrifice of truth and sincerity, virtue becomes a relative idea, having no other foundation than utility, and of that utility men pretend arbitrarily to judge, shaping it to their own convenience.

Women, I allow, may have different duties to fulfil; but they are *human* duties, and the principles that should regulate the discharge of them, I sturdily maintain, must be the same.

To become respectable, the exercise of their understanding is necessary, there is no other foundation for independence of character; I mean explicitly to say that they must only bow to the authority of reason, instead of being the *modest* slaves of opinion.

In the superior ranks of life how seldom do we meet with a man of superior abilities, or even common acquirements? The reason appears to me clear, the state they are born in was an unnatural one. The human character has ever been formed by the employments the individual, or class, pursues; and if the faculties are not sharpened by necessity, they must remain obtuse. The argument may fairly be extended to women; for, seldom occupied by serious business, the pursuit of pleasure gives that insignificancy to their character which renders the society of the *great* so insipid. The same want of firmness, produced by a similar cause, forces them both to fly from themselves to noisy pleasures, and artificial passions, till vanity takes place of every social affection, and the characteristics of humanity can scarcely be discerned. Such are the blessings of civil governments, as they are at present organized, that wealth and female softness equally tend to debase mankind, and are produced by the same cause; but allowing women to be rational creatures, they should be incited to acquire virtues which they may call their own, for how can a rational being be ennobled by anything that is not obtained by its *own* exertions? . . .

Of the Pernicious Effects Which Arise from the Unnatural Distinctions Established in Society

. . . though I consider that women in the common walks of life are called to fulfil the duties of wives and mothers, by religion and reason, I cannot help lamenting that women of a superior cast have not a road open by which they can pursue more extensive plans of usefulness and independence. I may excite laughter, by dropping a hint, which I mean to pursue, some future time, for I really think that women ought to have representatives, instead of being arbitrarily governed without having any direct share allowed them in the deliberations of government.

But, as the whole system of representation is now, in this country, only a convenient handle for despotism, they need not complain, for they are as well represented as a numerous class of hard working mechanics, who pay for the support of royalty when they can scarcely stop their children's mouths with bread. How are they represented whose very sweat supports the splendid stud of an heir apparent, or varnishes the chariot of some female favourite who looks down on shame? Taxes on the very necessaries of life, enable an endless tribe of idle princes and princesses to pass with stupid pomp before a gaping crowd, who almost worship the very parade which costs them so dear. This is mere gothic grandeur, something like the barbarous useless parade of having sentinels on horseback at Whitehall, which I could never view without a mixture of contempt and indignation. . . .

But what have women to do in society? I may be asked, but to loiter with easy grace; surely you would not condemn them all to suckle fools and chronicle small beer! No. Women might certainly study the art of healing, and be physicians as well as nurses. And midwifery, decency seems to allot to them, though I am afraid the word midwife, in our dictionaries, will soon give place to *accoucheur,* and one proof of the former delicacy of the sex be effaced from the language.

They might, also, study politics, and settle their benevolence on the broadest basis; for the reading of history will scarcely be more useful than the perusal of romances, if read as mere biography; if the character of the times, the political improvements, arts, &c. be not observed. In short, if it be not considered as the history of man; and not of particular men, who filled a niche in the temple of fame, and dropped into the black rolling stream of time, that silently sweeps all before it, into the shapeless void called—eternity. For shape, can it be called, "that shape hath none"?

Business of various kinds, they might likewise pursue, if they were educated in a more orderly manner, which might save many from common and legal prostitution. Women would not then marry for a support, as men accept of places under government, and neglect the implied duties; nor would an attempt to earn their own subsistence, a most laudable one! sink them almost to the level of those poor abandoned creatures who live by prostitution. For are not milliners and mantua-makers reckoned the next class? The few employments open to women, so far from being liberal, are menial; and when a superior education enables them to take charge of the education of children as governesses, they are not treated like the tutors of sons, though even clerical tutors are not always treated in a manner calculated to render them respectable in the eyes of their pupils, to say nothing of the private comfort of the individual. But as women educated like gentlewomen, are never designed for the humiliating situation which necessity sometimes forces them to fill, these situations are considered in the light of a degradation; and they know little of the human heart, who need to be told, that nothing so painfully sharpens sensibility as such a fall in life.

Some of these women might be restrained from marrying by a proper spirit or delicacy, and others may not have had it in their power to escape in this pitiful way from servitude; is not that government then very defective, and very unmindful of the happiness of one half of its members, that does not provide for honest, independent women, by encouraging them to fill respectable stations? But in order to render their private virtue a public benefit, they must have a civil existence in the state, married or single; else we shall continually see some worthy woman, whose sensibility has been rendered painfully acute by undeserved contempt, droop like "the lily broken down by a plow-share."

It is a melancholy truth; yet such is the blessed effect of civilization! the most respectable women are the most oppressed; and, unless they have understandings far superiour to the common run of understandings, taking in both sexes, they must, from being treated like contemptible beings, become contemptible. How many women thus waste life away the prey of discontent, who might have practised as physicians, regulated a farm, managed a shop, and stood erect, supported by their own industry, instead of hanging their heads surcharged with the dew of sensibility, that consumes the beauty to which it at first gave lustre; nay, I doubt whether pity and love are so near akin as poets feign, for I have seldom seen much comparison excited by the helplessness of females, unless they were fair; then, perhaps, pity was the soft handmaid of love, or the harbinger of lust. . . .

. . . I then would fain convince reasonable men of the importance of some of my remarks, and prevail on them to weigh dispassionately the whole tenor of my observations.—I appeal to their understandings; and, as a fellow-creature, claim, in the name of my sex, some interest in their hearts. I entreat them to assist to emancipate their companion, to make her a *help meet* for them!

Would men but generously snap our chains, and be content with rational fellowship instead of slavish obedience, they would find us more observant daughters, more affectionate sisters, more faithful wives, more reasonable mothers—in a word, better citizens. We should then love them with true affection, because we should learn to respect ourselves; and the peace of mind of a worthy man would not be interrupted by the idle vanity of his wife, nor the babes sent to nestle in a strange bosom, having never found a home in their mother's. . . .

On National Education

. . . True taste is ever the work of the understanding employed in observing natural effects; and till women have more understanding, it is vain to expect them to possess domestic taste. Their lively senses will ever be at work to harden their hearts, and the emotions struck out of them will continue to be vivid and transitory, unless a proper education store their mind with knowledge.

It is the want of domestic taste, and not the acquirement of knowledge, that takes women out of their families, and tears the smiling babe from the breast that ought to afford it nourishment. Women have been allowed to remain in ignorance, and slavish dependence, many, very many years, and still we hear of nothing but their fondness of pleasure and sway, their preference of rakes and soldiers, their childish attachment to toys, and the vanity that makes them value accomplishments more than virtues. . . .

Let an enlightened nation then try what effect reason would have to bring them back to nature, and their duty; and allowing them to share the advantages of education and government with man, see whether they will become better, as they grow wiser and become free. They cannot be injured by the experiment; for it is not in the power of man to render them more insignificant than they are at present.

To render this practicable, day schools, for particular ages, should be established by government, in which boys and girls might be educated together. The school for the younger children, from five to nine years of age, ought to be absolutely free and open to all classes. A sufficient number of masters should also be chosen by a select committee, in each parish, to whom any complaint of negligence, &c. might be made, if signed by six of the children's parents. . . .

. . . to prevent any of the distinctions of vanity, they should be dressed alike, and all obliged to submit to the same discipline, or leave the school. The school-room ought to be surrounded by a large piece of ground, in which the children might be usefully exercised, for at this age they should not be confined to any sedentary employment for more than an hour at a time. But these relaxations might all be rendered a part of elementary education, for many things improve and amuse the senses, when introduced as a kind of show, to the principles of which, dryly laid down, children would turn a deaf ear. For instance, botany, mechanics, and astronomy. Reading, writing, arithmetic, natural history, and some simple experiments in natural philosophy, might fill up the day; but these pursuits should never encroach on gymnastic plays in the open air. The elements of religion, history, the history of man, and politics, might also be taught by conversations, in the socratic form.

After the age of nine, girls and boys, intended for domestic employments, or mechanical trades, ought to be removed to other schools, and receive instruction, in some measure appropriated to the destination of each individual, the two sexes being still together in the morning; but in the afternoon, the girls should attend a school where plain-work, mantua-making, millinery, &c. would be their employment.

The young people of superior abilities, or fortune, might now be taught, in another school, the dead and living languages, the elements of science, and continue the study of history and politics, on a more extensive scale, which would not exclude polite literature.

Girls and boys still together? I hear some readers ask: yes. And I should not fear any other consequence than that some early attachment might take place; which, whilst it had the best effect on the moral character of the young people, might not perfectly agree with the views of the parents, for it will be a long time, I fear, before the world will be so far enlightened that parents, only anxious to render their children virtuous, shall allow them to choose companions for life themselves. . . .

In this plan of education the constitution of boys would not be ruined by the early debaucheries, which now make men so selfish, or girls rendered weak and vain, by indolence, and frivolous pursuits. But, I presuppose, that such a degree of equality should be established between the sexes as would shut out gallantry and coquetry, yet allow friendship and love to temper the heart for the discharge of higher duties.

These would be schools of morality—and the happiness of man, allowed to flow from the pure springs of duty and affection, what advances might not the human mind make? Society can only be happy and free in proportion as it is virtuous; but the present distinctions, established in society, corrode all private, and blast all public virtue.

I have already inveighed against the custom of confining girls to their needle, and shutting them out from all political and civil employments; for by thus narrowing their minds they are rendered unfit to fulfil the peculiar duties which nature has assigned them.

Only employed about the little incidents of the day, they necessarily grow up cunning. My very soul has often sickened at observing the sly tricks practised by women to gain some foolish thing on which their silly hearts were set. Not allowed to dispose of money, or call any thing their own, they learn to turn the market penny; or, should a husband offend, by staying from home, or give rise to some emotions of jealousy—a new gown, or any pretty bawble, smooths Juno's angry brow.

But these *littlenesses* would not degrade their character, if women were led to respect themselves, if political and moral subjects were opened to them; and I will venture to affirm that this is the only way to make them properly attentive to their domestic duties.—An active mind embraces the whole circle of its duties, and finds time enough for all. It is not, I assert, a bold attempt to emulate masculine virtues; it is not the enchantment of literary pursuits, or the steady investigation of scientific subjects, that leads women astray from duty. No, it is indolence and vanity—the love of pleasure and the love of sway, that will reign paramount in an empty mind. I say empty emphatically, because the education which women now receive scarcely deserves the name. For the little knowledge that they are led to acquire, during the important years of youth, is merely relative to accomplishments; and accomplishments without a bottom, for unless the understanding be cultivated, superficial and monotonous is every grace. Like the charms of a made up face, they only strike the senses in a crowd; but at home, wanting mind, they want variety. The consequence is obvious; in gay scenes of dissipation we meet the artificial mind and face, for those who fly from solitude dread, next to solitude, the domestic circle; not having it in their power to amuse or interest, they feel their own insignificance, or find nothing to amuse or interest themselves.

Besides, what can be more indelicate than a girl's *coming out* in the fashionable world? Which, in other words, is to bring to market a marriageable miss, whose person is taken from one public place to another, richly caparisoned. Yet, mixing in the giddy circle under restraint, these butterflies long to flutter at large, for the first affection of their souls is their own persons, to which their attention has been called with the most sedulous care whilst they were preparing for the period that decides their fate for life. Instead of pursuing this idle routine, sighing for tasteless shew, and heartless state, with what dignity would the youths of both sexes form attachments in the schools that I have cursorily pointed out; in which, as life advanced, dancing, music, and drawing, might be admitted as relaxations, for at these schools young people of fortune ought to remain, more or less, till they were of age. Those, who were designed for particular professions, might attend, three or four mornings in the week, the schools appropriated for their immediate instruction. . . .

I know that libertines will also exclaim, that woman would be unsexed by acquiring strength of body and mind, and that beauty, soft bewitching beauty! would no longer adorn the daughters of men. I am of a very different opinion, for I think that, on the contrary, we should then see dignified beauty, and true grace; to produce which, many powerful physical and moral causes would concur.—Not relaxed beauty, it is true, or the graces of helplessness; but such as appears to make us respect the human body as a majestic pile fit to receive a noble inhabitant, in the relics of antiquity. . . .

Besides, understanding is necessary to give variety and interest to sensual enjoyments, for low, indeed, in the intellectual scale, is the mind that can continue to love when neither virtue nor sense give a human appearance to an animal appetite. But sense will always preponderate; and if women be not, in general, brought more on a level with men, some superiour women, like the Greek courtezans, will assemble the men of abilities around them, and draw from their families many citizens, who would have stayed at home had their wives had more sense, or the graces which result from the exercise of understanding and fancy, the legitimate parents of taste. A woman of talents, if she be not absolutely ugly, will always obtain great power, raised by the weakness of her sex; and in proportion as men acquire virtue and delicacy, by the exertion of reason, they will look for both in women, but they can only acquire them in the same way that men do. . . .

I speak of the improvement and emancipation of the whole sex, for I know that the behaviour of a few women, who, by accident, or following a strong bent of nature, have acquired a portion of knowledge superiour to that of the rest of their sex, has often been overbearing; but there have been instances of women who, attaining knowledge, have not discarded modesty, nor have they always pedantically appeared to despise the ignorance which they laboured to disperse in their own minds. The exclamations then which any advice respecting female learning, commonly produces, especially from pretty women, often arise from envy. When they chance to see that even the lustre of their eyes, and the flippant

sportiveness of refined coquetry will not always secure them attention, during a whole evening, should a woman of a more cultivated
understanding endeavour to give a rational turn to the conversation, the common source of consolation is, that such women seldom get husbands. What arts have I not seen silly women use to
interrupt by *flirtation,* a very significant word to describe such a
manoeuvre, a rational conversation which made the men forget
that they were pretty women.

But, allowing what is very natural to man, that the possession
of rare abilities is really calculated to excite overweening pride—
disgusting in both men and women—in what a state of inferiority
must the female faculties have rusted when such a small portion of
knowledge as those women attained, who have sneeringly been
termed learned women, could be singular?—Sufficiently so to puff
up the possessor, and excite envy in her contemporaries, and some
of the other sex. Nay, has not a little rationality exposed many
women to the severest censure? I advert to well known facts, for I
have frequently heard women ridiculed, and every little weakness
exposed, only because they adopted the advice of some medical
men, and deviated from the beaten track in their mode of treating
their infants. I have actually heard this barbarous aversion to innovation carried still further, and a sensible woman stigmatized as an
unnatural mother, who has thus been wisely solicitous to preserve
the health of her children, when in the midst of her care she has
lost one by some of the casualties of infancy, which no prudence
can ward off. Her acquaintance have observed, that this was the
consequence of newfangled notions—the newfangled notions of
ease and cleanliness. And those who pretending to experience,
though they have long adhered to prejudices that have, according
to the opinion of the most sagacious physicians, thinned the human
race, almost rejoiced at the disaster that gave a kind of sanction to
prescription.

Indeed, if it were only on this account, the national education
of women is of the utmost consequence, for what a number of human sacrifices are made to that moloch prejudice! and in how
many ways are children destroyed by the lasciviousness of man?
The want of natural affection, in many women, who are drawn
from their duty by the admiration of men, and the ignorance of
others, render the infancy of man a much more perilous state than
that of brutes; yet men are unwilling to place women in situations
proper to enable them to acquire sufficient understanding to know
how even to nurse their babes.

So forcibly does this truth strike me, that I would rest the
whole tendency of my reasoning upon it, for whatever tends to in-

capacitate the maternal character, takes woman out of her sphere....

In public schools women, to guard against the errors of ignorance, should be taught the elements of anatomy and medicine, not only to enable them to take proper care of their own health, but to make them rational nurses of their infants, parents, and husbands; for the bills of mortality are swelled by the blunders of self-willed old women, who give nostrums of their own without knowing any thing of the human frame. It is likewise proper only in a domestic view, to make women acquainted with the anatomy of the mind, by allowing the sexes to associate together in every pursuit; and by leading them to observe the progress of the human understanding in the improvement of the sciences and arts; never forgetting the science of morality, or the study of the political history of mankind....

...The conclusion which I wish to draw, is obvious; make women rational creatures, and free citizens, and they will quickly become good wives, and mothers; that is—if men do not neglect the duties of husbands and fathers.

Discussing the advantages which a public and private education combined, as I have sketched, might rationally be expected to produce, I have dwelt most on such as are particularly relative to the female world, because I think the female world oppressed; yet the gangrene, which the vices engendered by oppression have produced, is not confined to the morbid part, but pervades society at large: so that when I wish to see my sex become more like moral agents, my heart bounds with the anticipation of the general diffusion of that sublime contentment which only morality can diffuse....

REFLECTING ON MEANING

1. What is the "false system of education" that Wollstonecraft describes? What kind of training does it offer to women? What does it lead women to value and to desire? In what ways does it result in either slavishness or tyranny? According to Wollstonecraft, what would be the "most perfect education"? How would it differ from the system she indicts?

2. A large section of Wollstonecraft's treatise is a reasoned response to Rousseau's views on women. From Wollstonecraft's rebuttal, what can you deduce about Rousseau's views? According to

Rousseau, what larger purpose do women serve in society? What does he think the goal of their education should be?

3. Wollstonecraft argues that true equality will make women better wives and mothers. Why does she repeatedly make this point? Do you think she is reinforcing sexist views on the role of women? Why or why not?

EXPLORING RHETORICAL STRATEGIES

1. Wollstonecraft states that her purpose is "to persuade women." To what extent do you agree that she addresses her argument to women exclusively? What evidence suggests that she also addresses men?

2. A crux of Wollstonecraft's argument is the comparison between women and "military men." What is the purpose of this extended analogy? What point does it allow Wollstonecraft to make about differences between women and men? How effective is this device?

3. Wollstonecraft speaks to us across a time span of nearly two centuries. Do you find her argument still relevant? Why or why not? How do you think modern readers would react to her essay if they assumed that its author was contemporary?

The Rights of Women

FREDERICK DOUGLASS

After attending a "Woman's Rights Convention" at Sen-
eca Falls, New York, Frederick Douglass—a former slave—wrote
and published this article in the July 28, 1848, edition of his
abolitionist newspaper, the North Star. *In it he argues for the*
equal treatment of women.

One of the most interesting events of the past week was the holding of what is technically styled a Woman's Rights Convention at Seneca Falls. The speaking, addresses, and resolutions of this extraordinary meeting was almost wholly conducted by women; and although they evidently felt themselves in a novel position, it is but simple justice to say that their whole proceedings were characterized by marked ability and dignity. No one present, we think, however much he might be disposed to differ from the views advanced by the leading speakers on that occasion, will fail to give them credit for brilliant talents and excellent dispositions. In this meeting, as in other deliberative assemblies, there were frequent differences of opinion and animated discussion; but in no case was there the slightest absence of good feeling and decorum. Several interesting documents setting forth the rights as well as the grievances of women were read. Among these was a Declaration of Sentiments to be regarded as the basis of a grand movement for attaining the civil, social, political, and religious rights of women. We should not do justice to our own convictions, or to the excellent persons connected with this infant movement, if we did not in this connection offer a few remarks on the general subject which the Convention met to consider and the objects they seek to attain. In doing so, we are not insensible that the bare mention of this truly important subject in any other than terms of contemptuous ridicule and scornful disfavor, is likely to excite against us the fury of bigotry and the folly of prejudice. A discussion of the rights of animals would be regarded with far more complacency by many of what are called the *wise* and the *good* of our land, than would a discussion of the rights of women. It is, in their estimation, to be guilty of evil thoughts, to think that woman is entitled to equal rights with man. Many who have at last made the discovery that the Negroes have some rights as well as other members of the human family, have yet to be convinced that women are entitled to any. Eight years ago a number of persons of this description actually abandoned the anti-slavery cause, lest by giving their influence in that direction they might possibly be giving countenance to the dangerous heresy that woman, in respect to rights, stands on equal footing with man. In the judgment of such persons the American slave system, with all its concomitant horrors, is less to be deplored that this *wicked* idea. It is perhaps needless to say, that we cherish little sympathy for such sentiments or respect for such prejudices. Standing as we do upon the watch-tower of human freedom, we cannot be deterred from an expression of our approbation of any movement, however humble, to improve and elevate the character of any members of the human family. While it is impossible for us to go into this subject at length, and dispose of the various objections which are often urged against such a doctrine as that of female equality, we are free to say that in respect to political rights, we hold women to be justly entitled to all we claim for men. We go farther, and express our conviction that all political rights which it is expedient for man to exercise, it is equally so for woman. All that distinguishes man as an intelligent and accountable being is equally true of woman, and if that government only is just which governs by the free consent of the governed, there can be no reason in the world for denying to woman the exercise of the elective franchise, or a hand in making and administering the laws of the land. Our doctrine is that "right is of no sex." We therefore bid the women engaged in this movement our humble Godspeed.

REFLECTING ON MEANING

1. Douglass begins his article by complimenting the proceedings of the Woman's Rights Convention at Seneca Falls, which he had attended the preceding week. He praises the convention participants for what attributes? What is the "Declaration of Sentiments"? What is its purpose?

2. This article was published in Douglass's abolitionist newspaper, the *North Star*. Which specific statements are directed against those abolitionists who wish to gain freedom for the slaves, but shy away from expressing sympathy to the women's rights movement? What does Douglass say happened eight years be-

fore? What is his opinion of the circumstances? How does Douglass use this occurrence to shape his argument?

3. Douglass writes, "Standing as we do upon the watch-tower of human freedom, we cannot be deterred from an expression of our approbation of any movement, however humble, to improve and elevate the character of any members of the human family." Do you think that Douglass is attempting to align the members of the antislavery movement with members of the women's movement? Why or why not? How convincing is his argument?

EXPLORING RHETORICAL STRATEGIES

1. Douglass, a slave until he was twenty-one years old, learned to read and write as a child under the instruction of his Northern mistress. At approximately age thirty, he wrote this piece, which uses the elevated and mature language of a highly educated person. What rhetorical effect might this sophisticated language have on his audience? How might an 1848 audience respond to such an articulate former slave?

2. Douglass argues that a "discussion of the rights of animals would be regarded with far more complacency by many of what are called the *wise* and the *good* of our land, than would a discussion of the rights of women." Who are the *wise* and *good* to whom Douglass refers? How does Douglass's use of irony underscore his argument?

3. How convincing is Douglass's call for equal rights for women? How might the responses of an audience comprised of white males be different from an audience composed of black males? How might an uneducated audience react to Douglass's discourse?

From The Subjection
of Women

JOHN STUART MILL

A nineteenth-century British philosopher and parliamentarian, John Stuart Mill was a powerful speaker for women's rights. In the following selection, an excerpt from The Subjection of Women *(1869), Mill argues that "the legal subordination of one sex to the other...is wrong in itself" and should be "replaced by a principle of perfect equality."*

1

The object of this Essay is to explain as clearly as I am able, the grounds of an opinion which I have held from the very earliest period when I had formed any opinions at all on social or political matters, and which, instead of being weakened or modified, has been constantly growing stronger by the progress of reflection and the experience of life: That the principle which regulates the existing social relations between the two sexes—the legal subordination of one sex to the other—is wrong in itself, and now one of the chief hindrances to human improvement; and that it ought to be replaced by a principle of perfect equality, admitting no power or privilege on the one side, nor disability on the other....

The generality of a practice is in some cases a strong presumption that it is, or at all events once was, conducive to laudable ends. This is the case, when the practice was first adopted, or afterwards kept up, as a means to such ends, and was grounded on experience of the mode in which they could be most effectually attained. If the authority of men over women, when first established, had been the result of a conscientious comparison between different modes of constituting the government of society; if, after trying various other modes of social organization—the government of women over men, equality between the two, and such mixed and divided modes of government as might be invented—it had been decided, on the testimony of experience, that the mode in which women are wholly under the rule of men, having no share at all in public concerns, and each in private being under the legal obligation of obedience to the man with whom she has associated her destiny, was the arrangement most conducive to the happiness and well being of both; its general adoption might then be fairly thought to be some evidence that, at the time when it was adopted, it was the best: though even then the considerations which recommended it may, like so many other primeval social facts of the greatest importance, have subsequently, in the course of ages, ceased to exist. But the state of the case is in every respect the reverse of this. In the first place, the opinion in favour of the present system, which entirely subordinates the weaker sex to the stronger, rests upon theory only; for there never has been trial made of any other: so that experience, in the sense in which it is vulgarly opposed to theory, cannot be pretended to have pronounced any verdict. And in the second place, the adoption of this system of inequality never was the result of deliberation, or forethought, or any social ideas, or any notion whatever of what conduced to the benefit of humanity or the good order of society. It arose simply from the fact that from the very earliest twilight of human society, every woman (owing to the value attached to her by men, combined with her inferiority in muscular strength) was found in a state of bondage to some man. Laws and systems of polity always begin by recognising the relations they find already existing between individuals. They convert what was a mere physical fact into a legal right, give it the sanction of society, and principally aim at the substitution of public and organized means of asserting and protecting these rights, instead of the irregular and lawless conflict of physical strength....

... We now live—that is to say, one or two of the most advanced nations of the world now live—in a state in which the law of the strongest seems to be entirely abandoned as the regulating principle of the world's affairs: nobody professes it, and, as regards most of the relations between human beings, nobody is permitted to practise it. When any one succeeds in doing so, it is under cover of some pretext which gives him the semblance of having some general social interest on his side. This being the ostensible state of things, people flatter themselves that the rule of mere force is ended; that the law of the strongest cannot be the reason of existence of anything which has remained in full operation down to the present time. However any of our present institutions may have begun, it can only, they think, have been preserved to this period of advanced civilization by a well-grounded feeling of its adaptation to human nature, and conduciveness to the general good. They do not understand the great vitality and durability of institutions which place right on the side of might; how intensely they are clung to; how the good as well as the bad propensities and sentiments of those who have power in their hands, become identified with retaining it; how slowly these bad institutions give way, one at a time, the weakest first, beginning with those which are least interwoven with the daily habits of life; and how very rarely those who have obtained legal power because they first had physical, have ever lost their hold of it until the physical power had passed over to the other side. Such shifting of the physical force not having taken place in the case of women; this fact, combined with all the peculiar and characteristic features of the particular case, made it certain from the first that this branch of the system of right founded on might, though softened in its most atrocious features at an earlier period than several of the others, would be the very last to disappear. It was inevitable that this one case of a social relation grounded on force, would survive through generations of institutions grounded on equal justice, an almost solitary exception to the general character of their laws and customs; but which, so long as it does not proclaim its own origin, and as discussion has not brought out its true character, is not felt to jar with modern civilization, any more than domestic slavery among the Greeks jarred with their notion of themselves as a free people....

... Whatever gratification of pride there is in the possession of power, and whatever personal interest in its exercise, is in this case not confined to a limited class, but common to the whole male sex. Instead of being, to most of its supporters, a thing desirable chiefly in the abstract, or, like the political ends usually contended for by factions, of little private importance to any but the leaders; it comes home to the person and hearth of every male head of a family, and of every one who looks forward to being so. The clodhopper exercises, or is to exercise, his share of the power equally with the highest nobleman. And the case is that in which the desire of power is the strongest: for every one who desires power, desires it most over those who are nearest to him, with whom his life is passed, with whom he has most concerns in common, and in whom any independence of his authority is oftenest likely to interfere with his individual preferences. If, in the other cases specified, powers manifestly grounded only on force, and having so much less to support them, are so slowly and with so much difficulty got rid of, much more must it be so with this, even if it rests on no better foundation than those. We must consider, too, that the possessors of the power have facilities in this case, greater than in any other, to prevent any uprising against it. Every one of the subjects lives under the very eye, and almost, it may be said, in the hands, of one of the masters—in closer intimacy with him than with any of her fellow-subjects; with no means of combining against him, no power of even locally overmastering him, and, on the other hand, with the strongest motives for seeking his favour and avoiding to give him offence. In struggles for political emancipation, everybody knows how often its champions are bought off by bribes, or daunted by terrors. In the case of women, each individual of the subject-class is in a chronic state of bribery and intimidation combined. In setting up the standard of resistance, a large number of the leaders, and still more of the followers, must make an almost complete sacrifice of the pleasures or the alleviations of their own individual lot. If ever any system of privilege and enforced subjection had its yoke tightly riveted on the necks of those who are kept down by it, this has. . . .

Some will object, that a comparison cannot fairly be made between the government of the male sex and the forms of unjust power which I have adduced in illustration of it, since these are arbitrary, and the effect of mere usurpation, while it on the contrary is natural. But was there ever any domination which did not appear natural to those who possessed it? There was a time when the division of mankind into two classes, a small one of masters and a numerous one of slaves, appeared, even to the most cultivated minds, to be a natural, and the only natural, condition of the human race. . . . The subjection of women to men being a universal custom, any departure from it quite naturally appears unnatural. But how entirely, even in this case, the feeling is dependent on custom, appears by ample experience. Nothing so much astonishes the people of distant parts of the world, when they first learn anything about England, as to be told that it is under a queen; the thing seems to them so unnatural as to be almost incredible. To Englishmen this does not seem in the least degree unnatural, because they are used to it; but they do feel it unnatural that women should be soldiers or Members of Parliament. In the feudal ages, on the contrary, war and politics were not thought unnatural to women, because not unusual; it seemed natural that women of the privileged classes should be of manly character, inferior in nothing but bodily strength to their husbands and fathers. . . .

But, it will be said, the rule of men over women differs from all these others in not being a rule of force: it is accepted voluntarily; women make no complaint, and are consenting parties to it. In the first place, a great number of women do not accept it. Ever since there have been women able to make their sentiments known by their writings (the only mode of publicity which society permits to them), an increasing number of them have recorded protests against their present social condition: and recently many thousands of them, headed by the most eminent women known to the public, have petitioned Parliament for their admission to the Parliamentary Suffrage. The claim of women to be educated as solidly, and in the same branches of knowledge, as men, is urged with growing intensity, and with a great prospect of success; while the demand for their admission into professions and occupations hitherto closed against them, becomes every year more urgent. Though there are not in this country, as there are in the United States, periodical Conventions and an organised party to agitate for the Rights of Women, there is a numerous and active society organized and managed by women, for the more limited object of obtaining the political franchise. Nor is it only in our own country and in America that women are beginning to protest, more or less collectively, against the disabilities under which they labour. . . . It is a political law of nature that those who are under any power of ancient origin, never begin by complaining of the power itself, but only of its oppressive exercise. There is never any want of women who complain of ill usage by their husbands. There would be infinitely more, if complaint were not the greatest of all provocatives to a repetition and increase of the ill usage. It is this which frustrates all attempts to maintain the power but protect the woman against its abuses. In no other case (except that of a child) is the person who has been proved judicially to have suffered an injury, replaced under the physical power of the culprit who inflicted it. Accordingly wives, even in the most extreme and protracted cases of bodily ill usage, hardly ever dare avail themselves of the laws made for their protection: and if, in a moment of irrepressible indignation, or by the interference of neighbours, they are induced to do so, their whole effort afterwards is to disclose as little as they can, and to beg off their tyrant from his merited chastisement.

All causes, social and natural, combine to make it unlikely that women should be collectively rebellious to the power of men. They are so far in a position different from all other subject classes, that their masters require something more from them than actual service. Men do not want solely the obedience of women, they want their sentiments. All men, except the most brutish, desire to have, in the woman most nearly connected with them, not a forced slave but a willing one, not a slave merely, but a favourite. They have therefore put everything in practice to enslave their minds. The masters of all other slaves rely, for maintaining obedience, on fear; either fear of themselves, or religious fears. The masters of women wanted more than simple obedience, and they turned the whole force of education to effect their purpose. All women are brought up from the very earliest years in the belief that their ideal of character is the very opposite to that of men; not self-will, and government by self-control, but submission, and yielding to the control of others. All the moralities tell them that it is the duty of women, and all the current sentimentalities that it is their nature, to live for others; to make complete abnegation of themselves, and to have no life but in their affections. And by their affections are meant the only ones they are allowed to have—those to the men with whom they are connected, or to the children who constitute an additional and indefeasible tie between them and a man. When we put together three things—first, the natural attraction between opposite sexes; secondly, the wife's entire dependence on the husband, every privilege or pleasure she has being either his gift, or depending entirely on his will; and lastly, that the principal object of human pursuit, consideration, and all objects of social ambition, can in general be sought or obtained by her only through him, it would be a miracle if the object of being attractive to men had not become the polar star of feminine education and formation of character. And, this great means of influence over the minds of women having been acquired, an instinct of selfishness made men avail themselves of it to the utmost as a means of holding women in subjection, by representing to them meekness, submissiveness, and resignation of all individual will into the hands of a man, as an essential part of sexual attractiveness. Can it be doubted that any of the other yokes which mankind have succeeded in breaking, would have subsisted till now if the same means had existed, and had been as sedulously used, to bow down their minds to it? . . .

The preceding considerations are amply sufficient to show that custom, however universal it may be, affords in this case no presumption, and ought not to create any prejudice, in favour of the arrangements which place women in social and political subjection to men. But I may go farther, and maintain that the course of history, and the tendencies of progressive human society, afford not only no presumption in favour of this system of inequality of rights, but a strong one against it; and that, so far as the whole course of human improvement up to this time, the whole stream of modern tendencies, warrants any inference on the subject, it is, that this relic of the past is discordant with the future, and must necessarily disappear. . . .

2

. . . I am far from pretending that wives are in general no better treated than slaves; but no slave is a slave to the same lengths, and in so full a sense of the word, as a wife is. Hardly any slave, except one immediately attached to the master's person, is a slave at all hours and all minutes; in general he has, like a soldier, his fixed task, and when it is done, or when he is off duty, he disposes, within certain limits, of his own time, and has a family life into which the master rarely intrudes. "Uncle Tom" under his first master had his own life in his "cabin," almost as much as any man whose work takes him away from home, is able to have in his own family. But it cannot be so with the wife. Above all, a female slave has (in Christian countries) an admitted right, and is considered under a moral obligation, to refuse to her master the last familiarity. Not so the wife: however brutal a tyrant she may unfortunately be chained to—though she may know that he hates her, though it may be his daily pleasure to torture her, and though she may feel it impossible not to loathe him—he can claim from her and enforce the lowest degradation of a human being, that of being made the instrument of an animal function contrary to her inclinations. While she is held in this worst description of slavery as to her own person, what is her position in regard to the children in whom she and her master have a joint interest? They are by law *his* children. He alone has any legal rights over them. Not one act can she do towards or in relation to them, except by delegation from him. Even after he is dead she is not their legal guardian, unless he by will has made her so. He could even send them away from her, and deprive her of the means of seeing or corresponding with them, until this power was in some degree restricted by Serjeant Talfourd's Act. This is her legal state. And from this state she has no means of withdrawing herself. If she leaves her husband, she can take nothing with her, neither her children nor anything which is rightfully her own. If he chooses, he can compel her to return, by law, or by physical force; or he may content himself with seizing for his own use anything which she may earn, or which may be given to her by her relations. It is only legal separation by a decree of a court of justice, which entitles her to live apart, without being forced back into the custody of an exasperated jailer—or which empowers her to apply any earnings to her own use, without fear that a man whom perhaps she has not seen for twenty years will pounce upon her some day and carry all off. This legal separation, until lately, the courts of justice would only give at an expense which made it inaccessible to any one out of the higher ranks. Even now it is only given in cases of desertion, or of the extreme of cruelty; and yet complaints are made every day that it is granted too easily. Surely, if a woman is denied any lot in life but that of being the personal body-servant of a despot, and is dependent for everything upon the chance of finding one who may be disposed to make a favourite of her instead of merely a drudge, it is a very cruel aggravation of her fate that she should be allowed to try this chance only once. The natural sequel and corollary from this state of things would be, that since her all in life depends upon obtaining a good master, she should be allowed to change again and again until she finds one. I am not saying that she ought to be allowed this privilege. That is a totally different consideration. The question of divorce, in the sense involving liberty of remarriage, is one into which it is foreign to my purpose to enter. All I now say is, that to those to whom nothing but servitude is allowed, the free choice of servitude is the only, though a most insufficient, alleviation. Its refusal completes the assimilation of the wife to the slave—and the slave under not the mildest form of slavery: for in some slave codes the slave could, under certain circumstances of ill usage, legally compel the master to sell him. But no amount of ill usage, without adultery superadded, will in England free a wife from her tormentor.

I have no desire to exaggerate, nor does the case stand in any need of exaggeration. I have described the wife's legal position, not her actual treatment. The laws of most countries are far worse than the people who execute them, and many of them are only able to remain laws by being seldom or never carried into effect. If married life were all that it might be expected to be, looking to the laws alone, society would be a hell upon earth. Happily there are both feelings and interests which in many men exclude, and in most, greatly temper, the impulses and propensities which lead to tyranny: and of those feelings, the tie which connects a man with his wife affords, in a normal state of things, incomparably the strongest example. The only tie which at all approaches to it, that between him and his children, tends, in all save exceptional cases, to strengthen, instead of conflicting with, the first. Because this is true; because men in general do not inflict, nor women suffer, all the misery which could be inflicted and suffered if the full power of tyranny with which the man is legally invested were acted on; the defenders of the existing form of the institution think that all its iniquity is justified, and that any complaint is merely quarrelling with the evil which is the price paid for every great good. But the mitigations in practice, which are compatible with maintaining in full legal force this or any other kind of tyranny, instead of being any apology for despotism, only serve to prove what power human nature possesses of reacting against the vilest institutions, and with what vitality the seeds of good as well as those of evil in human character diffuse and propagate themselves. Not a word can be said for despotism in the family which cannot be said for political despotism. . . .

3

On the other point which is involved in the just equality of women, their admissibility to all the functions and occupations hitherto retained as the monopoly of the stronger sex, I should anticipate no difficulty in convincing any one who has gone with me on the subject of the equality of women in the family. I believe that their disabilities elsewhere are only clung to in order to maintain their subordination in domestic life; because the generality of the male sex cannot yet tolerate the idea of living with an equal. Were it not for that, I think that almost every one, in the existing state of opinion in politics and political economy, would admit the injustice of excluding half the human race from the greater number of lucrative occupations, and from almost all high social functions; ordaining from their birth either that they are not, and cannot by any possibility become, fit for employments which are legally open to the stupidest and basest of the other sex, or else that however fit they may be, those employments shall be interdicted to them, in order to be preserved for the exclusive benefit of males. In the last two centuries, when (which was seldom the case) any reason beyond the mere existence of the fact was thought to be required to justify the disabilities of women, people seldom assigned as a reason their inferior mental capacity; which, in times when there was a real trial of personal faculties (from which all women were not excluded) in the struggles of public life, no one really believed in. The reason given in those days was not women's unfitness, but the interest of society, by which was meant the interest of men: just as the *raison d'etat,* meaning the convenience of the government, and the support of existing authority, was deemed a sufficient explanation and excuse for the most flagitious crimes. In the present day, power holds a smoother language, and whomsoever it oppresses, always pretends to do so for their own good: accordingly, when anything is forbidden to women, it is thought necessary to say, and desirable to believe, that they are incapable of doing it, and that they depart from their real path of success and happiness when they aspire to it. But to make this reason plausible (I do not say valid), those by whom it is urged must be prepared to carry it to a much greater length than any one ventures to do in the face of present experience. It is not sufficient to maintain that women on the average are less gifted than men on the average, with certain of the higher mental faculties, or that a smaller number of women than of men are fit for occupations and functions of the highest intellectual character. It is necessary to maintain that no women at all are fit for them, and that the most eminent women are inferior in mental faculties to the most mediocre of the men on whom those functions at present devolve. For if the performance of the function is decided either by competition, or by any mode of choice which secures regard to the public interest, there needs to be no apprehension that any important employments will fall into the hands of women inferior to average men, or to the average of their male competitors. The only result would be that there would be fewer women than men in such employments; a result certain to happen in any case, if only from the preference always likely to be felt by the majority of women for the one vocation in which there is nobody to compete with them. Now, the most determined depreciator of women will not venture to deny, that when we add the experience of recent times to that of ages past, women, and not a few merely, but many women, have proved themselves capable of everything, perhaps without a single exception, which is done by men, and of doing it successfully and creditably. The utmost that can be said is, that there are many things which none of them have succeeded in doing as well as they have been done by some men—many in which they have not reached the very highest rank. But there are extremely few, dependent only on mental faculties, in which they have not attained the rank next to the highest. Is not this enough, and much more than enough, to make it a tyranny to them, and a detriment to society, that they should not be allowed to compete with men for the exercise of these functions? Is it not a mere truism to say, that such functions are often filled by men far less fit for them than numbers of women, and who would be beaten by women in any fair field of competition? What difference does it make that there may be men somewhere, fully employed about other things, who may be still better qualified for the things in question than these women? Does not this take place in all competitions? Is there so great a superfluity of men fit for high duties, that society can afford to reject the service of any competent person? Are we so certain of always finding a man made to our hands for any duty or function of social importance which falls vacant, that we lose nothing by putting a ban upon one-half of mankind, and refusing beforehand to make their faculties available, however distinguished they may be? And even if we could do without them, would it be consistent with justice to refuse to them their fair share of honour and distinction, or to deny to them the equal moral right of all human beings to choose their occupation (short of injury to others) according to their own preferences, at their own risk? Nor is the injustice confined to them: it is shared by those who are in a position to benefit by their services. To ordain that any kind of persons shall not be physicians, or shall not be advocates, or shall not be Members of Parliament, is to injure not them only, but all who employ physicians or advocates, or elect Members of Parliament, and who are deprived of the stimulating effect of greater competition on the exertions of the competitors, as well as restricted to a narrower range of individual choice. . . .

4

. . . Think what it is to a boy, to grow up to manhood in the belief that without any merit or any exertion of his own, though he may be the most frivolous and empty or the most ignorant and stolid of mankind, by the mere fact of being born a male he is by right the superior of all and every one of an entire half of the human race: including probably some whose real superiority to himself he has daily or hourly occasion to feel; but even if in his whole conduct he habitually follows a woman's guidance, still, if he is a fool, she thinks that of course she is not, and cannot be, equal in ability and judgment to himself; and if he is not a fool, he does worse—he sees that she is superior to him, and believes that, notwithstanding her superiority, he is entitled to command and she is bound to obey. What must be the effect on his character, of this lesson? And men of the cultivated classes are often not aware how deeply it sinks into the immense majority of male minds. For, among right-feeling and well-bred people, the inequality is kept as much as possible out of sight; above all, out of sight of the children. As much obedience is required from boys to their mother as to their father: they are not permitted to domineer over their sisters, nor are they accustomed to see these postponed to them, but the contrary; the compensations of the chivalrous feeling being made prominent, while the servitude which requires them is kept in the background. Well brought-up youths in the higher classes thus often escape the bad influences of the situation in their early years, and only experience them when, arrived at manhood, they fall under the dominion of facts as they really exist. Such people are little aware, when a boy is differently brought up, how early the notion of his inherent superiority to a girl arises in his mind; how it grows with his growth and strengthens with his strength; how it is inoculated by one schoolboy upon another; how early the youth thinks himself superior to his mother, owing her perhaps forbearance, but no real respect; and how sublime and sultan-like a sense of superiority he feels, above all, over the woman whom he honours by admitting her to a partnership of his life. Is it imagined that all this does not pervert the whole manner of existence of the man, both as an individual and as a social being? . . .

. . . If no authority, not in its nature temporary, were allowed to one human being over another, society would not be employed in building up propensities with one hand which it has to curb with the other. The child would really, for the first time in man's existence on earth, be trained in the way he should go, and when he was old there would be a chance that he would not depart from it. But so long as the right of the strong to power over the weak rules in the very heart of society, the attempt to make the equal right of the weak the principle of its outward actions will always be an uphill struggle; for the law of justice, which is also that of Christianity, will never get possession of men's inmost sentiments; they will be working against it, even when bending to it.

The second benefit to be expected from giving to women the free use of their faculties, by leaving them the free choice of their employments, and opening to them the same field of occupation and the same prizes and encouragements as to other human beings, would be that of doubling the mass of mental faculties available for the higher service of humanity. Where there is now one person qualified to benefit mankind and promote the general improvement, as a public teacher, or an administrator of some branch of public or social affairs, there would then be a chance of two. . . .

. . . The association of men with women in daily life is much closer and more complete than it ever was before. Men's life is more domestic. Formerly, their pleasures and chosen occupations were among men, and in men's company: their wives had but a fragment of their lives. At the present time, the progress of civilisation, and the turn of opinion against the rough amusements and convivial excesses which formerly occupied most men in their hours of relaxation—together with (it must be said) the improved tone of modern feeling as to the reciprocity of duty which binds the husband towards the wife–have thrown the man very much more upon home and its inmates, for his personal and social pleasures: while the kind and degree of improvement which has been made in women's education, has made them in some degree capable of being his companions in ideas and mental tastes, while leaving them, in most cases, still hopelessly inferior to him. His desire of mental communion is thus in general satisfied by a communion from which he learns nothing. An unimproving and unstimulating companionship is substituted for (what he might otherwise have been obliged to seek) the society of his equals in powers and his fellows in the higher pursuits. We see, accordingly, that young men of the greatest promise generally cease to improve as soon as they marry, and, not improving, inevitably degenerate. If the wife does not push the husband forward, she always holds him back. He ceases to care for what she does not care for; he no longer desires, and ends by disliking and shunning, society congenial to his former aspirations, and which would now shame his falling-off from them; his higher faculties both of mind and heart cease to be called into activity. And this change coinciding with the new and selfish interests which are created by the family, after a few years he differs in no material respect from those who have never had wishes for anything but the common vanities and the common pecuniary objects.

What marriage may be in the case of two persons of cultivated faculties, identical in opinions and purposes, between whom there exists that best kind of equality, similarity of powers and capacities with reciprocal superiority in them–so that each can enjoy the luxury of looking up to the other, and can have alternately the pleasure of leading and of being led in the path of development–I will not attempt to describe. To those who can conceive it, there is no need; to those who cannot, it would appear the dream of an enthusiast. But I maintain, with the profoundest conviction, that this, and this only, is the ideal of marriage; and that all opinions, customs, and institutions which favour any other notion of it, or turn the conceptions and aspirations connected with it into any other direction, by whatever pretences they may be coloured, are relics of primitive barbarism. The moral regeneration of mankind will only really commence, when the most fundamental of the social relations is placed under the rule of equal justice, and when human beings learn to cultivate their strongest sympathy with an equal in rights and in cultivation.

Thus far, the benefits which it has appeared that the world would gain by ceasing to make sex a disqualification for privileges and a badge of subjection, are social rather than individual; consisting in an increase of the general fund of thinking and acting power, and an improvement in the general conditions of the association of men with women. But it would be a grievous understatement of the case to omit the most direct benefit of all, the unspeakable gain in private happiness to the liberated half of the species; the difference to them between a life of subjection to the will of others, and a life of rational freedom. After the primary necessities of food and raiment, freedom is the first and strongest want of human nature. . . .

When we consider the positive evil caused to the disqualified half of the human race by their disqualification—first in the loss of the most in spiriting and elevating kind of personal enjoyment, and next in the weariness, disappointment, and profound dissatisfaction with life, which are so often the substitute for it; one feels that among all the lessons which men require for carrying on the struggle against the inevitable imperfections of their lot on earth, there is no lesson which they more need, than not to add to the evils which nature inflicts, by their jealous and prejudiced restrictions on one another. Their vain fears only substitute other and worse evils for those which they are idly apprehensive of: while every restraint on the freedom of conduct of any of their human fellow-creatures (otherwise than by making them responsible for any evil actually caused by it), dries up *pro tanto* the principal fountain of human happiness, and leaves the species less rich, to an inappreciable degree, in all that makes life valuable to the individual human being.

REFLECTING ON MEANING

1. According to Mill, what is the nature of women's subjection? In what ways are they oppressed? Why don't they rise up against their oppressors? Why don't they resist? How does their subjection represent a "branch of the system of right founded on might," as Mill puts it?

2. What distinction does Mill make between nature and custom? What definitions does he provide for natural and unnatural? How do these conceptions relate to the difficulty of recognizing

women's oppression? How did their subjection come to seem so natural?

3. From a nineteenth-century perspective, Mill describes how women's subjection affects home and marriage. What observations does he make? To what extent are these observations valid today? How, if at all, does women's status influence family interactions in the present?

EXPLORING RHETORICAL STRATEGIES

1. What is Mill's main idea? Is he successful in making a convincing argument for it? Why or why not?

2. Mill effectively integrates opposing viewpoints in his essay. What are some of the opposing views he discusses? In what ways does he refute them? How does this strategy help him advance his own viewpoint?

3. What is the primary analogy Mill uses to illustrate the nature of women's subjection? In what ways does he extend this analogy? How does it help him make women's subjection seem less "natural"?

From Women and Economics

CHARLOTTE PERKINS GILMAN

---

*The nineteenth-century American feminist Charlotte Per-
kins Gilman examines the economic status of women in the following excerpt from her book* Women and Economics,
*published in 1898. She maintains that society places women in
a situation in which their only "personal profit" derives directly
from "their power to win and hold the other sex." Gilman outlines a system of child care that would release women from this
bondage and transform the mother from "home servant" to "social servant."*

T he economic status of the human race in any nation, at any
time, is governed mainly by the activities of the male: the
female obtains her share in the racial advance only through
him.

Studied individually, the facts are even more plainly visible,
more open and familiar. From the day laborer to the millionaire,
the wife's worn dress or flashing jewels, her low roof or her lordly
one, her weary feet or her rich equipage,—these speak of the economic ability of the husband. The comfort, the luxury, the necessities of life itself, which the woman receives, are obtained by the
husband, and given her by him. And, when the woman, left alone
with no man to "support" her, tries to meet her own economic necessities, the difficulties which confront her prove conclusively
what the general economic status of the woman is. . . . But we are
instantly confronted by the commonly received opinion that, although it must be admitted that men make and distribute the
wealth of the world, yet women earn their share of it as wives. This
assumes either that the husband is in the position of employer and
the wife as employee, or that marriage is a "partnership," and the
wife an equal factor with the husband in producing wealth. . . .

Women consume economic goods. What economic product
do they give in exchange for what they consume? The claim that
marriage is a partnership, in which the two persons married produce wealth which neither of them, separately, could produce, will
not bear examination. A man happy and comfortable can produce

more than one unhappy and uncomfortable, but this is as true of a father or son as of a husband. To take from a man any of the conditions which make him happy and strong is to cripple his industry, generally speaking. But those relatives who make him happy are not therefore his business partners, and entitled to share his income.

Grateful return for happiness conferred is not the method of exchange in a partnership. The comfort a man takes with his wife is not in the nature of a business partnership, nor are her frugality and industry. A housekeeper, in her place, might be as frugal, as industrious, but would not therefore be a partner. Man and wife are partners truly in their mutual obligation to their children,—their common love, duty, and service. But a manufacturer who marries, or a doctor, or a lawyer, does not take a partner in his business, when he takes a partner in parenthood, unless his wife is also a manufacturer, a doctor, or a lawyer. . . .

If the wife is not, then, truly a business partner, in what way does she earn from her husband the food, clothing, and shelter she receives at his hands? By house service, it will be instantly replied. This is the general misty idea upon the subject,—that women earn all they get, and more, by house service. Here we come to a very practical and definite economic ground. Although not producers of wealth, women serve in the final processes of preparation and distribution. Their labor in the household has a genuine economic value.

For a certain percentage of persons to serve other persons, in order that the ones so served may produce more, is a contribution not to be overlooked. The labor of women in the house, certainly, enables men to produce more wealth than they otherwise could; and in this way women are economic factors in society. But so are horses. The labor of horses enables men to produce more wealth than they otherwise could. The horse is an economic factor in society. But the horse is not economically independent, nor is the woman. . . .

The labor which the wife performs in the household is given as part of her functional duty, not as employment. The wife of the poor man, who works hard in a small house, doing all the work for the family, or the wife of the rich man, who wisely and gracefully manages a large house and administers its functions, each is entitled to fair pay for services rendered.

To take this ground and hold it honestly, wives, as earners through domestic service, are entitled to the wages of cooks, housemaids, nursemaids, seamstresses, or housekeepers, and to no more. This would of course reduce the spending money of the wives of the rich, and put it out of the power of the poor man to "support" a wife at all, unless, indeed, the poor man faced the situation fully, paid his wife her wages as house servant, and then she and he combined their funds in the support of their children. He would be keeping a servant: she would be helping keep the family. But nowhere on earth would there be "a rich woman" by these means. Even the highest class of private housekeeper, useful as her services are, does not accumulate a fortune. . . .

But the salient fact in this discussion is that, whatever the economic value of the domestic industry of women is, they do not get it. The women who do the most work get the least money, and the women who have the most money do the least work. Their labor is neither given nor taken as a factor in economic exchange. It is held to be their duty as women to do this work; and their economic status bears no relation to their domestic labors, unless an inverse one. Moreover, if they were thus fairly paid,—given what they earned, and no more,—all women working in this way would be reduced to the economic status of the house servant. Few women—or men either—care to face this condition. The ground that women earn their living by domestic labor is instantly forsaken, and we are told that they obtain their livelihood as mothers. This is a peculiar position. We speak of it commonly enough, and often with deep feeling, but without due analysis. . . .

If this is so, if motherhood is an exchangeable commodity given by women in payment for clothes and food, then we must of course find some relation between the quantity or quality of the motherhood and the quantity and quality of the pay. This being true, then the women who are not mothers have no economic status at all; and the economic status of those who are must be shown to be relative to their motherhood. This is obviously absurd. The childless wife has as much money as the mother of many,—more; for the children of the latter consume what would otherwise be hers; and the inefficient mother is no less provided for than the efficient one. Visibly, and upon the face of it, women are not maintained in economic prosperity proportioned to their motherhood. Motherhood bears no relation to their economic status. . . . The claim of motherhood as a factor in economic exchange is false today. But suppose it were true. Are we willing to hold this ground, even in theory? Are we willing to consider motherhood as a business, a form of commercial exchange? Are the cares and duties of the mother, her travail and her love, commodities to be exchanged for bread?

It is revolting so to consider them; and, if we dare face our own thoughts, and force them to their logical conclusion, we shall see that nothing could be more repugnant to human feeling, or more socially and individually injurious, than to make motherhood a trade. Driven off these alleged grounds of women's economic independence; shown that women, as a class, neither produce nor distribute wealth; that women, as individuals, labor mainly as house servants, are not paid as such, and would not be satisfied with such an economic status if they were so paid; that wives are not business partners or co-producers of wealth with their husbands, unless they actually practise the same profession; that they are not salaried as mothers, and that it would be unspeakably degrading if they were,—what remains to those who deny that women are supported by men? This. . .—that the function of maternity unfits a woman for economic production, and, therefore, it is right that she should be supported by her husband. . . .

. . . Because of her maternal duties, the human female is said to be unable to get her own living. As the maternal duties of other females do not unfit them for getting their own living and also the livings of their young, it would seem that the human maternal duties require the segregation of the entire energies of the mother to the service of the child during her entire adult life, or so large a proportion of them that not enough remains to devote to the individual interests of the mother. . . .

Is this the condition of human motherhood? Does the human mother, by her motherhood, thereby lose control of brain and body, lose power and skill and desire for any other work? Do we see before us the human race, with all its females segregated entirely to the uses of motherhood, consecrated, set apart, specially developed, spending every power of their nature on the service of their children?

We do not. We see the human mother worked far harder than a mare, laboring her life long in the service, not of her children only, but of men; husbands, brothers, fathers, whatever male relatives she has; for mother and sister also; for the church a little, if she is allowed; for society, if she is able; for charity and education and reform—working in many ways that are not the ways of motherhood.

It is not motherhood that keeps the housewife on her feet from dawn till dark; it is house service, not child service. Women work longer and harder than most men, and not solely in maternal duties. . . . Many mothers, even now, are wage-earners for the family, as well as bearers and rearers of it. And the women who are not so occupied, the women who belong to rich men,—here perhaps is the exhaustive devotion to maternity which is supposed to justify an admitted economic dependence. But we do not find it even among these. Women of ease and wealth provide for their children better care than the poor woman can; but they do not spend more time upon it themselves, nor more care and effort. They have other occupation.

In spite of her supposed segregation to maternal duties, the human female, the world over, works at extra-maternal duties for hours enough to provide her with an independent living, and then is denied independence on the ground that motherhood prevents her working! . . .

With the growth of civilization, we have gradually crystallized into law the visible necessity for feeding the helpless female; and even old women are maintained by their male relatives with a comfortable assurance. But to this day—save, indeed, for the increasing army of women wage-earners, who are changing the face of the world by their steady advance toward economic independence—the personal profit of women bears but too close a relation to their power to win and hold the other sex. From the odalisque with the most bracelets to the débutante with the most bouquets, the relation still holds good,—woman's economic profit comes through the power of sex-attraction.

When we confront this fact boldly and plainly in the open market of vice, we are sick with horror. When we see the same economic relation made permanent, established by law, sanctioned and sanctified by religion, covered with flowers and incense and all accumulated sentiment, we think it innocent, lovely, and right. The transient trade we think evil. The bargain for life we think good. But the biological effect remains the same. In both cases the female gets her food from the male by virtue of her sex-relationship to him. In both cases, perhaps even more in marriage because of its perfect acceptance of the situation, the female of genus homo, still living under natural law, is inexorably modified to sex in an increasing degree. . . .

Another instance of so grossly unjust, so palpable, so general an evil that it has occasionally aroused some protest even from our dull consciousness is this: the enforced attitude of the woman toward marriage. To the young girl, as has been previously stated, marriage is the one road to fortune, to life. She is born highly specialized as a female: she is carefully educated and trained to realize in all ways her sex-limitations and her sex-advantages. What she has to gain even as a child is largely gained by feminine tricks and charms. Her reading, both in history and fiction, treats of the same position for women; and romance and poetry give it absolute predominance. Pictorial art, music, the drama, society, everything, tells her that she is *she,* and that all depends on whom she marries. Where young boys plan for what they will achieve and attain, young girls plan for whom they will achieve and attain. . . .

With such a prospect as this before her; with an organization specially developed to this end; with an education adding every weight of precept and example, of wisdom and virtue, to the natural instincts; with a social environment the whole machinery of which is planned to give the girl a chance to see and to be seen, to provide her with "opportunities"; and with all the pressure of personal advantage and self-interest added to the sex-instinct,—what one would logically expect is a society full of desperate and eager husband-hunters, regarded with popular approval.

Not at all! Marriage is the woman's proper sphere, her divinely ordered place, her natural end. It is what she is born for, what she is trained for, what she is exhibited for. It is, moreover, her means of honorable livelihood and advancement. *But*–she must not even look as if she wanted it! She must not turn her hand over to get it. She must sit passive as the seasons go by, and her "chances" lessen with each year. Think of the strain on a highly sensitive nervous organism to have so much hang on one thing, to see the possibility of attaining it grow less and less yearly, and to be forbidden to take any step toward securing it! This she must bear with dignity and grace to the end. . . .

The cruel and absurd injustice of blaming the girl for not getting what she is allowed no effort to obtain seems unaccountable; but it becomes clear when viewed in connection with the sexuo-economic relation. Although marriage is a means of livelihood, it is not honest employment where one can offer one's labor without shame, but a relation where the support is given outright, and enforcement by law in return for the functional service of the woman, the "duties of wife and mother." Therefore no honorable woman can ask for it. . . .

. . . Half the human race is denied free productive expression, is forced to confine its productive human energies to the same channels as its reproductive sex-energies. Its creative skill is confined to the level of immediate personal bodily service, to the making of clothes and preparing of food for individuals. No social service is possible. While its power of production is checked, its power of consumption is inordinately increased by the showering upon it of the "unearned increment" of masculine gifts. For the woman there is, first, no free production allowed; and, second, no relation maintained between what she does produce and what she consumes. She is forbidden to make, but encouraged to take. Her industry is not the natural output of creative energy, not the work she does because she has the inner power and strength to do it; nor is her industry even the measure of her gain. She has, of course, the natural desire to consume; and to that is set no bar save the capacity or the will of her husband.

Thus we have painfully and laboriously evolved and carefully maintain among us an enormous class of non-productive consumers,—a class which is half the world, and mother of the other half. We have built into the constitution of the human race the habit and desire of taking, as divorced from its natural precursor and concomitant of making. . . . To consume food, to consume clothes, to consume houses and furniture and decorations and ornaments and amusements, to take and take and take forever,—from one man if they are virtuous, from many if they are vicious, but always to take and never to think of giving anything in return except their womanhood,—this is the enforced condition of the mothers of the race. What wonder that their sons go into business "for what there is in it"! What wonder that the world is full of the desire to get as much as possible and to give as little as possible! . . .

. . . [T]he consuming female, debarred from any free production, unable to estimate the labor involved in the making of what she so lightly destroys, and her consumption limited mainly to those things which minister to physical pleasure, creates a market for sensuous decoration and personal ornament, for all that is luxurious and enervating, and for a false and capricious variety in such supplies, which operates as a most deadly check to true industry and true art. As the priestess of the temple of consumption, as the limitless demander of things to use up, her economic influence is reactionary and injurious. Much, very much, of the current of useless production in which our economic energies run waste—man's strength poured out like water on the sand—depends on the creation and careful maintenance of this false market, this sink into which human labor vanishes with no return. Woman, in her false economic position, reacts injuriously upon industry, upon art, upon science, discovery, and progress. The sexuo-economic relation in its effect on the constitution of the individual keeps alive in us the instincts of savage individualism which we should otherwise have well outgrown. It sexualizes our industrial relation and commercializes our sex-relation. And, in the external effect upon the market, the over-sexed woman, in her unintelligent and ceaseless demands, hinders and perverts the economic development of the world. . . .

Economic independence for women necessarily involves a change in the home and family relation. But, if that change is for the advantage of individual and race, we need not fear it. It does not involve a change in the marriage relation except in withdrawing the element of economic dependence, nor in the relation of mother to child save to improve it. But it does involve the exercise of human faculty in women, in social service and exchange rather than in domestic service solely. This will of course require the introduction of some other form of living than that which now obtains. It will render impossible the present method of feeding the world by means of millions of private servants, and bringing up children by the same hand. . . .

Perhaps it is worth while to examine the nature of our feeling toward that social institution called "the family," and the probable effect upon it of the change in woman's economic status.

Marriage and "the family" are two institutions, not one, as is commonly supposed. We confuse the natural result of marriage in children, common to all forms of sex-union, with the family,–a purely social phenomenon. Marriage is a form of sex-union recognized and sanctioned by society. It is a relation between two or more persons, according to the custom of the country, and involves mutual obligations. Although made by us an economic relation, it is not essentially so, and will exist in much higher fulfillment after the economic phase is outgrown. . . .

The family is a decreasing survival of the earliest grouping known to man. Marriage is an increasing development of high social life, not fully evolved. So far from being identical with the family, it improves and strengthens in inverse ratio to the family. . . . There was no conception of marriage as a personal union for life of two well-matched individuals during the patriarchal era. Wives were valued merely for child-bearing. The family needed numbers of its own blood, especially males; and the man-child was the price of favor to women then. . . . Its bonds of union were of the loosest,– merely common paternity, with a miscellaneous maternity of inimical interests. Such a basis forever forbade any high individualization, and high individualization with its demands for a higher marriage forbids any numerical importance to the family. Marriage has risen and developed in social importance as the family has sunk and decreased. . . .

If there should be built and opened in any of our large cities today a commodious and well-served apartment house for professional women with families, it would be filled at once. The apartments would be without kitchens; but there would be a kitchen belonging to the house from which meals could be served to the families in their rooms or in a common dining-room, as preferred. It would be a home where the cleaning was done by efficient workers, not hired separately by the families, but engaged by the manager of the establishment; and a roof-garden, day nursery, and kindergarten, under well-trained professional nurses and teachers,

would insure proper care of the children. The demand for such provision is increasing daily, and must soon be met, not by a boarding-
house or a lodging-house, a hotel, a restaurant, or any makeshift
patching together of these; but by a permanent provision for the
needs of women and children, of family privacy with collective advantage. This must be offered on a business basis to prove a substantial business success; and it will so prove, for it is a growing
social need. . . .

. . . Many would so desire, keeping their own rooms, their
personal inner chambers, inviolate from other presence than that
of their nearest and dearest. . . . Of all popular paradoxes, none is
more nakedly absurd than to hear us prate of privacy in a place
where we cheerfully admit to our table-talk and to our door
service—yes, and to the making of our beds and to the handling of
our clothing—a complete stranger. . . .

This stranger all of us who can afford it summon to our
homes, . . . —with this observing and repeating army lodged in the
very bosom of the family, may we not smile a little bitterly at our
fond ideal of "the privacy of the home"? The swift progress of professional sweepers, dusters, and scrubbers, through rooms where
they were wanted, and when they were wanted, would be at least
no more injurious to privacy than the present method. Indeed, the
exclusion of the domestic servant, and, the entrance of woman on
a plane of interest at once more social and more personal, would
bring into the world a new conception of the sacredness of privacy,
a feeling for the rights of the individual as yet unknown.

In reconstructing in our minds the position of woman under
conditions of economic independence, it is most difficult to think
of her as a mother.

We are so unbrokenly accustomed to the old methods of
motherhood, so convinced that all its processes are interrelative
and indispensable, and that to alter one of them is to endanger the
whole relation, that we cannot conceive of any desirable change.

When definite plans for such change are suggested,—ways in
which babies might be better cared for than at present,—we either
deny the advantages of the change proposed or insist that these advantages can be reached under our present system. Just as in cooking we seek to train the private cook and to exalt and purify the
private taste, so in baby-culture we seek to train the individual
mother, and to call for better conditions in the private home; in
both cases ignoring the relation between our general system and its
particular phenomena. Though it may be shown, with clearness,
that in physical conditions the private house, as a place in which to
raise children, may be improved upon, yet all the more stoutly do

we protest that the mental life, the emotional life, of the home is the best possible environment for the young.

There was a time in human history when this was true. While progress derived its main impetus from the sex-passion, and the highest emotions were those that held us together in the family relation, such education and such surroundings as fostered and intensified these emotions were naturally the best. But in the stage into which we are now growing, when the family relation is only a part of life, and our highest duties lie between individuals in social relation, the child has new needs....

... [W]e have reached a stage where individual and racial progress is best served by the higher specialization of individuals and by a far wider sense of love and duty. This change renders the psychic condition of home life increasingly disadvantageous. We constantly hear of the inferior manners of the children of today, of the restlessness of the young, of the flat treason of deserting parents. It is visibly not so easy to live at home as it used to be. Our children are not more perversely constituted than the children of earlier ages, but the conditions in which they are reared are not suited to develop the qualities now needed in human beings.

This increasing friction between members of families should not be viewed with condemnation from a moral point of view, but studied with scientific interest. If our families are so relatively uncomfortable under present conditions, are there not conditions wherein the same families could be far more comfortable?... It is in the training of children... that the private home has ceased to be sufficient, or the isolated, primitive, dependent woman capable. Not that the mother does not have an intense and overpowering sense of loyalty and of duty; but it is duty to individuals, just as it was in the year one. What she is unable to follow, in her enforced industrial restriction, is the higher specialization of labor, and the honorable devotion of human lives to the development of their work....

She cannot teach what she does not know. She cannot in any sincerity uphold as a duty what she does not practise. The child learns more of the virtues needed in modern life—of fairness, of justice, of comradeship, of collective interest and action—in a common school than can be taught in the most perfect family circle. We may preach to our children as we will of the great duty of loving and serving one's neighbor; but what the baby is born into, what the child grows up to see and feel, is the concentration of one entire life—his mother's—upon the personal aggrandizement of one family, and the human service of another entire life—his father's—so warped and strained by the necessity of "supporting his family" that treason to society is the common price of comfort in the home. . . .

And this is the atmosphere in which the wholly home-bred, mother-taught child grows up. Why should not food and clothes and the comforts of his own people stand first in his young mind? Does he not see his mother, the all-loved, all-perfect one, peacefully spending her days in the arrangement of these things which his father's ceaseless labor has procured? Why should he not grow up to care for his own, to the neglect and willing injury of all the rest, when his earliest, deepest impressions are formed under such exclusive devotion?

It is not the home as a place of family life and love that injures the child, but as the centre of a tangled heap of industries, low in their ungraded condition, and lower still because they are wholly personal. Work the object of which is merely to serve one's self is the lowest. Work the object of which is merely to serve one's family is the next lowest. Work the object of which is to serve more and more people, in widening range. . . is social service in the fullest sense, and the highest form of service that we can reach. . . .

We suffer also, our lives long, from an intense self-consciousness, from a sensitiveness beyond all need; we demand measureless personal attention and devotion, because we have been born and reared in a very hot-bed of these qualities. A baby who spent certain hours of every day among other babies, being cared for because he was a baby, and not because he was "my baby," would grow to have a very different opinion of himself from that which is forced upon each new soul that comes among us by the ceaseless adoration of his own immediate family. What he needs to learn at once and for all, to learn softly and easily, but inexorably, is that he is one of many. We all dimly recognize this in our praise of large families, and in our saying that "an only child is apt to be selfish." So is an only family. The earlier and more easily a child can learn that human life means many people, and their behavior to one another, the happier and stronger and more useful his life will be.

This could be taught him with no difficulty whatever, under certain conditions, just as he is taught his present sensitiveness and egotism by the present conditions. It is not only temperature and diet and rest and exercise which affect the baby. "He does love to be noticed," we say. "He is never so happy as when he has a dozen worshippers around him." But what is the young soul learning all the while? What does he gather, as he sees and hears and slowly absorbs impressions? With the inflexible inferences of a clear, young brain, unsupplied with any counter-evidence until later in life, he learns that women are meant to wait on people, to get dinner, and sweep and pick up things; that men are made to bring home things, and are to be begged of according to circumstances; that babies are the object of concentrated admiration; that their hair, hands, feet, are specially attractive; that they are the heated focus of attention, to be passed from hand to hand, swung and danced and amused most violently, and also be laid aside and have nothing done to them, with no regard to their preference in either case. . . .

. . . [W]hile we flatter ourselves that things remain the same, they are changing under our very eyes from year to year, from day to day. Education, hiding itself behind a wall of books, but consisting more and more fully in the grouping of children and in the training of faculties never mentioned in the curriculum,– education, which is our human motherhood, has crept nearer and nearer to its true place, its best work,–the care and training of the little child. Some women there are, and some men, whose highest service to humanity is the care of children. Such should not concentrate their powers upon their own children alone,–a most questionable advantage,–but should be so placed that their talent and skill, their knowledge and experience, would benefit the largest number of children. . . .

As we now arrange life, our children must take their chances while babies, and live or die, improve or deteriorate, according to the mother to whom they chance to be born. An inefficient mother does not prevent a child from having a good college education; but the education of babyhood, the most important of all, is wholly in her hands. It is futile to say that mothers should be taught how to fulfil their duties. You cannot teach every mother to be a good school educator or a good college educator. Why should you expect every mother to be a good nursery educator?

The growth and change in home and family life goes steadily on under and over and through our prejudices and convictions; and the education of the child has changed and become a social function, while we still imagine the mother to be doing it all. . . .

We think no harm of motherhood because our darlings go out each day to spend long hours in school. The mother is not held neglectful, nor the child bereft. It is not called a "separation of mother and child." There would be no further harm or risk or loss in a babyhood passed among such changed surroundings and skilled service as should meet its needs more perfectly than it is possible for the mother to meet them alone at home.

Better surroundings and care for babies, better education, do not mean, as some mothers may imagine, that the tiny monthling is to be taught to read, or even that it is to be exposed to cabalistical arrangements of color and form and sound which shall mysteriously force the young intelligence to flower. It would mean, mainly, a far quieter and more peaceful life than is possible for the heavily loved and violently cared for baby in the busy household; and the impressions which it did meet would be planned and maintained with an intelligent appreciation of its mental powers. The mother would not be excluded, but supplemented, as she is now, by the teacher and the school. . . .

. . . The mother as a social servant instead of a home servant will not lack in true mother duty. She will love her child as well, perhaps better, when she is not in hourly contact with it, when she goes from its life to her own life, and back from her own life to its life, with ever new delight and power. She can keep the deep, thrilling joy of motherhood far fresher in her heart, far more vivid and open in voice and eyes and tender hands, when the hours of individual work give her mind another channel for her own part of the day. From her work, loved and honored though it is, she will return to the home life, the child life, with an eager, ceaseless pleasure, cleansed of all the fret and fraction and weariness that so mar it now.

REFLECTING ON MEANING

1. According to Gilman, why is it wrong to assume that women's economic power derives from their role in marriage partnerships, from their work in the household, or from their maternal duties? What is the actual source of their economic worth? Why does Gilman suggest that this situation should make us "sick with horror"? What is the role of marriage and family in this economic arrangement? What makes marriage a "means of livelihood" but "not honest employment"?

2. What point does Gilman make about the influence of women on general economic development? What does calling woman the "priestess of the temple of consumption" suggest about women's economic influence? Why does Gilman frame their influence in negative terms? Do you agree with her assessment? Why or why not?

3. Gilman asserts that "economic independence for women necessarily involves a change in the home and family relation." Why

is this the case, according to Gilman? What kinds of changes does she suggest? What effect does she believe these changes will have on child-raising methods? What will they accomplish for women in the long run?

EXPLORING RHETORICAL STRATEGIES

1. What is the main idea that Gilman expresses in this selection? How do her discussions of child care and of women as consumers relate to this larger idea?

2. Rather than beginning her discussion by stating what the basis of women's economic status is, Gilman presents and refutes views that run counter to her own. In other words, she works toward her thesis by a process of elimination. What is the effect of this strategy? Is it successful?

3. Gilman makes extensive use of rhetorical questions. What instances of this device can you identify? How do these questions help shape the development of her discussion? What do they suggest about her awareness of audience?

Awakening and Revolt

MARGARET SANGER

Margaret Sanger was a leader in the American birth control movement in the second decade of the twentieth century. She served as a catalyst for bringing the issue of contraception to the forefront, organizing international conferences and establishing many clinics. In "Awakening and Revolt," an excerpt from My Fight for Birth Control, *published in 1931, Sanger relates how her eyes were initially opened to the plight of women who had no way to prevent their own pregnancies.*

Early in the year 1912 I came to a sudden realization that my work as a nurse and my activities in social service were entirely palliative and consequently futile and useless to relieve the misery I saw all about me. . . .

Were it possible for me to depict the revolting conditions existing in the homes of some of the women I attended in that one year, one would find it hard to believe. There was at that time, and doubtless is still today, a sub-stratum of men and women whose lives are absolutely untouched by social agencies.

The way they live is almost beyond belief. They hate and fear any prying into their homes or into their lives. They resent being talked to. The women slink in and out of their homes on their way to market like rats from their holes. The men beat their wives sometimes black and blue, but no one interferes. The children are cuffed, kicked and chased about, but woe to the child who dares to tell tales out of the home! Crime or drink is often the source of this secret aloofness, usually there is something to hide, a skeleton in the closet somewhere. The men are sullen, unskilled workers, picking up odd jobs now and then, unemployed usually, sauntering in and out of the house at all hours of the day and night.

The women keep apart from other women in the neighborhood. Often they are suspected of picking a pocket or "lifting" an article when occasion arises. Pregnancy is an almost chronic condition amongst them. I knew one woman who had given birth to eight children with no professional care whatever. The last one was born in the kitchen, witnessed by a son of ten years who, under his mother's direction, cleaned the bed, wrapped the placenta and soiled articles in paper, and threw them out of the window into the court below. . . .

In this atmosphere abortions and birth become the main theme of conversation. On Saturday nights I have seen groups of fifty to one hundred women going into questionable offices well known in the community for cheap abortions. I asked several women what took place there, and they all gave the same reply: a quick examination, a probe inserted into the uterus and turned a few times to disturb the fertilized ovum, and then the woman was sent home. Usually the flow began the next day and often continued four or five weeks. Sometimes an ambulance carried the victim to the hospital for a curetage, and if she returned home at all she was looked upon as a lucky woman.

This state of things became a nightmare with me. There seemed no sense to it all, no reason for such waste of mother life, no right to exhaust women's vitality and to throw them on the scrap-heap before the age of thirty-five.

Everywhere I looked, misery and fear stalked—men fearful of losing their jobs, women fearful that even worse conditions might come upon them. The menace of another pregnancy hung like a sword over the head of every poor woman I came in contact with that year. The question which met me was always the same: What can I do to keep from it? or, What can I do to get out of this? Sometimes they talked among themselves bitterly.

"It's the rich that know the tricks," they'd say, "while we have all the kids." Then, if the women were Roman Catholics, they talked about "Yankee tricks," and asked me if I knew what the Protestants did to keep their families down. When I said that I didn't believe that the rich knew much more than they did I was laughed at and suspected of holding back information for money. They would nudge each other and say something about paying me before I left the case if I would reveal the "secret." . . .

Finally the thing began to shape itself, to become accumulative during the three weeks I spent in the home of a desperately sick woman living on Grand Street, a lower section of New York's East Side.

Mrs. Sacks was only twenty-eight years old; her husband, an unskilled worker, thirty-two. Three children, aged five, three and one, were none too strong nor sturdy, and it took all the earnings of the father and the ingenuity of the mother to keep them clean, provide them with air and proper food, and give them a chance to grow into decent manhood and womanhood.

Both parents were devoted to these children and to each other. The woman had become pregnant and had taken various drugs and purgatives, as advised by her neighbors. Then, in desperation, she had used some instrument lent to her by a friend. She was found prostrate on the floor amidst the crying children when her husband returned from work. Neighbors advised against the ambulance, and a friendly doctor was called. The husband would not hear of her going to a hospital, and as a little money had been saved in the bank a nurse was called and the battle for that precious life began.

It was in the middle of July. The three-room apartment was turned into a hospital for the dying patient. Never had I worked so fast, never so concentratedly as I did to keep alive that little mother. Neighbor women came and went during the day doing the odds and ends necessary for our comfort. The children were sent to friends and relatives and the doctor and I settled ourselves to outdo the force and power of an outraged nature.

Never had I known such conditions could exist. July's sultry days and nights were melted into a torpid inferno. Day after day, night after night, I slept only in brief snatches, ever too anxious about the condition of that feeble heart bravely carrying on, to stay long from the bedside of the patient. . . .

At the end of two weeks recovery was in sight, and at the end of three weeks I was preparing to leave the fragile patient to take up the ordinary duties of her life, including those of wifehood and motherhood. Everyone was congratulating her on her recovery. All the kindness of sympathetic and understanding neighbors poured in upon her in the shape of convalescent dishes, soups, custards, and drinks. Still she appeared to be despondent and worried. She seemed to sit apart in her thoughts as if she had no part in these congratulatory messages and endearing welcomes. I thought at first that she still retained some of her unconscious memories and dwelt upon them in her silences.

But as the hour for my departure came nearer, her anxiety increased, and finally with trembling voice she said: "Another baby will finish me, I suppose."

"It's too early to talk about that," I said, and resolved that I would turn the question over to the doctor for his advice. When he came I said: "Mrs. Sacks is worried about having another baby."

"She well might be," replied the doctor, and then he stood before her and said: "Any more such capers, young woman, and there will be no need to call me."

"Yes, yes—I know, Doctor," said the patient with trembling voice, "but," and she hesitated as if it took all of her courage to say it, "*what* can I do to prevent getting that way again?"

"Oh ho!" laughed the doctor good naturedly, "You want your cake while you eat it too, do you? Well, it can't be done." Then, familiarly slapping her on the back and picking up his hat and bag to depart, he said: "I'll tell you the only sure thing to do. Tell Jake to sleep on the roof!"

With those words he closed the door and went down the stairs, leaving us both petrified and stunned.

Tears sprang to my eyes, and a lump came in my throat as I looked at that face before me. It was stamped with sheer horror. I thought for a moment she might have gone insane, but she conquered her feelings, whatever they may have been, and turning to me in desperation said: "He can't understand, can he?—he's a man after all—but you do, don't you? You're a woman and you'll tell me the secret and I'll never tell it to a soul."

She clasped her hands as if in prayer, she leaned over and looked straight into my eyes and beseechingly implored me to tell her something—something *I really did not know.* It was like being on a rack and tortured for a crime one had not committed. To plead guilty would stop the agony; otherwise the rack kept turning.

I had to turn away from that imploring face. I could not answer her then. I quieted her as best I could. She saw that I was moved by the tears in my eyes. I promised that I would come back in a few days and tell her what she wanted to know. The few simple means of limiting the family like *coitus interruptus* or the condom were laughed at by the neighboring women when told these were the means used by men in the well-to-do families. That was not believed, and I knew such an answer would be swept aside as useless were I to tell her this at such a time.

A little later when she slept I left the house, and made up my mind that I'd keep away from those cases in the future. I felt helpless to do anything at all. I seemed chained hand and foot, and longed for an earthquake or a volcano to shake the world out of its lethargy into facing these monstrous atrocities.

The intelligent reasoning of the young mother—how to *prevent* getting that way again—how sensible, how just she had been—yes, I promised myself I'd go back and have a long talk with her and tell her more, and perhaps she would not laugh but would believe that those methods were all that were really known.

But time flew past, and weeks rolled into months. That wistful, appealing face haunted me day and night. I could not banish from my mind memories of that trembling voice begging so humbly for knowledge she had a right to have. I was about to retire one night three months later when the telephone rang and an agitated man's voice begged me to come at once to help his wife who was sick again. It was the husband of Mrs. Sacks, and I intuitively knew before I left the telephone that it was almost useless to go.

I dreaded to face that woman. I was tempted to send someone else in my place. I longed for an accident on the subway, or on the street—anything to prevent my going into that home. But on I went, just the same. I arrived a few minutes after the doctor, the same one who had given her such noble advice. The woman was dying. She was unconscious. She died within ten minutes after my arrival. It was the same result, the same story told a thousand times before—death from abortion. She had become pregnant, had used drugs, had then consulted a five-dollar professional abortionist, and death followed.

The doctor shook his head as he rose from listening for the heart beat. I knew she had already passed on; without a groan, a sigh or recognition of our belated presence she had gone into the Great Beyond as thousands of mothers go every year. I looked at that drawn face now stilled in death. I placed her thin hands across her breast and recalled how hard they had pleaded with me on that last memorable occasion of parting. The gentle woman, the devoted mother, the loving wife had passed on leaving behind her a frantic husband, helpless in his loneliness, bewildered in his helplessness as he paced up and down the room, hands clenching his head, moaning "My God! My God! My God!"

The Revolution came—but not as it has been pictured nor as history relates that revolutions have come. It came in my own life. It began in my very being as I walked home that night after I had closed the eyes and covered with a sheet the body of that little helpless mother whose life had been sacrificed to ignorance.

After I left that desolate house I walked and walked and walked; for hours and hours I kept on, bag in hand, thinking, regretting, dreading to stop; fearful of my conscience, dreading to face my own accusing soul. At three in the morning I arrived home still clutching a heavy load the weight of which I was quite unconscious.

I entered the house quietly, as was my custom, and looked out of the window down upon the dimly lighted, sleeping city. As I stood at the window and looked out, the miseries and problems of that sleeping city arose before me in a clear vision like a panorama: crowded homes, too many children; babies dying in infancy; mothers overworked; baby nurseries; children neglected and hungry—mothers so nervously wrought they could not give the little things the comfort nor care they needed; mothers half sick most of their lives—"always ailing, never failing"; women made into drudges; children working in cellars; children aged six and seven pushed into the labor market to help earn a living; another baby on the way; still another; yet another; a baby born dead—great relief; an older child dies—sorrow, but nevertheless relief—insurance helps; a mother's death—children scattered into institutions; the father, desperate, drunken; he slinks away to become an outcast in a society which has trapped him. . . .

. . . For hours I stood, motionless and tense, expecting something to happen. I watched the lights go out, I saw the darkness gradually give way to the first shimmer of dawn, and then a colorful sky heralded the rise of the sun. I knew a new day had come for me and a new world as well.

It was like an illumination. I could now see clearly the various social strata of our life; all its mass problems seemed to be centered around uncontrolled breeding. There was only one thing to be done: call out, start the alarm, set the heather on fire! Awaken the womanhood of America to free the motherhood of the world! I released from my almost paralyzed hand the nursing bag which unconsciously I had clutched, threw it across the room, tore the uniform from my body, flung it into a corner, and renounced all palliative work forever.

I would never go back again to nurse women's ailing bodies while their miseries were as vast as the stars. I was now finished with superficial cures, with doctors and nurses and social workers who were brought face to face with this overwhelming truth of women's needs and yet turned to pass on the other side. They must be made to see these facts. I resolved that women should have knowledge of contraception. They have every right to know about their own bodies. I would strike out—I would scream from the housetops. I would tell the world what was going on in the lives of these poor women. I *would* be heard. No matter what it should cost. *I would be heard.*

REFLECTING ON MEANING

1. What reasons does Sanger give to explain why she became dissatisfied with her work as a nurse? Why does she call this work "palliative"? How did the work she was later to do differ from her earlier work?

2. Sanger did not return to Mrs. Sacks in a few days, as she had promised she would. Why do you think she chose not to?

3. What does Sanger mean when she says that "the Revolution came"? In what ways was this revolution a personal one? What larger revolution is she also alluding to?

EXPLORING RHETORICAL STRATEGIES

1. What is the significance of the title of this selection? In what ways was Sanger's experience an awakening? In what ways was it also a revolt?

2. Sanger does a good job of showing what she saw as well as describing what she experienced. Where does she help her audience see for themselves what she saw? What does she accomplish in doing this?

3. What is the effect of the repetition in Sanger's concluding paragraph? In what ways does she use italics to lend an oral quality to her sentences? In what ways does she effectively express the depth of her commitment to the cause of birth control?

Birth Control–A Parent's Problem or Woman's?

MARGARET SANGER

In this excerpt from Woman and the New Race, *published in 1920, Margaret Sanger shifts away from the personal perspective of the preceding selection to argue that women must take responsibility for birth control.*

The problem of birth control has arisen directly from the effort of the feminine spirit to free itself from bondage. Woman herself has wrought that bondage through her reproductive powers and while enslaving herself has enslaved the world. The physical suffering to be relieved is chiefly woman's. Hers, too, is the love life that dies first under the blight of too prolific breeding. Within her is wrapped up the future of the race—it is hers to make or mar. All of these considerations point unmistakably to one fact—it is woman's duty as well as her privilege to lay hold of the means of freedom. Whatever men may do, she cannot escape the responsibility. For ages she has been deprived of the opportunity to meet this obligation. She is now emerging from her helplessness. Even as no one can share the suffering of the overburdened mother, so no one can do this work for her. Others may help, but she and she alone can free herself.

The basic freedom of the world is woman's freedom. A free race cannot be born of slave mothers. A woman enchained cannot choose but give a measure of that bondage to her sons and daughters. No woman can call herself free who does not own and control her body. No woman can call herself free until she can choose consciously whether she will or will not be a mother.

It does not greatly alter the case that some women call themselves free because they earn their own livings, while others profess freedom because they defy the conventions of sex relationship. She who earns her own living gains a sort of freedom that is not to be undervalued, but in quality and in quantity it is of little account beside the untrammeled choice of mating or not mating, of being a mother or not being a mother. She gains food and clothing and shelter, at least, without submitting to the charity of her companion, but the earning of her own living does not give her the development of her inner sex urge, far deeper and more powerful in its outworkings than any of these externals. In order to have that development, she must still meet and solve the problem of motherhood.

With the so-called "free" woman, who chooses a mate in defiance of convention, freedom is largely a question of character and audacity. If she does attain to an unrestricted choice of a mate, she is still in a position to be enslaved through her reproductive powers. Indeed, the pressure of law and custom upon the woman not legally married is likely to make her more of a slave than the woman fortunate enough to marry the man of her choice.

Look at it from any standpoint you will, suggest any solution you will, conventional or unconventional, sanctioned by law or in defiance of law, woman is in the same position, fundamentally, until she is able to determine for herself whether she will be a mother and to fix the number of her offspring. This unavoidable situation is alone enough to make birth control, first of all, a woman's problem. On the very face of the matter, voluntary motherhood is chiefly the concern of the woman.

It is persistently urged, however, that since sex expression is the act of two, the responsibility of controlling the results should not be placed upon woman alone. Is it fair, it is asked, to give her, instead of the man, the task of protecting herself when she is, perhaps, less rugged in physique than her mate, and has, at all events, the normal, periodic inconveniences of her sex?

We must examine this phase of her problem in two lights—that of the ideal, and of the conditions working toward the ideal. In an ideal society, no doubt, birth control would become the concern of the man as well as the woman. The hard, inescapable fact which we encounter to-day is that man has not only refused any such responsibility, but has individually and collectively sought to prevent woman from obtaining knowledge by which she could assume this responsibility for herself. She is still in the position of a dependent to-day because her mate has refused to consider her as an individual apart from his needs. She is still bound because she has in the past left the solution of the problem to him. Having left it to him, she finds that instead of rights, she has only such privileges as she has gained by petitioning, coaxing and cozening. Having left it to him, she is exploited, driven and enslaved to his desires.

While it is true that he suffers many evils as the consequence of this situation, she suffers vastly more. While it is true that he should be awakened to the cause of these evils, we know that they come home to her with crushing force every day. It is she who has the long burden of carrying, bearing and rearing the unwanted children. . . . It is her heart that the sight of the deformed, the subnormal, the undernourished, the overworked child smites first and oftenest and hardest. It is *her* love life that dies first in the fear of undesired pregnancy. It is her opportunity for self expression that perishes first and most hopelessly because of it. . . .

Conditions, rather than theories, facts, rather than dreams, govern the problem. They place it squarely upon the shoulders of woman. She has learned that whatever the moral responsibility of the man in this direction may be, he does not discharge it. She has learned that, lovable and considerate as the individual husband may be, she has nothing to expect from men in the mass, when they make laws and decree customs. She knows that regardless of what ought to be, the brutal, unavoidable fact is that she will never receive her freedom until she takes it for herself.

Having learned this much, she has yet something more to learn. Women are too much inclined to follow in the footsteps of men, to try to think as men think, to try to solve the general problems of life as men solve them. If after attaining their freedom, women accept conditions in the spheres of government, industry, art, morals and religion as they find them, they will be but taking a leaf out of man's book. The woman is not needed to do man's work. She is not needed to think man's thoughts. She need not fear that the masculine mind, almost universally dominant, will fail to take care of its own. Her mission is not to enhance the masculine spirit, but to express the feminine; hers is not to preserve a man-made world, but to create a human world by the infusion of the feminine element into all of its activities.

Woman must not accept; she must challenge. She must not be awed by that which has been built up around her; she must reverence that within her which struggles for expression. Her eyes must be less upon what is and more clearly upon what should be. She must listen only with a frankly questioning attitude to the dogmatized opinions of man-made society. When she chooses her new, free course of action, it must be in the light of her own opinion—of her own intuition. Only so can she give play to the feminine spirit. Only thus can she free her mate from the bondage which he wrought for himself when he wrought hers. Only thus can she restore to him that of which he robbed himself in restricting her. Only thus can she remake the world. . . .

Woman must have her freedom—the fundamental freedom of choosing whether or not she shall be a mother and how many children she will have. Regardless of what man's attitude may be, that problem is hers—and before it can be his, it is hers alone.

She goes through the vale of death alone, each time a babe is born. As it is the right neither of man nor the state to coerce her into this ordeal, so it is her right to decide whether she will endure it. That right to decide imposes upon her the duty of clearing the way to knowledge by which she may make and carry out the decision.

Birth control is woman's problem. The quicker she accepts it as hers and hers alone, the quicker will society respect motherhood. The quicker, too, will the world be made a fit place for her children to live.

REFLECTING ON MEANING

1. According to Sanger, why is birth control necessarily a concern of women but not of men? Do you agree that women should take complete responsibility for contraception? Should it be a joint responsibility shared by a man and a woman? Why or why not?

2. Sanger asserts that "no woman can call herself free who does not own and control her body." What does she mean? To what extent

does contraception provide such control? To what extent do you agree or disagree with Sanger's assertion? Why?

3. Attaining freedom, Sanger maintains, is not enough; rather, women must "challenge" the masculine world. What does she mean? According to Sanger, how would such an endeavor also free men?

EXPLORING RHETORICAL STRATEGIES

1. Sanger uses the language of slavery to describe mandatory pregnancy. Is her analogy appropriate? What rhetorical strength does she derive from it?

2. What is Sanger's tone in this excerpt? How does her tone reinforce her purpose? In what ways does the tone of this selection differ from that of "Awakening and Revolt"? What similarities do you see?

3. Part of the rhetorical strength of this selection derives from Sanger's effective use of repetition in sentence structure. How many instances of repetition can you find? What effect does it create?

Chapter 7 _____

RACE AND FEMININITY

Ain't I a Woman?

SOJOURNER TRUTH

Sojourner Truth (1795–1883) was a former slave and well-known abolitionist who gave the following speech at the Akron Women's Rights Convention in 1851. After hearing several "men of the cloth" explain why women were not the equal of men, Truth advanced to the podium and offered this brief, yet powerful rebuttal of their arguments.

Well, children, where there is so much racket there must be something out of kilter. I think that 'twixt the negroes of the South and the women at the North, all talking about rights, the white men will be in a fix pretty soon. But what's all this here talking about?

That man over there says that women need to be helped into carriages, and lifted over ditches, and to have the best place everywhere. Nobody ever helps me into carriages, or over mud-puddles, or gives me any best place! And ain't I a woman? Look at me! Look at my arm! I have ploughed and planted, and gathered into barns, and no man could head me! And ain't I a woman? I could work as much and eat as much as a man–when I could get it–and bear the lash as well! And ain't I a woman? I have borne thirteen children, and seen them most all sold off to slavery, and when I cried out with my mother's grief, none but Jesus heard me! And ain't I a woman?

Then they talk about this thing in the head; what's this they call it? [Intellect, someone whispers.] That's it, honey. What's that

got to do with women's rights or negro's rights? If my cup won't
hold but a pint, and yours holds a quart, wouldn't you be mean not
to let me have my little half-measure full?

Then that little man in black there, he says women can't have
as much rights as men, 'cause Christ wasn't a woman! Where did
your Christ come from? Where did your Christ come from? From
God and a woman! Man had nothing to do with Him.

If the first woman God ever made was strong enough to turn
the world upside down all alone, these women together ought to be
able to turn it back, and get it right side up again! And now they is
asking to do it, the men better let them.

Obliged to you for hearing me, and now old Sojourner ain't
got nothing more to say.

REFLECTING ON MEANING

1. In this essay, Sojourner Truth refutes four important arguments
by men who are opposed to equal rights for women: women are
fragile and helpless, men possess superior intellect, Christ was a
man, and Eve sinned against humanity. What are Truth's responses to these arguments? How does she invert each male argument and refute its supposed logic?

2. The early women's movement was peopled predominantly by
middle- and upper-class white women who wished to gain voting
rights. How does Truth's response to the assertion that women's
fragility and helplessness necessitate special treatment reveal the
intricacies of the issues of race and class? What lessons might
Truth be attempting to deliver to the middle- and upper-class
white feminists at the Akron Women's Rights Convention? Why
is the question, "And ain't I a woman?" such a powerful and appropriate rejoinder?

3. Why does Truth begin her speech by saying that "the white men
will be in a fix pretty soon"? To what historical circumstances is
she referring? How were the circumstances of blacks and
women similar and dissimilar in the mid-nineteenth century?
Near the end of her speech, she says, "And now they is asking to
do it, the men better let them." What does she mean by this?
Could this statement combined with her reference to Eve empower women? Could it be interpreted as a threat? Why or why
not?

EXPLORING RHETORICAL STRATEGIES

1. Sojourner Truth asks ten questions in the course of her speech. First, she states a fact; then, she asks a question. What is the rhetorical effect of this technique? Four times she asks, "And ain't I a woman?" Why? What unasked questions and unspoken answers might this essay create in the minds of the 1851 audience? How might a contemporary audience respond to this speech? Are these issues still relevant today?

2. Sojourner Truth, a slim black woman, was almost six feet tall. She begins this speech by addressing her audience as "children." Why would a former slave address a predominantly white audience in this way? What is the rhetorical effect of her references to members of her audience as "honey" and "that little man in black there"? At the end of her speech, she says, "Obliged to you for hearing me, and now old Sojourner ain't got nothing more to say." What response might her original audience have to this closing statement? What is the tone of this essay? What specific lines of this speech might a powerful speaker enhance?

3. Because Sojourner Truth never learned to read or write, this speech was recorded by the conference presider, Frances Gage, who made the claim that her speech changed the tide of the convention. Considering that this speech was a verbal response to arguments that Truth had just heard, how effective are her responses to each of the four arguments? In response to the religious arguments of the males in attendance, how might Truth's biblical explanations have influenced the opinions of the religious members of her audience?

Sisters Under the Skin?
Confronting Race and Sex

ELLEN WILLIS

Black feminists and white feminists need to come to a joint realization that the project of feminist solidarity involves eradicating both racism and sexism. Essayist Ellen Willis contends that the current divisiveness between these two groups is a result of misunderstandings and errors on both sides.

R ecently, at a feminist meeting, a black woman argued that in American society race is a more absolute division than sex, a more basic determinant of social identity. This started an intense discussion: if someone shook us out of a deep sleep and demanded that we define ourselves, what would we blurt out first? The black woman said "black woman." Most of the white women said "woman"; some said "lesbian." No one said "white person" or "white woman."

I'm not sure it makes sense to say that one social division is more absolute than another. I wonder if it isn't more a matter of different kinds of division. Most blacks and whites live in separate communities, in different social, cultural, and economic worlds, while most women and men share each other's daily, intimate lives and cooperate, even if unequally, in such elemental activities as fucking, procreating, and keeping a household going. On the other hand, a man and a woman can spend their lives together and have such disparate versions of their "common" experience that they might as well live on different planets. Do I feel more distant from black women than from white men? Everything else (class) being equal? (Except that it usually isn't.) In some ways yes, in some ways no. But whatever the objective truth, my sex feels more basic to my identity than my race. This is not surprising: in a sexist society it's impossible to take one's femaleness for granted; in a racist society whiteness is simply generic humanness, entirely unremarkable. Suppose, though, that a black revolution were to seriously challenge my racial privileges? Suppose I had to confront every day, every hour, the question of which side I'm on?

Such questions excite and disturb me. Like talk about sexuality, discussions of the racial-sexual nexus radiate danger and taboo—a sign that the participants are on to something. Lately such discussions, mostly initiated by black women, are happening more often. They raise the heartening possibility of connecting, and in the process revitalizing, the unhappily divergent discourses of feminism and black liberation. This could be the first step toward creating a new feminist radicalism, whose interracial, interclass bonds go deeper than lowest-common-denominator coalition politics.

One of the women at the meeting suggested that I read *Sally Hemmings,* Barbara Chase-Riboud's controversial historical novel about Thomas Jefferson's black mistress. I found it a devastating study of the psychology of masters and slaves, the politics of romantic love, the relations between black and white women, and the institution of the family. Much of its power lies in the way the author merges the race and sex of each character into a seamless whole, bringing home the point that to abstract these categories is already to falsify experience. So long as whiteness and maleness remain the norm, white women can think of themselves as "women," black men as "blacks"; but black women, doubly the Other, must be constantly aware of their dual identity at the same time that they suffer from both racial and sexual invisibility. In forcing the rest of us to see them, they also present us with new and far less tidy pictures of ourselves.

This suggests that confronting the oppression of black women means more than taking in new information or taking up new issues. It also means questioning the intellectual frameworks that the (male-dominated) black and (white-dominated) feminist movements have set up. If race and sex are experientially inseparable, can we (should we) still analyze them separately? If all women are subject to male supremacy—yet black and white women play out their relations with men (both inside and outside their own communities) in different ways—do they still have a common core of female experience, a common political oppression *as women?* Theoretically, the different situations of black women and black men should raise the same sort of question. But in practice black women have tended to single out their relation to white women and feminism as the more painful problematic issue. This subject is now bursting through a decade's sediment of sloganeering, ritualistic condemnations, and liberal apologies to inform some provocative new writing.

But first, I feel I have to say something about Angela Davis. Her *Women, Race and Class* may have been inspired by all this ferment, but the kindest judgment I can make is that it misses the

point. From Davis's orthodox Marxist perspective (still CP after all
these years!), in which economic relations determine all, while sexual relations have no material status and sexism is merely a set of
bad attitudes, the question of how racial and sexual politics interact
loses its meaning: Davis strips racism of its psychocultural dimension and treats it strictly as a form of economic exploitation; she
tends to ignore sexism altogether, except when invoking it as an
excuse for white bourgeois feminists to undermine the struggles of
black and working people. (For instance, she rightly condemns the
racism of white suffragists outraged at the prospect that black men
would get the vote before white women—but rationalizes the sexism that prompted black men to sell out women of both races by
agreeing that the black male vote should have priority. Black men's
"sexist attitudes," Davis argues, were "hardly a sound reason for ar-
resting the progress of the overall struggle for Black liberation"—
and never mind the effect on that struggle of denying the vote to
half the black population.) Still, it would be a mistake to simply dismiss Davis's book as an anachronism. In more subtle and ambiguous forms, its brand of left antifeminism continues to influence
women's thinking. Besides, Angela Davis is a public figure, and
Women, Race and Class will undoubtedly outsell both the books I'm
about to discuss.

    Gloria I. Joseph is black; Jill Lewis is white. In *Common Differ-
ences: Conflicts in Black and White Feminist Perspectives,* they attempt
to explore their separate histories, confront misunderstandings,
and move toward "collaborative struggle." The book has the flavor
of an open-ended political conversation; for the most part the authors write separate chapters, each commenting from her own perspective on various aspects of sexual politics. The result is uneven,
full of intellectual loose ends and contradictions, and both writers
have an unfortunate penchant for clotted, obfuscatory prose. But
Common Differences does help to clarify touchy areas of black-white
conflict. Joseph's chapters—which taught me a lot, especially about
black mothers and daughters—are a valuable counterweight (and
an implicit rebuke) to the tendency of white feminist theorists to
base their generalizations about the female condition on white
women's experience. In discussing black women's lives, Joseph
uses a time-honored feminist method: she records group discussions and individual comments, picks out common themes and
contradictions, and tries to draw conclusions. The immediacy of
this material exposes white feminist parochialism more effectively
than any abstract argument.

    Without denying the movement's shortcomings, Lewis sets
out to debunk the stereotype of the spoiled, elitist "women's

libber." The feminist movement, she maintains, deserves recognition as the only social movement to challenge the status of women as women. She argues that white feminists have been struggling toward a deeper understanding of race and class, and that even those sectors of the movement most narrowly oriented to white middle-class concerns "have engaged in and won concrete struggles that potentially open up new terrain for *all* women."

In their introduction, Joseph and Lewis agree that "as a political movement, women's liberation did and does touch on questions which in different ways affect *all* women's lives." But *Common Differences* is much more about difference than about commonality. In *Ain't I a Woman: Black Women and Feminism* Bell Hooks strides boldly beyond pluralism to the rockier ground of synthesis. While Hooks also stresses the uniqueness of black women's experience and the ways it has been discounted, her aim is to enlarge the theoretical framework of feminism. To this end she analyzes black women's condition in a historical context, tracing the basic patterns of black female oppression to slavery and developing three intertwined themes: black men's sexism, white women's racism, and the effect of white men's racial-sexual politics on the relations between black and white women. Hooks is a contentious writer, and I don't always agree with her contentions, but *Ain't I a Women* has an intellectual vitality and daring that should set new standards for the discussion of race and sex.

The central political question these books raise is why the contemporary feminist movement has been so white. Most critics of the movement have offered a simple answer: white feminists' racism has driven black women away. This indictment is true as far as it goes, but it already takes for granted facts that need explaining. Why, in the first place, was it primarily white women, rather than black women or both groups simultaneously, who felt impelled to mobilize against sexism? And why did so many politically conscious black women reject the movement (in some cases the very idea of feminism) out of hand, rather than insisting that it purge its theory and practice of racism, or organizing groups committed to a nonracist feminist politics? Antifeminist leftists have typically argued that sexual politics are inherently a white middle-class crotchet, irrelevant to women who are "really"–i.e., economically and racially–oppressed. Or else (this is Angela Davis's main strategy) they redefine feminism to mean women fighting together against racism and capitalism, and conclude that black and white working-class women have been the leaders of the *real* feminist struggle. Either way they imply that sexism is not a problem for black women, if indeed it is a problem at all.

Hooks, Joseph, and Lewis reject this idea. They assume that black women have a stake in women's liberation, and see white feminists' racism as part of a complex social history that has shaped black women's politics. Bell Hooks argues that estrangement between black and white women goes all the way back to slavery. The terms of the conflict, as she sees it, were defined by white men who applied racism to a Victorian sexual (and class) ideology that divided women into two categories: good (chaste, delicate, to be protected and idealized) and bad (licentious, unrefined, to be exploited and punished). While the white upper-class southern woman represented the feminine ideal, black female slaves were stigmatized, in schizoid fashion, both as bad women—therefore deserving to be raped and beaten—and as nonwomen: in doing the same work as men, black women threatened the ideology of female inferiority, a contradiction resolved by defining them as neuter beasts of burden.

At the same time, the white woman's power to collaborate in oppressing blacks softened and obscured the reality of her own inferior position. She exercised this power most directly over female slaves, whom she often treated with the special viciousness of the insecure boss. No doubt the degraded status of black women also reminded her, subconsciously at least, of what can happen to any female who provokes men into dropping the mask of patriarchal benevolence. As Hooks obsesses, the manifest cruelty of white women's own husbands, fathers, and brothers "served as a warning of what might be their fate should they not maintain a passive stance. Surely, it must have occurred to white women that were enslaved black women not available to bear the brunt of such intense antiwoman aggression, they themselves might have been the victims." As a result, the very identification that might have led white women to black women's defense probably had the opposite effect. White men's sexual pursuit of black women also exposed white women's humiliating position: they could neither prevent their husbands' behavior nor claim a comparable freedom for themselves. Instead they expressed their anger, salvaged their pride, and defended their own good-woman status by vilifying black women as seducers and sluts.

Hooks shows that what she calls the "devaluation of black womanhood" did not end with slavery but remains a potent source of black women's rage. Her account of how black women are systematically disparaged as whores, castrating matriarchs, and sexless mammies explains a crucial ingredient of black female hostility to the women's movement. Clearly, when white feminists ignored black female experience and in effect equated "woman" with "white woman," the insult had a double meaning for black

women: it suggested that we were not only reinforcing white supremacy but trying to have it both ways by preserving our monopoly on femininity and its rewards (respect, status, financial support)
while demanding the option of rejecting it. This perception of bad
faith fueled the angry denunciations of feminism as "white
women's business."

But envying white women's "femininity" is a trap for black
women, as Hooks is well aware. Idealization of the white woman's
status has tended to divert black women from demanding sexual
justice to attacking black men for their inability to support stay-at-
home wives. Many black women have endorsed black male demands for female subservience in the hope that at last they would
get a crack at the pedestal. At the same time, their envy of white
women has been mixed with contempt, an emotion that led some
black women to insist they didn't need a movement because they
were already liberated. Another illusion in Hooks's relentless catalogue: strength in adversity and the need to make a living are not
the same thing as freedom.

Gloria Joseph emphasizes the painful collisions of black and
female identity. As she says, "an individual cannot be two separate
entities." Yet black women suffer from two modes of oppression
and so are implicated, like it or not, in two social movements at
once. At best this involves a double burden, at worst a continuing
conflict of loyalties and priorities. Joseph shows that deep ambiva-
lences permeate black women's thinking—on black men (distrust
and antagonism mixed with solidarity, affection, and protective-
ness), on sex ("a 'desirable no-no,' an 'attractive nuisance'"), on
feminism itself (most of Joseph's respondents reject the movement
but endorse its goals). Her argument suggests that black women
have been slow to commit themselves to feminism—especially the
more radical aspects of sexual politics—for fear of weakening their
ties with the black community and the black struggle. Jill Lewis
points out that white middle-class women could focus singlemind-
edly on feminism because "they did not have the stakes of *racial*
unity or solidarity with White men that the Black women had with
Black men" and because their privileges left them "free of the survival struggles that are priorities for minority and working-class
women." If anything, class and racial privileges (particularly education) spurred their consciousness of sexual injustice by raising
expectations that were thwarted purely because they were women.

Ironically, Joseph exemplifies the dilemma she describes: like
many other black women who define themselves as feminists, she
draws the line at calling black men oppressors. While Joseph and
Lewis agree that black and white women are oppressed as women,

they uncritically assume that male supremacy is a product of white culture, and that the concept does not really apply to male-female relations among blacks, except insofar as all white institutions and values shape black life. Lewis asserts that institutionalized sexism in America was imported by European immigrants, as if Native American, African, and other nonwhite cultures were free of male dominance. In fact, no anthropologist, feminist or otherwise, has ever come up with convincing evidence of a culture in which some form of male dominance does not exist.

Lewis and Joseph argue that because black men do not have the same worldly power as white men, "Male dominance as a salient problematic factor in male-female sexual relationships cannot be considered as a universal trait applicable to all men." But Joseph's own descriptions of black women's attitudes toward sex, men, and marriage—not to mention their struggles to bring up children alone—belie this view. Rather, her evidence confirms that despite black men's economic and social subordination to whites they share with all men certain male supremacist prerogatives, including physical and sexual aggression, the assumption of male superiority, and refusal to share responsibility for child rearing and housework. Joseph and Lewis also make the puzzling claim that sexist repression is more severe for white women because "Black women can be kept in their places via racism alone." Does racism alone account for black women's oppression as mothers, workers (including domestic workers), welfare recipients, prostitutes, victims of rape and sexual exploitation?

All this adds up to a bad case of conceptual confusion. You can't simultaneously agree that black women need feminism and deny the basic premise of feminism—that men have power over women. Women who engage in this form of doublethink still have a toe or two in the camp of left antifeminism; while rejecting crude economism of the Angela Davis variety, they assume that sexism is perpetuated not by men in general but by a white capitalist ruling class.

Hooks insists on the reality of black male sexism. Discussing the experience of female slaves, she angrily refutes the cliché that "the most cruel and dehumanizing impact of slavery...was that black men were stripped of their masculinity." This idea, she argues, merely reflects the sexist assumption that men's experience is more important than women's and that "the worst that can happen to a man is that he be made to assume the social status of woman." In fact, though all slaves suffered brutal oppression, "black men were allowed to maintain some semblance of their societally defined masculine role." Noting that American blacks came from African patriarchal cultures, Hooks rejects the idea that black men learned sexism from whites and the myth (repeated once again by Angela Davis) that within the slave community men and women were equal. On the contrary, the slaves accepted the concept of male superiority, and black families maintained a sexual division of labor, with women doing the cooking, cleaning, and child care. Nor did slave-holders assign black men "women's work." Black women, however, were forced by their white masters to perform both "masculine" and "feminine" functions, working alongside black men at backbreaking labor in the fields, while also serving as houseworkers, breeders, and sexual objects.

Hooks implicitly links what she sees as black women's false consciousness about sexism with their political isolation: while the sexism of black male activists has forced black women to choose between asserting themselves as women and maintaining racial solidarity, the racism of white feminists has reinforced and justified that split. *Ain't I a Woman* describes how this combination of pressures undermined black women's efforts to participate in both 19th and 20th century feminist movements. In dissecting the rhetoric of the contemporary black and women's movements, Hooks shows how sexism has been promoted as a cure for racism, sisterhood as a rationale for ignoring it. Black power advocates, confusing liberation with the assertion of their "manhood," embraced a white man's contention that a black matriarchy was the cause of their problems, and called on black women to advance the black cause by being submissive; some even suggested that sexual equality was a white racist idea, indicative of the white man's effeteness and decadence. Black Muslims tried to reverse the racist Victorian paradigm, defining black women as the feminine ideal and white women as devils (and establishing rigid patriarchal families).

Meanwhile the early radical feminists were claiming that the division between men and women was the most basic social hierarchy, and that since men had ruled every known political system, racism was basically a male problem ("men dominate women, a few men dominate the rest"–Redstockings Manifesto). This analysis, which I and most of my political cohorts then subscribed to, has had a good deal of influence on the movement as a whole. It has two erroneous implications: that it's impossible for white women to oppress black men, and that racial conflict between black women and white women has no objective basis, but is (on both sides) an inauthentic antagonism that only serves the interests of men. Radical feminists understood, theoretically, that to build female unity white women had to oppose racism and change their own racist attitudes and behavior. We were sharply critical of lib-

eral feminists who defined women's freedom in terms of professional careers and formal equality within a racist, class-stratified
social system. Yet emotionally our belief that sex was a more basic
division than race allowed us to evade responsibility for racism. It
was tempting to imagine that simply by doing what we wanted
most passionately to do—build a radical feminist movement—we
would also be fighting racism; tempting, too, to play down how
much we benefited from being white. For a while feminism seemed
a way out of the classic bind of white middle-class radicals: we no
longer had to see ourselves as privileged people wondering where
we fit into the revolutionary struggle; we too were part of an oppressed class with a historic destiny.

Hooks's anger at this refusal to be accountable is well-
deserved. But when she gets down to specifics, she tends to over-
simplify and at times rewrite history. In her indictment of "white
upper and middle-class feminists" (Abby Rockefeller aside, who are
these upper-class feminists I keep hearing about?), the movement
becomes a monolith. The political differences between liberals and
radicals, the social conditions that allowed the former to co-opt and
isolate the latter, the fierce intramovement debates about race and
class are ignored or dismissed. White feminists' main aim, Hooks
charges, has been to join the male power structure; the movement
has posed no threat to the system.

This is silly. The women's movement has been no more or
less opportunistic than the black movement, the labor movement,
or any other mass movement successful enough to attract power
mongers. Feminists have not succeeded in making a revolution
(neither, I believe, has the rest of the left), but—as Jill Lewis ably argues—we did create a new political arena and set a revolutionary
process in motion. (Among other things, we established the political context in which a book like *Ain't I a Woman* can be written and
read.) The best measure of our threat to the system is the virulence
of the reaction against us.

Hooks also indulges in overkill when she tries to explain white
feminists' appropriation of female experience in terms of two different, even contradictory forms of racism. My own view is that the
right explanation is the obvious one: we were acting on the unconscious racist assumption that our experience was representative,
along with the impulse to gloss over racial specificities so as to keep
the "complication" of racism from marring our vision of female
unity. Hooks makes these points, but she also argues that white feminists have shared the racist/sexist perception of black women as
nonwomen. In the process she accuses white feminists of claiming
that black women are oppressed only by racism, not sexism, and

denying that black men can be oppressive. These charges are, to put it mildly, befuddling. If there was any point radical feminists insisted on it was that all women were oppressed because of their sex, and that all men had the power to oppress women. In response, antifeminist black women (along with black and white male leftists) made the arguments Hooks now puts in our mouths, and denounced us as racists for attributing a "white problem" to black people. Inevitably, many white women have echoed these arguments, but it's perverse to blame feminists for them.

In fact, white feminists have generally been quite conscious of black women *as women;* it's their blackness we've had trouble with. Straightforward reactionary racism exaggerates differences and denies commonalities; liberal racism, more typical of white feminists, does the opposite. Since the denial of black women's "femininity" is such a central issue for Hooks, she mistakenly assumes that protecting an exclusive claim to femininity is equally an issue for all white women. On the contrary, white feminists felt free to challenge received definitions of femininity because we took for granted our right to be considered women. And it was precisely because our claim to womanhood was not an issue for us that we were insensitive to black women's pain at being denied it by racial fiat. Many white feminists recognized that the division between white women and black women had something to do with good girls and bad girls. (Shulamith Firestone, in *The Dialetic of Sex,* discusses this idea at length.) What we didn't see was the asymmetry: we could decide to be bad, or play at being bad; black women had no choice.

Hooks's misperception of white feminists' psychology also leads her to argue that their analogies between women and blacks were designed "to evoke in the minds of racist white men an image of white womanhood being degraded" by association with black people, especially black men. Again, the "image of white womanhood" had much less resonance than Hooks imagines, either for white feminists or for the white liberal and leftist men who were our immediate targets. The main reason that '60s feminists relied so heavily on comparisons between sexism and racism is that white male politicos recognized the race issue as morally legitimate, while dismissing feminism as "a bunch of chicks with personal problems." If anything, we were trying to evoke in these men the same guilt about sexism that they already felt about racism; since we hadn't yet experienced the drawbacks of liberal guilt, we craved its validation. We also hoped, naively enough, to convince black men to renounce their sexism and identify with the feminist cause.

Hooks takes a hard line on analogies between women and blacks. She argues that they always imply a comparison between white women and black men, that they make black women invisible, obscure the issue of white women's racial privileges and divert attention from racism to white women's problems. Certainly racial-sexual analogies have been misused in all the ways Hooks cites, but I don't see these misuses as either invariable or necessary. Many feminists have made analogies between women and blacks in full awareness that they are talking about two overlapping groups; what they mean to compare is two sets of oppressive relations, male-female and white-black. And though the dynamics and effects of racism and sexism differ in important ways, the parallels—legal, social, ideological—do exist. Which is why antiracist movements have been so instrumental in stimulating feminist consciousness and revolt.

Hooks refuses to recognize this. Scoffing at the idea that abolitionism inspired the first feminist wave, she says, "No 19th century white woman could grow to maturity without an awareness of institutionalized sexism." But of course 19th century white women—and for that matter my generation of white women—did exactly that. It is the essence of institutionalized sexism to pose as the natural order; to experience male dominance is one thing, to understand that it is political, therefore changeable, is quite another. For me and most feminists I know, that politicizing process was very much influenced by the civil rights and black power movements. Conversely, though feminism was not a miraculous antidote to our racist impulses and illusions, it did increase our understanding of racism.

Surely, the answer to exploitative comparisons between women and blacks is not to deny the organic link between antisexist and antiracist politics. Here Hooks, too, gets trapped in contradictory thinking. She argues that the issues of racism and sexism cannot really be separated, yet she repeatedly singles out racism as an issue that is not only separate from sexism but prior to it. According to Hooks, "American society is one in which racial imperialism supersedes sexual imperialism," and all black people, black men included, are absolutely lower on the social scale than any white woman. In other words, it is illegitimate for feminists to regard sexism as a category that can, at least theoretically, be abstracted from (and compared to) racism; but no comparable stricture applies to black liberationists.

Gloria Joseph agrees that, "In the end, it is a question of priorities, and given the nature of racism in this country, it should be obvious that the Black liberation struggle claims first priority." Most black feminists whose views I know about take a similar position. It is easy to see why; because racism is intertwined with, and in part defined by class oppression, black people as a group suffer an excruciating combination of economic hardship and social indignity that white middle-class women and even most white working-class women escape. (Of course this does not necessarily hold true for individuals—it can be argued that a middle-class educated black man is a lot better off than a white welfare mother from an Appalachian rural slum.) Besides, as Hooks points out, women without the insulation of racial or class privilege are also the most vulnerable to sexist oppression: a white professional woman can buy liberation from housework by hiring a black maid; she can also (for the time being) buy the legal abortion Medicaid patients are denied.

Left antifeminists have often used this line of reasoning to suggest that sexual issues should wait until racism and poverty are abolished. Black feminists, by definition, have rejected that idea. But what then does it mean, in practical political terms, to say that despite the irreducibly dual character of black women's oppression, their sex is less immediate an issue than their race? Specifically, what does this imply for the prospect of an antiracist feminist movement, or, more modestly, "collaborative struggle"?

While Hooks never really focuses on strategic questions, Joseph and Lewis often write as if black and white women are on fundamentally separate tracks. They refer, for instance, to "White feminism," a concept as self-contradictory as, say, "male socialism"; while one can speak of a feminism limited and flawed by white racist bias, it is *feminism* only to the extent that it challenges the subjection of women as a group. (The mechanical pluralism underlying the notion of separate-but-equal "White" and "Black" feminisms also impels the authors to capitalize "White." Though capitalizing "Black" may make sense as a polemical device for asserting black pride, racial self-assertion by white people is something else again.) But in discussing abortion, Jill Lewis endorses a specific approach to integrating feminism with race and class struggle. The strategy she describes has developed as a response to the abortion backlash, but the basic idea could be applied to almost any feminist issue. Since I think it's both appealing and fallacious, I want to discuss it in some detail.

Lewis argues that to "isolate" abortion as an issue and defend it in terms of freedom for women betrays a white middle-class bias: since black women suffer not only from being denied safe abortions but from sterilization abuse, inadequate health care, and poverty—all of which impinge on their reproductive choices—a radical approach to "reproductive rights" must address all these concerns. The trouble with this logic is that abortion is not just one of many medical or social services being rolled back by Reaganism; nor does the present opposition to abortion stem from the same sources or political motives as pressure toward sterilization. Abortion is first of all the key issue of the new right's antifeminist campaign, the ground on which a larger battle over the very idea of women's liberation is being fought. In essence, the antiabortionists are arguing that women who assert their free agency and refuse to be defined by their childbearing capacity are immoral. (In contrast, no one defends poverty or forced sterilization on principle.) So long as this moral attack on women is gaining ground, presenting abortion primarily as a health or social welfare measure is ineffective because it evades the underlying issue. Our choice right now is to defend abortion as a pivotal issue of women's freedom, or lose the battle by default. This is not to belittle the urgency of opposing sterilization abuse (which is, among other things, another expression of contempt for black femaleness) or demanding better health care. Nor is it to deny that all these issues are linked in important ways. My point is only that the reproductive rights strategy does not resolve the touchy question of priorities. Rather, while purporting to cover all bases, it submerges sexual politics in an economic and social welfare program.

Is this good for black women? Gloria Joseph points out that on the issue of abortion rights, "Black women have even more at stake, since it is they who suffer more from illegal and abusive abortions." They also suffer more from having unwanted children under horrendous conditions. If a sexual-political strategy offers the only real chance to preserve legal abortion and restore public funding, it is clearly in black women's interest. Since black women are faced with so many urgent problems, they may well have other priorities, but it doesn't follow that white women who concentrate on abortion are indulging a racist bias. On the contrary they're doing a crucial job that will benefit all women in the end.

All this suggests that the question of whether racism is worse (or more basic, or more pressing) than sexism matters less than the fact that both are intolerable. I don't agree with the white feminists Bell Hooks castigates for dismissing racial differences on the grounds that "oppression cannot be measured." It's clear to me that in demonstrable ways, some oppressed people are worse off than others. But I do question whose interests are really served by the measuring. Once it's established that black women are the most victimized group, and that most black men are more victimized than most white women—then what?

In my experience, this kind of ranking does not lead to a politics of genuine liberation, based on mutual respect and cooperation among oppressed groups, but instead provokes a politics of *ressentiment,* competition, and guilt. Black men tend to react not by recognizing the sexual oppression of black women but by rationalizing their antifeminism as a legitimate response to white women's privileges. White women who are sensitive to the imputation of racism tend to become hesitant and apologetic about asserting feminist greivances. As for white women who can't see beyond their own immediate interests, attempts to demote them in the ranks of the oppressed do nothing but make them feel unjustly attacked and confirmed in their belief that sexual and racial equality are separate, competing causes. The ultimate results are to reinforce left antifeminism, weaken feminist militance, widen the split between the black and feminist movements, and play into the divide and conquer tactics of white men ("We can do something for blacks or for women, but not both, so you folks fight it out"). Black women, caught in the racial-sexual crossfire, stand to lose the most.

Insistence on a hierarchy of oppression never radicalizes people, because the impulse behind it is moralistic. Its object is to get the "lesser victims" to stop being selfish, to agree that their own pain (however deeply they may feel it) is less serious and less deserving of attention (including their own) than someone else's. Its appeal is that it allows people at the bottom of social hierarchies to turn the tables and rule over a moral hierarchy of suffering and powerlessness. But whatever the emotional comfort of righteousness, it's a poor substitute for real change. And we ought to know by now that effective radical movements are not based on self-abnegation; rather, they emerge from the understanding that unless we heal the divisions among us, none of us can win.

The logic of competing oppressions does not heal divisions but intensifies them, since it invites endless and absurd extension—for every person who has no shoes, there is always someone who has no feet. (One might ask, by this logic, what Bell Hooks has to complain about next to a woman from a dirt-poor Third World country who was sold to her husband and had her clitoris cut off at age four.) White women will not become committed allies of black women because they're told that their own suffering is unimportant. What white women must be convinced of is that it's impossible to have it both ways—that the privileges we cling to are an insuperable obstacle to the freedom and equality we long for. We need to learn this lesson again and again. Good books help.

REFLECTING ON MEANING

1. Willis argues that "black women, doubly the Other, must be constantly aware of their dual identity at the same time that they suf-

fer from both racial and sexual invisibility." What does Willis mean? How does she illustrate this notion? Why aren't black men "doubly the Other"?

2. After discussing the work of several important feminist critics—Angela Davis, bell hooks, and Gloria I. Joseph and Jill Lewis—Willis proposes that some "conceptual confusion" exists. What is this confusion? What is the "doublethink" that some of these critics are engaging in? In what ways does Willis agree with hooks? On what issues does she disagree? How does hooks's opinion on the source of black men's sexism differ from the position taken by Davis?

3. According to Willis, in what ways have white feminists been insensitive to black women's issues? Why is the abortion issue so important for both black and white women? Willis suggests that the divisiveness between black and white women needs to be healed, or no one can win. Why would the "logic of competing oppressions" prevent solidarity? Do you agree or disagree with this position? Why or why not?

EXPLORING RHETORICAL STRATEGIES

1. A primary question raised by Willis's essay is whether "racism is worse (or more basic, or more pressing) than sexism." Is her juxtaposition and intermingling of the positions taken by Davis, hooks, Joseph, and Lewis effective in answering this question? At the end of the essay, how does Willis herself answer this question?

2. What is the purpose of this essay? What is the main point that Willis is trying to make? Who is Willis's intended audience: black feminists, white feminists, or both? What details of the essay reveal Willis's intention?

3. Through the course of her essay, Willis has critiqued the work of several writers. How might her last line, "Good books help," be interpreted? Is she being ironic or serious?

Invisibility Is an Unnatural Disaster:
Reflections of an Asian American Woman

MITSUYE YAMADA

How have Asian American women been rendered invisible in American society? Poet and essayist Mitsuye Yamada reflects on this question by relating her personal experience of this "unnatural disaster." She considers her own history of passive resistance and "resigned acceptance" to stereotypes and calls for Asian American women to gain recognition by asserting their own voices.

L ast year for the Asian segment of the Ethnic American Literature course I was teaching, I selected a new anthology entitled *Aiiieeeee!* compiled by a group of outspoken Asian American writers. During the discussion of the long but thought-provoking introduction to this anthology, one of my students blurted out that she was offended by its militant tone and that as a white person she was tired of always being blamed for the oppression of all the minorities. I noticed several of her classmates' eyes nodding in tacit agreement. A discussion of the "militant" voices in some of the other writings we had read in the course ensued. Surely, I pointed out, some of these other writings have been just as, if not more, militant as the words in this introduction? Had they been offended by those also but failed to express their feelings about them? To my surprise, they said they were not offended by any of the Black American, Chicano or American Indian writings, but were hard-pressed to explain why when I asked for an explanation. A little further discussion revealed that they "understood" the anger expressed by the Black and Chicanos and they "empathized" with the frustrations and sorrow expressed by the American Indian. But the Asian Americans??

Then finally, one student said it for all of them: "It made me angry. *Their* anger made *me* angry, because I didn't even know the Asian Americans felt oppressed. I didn't expect their anger."

At this time I was involved in an academic due process procedure begun as a result of a grievance I had filed the previous semester against the administrators at my college. I had filed a grievance for violation of my rights as a teacher who had worked in the district for almost eleven years. My student's remark "Their anger made me angry. . . I didn't expect their anger," explained for me the reactions of some of my own colleagues as well as the reactions of the administrators during those previous months. The grievance procedure was a time-consuming and emotionally draining process, but the basic principle was too important for me to ignore. That basic principle was that I, an individual teacher, do have certain rights which are given and my superiors cannot, should not, violate them with impunity. When this was pointed out to them, however, they responded with shocked surprise that I, of all people, would take them to task for violation of what was clearly written policy in our college district. They all seemed to exclaim, "We don't understand this; this is so uncharacteristic of her; she seemed such a nice person, so polite, so obedient, so non-trouble-making." What was even more surprising was once they were forced to acknowledge that I was determined to start the due process action, they assumed I was not doing it on my own. One of the administrators suggested someone must have pushed me into this, undoubtedly some of "those feminists" on our campus, he said wryly.

In this age when women are clearly making themselves visible on all fronts, I, an Asian American woman, am still functioning as a "front for those feminists" and therefore invisible. The realization of this sinks in slowly. Asian Americans as a whole are finally coming to claim their own, demanding that they be included in the multicultural history of our country. I like to think, in spite of my administrator's myopia, that the most stereotyped minority of them all, the Asian American woman, is just now emerging to become part of that group. It took forever. Perhaps it is important to ask ourselves why it took so long. We should ask ourselves this question just when we think we are emerging as a viable minority in the fabric of our society. I should add to my student's words, "because I didn't even know they felt oppressed," that it took this long because we Asian American women have not admitted to ourselves that we *were* oppressed. We, the visible minority that is invisible.

I say this because until a few years ago I have been an Asian American woman working among non-Asians in an educational institution where most of the decision-makers were men[1]; an Asian American woman thriving under the smug illusion that I was *not* the stereotypic image of the Asian woman because I had a career teaching English in a community college. I did not think anything assertive was necessary to make my point. People who know me, I reasoned, the ones who count, know who I am and what I think. Thus, even when what I considered a veiled racist remark was made in a casual social setting, I would "let it go" because it was pointless to argue with people who didn't even know their remark was racist. I had supposed that I was practicing passive resistance while being stereotyped, but it was so passive no one noticed I was resisting; it was so much my expected role that it ultimately rendered me invisible.

My experience leads me to believe that contrary to what I thought, I had actually been contributing to my own stereotyping. Like the hero in Ralph Ellison's novel *The Invisible Man,* I had become invisible to white Americans, and it clung to me like a bad habit. Like most bad habits, this one crept up on me because I took it in minute doses like Mithradates' poison and my mind and body adapted so well to it I hardly noticed it was there.

For the past eleven years I have busied myself with the usual chores of an English teacher, a wife of a research chemist, and a mother of four rapidly growing children. I hadn't even done much to shatter this particular stereotype: the middle class woman happy to be bringing home the extra income and quietly fitting into the man's world of work. When the Asian American woman is lulled into believing that people perceive her as being different from other Asian women (the submissive, subservient, ready-to-please, easy-to-get-along-with Asian woman), she is kept comfortably content with the state of things. She becomes ineffectual in the milieu in which she moves. The seemingly apolitical middle class woman and the apolitical Asian woman constituted a double invisibility.

I had created an underground culture of survival for myself and had become in the eyes of others the person I was trying not to be. Because I was permitted to go to college, permitted to take a stab at a career or two along the way, given "free choice" to marry and have a family, given a "choice" to eventually do both, I had assumed I was more or less free, not realizing that those who are free make and take choices; they do not choose from options proffered by "those out there."

I, personally, had not "emerged" until I was almost fifty years old. Apparently through a long conditioning process, I had learned how *not* to be seen for what I am. A long history of ineffectual activities had been, I realize now, initiation rites toward my eventual invisibility. The training begins in childhood; and for women and minorities, whatever is started in childhood is continued throughout their adult lives. I first recognized just how invisible I was in my first real confrontation with my parents a few years after the outbreak of World War II.

During the early years of the war, my older brother, Mike, and I left the concentration camp in Idaho to work and study at the University of Cincinnati. My parents came to Cincinnati soon after my father's release from Internment Camp (these were POW camps to which many of the Issei[2] men, leaders in their communities, were sent by the FBI), and worked as domestics in the suburbs. I did not see them too often because by this time I had met and was much influenced by a pacifist who was out on a "furlough" from a conscientious objectors' camp in Trenton, North Dakota. When my parents learned about my "boy friend" they were appalled and frightened. After all, this was the period when everyone in the country was expected to be one-hundred percent behind the war effort, and the Nisei[3] boys who had volunteered for the Armed Forces were out there fighting and dying to prove how American we really were. However, during interminable arguments with my father and overheard arguments between my parents, I was devastated to learn they were not so much concerned about my having become a pacifist, but they were more concerned about the possibility of my marrying one. They were understandably frightened (my father's prison years of course were still fresh on his mind) about repercussions on the rest of the family. In an attempt to make my father understand me, I argued that even if I didn't marry him, I'd still be a pacifist; but my father reassured me that it was "all right" for me to be a pacifist because as a Japanese national and a "girl" *it didn't make any difference to anyone.* In frustration I remember shouting, "But can't you see, *I'm* philosophically committed to the pacifist cause," but he dismissed this with "In my college days we used to call philosophy, foolosophy," and that was the end of that. When they were finally convinced I was not going to marry "my pacifist," the subject was dropped and we never discussed it again.

As if to confirm my father's assessment of the harmlessness of my opinions, my brother Mike, an American citizen, was suddenly expelled from the University of Cincinnati while I, "an enemy alien," was permitted to stay. We assumed that his stand as a pacifist, although he was classified a 4-F because of his health, contributed to his expulsion. We were told the Air Force was conducting sensitive wartime research on campus and requested his removal, but they apparently felt my presence on campus was not as threatening.

I left Cincinnati in 1945, hoping to leave behind this and other unpleasant memories gathered there during the war years, and plunged right into the politically active atmosphere at New York University where students, many of them returning veterans, were continuously promoting one cause or other by making speeches in Washington Square, passing out petitions, or staging demonstrations. On one occasion, I tagged along with a group of students who took a train to Albany to demonstrate on the steps of the State Capitol. I think I was the only Asian in this group of predominantly Jewish students from NYU. People who passed us were amused and shouted "Go home and grow up." I suppose Governor Dewey, who refused to see us, assumed we were a group of adolescents without a cause as most college students were considered to be during those days. It appears they weren't expecting any results from our demonstration. There were no newspersons, no security persons, no police. No one tried to stop us from doing what we were doing. We simply did "our thing" and went back to our studies until next time, and my father's words were again confirmed: it made no difference to anyone, being a young student demonstrator in peacetime, 1947.

Not only the young, but those who feel powerless over their own lives know what it is like not to make a difference on anyone or anything. The poor know it only too well, and we women have known it since we were little girls. The most insidious part of this conditioning process, I realize now, was that we have been trained not to expect a response in ways that mattered. We may be listened to and responded to with placating words and gestures, but our psychological mind set has already told us time and again that we were born into a ready-made world into which we must fit ourselves, and that many of us do it very well.

This mind set is the result of not believing that the political and social forces affecting our lives are determined by some person, or a group of persons, probably sitting behind a desk or around a conference table.

Just recently I read an article about "the remarkable track record of success" of the Nisei in the United States. One Nisei was quoted as saying he attributed our stamina and endurance to our ancestors whose characters had been shaped, he said, by their living in a country which has been constantly besieged by all manner of natural disasters, such as earthquakes and hurricanes. He said the Nisei has inherited a steely will, a will to endure and hence, to survive.

This evolutionary explanation disturbs me, because it equates the "act of God" (i.e., natural disasters) to the "act of man" (i.e., the war, the evacuation). The former is not within our power to alter, but the latter, I should think, is. By putting the "acts of God" on par with the acts of man, we shrug off personal responsibilities.

I have, for too long a period of time accepted the opinion of others (even though they were directly affecting my life) as if they were objective events totally out of my control. Because I separated such opinions from the persons who were making them, I accepted them the way I accepted natural disasters; and I endured them as inevitable. I have tried to cope with people whose points of view alarmed me in the same way that I had adjusted to natural phenomena, such as hurricanes, which plowed into my life from time to time. I would readjust my dismantled feelings in the same way that we repaired the broken shutters after the storm. The Japanese have an all-purpose expression in their language for this attitude of resigned acceptance: "Shikataganai." "It can't be helped." "There's nothing I can do about it." It is said with the shrug of the shoulders and tone of finality, perhaps not unlike the "those-were-my-orders" tone that was used at the Nuremberg trials. With all the sociological studies that have been made about the causes of the evacuations of the Japanese Americans during World War II, we should know by now that "they" knew that the West Coast Japanese Americans would go without too much protest, and of course, "they" were right, for most of us (with the exception of those notable few), resigned to our fate, albeit bewildered and not willingly. We were not perceived by our government as responsive Americans; we were objects that happened to be standing in the path of the storm.

Perhaps this kind of acceptance is a way of coping with the "real" world. One stands against the wind for a time, and then succumbs eventually because there is no point to being stubborn against all odds. The wind will not respond to entreaties anyway, one reasons; one should have sense enough to know that. I'm not ready to accept this evolutionary reasoning. It is too rigid for me; I would like to think that my new awareness is going to make me more visible than ever, and to allow me to make some changes in the "man made disaster" I live in at the present time. Part of being visible is refusing to separate the actors from their actions, and demanding that they be responsible for them.

By now, riding along with the minorities' and women's movements, I think we are making a wedge into the main body of American life, but people are still looking right through and around us, assuming we are simply tagging along. Asian American women still remain in the background and we are heard but not really listened to. Like Musak, they think we are piped into the air-waves by someone else. We must remember that one of the most insidious ways of keeping women and minorities powerless is to let them only talk about harmless and inconsequential subjects, or let them speak freely and not listen to them with serious intent.

We need to raise our voices a little more, even as they say to us "This is so uncharacteristic of you." To finally recognize our own invisibility is to finally be on the path toward visibility. Invisibility is not a natural state for anyone.

NOTES

1. It is hoped this will change now that a black woman is Chancellor of our college district.
2. Issei—Immigrant Japanese, living in the U.S.
3. Nisei—Second generation Japanese, born in the U.S.

REFLECTING ON MEANING

1. This essay begins with Yamada's account of her students' reactions to writings by Asian Americans. One student commented, "It made me angry. *Their* anger made *me* angry, because I didn't even know the Asian Americans felt oppressed. I didn't expect their anger." How did this student's response help Yamada to understand her colleagues' and administrators' responses to the grievance that she had filed against the administrators of her college? What incorrect assumption did one of the administrators make about the impetus for Yamada's instigation of the due-process action? How does this assumption relate to this essay's thesis?

2. Yamada contends that the Asian American woman is the "most stereotyped minority of them all." What are some of the popular stereotypes made about Asian American women? How are Asian American women rendered invisible? How did Yamada's "passive resistance" contribute to her own stereotyping? When Yamada says, "I had assumed I was more or less free, not realizing that those who are free make and take choices; they do not choose from options proffered by 'those out there,'" what does she mean?

3. Yamada relates her "long history of ineffectual activities" that were really "initiation rites toward my eventual invisibility." What examples does she provide to illustrate this point?

4. This essay makes a distinction between "acts of God" (natural disasters like hurricanes) and "acts of man" (the war and the evacuation of the Japanese). How does Yamada's former attitude of resigned acceptance to the inappropriate actions or words of others relate to her discussion of natural disasters? How is her reaction to stereotypes and prejudices different now? What does she mean when she says, "We need to raise our voices a little more"?

EXPLORING RHETORICAL STRATEGIES

1. Who is Yamada's intended audience? Is she primarily targeting Asian American women or the people who treat them as invisi-

ble? What is her purpose in this essay? How might Yamada's students, colleagues, college administrators, and family react to her narratives about them?

2. Yamada constructs her essay using the metaphor of natural versus unnatural disasters. How effective is this metaphor? How does her discussion of the years surrounding WW II support both this metaphor and her thesis?

3. This essay is predominantly an autobiographical narrative describing Yamada's experiences and reflections on her own invisibility. How effective is her use of the personal pronoun "I"? What persona does she construct for herself? Is this essay convincing? What is your emotional response to her argument?

Racism and Feminism

BELL HOOKS

Feminist author and theorist bell hooks discusses how racism has historically permeated the women's liberation movement and has created an arena where "white and black women compete to be the chosen female group." In order for change to occur and solidarity to unite all women, liberation must cease to be based on obtaining the power that white men have.

I am a black woman. I attended all-black public schools. I grew up in the south where all around me was the fact of racial discrimination, hatred, and forced segregation. Yet my education as to the politics of race in American society was not that different from that of white female students I met in integrated high schools, in college, or in various women's groups. The majority of us understood racism as a social evil perpetuated by prejudiced white people that could be overcome through bonding between blacks and liberal whites, through militant protest, changing of laws or racial integration. Higher educational institutions did nothing to increase our limited understanding of racism as a political ideology. Instead professors systematically denied us truth, teaching us to accept racial polarity in the form of white supremacy and sexual polarity in the form of male dominance.

American women have been socialized, even brainwashed, to accept a version of American history that was created to uphold and maintain racial imperialism in the form of white supremacy and sexual imperialism in the form of patriarchy. One measure of the success of such indoctrination is that we perpetuate both consciously and unconsciously the very evils that oppress us. I am certain that the black female sixth grade teacher who taught us history, who taught us to identify with the American government, who loved those students who could best recite the pledge of allegiance to the American flag was not aware of the contradiction; that we should love this government that segregated us, that failed to send schools with all black students supplies that went to schools with only white pupils. Unknowingly she implanted in our psyches a seed of the racial imperialism that would keep us forever in bondage. For how does one overthrow, change, or even challenge a system that you have been taught to admire, to love, to believe in? Her innocence does not change the reality that she was teaching black children to embrace the very system that oppressed us, that she encouraged us to support it, to stand in awe of it, to die for it.

That American women, irrespective of their education, economic status, or racial identification, have undergone years of sexist and racist socialization that has taught us to blindly trust our knowledge of history and its effect on present reality, even though that knowledge has been formed and shaped by an oppressive system, is nowhere more evident than in the recent feminist movement. The group of college-educated white middle and upper class women who came together to organize a women's movement brought a new energy to the concept of women's rights in America. They were not merely advocating social equality with men. They demanded a transformation of society, a revolution, a change in the American social structure. Yet as they attempted to take feminism beyond the realm of radical rhetoric and into the realm of American life, they revealed that they had not changed, had not undone the sexist and racist brainwashing that had taught them to regard women like themselves as Others. Consequently, the Sisterhood they talked about has not become a reality, and the women's movement they envisioned would have a transformative effect on American culture has not emerged. Instead, the hierarchical pattern of race and sex relationships already established in American society merely took a different form under "feminism": the form of women being classed as an oppressed group under affirmative action programs further perpetuating the myth that the social status of all women in America is the same; the form of women's studies programs being established with all-white faculty teaching literature almost exclusively by white women about white women and frequently from racist perspectives; the form of white women writing books that purport to be about the experience of American women when in fact they concentrate solely on the experience of white women; and finally the form of endless argument and debate as to whether or not racism was a feminist issue.

Every women's movement in America from its earliest origin to the present day has been built on a racist foundation—a fact which in no way invalidates feminism as a political ideology. The racial apartheid social structure that characterized 19th and early 20th century American life was mirrored in the women's rights movement. The first white women's rights advocates were never seeking social equality for all women; they were seeking social equality for white women. Because many 19th century white women's rights advocates were also active in the abolitionist movement, it is often assumed they were anti-racist. Historiographers and especially recent feminist writing have created a version of American history in which white women's rights advocates are presented as champions of oppressed black people. This fierce romanticism has informed most studies of the abolitionist movement. In contemporary times there is a general tendency to equate abolitionism with a repudiation of racism. In actuality, most white abolitionists, male and female, though vehement in their antislavery protest, were totally opposed to granting social equality to black people. Joel Kovel, in his study *White Racism: A Psychohistory,* emphasizes that the "actual aim of the reform movement, so nobly and bravely begun, was not the liberation of the black, but the fortification of the white, conscience and all."

It is a commonly accepted belief that white female reformist empathy with the oppressed black slave, coupled with her recognition that she was powerless to end slavery, led to the development of a feminist consciousness and feminist revolt. Contemporary historiographers and in particular white female scholars accept the theory that the white women's rights advocates' feelings of solidarity with black slaves were an indication that they were anti-racist and were supportive of social equality of blacks. It is this glorification of the role white women played that leads Adrienne Rich to assert:

> ...It is important for white feminists to remember that— despite lack of constitutional citizenship, educational deprivation, economic bondage to men, laws and customs forbidding

women to speak in public or to disobey fathers, husbands, and brothers—our white foresisters have, in Lillian Smith's words, repeatedly been "disloyal to civilization" and have "smelled death in the word 'segregation,'" often defying patriarchy for the first time, not on their own behalf but for the sake of black men, women, and children. We have a strong anti-racist female tradition despite all efforts by the white patriarchy to polarize its creature-objects, creating dichotomies of privilege and caste, skin color, and age and condition of servitude.

There is little historical evidence to document Rich's assertion that white women as a collective group or white women's rights advocates are part of an anti-racist tradition. When white women reformers in the 1830s chose to work to free the slave, they were motivated by religious sentiment. They attacked slavery, not racism. The basis of their attack was moral reform. That they were not demanding social equality for black people is an indication that they remained committed to white racist supremacy despite their anti-slavery work. While they strongly advocated an end to slavery, they never advocated a change in the racial hierarchy that allowed their caste status to be higher than that of black women or men. In fact, they wanted that hierarchy to be maintained. Consequently, the white women's rights movement which had a lukewarm beginning in earlier reform activities emerged in full force in the wake of efforts to gain rights for black people precisely because white women wanted to see no change in the social status of blacks until they were assured that their demands for more rights were met.

White women's rights advocate and abolitionist Abby Kelly's comment, "We have good cause to be grateful to the slave for the benefit we have received to ourselves, in working for him. In striving to strike his irons off, we found most surely, that we were manacled ourselves," is often quoted by scholars as evidence that white women became conscious of their own limited rights as they worked to end slavery. Despite popular 19th century rhetoric, the notion that white women had to learn from their efforts to free the slave of their own limited rights is simply erroneous. No 19th century white woman could grow to maturity without an awareness of institutionalized sexism. White women did learn via their efforts to free the slave that white men were willing to advocate rights for blacks while denouncing rights for women. As a result of negative reaction to their reform activity and public effort to curtail and prevent their anti-slavery work, they were forced to acknowledge that without outspoken demands for equal rights with white men they might ultimately be lumped in the same social category with blacks—or even worse, black men might gain a higher social status than theirs.

It did not enhance the cause of oppressed black slaves for white women to make synonymous their plight and the plight of the slave. Despite Abby Klein's dramatic statement, there was very little if any similarity between the day-to-day life experiences of white women and the day-to-day experiences of the black slave. Theoretically, the white woman's legal status under patriarchy may have been that of "property," but she was in no way subjected to the de-humanization and brutal oppression that was the lot of the slave. When white reformers made synonymous the impact of sexism on their lives, they were not revealing an awareness of or sensitivity to the slave's lot; they were simply appropriating the horror of the slave experience to enhance their own cause.

The fact that the majority of white women reformers did not feel political solidarity with black people was made evident in the conflict over the vote. When it appeared that white men might grant black men the right to vote while leaving white women disenfranchised, white suffragists did not respond as a group by demanding that all women and men deserved the right to vote. They simply expressed anger and outrage that white men were more committed to maintaining sexual hierarchies than racial hierarchies in the political arena. Ardent white women's rights advocates like Elizabeth Cady Stanton who had never before argued for women's rights on a racially imperialistic platform expressed outrage that inferior "niggers" should be granted the vote while "superior" white women remained disenfranchised. Stanton argued:

> If Saxon men have legislated thus for their own mothers, wives and daughters, what can we hope for at the hands of Chinese, Indians, and Africans?... I protest against the enfranchisement of another man of any race or clime until the daughters of Jefferson, Hancock, and Adams are crowned with their rights.

White suffragists felt that white men were insulting white womanhood by refusing to grant them privileges that were to be granted black men. They admonished white men not for their sexism but for their willingness to allow sexism to overshadow racial alliances. Stanton, along with other white women's rights supporters, did not want to see blacks enslaved, but neither did she wish to see the status of black people improved while the status of white women remained the same.

Animosity between black and white women's liberationists was not due solely to disagreement over racism within the women's movement; it was the end result of years of jealousy, envy, competition, and anger between the two groups. Conflict between black and white women did not begin with the 20th century women's movement. It began during slavery. The social status of white women in America has to a large extent been determined by white people's relationship to black people. It was the enslavement of African people in colonized America that marked the beginning of a change in the social status of white women. Prior to slavery, patriarchal law decreed white women were lowly inferior beings, the subordinate group in society. The subjugation of black people allowed them to vacate their despised position and assume the role of a superior.

Consequently, it can be easily argued that even though white men institutionalized slavery, white women were its most immediate beneficiaries. Slavery in no way altered the hierarchical social status of the white male but it created a new status for the white female. The only way that her new status could be maintained was through the constant assertion of her superiority over the black woman and man. All too often colonial white women, particularly those who were slave mistresses, chose to differentiate their status from the slave's by treating the slave in a brutal and cruel manner. It was in her relationship to the black female slave that the white woman could best assert her power. Individual black slave women were quick to learn that sex-role differentiation did not mean that the white mistress was not to be regarded as an authority figure. Because they had been socialized via patriarchy to respect male authority and resent female authority, black women were reluctant to acknowledge the "power" of the white mistress. When the enslaved black woman expressed contempt and disregard for white female authority, the white mistress often resorted to brutal punishment to assert her authority. But even brutal punishment could not change the fact that black women were not inclined to regard the white female with the awe and respect they showed to the white male.

By flaunting their sexual lust for the bodies of black women and their preference for them as sexual partners, white men successfully pitted white women and enslaved black women against one another. In most instances, the white mistress did not envy the black female slave her role as sexual object; she feared only that her newly acquired social status might be threatened by white male sexual interaction with black women. His sexual involvement with black women (even if that involvement was rape) in effect reminded the white female of her subordinate position in relationship to him. For he could exercise his power as racial imperialist and sexual imperialist to rape or seduce black women, while white women were not free to rape or seduce black men without fear of punishment. Though the white female might condemn the actions of a white male who chose to interact sexually with black female slaves, she was unable to dictate to him proper behavior. Nor could she retaliate by engaging in sexual relationships with enslaved or free black men. Not surprisingly, she directed her anger and rage at the enslaved black women. In those cases where emotional ties developed between white men and black female slaves, white mistresses would go to great lengths to punish the female. Severe beatings were the method most white women used to punish black female slaves. Often in a jealous rage a mistress might use disfigurement to punish a lusted-after black female slave. The mistress might cut off her breast, blind an eye, or cut off another body part. Such treatment naturally caused hostility between white women and enslaved black women. To the enslaved black woman, the white mistress living in relative comfort was the representative symbol of white womanhood. She was both envied and despised—envied for her material comfort, despised because she felt little concern or compassion for the slave woman's lot. Since the white woman's privileged social status could not exist if a group of women were present to assume the lowly position she had abdicated, it follows that black and white women would be at odds with one another. If the white woman struggled to change the lot of the black slave woman, her own social position on the race-sex hierarchy would be altered.

Manumission did not bring an end to conflicts between black and white women; it heightened them. To maintain the apartheid structure slavery had institutionalized, white colonizers, male and female, created a variety of myths and stereotypes to differentiate the status of black women from that of white women. White racists and even some black people who had absorbed the colonizer's mentality depicted the white woman as a symbol of perfect womanhood and encouraged black women to strive to attain such perfection by using the white female as her model. The jealousy and envy of white women that had erupted in the black woman's consciousness during slavery was deliberately encouraged by the dominant white culture. Advertisements, newspaper articles, books, etc., were constant reminders to black women of the difference between their social status and that of white women, and they bitterly resented it. Nowhere was this dichotomy as clearly demonstrated as in the materially privileged white household where the black female domestic worked as an employee of the white family. In these relationships, black women workers were exploited to enhance the social standing of white families. In the white community, employing domestic help was a sign of material privilege and the person who directly benefited from a servant's work was the white woman, since without the servant she would have performed domestic chores. Not surprisingly, the black female domestic tended to see the white female as her "boss," her oppressor, not the white male whose earnings usually paid her wage.

Throughout American history white men have deliberately promoted hostility and divisiveness between white and black women. The white patriarchal power structure pits the two groups against each other, preventing the growth of solidarity between women and ensuring that women's status as a subordinate group under patriarchy remains intact. To this end, white men have supported changes in the white woman's social standing only if there exists another female group to assume that role. Consequently, the white patriarch undergoes no radical change in his sexist assumption that woman is inherently inferior. He neither relinquishes his dominant position nor alters the patriarchal structure of society. He is, however, able to convince many white women that fundamental changes in "woman's status" have occurred because he has successfully socialized her, via racism, to assume that no connection exists between her and black women.

Because women's liberation has been equated with gaining privileges within the white male power structure, white men—and not women, either white or black—have dictated the terms by which women are allowed entrance into the system. One of the terms male patriarchs have set is that one group of women is granted privileges that they obtain by actively supporting the oppression and exploitation of other groups of women. White and black women have been socialized to accept and honor these terms, hence the fierce competition between the two groups; a competition that has always been centered in the arena of sexual politics, with white and black women competing against one another for male favor. This competition is part of an overall battle between various groups of women to be the chosen female group.

The contemporary move toward feminist revolution was continually undermined by competition between various factions. In regards to race, the women's movement has become simply another arena in which white and black women compete to be the chosen female group. This power struggle has not been resolved by the formation of opposing interest groups. Such groups are symptomatic of the problem and are no solution. Black and white women have for so long allowed their idea of liberation to be formed by the existing status quo that they have not yet devised a strategy by which we can come together. They have had only a slave's idea of freedom. And to the slave, the master's way of life represents the ideal free lifestyle.

Women's liberationists, white and black, will always be at odds with one another as long as our idea of liberation is based on having the power white men have. For that power denies unity, denies common connections, and is inherently divisive. It is woman's acceptance of divisiveness as a natural order that has caused black and white women to cling religiously to the belief that bonding across racial boundaries is impossible, to passively accept the notion that the distances that separate women are immutable.

REFLECTING ON MEANING

1. Hooks contends that "Every women's movement in America from its earliest origin to the present day has been built on a racist foundation—a fact which in no way invalidates feminism as a political ideology." What examples does she provide to support this statement? How has history reinscribed racist ideology, even in the early work of abolitionists?

2. Hooks argues that the early female abolitionists were motivated only by religious sentiment, not by antiracism. According to hooks, why didn't the early abolitionists demand social equality for black people? What did white women learn "via their efforts to free the slave"? What did the conflict about the vote reveal about political solidarity between white women and black people?

3. When did conflict between black women and white women begin? How has the social status of white women been elevated by the subjugation of black people? How would you characterize the relationship between white mistresses and their black male and female slaves? How did white mistresses react to their husband's lust for black female slaves? What types of punishments were inflicted on black female slaves who developed emotional ties to their white masters?

4. Hooks contends, "Throughout American history white men have deliberately promoted hostility and divisiveness between white and black women," which prevents the solidarity of women and ensures their continued status as subordinates. How has the women's movement proven itself to be "another arena in which white and black women compete to be the chosen female

group"? What needs to happen for bonding to occur across racial boundaries? What does hooks mean when she says that black and white women "have had only a slave's idea of freedom"?

EXPLORING RHETORICAL STRATEGIES

1. Bell hooks, like e. e. cummings and others, chooses to write her name using all lowercase letters. Why might she choose to do this? What statement might she be making about traditional rules of capitalization? How might this practice align with her feminist philosophy?

2. Hooks begins her essay by writing, "I am a black woman;" then, she briefly discusses her childhood and education. Using her black, female, sixth-grade teacher as an example, she illustrates how American women are socialized and brainwashed into believing a version of American history that reinforces white supremacist patriarchy. How effective is her use of the personal *I* in her argument? Do you agree or disagree with her description of the socialization of American students? Why or why not?

3. Analyze the rhetoric of the quotations by Abby Kelly and Elizabeth Cady Stanton. What white supremacist ideologies might they reveal?

TAKING A STAND
QUESTIONS FOR CONSIDERATION

1. In describing historical conditions for women and making proposals for change, several authors in this part define what full
   freedom for women would entail. Survey the essays of at least
   four authors and deduce their definitions of freedom for women.
   What do their definitions have in common? How do they differ?
   Which definition do you consider most fundamental to the issue
   of women's freedom? Why? You may wish to review essays by
   McGuigan, Millett, Wollstonecraft, Douglass, Mill, Gilman,
   Sanger, and hooks.

2. Has the status of women changed over the centuries? Drawing
   on the historical insights offered by at least three authors, argue
   that significant headway toward equality for women has or has
   not been made in the twentieth century. Amply describe past
   conditions, and explain in detail how women's status has or has
   not changed. In exploring this issue, be sure to consider the extent to which the questions raised in the selection from Plato's
   Republic are still relevant today.

3. Mill and McGuigan suggest that women's intellectual achievements have been limited by social and economic oppression.
   How do both of these authors explain why women have not been
   more successful in intellectual endeavors? Do you agree or disagree that women's achievements in these areas have been handicapped by circumstance? To what extent are current conditions
   perhaps more conducive to such achievements?

4. Historically, white women have enjoyed certain privileges not
   granted to women of color. However, some feminists argue that
   these privileges only make white women even more dependent
   on patriarchy. After reviewing the essays by Truth, Willis, Yamada, and hooks, develop a response to this argument. Are
   white women who continue to support the patriarchy complici-
   tous in their own subjugation? Why or why, not? How might a
   reconsideration of sexism conjoined with an analysis of racism
   help to assist the feminist political project?

5. Daly traces the origin of women's oppression to the Bible and
   the church fathers, whereas Pope Pius XI's encyclical summarizes the views of the Catholic church as they stood as recently as
   1930. Drawing on Daly's survey and the papal encyclical, determine the extent to which the church's views changed over the

centuries. Do you agree or disagree that Christian religions have reinforced and continue to reinforce women's oppression? Why?

6. Wollstonecraft, McGuigan, and Mill examine women's education. What are their conclusions? What do they suggest? Has women's access to a real education changed over the centuries? What does Millett say about the education of women? In shaping your response, you may want to consider the essays in Part IV by Horner, Rich, and Thomas.

7. Kate Millett defines *Bisex* as "the end of enforced perverse heterosexuality" and argues that it would be a desirable result of a sexual revolution. Several other authors in this text—McIntosh, White, Weitz, and Hopkins (Part I) and Lorde (Part III) discuss our society's heterosexist ideology and offer new ways of thinking about homosexuality. After reviewing these authors' works, summarize their main arguments and discuss the pros and cons of their suggestions for social change. Is the current gay rights movement effective? What important rights have homosexuals recently earned? Do you think that homosexuals should be treated in the same way as heterosexuals? Why or why not? Is the gay rights movement any different from the women's movement or the antislavery movement?

8. The metaphor of invisibility is a useful tool for feminist analysis. Several authors in this section either explicitly or implicitly refer to female invisibility. Consider the essays by Truth, Willis, Yamada, and hooks to construct a discussion of various ways in which some, if not all, women are rendered invisible by society.

Part III

Language and Sexism

Many dialect experts contend that language shapes reality, that how we talk or write about a subject dictates the way in which we think about it. These experts also argue that what a society "thinks" about a subject changes as its language about that subject changes. These notions are central concerns of feminist scholars who have demonstrated that the English language is especially sexist, because it tends to acknowledge male experience and values while trivializing female experience and values. The essays in Part III examine the role of language in reinforcing sexist assumptions, but they also imply that such attitudes can change if we alter our speech.

The authors of the first group of essays, under the heading "Sexist Language," analyze the kinds of linguistic discrimination inherent in the English language. Casey Miller and Kate Swift enumerate instances of linguistic sexism and conclude that such language ignores women as persons. Alleen Pace Nilsen examines dictionary definitions to show how words influence culture. Miller and Swift, in another essay, point out that in our society women's names are less important than men's. Finally, Audre Lorde takes to task feminist language and writing practices that reinscibe heterosexism and racism.

In the second group of essays, several authors examine the role of conversation. Gloria Steinem summarizes research on the "politics of conversation" and the effects of masculine and feminine styles of conversation. Similarly, Anne Roiphe evaluates several "genderspeak" books and the criticisms leveled against them. While most conversation research has explored the politics of female-male interaction, Lynet Uttal focuses on feminist-feminist interaction by analyzing conversations within both Women of Color and Anglo feminist groups.

Although it remains to be seen whether sexist attitudes will diminish as the English language becomes less gender-biased, what is certain is that authors such as those represented in Part III have made great inroads in raising consciousness about the politics of conversation and language's powerful effects on both its speakers and listeners. Only by reevaluating how male-dominated English really is and by actively listening to an individual's differences can feminists hope to instigate change.

Chapter 8 _____

SEXIST LANGUAGE

One Small Step for Genkind

CASEY MILLER AND KATE SWIFT

In this essay language experts Casey Miller and Kate Swift contend that the English language "operates to keep women invisible." They survey instances of sexism and call for linguistic reform that will acknowledge women as "real people."

A riddle is making the rounds that goes like this: A man and his young son were in an automobile accident. The father was killed and the son, who was critically injured, was rushed to a hospital. As attendants wheeled the unconscious boy into the emergency room, the doctor on duty looked down at him and said, "My God, it's my son!" What was the relationship of the doctor to the injured boy?

If the answer doesn't jump to your mind, another riddle that has been around a lot longer might help: The blind beggar had a brother. The blind beggar's brother died. The brother who died had no brother. What relation was the blind beggar to the blind beggar's brother?

As with all riddles, the answers are obvious once you see them: The doctor was the boy's mother and the beggar was her brother's sister. Then why doesn't everyone solve them immediately? Mainly because our language, like the culture it reflects, is male oriented. To say that a woman in medicine is an exception is simply to confirm that statement. Thousands of doctors are women, but in order to be seen in the mind's eye, they must be called women doctors.

Except for words that refer to females by definition (mother, actress, Congresswoman), and words for occupations traditionally held by females (nurse, secretary, prostitute), the English language defines everyone as male. The hypothetical person ("if a man can walk 10 miles in two hours . . . "), the average person ("the man in the street") and the active person ("the man on the move") are male. The assumption is that unless otherwise identified, people in general—including doctors and beggars—are men. It is a semantic mechanism that operates to keep women invisible: *man* and *mankind* represent everyone; *he* in generalized use refers to either sex; the "land where our fathers died" is also the land of our mothers— although they go unsung. As the beetle-browed and mustachioed man in a Steig cartoon says to his two male drinking companions, "When I speak of mankind, one thing I *don't* mean is womankind."

Semantically speaking, woman is not one with the species of man, but a distinct subspecies. "Man," says the 1971 edition of the Britannica Junior Encyclopedia, "is the highest form of life on earth. His superior intelligence, combined with certain physical characteristics, have enabled man to achieve things that are impossible for other animals." (The prose style has something in common with the report of a research team describing its studies on "the development of the uterus in rats, guinea pigs and men.") As though quoting the Steig character, still speaking to his friends in McSorley's, the Junior Encyclopedia continues: "Man must invent most of his behavior, because he lacks the instincts of lower animals. . . . Most of the things he learns have been handed down from his ancestors by language and symbols rather than by biological inheritance."

Considering that for the last 5,000 years society has been patriarchal, that statement explains a lot. It explains why Eve was made from Adam's rib instead of the other way around, and who invented all those Adam-rib words like *fe*male and *wo*man in the first place. It also explains why, when it is necessary to mention woman, the language makes her a lower caste, a class separate from the rest of man; why it works to "keep her in her place."

This inheritance through language and other symbols begins in the home (also called a man's castle) where man and wife (not husband and wife, or man and woman) live for a while with their children. It is reinforced by religious training, the educational system, the press, government, commerce and the law. As Andrew Greeley wrote not long ago in his magazine, "man is a symbol-creating animal. He orders and interprets his reality by his symbols, and he uses the symbols to reconstruct that reality."

Consider some of the reconstructed realities of American history. When school children learn from their textbooks that the

early colonists gained valuable experience in governing themselves, they are not told that the early colonists who were women
were denied the privilege of self-government; when they learn that
in the 18th century the average man had to manufacture many of
the things he and his family needed, they are not told that this "average man" was often a woman who manufactured much of what
she and her family needed. Young people learn that intrepid pioneers crossed the country in covered wagons with their wives, children and cattle; they do not learn that women themselves were
intrepid pioneers rather than part of the baggage.

In a paper published this year in Los Angeles as a guide for
authors and editors of social-studies textbooks, Elizabeth Burr,
Susan Dunn and Norma Farquhar document unintentional skew-
ings of this kind that occur either because women are not specifi
cally mentioned as affecting or being affected by historical events,
or because they are discussed in terms of outdated assumptions.
"One never sees a picture of women captioned simply 'farmers' or
'pioneers,'" they point out. The subspecies nomenclature that requires a caption to read "women farmers" or "women pioneers" is
extended to impose certain jobs on women by definition. The text-
book guide gives as an example the word *housewife,* which it says
not only "suggests that domestic chores are the exclusive burden of
females," but gives "female students the idea that they were born to
keep house and teaches male students that they are automatically
entitled to laundry, cooking and housecleaning services from the
women in their families."

Sexist language is any language that expresses such stereotyped attitudes and expectations, or that assumes the inherent superiority of one sex over the other. When a woman says of her
husband, who has drawn up plans for a new bedroom wing and left
out closets, "Just like a man," her language is as sexist as the man's
who says, after his wife has changed her mind about needing the
new wing after all, "Just like a woman."

Male and female are not sexist words, but masculine and
feminine almost always are. Male and female can be applied objectively to individual people and animals and, by extension, to
things. When electricians and plumbers talk about male and female couplings, everyone knows or can figure out what they mean.
The terms are graphic and culture free.

Masculine and feminine, however, are as sexist as any words
can be, since it is almost impossible to use them without invoking
cultural stereotypes. When people construct lists of "masculine"
and "feminine" traits they almost always end up making assumptions that have nothing to do with innate differences between the

sexes. We have a friend who happens to be going through the process of pinning down this very phenomenon. He is 7 years old and his question concerns why his coats and shirts button left over right while his sister's button the other way. He assumes it must have something to do with the differences between boys and girls, but he can't see how.

What our friend has yet to grasp is that the way you button your coat, like most sex-differentiated customs, has nothing to do with real differences but much to do with what society wants you to feel about yourself as a male or female person. Society decrees that it is appropriate for girls to dress differently from boys, to act differently, and to think differently. Boys must be masculine, whatever that means, and girls must be feminine.

Unabridged dictionaries are a good source for finding out what society decrees to be appropriate, though less by definition than by their choice of associations and illustrations. Words associated with males—*manly, virile* and *masculine,* for example—are defined through a broad range of positive attributes like strength, courage, directness and independence, and they are illustrated through such examples of contemporary usage as "a manly determination to face what comes," "a virile literary style," "a masculine love of sports." Corresponding words associated with females are defined with fewer attributes (though weakness is often one of them) and the examples given are generally negative if not clearly pejorative: "feminine wiles," "womanish tears," "a womanlike lack of promptness," "convinced that drawing was a waste of time, if not downright womanly."

Male-associated words are frequently applied to females to describe something that is either incongruous ("a mannish voice") or presumably commendable ("a masculine mind," "she took it like a man"), but female-associated words are unreservedly derogatory when applied to males, and are sometimes abusive to females as well. The opposite of "masculine" is "effeminate," although the opposite of "feminine" is simply "unfeminine."

One dictionary, after defining the word *womanish* as "suitable to or resembling a woman," further defines it as "unsuitable to a man or to a strong character of either sex." Words derived from "sister" and "brother" provide another apt example, for whereas "sissy," applied either to a male or female, conveys the message that sisters are expected to be timid and cowardly, "buddy" makes clear that brothers are friends.

The subtle disparagement of females and corresponding approbation of males wrapped up in many English words is painfully illustrated by "tomboy." Here is an instance where a girl who likes sports and the out-of-doors, who is curious about how things work, who is adventurous and bold instead of passive, is defined in terms of something she is not—a boy. By denying that she can be the person she is and still be a girl, the word surreptitiously undermines her sense of identity: it says she is unnatural. A "tomboy," as defined by one dictionary, is a "girl, especially a young girl, who behaves like a spirited boy." But who makes the judgment that she is acting like a spirited boy, not a spirited girl? Can it be a coincidence that in the case of the dictionary just quoted the editor, executive editor, managing editor, general manager, all six members of the Board of Linguists, the usage editor, science editor, all six general editors of definitions, and 94 out of the 104 distinguished experts consulted on usage—are men?

It isn't enough to say that any invidious comparisons and stereotypes lexicographers perpetuate are already present in the culture. There are ways to define words like womanly and tomboy that don't put women down, though the tradition has been otherwise. Samuel Johnson, the lexicographer, was the same Dr. Johnson who said, "A woman preaching is like a dog's walking on his hind legs. It is not done well; but you are surprised to find it done at all."

Possibly because of the negative images associated with womanish and womanlike, and with expressions like "woman driver" and "woman of the street," the word woman dropped out of fashion for a time. The women at the office and the women on the assembly line and the women one first knew in school all became ladies or girls or gals. Now a countermovement, supported by the very term women's liberation, is putting back into words like woman and sister and sisterhood the meaning they were losing by default. It is as though, in the nick of time, women had seen that the language itself could destroy them.

Some long-standing conventions of the news media add insult to injury. When a woman or girl makes news, her sex is identified at the beginning of a story, if possible in the headline or its equivalent. The assumption, apparently, is that whatever event or action is being reported, a woman's involvement is less common and therefore more newsworthy than a man's. If the story is about achievement, the implication is: "pretty good for a woman." And because people are assumed to be male unless otherwise identified, the media have developed a special and extensive vocabulary to avoid the constant repetition of "woman." The results, "Grandmother Wins Nobel Prize," "Blonde Hijacks Airliner," "Housewife to Run for Congress," convey the kind of information that would be ludicrous in comparable headlines if the subjects were men. Why, if "Unsalaried Husband to Run for Congress" is unacceptable to editors, do women have to keep explaining that to describe them through external or superficial concerns reflects a sexist view of women as decorative objects, breeding machines and extensions of men, not real people?

Members of the Chicago chapter of the National Organization for Women recently studied the newspapers in their area and drew up a set of guidelines for the press. These include cutting out descriptions of the "clothes, physical features, dating life and marital status of women where such references would be considered inappropriate if about men"; using language in such a way as to include women in copy that refers to homeowners, scientists and business people where "newspaper descriptions often convey the idea that all such persons are male"; and displaying the same discretion in printing generalizations about women as would be shown toward racial, religious and ethnic groups. "Our concern with what we are called may seem trivial to some people," the women said, "but we regard the old usages as symbolic of women's position within this society."

The assumption that an adult woman is flattered by being called a girl is matched by the notion that a woman in a menial or poorly paid job finds compensation in being called a lady. Ethel Strainchamps has pointed out that since lady is used as an adjective with nouns designating both high and low occupations (lady wrestler, lady barber, lady doctor, lady judge), some writers assume they can use the noun form without betraying value judgments. Not so, Strainchamps says, rolling the issue into a spitball: "You may write, 'He addressed the Republican ladies,' or 'The Democratic ladies convened'... but I have never seen 'the Communist ladies' or 'the Black Panther ladies' in print."

Thoughtful writers and editors have begun to repudiate some of the old usages. "Divorcée," "grandmother" and "blonde," along with "vivacious" "pert," "dimpled" and "cute," were dumped by the Washington Post in the spring of 1970 by the executive editor, Benjamin Bradlee. In a memo to his staff, Bradlee wrote, "The meaningful equality and dignity of women is properly under scrutiny today... because this equality has been less than meaningful and the dignity not always free of stereotype and condescension."

What women have been called in the press—or at least the part that operates above ground—is only a fraction of the infinite variety of alternatives to "women" used in the subcultures of the English-speaking world. Beyond "chicks," "dolls," "dames," "babes," "skirts" and "broads" are the words and phrases in which women are reduced to their sexuality and nothing more. It would be hard to think of another area of language in which the human mind has been so fertile in devising and borrowing abusive terms. In "The Female Eunuch," Germaine Greer devotes four pages to anatomical terms and words for animals, vegetables, fruits, baked goods, implements and receptacles, all of which are used to dehumanize the female person. Jean Faust, in an article aptly called "Words That Oppress," suggests that the effort to diminish women through language is rooted in a male fear of sexual inadequacy. "Woman is made to feel guilty for and akin to natural disasters," she writes; "hurricanes and typhoons are named after her. Any negative or threatening force is given a feminine name. If a man runs into bad luck climbing up the ladder of success (a male-invented game), he refers to the 'bitch goddess' success."

The sexual overtones in the ancient and no doubt honorable custom of calling ships "she" have become more explicit and less honorable in an age of air travel: "I'm Karen. Fly me." Attitudes of ridicule, contempt and disgust toward female sexuality have spawned a rich glossary of insults and epithets not found in dictionaries. And the usage in which four-letter words meaning copulate are interchangeable with cheat, attack and destroy can scarcely be unrelated to the savagery of rape.

In her updating of Ibsen's "A Doll's House," Clare Boothe Luce has Nora tell her husband she is pregnant—"In the way only men are supposed to get pregnant." "Men, pregnant?" he says, and she nods; "With ideas. Pregnancies there [*she taps his head*] are masculine. And a very superior form of labor. Pregnancies here [*taps her tummy*] are feminine—a very inferior form of labor."

Public outcry followed a revised translation of the New Testament describing Mary as "pregnant" instead of "great with child." The objections were made in part on esthetic grounds: there is no attractive adjective in modern English for a woman who is about to give birth. A less obvious reason was that replacing the euphemism with a biological term undermined religious teaching. The initiative and generative power in the conception of Jesus are understood to be God's; Mary, the mother, was a vessel only.

Whether influenced by this teaching or not, the language of human reproduction lags several centuries behind scientific understanding. The male's contribution to procreation is still described as though it were the entire seed from which a new life grows: the initiative and generative power involved in the process are thought of as masculine, receptivity and nurturance as feminine. "Seminal" remains a synonym for "highly original," and there is no comparable word to describe the female's equivalent contribution.

An entire mythology has grown from this biological misunderstanding and its semantic legacy; its embodiment in laws that for centuries made women nonpersons was a key target of the 19th-century feminist movement. Today, more than 50 years after women finally won the basic democratic right to vote, the word "liberation" itself, when applied to women, means something less than when used of other groups of people. An advertisement for the N.B.C. news department listed Women's Liberation along with crime in the streets and the Vietnam war as "bad news." Asked for his views on Women's Liberation, a highly placed politician was quoted as saying, "Let me make one thing perfectly clear. I wouldn't want to wake up next to a lady pipe-fitter."

One of the most surprising challenges to our male-dominated culture is coming from within organized religion, where the issues are being stated, in part, by confronting the implications of traditional language. What a growing number of theologians and scholars are saying is that the myths of the Judeo-Christian tradition, being the products of patriarchy, must be reexamined, and that the concept of an exclusively male ministry and the image of a male god have become idolatrous.

Women are naturally in the forefront of this movement, both in their efforts to gain ordination and full equality and through their contributions to theological reform, although both these efforts are often subtly diminished. When the Rev. Barbara Anderson was ordained by the American Lutheran Church, one newspaper printed her picture over a caption headed "Happy Girl." Newsweek's report of a protest staged last December [1971] by women divinity students at Harvard was jocular ("another tilt at the windmill") and sarcastic: "Every time anyone in the room lapsed into what [the students] regarded as male chauvinism—such as using the word 'mankind' to describe the human race in general—the outraged women ...drowned out the offender with earpiercing blasts from party-favor kazoos.... What annoyed the women most was the universal custom of referring to God as 'He.'"

The tone of the report was not merely unfunny; it missed the connection between increasingly outmoded theological language and the accelerating number of women (and men) who are dropping out of organized religion, both Jewish and Christian. For language, including pronouns, can be used to construct a reality that simply mirrors society's assumptions. To women who are committed to the reality of religious faith, the effect is doubly painful. Professor Harvey Cox, in whose classroom the protest took place, stated the issue directly: The women, he said, were raising the "basic theological question of whether God is more adequately thought of in personal or suprapersonal terms."

Toward the end of Don McLean's remarkable ballad "American Pie," a song filled with the imagery of abandonment and disillusion, there is a stanza that must strike many women to the quick. The church bells are broken, the music has died; then:

> And the three men I admire most,
> The Father, Son and the Holy Ghost,
> They caught the last train for the Coast—
> The day the music died.

Three men I admired most. There they go, briefcases in hand and topcoats buttoned left over right, walking down the long cold platform under the city, past the baggage wagons and the hissing steam onto the Pullman. Bye, bye God—all three of you—made in the image of male supremacy. Maybe out there in L.A. where the weather is warmer, someone can believe in you again.

The Roman Catholic theologian Elizabeth Farians says "the bad theology of an overmasculinized church continues to be one of the root causes of women's oppression." The definition of oppression is "to crush or burden by abuse of power or authority; burden spiritually or mentally as if by pressure."

When language oppresses, it does so by any means that disparage and belittle. Until well into the 20th century, one of the ways English was manipulated to disparage women was through the addition of feminine endings to nonsexual words. Thus a woman who aspired to be a poet was excluded from the company of real poets by the label poetess, and a women who piloted an airplane was denied full status as an aviator by being called an aviatrix. At about the time poetess, aviatrix, and similar Adamribbisms were dropping out of use, H. W. Fowler was urging that they be revived. "With the coming expansion of women's vocations," he wrote in the first edition (1926) of "Modern English Usage," "feminines for vocation-words are a special need of the future." There can be no doubt he subsconsciously recognized the relative status implied in the -*ess* designations. His criticism of a woman who wished to be known as an author rather than an authoress was that she had no need "to raise herself to the level of the male author by asserting her right to his name."

Who has the prior right to a name? The question has an interesting bearing on words that were once applied to men alone, or to both men and women, but now, having acquired abusive associations, are assigned to women exclusively. Spinster is a gentle case in point. Prostitute and many of its synonyms illustrate the phenomenon better. If Fowler had chosen to record the changing usage of harlot from hired man (in Chaucer's time) through rascal and entertainer to its present definition, would he have maintained that the female harlot is trying to raise herself to the level of the male harlot by asserting her right to his name? Or would he have plugged for harlotress?

The demise of most -ess endings came about before the start of the new feminist movement. In the second edition of "Modern English Usage," published in 1965, Sir Ernest Gowers frankly admitted what his predecessors had been up to. "Feminine designations," he wrote, "seem now to be falling into disuse. Perhaps the explanation of this paradox is that it symbolizes the victory of women in their struggle for equal rights; it reflects the abandonment by men of those ideas about women in the professions that moved Dr. Johnson to his rude remark about women preachers."

If Sir Ernest's optimism can be justified, why is there a movement back to feminine endings in such words as chairwoman, councilwoman and congresswoman? Betty Hudson, of Madison, Conn., is campaigning for the adoption of "selectwoman" as the legal title for a female member of that town's executive body. To have to address a woman as "Selectman," she maintains, "is not only bad grammar and bad biology, but it implies that politics is still, or should be, a man's business." A valid argument, and one that was, predictably, countered by ridicule, the surefire weapon for undercutting achievement. When the head of the Federal Maritime Commission, Helen D. Bentley, was named "Man of the Year" by an association of shipping interests, she wisely refused to be drawn into light-hearted debate with interviewers who wanted to make the award's name a humorous issue. Some women, of course, have yet to learn they are invisible. An 8-year-old who visited the American Museum of Natural History with her Brownie Scout troop went through the impressive exhibit on pollution and overpopulation called "Can Man Survive?" Asked afterward, "Well, can he?" she answered, "I don't know about him, but we're working on it in Brownies."

Nowhere are women rendered more invisible by language than in politics. The United States Constitution, in describing the qualifications for Representative, Senator and President, refers to each as *he*. No wonder Shirley Chisholm, the first woman since 1888 to make a try for the Presidential nomination of a major party, has found it difficult to be taken seriously. The observation by Andrew Greeley already quoted—that "man" uses "his symbols" to reconstruct "his reality"—was not made in reference to the symbols of language but to the symbolic impact the "nomination of a black man for Vice-Presidency" would have on race relations in the United States. Did the author assume the generic term "man" would of course be construed to include "woman"? Or did he deliberately use a semantic device to exclude Shirley Chisholm without having to be explicit?

Either way, his words construct a reality in which women are ignored. As much as any other factor in our language, the ambiguous meaning of *man* serves to deny women recognition as people. In a recent magazine article, we discussed the similar effect on women of the generic pronoun *he,* which we proposed to replace by a new common gender pronoun *tey.* We were immediately told, by a number of authorities, that we were dabbling in the serious business of linguistics, and the message that reached us from these scholars was loud and clear: It - is - absolutely - impossible - for - anyone - to - introduce - a - new - word - into - the - language - just - because - there - is - a need - for - it, so - stop - wasting - your - time.

When words are suggested like "herstory" (for history), "sportsoneship" (for sportsmanship) and "mistresspiece" (for the work of a Virginia Woolf) one suspects a not-too-subtle attempt to make the whole language problem look silly. But unless Alexander Pope, when he wrote "The proper study of mankind is man," meant that women should be relegated to the footnotes (or, as George Orwell might have put it, "All men are equal, but men are more equal than women"), viable new words will surely someday supersede the old.

Without apologies to Freud, the great majority of women do not wish in their hearts that they were men. If having grown up with a language that tells them they are at the same time men and not men raises psychic doubts for women, the doubts are not of their sexual identity but of their human identity. Perhaps the present unrest surfacing in the Women's Movement is part of an evolutionary change in our particular form of life—the one form of all in the animal and plant kingdoms that orders and interprets its reality by symbols. The achievements of the species called man have brought us to the brink of self-destruction. If the species survives into the next century with the expectation of going on, it may only be because we have become part of what Harlow Shapley calls the psychozoic kingdom, where brain overshadows brawn and rationality has replaced superstition.

Searching the roots of Western civilization for a word to call this new species of man and woman, someone might come up with *gen,* as in genesis and generic. With such a word, *man* could be used exclusively for males as *woman* is used for females, for gen would include both sexes. Like the words deer and bison, gen would be both plural and singular. Like progenitor, progeny, and generation, it would convey continuity. Gen would express the warmth and generalized sexuality of generous, gentle, and genuine; the specific sexuality of genital and genetic. In the new family of gen, girls and boys would grow to genhood, and to speak of genkind would be to include all the people of the earth.

REFLECTING ON MEANING

1. Miller and Swift argue that the English language is sexist in several ways: (a) it assumes that "unless otherwise identified, people in general ... are men"; (b) it represents women as a kind of "subspecies"; (c) it depicts women in negative terms; and (d) it reduces women "to their sexuality and nothing more." What examples do the authors provide to support each assertion? Do you find their assertions convincing? Why or why not?

2. What are some examples of sexist language that men use? That women use? Do men and women use sexist language in reference to persons of the same gender? According to Miller and Swift, why doesn't a speaker's gender determine whether an utterance is sexist?

3. What do you think of Miller and Swift's solution to the problem of sexism in language? How viable is their solution? Is it possible to change the English language? Would doing so change cultural attitudes and assumptions about gender?

EXPLORING RHETORICAL STRATEGIES

1. What is the effect of the riddles with which Miller and Swift begin their essay? Were you able to solve them? How do these riddles both illuminate the problem of sexism in English and implicate the reader in it?

2. What famous words does the title "One Small Step for Genkind" echo? What is the connection between this historic event and the essay's thesis? How does the title provide an ironic commentary on the idea of human progress?

3. This essay originally appeared in 1972 in the *New York Times Magazine*. Are the ideas it presents still controversial? Are they still relevant? Has the English language changed to the extent that Miller and Swift's argument no longer seems necessary?

Sexism in English:
A 1990s Update

ALLEEN PACE NILSEN

What can language reveal about society? According to English professor Alleen Pace Nilsen, language is "like an X-ray" that provides "visible evidence of invisible thoughts." In this essay, Nilsen reports on the results of her two-decade-long investigation of American English usage, a study that illuminates many of the "invisible" sexist assumptions operating in society at large.

T wenty years ago I embarked on a study of the sexism inherent in American English. I had just returned to Ann Arbor, Michigan, after living for two years (1967–69) in Kabul, Afghanistan, where I had begun to look critically at the role society assigned to women. The Afghan version of the *chaderi* prescribed for Moslem women was particularly confining. Afghan jokes and folklore were blatantly sexist, such as this proverb: "If you see an old man, sit down and take a lesson; if you see an old woman, throw a stone."

But it wasn't only the native culture that made me question women's roles, it was also the American community.

Most of the American women were like myself–wives and mothers whose husbands were either career diplomats, employees of USAID, or college professors who had been recruited to work on various contract teams. We were suddenly bereft of our traditional roles: some of us became alcoholics, others got very good at bridge, while still others searched desperately for ways to contribute either to our families or to the Afghans. The local economy provided few jobs for women and certainly none for foreigners; we were isolated from former friends and the social goals we had grown up with.

When I returned in the fall of 1969 to the University of Michigan in Ann Arbor, I was surprised to find that many other women were also questioning the expectations they had grown up with. In the spring of 1970, a women's conference was announced. I hired a babysitter and attended, but I returned home more troubled than ever. The militancy of these women frightened me. Since I wasn't ready for a revolution, I decided I would have my own feminist movement. I would study the English language and see what it could tell me about sexism. I started reading a desk dictionary and making notecards on every entry that seemed to tell something about male and female. I soon had a dog-eared dictionary, along with a collection of note cards filling two shoe boxes.

Ironically, I started reading the dictionary because I wanted to avoid getting involved in social issues, but what happened was that my notecards brought me right back to looking at society. Language and society are as intertwined as a chicken and an egg. The language a culture uses is telltale evidence of the values and beliefs of that culture. And because there is a lag in how fast a language changes—new words can easily be introduced, but it takes a long time for old words and usages to disappear—a careful look at English will reveal the attitudes that our ancestors held and that we as a culture are therefore predisposed to hold. My notecards revealed three main points. Friends have offered the opinion that I didn't need to read the dictionary to learn such obvious facts. Nevertheless, it was interesting to have linguistic evidence of sociological observations.

Women Are Sexy; Men Are Successful

First, in American culture a woman is valued for the attractiveness and sexiness of her body, while a man is valued for his physical strength and accomplishments. A woman is sexy. A man is successful.

A persuasive piece of evidence supporting this view are the eponyms—words that have come from someone's name—found in English. I had a two-and-a-half-inch stack of cards taken from men's names but less than a half-inch stack from women's names, and most of those came from Greek mythology. In the words that came into American English since we separated from Britain, there are many eponyms based on the names of famous American men: *Bartlett pear, boysenberry, diesel engine, Franklin stove, Ferris wheel, Gatling gun, mason jar, sideburns, sousaphone, Schick test,* and *Winchester rifle.* The only common eponyms taken from American women's names are *Alice blue* (after Alice Roosevelt Longworth), *bloomers* (after Amelia Jenks Bloomer), and *Mae West jacket* (after the buxom actress). Two out of the three feminine eponyms relate closely to a woman's physical anatomy, while the masculine eponyms (except for *sideburns* after General Burnsides) have nothing to do with the namesake's body but, instead, honor the man for an accomplishment of some kind.

Although in Greek mythology women played a bigger role than they did in the biblical stories of the Judeo-Christian cultures and so the names of goddesses are accepted parts of the language in such place names as Pomona from the goddess of fruit and Athens from Athena and in such common words as *cereal* from Ceres, *psychology* from Psyche, and *arachnoid* from Arachne, the same tendency to think of women in relation to sexuality is seen in the eponyms *aphrodisiac* from Aphrodite, the Greek name for the goddess of love and beauty, and *venereal disease* from Venus, the Roman name for Aphrodite.

Another interesting word from Greek mythology is *Amazon.* According to Greek folk etymology, the *a* means "without" as in *atypical* or *amoral,* while *mazon* comes from *mazos* meaning "breast" as still seen in *mastectomy.* In the Greek legend, Amazon women cut off their right breasts so that they could better shoot their bows. Apparently, the storytellers had a feeling that for women to play the active, "masculine" role the Amazons adopted for themselves, they had to trade in part of their femininity.

This preoccupation with women's breasts is not limited to ancient stories. As a volunteer for the University of Wisconsin's *Dictionary of American Regional English (DARE),* I read a western trapper's diary from the 1930s. I was to make notes of any unusual usages or language patterns. My most interesting finding was that the trapper referred to a range of mountains as *The Teats,* a metaphor based on the similarity between the shapes of the mountains and women's breasts. Because today we use the French wording, *The Grand Tetons,* the metaphor isn't as obvious, but I wrote to mapmakers and found the following listings: *Nippletop* and *Little Nipple Top* near Mount Marcy in the Adirondacks; *Nipple Mountain* in Archuleta County, Colorado; *Nipple Peak* in Coke County, Texas; *Nipple Butte* in Pennington, South Dakota; *Squaw Peak* in Placer County, California (and many other locations); *Maiden's Peak* and *Squaw Tit* (they're the same mountain) in the Cascade Range in Oregon; *Mary's Nipple* near Salt Lake City, Utah; and *Jane Russell Peaks* near Stark, New Hampshire.

Except for the movie star Jane Russell, the women being referred to are anonymous—it's only a sexual part of their body that is mentioned. When topographical features are named after men, it's probably not going to be to draw attention to a sexual part of their bodies but instead to honor individuals for an accomplishment. For example, no one thinks of a part of the male body when hearing a reference to Pike's Peak, Colorado, or Jackson Hole, Wyoming.

Going back to what I learned from my dictionary cards, I was surprised to realize how many pairs of words we have in which the feminine word has acquired sexual connotations while the masculine word retains a serious businesslike aura. For example, a *callboy* is the person who calls actors when it is time for them to go on stage, but a *call girl* is a prostitute. Compare *sir* and *madam*. *Sir* is a term of respect, while *madam* has acquired the specialized meaning of a brothel manager. Something similar has happened to *master* and *mistress*. Would you rather have a painting by an *old master* or an *old mistress?*

It's because the word *woman* had sexual connotations, as in "She's his woman," that people began avoiding its use, hence such terminology as *ladies' room, lady of the house,* and *girls' school* or *school for young ladies.* Feminists, who ask that people use the term *woman* rather than *girl* or *lady,* are rejecting the idea that *woman* is primarily a sexual term. They have been at least partially successful in that today *woman* is commonly used to communicate gender without intending implications about sexuality.

I found two hundred pairs of words with masculine and feminine forms, e.g., *heir-heiress, hero-heroine, steward-stewardess, usher-usherette.* In nearly all such pairs, the masculine word is considered the base, with some kind of a feminine suffix being added. The masculine form is the one from which compounds are made, e.g., from *king-queen* comes *kingdom* but not *queendom,* from *sportsman-sportslady* comes *sportsmanship* but not *sportsladyship.* There is one—and only one—semantic area in which the masculine word is not the base or more powerful word. This is in the area dealing with sex and marriage. When someone refers to a *virgin,* a listener will probably think of a female, unless the speaker specifies *male* or uses a masculine pronoun. The same is true for *prostitute.*

In relation to marriage, there is much linguistic evidence showing that weddings are more important to women than to men. A woman cherishes the wedding and is considered a bride for a whole year, but a man is referred to as a groom only on the day of the wedding. The word *bride* appears in *bridal attendant, bridal gown, bridesmaid, bridal shower,* and even *bridegroom. Groom* comes from the Middle English *grom,* meaning "man," and in the sense is seldom used outside of the wedding. With most pairs of male/female words, people habitually put the masculine word first, *Mr. and Mrs., his and hers, boys and girls, men and women, kings and queens, brothers and sisters, guys and dolls,* and *host and hostess,* but it is the *bride and groom* who are talked about, not the *groom and bride.*

The importance of marriage to a woman is also shown by the fact that when a marriage ends in death, the woman gets the title of *widow.* A man gets the derived title of *widower.* This term is not used in other phrases or contexts, but *widow* is seen in *widowhood, widow's peak,* and *widow's walk.* A *widow* in a card game is an extra hand of cards, while in typesetting it is an extra line of type.

How changing cultural ideas bring changes to language is clearly visible in this semantic area. The feminist movement has caused the differences between the sexes to be downplayed, and since I did my dictionary study two decades ago, the word *singles* has largely replaced such sex specific and value-laden terms as *bachelor, old maid, spinster, divorcée, widow,* and *widower.* And in 1970 I wrote that when a man is called *a professional* he is thought to be a doctor or a lawyer, but when people hear a woman referred to as a *professional* they are likely to think of a prostitute. That's not as true today because so many women have become doctors and lawyers that it's no longer incongruous to think of women in those professional roles.

Another change that has taken place is in wedding announcements. They used to be sent out from the bride's parents and did not even give the name of the groom's parents. Today, most couples choose to list either all or none of the parents' names. Also it is now much more likely that both the bride and groom's picture will be in the newspaper, while a decade ago only the bride's picture was published on the "Women's" or the "Society" page. Even the traditional wording of the wedding ceremony is being changed. Many officials now pronounce the couple "husband and wife" instead of the old "man and wife," and they ask the bride if she promises "to love, honor, and cherish," instead of "to love, honor, and obey."

Women Are Passive; Men Are Active

The wording of the wedding ceremony also relates to the second point that my cards showed, which is that women are expected to play a passive or weak role while men play an active or strong role. In the traditional ceremony, the official asks, "Who gives the bride away?" and the father answers, "I do." Some fathers answer, "Her mother and I do," but that doesn't solve the problem inherent in the question. The idea that a bride is something to be handed over from one man to another bothers people because it goes back to the days when a man's servants, his children, and his wife were all considered to be his property. They were known by his name because they belonged to him, and he was responsible for their actions and their debts.

The grammar used in talking or writing about weddings as well as other sexual relationships shows the expectation of men playing the active role. Men *wed* women while women *become* brides of men. A man *possesses* a woman; he *deflowers* her; he *performs;* he *scores;* he *takes away* her virginity. Although a woman can *seduce* a man, she cannot offer him her virginity. When talking about virginity, the only way to make the woman the actor in the sentence is to say that "She lost her virginity," but people lose things by accident rather than by purposeful actions, and so she's only the grammatical, not the real-life, actor.

The reason that women tried to bring the term *Ms.* into the language to replace *Miss* and *Mrs.* relates to this point. Married women resent being identified only under their husband's names. For example, when Susan Glascoe did something newsworthy, she would be identified in the newspaper only as Mrs. John Glascoe. The dictionary cards showed what appeared to be an attitude on the part of the editors that it was almost indecent to let a respectable woman's name march unaccompanied across the pages of a dictionary. Women were listed with male names whether or not the male contributed to the woman's reason for being in the dictionary or in his own right was as famous as the woman. For example, Charlotte Brontë was identified as Mrs. Arthur B. Nicholls, Amelia Earhart as Mrs. George Palmer Putnam, Helen Hayes as Mrs. Charles MacArthur, Jenny Lind as Mme. Otto Goldschmit, Cornelia Otis Skinner as the daughter of Otis, Harriet Beecher Stowe as the sister of Henry Ward Beecher, and Edith Sitwell as the sister of Osbert and Sacheverell. A very small number of women got into the dictionary without the benefit of a masculine escort. They were rebels and crusaders: temperance leaders Frances Elizabeth Caroline Willard and Carry Nation, women's rights leaders Carrie Chapman Catt and Elizabeth Cady Stanton, birth control educator Margaret Sanger, religious leader Mary Baker Eddy, and slaves Harriet Tubman and Phillis Wheatley.

Etiquette books used to teach that if a woman had *Mrs.* in front of her name, then the husband's name should follow because *Mrs.* is an abbreviated form of *Mistress* and a woman couldn't be a mistress of herself. As with many arguments about "correct" language usage, this isn't very logical because *Miss* is also an abbreviation of *Mistress*. Feminists hoped to simplify matters by introducing *Ms.* as an alternative to both *Mrs.* and *Miss,* but what happened is that *Ms.* largely replaced *Miss,* to become a catch-all business title for women. Many married women still prefer the title *Mrs.,* and some resent being addressed with the term *Ms.* As one frustrated newspaper reporter complained, "Before I can write about a woman, I have to know not only her marital status but also her political philosophy." The result of such complications may contribute to the demise of titles, which are already being ignored by many computer programmers who find it more efficient to simply use names, for example in a business letter: "Dear Joan Garcia," instead of "Dear Mrs. Joan Garcia," "Dear Ms. Garcia," or "Dear Mrs. Louis Garcia."

The titles given to royalty provide an example of how males can be disadvantaged by the assumption that they are always to play the more powerful role. In British royalty, when a male holds a title, his wife is automatically given the feminine equivalent. But the reverse is not true. For example, a *count* is a high political officer with a *countess* being his wife. The same is true for a *duke* and a *duchess* and a *king* and a *queen*. But when a female holds the royal title, the man she marries does not automatically acquire the matching title. For example, Queen Elizabeth's husband has the title of *prince* rather than *king*, but if Prince Charles should become king while he is still married to Lady or Princess Diana, she will be known as the queen. The reasoning appears to be that since masculine words are stronger, they are reserved for true heirs and withheld from males coming into the royal family by marriage. If Prince Philip were called *King Philip*, it would be much easier for British subjects to forget where the true power lies.

The names that people give their children show the hopes and dreams they have for them, and when we look at the differences between male and female names in a culture, we can see the cumulative expectations of that culture. In our culture girls often have names taken from small, aesthetically pleasing items, e.g., *Ruby, Jewel,* and *Pearl. Esther* and *Stella* mean "star," *Ada* means "ornament," and *Vanessa* means "butterfly." Boys are more likely to be given names with meanings of power and strength, e.g., *Neil* means "champion," *Martin* is from Mars, the God of War, *Raymond* means "wise protection," *Harold* means "chief of the army," *Ira* means "vigilant," *Rex* means "king," and *Richard* means "strong king."

We see similar differences in food metaphors. Food is a passive substance just sitting there waiting to be eaten. Many people have recognized this and so no longer feel comfortable describing women as "delectable morsels." However, when I was a teenager, it was considered a compliment to refer to a girl (we didn't call anyone a woman until she was middle-aged) as a *cute tomato,* a *peach,* a *dish,* a *cookie, honey, sugar,* or *sweetie-pie.* When being affectionate, women will occasionally call a man *honey* or *sweetie,* but in general, food metaphors are used much less often with men than with women. If a man is called *a fruit,* his masculinity is being questioned. But it's perfectly acceptable to use a food metaphor if the food is heavier and more substantive than that used for women. For example pin-up pictures of women have long been known as *cheesecake,* but when Burt Reynolds posed for a nude centerfold the picture was immediately dubbed *beefcake,* cf. *a hunk of meat.* That such sexual references to men have come into the language is another reflection of how society is beginning to lessen the differences between their attitudes toward men and women.

Something similar to the *fruit* metaphor happens with references to plants. We insult a man by calling him a *pansy,* but it wasn't considered particularly insulting to talk about a girl being a *wall-flower,* a *clinging vine,* or a *shrinking violet,* or to give girls such names as *Ivy, Rose, Lily, Iris, Daisy, Camellia, Heather,* and *Flora.* A plant metaphor can be used with a man if the plant is big and strong, for example, Andrew Jackson's nickname of *Old Hickory.* Also, the phrases *blooming idiots* and *budding geniuses* can be used with either sex, but notice how they are based on the most active thing a plant can do which is to bloom or bud.

Animal metaphors also illustrate the different expectations for males and females. Men are referred to as *studs, bucks,* and *wolves* while women are referred to with such metaphors as *kitten, bunny, beaver, bird, chick,* and *lamb.* In the 1950s we said that boys went *tomcatting,* but today it's just *catting around* and both boys and girls do it. When the term *foxy,* meaning that someone was sexy, first became popular it was used only for girls, but now someone of either sex can be described as *a fox.* Some animal metaphors that are used predominantly with men have negative connotations based on the size and/or strength of the animals, e.g., *beast, bull-headed, jackass, rat, loanshark,* and *vulture.* Negative metaphors used with women are based on smaller animals, e.g., *social butterfly, mousy, catty,* and *vixen.* The feminine terms connote action, but not the same kind of large scale action as with the masculine terms.

Women Are Connected with Negative Connotations; Men with Positive Connotations

The final point that my notecards illustrated was how many positive connotations are associated with the concept of masculine, while there are either trivial or negative connotations connected with the corresponding feminine concept. An example from the animal metaphors makes a good illustration. The word *shrew* taken from the name of a small but especially vicious animal was defined in my dictionary as "an ill-tempered scolding woman," but the word *shrewd* taken from the same root was defined as "marked by clever, discerning awareness" and was illustrated with the phrase "a shrewd businessman."

Early in life, children are conditioned to the superiority of the masculine role. As child psychologists point out, little girls have much more freedom to experiment with sex roles than do little boys. If a little girl acts like a *tomboy,* most parents have mixed feelings, being at least partially proud. But if their little boy acts like a *sissy* (derived from *sister*), they call a psychologist. It's perfectly acceptable for a little girl to sleep in the crib that was purchased for her brother, to wear his hand-me-down jeans and shirts, and to ride the bicycle that he has outgrown. But few parents would put a boy baby in a white and gold crib decorated with frills and lace, and virtually no parents would have their little boys wear his sister's hand-me-down dresses, nor would they have their son ride a girl's pink bicycle with a flower-bedecked basket. The proper names given to girls and boys show this same attitude. Girls can have "boy" names—*Chris, Craig, Jo, Kelly, Shawn, Teri, Toni,* and *Sam*—but it doesn't work the other way around. A couple of generations ago, *Beverly, Francis, Hazel, Marion,* and *Shirley* were common boys' names. As parents gave these names to more and more girls, they fell into disuse for males, and some older men who have these names prefer to go by their initials or by such abbreviated forms as *Haze* or *Shirl.*

When a little girl is told to *be a lady,* she is being told to sit with her knees together and to be quiet and dainty. But when a little boy is told to *be a man* he is being told to be noble, strong, and virtuous—to have all the qualities that the speaker looks on as desirable. The concept of manliness has such positive connotations that it used to be a compliment to call someone a *he-man,* to say that he was doubly a man. Today many people are more ambivalent about this term and respond to it much as they do to the word *macho.* But calling someone a *manly man* or a *virile man* is nearly always meant as a compliment. *Virile* comes from the Indo-European *vir* meaning "man," which is also the basis of *virtuous.* Contrast the positive connotations of both *virile* and *virtuous* with the negative connotations of *hysterical.* The Greeks took this latter word from their name for *uterus* (as still seen in *hysterectomy*). They thought that women were the only ones who experienced uncontrolled emotional outbursts, and so the condition must have something to do with a part of the body that only women have.

Differences in the connotations between positive male and negative female connotations can be seen in several pairs of words that differ denotatively only in the matter of sex. *Bachelor* as compared to *spinster* or *old maid* has such positive connotations that women try to adopt them by using the term *bachelor-girl* or *bachelorette.* *Old maid* is so negative that it's the basis for metaphors: pretentious and fussy old men are called *old maids,* as are the leftover kernels of unpopped popcorn, and the last card in a popular children's game.

Patron and *matron* (Middle English for *father* and *mother*) have such different levels of prestige that women try to borrow the more positive masculine connotations with the word *patroness,* literally "female father." Such a peculiar term came about because of the high prestige attached to *patron* in such phrases as *a patron of the arts* or *a patron saint. Matron* is more apt to be used in talking about a woman in charge of a jail or a public restroom.

When men are doing jobs that women often do, we apparently try to pay the men extra by giving them fancy titles, for example, a male cook is more likely to be called a *chef* while a male seamstress will get the title of *tailor.* The armed forces have a special problem in that they recruit under such slogans as "The Marine Corps builds men!" and "Join the Army! Become a Man." Once the recruits are enlisted, they find themselves doing much of the work that has been traditionally thought of as "women's work." The solution to getting the work done and not insulting anyone's masculinity was to change the titles as shown below:

waitress	orderly
nurse	medic or corpsman
secretary	clerk-typist
assistant	adjutant
dishwasher or kitchen helper	KP (kitchen police)

Compare *brave* and *squaw.* Early settlers in America truly admired Indian men and hence named them with a word that carried connotations of youth, vigor, courage. But they used the Algonquin's name for "woman" and over the years it developed almost opposite connotations to those of *brave. Wizard* and *witch* contrast almost as much. The masculine *wizard* implies skill and wisdom combined with magic, while the feminine *witch* implies evil intentions combined with magic. Part of the unattractiveness of both *witch* and *squaw* is that they have been used so often to refer to old women, something with which our culture is particularly uncomfortable, just as the Afghans were. Imagine my surprise when I ran across the phrases *grandfatherly advice* and *old wives' tales* and realized that the underlying implication is the same as the Afghan proverb about old men being worth listening to while old women talk only foolishness.

Other terms that show how negatively we view old women as compared to young women are *old nag* as compared to *filly, old crow* or *old bat* as compared to *bird,* and of being *catty* as compared to being *kittenish.* There is no matching set of metaphors for men. The chicken metaphor tells the whole story of a woman's life. In her youth she is a *chick*. Then she marries and begins *feathering her nest*. Soon she begins feeling *cooped up,* so she goes to *hen parties* where she *cackles* with her friends. Then she has her *brood,* begins to *hen-peck* her husband, and finally turns into an *old biddy*.

I embarked on my study of the dictionary not with the intention of prescribing language change but simply to see what the language would tell me about sexism. Nevertheless I have been both surprised and pleased as I've watched the changes that have occurred over the past two decades. I'm one of those linguists who believes that new language customs will cause a new generation of speakers to grow up with different expectations. This is why I'm happy about people's efforts to use inclusive language, to say *he or she* or *they* when speaking about individuals whose names they do not know. I'm glad that leading publishers have developed guidelines to help writers use language that is fair to both sexes, and I'm glad that most newspapers and magazines list women by their own names instead of only by their husbands' names and that educated and thoughtful people no longer begin their business letters with "Dear Sir" or "Gentlemen," but instead use a memo form or begin with such salutations as "Dear Colleagues," "Dear Reader," or "Dear Committee Members." I'm also glad that such words as *poetess, authoress, conductress,* and *aviatrix* now sound quaint and old-fashioned and that *chairman* is giving way to *chair* or *head, mailman* to *mail carrier, clergyman* to *clergy,* and *stewardess* to *flight attendant*. I was also pleased when the National Oceanic and Atmospheric Administration bowed to feminist complaints and in the late 1970s began to alternate men's and women's names for hurricanes. However, I wasn't so pleased to discover that the change did not immediately erase sexist thoughts from everyone's mind, as shown by a headline about Hurricane David in a 1979 New York tabloid, "David Rapes Virgin Islands." More recently a similar metaphor appeared in a headline in the *Arizona Republic* about Hurricane Charlie, "Charlie Quits Carolinas, Flirts with Virginia."

What these incidents show is that sexism is not something existing independently in American English or in the particular dictionary that I happened to read. Rather, it exists in people's minds. Language is like an X ray in providing visible evidence of invisible thoughts. The best thing about people being interested in and discussing sexist language is that as they make conscious decisions about what pronouns they will use, what jokes they will tell or laugh at, how they will write their names, or how they will begin their letters, they are forced to think about the underlying issue of sexism. This is good because as a problem that begins in people's assumptions and expectations, it's a problem that will be solved only when a great many people have given it a great deal of thought.

REFLECTING ON MEANING

1. Through analyzing language usage, Nilsen identifies three cultural assumptions about women and men:

   - "In American culture a woman is valued for the attractiveness and sexiness of her body, while a man is valued for his physical strengths and accomplishments. A woman is sexy. A man is successful."

   - "Women are expected to play a passive or weak role while men play an active or strong role."

   - "Many positive connotations are associated with the concept of masculine, while there are either trivial or negative connotations connected with the corresponding feminine concept."

   What evidence does she provide to support these assertions? Do you think that her inferences about language are reasonable? Why or why not?

2. Nilsen lists several word pairs whose feminine elements carry sexual connotations, whereas their masculine counterparts convey a "serious businesslike aura." What are some of these word pairs? Do you agree or disagree with Nilsen's conclusions about these words? According to Nilsen, how are such word pairs beginning to reflect social change?

3. Nilsen explores the relationship between society and language, asserting that they are "as intertwined as a chicken and an egg." What does she mean? Do you agree with her viewpoint? Why or why not? How might sexist language not only reflect but reinforce sexism in society? How do the connections between language and society help explain why Nilsen's note cards brought her "right back to looking at society"?

EXPLORING RHETORICAL STRATEGIES

1. Nilsen begins her essay by describing the personal and political events that spurred her interest in sexist language. Why does she

preface her observations on the English language with this kind of introduction? What do the events she describes have to do with her topic? How does this information advance her thesis about language and society?

2. What principle does Nilsen use to structure the body of her essay? In what format does she present her main points, secondary points, and evidence? How does this structure facilitate a reader's understanding of and response to her argument?

3. Nilsen provides numerous pieces of evidence from a dictionary to support her assertions; in fact, the essay nearly becomes a catalogue of specific examples. Why does she include so many examples? What considerations about her topic and audience may have persuaded her to provide this much evidence to illustrate her assertions?

Women and Names

CASEY MILLER AND KATE SWIFT

Names are powerful symbols of identity in society. Yet, as Casey Miller and Kate Swift point out, "women's names are less important than men's"—so much so that women routinely surrender them when they marry. This custom as well as others, they argue, "reinforces the powerful myth that pervades the rest of our language—the myth that the human race is essentially male."

The photograph of the three bright, good-looking young people in the Army recruitment ad catches the eye. All three have a certain flair, and one knows just by looking at the picture that they are enjoying life and glad they joined up. They are typical Americans, symbols of the kind of people the modern Army is looking for. The one closest to the camera is a white male. His name, as can be seen from the neat identification tag pinned to the right pocket of his regulation blouse, is Spurgeon. Behind him and slightly to the left is a young black man. He is wearing a decoration of some kind, and his name is Sort–. Perhaps it is Sorter or Sortman–only the first four letters show. A young woman, who is also white, stands behind Spurgeon on the other side. She is smiling and her eyes shine; she looks capable. She is probably wearing a name tag too, but because Spurgeon is standing between her and the camera, her name is hidden. She is completely anonymous.

The picture is not a candid shot; it was carefully posed. The three models were chosen from thousands of possible recruits. They are the same height; they all have dark hair and are smiling into the camera. They look like students, and the copy says the Army will pay 75 per cent of their tuition if they work for a college degree. It is no accident that two are white, one black, or that two are male, one female. Nor is it an accident that Spurgeon stands in front of the others at the apex of a triangle, or that, since someone had to be anonymous, the woman was chosen.[1]

In our society women's names are less important than men's. The reasons why are not hard to identify, but the consequences for both men and women are more far-reaching than members of either sex, with a few notable exceptions, have been prepared to admit or even, until recently, to examine. Like other words, names are symbols; unlike other words, what they symbolize is unique. A thousand John Does and Jane Roes may live and die, but no bearer of those names has the same inheritance, the same history, or the same fears and expectations as any other. It therefore seems legitimate to ask what effect our naming customs have on girls and boys and on the women and men they grow into. Are the symbol-words that become our names more powerful than other words?

Few people can remember learning to talk. The mystery of language is rarely revealed in a single moment of electrifying insight like Helen Keller's, when suddenly, at the age of seven, the deaf and blind child realized for the first time the connection between the finger signals for w-a-t-e-r her teacher was tapping into her palm and "the wonderful cool something" that flowed from the pump spout onto her other hand.[2]

From what scholars report about the way children normally acquire speech, it seems probable that "learning to talk" is actually the measured release, in conjunction with experience, of an innate capacity for language that is common to all human beings.[3] We are no more likely to remember the process than we are to remember growing taller. What one may remember is a particular moment– seeing the yardstick exactly even with the latest pencil line marking one's height on the door jamb or learning a word for some particular something one had been aware of but could not name: tapioca, perhaps, or charisma, or a cotter pin. Anyone who has ever said, "so *that's* what those things are called," knows the experience.

When children are first learning to talk they go through a series of similar experiences. The very act of learning what a person or thing is called brings the object into the child's ken in a new way. It has been made specific. Later, the specific will also become general, as when the child calls any small, furry animal a "kitty." Words are symbols; their meanings can be extended.

Amanda, who is twenty months old, has spurts of learning names. "Mum," she says to her mother while pointing to the box. "Mum," she says again, pointing to the doorknob. "What is it?" she is asking without using words. "Tell me its name." When she calls her mother by a name, she knows her mother will respond to it. She knows that she, Amanda, has a name. It is important to her, for she has already become aware of herself as a thing different from everything else. As a psychologist might put it, her ego is emerging. Hearing her name, being called by it, is part of the process.

Amanda makes certain sounds, naming food or her bottle, that tell her parents she is hungry or thirsty. Before long she will speak of herself in the third person: "'Manda want apple." "'Manda come too." She may repeat her name over and over, perhaps mixing it with nonsense syllables. It is like a charm. It may be the first word she learns to spell. She will delight in seeing the letters of her name, this extension of herself, on her toothbrush or drinking mug. They belong to her, not to her brother or to her mother or father.

When children begin to play with other children and when they finally go to school, their names take on a public dimension. The child with a "funny" name is usually in for trouble, but most kids are proud of their names and want to write them on their books and pads and homework. There was a time when older children carved their names or initials on trees. Now that there are so many people and so few trees, the spray can has taken over from the jackknife, but the impulse to put one's identifying mark where all the world can see it is as strong as ever. The popularity of commercially produced name-on objects of every kind, from tee-shirts to miniature license plates, also attests to the importance youngsters (and a lot of grown-ups too) place on claiming and proclaiming their names.

Given names are much older than surnames, of course, probably as old as language itself. One can imagine that as soon as our ancient forebears started using sounds to represent actions or objects, they also began to distinguish each other in the same way. One might even speculate that the people who most often assigned sounds to others were those who produced and cared for the group's new members. Commenting on the assumption of philologists that the exchange of meaningful vocal sounds began among males as they worked and hunted together—hence the so-called "yo-heave-ho" and "bow-wow" theories of language origin—Ethel Strainchamps, a psycholinguist, notes that most philologists have in the past been men. Considering the importance to human survival of communication between mother and child when open fires, venomous reptiles, and other hazards were everywhere, "it might have occurred to a woman that a 'no-no' theory was more likely," Strainchamps says.[4] Perhaps her suggestion should be taken a step further: who knows that it was not the creative effort of women, striving to communicate with each new baby, calling it by a separate and distinguishing sound, that freed the primordial human mind from the prison of animal grunts and led in time to the development of language?

Inevitably, some people dislike the names they have been given, and many children go through a phase of wanting to be called something else. For no apparent reason Anne announces that her name is really Koko and she will not answer to any other. For months nothing will change her resolve. She is Koko—and then one day she is Anne again. But if Cecil decides he wants to be called Jim, or Fanny elects to be known as Jill, the reasons may be less obscure: names do seem to give off vibrations of a sort, and other people's response to your name becomes a part of their response to you. Some psychologists think that given names are signals of parental expectations: children get the message and act on it either positively or negatively. One study claims to show, for example, that names can be "active" or "passive." If you call your son Mac or Bart he will become a more active person than if you call him Winthrop or Egbert. Your daughter is more likely to be outgoing and confident, according to this theory, if you call her Jody rather than Letitia. It follows, though, that if Jody prefers to be called Letitia, she is letting it be known that she sees herself in a more passive and dependent way than you anticipated.[5]

Last names, too, can be positive or negative. Some carry a mystique of greatness or honor: Randolph, Diaz, Morgenthau, Saltonstall. Others are cumbersome, or they invite cruel or tasteless jokes. Many people decide, for one reason or another, to change their last names, but a great many more take pride today in being identified as a Klein or a Mackenzie, a Giordano or a Westervelt. The first-and-last-name mix which a person grows up with—that combination of particular and general, of personal and traditional—is not lightly exchanged for another.

Whether a name is self-chosen or bestowed at birth, making it one's own is an act of self-definition. When a former Cabinet member who had been involved in the Watergate scandal asked the Senate investigating committee to give back his good name, he was speaking metaphorically, for no one had taken his name away. What he had lost, justly or unjustly, was his public image as a person of integrity and a servant of the people. One's name also represents one's sense of power and self-direction. "I'm so tired I don't know my own name" is a statement of confusion and fatigue. *Your* name, the beginning of your answer to "Who am I?" is the outermost of the many layers of identity reaching inward to the real you. It is one of the significant differences between you and, let's say, a rose, which is named but does not know it. Yet it is one of the things a little girl grows up knowing she will be expected to lose if she marries.

The loss of women's last names may seem compensated for by a custom in first-naming that allows girls to be called by a version of their fathers' names, so that—after a fashion, at least—continuity is restored. In this post-Freudian age it would be bad form to give a boy a version of his mother's first name. Nevertheless, if a couple named Henrietta and Frank should decide to call their son Henry, chances are an earlier Henry, after whom Henrietta was named, provides the necessary male for him to identify with. In any case, the name has come back into its own: it stands four-square and solid, which is seldom true of the derivative names given to girls. The strength of John is preserved in Joan and Jean, but these are exceptions. Names like Georgette and Georgina, Josephine, Paulette and Pauline, beautiful as they may sound, are diminutives. They are copies, not originals, and like so many other words applied to women, they can be diminishing.

A man in most Western societies can not only keep his name for his lifetime but he can pass it on intact to his son, who in turn can pass it on to *his* son. The use of a surname as a given name is also usually reserved for males, presumably on the grounds that such names do not have a sufficiently "feminine" sound for the "weaker sex." When tradition permits the giving of a family surname to daughters, as in the American South, a woman can at least retain her identification with that branch of her family. Once a surname has gained popularity as a girl's name, however, it is likely to face extinction as a boy's name. Shirley, for example, an old Yorkshire family name meaning "shire meadow," was once given as a first name only to boys. Not until Charlotte Brontë wrote *Shirley*—a novel published in 1849, whose central character, Shirley Keeldar, was modeled on Charlotte's sister Emily—was it used for a girl.[6] Since then, Shirley has become popular as a girl's name but has dropped out of use as a boy's. Names like Leslie, Beverly, Evelyn, and Sidney may be traveling the same route. Once they have become popular as women's names, their histories as surnames are forgotten, and before long they may be given to girls exclusively.

In English, names like Charity, Constance, Patience, Faith, Hope, Prudence, and Honor no longer have popular equivalents for males, as they often do in other languages. The qualities described are not limited to females, of course, and yet to name a son Honor or Charity, even if doing so breaks no objective rule, would somehow run counter to social expectations. This may be true in part because such names are subjective, expressing more intimately than would seem appropriate for a boy the parents' expectations for their offspring. Or the principle that applied in the case of Shirley may apply here, for once a name or a word becomes associated with women, it is rarely again considered suitable for men.

One of the most useful functions of a given name is to serve as a quick identifier of sex. Nearly everyone, whether they admit it or not, is interested in knowing what sex an unknown person is. You get a postcard from a friend saying he will be stopping by to see you next week with someone named Lee, and chances are the first question that pops into your mind is not whether Lee is young or old, black or white, clever or dull, but whether Lee will turn out to be female or male. Still, natural curiosity does not entirely explain the annoyance or embarrassment some people seem to feel when women have names that are not specifically female by tradition or why names that become associated with women are thenceforth out of bounds for men.

If quick sex identification were the only consideration, the long male tradition of using initials in place of first names would not have come about. People with names like J. P. Morgan, P. T. Barnum, and L. L. Bean were always male–or were they? No one could stop women from sneaking under the flap of *that* tent, and in fact so many did that the practice had to be disallowed. In the early years of this century Columbia University, which in its academic bulletins identified male faculty members only by their surnames and initials, wrote out the names of women faculty members in full–lest anyone unintentionally enroll in a course taught by a woman.[7]

Perhaps it is because of the transience of women's last names that their first names seem often to be considered the logical, appropriate, or even polite counterpart of men's surnames, and the news media frequently reflect this feeling. When Secretary of State Henry Kissinger and Nancy Maginnis were married, many news stories called them "Kissinger and Nancy" after the first paragraph. The usage is so accepted, and its belittling implications so subliminal, that it often persists in defiance of changes taking place all about it. In a magazine story on the atypical career choices of six graduate students, the subhead read "Stereotypes fade as men and women students . . . prepare to enter fields previously dominated almost exclusively by the opposite sex." Three women going into dentistry, business administration, and law were introduced by their full names, as were three men whose fields of study were nursing, library science, and primary education. The men were then referred to as Groves, White, and Fondow, while the women became Fran, Carol, and Pam.[8]

Children, servants, and other presumed inferiors are apt to be first-named by adults and employers and by anyone else who is older, richer, or otherwise assumed to be superior. In turn, those in the first category are expected to address those in the second by their last names prefixed with an appropriate social or professional title. People on a fairly equal footing, however, either first-name each other or by mutual if unspoken agreement use a more formal mode of address.

As it happens, even though the average full-time working woman in the United States is slightly older than the average man who is employed full-time, she makes only slightly more than half the salary he makes.[9] This may explain why a great many more women than men are called by their first names on the job and why, in offices where most of the senior and junior executives are men and most of the secretaries and clerks are women, the first-naming of all women—including executives, if any—easily becomes habitual. Or it could be that women are at least slightly less impressed by the thought of their own importance, slightly more inclined to meet their colleagues and employees on equal terms. When a reporter asked newly elected Governor Ella Grasso of Connecticut what she wanted to be called and she answered, "People usually call me Ella," a new benchmark for informality must have been set in the other forty-nine state capitals. Unless men respond in the same spirit, however, without taking advantage of what is essentially an act of generosity, women like Governor Grasso will have made a useless sacrifice, jeopardizing both their identity and their prestige.

In the whole name game, it is society's sanction of patronymy that most diminishes the importance of women's names—and that sanction is social only, not legal. In the United States no state except Hawaii legally requires a woman to take her husband's name when she marries, although social pressures in the other states are almost as compelling.[10] The very fact that until recently few women giving up their names realized they were not required to do so shows how universal the expectation is. Any married couple who agree that the wife will keep her own name are in for harassment, no matter how legal their stand: family, friends, the Internal Revenue Service, state and local agencies like motor vehicle departments and voter registrars, hotels, credit agencies, insurance companies are all apt to exert pressure on them to conform. One judge is quoted as saying to a married woman who wanted to revert to her birth name, "If you didn't want his name, why did you get married? Why didn't you live with him instead?"[11] To thus equate marriage with the desire of some women to be called "Mrs." and the desire of some men to have "a Mrs." is insulting to both sexes; yet the equation is so widely accepted that few young people growing up in Western societies think in any different terms.

The judge just quoted was, in effect, defining what a family is in a patronymical society like ours where only males are assured permanent surnames they can pass on to their children. Women are said to "marry into" families, and families are said to "die out" if an all-female generation occurs. The word family, which comes from the Latin *famulus,* meaning a servant or slave, is itself a reminder that wives and children, along with servants, were historically part of man's property. When black Americans discard the names of the slaveholders who owned their forebears, they are consciously disassociating their sense of identity from the property status in which their ancestors were held. To adopt an African name is one way of identifying with freedom and eradicating a link to bondage. The lot of married women in Western society today can hardly be called bondage, but to the degree that people's names are a part of themselves, giving them up, no matter how willingly, is tantamount to giving up some part of personal, legal, and social autonomy.

Since a surname defines a family and identifies its members, a man who marries and has children extends his family, but a woman in marrying gives up her "own" family and joins in extending another's. She may be fully aware that she brings to her new family—to her children and grandchildren—the genetic and cultural heritage of her parents and grandparents, but the lineages she can trace are ultimately paternal. Anyone who decides to look up their ancestors through marriage and birth records in town halls and genealogical societies may find paternal lines going back ten or fifteen generations or more, whereas with few exceptions maternal ones end after two or three. The exceptions are interesting for they emphasize how important the lost information from maternal lines really is. Stephen Birmingham, writing about America's blue-blooded families, notes that "'Who is she?' as a question may mean, 'What was her maiden name?' It may also mean what was her mother's maiden name, and what was her grandmother's maiden name, and so on."[12] Blue bloods, in other words, care a lot about "maiden names," and rightly so, considering that the inputs of maternal genes and culture have as great an effect on offspring as paternal inputs.

Obviously we all have as many female ancestors as male ancestors, but maternal lineages, marked with name changes in every generation, are far more difficult to trace. To most of us the identity of our mother's mother's mother's mother, and that of *her* mother, and on back, are lost forever. How is one affected by this fading out of female ancestors whose names have disappeared from memory and the genealogical records? Research on the subject is not readily available, if it exists at all, but it seems likely that daughters are affected somewhat differently from sons. If it is emotionally healthy, as psychologists believe, for a child to identify with the parent of the same sex, would it not also be healthy for a child to identify with ancestors of the same sex?

A boy, knowing he comes from a long line of males bearing the name Wheelwright, for example, can identify with his forefathers: Johnny Wheelwright in the 1970s, if he wants to, can imagine some medieval John in whose workshop the finest wheels in the land were fashioned, a John who had a son, who had a son, who had a son, until at last Johnny Wheelwright himself was born. No line of identifiable foremothers stretches back into the past to which his sister Mary can lay claim. Like Johnny, she is a Wheelwright, assigned by patronymy to descent from males. What neither boy nor girl will ever be able to trace is their equally direct descent from, let's say, a woman known as the Healer, a woman whose daughter's daughter's daughter, through the generations, passed on the skilled hands which both John and Mary may have inherited.

Imagine, in contrast to Johnny Wheelwright, a hypothetical woman of today whose name is Elizabeth Jones. If you were to ask, in the manner of a blue blood, "Who is she?" you might be told, "She was a Fliegendorf. Her people were Pennsylvania Dutch farmers who came over from Schleswig-Holstein in the seventeenth century." Actually, that tells a fraction of the story. This hypothetical Elizabeth Jones's mother—who met her father at an Army post during the Second World War—was a Woslewski whose father emigrated from Poland as a boy, lived in Chicago, and there married a Quinn whose mother came from Canada and was a Valliére. The mother of that Valliére was the great-great-granddaughter of a woman whose given name was the equivalent of "Deep Water" and who belonged to a group of native North Americans called the Têtes de Boule by French explorers.

Elizabeth Jones's father's mother, in Pennsylvania, had been a Bruhofer, whose mother had been a Gruber, whose mother, a Powell, was born in Georgia and was the great-great-granddaughter of a woman brought to this country from Africa in the hold of a slave ship.

Thus, although Elizabeth Jones is said to have been a Fliegendorf whose people came from Schleswig-Holstein in the sixteen hundreds, fewer than 5 per cent of her two thousand or so direct ancestors who were alive in that century had any connection with Schleswig-Holstein, and only one of those who made the passage to America was born with the name Fliegendorf. The same may be said, of course, of Elizabeth Jones's brother, Ed Fliegendorf's relationship to the Fliegendorf family or Johnny Wheelwright's relationship to the bearers of his name. Yet so strong is our identification with the name we inherit at birth that we tend to forget both the rich ethnic mix most of us carry in our genes and the arbitrary definition of "family" that ultimately links us only to the male line of descent.

This concept of family is one of the reasons why most societies through most of history have placed greater value on the birth of a male child than of a female child. Ours is no exception. A recent survey reported in *Psychology Today* showed that a higher percentage of prospective parents in the United States would prefer to have a son than a daughter as a first or only child. The percentage who feel this way, however, has dropped from what it was only twenty years ago.[13] Responding to the report, a reader expressed his opinion that the change could be attributed to "a breakdown in the home-and-family ideal" among young parents today. "The son," he wrote in a letter to the editor, "and in particular the eldest son, is strongly tied to the archetypal family; first as its prime agent of continuation, and also as the future guardian and master of the home."[14] Here, then, family and name are seen as synonymous, the male is the prime if not only progenitor, and even the order of birth among male children affects the model of an ideal family.

One could not ask for a better example of how patronymy reinforces the powerful myth that pervades the rest of our language—the myth that the human race is essentially male. The obvious first reaction to such a statement may be to say, "But that's absurd. No one thinks of the race as essentially male." And yet we do. As the social critic Elizabeth Janeway has pointed out, a myth does not really describe a situation; rather, it tries to bring about what it declares to exist.[15]

A childless couple adopted a baby girl. When asked why they chose a girl rather than a boy, they explained that if she did not live up to their expectations because of her genetic heritage, "at least she won't carry on the family." Journalist Mike McGrady states the myth of racial maleness even more tellingly in an article about sperm banking: "One customer...gave a reason for depositing sperm that may foreshadow the future: it was to carry on the family line should his male offspring prove sterile. What we are talking about here," McGrady said, "is not fertility insurance but immortality insurance."[16] This customer, then, believes he cannot be linked to future generations through his female offspring, should they prove fertile. His immortality, one must conclude, is not in his sperm or his genes but in his name.

"One's name and strong devotion to it," wrote an Austrian philosopher, Otto Weininger, around the turn of the century, "are even more dependent on personality than is the sense of property.... Women are not bound to their names with any strong bond. When they marry they give up their own name and assume that of their husband without any sense of loss.... The fundamental namelessness of the woman is simply a sign of her undifferentiated personality."[17] Weininger, whose book *Sex and Character* had a brief but powerful influence on popular psychology, is of historical interest because he articulated the myth of humanity's maleness at a time when the first wave of feminism was beginning to be taken seriously by governments, trade unions, and other institutions in England and the United States as well as in Europe. In describing the "fundamental namelessness" of woman as "a sign of her undifferentiated personality," Weininger was building support for his premise that "women have no existence and no essence ... no share in ontological reality, no relation to the thing-in-itself, which, in the deepest interpretation, is the absolute, is God."[18]

Otto Weininger was aware of the movement for women's rights and was deeply disturbed by it. He may well have heard of the noted American feminist Lucy Stone, whose decision to keep her birth name when she married Henry Blackwell in 1855 had created consternation on both sides of the Atlantic. An eloquent speaker with a free and fearless spirit, Stone was widely known as an antislavery crusader. After the Civil War her organizing efforts helped secure passage of the Fourteenth Amendment, which extended the vote to freed slaves who were men. She devoted the rest of her long, productive life to the cause of suffrage for women and founded and edited the *Woman's Journal,* for forty-seven years the major weekly newspaper of the women's movement.

It is especially relevant that among Lucy Stone's many important contributions to history she is best known today for her refusal to give up her name, Her explanation, "My name is the symbol of my identity and must not be lost," was a real shocker to anyone who had not considered the possibility that a married woman could have an individual identity—and in the nineteenth century that meant almost everyone. The law did not recognize such a possibility, as the famous English jurist William Blackstone made clear when he summarized the rule of "coverture," influencing both British and American law for well over a hundred years. "By marriage," he wrote, "the husband and wife are one person in the law—that is, the very being or legal existence of the woman is suspended during the marriage...."[19]

The suspended existence of the married woman came to be well symbolized in the total submersion of a wife's identity in her husband's name—preceded by "Mrs." The use of designations like "Mrs. John Jones" does not go back much before 1800. Martha Washington would have been mystified to receive a letter addressed to "Mrs. George Washington," for at that time the written abbreviation *Mrs.,* a social title applied to any adult woman, was used interchangeably with its spelled-out form *mistress* and was probably pronounced the same way. "Mistress George" would have made little sense.

Lucy Stone's example was followed in the late nineteenth and early twentieth centuries by small but increasing numbers of women, mostly professional writers, artists, and scientists. The Lucy Stone League, founded in New York in 1921, was the first organization to help women with the legal and bureaucratic difficulties involved in keeping their names after marriage. Its early leaders included Jane Grant, co-founder with her first husband, Harold Ross, of the *New Yorker* magazine, and journalist Ruth Hale who in 1926 asked rhetorically how men would respond to the suggestion that they give up *their* names. The suggestion does not often arise, but a psychologist recently described the reaction of one husband and father when someone in his family raised the possibility of changing the family name because they didn't like it:

"He suddenly realized that it was a traumatic thing for him to consider giving up his last name," according to Dr. Jack Sawyer of Northwestern University. "He said he'd never realized before that 'only men have real names in our society, women don't.' And it bothered him also that his name should be a matter of such consequence for him. He worried about his professional standing, colleagues trying to contact him—all kinds of things that women face as a matter of course when they get married. Men have accepted the permanency of their names as one of the rights of being male, and it was the first time he realized how much his name was part of his masculine self-image."[20]

Lucy Stone, whose self-image was comfortably female but not feminine, agreed to be known as Mrs. Stone after her marriage. Through this compromise with custom she avoided the somewhat schizophrenic situation many well-known women face when they use their birth names professionally and their husbands' names socially, thus becoming both Miss Somebody and Mrs. Somebody Else. The Pulitzer prize–winning novelist Jean Stafford wants to be "saluted as *Miss* Stafford if the subject at hand has to do with me and my business or as *Mrs.* Liebling if inquiries are being made about my late husband."[21] Miss Stafford objects to being addressed as "Ms.," a title that Lucy Stone would probably have welcomed had it existed in her time.

During the nearly two centuries in which the use of the distinguishing marital labels Miss or Mrs. for women was rigidly enforced by custom, the labels tended to become parts of women's names, in effect replacing their given names. A boarding school founded by Sarah Porter in Farmington, Connecticut, soon became known as Miss Porter's School. After the actress Minnie Maddern married Harrison Grey Fiske, she became famous as Mrs. Fiske. In the following classroom dialogue, the columnist Ellen Cohn provides a classic example of how the custom works:

> *Question:* Who is credited with discovering radium?
> *Answer* (all together): Madam Curie.
> *Teacher:* Well, class, the woman (who was indeed married to a man named Pierre Curie) had a first name all her own. From now on let's call her Marie Curie.
> *Question:* Can Madam Curie ever be appropriately used?
> *Answer:* Of course. Whenever the inventor of the telephone is called Mr. Bell.[22]

Through the transience and fragmentation that have traditionally characterized women's names, some part of the human female self-image has been sacrificed. It is hardly surprising, therefore, that the second wave of feminist consciousness brought a serious challenge to patronymy and to the assignment of distinguishing marital labels to women. To be named and defined by someone else is to accept an imposed identity—to agree that the way others see us is the way we really are. Naming conventions, like the rest of language, have been shaped to meet the interests of society, and in patriarchal societies the shapers have been men. What is happening now in language seems simply to reflect the fact that, in the words of Dr. Pauli Murray, "women are seeking their own image of themselves nurtured from within rather than imposed from without."[23]

NOTES

1. The recruitment ad appeared in the September 30, 1974, issue of *Time* magazine, pp. 84–85. By the following year, similar ads were posed in such a way that the name of each recruit was visible.
2. Helen Keller, *The Story of My Life,* Garden City, N.Y., Doubleday & Company, 1955, p. 36. (First published in 1902.)
3. Eric H. Lenneberg, "On Explaining Language," *Science,* May 9, 1969, pp. 635–43.
4. Ethel Strainchamps, "Our Sexist Language," in Vivian Gornick and Barbara K. Moran, eds., *Woman in Sexist Society,* New York, Basic Books, 1971, p. 247.
5. The study by James Bruning and William Albott, reported in the March 1974 issue of *Human Behavior,* was described by Melvin Maddocks, the Christian Science Monitor News Service, and reprinted in the *Middletown* (Conn.) *Press,* June 26, 1974.
6. Linwood Sleigh and Charles Johnson, *Apollo Book of Girls' Names,* New York, Thomas Y. Crowell Company, 1962, p. 194.
7. Alice H. Bonnell, "Women at Columbia: The Long March to Equal Opportunities," Columbia Reports, May 1972.
8. University of North Carolina News Bureau press release reprinted in the university's *Alumni Review,* November 1971.
9. Based on figures reported in *The World Almanac & Book of Facts 1975,* New York, Newspaper Enterprise Association, 1974.
10. "Booklet for Women Who Wish to Determine Their Own Names After Marriage," Barrington, Ill., Center for a Woman's Own Name, 1974, p. 7.
11. Quoted by Carmen Rubio in "Staying Single–In Name Only," *Sunday, The Hartford Courant Magazine,* February 2, 1975.
12. Stephen Birmingham, *The Right People: A Portrait of the American Social Establishment,* Boston, Little, Brown and Company, 1968, p. 9.
13. "Newsline," *Psychology Today,* August 1974, p. 29.
14. Robert T. Means, Jr., Letter to the Editor, *Psychology Today,* November 1974, p. 14.
15. Elizabeth Janeway, *Man's World, Woman's Place: A Study in Social Mythology,* New York, A Delta Book, Dell Publishing Company, 1971, p. 337.
16. Mike McGrady, "Family Banking," *New York* magazine, June 12, 1972, p. 42.
17. Otto Weininger, *Sex and Character,* New York, G. P. Putnam's Sons, 1906, p. 206. This is the "authorized translation from the sixth German edition"; also published in London by William Heinemann.

18. Ibid., p. 286.
19. Quoted by Lucy Komisar, *The New Feminism,* New York, Warner Paperback Library, 1971, p. 81. Blackstone's *Commentaries* was first published in 1765–69.
20. Arline Brecher, "Male Lib: The Men Who Want Human Liberation: An Interview with Psychologist Jack Sawyer," *New Woman,* February 1972, p. 73.
21. Jean Stafford, "Don't Use Ms. with Miss Stafford, Unless You Mean ms.," *New York Times,* September 21, 1973, p. 36.
22. Ellen Cohn, "The Liberated Woman," *New York Sunday News* magazine, June 17, 1973, p. 4.
23. Pauli Murray, testimony before Rep. Edith Green's Special Subcommittee on Education in Support of Section 805 of H.R. 16098, June 19, 1970, U.S. Government Printing Office, 1970.

REFLECTING ON MEANING

1. "In our society women's names are less important than men's. The reasons why are not hard to identify, but the consequences for both men and women are more far-reaching than members of either sex . . . have been prepared to admit or even, until recently, to examine." What are some of these consequences, according to Miller and Swift?

2. What are some of the naming customs that Miller and Swift discuss? What does a person's name represent to him or her? What does it represent in society? What connections between name and identity do Miller and Swift make?

3. According to Miller and Swift, "first-naming" often reflects a power inequity between women and men. What is first-naming? In what situations does it occur? Do you agree that it trivializes women and their accomplishments? Why or why not?

4. Miller and Swift trace a link between our conception of family and male surnames. What is this link? How does it influence the way we think about "family"? Why do Miller and Swift implicate it in the "suspended existence of the married woman"? What do they mean?

EXPLORING RHETORICAL STRATEGIES

1. Miller and Swift begin their essay by describing a recruitment ad. In what ways does the ad relate to their thesis? How does it

provide a springboard for the rest of the essay? Why do they say that the ad's format did not occur by accident?

2. Although Miller and Swift's essay focuses on women and names, they make a larger point about the English language. What is this point? How do their assertions about names support this point?

3. What different kinds of evidence do Miller and Swift offer to support their assertions?

The Master's Tools Will Never Dismantle the Master's House

AUDRE LORDE

In this essay from her panel presentation at the Second Sex Conference in New York in 1979, poet Audre Lorde makes provocative statements about the racist, classist, and homophobic positions adopted by many white feminists. By ignoring the perspectives of lesbian and Third World women, feminists are mistakenly using patriarchal tools in their attempts to dismantle patriarchy.

I agreed to take part in a New York University Institute for the Humanities conference a year ago, with the understanding that I would be commenting upon papers dealing with the role of difference within the lives of american women; difference of race, sexuality, class, and age. For the absence of these considerations weakens any feminist discussion of the personal and the political.

It is a particular academic arrogance to assume any discussion of feminist theory in this time and in this place without examining our many differences, and without a significant input from poor women, black and third world women, and lesbians. And yet, I stand here as a black lesbian feminist, having been invited to comment within the only panel at this conference where the input of black feminists and lesbians is represented. What this says about the vision of this conference is sad, in a country where racism, sexism and homophobia are inseparable. To read this program is to assume that lesbian and black women have nothing to say of existentialism, the erotic, women's culture and silence, developing feminist theory, or heterosexuality and power. And what does it mean in personal and political terms when even the two black women who did present here were literally found at the last hour? What does it mean when the tools of a racist patriarchy are used to examine the fruits of that same patriarchy? It means that only the most narrow perimeters of change are possible and allowable.

The absence of any consideration of lesbian consciousness or the consciousness of third world women leaves a serious gap within this conference and within the papers presented here. For example, in a paper on material relationships between women, I was conscious of an either/or model of nurturing which totally dismissed my knowledge as a black lesbian. In this paper there was no examination of mutuality between women, no systems of shared support, no interdependence as exists between lesbians and women-identified women. Yet it is only in the patriarchal model of nurturance that women "who attempt to emancipate themselves pay perhaps too high a price for the results," as this paper states.

For women, the need and desire to nurture each other is not pathological but redemptive, and it is within that knowledge that our real power is rediscovered. It is this real connection which is so feared by a patriarchal world. For it is only under a patriarchal structure that maternity is the only social power open to women.

Interdependency between women is the only way to the freedom which allows the "I" to "be," not in order to be used, but in order to be creative. This is a difference between the passive "be" and the active "being."

Advocating the mere tolerance of difference between women is the grossest reformism. It is a total denial of the creative function of difference in our lives. For difference must be not merely tolerated, but seen as a fund of necessary polarities between which our creativity can spark like a dialectic. Only then does the necessity for interdependency become unthreatening. Only within that interdependency of different strengths, acknowledged and equal, can the power to seek new ways to actively "be" in the world generate, as well as the courage and sustenance to act where there are no charters.

Within the interdependence of mutual (non-dominant) differences lies that security which enables us to descend into the chaos of knowledge and return with true visions of our future, along with the concomitant power to effect those changes which can bring that future into being. Difference is that raw and powerful connection from which our personal power is forged.

As women, we have been taught to either ignore our differences or to view them as causes for separation and suspicion rather than as forces for change. Without community, there is no liberation, only the most vulnerable and temporary armistice between an individual and her oppression. But community must not mean a shedding of our differences, nor the pathetic pretense that these differences do not exist.

Those of us who stand outside the circle of this society's definition of acceptable women; those of us who have been forged in the crucibles of difference: those of us who are poor, who are lesbians, who are black, who are older, know that *survival is not an academic skill.* It is learning how to stand alone, unpopular and sometimes reviled, and how to make common cause with those others identified as outside the structures, in order to define and seek a world in which we can all flourish. It is learning how to take our differences and make them strengths. *For the master's tools will never dismantle the master's house.* They may allow us temporarily to beat him at his own game, but they will never enable us to bring about genuine change. And this fact is only threatening to those women who still define the master's house as their only source of support.

Poor and third world women know there is a difference between the daily manifestations and dehumanizations of marital slavery and prostitution, because it is our daughters who line 42nd Street. The Black panelists' observation about the effects of relative powerlessness and the differences of relationship between black women and men from white women and men illustrate some of our unique problems as black feminists. If white american feminist theory need not deal with the differences between us, and the resulting difference in aspects of our oppressions, then what do you do with the fact that the women who clean your houses and tend your children while you attend conferences on feminist theory are, for the most part, poor and third world women? What is the theory behind racist feminism?

In a world of possibility for us all, our personal visions help lay the groundwork for political action. The failure of the academic feminists to recognize difference as a crucial strength is a failure to reach beyond the first patriarchal lesson. Divide and conquer, in our world, must become define and empower.

Why weren't other black women and third world women found to participate in this conference? Why were two phone calls to me considered a consultation? Am I the only possible source of names of black feminists? And although the black panelist's paper ends on an important and powerful connection of love between women, what about interracial cooperation between feminists who don't love each other?

In academic feminist circles, the answer to these questions is often "We did not know who to ask." But that is the same evasion of responsibility, the same cop-out, that keeps black women's art out of women's exhibitions, black women's work out of most feminist publications except for the occasional "Special Third World Women's Issue,"[1] and black women's texts off of your reading lists. But as Adrienne Rich pointed out in a recent talk, white feminists have educated themselves about such an enormous amount over the past ten years, how come you haven't also educated yourselves about black women and the differences between us—white and black—when it is key to our survival as a movement?

Women of today are still being called upon to stretch across the gap of male ignorance, and to educate men as to our existence and our needs. This is an old and primary tool of all oppressors to keep the oppressed occupied with the master's concerns. Now we hear that it is the task of black and third world women to educate white women, in the face of tremendous resistance, as to our existence, our differences, our relative roles in our joint survival. This is a diversion of energies and a tragic repetition of racist patriarchal thought.

Simone DeBeauvoir once said:

> "It is in the knowledge of the genuine conditions of our lives that we must draw our strength to live and our reasons for acting."

Racism and homophobia are real conditions of all our lives in this place and this time. *I urge each one of us here to reach down into that deep place of knowledge inside herself and touch that terror and loathing of any difference that lives there. See whose face it wears.* Then the personal as the political can begin to illuminate all our choices.

NOTE

1. *Conditions* of Brooklyn, NY, is a major exception. It has fairly consistently published the work of women of color before it was "fashionable" to do so. (editor's note)

REFLECTING ON MEANING

1. This essay is a conference paper from a panel presentation that Lorde made in New York in 1979. What are Lorde's opinions of the panels and the papers presented at this conference? Although she does not specifically use the word *tokenism* in her

critique of either this conference or feminism in general, which of Lorde's comments suggest that she is concerned with this issue?

2. Explain the title of this essay. What are "the master's tools"? What is "the master's house"? Why can't the master's tools dismantle the master's house? Why is Lorde's argument "threatening to those women who still define the master's house as their only source of power"?

3. Why is Lorde upset by the "absence of any consideration of lesbian consciousness or the consciousness of third world women"? Why is it important to consider the consciousness of these marginalized women? Lorde argues that expecting women of color to educate white women constitutes a tragic repetition of racist thought. Explain this position. If women of color don't educate white women, who will?

4. Lorde contends that academic feminists have failed to "recognize difference as a crucial strength ... that raw and powerful connection from which our personal power is forged." How could a recognition of difference aid feminists in their search for equality? Would acknowledging difference undermine and subvert a group's solidarity? Why should white heterosexual feminists be concerned with the issues of black lesbian feminists?

EXPLORING RHETORICAL STRATEGIES

1. Who is the intended audience for this essay? Is Lorde addressing all feminists, or just white academic feminists? When Lorde says, "those of us," to whom is she referring? How might white feminists and feminists of color vary in their responses to her argument?

2. What is the tone of this essay? Do you find it harsh and accusatory? Do any of Lorde's statements or questions appear to be accusations or condemnations? Do you think that this essay offended its original audience? What is your reaction to this essay?

3. What are the main points that Lorde makes? What evidence does she provide to support her assertions? Do you agree with her arguments or not?

Chapter 9 _____

CONVERSATION AND GENDER

Men and Women Talking

GLORIA STEINEM

In this selection, activist Gloria Steinem takes a contro-versial look at the "politics of conversation"—the dynamics of communication between women and men. Her essay debunks several common myths about women and outlines strategies for subverting the hierarchy of gender that influences everyday con-versation.

Once upon a time (that is, just a few years ago), psychologists believed that the way we chose to communicate was largely a function of personality. If certain conversational styles turned out to be more common to one sex than the other (more abstract and aggressive talk for men, for instance, more personal and equivocal talk for women), then this was just another tribute to the influence of biology on personality.

Consciously or otherwise, feminists have challenged this assumption from the beginning. Many of us learned a big lesson in the sixties when our generation spoke out on the injustices of war, as well as of race and class; yet women who used exactly the same words and style as our male counterparts were less likely to be listened to or to be taken seriously. When we tried to talk about this and other frustrations, the lack of listening got worse, with opposition and even ridicule just around every corner. Only women's own meetings and truth telling began to confirm what we had thought

each of us was alone in experiencing. It was also those early consciousness-raising groups that began to develop a more cooperative, less combative way of talking, an alternative style that many
women have maintained and been strengthened by ever since.

The problem is that this culturally different form has remained an almost totally female event. True, it has helped many,
many women arrive at understanding each other and working out
strategies for action. But as an influence on the culturally male style
of public talking, it has remained almost as removed as its more domestic versions of the past.

One reason for our decade or so of delay in challenging existing styles of talking makes good tactical sense. Our first task was to
change the words themselves. We did not feel included (and usage
studies showed that, factually, we were not) in hundreds of such
supposedly generic terms as *mankind* and *he, the brotherhood of man*
and *statesman*. Nor could we fail to see the racial parallels to being
identified as "girls" at advanced ages, or with first names only, or
by our personal connection (or lack of one) to a member of the
dominant group.

Hard as it was (and still is), this radical act of seizing the power
to name ourselves and our experience was easier than taking on
the politics of conversation. Documenting society-wide patterns of
talking required expensive research and surveys. Documenting the
sexism in words, and even conjuring up alternatives, took only one
courageous woman scholar and a dictionary (for instance, *Guidelines for Equal Treatment of the Sexes,* the pioneering work of Alma
Graham for McGraw-Hill). That was one good economic reason
why such works were among the first and best by feminist scholars.

In retrospect, the second cause for delay makes less feminist
sense—the long popularity of assertiveness training. Though most
women needed to be more assertive (or even more aggressive,
though that word was considered too controversial), many of these
courses taught women how to play the existing game, not how to
change the rules. Unlike the feminist assault on sexist language,
which demanded new behavior from men, too, assertiveness training was more reformist than revolutionary. It pushed one-way
change for women only, thus seeming to confirm masculine-style
communication as the only adult model or the most effective one.
Certainly, many individual women were helped, and many men
were confronted with the educational experience of an assertive
woman, but the larger impact was usually to flatter the existing
masculine game of talk-politics by imitating it.

Since then, however, a few feminist scholars have had the time
and resources to document conversational patterns of mixed and

single-sex groups, both here and in Europe. Traditional scholarship, influenced by feminism, has also begun to look at conversational styles as functions of power and environment. For instance, employees pursue topics raised by their employers more than the reverse, older people feel free to interrupt younger ones, and subordinates are more polite than bosses. Since women share all those conversational habits of the less powerful, even across the many lines of class and status that divide us, how accidental can that be?

Even the new feminist-influenced research has a long way to go in neutralizing the masculine bias of existing studies. For instance, *talking* is assumed to be the important and positive act, while *listening,* certainly a productive function, is the subject of almost no studies at all.

Nonetheless, there is enough new scholarship to document different styles, to point out some deficiencies in the masculine model of communicating, and to give us some ideas on how to create a synthesis of both that could provide a much wider range of alternatives for women *and* for men.

I

Have you assumed that women talk more than men—and thus may dominate in discussion if nowhere else? If so, you're not alone. Researchers of sex differences in language started out with that assumption. So did many feminists, who often explained women's supposedly greater penchant for talking as compensation for a lack of power to act.

In fact, however, when Dale Spender, an English feminist and scholar, surveyed studies of talkativeness for her recent book, *Man Made Language,* she concluded that "perhaps in more than any other research area, findings were in complete contradiction with the stereotype. . . . There has not been one study which provides evidence that women talk more than men, and there have been numerous studies which indicate that men talk more than women."

Her conclusion held true regardless of whether the study in question asked individuals to talk into a tape recorder with no group interaction; or compared men and women talking on television; or measured amounts of talk in mixed groups (even among male and female state legislators); or involved group discussions of a subject on which women might be expected to have more expertise. (At a London workshop on sexism and education, for instance, the five men present managed to talk more than their thirty-two female colleagues combined.)

Some studies of male silence in heterosexual couples might seem to counter these results, but Spender's research supports their conclusion that a major portion of female talk in such one-to-one situations is devoted to drawing the man out, asking questions, introducing multiple subjects until one is accepted by him, or demonstrating interest in the subjects he introduces. Clearly, male silence (or silence from a member of any dominant group) is not necessarily the same as listening. It might mean a rejection of the speaker, a refusal to become vulnerable through self-revelation, or a decision that this conversation is not worthwhile. Similarly, talking by the subordinate group is not necessarily an evidence of power. Its motive may be a Scheherazade-like need to intrigue and thus survive, or simply to explain and justify one's actions.

In addition to a generally greater volume of talk, however, men interrupt women more often than vice versa. This is true both in groups and in couples. Male interruptions of women also bring less social punishment than female interruptions of men. Men also interrupt women more often than women interrupt each other.

Moreover, males are more likely to police the subject matter of conversation in mixed-sex groups. One study of working-class families showed that women might venture into such "masculine" topics as politics or sports, and men might join "feminine" discussions of domestic events, but in both cases, it was the men who ridiculed or otherwise straightened out nonconformers who went too far. Even in that London workshop on sexism, for instance, the concrete experiences of the female participants were suppressed in favor of the abstract, general conclusions on sexism that were preferred by the men. The few males present set the style for all the females.

How did the myth of female talkativeness and conversational dominance get started? Why has this supposed female ability been so accepted that many sociologists, and a few battered women themselves, have even accepted it as a justification for some men's violence against their wives?

The uncomfortable truth seems to be that the amount of talk by women has been measured less against the amount of men's talk than against the expectation of female silence.

Indeed, women who accept and set out to disprove the myth of the talkative woman may pay the highest price of all. In attempting to be the exceptions, we silence ourselves. If that is so, measuring our personal behavior against real situations and real studies should come as a relief, a confirmation of unspoken feelings.

We are not crazy for instance, if we feel that, when we finally do take the conversational floor in a group, we are out there in exposed verbal flight, like fearful soloists plucked from the chorus. We are not crazy to feel that years of unspoken thoughts are bottled up inside our heads, and come rushing out in a way that may make it hard to speak calmly even when we finally have the chance.

Once we give up searching for approval for stifling our thoughts, or by imitating the male norm of abstract, assertive communicating, we often find it easier to simply say what needs to be said, and thus to earn respect and approval. Losing self-consciousness and fear allows us to focus on the content of what we are saying instead of on ourselves.

Women's well-developed skill as listeners, perhaps the real source of our much-vaunted "intuition," should not be left behind. We must retain it for ourselves and teach it to men by bringing it with us into our work and daily lives, but that will only happen if we affirm its value. Female culture does have a great deal to contribute to the dominant one. Furthermore, women might feel better about talking equally, selecting subjects, and even interrupting occasionally if we took the reasonable attitude that we are helping men to become attentive and retentive listeners, too. We are paying them the honor of communicating as honestly as we can and treating them as we would want to be treated. After all, if more men gained sensitive listening skills, they would have "intuition," too.

These are practical exercises for achieving a change in the balance of talk. Try tape-recording a dinner-table conversation or meeting (in the guise of recording facts, so participants don't become self-conscious about their talk politics), then play the tape back to the same group, and ask them to add up the number of minutes talked, interruptions, and subject introductions for each gender. Or give a dozen poker chips to each participant in a discussion, and require that one chip be given up each time a person speaks. Or break the silence barrier for those who rarely talk by going around the room once at the beginning of each meeting, consciousness-raising-style, with a question that each participant must answer personally, even if it's only a self-introduction. (It is said that the British Labour party was born only after representatives of its warring factions spent an hour moving their conference table into a larger room. That one communal act broke down individual isolation, just as one round of communal speaking helps break the ice.)

If such methods require more advance planning or influence on the group than you can muster, or if you're trying to sensitize just one person, try some individual acts. Discussing the results of studies on who talks more can produce some very healthy self-consciousness in both women and men. If one group member speaks rarely, try addressing more of your own remarks to her (or him) directly. On the other hand, if one man (or woman) is a domineering interrupter, try objecting directly, interrupting in return, timing the minutes of his or her talk, or just being inattentive. If someone cuts you off, say with humor, "That's one," then promise some conspicuous act when the interruptions get to three. Keep score on "successful" topic introductions, add them up by gender, and announce them at the discussion's end.

If questions and comments following a lecture come mostly from men, stand up and say so. It may be a learning moment for everyone. The prevalence of male speakers in mixed audiences has caused some feminist lecturers to reserve equal time for questions from women only.

To demonstrate the importance of listening as a positive act, try giving a quiz on the content of female and male speakers. Hopefully you *won't* discover the usual: that men often remember what male speakers say better than they remember female speakers' content; that women often remember male content better, too, but that women listen and retain the words of *both* sexes somewhat better than men do.

Check the talk politics concealed in your own behavior. Does your anxiety level go up (and your hostess instincts quiver) when women are talking and men are listening, but not the reverse? For instance, men often seem to feel okay about "talking shop" for hours while women listen, but women seem able to talk in men's presence for only a short time before feeling anxious, apologizing, and encouraging the men to speak. If you start to feel wrongly uncomfortable about making males listen, try this exercise: *keep on talking,* and encourage your sisters to do the same. Honor men by treating them as honestly as you treat women. You will be allowing them to learn.

II

Here are three popular assumptions: (1) Women talk about themselves, personalize, and gossip more than men do. (2) Men would rather talk to groups of men than to mixed groups, and women prefer mixed groups to all-female ones. (3) Women speakers and women's issues are hampered by the feminine style of their presentation. As you've probably guessed by now, most evidence is to the contrary of all three beliefs.

After recording the conversational themes of single-sex and mixed-sex groups, for instance, social psychologist Elizabeth Aries found that men in all-male groups were more likely to talk about themselves than were women in all-female ones. Men were also more likely to use self-mentions to demonstrate superiority or aggressiveness, while women used them to share an emotional reaction to what was being said by others.

Phil Donahue, one of the country's most experienced interviewers, capsulizes the cultural difference between men and women this way: "If you're in a social situation, and women are talking to each other, and one woman says, 'I was hit by a car today,' all the other women will say, 'You're kidding! What happened? Where? Are you all right?' In the same situation with males, one male says, 'I was hit by a car today.' I guarantee you that there will be another male in the group who will say, 'Wait till I tell you what happened to *me.*'"

If quantity of talking about oneself is a measure of "personalizing," and self-aggrandizement through invoking the weakness of others is one characteristic of gossip, then men may be far more "gossipy" than women—especially when one includes sexual bragging.

In addition, subjects introduced by males in mixed groups are far more likely to "succeed" than subjects introduced by women, and, as Aries concluded, women in mixed groups are more likely to interact with men than with other women. Thus, it's not unreasonable to conclude that mixed groups spend more time discussing the lives and interests of male participants than of female ones.

On the other hand, research by Aries and others shows that women are more likely to discuss human relationships. Since "relationships" often fall under "gossip" in men's view, this may account for the frequent male observation that women "personalize" everything. Lecturers often comment, for instance, that women in an audience ask practical questions about their own lives, while men ask abstract questions about groups or policies. When the subject is feminism, women tend to ask about practical problems. Men are more likely to say something like, "But how will feminism impact the American family?"

To quote Donahue, who deals with mostly female audiences: "I've always felt a little anxious about the possibility of a program at night with a male audience. The problem as I perceive it—and this is a generalization—is that men tend to give you a speech, whereas women will ask a question and then listen for the answer and make another contribution to the dialogue. In countless situations I have a male in my audience stand up and say in effect, 'I don't know what you're arguing about; here's the answer to this thing.' And then proceed to give a mini-speech."

Aries also documented the more cooperative, rotating style of talk and leadership in women-only groups: the conscious or unconscious habit of "taking turns." As a result, women actually prefer talking in their own single-sex groups for the concrete advantages of both having a conversational turn and being listened to. On the other hand, she confirmed research that shows male-only groups to have more stable hierarchies, with the same one or several talkers dominating most of the time.

As Aries points out, no wonder men prefer the variation and opportunity of mixed-sex audiences. They combine the seriousness of a male presence with more choice of styles—and, as Spender adds caustically, the assurance of at least some noncompetitive listeners.

Women's more gentle delivery, "feminine" choice of adjectives, and greater attention to grammar and politeness have been heavily criticized. Linguist Robin Lakoff pioneered the exposure of "ladylike" speech as a double bind that is both required of little girls, and used as a reason why, as adults, they may not be seen as forceful or serious. (Even Lakoff seems to assume, however, that female speech is to be criticized as the deficient form, while male speech is the norm and thus escapes equal comment.) Sociologist Arlie Hochschild also cites some survival techniques of racial minorities that women of all races seem to share: playing dumb and dissembling, for instance, or expressing frequent approval of others.

But whether this criticism of female speech patterns is justified or not, there is also evidence that a rejection of the way a woman speaks is often a way of blaming or dismissing her without dealing with the content of what she is saying.

For instance, women speakers are more likely to hear some version of "You have a good point, but you're not making it effectively," or "Your style is too aggressive/weak/loud/quiet." It is with such paternalistic criticisms that male politicians often dismiss the serious message of a female colleague, or that husbands turn aside the content of arguments made by their wives.

It is also such criticisms that allow women candidates to be rejected without dealing with the substance of the issues they raise. When Bella Abzug of New York and Gloria Schaeffer of Connecticut both ran for political office in one recent year, each was said to have a personal style that would prevent her from being an effective senator: Abzug because she was "too abrasive and aggressive, and Schaeffer because she was "too ladylike and quiet." Style was made the central issue by the press, and thus became one in the public-opinion polls. Both were defeated.

There are three anomalies that give away this supposedly "helpful" criticism. First, it is rarely used when a woman's message is not challenging to male power. (How often are women criticized for being too fierce in defense of their families? How often was Phyllis Schlafly criticized for being too aggressive in her opposition to the Equal Rights Amendment?) Second, the criticism is rarely accompanied by real support, even when the critic presents himself (or herself) as sympathetic. (Women political candidates say they often get critiques of their fund-raising techniques instead of cash, even from people who agree with them on issues.) Finally, almost everyone, regardless of status, feels a right to criticize. (Women professors report criticism of their teaching style from young students, as do women bosses from their employees.)

Just as there is a conversational topic that men in a group often find more compelling than any introduced by a woman (even when it's exactly the same topic, but *re*introduced by a man), or a political issue that is "more important" than any of concern to women, so there is usually a better, more effective style than the one a woman happens to be using.

Men *would* support us, we are told, if only we learned how to ask for their support in the right way. It's a subtle and effective way of blaming the victim.

What can we do to break through these stereotypes? Keeping notes for one meeting or one week on the male/female ratio of gossip or self-mentions could be educational. Declaring a day's moratorium on all words that end in "-tion" and all generalities might encourage men to state their personal beliefs *without* disguising them as general conclusions.

As a personal exercise, try countering slippery abstractions with tangible examples. When David Susskind and Germaine Greer were guests on the same television talk show, for instance, Susskind used general, pseudoscientific statements about women's monthly emotional changes as a way of excusing the injustices cited by this very intelligent woman. Finally, Greer turned politely to Susskind and said. "Tell me, David. Can you tell if I'm menstruating right now—or not?" She not only eliminated any doubts raised by Susskind's statements, but subdued his pugnacious style for the rest of the show.

Men themselves are working to break down the generalities and competitiveness that a male-dominant culture has imposed on them. Some are meeting in all-male consciousness-raising groups, learning how to communicate more openly and personally among themselves.

Many women are also trying to break down the barriers we ourselves maintain. For instance, women's preference for talking to one another has a great deal to do with the shorthand that shared experience provides. Furthermore, the less powerful group usually knows the powerful one much better than vice versa—blacks have had to understand whites in order to survive, women have had to know men—yet the powerful group can afford to regard the less powerful one as a mystery. Indeed, the idea of differentness and the Mysterious Other may be necessary justifications for the power imbalance and the lack of empathy it requires.

One result is that, even when the powerful group *wants* to listen, the other may despair of talking: it's just too much trouble to explain. Recognizing this unequal knowledge encourages women to talk about themselves to men, at least to match the time they spend talking about themselves. After all, they cannot read our minds.

On issues of style, role reversals are enlightening. For instance, ask a man who is critical of "aggressive" women to try to argue a serious political point while speaking "like a lady." A woman candidate might also ask critics to write a speech in the style they think she should use. Responding in kind can create a quick reversal. There's a certain satisfaction to saying, in the middle of a man's impassioned speech: "I suppose you have a point to make, but you're not expressing it well. Now, if you just used more personal examples. If you changed your language, your timing, and perhaps your suit. . . ."

Finally, if all talk fails, try putting the same message in writing. The point is to get your message across, whether or not the man in question can separate it from the medium.

III

Women's higher-pitched voices and men's lower ones are the result of physiology. Because deep voices are more pleasant and authoritative, women speakers will always have a problem. Besides, female facial expressions and gestures aren't as forceful . . . and so on. It's true that tone of voice is partly created by throat construction and the resonance of bones. Though there is a big area of male-female overlap in voice tone, as well as in size, strength, and other physical attributes, we assume that all men will have a much deeper pitch than all women.

In fact, however, no one knows exactly how much of our speaking voices are imitative and culturally produced. Studies of young boys before puberty show that their vocal tones may deepen *even before physiological changes can account for it.* They are imitating the way the males around them speak. Dale Spender cites a study of males who were not mute, but who were born deaf and thus unable to imitate sound. Some of them never went through an adolescent voice change at all.

Whatever the mix of physiological and cultural factors, however, the important point is that the *acceptance* of vocal tone is definitely cultural and therefore subject to change.

In Japan, for instance, a woman's traditionally high-pitched, soft speaking voice is considered a very important sexual attribute. (When asked in a public-opinion poll what attribute they found most attractive in women, the majority of Japanese men said "voice.") Though trained to speak in upper registers, Japanese women, like many of their sisters around the world, often speak in lower tones when men are not present. They may even change their language as well. (A reporter's tapes of Japanese schoolgirls talking among themselves caused a scandal. They were using masculine word endings and verbs in a country where the language is divided into formally masculine and feminine forms.) Thus, Japanese men may find a high voice attractive not for itself but for its tribute to a traditional subservience.

Some American women also cultivate a high, childish, or whispery voice à la Marilyn Monroe. We may sense that a woman is talking to a man on the other end of the phone, or a man to a woman, because she lightens her normal tone and he deepens his.

A childlike or "feminine" vocal style becomes a drawback, however, when women try for any adult or powerful role. Female reporters were kept out of television and radio for years by the argument that their voices were too high, grating, or nonauthoritative to speak the news credibly. Even now, women's voices may be thought more suitable for human interest and "soft news," while men still announce "hard news." In the early days of television, women were allowed to do the weather reports—very sexily. When meteorology and weather maps became the vogue, however, most stations switched to men. Even now, 85 percent of all voice-overs on television ads, including those for women's products, are done by men. Even on floor wax and detergents, men are likely to be the voices of expertise and authority.

In the long run, however, men may suffer more from cultural restrictions on tone of voice than women do. Linguist Ruth Brend's study of male and female intonation patterns in the United States, for instance, disclosed four contrasting levels used by women in normal speech, but only three levels used by men. This isn't a result of physiology: men also have at least four levels available to them, but they rarely use the highest one. Thus, women may speak publicly in both high and low tones with some degree of social acceptability, but men must use their lower tones only. It's okay to flatter the ruling class with imitation, just as it's okay for women to wear pants or for blacks to speak and dress like Establishment whites, but it's less okay for men to wear feminine clothes, for whites to adopt black speech and street style, or for men to imitate or sound like women. (Such upper-class exceptions as the female-impersonating shows put on by the Hasty Pudding Club at Harvard or by the very rich men of the Bohemian Grove in California seem to indicate that even ridicule of women requires security. It's much less likely to happen at the working-class level of bowling clubs and bars.)

As the price of "masculinity," men as a group are losing variety in their speech and an ability to express a full range of emotions. The higher proportion of masculine monotones is also a penalty to the public ear.

In the same way, physical expressiveness may be viewed as "feminine." Women can be vivacious. We are allowed more varieties of facial expression and gestures. Men must be rocklike. Certainly, some emotive and expressive men are being imprisoned by that belief.

The down side is that women's greater range of expression is also used to ridicule females as emotionally unstable. That sad point is made by Nancy Henley in *Body Politics: Power, Sex, and Nonverbal Communication.* "Women's facial expressivity," she explains, "has been allowed a wider range than men's, encompassing within the sex stereotype not only pleasant expressions, but negative ones like crying." Since males are encouraged to leave crying and other emotional expression in their childhoods, females who retain this human ability are often compared to children.

Nonetheless, women's wider range also allows us to recognize more physical expression when we see it. Henley refers to a study showing that women of all races and black men usually do better than white men at identifying nonverbal emotional clues. We're both less imprisoned by the rocklike mask of being in control, and more needful of the survival skill of paying attention.

In short, women need to affirm and expand expressiveness, but men are also missing some major ways of signalling the world and getting signals back.

You can't change vocal cords (theirs or ours), but you can make sure they're being well used. Tape-record women talking together, then record the same people talking to men. It's a good way to find out whether we're sending out geishalike tonal clues. Some women are neglecting our lower range. Others, especially when trying to be taken seriously, are overcompensating for supposed emotionalism by narrowing to a "reasonable" monotone. Men may also change under pressure of taped evidence: for instance, the contrast between their dullness when talking with men and their expressiveness when talking to children. Many actors, female and male, are living testimonials to how much and how quickly—with effort, exercise, and freedom—a vocal range can change.

Most important, remember that there is nothing *wrong* with women's voices, and no subject or emotion they cannot convey. This is especially important for women who are lonely tokens. The first women in law and business schools, the board room, or the assembly line, often report that the sound of their own voices comes as a shock—a major barrier to reciting in class, speaking up on policy, or arguing in union meetings. It may take a while for words said in a female voice to be taken seriously, but a head-turning response to the unusual sound is also a tribute to its owner as a courageous pioneer.

The advent of video recorders is a major breakthrough in understanding and changing our nonverbal expressions. Watching the incontrovertible evidence of how we come across to others can be more useful than years of psychiatry. Many men and boys could also benefit from such expressiveness exercises as a game of charades, or communicating with children. Women and girls can free body movements through sports, a conscious effort to take up more space when sitting or standing, and using body language we may not use only when relaxed with other women. Many of us could benefit from watching female impersonators and learning the many ways in which we have been trained to be female impersonators, too.

The point is not that one gender's cultural style is superior to the other's. The current "feminine" style of communicating may be better suited to, say, the performing arts, medical diagnosis, and conflict resolution. It has perfected emotional expressiveness, careful listening, and a way of leaving an adversary with dignity intact. The current "masculine" style may be better suited to, say, procedural instruction, surgical teams and other situations requiring hierarchical command, and job interviews. It has perfected linear and abstract thinking, quick commands, and a willingness to speak well of oneself or present views with assertiveness. But we will never achieve this full human circle of expression if women imitate the male "adult" style. We have to teach as well as learn.

A feminist assault on the politics of talking, and listening, is a radical act. It's a way of transforming the cultural vessel in which both instant communication and long-term anthropological change are carried. Unlike the written word, or visual imagery, or any form of communication divorced from our presence, talking and listening won't allow us to hide. There is no neutral page, image, sound, or even a genderless name to protect us. We are demanding to be accepted and understood by all the senses and for our whole selves.

That's precisely what makes the change so difficult. And so crucial.

REFLECTING ON MEANING

1. Steinem presents several prevalent social myths about women and conversation. What are these myths? Are they still prevalent today?

2. Steinem's summary of research into the "politics of conversation" addresses several important topics: the roles women and men play in mixed-gender conversation, the different ways men and women are perceived in mixed-gender conversation, and the physiology of speech in relation to social values. According to Steinem, what does research suggest about these issues?

3. Steinem also cites research that suggests men and women have very different conversational styles. What differences does she point out? What is the "masculine" style? What is the "feminine" style?

EXPLORING RHETORICAL STRATEGIES

1. Steinem begins her essay with the words "Once upon a time (that is, just a few years ago) . . . " What is the significance of this opening? What does this allusion suggest about her perspective on her topic?

2. The essay seems to have multiple purposes. What evidence can you find to delineate these various purposes? Does Steinem successfully fulfill all of them? In what ways?

3. What evidence of Steinem's intended audience can you find? How might women and men respond differently to her essay? How might Steinem need to change her discussion to address an audience of the opposite gender?

Talking Trouble

ANNE ROIPHE

Are women essentially *different from men, or have they just learned different rules of social behavior? In this essay, Anne Roiphe considers both sides of the essentialist/social constructionism debate about the origin of men's and women's differing communication styles.*

It is a highly public yet intensely personal debate. Psychologists, sociologists, feminist theorists, talk-show hosts, pop-culture writers and academics are lining up to throw rotten tomatoes at each other. There's a lot at stake, and we don't want to be wrong about this one.

Women's management style is or is not significantly different from men's. Women do or do not suffer in the workplace from gender differences. Are you a more accommodating, cooperative, "we" sort of person than your male colleague? Is his style of grabbing attention and credit, interrupting you and defining his turf giving him the promotion that you deserve? Do you speak softly, hesitantly, hedgingly (um, maybe, perhaps?), while he swears, shouts, pounds his desk and makes clear, affirmative statements? As you try to avoid the word that rhymes with witch, are you muffling yourself, clipping your own wings? Do you want to be liked, while he wants to be top dog?

The big question behind the others in this: Are women *essentially* different from men? Have little girls learned different rules of social behavior from little boys, or is there something else that constantly stymies women in the workplace?

The answers aren't as easy as they seem. Social science always sounds true, but often isn't. The experts have a long track record of misinforming us. Once upon a time, they thought women didn't have the physical strength to get a college education, and they had the charts to prove it. They have biases, they miscount, they miss the forest for the trees. And when they disagree, we have to be especially wary.

This particular debate began with a psychologist, Robin Lakoff, who proposed in her 1975 book *Language and Woman's Place* that women characteristically use a speech style that is hesitant, ingratiating and indirect. Across the country, graduate students set out to prove—or disprove—her point. Now we have Deborah Tannen, a sociolinguistics professor at Georgetown University and author of *You Just Don't Understand,* which has been a best-seller since its publication in 1990, when it topped the hit parade of cocktail-party conversations with its examples of how gender affects communication style. Tannen made the case that little girls playing in groups learn to blend in, be sensitive to one another's feelings, avoid boasting; that they are punished by exclusion when they are bossy. Little boys, she observed, are primarily concerned with dominance and are rewarded for being the boss—whether in Little League or in the gang selling lemonade on the corner. Boy groups, she said, are always about who's up and who's down. Girl groups are about including everyone and at least feigning niceness. Men are the people of the ladder, and women are the people of the circle.

Now Tannen has written a second book, out this month [Oct. 1994], called *Talking from 9 to 5.* It extends her thesis into the workplace, and it overflows with convincing anecdotes—some as funny as they are depressing—about how women's language choices and patterns of speech constantly undercut them on the job. The book offers valuable observations for anyone who goes to work, male or female, but there are two sides to this story and Tannen's critics can be as convincing as she is.

For *Talking from 9 to 5,* Tannen has watched, taped and analyzed men and women talking to one another in a wide variety of work settings. What she sees consistently is women asking questions instead of making declarations, saying *we* instead of *I,* allowing others to snatch their glory and take their raises. What she sees is women who have been socialized not to brag losing credit for their own accomplishments. She does not blame men for inherent sexism or chauvinism, but sees the problem in terms of misunderstanding due to opposing male and female verbal styles, developed in childhoods spent playing largely with our own sex. Tannen describes a case in which two co-workers who are friendly with each other are asked to do a marketing survey together. The man begins by telling the woman which categories he wants to research, assuming that she will simply accept what's left. The woman is taken aback, and tells him so; she expected that they would tell each other what they wanted to cover and then compromise. After this initial verbal stumble, they are able to negotiate.

Tannen also described a worrisome female inability to stand out in a crowd, get to know the boss, trumpet accomplishments. She says that men more often allow problems to happen and then charge forward like white knights to solve them, making themselves look good in the process. Women, by contrast, spend a lot of time anticipating and preventing problems—and consequently rarely get credit when nothing goes wrong. Tannen points out that when women talk in hesitant, tentative ways, they may be trying to camouflage their position or soften the impact of what they are saying for the sake of their listeners, but their approach can make them appear to lack confidence. She observes that men speak more often, interrupt more, take up more meeting time and turn up the volume when they hold forth. This style, while not earning you points from Miss Manners, does seem to impress others, including the boss, and makes it less likely that the more deferential or indirect women in the room will be recognized for their contributions. In one case, a woman's talent for self-deprecation allowed a meeting's participants, including Tannen herself, to come away thinking that the most senior man present—who had only supported the excellent suggestions of this woman—had contributed most to the discussion. Tannen didn't recognize her mistaken assumption until she typed up her notes of the meeting.

Also in Tannen's camp is psychologist John Gray, who wrote *Men Are from Mars, Women Are from Venus.* This pop best-seller, which has sold more than a million copies since its publication in 1992, goes beyond Tannen's hypothesis to announce that we are so different from each other that—well, you read the loopy title. Gray, like Tannen, hears the static on our wave lengths and tries to explain how our inability to receive each other's signals causes trouble at home as well as on the job. And he says things that seem right on a gut level: Men want to be trusted and admired, not improved; women want to be listened to and given emotional support, not solutions.

While his observations on how frightened men are—and how insecure both sexes are—seem accurate, Gray's answers tend to be mechanical and broad. Truth is, we're all complex, elusive, sometimes self-destructive souls. We're much harder to pin down than Gray maintains. His oversimplications fall apart in the heat of real life. Not every woman, for instance, wants only comfort when she tells her husband that she has been passed over for promotion. She may also want him to be a sounding board, to think though a plan of action with her. The so-called male focus on action may be the most comforting response of all in such cases.

Following the mega-success of Tannen's book, a flood of similarly titled mass-market tomes has nearly drowned us: *Breaking Through Male Silence; Genderflex; How Can I Get Through to You?; Miscommunication and Problematic Talk;* and *Communicate with Confidence!*

Like all schematic solutions, each contains a kernel of truth but can't be applied across the board. My grandmother told me to wash my hands before eating unless I was starving: good advice, but not sufficient for all dinner encounters.

Despite the proliferation and popularity of these "gender-speak" books, there are critics who dispute aspects of the theories. One of the most articulate debunkers is Mary Crawford, a psychology professor at the University of South Carolina. In her book, *Talking Differences,* also out this fall, she disputes the accuracy of previous academic research and says that Tannen has failed to thoroughly analyze the power issues involved in speech and the difference that role and status make in how people use language. In fairness, Tannen does say that senior-level participants are freer to speak in meetings, since they have less to lose in that setting than subordinates do. But Crawford attacks the idea that there is something essentially female in submissive, blurred language. She does not accept the notion that little girls' groups are inclusive and nonhierarchical, arguing that the gender-difference proponents are ignoring factors of age, social class and sexual orientation.

Crawford, who believes that society shapes us, says we learn patterns of speech in a crucible of social actions. The explanations for how we behave are not in our nature but in our world. She asserts that speech patterns depend more on social status and the power relation between speaker and listener than on gender. She maintains that not every interruption is an act of dominance and not every hedge (well, maybe not) is an admission of weakness.

What particularly galls Crawford is that Tannen's view puts the burden of change on the backs of women, rather than seeing the cultural responsibility for our displacement in the corporate world. She feels that finding the right way to ask for something doesn't mean that you will get it. She finds it hard to accept that the nature of our childhood play groups is so important to us as adults. She cites studies that show that if someone cuts in a line, males and females protest with equal vociferousness. In one psychologist's rather mean-spirited study, young men and women hesitated for the same period of time and then were equally adamant in telling a fellow student to stop playing loud music while they were taking an exam.

Crawford and those who agree with her dislike all this talk about "women's style" because they are worried that it diverts us from real group political action. They are concerned that we will assume that it's our fault that we haven't been promoted. Myra Stober, a workplace-issues expert and a Stanford University dean, has said, "I just don't see any good evidence [based on the studies I've looked at] for the difference perspective. [The notion of gender-speak] glorifies existing stereotypes of female behavior." An Emory University study finds few communication differences between men and women in positions of leadership. "There's a scary orthodoxy about this," Jeffrey Sonnenfeld, who runs the Center for Leadership and Career Studies at Emory's business school in Atlanta has noted. "It dictates that all women should behave in a certain way."

Rozanne Ridgeway, the former U.S. ambassador to Finland, made much the same point at a roundtable on female leadership styles sponsored by Sara Lee earlier this year. "Job responsibilities," she pointed out, "can dictate style." Ridgeway went on to say that when she led international delegations, "my state of inclusiveness had nothing to do with my being female ... [but] with the fact that each of the eighty men on my side of the table had the power to sink the outcome of any negotiation." On the other hand, when she works with enlisted men, she says, she takes a militaristic, hierarchical stance.

Feminist socialist Cynthia Fuchs Epstein, author of *Deceptive Distinctions,* a seminal book, published in 1988, which argues that most gender distinctions are socially constructed and superficial, says, "The emphasis on female management style is reductionist and simplistic. All the studies give contradictory results; they were done with young college students, and what they have measured are, in fact, very tiny differences. Most of the studies have not been borne out by research. In fact, all the evidence indicates that there is more variation between *people* than between *sexes*."

Sheila Wellington, the director of Catalyst, a corporate-research firm that focuses on women's issues, is also irritated by all this gender-style talk. "I think to focus on difference is to grab the wrong end of the stick," she says. Like Stober, she worries that if we buy into the notion that women are supposed to act one way or another, we will just perpetuate stereotypes. "This information about women's behaviors will be translated to the detriment of women," says Wellington. "The inevitable effect of the 'feminine' style will be stereotyping. And in the end, all stereotypes are limiting–be they positive or negative. They are disabling, divisive. Women must be empowered to develop personal styles that allow them to be effective."

So what do *we* figure, you and I, who are not gladiators in this fight? Since most of us are not social scientists, we can't evaluate the methodology of a given experiment. But we can be skeptical of results, gleaned from college-age kids, that can easily be skewed to demonstrate whatever the researcher wishes. Overall, all these authors sound reasonable–bestsellers and academics alike–and the supporting studies of both sides are somewhat convincing. But both sides can't be right–can they?

Common sense tells us that women in general do have to seek and use authority somewhat differently than men do. Men can order other people around without risking their masculinity, while women are often in trouble if their culturally defined femininity is brazenly abandoned. Common sense tells us that, whether by nature or by nurture, whether it happened in our Girl Scout troop or in the womb, we do not fear expressing emotions as much as men do, and we are more cautious about direct assertion. Tannen is right: We're *not* comfortable talking ourselves up, and some of us find it difficult to issue orders.

Some of us, of course, don't. Common sense also tells us that women arrive at their jobs with varying levels of confidence and highly diverse personal styles. One flirts, one schemes, one drives forward like a Mack truck. So do men. The smartest of both sexes probably use all these techniques at different times, to one degree or another. Tannen's advice to listen to ourselves is sound; if our way of speaking or comporting ourselves on the job is self-defeating, we should change it. It is not blaming the victim to figure out a way to climb over a wall. You can bet that the top medical student who told Tannen about a low evaluation she received from a supervising doctor–simply, she later learned, because she asked more questions than her peers–learned to ask less and wonder more. If we don't speak up enough, if we're afraid to interrupt and seize our space at the conference table, if we're having trouble making ourselves clear, then we should try to change. What's wrong with accepting some sensible advice?

On the other hand, Crawford and company are also right. This cannot be a simple matter of women's ineffectiveness taught around the campfire. It's harmful and stupid to think that the barriers many of us still face in the work world are ones we built ourselves. They are the result of longstanding inequities. We sound deferential because, for the most part, we *don't* have the power. This is not a simple male-versus-female issue. It's about who controls the marbles in any given workplace. I am fairly certain that most women CEOs don't sound like shrinking violets, and just as certain that men without power sound deferential. "Yes, sir," they say.

We need to think of ourselves as a political movement, as generations in the process of a still-new revolution. I'll bet anything that my daughters aren't anywhere near as nice in a meeting as I am, and I'll bet that I'm not as quiet as my best friend. As Epstein rightly points out, "The notion at the base of this debate is that women have a single personality." The generation brought up with the assumption that they can become anything they want is bound to use less hedging language than my mother's generation did.

Women have always been as competitive as men, as desirous of the top prize, as capable of asserting, inventing, pushing, getting what they want, as men: Scarlett O'Hara was nobody's wimp. The prize has just been different, and our battlefield has been socially framed as domestic or personal until very recently. Now that we can range across the culture, we will lope along, some of us racing, some of us walking. Just like men.

Not long ago, when my daughter was rushed to the hospital with an ectopic pregnancy, the staff would not operate until they had verified the diagnosis with a sonogram. Hours passed. My daughter was in great pain. I kept asking the nurses to check with the doctors. I asked very politely. I thought, "I'd better be nice or they'll ignore me." Nothing happened. Then my husband arrived and began yelling. My daughter was in shock. The doctors came running. Her life was saved not because of my deference to authority, but because he raised hell.

I learned something that day. Next time, *I'll* yell. I like to think that my error was generational and that the feminist movement will make all of us more direct, more confrontational and more able to yell when the occasion demands it.

Meanwhile, both the Tannen and Crawford positions have something to offer us. If our speech is confused or sends the wrong message to the Big Cheese, we can alter how we speak. Why not? Seems like a good idea; do it. And we do have to consider female social parameters in office behavior. It's all right to swear like the guys, but we can't suddenly start spewing baseball statistics unless we really love them, and few of us really do. We would sound silly talking in a way that seems unnatural to us. We have to find our own style—dominant, effective, noticed, yet still human, recognizably human. We *are* gendered, and while we do not know what gender makes us do or exactly why, we do know that gender infuses our personal gifts with its particular essence. I think while the sociologists argue this one out, we shouldn't worry about being too feminine or too masculine. What we have to worry about is being damned good at what we do and finding a style that is both effective and comfortable. If that involves being cooperative, likable, friendly, so be it. If the moment calls for cutting throats, we ought to be able to slash with the best of them.

I once met Rosario Murillo, the wife of Daniel Ortega, the former Nicaraguan president, and a former Sandinista rebel herself. She wore stiletto heels and bright red lipstick. She was rumored to have killed an enemy general with a knife. "Wow," I thought. "She's beautiful, sexy, brainy... and dangerous." Mary Crawford is a little on the grim, righteous side. Deborah Tannen is very earnest. Murillo was just right; tough and feminine at the same time. My life would be perfect if I had all three as personal trainers.

REFLECTING ON MEANING

1. Roiphe asks two important questions: "Are women *essentially* different from men?" and "Have little girls learned different rules of social behavior from little boys, or is there something else that constantly stymies women in the workplace?" What answers does Roiphe offer for these questions? Consider the various "genderspeak" books that Roiphe summarizes: Robin Lakoff's *Language and Women's Place,* Deborah Tannen's *You Just Don't Understand* and *Talking From 9 to 5,* and John Gray's *Men Are from Mars, Women Are from Venus.* How do each of these books explain the differences between the conversational styles of women and men?

2. How does Roiphe contrast the "genderspeak" books with the work of their critics? Explain the argument presented in Mary Crawford's *Talking Differences.* Why is the issue of power so important to Crawford's position? What particularly "galls" Crawford about Tannen's view? What important insights are offered in Cynthia Fuchs Epstein's *Deceptive Distinctions* and the research of Sheila Wellington?

3. After discussing the issues raised by both sides of the debate about the source of women's and men's differing conversational styles, Roiphe concludes that each side has something important to contribute. What conclusions does she reach? What useful observations does she make about power within relationships?

4. Roiphe argues that women "shouldn't worry about being too feminine or too masculine. What we have to worry about is being damned good at what we do and finding a style that is both effective and comfortable." How does this statement incorporate elements from both the essentialist and the social constructionist view of communication styles?

EXPLORING RHETORICAL STRATEGIES

1. What are two possible ways of interpreting the title of this essay, "Talking Trouble"? How do each of these interpretations illumi-

nate Roiphe's discussion of male and female conversational styles? In the second paragraph of her essay, Roiphe begins with two contradictory statements about women, then she offers a long series of questions to consider. How effective is this strategy of introducing her subject? After reading her questions, what position do you think she will take? Are you surprised by the conclusions she makes? How effectively does she answer her own questions?

2. This piece was originally published in *Working Woman* magazine in October 1994. Why was it an appropriate topic for that specific audience at that specific time? Describe the authorial voice that Roiphe adopts. Is it convincing? How useful are Roiphe's arguments for a contemporary audience? What other "gender-speak" books have appeared since 1994? Do they offer any new insights on women's or men's conversational styles?

3. Consider Roiphe's juxtaposition of social science research and autobiographical narrative. What rhetorical effect does this intermingling of genres produce? What is Roiphe's purpose in mentioning her daughter's ectopic pregnancy? Why does she close her essay by saying that "life would be perfect" if she had Deborah Tannen, Mary Crawford, and Rosario Crawford (a former Sandinista rebel) as her personal trainers?

Nods That Silence

LYNET UTTAL

Women's studies professor Lynet Uttal compares the politics of conversation within both Anglo feminist groups and Women of Color feminist groups, proposing a redefinition of feminist sisterhood that acknowledges both differences and disagreement.

I have participated regularly in Anglo feminist groups and Women of Color feminist groups for almost a decade now, and I am still wondering why each engages me so differently. In the Anglo feminist groups, I feel distanced and disconnected from the ways things get done. My relationships with the other women are always smooth and politely managed. I always feel that my presence is welcomed, but I usually don't agree wholeheartedly with the ideas, the analyses and the organizational tactics. Yet I continue to participate because I am concerned with many of the issues these groups address.

In contrast, my experiences in groups with women from many different racial/ethnic groups have been more connected while at the same time more conflictual. I feel much more understanding from these women, and membership in the ideas we pursue together, even though I more frequently find myself frustrated and heated up.

The major disagreement I have with the practices of Anglo feminist groups is the strong message they send out that our discussions need to be smooth, orderly, efficient and supportive. The idea is that we are not going to do to one another what men have always done to us—we are not going to silence one another nor be competitive. Instead, we are going to provide a space which is supportive and respectful of different opinions. We are not going to trash each other. So we tell ourselves to make space for everyone to talk. Nod supportively. We each have the right to speak after being silenced for so long.

But are we being supportive and respectful when we hear but fail to listen to one another? As I sit and listen in Anglo feminist groups, I often wonder if we are silencing ourselves in yet another way. When someone speaks and says something I don't fully understand or agree with, I search the faces of others in the group to see if they understand and are really in agreement with the speaker, or if they are silently acquiescing to the person speaking only to be supportive? I see some heads nodding, yet I see many others still, frozen, holding their thoughts inside because they don't feel it's okay to speak up and ask for clarification or disagree. Every time I try to verbalize my thoughts, I think over and over again in my head how to state my thoughts diplomatically. Yet even with this careful attention to words, after I speak I always end up feeling that I have breached a code of conduct. I always regret ever having spoken. When my over-rehearsed thoughts come bursting out, the sea of heads nods politely, acknowledging my right to speak, but it appears that their souls have failed to listen to what I have said.

These groups seem to gain their strength from a collectivity of women who are generally in agreement with one another. Those are the ones who come back again and again. Others come for awhile, remain quiet and then silently disappear without ever having been missed because they were never noticed. A few attempt to speak up. But they too fade away, silenced and subtly excluded by blank looks of "supportive" listening.

Yet without more interactive discussions in Anglo feminist groups, these "safe" spaces have set limits on how much we can learn from participating in these groups. Little can be carried over to other parts of our lives in an effective way. So if this is all that feminist sisterhood is about—protecting ourselves from any differences, maintaining at all costs an image of solidarity—it's a fruitless practice that leaves us at a standstill.

I worry constantly about this issue of hearing without listening. I have become even more concerned recently because Anglo middle-class feminist groups are actively recruiting women of color. Can a sisterhood that has historically provided safe and supportive spaces based on the commonalities between women also provide room for dialogue between women's differences? Thinking about the consciousness-raising groups of the sixties, I wonder how many women came to these groups and didn't stay. I hear that the groups were powerful because women were given a voice and learned strength from finding others who had their same struggles. Or was this an illusion which resulted when those who differed didn't stick around? Did practices of aligning around common experiences silence some women then, too?

I felt tremendous relief when I read Bonnie Thornton Dill's discussion on the problems of "sisterhood" in the women's movement.[1] She wrote that the political practice of sisterhood is based on bonding around common experiences. This concept assumes that all women in all societies experience patriarchal subordination in the same way. The experiences of Anglo middle-class women have defined what these commonalities are in the contemporary women's movement and have ignored how race and class dynamics create different experience for other women. She verbalized what I had sensed all along.

We are limited when we organize women's groups around assumed and certain sets of shared experiences. Instead of simply reproducing our past shared experiences, I think that we need to create new shared understandings by working with one another in women's groups. We need to learn more about each other. We need to ask each other, "How are you making sense of this situation?" "What's going on with you?" and "What do you think should be done?" and then negotiate a path we can all walk together. But in order for this to happen we must stop politely and passively hearing one another. We need to begin to actively listen and discuss our differences as well as our similarities so that we may accomplish what this sisterhood stuff is really supposed to be all about.

When I speak, I am tired of getting polite nods which hear me, but don't tell me if anyone is really listening. I am tired of the polite silences and the lack of responses or requests for clarification. I am tired of feeling that my words were given space, but they might as well have not been said because they didn't get built upon or incorporated into the conversation. I can feel the polite bridge built from the speaker before me, over my words, to the next speaker—a useless bridge because the ideas under it are already dried up by the silence from the banks.

The sisterhood I envision would mean *creating* a sense of unity that comes from all of us working together, building on our diverse experiences. But how is this going to happen? How do we learn to listen as well as hear one another? How can we learn to validate one another while at the same time provide room for questioning and expressing disagreement and misunderstanding? How can we do all this without seeming unsupportive and too competitive?

I believe it means that we have to be allowed to "get messy." A polite nod does not incorporate ideas into an ongoing discussion. Nods of validation simply further silence women by not giving serious consideration to what has just been said. No one is listening when they have no responses. Nor does it help any of us to question our own beliefs. On the other hand, a question or response lets me know that someone is listening to me and working with me to understand. Instead of a patronizing nod, I prefer the query which makes my comments a building block in the discussion. Laughter and disagreements are also responses which help us think further.

In each of the Women of Color groups I have been in, there is always a great deal of confusion caused by disagreements. Our ideas are threads that don't always weave together and colors that clash. Our ideas of how to structure time come into conflict. Some of us are very goal-directed and want to be efficient with our time together. Others of us are more willing to sacrifice efficiency in order to figure things out carefully. The distinction between Anglo feminist groups and Women of Color feminist groups is that differences are more explicitly acknowledged in discussions in Women of Color groups. By discussing them, these differences become less threatening and conflictual.

Our shared efforts to figure out the differences make us feel closer to women whom we each initially perceived as "others." There is a genuine commitment to work through the confusion no matter how much time it takes. It comes in the form of questions, hurt feelings, taking sides, feeling frustrated, and "aha, so that's what you mean. Okay." expressions. It doesn't always work out. Sometimes we stop with hurt feelings. But just as frequently we plow through the confusion as a group, putting ideas in order and creating a shared picture which we all can see. And all of this is possible because disagreements and confusion are not received as invalidation of our individual ideas.

As women's groups (especially Anglo women's groups) become more established and more institutionalized, I think we need to be careful of how we are going to incorporate diversity. Especially if becoming more established means becoming more bureaucratized and hierarchical in our way of making decisions. Incorporating diversity, if it is going to be successful, will require a great deal more of active listening, instead of passive hearing. It is going to require more active discussion instead of turn-taking, space-given talking. It's going to mean expressing disagreements, asking for clarifications and incorporating our differences in creating a shared vision together. A "sisterhood" that I want to belong to allows me to be different and still be able to work together. To this sisterhood, I will bring my individual history, listen to others' stories and know that we are building a foundation together.

NOTE

1. Bonnie Thornton Dill, "Race, Class and Gender: Prospects for an All-Inclusive Sisterhood," *Feminist Studies* 9, no. 1 (1983): 131–150.

REFLECTING ON MEANING

1. What major disagreement does Uttal have with how conversation is conducted within Anglo feminist groups? How have her experiences with Anglo feminist groups differed from her experiences with Women of Color feminist groups? How do Anglo feminist groups seem to gain their strength? What are the "safe" spaces constructed within these groups?

2. Uttal discusses the idea of "hearing without listening." What does this mean? How does this idea relate to consciousness-raising groups of the 1960s? Who currently defines common experiences in the contemporary women's movement? What is Uttal's opinion of this? What alternative model does she suggest will counter the practice of erasing individual differences?

3. Uttal proposes that feminists "must stop politely and passively hearing one another." Instead, what do feminists need to do? What type of sisterhood does she envision? What does she mean when she says that "we have to be allowed to get messy"? Uttal argues that when differences are discussed, they become less threatening and conflictual. How could a "messy" discussion of differences increase solidarity? According to Uttal, why would "active discussion" be preferable to "turn-taking" and "space-given talking"?

EXPLORING RHETORICAL STRATEGIES

1. Uttal's title, "Nods That Silence," describes what practice? Does her description of the conversations in Anglo feminist groups and Women of Color feminist groups effectively support her assertions? Do you agree or disagree with her argument that these two groups can be characterized in this way? Why?

2. This essay first appeared in the 1990 book *Making Face, Making Soul: Creative and Critical Perspectives by Feminists of Color.* Who is Uttal's intended audience? How might the audience response of an Anglo feminist differ from that of a Woman of Color feminist? Does Uttal risk alienating Anglo feminists with her description of their conversational practices? Why or why not?

3. Uttal begins her argument by discussing the reason behind Anglo feminists' harmonious conversational techniques. She then proceeds to point out the flaws in this way of thinking about conversation. Is her position valid? Does she offer sufficient evidence to support this position? Why or why not?

TAKING A STAND
QUESTIONS FOR CONSIDERATION

1. The authors represented in this part explore the nature and effect of sexism in the English language. Do you agree that English is inherently sexist? Why or why not? Summarize the views of at least two authors on the nature of sexism in the English language, and explain why you agree or disagree.

2. Miller and Swift, Nilsen, and Lorde suggest that sexism in the English language has profound consequences. What effect does linguistic sexism have on society? What problems does it create for women? In what ways, if any, does it contribute to their oppression? Survey the viewpoints of at least two authors and argue that sexism in the English language is or is not a serious problem.

3. A key point in the debate about sexism in language is whether language simply reflects cultural assumptions about gender or whether it actually creates and perpetuates sexist attitudes. Drawing on the two essays by Miller and Swift and the essay by Nilsen, determine your stand on this issue. Does sexism in English mirror or create sexist attitudes in society? What implications for change does your position suggest? Why?

4. Both Lorde and Uttal are concerned with the sexist language and thinking practices adopted by many Anglo feminists. What are the similarities and differences in Lorde's and Uttal's positions? How do they each contend with the issues of race, class, and sexuality? Why is the importance of acknowledging difference so central to both of their essays?

5. The two essays by Miller and Swift and the essay by Nilsen explore words, their origins, and their changing definitions to support the contention that English is indeed a sexist language. How does vocabulary reveal such cultural assumptions? Isn't a dictionary supposed to be unbiased, even objective? What do these authors' analyses of vocabulary suggest about the nature of reality? What enormous power does language possess?

6. What are some of the ways in which women and men have attempted to neutralize sexist bias in the English language? Summarize and evaluate the efforts and proposals described by at least two authors in Part III, and present your own plan for change. In what ways is your plan similar to theirs? How does your plan differ? What makes your plan more effective?

7. Miller and Swift argue that naming customs reflect and reinforce sexist attitudes. Some women have attempted to overcome this problem when they marry by maintaining their maiden name, adopting a hyphenated surname, or creating an original surname. What is your opinion of each of these solutions? What problems arise when a married couple has a child? What would you do to change naming customs to make them less biased? Consider the undermining of women's identity that Miller and Swift describe, and propose a solution that would make naming customs gender-neutral.

8. Both Steinem and Roiphe are less concerned with the English language than with the ways in which women talk with others. What do you think about their conclusions on the ways women interact with men? Do you agree with Steinem's contention that men interrupt women more often than the reverse? Do you agree with Roiphe's statement that "women, in general, do have to seek and use authority somewhat differently than men do"? To what extent is conversation influenced by social attitudes about gender? In shaping your response, consider your own personal experiences and observations, and closely observe men and women talking. What patterns do you notice? After reading these essays, do you support the essentialist or the social constructionist view of communication styles? Or do you have another explanation for the differences in women's and men's communication techniques?

Part IV_____

Gender and Social Institutions

As people become increasingly sensitive to the powerful role gender plays in almost every aspect of life, more and more attention is being focused on its effect to influence such cherished social institutions as the educational system, the family, and the workplace. In fact, these institutions serve as barometers of how much influence changing gender roles have had in society. The essays in Part IV address each of these institutions by focusing on the different experiences and expectations for women and men in our society.

The authors of the first group of essays, "Education," examine the influence of sexism on the educational experiences of women. Matina Horner's research demonstrates that women confront a "psychological barrier" to achievement in that they often fear both failure *and* success. Adrienne Rich suggests that women will not receive a true education until substantive changes are made in the educational system. Finally, M. Carey Thomas provides a historical perspective in describing how female students at the turn of the last century sometimes experienced debilitating anxiety, insecurity, and diffidence.

In the second group of essays, "Work," gender roles in various work situations are examined. Judy Syfers defines the traditional role of wife as that of a servant whose main responsibility is to support her husband. In his attempt to reverse discriminatory gender roles, Rick Greenberg recounts how he traded his job for "house fatherhood" with its subsequent pleasures and frustrations. Pat Mainardi considers how women are "brainwashed" by men into feeling guilty about not performing housework. Finally, Deborah Tannen–using a clothing metaphor to describe how women are "marked" in the workplace–considers how women's business styles differ from men's.

Together, these essays suggest some of the ways in which gender operates within social institutions, and they illustrate that as our conceptions of gender change, so too do those institutions. Although the changes have been largely positive, the essays in this section demonstrate that major, substantive change is needed in our basic attitudes toward gender before our major social institutions will provide men and women with equally beneficial experiences.

Chapter 10 _____

EDUCATION

Fail: Bright Woman

MATINA HORNER

Achievement motivation is an area that researchers have explored extensively, but as educator Matina Horner points out, these investigations have largely studied men. Setting out to rectify this omission, Horner conducted a study to "explore the basis for sex differences in achievement motivation." The results of her research are startling: afraid of failure and success, women face a "psychological barrier" to achievement.

Consider Phil, a bright young college sophomore. He has always done well in school, he is in the honors program, he has wanted to be a doctor as long as he can remember. We ask him to tell us a story based on one clue: *"After first-term finals, John finds himself at the top of his medical school class."* Phil writes:

> John is a conscientious young man who worked hard. He is pleased with himself. John has always wanted to go into medicine and is very dedicated.... John continues working hard and eventually graduates at the top of his class.

Now consider Monica, another honors student. She too has always done well and she too has visions of a flourishing career. We give her the same clue, but with "Anne" as the successful student—*after first-term finals, Anne finds herself at the top of her medical school class.* Instead of identifying with Anne's triumph, Monica tells a bizarre tale:

> Anne starts proclaiming her surprise and joy. Her fellow class-
> mates are so disgusted with her behavior that they jump on her
> in a body and beat her. She is maimed for life.

Next we ask Monica and Phil to work on a series of achievement tests by themselves. Monica scores higher than Phil. Finally we get them together, competing against each other on the same kind of tests. Phil performs magnificently, but Monica dissolves into a bundle of nerves.

The glaring contrast between the two stories and the dramatic changes in performance in competitive situations illustrate important differences between men and women in reacting to achievement.

In 1953, David McClelland, John Atkinson and colleagues published the first major work on the "achievement motive." Through the use of the Thematic Apperception Test (TAT), they were able to isolate the psychological characteristic of a *need to achieve.* This seemed to be an internalized standard of excellence, motivating the individual to do well in any achievement-oriented situation involving intelligence and leadership ability. Subsequent investigators studied innumerable facets of achievement motivation: how it is instilled in children, how it is expressed, how it relates to social class, even how it is connected to the rise and fall of civilizations. The result of all this research is an impressive and a theoretically consistent body of data about the achievement motive—in men.

Women, however, are conspicuously absent from almost all of the studies. In the few cases where the ladies were included, the results were contradictory or confusing. So women were eventually left out altogether. The predominantly male researchers apparently decided, as Freud had before them, that the only way to understand woman was to turn to the poets. Atkinson's 1958 book, *Motives in Fantasy, Action and Society,* is an 800-page compilation of all of the theories and facts on achievement motivation in men. Women got a footnote, reflecting the state of the science.

To help remedy this lopsided state of affairs, I undertook to explore the basis for sex differences in achievement motivation. But where to begin?

My first clue came from the one consistent finding on the women: they get higher test-anxiety scores than do the men. Eleanor Maccoby has suggested that the girl who is motivated to achieve is defying conventions of what girls "should" do. As a result, the intellectual woman pays a price in anxiety. Margaret Mead concurs, noting that intense intellectual striving can be viewed as "competitively aggressive behavior." And of course Freud thought that the whole essence of femininity lay in repressing aggressiveness (and hence intellectuality).

Thus consciously or unconsciously the girl equates intellectual achievement with loss of femininity. A bright woman is caught in a double bind. In testing and other achievement-oriented situations she worries not only about failure, but also about success. If she fails, she is not living up to her own standards of performance; if she succeeds, she is not living up to societal expectations about the female role. Men in our society do not experience this kind of ambivalence, because they are not only permitted but actively encouraged to do well.

For women, then, the desire to achieve is often contaminated by what I call the *motive to avoid success*. I define it as the fear that success in competitive achievement situations will lead to negative consequences, such as unpopularity and loss of femininity. This motive, like the achievement motive itself, is a stable disposition within the person, acquired early in life along with other sex-role standards. When fear of success conflicts with a desire to be successful, the result is an inhibition of achievement motivation.

I began my study with several hypotheses about the motive to avoid success:

1. Of course, it would be far more characteristic of women than of men.
2. It would be more characteristic of women who are capable of success and who are career-oriented than of women not so motivated. Women who are not seeking success should not, after all, be threatened by it.
3. I anticipated that the anxiety over success would be greater in competitive situations (when one's intellectual performance is evaluated against someone else's) than in noncompetitive ones (when one works alone). The aggressive, masculine aspects of achievement striving are certainly more pronounced in competitive settings, particularly when the opponent is male. Women's anxiety should therefore be greatest when they compete with men.

I administered the standard TAT achievement motivation measures to a sample of 90 girls and 88 boys, all undergraduates at the University of Michigan. In addition, I asked each to tell a story based on the clue described before: *After first-term finals, John (Anne) finds himself (herself) at the top of his (her) medical school class.* The girls wrote about Anne, the boys about John.

Their stories were scored for "motive to avoid success" if they expressed any negative imagery that reflected concern about doing well. Generally, such imagery fell into three categories:

1. The most frequent Anne story reflected strong fears of social rejection as a result of success. The girls in this group showed anxiety about becoming unpopular, unmarriageable and lonely.

   > Anne is an acne-faced bookworm. She runs to the bulletin board and finds she's at the top. As usual she smarts off. A chorus of groans is the rest of the class's reply.... She studies 12 hours a day, and lives at home to save money. "Well it certainly paid off. All the Friday and Saturday nights without dates, fun—I'll be the best woman doctor alive." And yet a twinge of sadness comes thru—she wonders what she really has. . . .

   > Although Anne is happy with her success she fears what will happen to her social life. The male med. students don't seem to think very highly of a female who has beaten them in their field. . . . She will be a proud and successful but alas a very *lonely* doctor.

   > Anne doesn't want to be number one in her class . . . she feels she shouldn't rank so high because of social reasons. She drops down to ninth in the class and then marries the boy who graduates number one.

   > Anne is pretty darn proud of herself, but everyone hates and envies her.

2. Girls in the second category were less concerned with issues of social approval or disapproval; they were more worried about definitions of womanhood. Their stories expressed guilt and despair over success, and doubts about their femininity or normality.

   > Unfortunately Anne no longer feels so certain that she really wants to be a doctor. She is worried about herself and wonders if perhaps she isn't normal. . . . Anne decides not to continue with her medical work but to take courses that have a deeper personal meaning for her.

   > Anne feels guilty. . . . She will finally have a nervous breakdown and quit medical school and marry a successful young doctor.

Anne is pleased. She had worked extraordinarily hard and her grades showed it. "It is not enough," Anne thinks. "I am not happy." She didn't even want to be a doctor. She is not sure what she wants. Anne says to hell with the whole business and goes into social work—not hardly as glamorous, prestigious or lucrative; but she is happy.

3. The third group of stories did not even try to confront the ambivalence about doing well. Girls in this category simply denied the possibility that any mere woman could be so successful. Some of them completely changed the content of the clue, or distorted it, or refused to believe it, or absolved Anne of responsibility for her success. These stories were remarkable for their psychological ingenuity:

> Anne is a *code name* for a nonexistent person created by a group of med. students. They take turns writing exams for Anne.

> Anne is really happy she's on top, though *Tom is higher than she*—though that's as it should be.... Anne doesn't mind Tom winning.

> Anne is talking to her counselor. Counselor says she will make a fine *nurse*.

> It was *luck* that Anne came out on top because she didn't want to go to medical school anyway.

Fifty-nine girls—over 65 percent—told stories that fell into one or another of the above categories. But only eight boys, fewer than 10 percent, showed evidence of the motive to avoid success. (These differences are significant at better than the .0005 level.) In fact, sometimes I think that most of the young men in the sample were incipient Horatio Algers. They expressed unequivocal delight at John's success (clearly John had worked hard for it), and projected a grand and glorious future for him. There was none of the hostility, bitterness and ambivalence that the girls felt for Anne. In short, the differences between male and female stories based on essentially the same clue were enormous.

Two of the stories are particularly revealing examples of this male-female contrast. The girls insisted that Anne give up her career for marriage:

> Anne has a boyfriend, Carl, in the same class and they are quite serious.... She wants him to be scholastically higher than she is. Anne will deliberately lower her academic standing the next

term, while she does all she subtly can to help Carl. His grades come up and Anne soon drops out of medical school. They marry and he goes on in school while she raises their family.

But of course the boys would ask John to do no such thing:

John has worked very hard and his long hours of study have paid off.... He is thinking about his girl, Cheri, whom he will marry at the end of med. school. He realizes he can give her all the things she desires after he becomes established. He will go on in med. school and be successful in the long run.

Success inhibits social life for the girls; it enhances social life for the boys.

Earlier I suggested that the motive to avoid success is especially aroused in competitive situations. In the second part of this study I wanted to see whether the aggressive overtones of competition against men scared the girls away. Would competition raise their anxiety about success and thus lower their performance?

First I put all of the students together in a large competitive group, and gave them a series of achievement tests (verbal and arithmetic). I then assigned them randomly to one of three other experimental conditions. One-third worked on a similar set of tests, each in competition with a member of the same sex. One-third competed against a member of the opposite sex. The last third worked by themselves, a non-competitive condition.

Ability is an important factor in achievement motivation research. If you want to compare two persons on the strength of their *motivation* to succeed, how do you know that any differences in performance are not due to initial differences in *ability* to succeed? One way of avoiding this problem is to use each subject as his own control; that is, the performance of an individual working alone can be compared with his score in competition. Ability thus remains constant; any change in score must be due to motivational factors. This control over ability was, of course, possible only for the last third of my subjects: the 30 girls and 30 boys who had worked alone *and* in the large group competition. I decided to look at their scores first.

Performance changed dramatically over the two situations. A large number of men did far better when they were in competition than when they worked alone. For the women the reverse was true. Fewer than one-third of the women, but more than two-thirds of the men, got significantly higher scores in competition.

When we looked at just the girls in terms of the motive to avoid success, the comparisons were even more striking. As predicted, the students who felt ambivalent or anxious about doing well turned in their best scores when they worked by themselves. Seventy-seven percent of the girls who feared success did better alone than in competition. Women who were low on the motive, however, behaved more like the men: 93 percent of them got higher scores in competition. (Results significant at the .005.)

Female Fear of Success and Performance

	Perform Better Working Alone	Perform Better in Competition
High fear of success	13	4
Low fear of success	1	12

As a final test of motivational differences, I asked the students to indicate on a scale from 1 to 100 "How important was it for you to do well in this situation?" The high-fear-of-success girls said that it was much more important for them to do well when they worked alone than when they worked in either kind of competition. For the low-fear girls, such differences were not statistically significant. Their test scores were higher in competition, as we saw, and they thought that it was important to succeed no matter what the setting. And in all experimental conditions—working alone, or in competition against males or females—high-fear women consistently lagged behind their fearless comrades on the importance of doing well.

The findings suggest that most women will fully explore their intellectual potential only when they do not need to compete—and least of all when they are competing with men. This was most true of women with a strong anxiety about success. Unfortunately, these are often the same women who could be very successful if they were free from that anxiety. The girls in my sample who feared success also tended to have high intellectual ability and histories of academic success. (It is interesting to note that all but two of these girls were majoring in the humanities and in spite of very high grade points aspired to traditional female careers: housewife, mother, nurse, schoolteacher. Girls who did not fear success, however, were aspiring to graduate degrees and careers in such scientific areas as math, physics and chemistry.)

We can see from this small study that achievement motivation in women is much more complex than the same drive in men. Most men do not find many inhibiting forces in their path if they are able and motivated to succeed. As a result, they are not threatened by competition; in fact, surpassing an opponent is a source of pride and enhanced masculinity.

If a woman sets out to do well, however, she bumps into a number of obstacles. She learns that it really isn't ladylike to be too intellectual. She is warned that men will treat her with distrustful tolerance at best, and outright prejudice at worst, if she pursues a career. She learns the truth of Samuel Johnson's comment, "A man is in general better pleased when he has a good dinner upon his table, than when his wife talks Greek." So she doesn't learn Greek, and the motive to avoid success is born.

In recent years many legal and educational barriers to female achievement have been removed; but it is clear that a psychological barrier remains. The motive to avoid success has an all-too-important influence on the intellectual and professional lives of women in our society. But perhaps there is cause for optimism. Monica may have had Anne maimed for life, but a few of the girls forecast a happier future for our medical student. Said one:

> Anne is quite a lady—not only is she tops academically, but she is liked and admired by her fellow students—quite a trick in a man-dominated field. She is brilliant—but she is also a woman. She will continue to be at or near the top. And . . . always a lady.

REFLECTING ON MEANING

1. Horner's study consisted of several distinct tests, each designed to answer a specific question. What questions was she trying to answer? How did she go about answering each one? What did she discover about achievement motivation in women and men?

2. "The findings suggest that most women will fully explore their intellectual potential only when they do not need to compete—and least of all when they are competing with men." What does this statement suggest to you about women and professional success? What does it suggest about education? How might the educational system be made more advantageous for women?

3. "In recent years many legal and educational barriers to female achievement have been removed; but it is clear that a psychological barrier remains." What barrier does Horner refer to? Why does she consider it a psychological barrier? What does this statement suggest about the nature of gender-based behavior?

What does it suggest about the nature of sexism? Why haven't legal and educational advances in the last twenty years resolved the problem of sexism?

EXPLORING RHETORICAL STRATEGIES

1. Horner begins and ends her essay by citing responses from her experimental study. Why does she open and close in this way? What effect did the disparity between the responses quoted at the beginning of the selection have on you? What effect did the concluding response have on you?

2. Horner's essay originally appeared in 1969 in *Psychology Today*. Based on her essay, what can you surmise about the readers of that magazine? What expectations might they have about reporting on experimental studies? Why do you think Horner described her methodology so extensively?

3. Horner explains why she conducted her study, but why—beyond reporting her conclusions—did she write this essay? What was her purpose? Was she trying to pass on information about her work or to advance a viewpoint? What does her tone reveal about her likely intentions?

Taking Women Students Seriously

ADRIENNE RICH

In this essay, originally presented as an address at a meeting on women's education, poet and author Adrienne Rich describes the influence that sexism has on the educational experiences of women at the postsecondary level. The essay is an impassioned plea to begin the process of change that must take place before women can truly become educated as women.

I see my function here today as one of trying to create a context, delineate a background, against which we might talk about women as students and students as women. I would like to speak for a while about this background, and then I hope that we can have, not so much a question period, as a raising of concerns, a sharing of questions for which we as yet may have no answers, an opening of conversations which will go on and on.

When I went to teach at Douglass, a women's college, it was with a particular background which I would like briefly to describe to you. I had graduated from an all-girls' school in the 1940s, where the head and the majority of the faculty were independent, unmarried women. One or two held doctorates, but had been forced by the Depression (and by the fact that they were women) to take secondary school teaching jobs. These women cared a great deal about the life of the mind, and they gave a great deal of time and energy—beyond any limit of teaching hours—to those of us who showed special intellectual interest or ability. We were taken to libraries, art museums, lectures at neighboring colleges, set to work on extra research projects, given extra French or Latin reading. Although we sometimes felt "pushed" by them, we held those women in a kind of respect which even then we dimly perceived was not generally accorded to women in the world at large. They were vital individuals, defined not by their relationships but by their personalities; and although under the pressure of the culture we were all certain we wanted to get married, their lives did not appear empty or dreary to us. In a kind of cognitive dissonance, we knew they were "old maids" and therefore supposed to be bitter and lonely;

yet we saw them vigorously involved with life. But despite their existence as alternate models of women, the *content* of the education they gave us in no way prepared us to survive as women in a world organized by and for men.

From that school, I went on to Radcliffe, congratulating myself that now I would have great men as my teachers. From 1947 to 1951, when I graduated, I never saw a single woman on a lecture platform, or in front of a class, except when a woman graduate student gave a paper on a special topic. The "great men" talked of other "great men," of the nature of Man, the history of Mankind, the future of Man; and never again was I to experience, from a teacher, the kind of prodding, the insistence that my best could be even better, that I had known in high school. Women students were simply not taken very seriously. Harvard's message to women was an elite mystification: we were, of course, part of Mankind; we were special, achieving women, or we would not have been there; but of course our real goal was to marry—if possible, a Harvard graduate.

In the late sixties, I began teaching at the City College of New York—a crowded, public, urban, multiracial institution as far removed from Harvard as possible. I went there to teach writing in the SEEK [Search for Education, Elevation, and Knowledge] Program, which predated Open Admissions and which was then a kind of model for programs designed to open up higher education to poor, black, and Third World students. Although during the next few years we were to see the original concept of SEEK diluted, then violently attacked and betrayed, it was for a short time an extraordinary and intense teaching and learning environment. The characteristics of this environment were a deep commitment on the part of teachers to the minds of their students; a constant, active effort to create or discover the conditions for learning, and to educate ourselves to meet the needs of the new college population; a philosophical attitude based on open discussion of racism, oppression, and the politics of literature and language; and a belief that learning in the classroom could not be isolated from the student's experience as a member of an urban minority group in white America. Here are some of the kinds of questions we, as teachers of writing, found ourselves asking:

1. What has been the student's experience of education in the inadequate, often abusively racist public school system, which rewards passivity and treats a questioning attitude or independent mind as a behavior problem? What has been her or his experience in a society that consistently undermines the selfhood of the

poor and the nonwhite? How can such a student gain that sense
of self which is necessary for active participation in education?
What does all this mean for us as teachers?

2. How do we go about teaching a canon of literature which has
   consistently excluded or depreciated nonwhite experience?
3. How can we connect the process of learning to write well with
   the student's own reality, and not simply teach her/him how to
   write acceptable lies in standard English?

When I went to teach at Douglass College in 1976, and in
teaching women's writing workshops elsewhere, I came to perceive stunning parallels to the questions I had first encountered in
teaching the so-called disadvantaged students at City. But in this instance, and against the specific background of the women's movement, the questions framed themselves like this:

1. What has been the student's experience of education in schools
   which reward female passivity, indoctrinate girls and boys in stereotypic sex roles, and do not take the female mind seriously?
   How does a woman gain a sense of her *self* in a system—in this
   case, patriarchal capitalism—which devalues work done by
   women, denies the importance and uniqueness of female experience, and is physically violent toward women? What does this
   mean for a woman teacher?
2. How do we, as women, teach women students a canon of literature which has consistently excluded or depreciated female experience, and which often expresses hostility to women and
   validates violence against us?
3. How can we teach women to move beyond the desire for male
   approval and getting "good grades" and seek and write their own
   truths that the culture has distorted or made taboo? (For women,
   of course, language itself is exclusive: I want to say more about
   this further on.)

In teaching women, we have two choices: to lend our weight to
the forces that indoctrinate women to passivity, self-depreciation,
and a sense of powerlessness, in which case the issue of "taking
women students seriously" is a moot one; or to consider what we
have to work against, as well as with, in ourselves, in our students,
in the content of the curriculum, in the structure of the institution,
in the society at large. And this means, first of all, taking ourselves
seriously: Recognizing that central responsibility of a woman to
herself, without which we remain always the Other, the defined,
the object, the victim; believing that there is a unique quality of val-
idation, affirmation, challenge, support, that one woman can offer

another. Believing in the value and significance of women's experience, traditions, perceptions. Thinking of ourselves seriously, not as one of the boys, not as neuters, or androgynes, but *as women.*

Suppose we were to ask ourselves, simply: What does a woman need to know? Does she not, as a self-conscious, self-defining human being, need a knowledge of her own history, her much-politicized biology, an awareness of the creative work of women of the past, the skills and crafts and techniques and powers exercised by women in different times and cultures, a knowledge of women's rebellions and organized movements against our oppression and how they have been routed or diminished? Without such knowledge women live and have lived without context, vulnerable to the projections of male fantasy, male prescriptions for us, estranged from our own experience because our education has not reflected or echoed it. I would suggest that not biology, but ignorance of our selves, has been the key to our powerlessness.

But the university curriculum, the high-school curriculum, do not provide this kind of knowledge for women, the knowledge of Womankind, whose experience has been so profoundly different from that of Mankind. Only in the precariously budgeted, much-condescended-to area of women's studies is such knowledge available to women students. Only there can they learn about the lives and work of women other than the few select women who are included in the "mainstream" texts, usually misrepresented even when they do appear. Some students, at some institutions, manage to take a majority of courses in women's studies, but the message from on high is that this is self-indulgence, soft-core education: the "real" learning is the study of Mankind.

If there is any misleading concept, it is that of "coeducation": that because women and men are sitting in the same classrooms, hearing the same lectures, reading the same books, performing the same laboratory experiments, they are receiving an equal education. They are not, first because the content of education itself validates men even as it invalidates women. Its very message is that men have been the shapers and thinkers of the world, and that this is only natural. The bias of higher education, including the so-called sciences, is white and male, racist and sexist; and this bias is expressed in both subtle and blatant ways. I have mentioned already the exclusiveness of grammar itself: "The student should test himself on the above questions"; "The poet is representative. He stands among partial men for the complete man." Despite a few halfhearted departures from custom, what the linguist Wendy Martyna has named "He-Man" grammar prevails throughout the culture. The efforts of feminists to reveal the profound ontological

implications of sexist grammar are routinely ridiculed by academi-
cians and journalists, including the professedly liberal *Times* columnist Tom Wicker and the professed humanist Jacques Barzun.
Sexist grammar burns into the brains of little girls and young
women a message that the male is the norm, the standard, the central figure beside which we are the deviants, the marginal, the dependent variables. It lays the foundation for androcentric thinking,
and leaves men safe in their solipsistic tunnel-vision.

Women and men do not receive an equal education because
outside the classroom women are perceived not as sovereign beings
but as prey. The growing incidence of rape on and off the campus
may or may not be fed by the proliferations of pornographic magazines and X-rated films available to young males in fraternities and
student unions; but it is certainly occurring in a context of widespread images of sexual violence against women, on billboards and
in so-called high art. More subtle, more daily than rape is the verbal
abuse experienced by the woman student on many campuses—
Rutgers for example—where, traversing a street lined with fraternity
houses, she must run a gauntlet of male commentary and verbal assault. The undermining of self, of a woman's sense of her right to occupy space and walk freely in the world, is deeply relevant to
education. The capacity to think independently, to take intellectual
risks, to assert ourselves mentally, is inseparable from our physical
way of being in the world, our feelings of personal integrity. If it is
dangerous for me to walk home late of an evening from the library,
because I am a woman and can be raped, how self-possessed, how exu-
berant can I feel as I sit working in that library? How much of my
working energy is drained by the subliminal knowledge that, as a
woman, I test my physical right to exist each time I go out alone? Of
this knowledge, Susan Griffin has written:

> ... more than rape itself, the fear of rape permeates our lives.
> And what does one do from day to day, with *this* experience,
> which says, without words and directly to the heart, *your exist-
> ence, your experience, may end at any moment.* Your experience
> may end, and the best defense against this is not to be, to deny
> being in the body, as a self, to ... avert your gaze, make your-
> self, as a presence in the world, less felt.

Finally, rape of the mind. Women students are more and
more often now reporting sexual overtures by male professors—
one part of our overall growing consciousness of sexual harassment in the workplace. At Yale a legal suit has been brought
against the university by a group of women demanding an explicit
policy against sexual advances toward female students by male

professors. Most young women experience a profound mixture of humiliation and intellectual self-doubt over seductive gestures by men who have the power to award grades, open doors to grants and graduate school, or extend special knowledge and training. Even if turned aside, such gestures constitute mental rape, destructive to a woman's ego. They are acts of domination, as despicable as the molestation of the daughter by the father.

But long before entering college the woman student has experienced her alien identity in a world which misnames her, turns her to its own uses, denying her the resources she needs to become self-affirming, self-defined. The nuclear family teaches her that relationships are more important than selfhood or work; that "whether the phone rings for you, and how often," having the right clothes, doing the dishes, take precedence over study or solitude; that too much intelligence or intensity may make her unmarriageable; that marriage and children—service to others—are, finally, the points on which her life will be judged a success or a failure. In high school, the polarization between feminine attractiveness and independent intelligence comes to an absolute. Meanwhile, the culture resounds with messages. During Solar Energy Week in New York I saw young women wearing "ecology" T-shirts with the legend: CLEAN, CHEAP, AND AVAILABLE; a reminder of the 1960s antiwar button which read: CHICKS SAY YES TO MEN WHO SAY NO. Department store windows feature female mannequins in chains, pinned to the wall with legs spread, smiling in positions of torture. Feminists are depicted in the media as "shrill," "strident," "puritanical," or "humorless," and the lesbian choice—the choice of the woman-identified woman—as pathological or sinister. The young woman sitting in the philosophy classroom, the political science lecture, is already gripped by tensions between her nascent sense of self-worth, and the battering force of messages like these.

Look at a classroom: look at the many kinds of women's faces, postures, expressions. Listen to the women's voices. Listen to the silences, the unasked questions, the blanks. Listen to the small, soft voices, often courageously trying to speak up, voices of women taught early that tones of confidence, challenge, anger, or assertiveness, are strident and unfeminine. Listen to the voices of the women and the voices of the men; observe the space men allow themselves, physically and verbally, the male assumption that people will listen, even when the majority of the group is female. Look at the faces of the silent, and of those who speak. Listen to a woman groping for language in which to express what is on her mind, sensing that the terms of academic discourse are not her language, trying to cut down her thought to the dimensions of a discourse not intended for her (*for it is not fitting that a woman speak in public*); or reading her paper aloud at breakneck speed, throwing her words away, deprecating her own work by a reflex prejudgment: *I do not deserve to take up time and space.*

As women teachers, we can either deny the importance of this context in which women students think, write, read, study, project their own futures; or try to work with it. We can either teach passively, accepting these conditions, or actively, helping our students identify and resist them.

One important thing we can do is *discuss* the context. And this need not happen only in a women's studies course; it can happen anywhere. We can refuse to accept passive, obedient learning and insist upon critical thinking. We can become harder on our women students, giving them the kinds of "cultural prodding" that men receive, but on different terms and in a different style. Most young women need to have their intellectual lives, their work, legitimized against the claims of family, relationships, the old message that a woman is always available for service to others. We need to keep our standards very high, not to accept a woman's preconceived sense of her limitations; we need to be hard to please, while supportive of risk-taking, because self-respect often comes only when exacting standards have been met. At a time when adult literacy is generally low, we need to demand more, not less, of women, both for the sake of their futures as thinking beings, and because historically women have always had to be better than men to do half as well. A romantic sloppiness, an inspired lack of rigor, a self-indulgent incoherence, are symptoms of female self-deprecation. We should help our women students to look very critically at such symptoms, and to understand where they are rooted.

Nor does this mean we should be training women students to "think like men." Men in general think badly: in disjuncture from their personal lives, claiming objectivity where the most irrational passions seethe, losing, as Virginia Woolf observed, their senses in the pursuit of professionalism. It is not easy to think like a woman in a man's world, in the world of the professions; yet the capacity to do that is a strength which we can try to help our students develop. To think like a woman in a man's world means thinking critically, refusing to accept the givens, making connections between facts and ideas which men have left unconnected. It means remembering that every mind resides in a body; remaining accountable to the female bodies in which we live; constantly retesting given hypotheses against lived experience. It means a constant critique of language, for as Wittgenstein (no feminist) observed, "The limits of my language are the limits of my world." And it means that most difficult thing of all: listening and watching in art and literature, in the social sciences, in all the descriptions we are given of the world, for the silences, the absences, the nameless, the unspoken, the encoded—for there we will find the true knowledge of women. And in breaking those silences, naming our selves, uncovering the hidden, making ourselves present, we begin to define a reality which resonates to *us,* which affirms *our* being, which allows the woman teacher and the woman student alike to take ourselves, and each other, seriously: meaning, to begin taking charge of our lives.

REFLECTING ON MEANING

1. According to Rich, what is the message the educational system conveys to women? How do university curricula, the composition of university faculties, and the interaction between faculty members and women students contribute to this message? Do you agree or disagree with Rich's observations? Why? What has been your experience in higher education so far?

2. Why does Rich find "coeducation" such a misleading concept? What does the term imply about the nature of education for women and men? What does it reveal about what matters where men and women are concerned? In what ways does it reinforce the gender-based hierarchy in society?

3. Rich states that "outside the classroom women are perceived not as sovereign beings but as prey." What does she mean? What connection is she making between the fear of rape and women students and their educational pursuits at the university? What does she mean by "rape of the mind"?

4. Why does Rich caution against teaching women to "think like men"? What does she mean when she says women must learn to "think like a woman in a man's world"? What kind of educational goals is she urging? What kinds of changes would her goals bring about in university curricula and classrooms?

EXPLORING RHETORICAL STRATEGIES

1. Rich's essay contains much evidence of its original form as a public address to a specific audience. What contributes to the "oral" quality of the essay? What evidence can you find of the composition of the original audience? Who are the people Rich addressed at the meeting where she originally delivered this talk?

2. Rich begins her critique of postsecondary education by outlining her own career as a student and a professor. Why does she do this? How does her recounting her background establish her credibility? What does it help her achieve in relation to her audience?

3. Near the end of her essay, Rich asks her audience to visualize a classroom and to listen to the voices there. What is the effect of her repeated injunctions to her audience to "listen"? How do these injunctions provide a foundation for the plea with which she concludes her essay: that her audience begin to "discuss" the problem and work toward "breaking those silences" that place women at a disadvantage in education?

Educated Woman

M. CAREY THOMAS

A former president of Bryn Mawr College, M. Carey Thomas lived from 1857 to 1935. In this excerpt from The Educated Woman in America, *Thomas depicts the insecurity and anxiety that women who wished to go to college once experienced and the conditions that reinforced their negative self-images. From her perspective in the past, she looks forward to a brighter future for women in postsecondary education and the great "social changes which are preparing the way for the coming economic independence of women."*

The passionate desire of women of my generation for higher education was accompanied thruout its course by the awful doubt, felt by women themselves as well as by men, as to whether women as a sex were physically and mentally fit for it. I think I can best make this clear to you if I refer briefly to my own experience. I cannot remember the time when I was not sure that studying and going to college were the things above all others which I wished to do. I was always wondering whether it could be really true, as everyone thought, that boys were cleverer than girls. Indeed, I cared so much that I never dared to ask any grown-up person the direct question, not even my father or mother, because I feared to hear the reply. I remember often praying about it, and begging God that if it were true that because I was a girl I could not successfully master Greek and go to college and understand things to kill me at once, as I could not bear to live in such an unjust world. When I was a little older I read the Bible entirely thru with passionate eagerness because I had heard it said that it proved that women were inferior to men. Those were not the days of the higher criticism. I can remember weeping over the account of Adam and Eve because it seemed to me that the curse pronounced on Eve might imperil girls' going to college; and to this day I can never read many parts of the Pauline epistles without feeling again the sinking of the heart with which I used to hurry over the verses referring to women's keeping silence in the churches and asking their husbands at home. I searched not only the Bible, but all other books I could get for light on the woman question. I read Milton with rage and indignation. Even as a child I knew him for the woman hater he was. The splendor of Shakespeare was obscured to me then by the lack of intellectual power in his greatest women characters. Even now it seems to me that only Isabella in *Measure for Measure* thinks greatly, and weighs her actions greatly, like a Hamlet or a Brutus.

I can well remember one endless scorching summer's day when sitting in a hammock under the trees with a French dictionary, blinded by tears more burning than the July sun, I translated the most indecent book I have ever read, Michelet's famous—were it not now forgotten, I should be able to say infamous—book on woman, *La femme*. I was beside myself with terror lest it might prove true that I myself was so vile and pathological a thing. Between that summer's day in 1874 and a certain day in the autumn in 1904, thirty years had elapsed. Altho during these thirty years I had read in every language every book on women that I could obtain, I had never chanced again upon a book that seemed to me so to degrade me in my womanhood as the seventh and seventeenth chapters on women and women's education, of President Stanley Hall's *Adolescence*. Michelet's sickening sentimentality and horrible oversexuality seemed to me to breathe again from every psuedo-scientific page. But how vast the difference between then and now in my feelings, and in the feelings of every woman who has had to do with the education of girls! Then I was terror-struck lest I, and every other woman with me, were doomed to live as pathological invalids in a universe merciless to women as a sex. Now we know that it is not we, but the man who believes such things about us, who is himself pathological, blinded by neurotic mists of sex, unable to see that women form one-half of the kindly race of normal, healthy human creatures in the world; that women, like men, are quickened and in-spired by the same study of the great traditions of their race, by the same love of learning, the same love of science, the same love of ab-stract truth; that women, like men, are immeasurably benefited, physically, mentally, and morally, and are made vastly better moth-ers, as men are made vastly better fathers, by subordinating the dis-tracting instincts of sex to the simple human fellowship of similar education and similar intellectual and social ideals.

It was not to be wondered at that we were uncertain in those old days as to the ultimate result of women's education. Before I myself went to college I had never seen but one college woman. I had heard that such a woman was staying at the house of an ac-quaintance. I went to see her with fear. Even if she had appeared in hoofs and horns I was determined to go to college all the same. But it was a relief to find this Vassar graduate tall and handsome and dressed like other women. When, five years later, I went to Leipzig to study after I had been graduated from Cornell, my mother used to write me that my name was never mentioned to her by the women of her acquaintance. I was thought by them to be as much of a disgrace to my family as if I had eloped with the coachman. Now, women who have been to college are as plentiful as blackber-ries on summer hedges. Even my native city of Baltimore is full of them, and women who have in addition studied in Germany are re-garded with becoming deference by the very Baltimore women who disapproved of me.

During the quarter of the century of the existence of the As-sociation of Collegiate Alumnae two generations of college women have reached mature life, and the older generation is now just pass-ing off the stage. We are therefore better prepared than ever before to give an account of what has been definitely accomplished, and to predict what will be the tendencies of women's college and uni-versity education in the future.

The curriculum of our women's colleges has steadily stiffened. Women, both in separate, and in coeducational colleges, seem to prefer the old-fashioned, so-called disciplinary studies. They dis-regard the so-called accomplishments. I believe that today more women than men are receiving a thoro college education, even al-tho in most cases they are receiving it sitting side by side with men in the same college lecture rooms.

We are now living in the midst of great and, I believe on the whole beneficent, social changes which are preparing the way for the coming economic independence of women.

In order to prepare for this economic independence, we should expect to see what is now taking place. Colleges for women and college departments of coeducational universities are attended by ever-increasing numbers of women students. In seven of the largest western universities women already outnumber men in the college departments....

Just because women have shown such an aptitude for a true college education and such delight in it, we must be careful to maintain it for them in its integrity. We must see to it that its disciplinary quality is not lowered by the insertion of so-called practical courses which are falsely supposed to prepare for life. Women are rapidly coming to control women's college education. It rests with us to decide whether we shall barter for a mess of pottage the inheritance of the girls of this generation which the girls of my generation agonized to obtain for themselves and for other girls.

REFLECTING ON MEANING

1. According to Thomas, why did women of her generation suffer such "awful doubt," such insecurity and anxiety about whether they were "physically and mentally fit" for higher education? What was the nature of her own self-doubt? Why wasn't she able to dismiss without a second thought the notion that being a woman made her unfit for such an endeavor?

2. Thomas recalls the "rage and indignation" with which she read the poet Milton, "weeping" over the biblical story of Adam and Eve, and missing the greatness of Shakespeare. She also expresses the terror that various books on women caused her. What exactly did she find so distressing about these works? What caused her to react to them in this way? Why would these works affect the way she perceived herself?

3. How would you describe the optimism Thomas expresses about conditions at the time this selection was written? What is she optimistic about? In what ways is her optimism justified? What does she seem to have reservations about? From the perspective of today, how would you evaluate her forecast for the future of women in higher education?

EXPLORING RHETORICAL STRATEGIES

1. What is Thomas's purpose in this short excerpt from her book? What is the idea she is trying to express?

2. Thomas's description of her generation's anxiety about higher education is framed in largely subjective terms: her own experiences, feelings, and reactions to very private events. Do you think this strategy strengthens or weakens the picture she paints? Why? Does such subjective experience support her observations about women in general? Why or why not?

3. In these few paragraphs. Thomas manages to look back to the past, to observe the present, and to look forward to the future. How does she integrate all of these perspectives into her essay? How does each perspective provide a foundation for the other?

Chapter 11 ——————————

WORK

I Want a Wife

JUDY SYFERS

Judy Syfers examines the family role of the wife in this satirical essay. Both humorous and thought-provoking, her treatment of the subject pivots on a comparison between wives and servants. Syfers concludes that it would be unreasonable for anyone, including women, not to want a wife.

I belong to that classification of people known as wives. I am A Wife. And, not altogether incidentally, I am a mother.

Not too long ago a male friend of mine appeared on the scene fresh from a recent divorce. He had one child, who is, of course, with his ex-wife. He is looking for another wife. As I thought about him while I was ironing one evening, it suddenly occurred to me that I, too, would like to have a wife. Why do I want a wife?

I would like to go back to school so that I can become economically independent, support myself, and, if need be, support those dependent upon me. I want a wife who will work and send me to school. And while I am going to school I want a wife to take care of my children. I want a wife to keep track of the children's doctor and dentist appointments. And to keep track of mine, too. I want a wife to make sure my children eat properly and are kept clean. I want a wife who will wash the children's clothes and keep them mended. I want a wife who is a good nurturant attendant to my children, who arranges for their schooling, makes sure that they have an adequate social life with their peers, takes them to the park, the zoo, etc. I want a wife who takes care of the children when they are sick, a wife who arranges to be around when the children need special care, because, of course, I cannot miss classes at school. My wife must arrange to lose time at work and not lose the job. It may mean a small cut in my wife's income from time to time, but I guess I can tolerate that. Needless to say, my wife will arrange and pay for the care of the children while my wife is working.

I want a wife who will take care of *my* physical needs. I want a wife who will keep my house clean. A wife who will pick up after my children, a wife who will pick up after me. I want a wife who will keep my clothes clean, ironed, mended, replaced when need be, and who will see to it that my personal things are kept in their proper place so that I can find what I need the minute I need it. I want a wife who cooks the meals, a wife who is a *good* cook. I want a wife who will plan the menus, do the necessary grocery shopping, prepare the meals, serve them pleasantly, and then do the cleaning up while I do my studying. I want a wife who will care for me when I am sick and sympathize with my pain and loss of time from school. I want a wife to go along when our family takes a vacation so that someone can continue to care for me and my children when I need a rest and change of scene.

I want a wife who will not bother me with rambling complaints about a wife's duties. But I want a wife who will listen to me when I feel the need to explain a rather difficult point I have come across in my course of studies. And I want a wife who will type my papers for me when I have written them.

I want a wife who will take care of the details of my social life. When my wife and I are invited out by my friends, I want a wife who will take care of the babysitting arrangements. When I meet people at school that I like and want to entertain, I want a wife who will have the house clean, will prepare a special meal, serve it to me and my friends and not interrupt when I talk about things that interest me and my friends. I want a wife who will have arranged that the children are fed and ready for bed before my guests arrive so that the children do not bother us. I want a wife who takes care of the needs of my guests so that they feel comfortable, who makes sure that they have an ashtray, that they are passed the hors d'oeuvres, that they are offered a second helping of the food, that their wine glasses are replenished when necessary, that their coffee is served to them as they like it. And I want a wife who knows that sometimes I need a night out by myself.

I want a wife who is sensitive to my sexual needs, a wife who makes love passionately and eagerly when I feel like it, a wife who makes sure that I am satisfied. And, of course, I want a wife who will not demand sexual attention when I am not in the mood for it. I want a wife who assumes the complete responsibility for birth control, because I do not want more children. I want a wife who will remain sexually faithful to me so that I do not have to clutter up my intellectual life with jealousies. And I want a wife who understands that *my* sexual needs may entail more than strict adherence to monogamy. I must, after all, be able to relate to people as fully as possible.

If, by chance, I find another person more suitable as a wife than the wife I already have, I want the liberty to replace my present wife with another one. Naturally, I will expect a fresh, new life; my wife will take the children and be solely responsible for them so that I am left free.

When I am through with school and have a job, I want my wife to quit working and remain at home so that my wife can more fully and completely take care of a wife's duties.

My God, who *wouldn't* want a wife?

REFLECTING ON MEANING

1. In her first sentence, Syfers establishes wives as a separate class of people who are expected to fulfill certain obligations within the family unit. Are wives indeed a separate class of people? To what extent do you find Syfers's delineation of wives reasonable?

2. Syfers is clearly satirizing a male attitude. What is this attitude? How prevalent is it? In what ways, if any, has she depicted it accurately?

3. According to Syfers, what specific jobs do women perform for their husbands? How does she categorize these jobs? Do you agree that women are expected to perform these many tasks? Why or why not?

EXPLORING RHETORICAL STRATEGIES

1. How would you describe the tone of Syfers's essay? What strategies does she use to achieve her tone? How does her tone contribute to the persona that she constructs? How would you describe this persona?

2. The list of responsibilities that Syfers compiles sounds rather like a job description. What is the cumulative effect of her inventory

of responsibilities? In what ways does this listing strategy help her make her point about wives?

3. Syfers makes effective use of rhetorical questions in two places in her essay: near the beginning, when she asks "Why do I want a wife?" and at the end, when she closes the essay with a one-sentence paragraph asking "My God, who *wouldn't* want a wife?" How do these two questions contribute to the overall essay? How do they "frame" the essay?

Escaping the Daily Grind for Life as a House Father

RICK GREENBERG

Rick Greenberg tells of leaving his job—"escaping the treadmill"—and taking on the duties and responsibilities of "house fatherhood." His account of his experience illuminates the difficulties and also the joys of reversing traditional gender roles with his wife, certainly a radical step in today's society.

You on vacation?" my neighbor asked.

My 15-month-old son and I were passing her yard on our daily hike through the neighborhood. It was a weekday afternoon and I was the only working-age male in sight.

"I'm uh ... working out of my house now," I told her.

Thus was born my favorite euphemism for house fatherhood, one of those new life-style occupations that is never merely mentioned. Explained, yes. Defended. Even rhapsodized about. I was tongue-tied then, but no longer. People are curious and I've learned to oblige.

I joined up earlier this year when I quit my job—a dead-end, ulcer-producing affair that had dragged on interminably. I left to be with my son until something better came along. And if nothing did, I'd be with him indefinitely.

This was no simple transition. I had never known a house father, never met one. I'd only read about them. They were another news magazine trend. Being a traditionalist, I never dreamed I'd take the plunge.

But as the job got worse, I gave it serious thought. And more thought. And in the end, I still felt ambivalent. This was a radical change that seemed to carry as many drawbacks as benefits. My dislike for work finally pushed me over the edge. That, and the fact that we had enough money to get by.

Escaping the treadmill was a bold stroke. I had shattered my lethargy and stopped whining, and for that I was proud.

Some friends said they were envious. Of course they weren't quitting one job without one waiting–the ultimate in middle-class taboos. That ran through my mind as I triumphantly, and without notice, tossed the letter of resignation on my boss' desk. Then I walked away wobbly-kneed.

The initial trauma of quitting, however, was mitigated by my eagerness to raise our son. Mine was the classic father's lament. I felt excluded. I had become "the man who got home after dark," that other person besides Mama. It hurt when I couldn't quiet his crying.

I sensed that staying home would be therapeutic. The chronic competitiveness and aggressiveness that had served me well as a daily journalist would subside. Something better would emerge, something less obnoxious. My ulcer would heal. Instead of beating deadlines, I'd be doing something important for a change. This was heresy coming from a newspaper gypsy, but it rang true.

There was unease, too. I'd be adrift, stripped of the home-office-home routine that had defined my existence for more than a decade. No more earning a living. No benchmarks. Time would be seamless. Would Friday afternoons feel the same?

The newness of it was scary.

Until my resignation, my wife and I typified today's baby-boomer couples, the want-it-all generation. We had two salaries, a full-time nanny and guilt pangs over practicing parenthood by proxy.

Now, my wife brings home the paychecks, the office problems and thanks for good work on the domestic front. With me at home, her work hours are more flexible. Nanny-less, I change diapers, prepare meals and do all the rest. And I wonder what comes next.

What if I don't find another job? My field is tight. At 34, I'm not getting any more marketable and being out of work doesn't help.

As my father asked incredulously: "Is this going to be what you do?"

Perhaps. I don't know. I wonder myself. It's even more baffling to my father, the veteran of a long and traditional 9-to-5 career. For most of it, my mother stayed home. My father doesn't believe in trends. All he knows is that his only son–with whom he

shares so many traits—has violated the natural order of men providing and women raising children. In his view, I've shown weakness
and immaturity by succumbing to a bad job.

But he's trying to understand, and I think he will.

I'm trying to understand it myself. House fatherhood has
been humbling, rewarding and unnerving.

"It's different," I tell friends. "Different."

Imagine never having to leave home for the office in the morning. That's how different. No dress-up, no commute. Just tumble out
of bed and you're there. House fathering is not for claustrophobics.

I find myself enjoying early morning shopping. My son and I
arrive right after the supermarket opens. The place is almost
empty. For the next hour we glide dreamily, cruising the aisles to a
Muzak accompaniment. This is my idyll. My son likes it, too; he's
fascinated by the spectacle.

Housekeeping still doesn't seem like work, and that's by design. I've mastered the art of doing just enough chores to get by.
This leaves me enough free time. Time to read and write and day-
dream. Time with my son. Time to think about the structure.

So much time, and so little traditional structure, that the days
sometimes blur together. I remember on Sunday nights literally
dreading the approaching work week, the grind. Today, the close
of the weekend still triggers a shiver of apprehension; I now face
the prospect of a week without tangible accomplishments, a void.

On our hikes to the playground, I can feel my old identity fading. All around are people with a mission, a sense of purpose.
Workers. And then there's the rest of us—the stroller and backpack
contingent. The moms, the nannies, and me. I wonder if I've
crossed over a line never to return.

Still, the ulcer seems to be healing. I take pride in laying out
a good dinner for the family and in pampering my wife after a
tough day at the office. I love reading to my son. Running errands
isn't even so bad. A lot of what had been drudgery or trivia is taking on new meaning; maybe I'm mellowing.

Which is ironic. To be a truly committed and effective at-
home parent, there must be this change—a softening, a contentment with small pleasures, the outwardly mundane. This is a time
of reduced demands and lowered expectations. Progress is gradual, often agonizingly so. Patience is essential. Ambition and competitiveness are anathema. Yet eliminating these last two qualities—
losing the edge—could ruin my chances of resurrecting my career.
I can't have it both ways.

The conflict has yet to be resolved. And it won't be unless I
make a firm commitment and choose one life style over the other.
I'm not yet ready for that decision.

In the meantime, a wonderful change is taking place in our home. Amid all the uncertainties, my son and I have gotten to know each other. He can't put a phrase together, but he confides in me. It can be nothing more than a grin or a devilish look. He tries new words on me, new shtick. We roll around a lot; we crack each other up. I'm no longer the third wheel, the man who gets home after dark. Now, I'm as much a part of his life as his mother is. I, too, can stop his crying. So far, that has made the experiment worthwhile.

REFLECTING ON MEANING

1. What does Greenberg's initial defensiveness about his new role in the family suggest about the way others perceived him? Why did his neighbor assume he was on vacation? Why did his father react so negatively to his new status? How do you think most women and men would react? What is your reaction?

2. Greenberg clearly sees himself as apart from the mainstream of society, the "people with a mission, a sense of purpose," the people who would consider it unspeakable not to work. How does the family unit relate to these values? What roles are outlined for women and men in the family? In what ways is a person occupied with child rearing a person without a mission or a sense of purpose?

3. "I can't have it both ways," Greenberg laments, echoing the dilemma that most women face: choosing between a career and a family. Is it possible to have both? What obstacles confront a person who tries to have it both ways? How do men in most cases manage to juggle both?

EXPLORING RHETORICAL STRATEGIES

1. Greenberg begins his essay with an anecdote about a neighbor. Is this an effective way to begin? Why or why not? How does the anecdote help him illustrate his thesis?

2. The essay contains the occasional "sentence fragment"—a group of words punctuated as a sentence but lacking an element considered necessary to a sentence, such as a subject or a finite verb. In addition, Greenberg uses one-sentence paragraphs. Both devices are often regarded as incorrect. How many instances of

each device can you identify? In what ways does Greenberg use these devices to his benefit?

3. Greenberg's essay is organized so that the present conflict he faces isn't addressed until the conclusion. Why do you think he delays telling about this conflict until the end of the essay? What effect does he achieve in doing so?

The Politics of Housework

PAT MAINARDI

How have women been brainwashed into believing that housework is their duty? Essayist Pat Mainardi combines humor and irony in her discussion of the source of women's guilt about housework.

Though women do not complain of the power of husbands, each complains of her own husband, or of the husbands of her friends. It is the same in all other cases of servitude; at least in the commencement of the emancipatory movement. The serfs did not at first complain of the power of the lords, but only of their tyranny.

    –John Stuart Mill, *On the Subjection of Women*

Liberated women—very different from women's liberation! The first signals all kinds of goodies, to warm the hearts (not to mention other parts) of the most radical men. The other signals—*housework*. The first brings sex without marriage, sex before marriage, cozy housekeeping arrangements ("You see, I'm living with this chick") and the self-content of knowing that you're not the kind of man who wants a doormat instead of a woman. That will come later. After all, who wants that old commodity anymore, the Standard American Housewife, all husband, home and kids. The New Commodity, the Liberated Woman, has sex a lot and has a Career, preferably something that can be fitted in with the household chores—like dancing, pottery, or painting.

On the other hand is women's liberation—and housework. What? You say this is all trivial? Wonderful! That's what I thought.

It seemed perfectly reasonable. We both had careers, both had to work a couple of days a week to earn enough to live on, so why shouldn't we share the housework? So I suggested it to my mate and he agreed—most men are too hip to turn you down flat. "You're right," he said, "It's only fair."

Then an interesting thing happened. I can only explain it by stating that we women have been brainwashed more than even we can imagine. Probably too many years of seeing television women in ecstasy over their shiny waxed floors or breaking down over their dirty shirt collars. Men have no such conditioning. They recognize the essential fact of housework right from the very beginning. Which is that it stinks. Here's my list of dirty chores: buying groceries, carting them home and putting them away; cooking meals and washing dishes and pots; doing the laundry, digging out the place when things get out of control; washing floors. The list could go on but the sheer necessities are bad enough. All of us have to do these things, or get someone else to do them for us. The longer my husband contemplated these chores the more repulsed he became, and so proceeded the change from the normally sweet considerate Dr. Jekyll into the crafty Mr. Hyde who would stop at nothing to avoid the horrors of—*housework*. As he felt himself backed into a corner laden with dirty dishes, brooms, mops, and reeking garbage, his front teeth grew longer and pointier, his fingernails haggled and his eyes grew wild. Housework trivial? Not on your life! Just try to share the burden.

So ensued a dialogue that's been going on for several years. Here are some of the high points:

> "I don't mind sharing the housework, but I don't do it very well. We should each do the things we're best at."
> *Meaning:* Unfortunately I'm no good at things like washing dishes or cooking. What I do best is a little light carpentry, changing light bulbs, moving furniture (*how often do you move furniture?*).
> *Also Meaning:* Historically the lower classes (black men and us) have had hundreds of years experience doing menial jobs. It would be a waste of manpower to train someone else to do them now.
> *Also Meaning:* I don't like the dull stupid boring jobs, so you should do them.

> "I don't mind sharing the work, but you'll have to show me how to do it."
> *Meaning:* I ask a lot of questions and you'll have to show me everything everytime I do it because I don't remember so good. Also don't try to sit down and read while I'm doing my jobs

because I'm going to annoy [the] hell out of you until it's easier to do them yourself.

"We used to be so happy?" (Said whenever it was his turn to do something.)
Meaning. I used to be so happy.
Meaning: Life without housework is bliss. (*No quarrel here. Perfect agreement.*)

"We have different standards, and why should I have to work to your standards? That's unfair."
Meaning: If I begin to get bugged by the dirt and crap I will say "This place sure is a sty" or "How can anyone live like this?" and wait for your reaction. I know that all women have a sore called "Guilt over a messy house" or "Household work is ultimately my responsibility." I know that men have caused that sore—if anyone visits and the place is a sty, they're not going to leave and say, "He sure is a lousy housekeeper." You'll take the rap in any case. I can outwait you.
Also Meaning: I can provoke innumerable scenes over the housework issue. Eventually doing all the housework yourself will be less painful to you than trying to get me to do half. Or I'll suggest we get a maid. She will do my share of the work. You will do yours. It's women's work.

"I've got nothing against sharing the housework, but you can't make me do it on your schedule."
Meaning: Passive resistance. I'll do it when I damned well please, if at all. If my job is doing dishes, it's easier to do them once a week. If taking out laundry, once a month. If washing the floors, once a year. If you don't like it, do it yourself oftener, and then I won't do it at all.

"I *hate* it more than you. You don't mind it so much.'
Meaning: Housework is garbage work. It's the worst crap I've ever done. It's degrading and humiliating for someone of *my* intelligence to do it. But for someone of *your* intelligence . . .

"Housework is too trivial to even talk about."
Meaning: It's even more trivial to do. Housework is beneath my status. My purpose in life is to deal with matters of significance. Yours is to deal with matters of insignificance. You should do the housework.

"This problem of housework is not a man-woman problem! In any relationship between two people one is going to have a stronger personality and dominate."
Meaning: That stronger personality had better be *me*.

"In animal societies, wolves, for example, the top animal is usually a male even where he is not chosen for brute strength

but on the basis of cunning and intelligence. Isn't that interesting?"
Meaning: I have historical, psychological, anthropological, and biological justification for keeping you down. How can you ask the top wolf to be equal?

"Women's liberation isn't really a political movement."
Meaning: The Revolution is coming too close to home.
Also Meaning: I am only interested in how I am oppressed, not how I oppress others. Therefore the war, the draft, and the university are political. Women's liberation is not.

"Man's accomplishments have always depended on getting help from other people, mostly women. What great man would have accomplished what he did if be had to do his own housework?
Meaning: Oppression is built into the System and I, as the white American male receive the benefits of this System. I don't want to give them up.

Postscript

Participatory democracy begins at home. If you are planning to implement your politics, there are certain things to remember.

1. He *is* feeling it more than you. He's losing some leisure and you're gaining it. The measure of your oppression is his resistance.
2. A great many American men are not accustomed to doing monotonous repetitive work which never ushers in any lasting let alone important achievement. This is why they would rather repair a cabinet than wash dishes. If human endeavors are like a pyramid with man's highest achievements at the top, then keeping oneself alive is at the bottom. Men have always had servants (us) to take care of this bottom strata of life while they have confined their efforts to the rarefied upper regions. It is thus ironic when they ask of women—where are your great painters, statesmen, etc? Mme. Matisse ran a millinery shop so he could paint. Mrs. Martin Luther King kept his house and raised his babies.
3. It is a traumatizing experience for someone who has always thought of himself as being against any oppression or exploitation of one human being by another to realize that in his daily life he has been accepting and implementing (and benefiting from) this exploitation; that his rationalization is little different from that of the racist who says "Black people don't feel pain" (women don't mind doing the shitwork); and that the oldest form of oppression in history has been the oppression of 50 percent of the population by the other 50 percent.

4. Arm yourself with some knowledge of the psychology of oppressed peoples everywhere, and a few facts about the animal
kingdom. I admit playing top wolf or who runs the gorillas is silly
but as a last resort men bring it up all the time. Talk about bees.
If you feel really hostile bring up the sex life of spiders. They
have sex. She bites off his head.

The psychology of oppressed people is not silly. Jews, immigrants, black men, and all women have employed the same
psychological mechanisms to survive: admiring the oppressor,
glorifying the oppressor, wanting to be like the oppressor, wanting the oppressor to like them, mostly because the oppressor
held all the power.

5. In a sense, all men everywhere are slightly schizoid—divorced
from the reality of maintaining life. This makes it easier for them
to play games with it. It is almost a cliché that women feel greater
grief at sending a son off to war or losing him to that war because
they bore him, suckled him, and raised him. The men who fo-
ment those wars did none of those things and have a more superficial estimate of the worth of human life. One hour a day is a low
estimate of the amount of time one has to spend "keeping" oneself. By foisting this off on others, man gains seven hours a week—
one working day more to play with his mind and not his human
needs. Over the course of generations it is easy to see whence
evolved the horrifying abstractions of modern life.

6. With the death of each form of oppression, life changes and new
forms evolve. English aristocrats at the turn of the century were
horrified at the idea of enfranchising working men—were sure
that it signaled the death of civilization and a return to barbarism. Some working men were even deceived by this line. Similarly with the minimum wage, abolition of slavery, and female
suffrage. Life changes but it goes on. Don't fall for any line about
the death of everything if men take a turn at the dishes. They will
imply that you are holding back the Revolution (their Revolution). But you are advancing it (your Revolution).

7. Keep checking up. Periodically consider who's actually *doing* the
jobs. These things have a way of backsliding so that a year later
once again the woman is doing everything. After a year make a
list of jobs the man has rarely if ever done. You will find cleaning
pots, toilets, refrigerators and ovens high on the list. Use time
sheets if necessary. He will accuse you of being petty. He is above
that sort of thing—(housework). Bear in mind what the worst jobs
are, namely the ones that have to be done every day or several
times a day. Also the ones that are dirty—it's more pleasant to
pick up books, newspapers, etc. than to wash dishes. Alternate
the bad jobs. It's the daily grind that gets you down. Also make
sure that you don't have the responsibility for the housework
with occasional help from him. "I'll cook dinner for you tonight"

implies it's really your job and isn't he a nice guy to do some of it for you.

8. Most men had a rich and rewarding bachelor life during which they did not starve or become encrusted with crud or buried under the litter. There is a taboo that says that women mustn't strain themselves in the presence of men: we haul around 50 pounds of groceries if we have to but aren't allowed to open a jar if there is someone around to do it for us. The reverse side of the coin is that men aren't supposed to be able to take care of themselves without a woman. Both are excuses for making women do the housework.

9. Beware of the double whammy. He won't do the little things he always did because you're now a "Liberated Woman," right? Of course he won't do anything else either...

I was just finishing this when my husband came in and asked what I was doing. Writing a paper on housework. Housework? He said, *Housework?* Oh my god how trivial can you get. A paper on housework.

Little Politics of Housework Quiz

The lowest job in the army, used as punishment is: (a) working 9–5 (b) kitchen duty (K.P.).

When a man lives with his family, his: (a) father (b) mother does his housework.

When he lives with a woman, (a) he (b) she does the housework.

(a) His son (b) his daughter learns [in] preschool how much fun it is to iron daddy's handkerchief.

From the *New York Times,* 9/21/69: "Former Greek Official George Mylonas pays the penalty for differing with the ruling junta in Athens by performing household chores on the island of Amorgos where he lives in forced exile" (with hilarious photo of a miserable Mylonas carrying his own water). What the *Times* means is that he ought to have (a) indoor plumbing (b) a maid.

Dr. Spock said (*Redbook* 3/69): "Biologically and temperamentally I believe, women were made to be concerned first and foremost with child care, husband and home care." Think about: (a) *who* made us (b) why? (c) what is the effect on their lives (d) what is the effect on our lives?

From *Time* 1/5/70, "Like their American counterparts, many housing project housewives are said to suffer from neurosis. And for the first time in Japanese history, many young husbands today complain of being henpecked. Their wives are beginning to demand detailed explanations when they don't come home straight from work and some Japanese males nowadays are even compelled to do housework." According to *Time,* women become neurotic: (a) when they are forced to do the maintenance work for the male caste all day every day of their lives or (b) when they no longer want to do the maintenance work for the male caste all day every day of their lives.

REFLECTING ON MEANING

1. How does Mainardi differentiate between "liberated women" and "women's liberation"? Why might men prefer "liberated women"? How is "women's liberation" connected to housework? In what ways have women been "brainwashed more than we can imagine"? Why aren't men subjected to the same conditioning as women?

2. Mainardi describes her husband's transformation as he contemplates sharing household chores from the "normally sweet and considerate Dr. Jekyll into the crafty Mr. Hyde who would stop at nothing to avoid the horrors of housework." What arguments does Mainardi's husband use to problematize the sharing of housework? What clever psychological weapons does he utilize? How do these arguments serve to instill guilt in his wife?

3. What do the following statements reveal about women's conditioning? "We used to be so happy," "We have different standards," "I hate it more than you," "Housework is too trivial to even talk about," and "Women's liberation isn't really a political movement." How do they illustrate the brainwashing of women?

EXPLORING RHETORICAL STRATEGIES

1. What is the effect of opening the essay with a quotation from John Stuart Mill? What does it lead you to expect from Mainardi's essay? How well does her argument fulfill your expectations?

2. How does the format of the essay—introduction, dialogue between Mainardi and her husband, "postscript" of advice, and the closing quotation from *Time*—contribute to its overall effectiveness?

3. This essay was originally published in 1970. Is the issue of sharing household responsibilities still an important concern of women? How does Mainardi's use of humor and irony make this essay rhetorically effective? What is your emotional response to this essay?

Marked:
Women in the Workplace

DEBORAH TANNEN

Because men represent the norm in a patriarchal society, all women are "marked" by their deviation from this norm. In the workplace, women and men display different styles of communicating and interacting. Linguist Deborah Tannen argues that women shouldn't simply try to replicate men's styles; instead, both men and women should highlight their own positive character traits and develop a unique style.

S ome years ago I was at a small working conference of four women and eight men. Instead of concentrating on the discussion, I found myself looking at the three other women at the table, thinking how each had a different style and how each style was coherent.

One woman had dark brown hair in a classic style that was a cross between Cleopatra and Plain Jane. The severity of her straight hair was softened by wavy bangs and ends that turned under. Because she was beautiful, the effect was more Cleopatra than plain.

The second woman was older, full of dignity and composure. Her hair was cut in a fashionable style that left her with only one eye, thanks to a side part that let a curtain of hair fall across half her face. As she looked down to read her prepared paper, the hair robbed her of binocular vision and created a barrier between her and the listeners.

The third woman's hair was wild, a frosted blond avalanche falling over and beyond her shoulders. When she spoke, she frequently tossed her head, thus calling attention to her hair and away from her lecture.

Then there was makeup. The first woman wore facial cover that made her skin smooth and pale, a black line under each eye, and mascara that darkened her already dark lashes. The second wore only a light gloss on her lips and a hint of shadow on her eyes. The third had blue bands under her eyes, dark blue shadow, mascara, bright red lipstick, and rouge; her fingernails also flashed red.

I considered the clothes each woman had worn on the three days of the conference: In the first case, man-tailored suits in primary colors with solid-color blouses. In the second, casual but stylish black T-shirt, a floppy collarless jacket and baggy slacks or skirt in neutral colors. The third wore a sexy jumpsuit; tight sleeveless jersey and tight yellow slacks; a dress with gaping armholes and an indulged tendency to fall off one shoulder.

Shoes? The first woman wore string sandals with medium heels; the second, sensible, comfortable walking shoes; the third, pumps with spike heels. You can fill in the jewelry, scarves, shawls, sweaters—or lack of them.

As I amused myself finding patterns and coherence in these styles and choices, I suddenly wondered why I was scrutinizing only the women. I scanned the table to get a fix on the styles of the eight men. And then I knew why I wasn't studying them. The men's styles were unmarked.

The term "marked" is a staple of linguistic theory. It refers to the way language alters the base meaning of a word by adding something—a little linguistic addition that has no meaning on its own. The unmarked form of a word carries the meaning that goes without saying, what you think of when you're not thinking anything special.

The unmarked tense of verbs in English is the present—for example, *visit*. To indicate past, you have to mark the verb for "past" by adding *ed* to yield *visited*. For future, you add a word: *will visit*. Nouns are presumed to be singular until marked for plural. To convey the idea of more than one, we typically add something, usually *s* or *es*. More than one *visit* becomes *visits,* and one *dish* becomes two *dishes,* thanks to the plural marking.

The unmarked forms of most English words also convey "male." Being male is the unmarked case. We have endings, such as *ess* and *ette,* to mark words as female. Unfortunately, marking words for female also, by association, tends to mark them for frivolousness. Would you feel safe entrusting your life to a doctorette? This is why many poets and actors who happen to be female object to the marked forms "poetess" and "actress." Alfre Woodard, an Oscar nominee for Best Supporting Actress, says she identifies herself as an actor because "actresses worry about eyelashes and cellulite, and women who are actors worry about the characters we are playing." Any marked form can pick up extra meaning beyond what the marking is intended to denote. The extra meanings carried by gender markers reflect the traditional associations with the female gender: not quite serious, often sexual.

I was able to identify the styles and types of the women at the conference because each of us had to make decisions about hair, clothing, makeup and accessories, and each of those decisions carried meaning. Every style available to us was marked. Of course, the men in our group had to make decisions too, but their choices carried far less meaning. The men could have chosen styles that were marked, but they didn't have to, and in this group, none did. Unlike the women, they had the option of being unmarked.

I took account of the men's clothes. There could have been a cowboy shirt with string tie or a three-piece suit or a necklaced hippie in jeans. But there wasn't. All eight men wore brown or blue slacks and standard-style shirts of light colors.

No man wore sandals or boots; their shoes were dark, closed, comfortable, and flat. In short, unmarked.

Although no man wore makeup, you couldn't say the men didn't wear makeup in the sense that you could say a woman didn't wear makeup. For men, no makeup is unmarked.

I asked myself what style we women could have adopted that would have been unmarked, like the men's. The answer was: none. There is no unmarked woman.

There is no woman's hairstyle that could be called "standard," that says nothing about her. The range of women's hairstyles is staggering, but if a woman's hair has no particular style, this in itself is taken as a statement that she doesn't care how she looks—an eloquent message that can disqualify a woman for many positions.

Women have to choose between shoes that are comfortable and shoes that are deemed attractive. When our group had to make an unexpected trek, the woman who wore flat laced shoes arrived first. The last to arrive was the woman with spike heels, her shoes in her hand and a handful of men around her.

If a woman's clothes are tight or revealing (in other words, sexy), it sends a message—an intended one of wanting to be attractive but also a possibly unintended one of availability. But if her clothes are not sexy, that too sends a message, lent meaning by the knowledge that they could have been. In her book *Women Lawyers,* Mona Harrington quotes a woman who, despite being a partner in her firm, found herself slipping into this fault line when she got an unexpected call to go to court right away. As she headed out the door, a young (male) associate said to her, "Hadn't you better button your blouse?" She was caught completely off guard. "My blouse wasn't buttoned unusually low," the woman told Harrington. "And this was not a conservative guy. But he thought one more button was necessary for court." And here's the rub: "I started wondering if my authority was being undermined by one button."

A woman wearing bright colors calls attention to herself, but if she avoids bright colors, she has (as my choice of verb in this sentence suggests) avoided something. Heavy makeup calls attention to the wearer as someone who wants to be attractive. Light makeup tries to be attractive without being alluring. There are thousands of products from which makeup must be chosen and myriad ways of applying them. Yet no makeup at all is anything but unmarked. Some men even see it as a hostile refusal to please them. Women who ordinarily do not wear makeup can be surprised by the trans-forming effect of putting it on. In a book titled *Face Value,* my col-league Robin Lakoff noted the increased attention she got from men when she went forth from a television station still profession-ally made-up.

Women can't even fill out a form without telling stories about themselves. Most application forms now give four choices for titles. Men have one to choose—"Mr."—so their choice carries no meaning other than to say they are male. But women must choose among three, each of them marked. A woman who checks the box for "Mrs." or "Miss" communicates not only whether she has been married but also that she has conservative tastes in forms of ad-dress, and probably other conservative values as well. Checking "Ms." declines to let on about marriage (whereas "Mr." declines nothing since nothing was asked), but it also marks the woman who checks it on her form as either liberated or rebellious, depending on the attitudes and assumptions of the one making the judgment.

I sometimes try to duck these variously marked choices by giv-ing my title as "Dr."—and thereby risk marking myself as either up-pity (hence sarcastic responses like "Excuse *me*!") or an overachiever (hence reactions of congratulatory surprise, like "Good for you!").

All married women's surnames are marked. If a woman takes her husband's name, she announces to the world that she is mar-ried and also that she is traditional in her values, according to some observers. To others it will indicate that she is less herself, more identified by her husband's identity. If she does not take her hus-band's name, this too is marked, seen as worthy of comment: She has *done* something; she has "kept her own name." Though a man can do exactly the same thing—and usually does—he is never said to have "kept his own name," because it never occurs to anyone that he might have given it up. For him, but not for her, using his own name is unmarked.

A married woman who wants to have her cake and eat it too may use her surname plus his. But this too announces that she is or has been married and often results in a tongue-tying string that makes life miserable for anyone who needs to alphabetize it. In a list (Harvey O'Donovan, Jonathon Feldman, Stephanie Woodbury McGillicutty), the woman's multiple name stands out. It is marked.

Pronouns conspire in this pattern as well. Grammar books tell us that "he" means "he or she" and that "she" is used only if a referent is specifically female. But this touting of "he" as the sex-indefinite pronoun is an innovation introduced into English by grammarians in the eighteenth and nineteenth centuries, according to Peter Mühlhäusler and Rom Harré in their book *Pronouns and People*. From at least about the year 1500, the correct sex-indefinite pronoun was "they," as it still is in casual spoken English. In other words, the female was declared by grammarians to be the marked case.

Looking at the men and women sitting around the conference table, I was amazed at how different our worlds were. Though men have to make choices too, and men's clothing styles may be less neutral now than they once were, nonetheless the parameters within which men must choose when dressing for work—the cut, fabric, or shade of jackets, shirts, and pants, and even the one area in which they are able to go a little wild, ties—are much narrower than the riotous range of colors and styles from which women must choose. For women, decisions about whether to wear a skirt, slacks, or a dress is only the start; the length of skirts can range from just above the floor to just below the hips, and the array of colors to choose from would make a rainbow look drab. But even this contrast in the range from which men and women must choose is irrelevant to the crucial point: A man can choose a style that will not attract attention or subject him to any particular interpretation, but a woman can't. Whatever she wears, whatever she calls herself, however she talks, will be fodder for interpretation about her character and competence. In a setting where most of the players are men, there is no unmarked woman.

This does not mean that men have complete freedom when it comes to dress. Quite the contrary—they have much less freedom than women have to express their personalities in their choice of fabrics, colors, styles, and jewelry. But the one freedom they have that women don't is the point of this discussion—the freedom to be unmarked.

That clothing is a metaphor for women's being marked was noticed by David Finkel, a journalist who wrote an article about women in Congress for *The Washington Post Magazine*. He used the contrast between women's and men's dress to open his article by describing the members coming through the doors to the floor of the U.S. House of Representatives:

> So many men, so many suits. Dark suits. Solid suits. Blue suits that look gray, gray suits that look blue. There's Tom Foley—he's in one, and Bob Michel, and Steny Hoyer, and Fred Grandy, and Dick Durbin, and dozens, make that hundreds, more.

So many suits, so many white shirts. And dark ties. And five o'clock shadows. And short haircuts. And loosening jowls. And big, visible ears.

So many, many men.

. . .

And still the members continue to pour through the doors–gray, grayer, grayest–until the moment when, emerging into this humidor, comes a surprise:

The color red.

It is Susan Molinari, a first-termer from New York . . .

Now, turquoise. It is Barbara Boxer . . .

Now, paisley. It is Jill Long . . .

Embroidering his color-of-clothing metaphor, Finkel, whose article appeared in May 1992, concluded, "Of the 435 members of the House of Representatives, 29 are women, which means that if Congress is a gray flannel suit, the women of Congress are no more than a handful of spots on the lapel."

When Is Sexism Realism?

If women are marked in our culture, their very presence in professional roles is, more often than not, marked. Many work settings, just like families, come with ready-made roles prescribed by gender, and the ones women are expected to fill are typically support roles. It was not long ago when medical offices and hospitals were peopled by men who were doctors and orderlies and women who were nurses and clerical workers, just as most offices were composed of men who ran the business and women who served them as receptionists, clerks, and secretaries. All members of Congress were men, and women found in the Capitol Building were aides and staff members. When a woman or man enters a setting in an atypical role, that expectation is always a backdrop to the scene.

All the freshmen women in Congress have had to contend with being mistaken for staff, even though they wear pins on their lapels identifying them as members. For her book *A Woman's Place,* Congresswoman Marjorie Margolies-Mezvinsky interviewed her female colleagues about their experiences. One congresswoman approached a security checkpoint with two congressmen when a guard stopped only her and told her to go through the metal detector. When Congresswoman Maria Cantwell needed to get into her office after hours, the guard wanted to know which member she worked for. But her press secretary, Larry West, has gone through the gate unthinkingly without being stopped. When Congresswoman Lynn Schenk attended a reception with a male aide, the host graciously held out his hand to the aide and said, "Oh, Congressman Schenk."

You don't have to be in Congress to have experiences like that. A woman who owned her own business found that if she took any man along on business trips, regardless of whether he was her vice president or her assistant, people she met tended to address themselves to him, certain that he must be the one with power and she his helper. A double-bass player had a similar experience when she arrived for an audition with a male accompanist. The people who greeted them assumed she was the accompanist. A woman who heads a research firm and holds a doctorate finds she is frequently addressed as "Mrs.," while her assistant, who holds only a master's degree, is addressed as "Dr."

One evening after hours, I was working in my office at Georgetown University. Faculty offices in my building are lined up on both sides of a corridor, with cubicles in the corridor for secretaries and graduate-student assistants. Outside each office is a nameplate with the professor's title and last name. The quiet of the after-hours corridor was interrupted when a woman came to my door and asked if she could use my phone. I was surprised but glad to oblige, and explained that she had to dial "9." She made the call, thanked me, and left. A few minutes later, she reappeared and asked if I had any correction fluid. Again surprised, but still happy to be of help, I looked in my desk drawer but had to disappoint her: Since my typewriter was self-correcting, I had none. My patience began to waver, but my puzzlement was banished when the woman bounded into my office for the third and final time to ask if I was Dr. Murphy's secretary, in which case she would like to leave with me the paper she was turning in to him.

I doubt this woman would have imposed on my time and space to use my telephone and borrow correction fluid if she had known I was a professor, even though I would not have minded had she done so. At least she would probably have been more deferential in intruding. And the experience certainly gave me a taste of how hard it must be for receptionists to get any work done, as everyone regards them as perpetually interruptible. But what amused and amazed me was that my being female had overridden so many clues to my position: My office was along the wall, it was fully enclosed like all faculty offices, my name and title were on the door, and I was working after five, the hour when offices close and secretaries go home. But all these clues were nothing next to the master clue of gender: In the university environment, she expected that professors were men and women were secretaries. Statistics were on her side: Of the eighteen members of my department at the time, sixteen were men; of the five members of Dr. Murphy's department, four were men. So she was simply trusting the world to be as she knew it was.

It is not particularly ironic or surprising that the student who mistook me for a secretary was female. Women are no less prone to assume that people will adhere to the norm than are men. And this includes women who themselves are exceptions. A woman physician who works in a specialty in which few of her colleagues are female told me of her annoyance when she telephones a colleague, identifies herself as "Dr. Jones calling for Dr. Smith," and is told by Dr. Smith's receptionist, "I'll go get Dr. Smith while you put Dr. Jones on the line." But this same woman catches herself referring to her patients' general practitioners as "he," even though she ought to know better than anyone that a physician could be a woman.

Children seem to pick up norms as surely as adults do. A woman who was not only a doctor but a professor at a medical school was surprised when her five-year-old said to her, "You're not a doctor, Mommy. You're a nurse." Intent on impressing her daughter, she said, "Yes, I am a doctor. In fact, I teach other doctors how to be doctors." The little girl thought about this as she incorporated the knowledge into her worldview. "Oh," she said. "But you only teach women doctors." (Conversely, male nurses must deal with being mistaken for doctors, and men who work as assistants must deal with being mistaken for their boss.)

Another of my favorite stories in this mode is about my colleague who made a plane reservation for herself and replied to the question "Is that Mrs. or Miss?" by giving her title: "It's Dr." So the agent asked, "Will the doctor be needing a rental car when he arrives?" Her attempt to reframe her answer to avoid revealing her marital status resulted in the agent reframing her as a secretary.

I relate these stories not to argue that sexism is rampant and that we should all try to bear in mind that roles are changing, although I believe these statements to be true. I am inclined to be indulgent of such errors, even though I am made uncomfortable when they happen to me, because I myself have been guilty of them. I recall an occasion when I gave a talk to a gathering of women physicians, and then signed books. The woman who organized the signing told me to save one book because she had met a doctor in the elevator who couldn't make it to the talk but asked to have a book signed nonetheless. I was pleased to oblige and asked, pen poised, to whom I should sign the book—and was surprised when I heard a woman's name. Even though I had just spent the evening with a room full of doctors who were all women, in my mind "a doctor" had called up the image of a man.

So long as women are a minority of professional ranks, we cannot be surprised if people assume the world is as it is. I mention these stories to give a sense of what the world is like for people who are exceptions to expectations—every moment they live in the unexpected role, they must struggle against others' assumptions that do not apply to them, much like gay men and lesbians with regard to their sexual orientation, and, as Ellis Cose documents in his book *The Rage of a Privileged Class,* much like middle-class black professionals in most American settings.

One particular burden of this pattern for a woman in a position of authority is that she must deal with incursions on her time, as others make automatic assumptions that her time is more expendable, although she also may benefit from hearing more information because people find her "approachable." There is a sense in which every woman is seen as a receptionist–available to give information and help, perennially interruptible. A woman surgeon complained that although she has very good relations with the nurses in her hospital, they simply do not wait on her the way they wait on her male colleagues. (The very fact that I must say "woman surgeon" and "male nurse" reflects this dilemma: All surgeons are presumed male, all nurses presumed female, unless proven otherwise. In other words, the unmarked surgeon is male, the unmarked nurse female.)

Expect the Expected

We approach new perceptions by measuring them against our past experience. This is a necessary process that makes it possible for us to get through life without regarding each incoming perception as brand-new. It works very well when the world we encounter is behaving as the world has done in the past but leads us astray when the world is new. And right now, we are all learning to deal with a world that is changing much faster than our expectations can keep up with.

A man was walking by a construction site in a large, busy city, absentmindedly surveying the scene, when his eyes met a surprise: The person sitting way up in the cab of a huge derrick, calmly making the crane grab mouthfuls of dirt, was a woman. He cheerfully called out to her, "Hey Mama, what's for supper?" It seemed to him a clever joke, and of course it was fleeting and not particularly well thought out, but in a wink he had reminded her that she was out of her place—which was in the kitchen.

If someone walks into a hospital and expects the doctors to be men and the nurses to be women—which means, by implication, that the women in white coats will be nurses and the men in white coats will be doctors—it will still be true most of the time. But it is not *always* true, and that is a problem for the women who are doctors and the men who are nurses and the patients who need to know which is which. When our expectations are not met, we call it sexism—responding to old patterns of gender that no longer apply, or no longer apply in all instances.

We are no less likely to respond to others according to expectations that we ourselves do not fit. I recall meeting a journalist years ago who had taken an interest in an article I had written about New York Jewish conversational style—an article in which I had identified myself as a native speaker of that style. As I waited for him outside the appointed restaurant, I saw him approach (I knew who he was because I had heard him give a talk) and saw his eyes run unseeing over me, as he looked for Deborah Tannen. When I identified myself, he said he didn't expect me to be blond, since he was looking for a fellow Jew—and then he laughed, because of all the times he himself had been told he didn't look like what people expected, because he too is a blond Jew.

What I am getting at is that there is no point in blaming those who expect the world to continue as it has been in the past, but we should not let anyone off the hook either—including ourselves. We must continually remind ourselves that the world is changing, and women and men no longer can be depended upon to stay in the narrowly prescribed roles we were consigned to in the past. But we must also be on guard for signs that such expectations are getting in our way. One of the major ways that expectations impede us is in the strong associations we have of how women and men should speak and behave. With women entering situations that were previously all male, where established norms for behavior are based on the ways men behaved in those roles, expectations must give way—either expectations for how someone in that role should behave, or expectations of the women who move into those roles. Which will it be? Will women change their ways of talking to fit existing norms, or will they change the norms—establish new expectations for the roles they come to fill?

"Your Style or Mine?"

There is a mountain of research attesting that when females and males get together in groups, the females are more likely to change their styles to adapt to the presence of males—whether they are adults or children. Psychologist Eleanor Maccoby cites studies by Linda Carli and by Judith Hall and Karen Braunwald showing that when women are with men, they become more like men: They raise their voices, interrupt, and otherwise become more assertive. But, Maccoby continues,

> there is also evidence that they carry over some of their well-practiced female-style behaviors, sometimes in exaggerated form. Women may wait for a turn to speak that does not come,

and thus they may end up talking less than they would in a women's group. They smile more than the men do, agree more often with what others have said, and give nonverbal signals of attentiveness to what others—perhaps especially the men—are saying (Duncan and Fiske 1977). In some writings this female behavior has been referred to as "silent applause."

Psychologist Campbell Leaper observed girls' tendency to adapt to boys' styles in his study of 138 children playing in pairs at the ages of five and seven. Although "collaborative" speech accounted for the majority of all the children's speech, whether or not they were talking to other children of the same sex, there were nonetheless differences in degree. He found collaborative and co-operative exchanges to be more frequent when girls played with girls, and controlling and domineering exchanges more frequent when boys played with boys, especially when the children were older. Boys were less likely than girls to adopt strategies typical of the other sex when they played co-ed. When girls played with boys, they used more controlling speech than when they played with girls. Leaper suspects this occurred because the boys tended to ignore the girls' polite speech. Again, we get a glimpse of the ritual nature of conversation. The girls' strategies worked best when used with other girls who shared the same strategies. When they used these strategies with boys, they didn't work as well, so the girls had to adapt to the boys' style to get results.

The tendency of women to adapt their styles to men's has been found even on the most small-scale and personal level. Donna Johnson and Duane Roen examined peer-review letters written by graduate students to fellow students whose term papers they had evaluated. The results showed that women students used slightly more positive evaluation terms, such as "interesting" and "helpful," than the men, but the most striking finding was that the women offered positive evaluation terms far more frequently *to other women* than they did to men, whereas the men offered only slightly more such terms to women than to other men. In other words, the women adjusted more in response to whether they were addressing another woman or a man. (An indirect result of this pattern was that men received the least praise, whether they were talking to other men or to women.)

"Why Can't a Woman Be More Like a Man?"

There are many ways that women entering the world of work are entering "the men's house," to use the phrase coined by Captain

Carol Barkalow as the title of her book about her military career. The very language spoken is often based on metaphors from sports or from the military, terms that are just idioms to many women, not references to worlds they have either inhabited or observed with much alacrity. Such expressions as "stick to your guns," "under the gun," "calling the shots," "an uphill battle," "a level playing field," "a judgment call," "start the ball rolling," "a curveball," "the ball's in their court," "batting a thousand," "struck out," "getting flak," "the whole nine yards," "in the ballpark," and "deep-six it" are part of our everyday vocabulary. (The list could go on and on.) Author Mark Richard recalls that when he was a struggling writer living in Virginia Beach, the fiction editor of a national magazine told him, "You want to play hardball fiction? You've got to come to New York."

In some cases, women (or men) not very familiar with sports may know how an expression is used without knowing its source. In others, a lack of familiarity with sports can lead to a failure of comprehension. A woman was told by her lawyer that according to a contract they were negotiating, "they can't sell you to Buffalo." She had to ask what he meant by that.

This is an area in which, it seems, women are already beginning to do things their own way, using metaphors from cooking, birthing, and sewing along with those from war and sports. For example, a woman discussing her plans for a company that would produce a series of videotapes said, "I'd like to be able to pop them out—not like breadsticks, but like babies." The 1994 Poet Laureate of the United States, Rita Dove, compared a poem to a bouillon cube, because it's concentrated, portable, and useful. A woman described an editorial project she was working on as being like needlepoint, in the sense that it required close attention to detail.

Although there is evidence that women do adapt their styles to those of men when they find themselves in interaction with men, they rarely adopt men's styles whole-hog. And it is well that they don't, because men and women who model their behavior on someone of the other gender often get a very different reaction than their role models get. In a workplace situation, it is frequently a man who has been the model, while a woman who tries to behave like him is distressed to find that the reaction she gets is very different.

A dramatic example of this phenomenon happened to Captain Carol Barkalow. One of the first women to attend West Point, Captain Barkalow rose to the position of company commander at Fort Lee in Virginia. In her attempt to make herself more like a male commanding officer, she took up bodybuilding. What better way to challenge the unfair assumption that women are not as strong as men, not strong enough to lead their unit? She did so well that she won second place in a bodybuilding competition.

Two months before Captain Barkalow was to take her command, news of her triumph was published in the post newspaper, along with the standard championship photograph in which she posed standing beside her trophy, clad in a bikini designed to show off the muscles she had worked so hard to develop. And this photograph very nearly cost her the command and her career. In the words of the brigade commander, "She had become the masturbatory fantasy of every goddamned male noncommissioned officer in the company." Her attempt to enhance her image in a male domain—the strength of her muscles—was interpreted sexually because a photograph of a woman posing in a bikini, even though the pose she struck was designed to look powerful rather than seductive, brought to mind an image not of fitness and strength but of a pinup. This is a particularly dramatic example of what Captain Barkalow learned during her years in the military, as she explains in her book: She could not be an officer in the same way that men were; she had to find her own way, a way that fulfilled the requirements of her job as a military officer without violating too many expectations for how a woman should be.

Change Others by Adapting Your Style

In talking to women physicians, I heard two different and conflicting themes repeated. From some, I heard that nurses were a problem. They simply did not give the women physicians the same respect they gave to male doctors; they would not do for them what they do for the men. From others, I heard that nurses were their best allies. The nurses they worked with would do anything for them, and more than once saved their skins. Which was the truth about how nurses, who are almost all women, tend to treat women doctors?

A possible explanation was offered by a prominent surgeon who was one of the few women in her specialty. She explained that when she first became a surgeon, she modeled her behavior on that of the male surgeons who had been her teachers. Having seen that the operating room functioned like the military, with the surgeon the captain, she tried barking orders like the other surgeons. But she found it didn't work. No one would take orders from her. So she had to change her style, finding ways of being firm that did not sound as authoritarian. And this, she believes, explains the different experiences women physicians reported having with nurses. If you try to be authoritarian, like many of your male colleagues are, it won't work with most nurses, but if you ally yourself with them and respect them as professional colleagues, they will be your best allies.

This seemed to offer a possible solution to the puzzle: Different women doctors may have different impressions of how nurses treat women doctors because of the different ways they treat nurses. It is interesting to note that men as doctors can choose whether or not they wish to adopt an authoritarian or even an imperious style without suffering a loss of service from nurses, but women doctors cannot. It is also instructive to consider the role that women play in ensuring that other women adhere to the norms for female interaction, just as men exert pressure on other men to behave according to norms for male interaction.

Indeed, there is ample evidence that women tend to speak differently from men, not in an absolutely predictable pattern but as a matter of degree. Allowing for the exceptions of individuals, and the great range of personal and cultural styles, there is nonetheless evidence (for example in the work of Candace West and of Nancy Ainsworth-Vaughn) that women physicians tend to talk differently to their patients than male doctors do, and that women lawyers tend to operate differently from men. But many are not aware that they are doing things differently, and those who are aware of it may be reluctant to admit it, since deviating from accepted norms always carries a price.

Linguist Barbara Johnstone interviewed four prominent and successful Texas women, because she was interested in how they thought their being women affected their public-speaking styles. But when Johnstone interviewed them, all four denied that their being female affected their ways of speaking. For example, an attorney said, " . . . people have told me that they think that I'm successful in the courtroom because I can identify with the jury, that the juries like me. And I haven't ever figured out why, except that . . . I try to smile, and I try to just be myself. And I don't put on any airs." Although I do not doubt that this attorney is indeed just being herself, it is nonetheless well documented that women tend to smile more than men. And placing value on not putting on airs sounds quite a bit like the assumption that a person should not flaunt her authority that typifies the way many women talk about management. (I offer evidence of this in Chapter Six.) Interestingly, all four women Johnstone interviewed spoke with pride of how their styles were influenced by their being Texan.

Mona Harrington writes of three women who left large law firms to start their own "alternative" firm specializing in commercial litigation. They determined to do things differently from the ways things were done in the large firms where they had worked before—both in managing their relationships with each other and in doing work for their clients.

In terms of interoffice relations, in the women's firm all partners make decisions together at meetings, have offices equal in size, and divide money earned equally among them, regardless of who brought in the client or who worked on the case. In terms of their working styles, the women told Harrington that they represent clients not by being as aggressive and confrontational as possible, but by listening, observing, and better "reading" opponents. One pointed out that in taking depositions, they get better results by adopting a "quiet, sympathetic approach," charming witnesses into forgetting that the attorney deposing them is their adversary, than by grilling witnesses and attacking them.

Yet when interviewed by the press about their approach, these same women do not mention their different styles, not even to explain how well they work. Just the opposite, they stress that they are "tough" litigators and seasoned veterans of traditionally contentious legal settings. The reason, they explained to Harrington, is that if they told the truth about their styles, they would be dismissed as soft and weak. Their conclusion has been that you can't talk about it; you have to just *be* it, and get a reputation based on results.

A Braid Is a Stronger Rope

Although I describe patterns of women's and men's typical (not universal) styles, and show that styles expected of women can work against them in work settings, I would not advise women to adopt men's styles to succeed—although in some cases, in some ways, this might work. In general, that advice is no more practical than advising women to go to work dressed in men's clothes. Instead, I would argue for flexibility and mutual understanding. The frustration of both genders will be reduced, and companies as well as individuals will benefit, if women and men (like Easterners and Southerners, old and young, and people of different classes and ethnic backgrounds) understand each other's styles. Once you understand what is happening to you, you can experiment on your own, trying new ways of behaving to solve your problems. Of course, all problems will not summarily disappear, but the sense of puzzlement and lack of control will at least subside.

Another reason it would be a mistake for women to try to behave like men is that businesses need to communicate with clients of different sorts, including more and more women. For instance, newspapers need to appeal to women as readers in order to sell newspapers, so it would do them no good to hire a slew of women who are just like men. I sometimes give the example of a woman who worked at an appraisal firm. One of her colleagues told her he had just gotten a very strange call from a client. After identifying herself, the client simply told him that she would be going on vacation that week and hung up, without giving him any comprehensible reason for her call. The woman who told me this said she was pretty sure she understood what this was about and called the client back to apologize for the slight delay in the appraisal she had ordered and reassure her that it would be ready when she returned from her vacation.

The appraiser also told me that she had been nonplussed by a client who called her up and began angrily berating her because his appraisal was late. Taken aback by the verbal assault, which seemed to her unacceptable in the context of a business relationship, she had become tongue-tied and unable to give him the assurances she had just given the other client, so she had her colleague call the man back and deal with him. This example shows how pointless it would be to ask which appraiser's style was "best." Each one was best at dealing with certain clients. Rather than trying to determine which style is best and hire a staff with uniform styles, the company clearly is benefiting from having a range of styles among its sales staff.

Nobody Nowhere was the first book by Donna Williams, the remarkable woman with autism, in which she describes her experience as a child and young adult, explaining what autism feels like from the inside and how she was able to function within its constraints. Among the effects of autism is increased sensitivity to all incoming sensory information, and an inability to process this information in a coherent way. In her second book, *Somebody Somewhere,* Williams recounts her continuing efforts to make contact with the world outside, including the events surrounding the publication of her first book. When an agent went in search of a publisher for *Nobody Nowhere,* he found not one but two major companies that wanted to publish the book, so the author had to choose between them. Williams's description of her meetings with the two publishers' emissaries is instructive. She met them in the home of her landlords, a couple named Mr. and Mrs. Miller.

> Tall and square, the first one resembled an insurance salesman. As he entered the Millers' place, he handed me an advertising catalogue for his company. I examined the picture of the ocean on the cover. What am I meant to do with this? I wondered.
>
> . . .
>
> He spoke confidently. Yet he was too self-assured and his ego dwarfed mine by comparison. . . . He took Mr. Miller aside to discuss the deal. I realized he considered me more as an odd-

ity with some intelligent bits rather than an equal human being. I smiled to myself. One down, one to go.

The next publisher had bright red hair and looked like the children's storybook character Holly Hobbie. She had a whisper of a voice to match. She was stiff as a board and shook like a sparrow confronted by a cat. I liked her even though her anxiety made me feel I was a psychopath. She was not at all self-assured, so there was enough social space to find myself present in her company. It is hard to make a decision when your body and voice are present but your sense of self is absent. Holly Hobbie made it easier.

She was about to go. I remembered the other guy with the company advertising catalogue. "Do you have anything to give me?" I asked. "Yes," she replied, producing three glossy picture books of landscapes of the Australian outback and tales of childhood and the plight of Australian Aborigines. This woman knew she was taking a person on board, not just a meal ticket. I decided to work with her. The book was on the road to publication.

Imagine a publishing executive making a decision about which of two individuals to hire: One is extremely confident and self-assured; the other is so lacking in confidence that when faced with an atypical author, she shakes visibly. The first is straightforward; the second speaks in a whisper. The first goes to a business meeting ready to talk deals with someone capable of understanding what he's talking about; the second comes armed with picture books. But the confident, self-assured, straight-talking publisher lost the book that turned out to be an international best-seller, and the quaking, whispering, picture-book-bearing publisher landed it.

Donna Williams is an unusual author. But there are many authors, or clients in other businesses, who would be more comfortable with a less assured style that does not overwhelm them. And there are many women who would be put off by someone who addresses himself to their landlord—or any man who happens to be present—rather than to her. Companies that have a uniform model of a "good" style employee will end up with a staff equipped to perform well when talking to individuals with some styles but not others. The company that is able to accommodate employees with a range of styles will have far more flexibility in dealing with customers whose styles also cover a range.

Not only customers, but the employees within a company, no longer come from the same mold. Bringing together people of different ethnic and class backgrounds, from different parts of the country and the world, all with their own personalities, inevitably results in a mix of conversational styles within the organization as well. Making the workplace more amenable to people with a range of styles will benefit not only women but everyone; not all men have the same style, and not all men have styles that are rewarded in traditional business environments. If more people's styles are accommodated, more talents and ideas will be available to the company.

Will Talk About Gender Differences Polarize?

Some people fear that putting people into two categories by talking about "women" and "men" can drive a wedge between us, polarizing us even more. This is a serious concern. I know of at least one instance in which that is exactly what happened. A female executive at a large accounting firm was so well thought of by her firm that they sent her to a weeklong executive-training seminar at the company's expense. Not surprisingly, considering the small number of women at her level, she was the only woman at the seminar, which was composed of high-ranking executives from a variety of the corporation's wide-ranging divisions. This did not surprise or faze her, since she was used to being the only woman among men.

All went well for the first three days of the seminar. But on the fourth, the leaders turned their attention to issues of gender. Suddenly, everyone who had been looking at her as "one of us" began to look at her differently—as a woman, "one of them." She was repeatedly singled out and asked to relate her experiences and impressions, something she did not feel she could do honestly, since she had no reason to believe they would understand or accept what she was talking about. When they said confidently that they were sure there was no discrimination against women in their company, that if women did not get promoted it was simply because they didn't merit promotion, she did not feel she could object. Worst of all, she had to listen to one after another of her colleagues express what she found to be offensive opinions about women's abilities. By the end of the day, she was so demoralized that she was questioning whether she wanted to continue to work for this company at all. Whereas she had started out feeling completely comfortable, not thinking of herself as different from the men, the discussion of gender issues made her acutely aware of how different she was and convinced her she could never again fit comfortably into this group.

The group in which this occurred was made up of people from far-flung offices, not many of whom were from her own home office. As a result, she was able eventually to get past the experience, and it did not poison her day-to-day relationships at work. If a similar workshop had been held among her daily co-workers, it could have been much more destructive. And the saddest part is that the unfortunate outcome resulted from a program designed to help. As anthropologist Gregory Bateson explained in his work on cybernetics, any time people interfere with a system to change it, they risk making things worse, because they don't understand all the elements in the system and how they interrelate.

But the alternative, doing nothing, is not a viable one, because the situation as it is will have to change. In the case of women in the workplace, the situation is changing, whether we talk about it or not. And the hope that all we had to do was open the doors and let women in has simply not been borne out. Twenty years after women began receiving MBAs and entering businesses where they had not been before, they still make up only a small percentage of higher-level executives. The "pipeline" argument has simply not panned out. Years after women entered the pipeline, they just aren't coming through the other end in proportion to their numbers going in. Instead, more and more women are leaving the corporate world, in greater numbers than men, either to start their own businesses, to be independent contractors, or to do other things entirely. (For example, a 1993 survey of those who received MBAs from Stanford University over the preceding ten-year period found that 22% of the women, as compared to 8% of the men, had left large corporations to start their own businesses.) Some of this may be a privilege that men too would take advantage of if they had the chance. But a lot of women are seeking alternatives simply because they tire of feeling like strangers in a strange land when they go to work each day. In a word, they tire of being marked.

Simply opening the doors and letting in women, or any individuals whose styles do not conform to those already in place, is not enough. As the experience of the executive at the training seminar showed, neither are localized efforts at diversity training, though surely these can help if they are done well. Finally, we can't just tell individuals that they should simply talk one way or another, as if ways of talking were hats you can put on when you enter an office and take off when you leave. For one thing, if you try to adopt a style that does not come naturally to you, you leave behind your intuitions and may well behave in ways inappropriate in any style or betray the discomfort you actually feel. Most important, we do not regard the way we talk—how we say what we mean, how we show consideration or frustration to others—as superficial, masks to be donned and doffed at will. Comprehensive training and awareness are needed, until everyone is working to make the workplace a world where differing styles are understood and appreciated.

REFLECTING ON MEANING

1. In linguistic theory, what is meant by the term *marked?* How does Tannen use a clothing metaphor to illustrate how all women are marked? Why aren't men similarly marked by their clothing?

2. What kinds of professional roles are women expected to fill? In what sense is every woman "seen as a receptionist"? What kinds of jobs have women traditionally occupied?

3. Why are women more likely to change their style of communicating and interacting within a mixed group? Tannen says, "I would not advise women to adopt men's styles to succeed." What are her reasons for this assertion? How will companies benefit from having employees with different styles? Men have traditionally dominated the workplace. If women don't become more assertive, aggressive, and competitive in their business relations, won't they suffer for it?

4. Tannen argues that "if you try to adopt a style that does not come naturally to you, you leave behind your intuitions and may well behave in ways inappropriate in any style or betray the discomfort you actually feel." Is she suggesting that women and men possess "natural" styles related to their specific sex rather than qualities learned as a result of social conditioning? Why or why not? Are there any problems with Tannen's statement?

EXPLORING RHETORICAL STRATEGIES

1. Why does Tannen begin her essay with a lengthy description of the clothing, makeup, and hair styles of the three business-women? How effectively does it illustrate her discussion of "marked"? She argues that a businessman could dress any way he pleases and he would not be considered marked. Do you agree or disagree? Why or why not?

2. Tannen uses numerous stories throughout her essay to illustrate certain points. Explain the rhetorical purpose of the following stories: the Georgetown University student assuming that Tannen was a secretary; the woman making plane reservations; the female bodybuilder; relationships between nurses and doctors; male and female publishing agents; and the female executive asked to speak for all women in an all-male training seminar.

3. What is Tannen's intended audience? How might an audience of business people react differently from an audience of radical feminists? What is your overall response to this essay?

TAKING A STAND
QUESTIONS FOR CONSIDERATION

1. In this part, several essays suggest that social institutions—namely, the educational system, the home, the family, and marriage—reinforce gender-based social stereotypes and women's oppression. Pick one of these institutions, summarize the observations of the appropriate authors, and draw your own conclusions. To what extent does the institution reinforce these roles? In what ways? To what extent does it, perhaps, simply reflect rather than shape them? What exactly is the nature of the cause-effect relationship at work in this case? In what ways, if any, does the institution create similar problems for men? In shaping your response, also consider the essays by Gilman and Wollstonecraft in Part II.

2. Is the educational system in the United States sexist? Horner, Rich, and Thomas all suggest that it is. Write an essay in which you summarize the views of these authors, and either refute or confirm their viewpoints. In exploring this issue, draw on your own observations and experiences as a student, and survey both male and female students to determine if women and men do, in fact, have different experiences in educational institutions. What patterns, if any, emerge from your data? You might want to refer to Millett's essay in Part II.

3. Rich identifies a problem in the educational system and outlines changes that would make it more responsive to women's needs. To what extent does she accurately pinpoint the problem? To what extent does her solution resolve the problem? Begin with a summary of Rich's viewpoint, identify what you see as the central problem in women's education, and design an educational system that would resolve it. In outlining the problem that you identify, consider Horner's conclusions about women and competition.

4. To pursue a career or to have a family—this is a choice that many women face. While Syfers explores the forced limitations placed on wives, Greenberg claims that he, too, struggles with the professional consequences of his decision to remain home to care for his family. As he puts it, "I can't have it both ways." What are the differences, if any, in Greenberg's and Syfers's situations? To what extent is the career vs. family dilemma limited to women? To what extent is it a choice that men must make as well? In shaping your response, consider the ways in which this dilemma has affected or might affect your own life plans. You might also consider Mainardi's discussion of housework.

5. Syfers, Mainardi, and Greenberg present contradictory views of housework. According to Syfers and Mainardi, it symbolizes women's servitude. Greenberg, however, doesn't have any problem with housework; in fact, he claims that "housework still doesn't seem like work." What accounts for the differing perspectives of these authors? Why do Syfers and Mainardi find housework empty and degrading, whereas Greenberg actually seems to enjoy it? Summarize the attitudes of these authors, and take a stand on this issue. What different solutions do these authors offer to the problem of housework?

6. In Chapter 11, the authors consider two environments in which women are employed: in the home and in the business arena. How are women regarded in each working situation? Is one job privileged over another? If so, what ideological factors influence this privileging? Has the position of women improved or deteriorated over time? What might the future of these working environments be?

7. Marriage and parenthood are two of our society's most revered institutions. Syfers and Mainardi discuss the difficult work that wives are expected to do, while Greenberg talks about his experiences as a "house father." What are the images of marriage and parenthood promoted in our society? To what extent are they illusion or reality? What is the social significance of motherhood and fatherhood? How do our concepts of these institutions shape our lives? In exploring these issues, you may also wish to consider White's perspectives on marriage in Part I.

8. Deborah Tannen uses the terms *marked* and *unmarked* to explain how women become recognized as different from men. Define both of these terms. Then, describe how being "marked" can alter the experiences of females in educational settings, home environments, and the business world. Review all the essays in this section to assist you with this discussion. You may also wish to consider de Beauvoir's essay in Part I.

Part V ⎯⎯⎯⎯⎯⎯

Sexism and the Status of Women

Besides the emotional or psychological by-products of sexism—such as feelings of inferiority, helplessness, and lowered self-esteem—discrimination produces serious, concrete consequences for many women. Simply because of their sex, women are often the victims of both culturally sanctioned and illegal forms of physical abuse. Part V looks at how sexual discrimination affects women in various global and cultural settings and produces debilitating social powerlessness.

The first group of essays, "Cultural Violence," focuses on how cultural sexism causes both mental and physical damage to women. Philip Goldberg begins by arguing that many women see their own sex as inferior and thus discriminate against other women. According to Brigid Brophy, women are still oppressed by a male-dominated society, even though their oppression is no longer as obvious as it once was. Claiming that powerlessness "corrupts women's hearts," Ellen Goodman discusses the health of women in clerical positions. Finally, Diane Johnson explores the ultimate form of discrimination and powerlessness: rape.

In "Global Perspectives," the second group of essays, the authors consider various cultural forms of discrimination against women and the subsequent powerlessness and physical violence that may result. Cherry and Charles Lindholm describe the custom of *purdah*—the institution of female seclusion—as it is practiced by Moslems in the Middle East. Mary Daly graphically reveals the horrors of female genital mutilation as it has been and continues to be practiced in many parts of the world. Reporting on the lucrative mail-order bride business, John Krich considers the implications of arranged marriages between men in the United States and women from Asia.

Although many of the authors represented in Part V acknowledge that some advances have been made in curbing cultural and global discrimination against women, some believe that this progress is more apparent than real. Certainly the cumulative picture of powerlessness and violence against women portrayed in these essays is a sobering indication of how much remains to be done before men and women can enjoy equal status.

Chapter 12

CULTURAL VIOLENCE

Are Women Prejudiced Against Women?

PHILIP GOLDBERG

Most people would agree that men perceive and evaluate women and men differently—such is the basis for claims of discrimination and sexism. Professor of psychology Philip Goldberg argues, however, that women do the same—that "women do consider their own sex inferior." In the following essay, Goldberg describes and reports on an experiment that led him to this conclusion, a study in which women evaluated identical articles attributed to hypothetical male and female authors.

W oman," advised Aristotle, "may be said to be an inferior man."

Because he was a man, Aristotle was probably biased. But what do women themselves think? Do they, consciously or unconsciously, consider their own sex inferior? And if so, does this belief prejudice them against other women—that is, make them view women, simply because they *are* women, as less competent than men?

According to a study conducted by myself and my associates, the answer to both questions is Yes. Women *do* consider their own sex inferior. And even when the facts give no support to this belief, they will persist in downgrading the competence—in particular, the intellectual and professional competence—of their fellow females.

Over the years, psychologists and psychiatrists have shown that both sexes consistently value men more highly than women. Characteristics considered male are usually praised: those considered female are usually criticized. In 1957 A. C. Sheriffs and J. P. McKee noted that "women are regarded as guilty of snobbery and irrational and unpleasant emotionality." Consistent with this report, E. G. French and G. S. Lesser found in 1964 that "women who value intellectual attainment feel they must reject the woman's role"—intellectual accomplishment apparently being considered, even among intellectual women, a masculine preserve. In addition, ardent feminists like Simone de Beauvoir and Betty Friedan believe that men, in important ways, are superior to women.

Now, is this belief simply prejudice, or are the characteristics and achievements of women really inferior to those of men? In answering this question, we need to draw some careful distinctions.

Different or Inferior?

Most important, we need to recognize that there are two distinct dimensions to the issue of sex differences. The first question is whether sex differences exist at all, apart from the obvious physical ones. The answer to this question seems to be a unanimous Yes—men, women, and social scientists agree that, psychologically and emotionally as well as physically, women *are* different from men.

But is being different the same as being inferior? It is quite possible to perceive a difference accurately but to value it inaccurately. Do women automatically view their differences from men as *deficiencies*? The evidence is that they do, and that this value judgment opens the door to anti-female prejudice. For if someone (male or female) concludes that women are inferior, his perceptions of women—their personalities, behavior, abilities, and accomplishments—will tend to be colored by his low expectations of women.

As Gordon W. Allport has pointed out in *The Nature of Prejudice,* whatever the facts about sex differences, anti-feminism—like any other prejudice—*distorts perception and experience*. What defines anti-feminism is not so much believing that women are inferior, as allowing that belief to distort one's perceptions of women. More generally, it is not the partiality itself, but the distortion born of that partiality, that defines prejudice.

Thus, an anti-Semite watching a Jew may see devious or sneaky behavior. But, in a Christian, he would regard such behavior only as quiet, reserved, or perhaps even shy. Prejudice is self-sustaining: It continually distorts the "evidence" on which the prejudiced person claims to base his beliefs. Allport makes it clear that anti-feminism, like anti-Semitism or any other prejudice, consistently twists the "evidence" of experience. We see not what is there, but what we *expect* to see.

The purpose of our study was to investigate whether there is real prejudice by women against women—whether perception itself is distorted unfavorably. Specifically, will women evaluate a professional article with a jaundiced eye when they think it is the work of a woman, but praise the same article when they think its author is a man? Our hypotheses were:

- Even when the work is identical, women value the professional work of men more highly than that of women.
- But when the professional field happens to be one traditionally reserved for women (nursing, dietetics), this tendency will be reversed, or at least greatly diminished.

Some 140 college girls, selected at random, were our subjects. One hundred were used for preliminary work; 40 participated in the experiment proper.

To test the second hypothesis, we gave the 100 girls a list of 50 occupations and asked them to rate "the degree to which you associate the field with men or with women." We found that law and city planning were fields strongly associated with men, elementary-school teaching and dietetics were fields strongly associated with women, and two fields—linguistics and art history—were chosen as neutrals, not strongly associated with either sex.

Now we were ready for the main experiment. From the professional literature of each of these six fields, we took one article. The articles were edited and abridged to about 1500 words, then combined into two equal sets of booklets. The crucial manipulation had to do with the authors' names—the same article bore a male name in one set of booklets, a female name in the other set. An example: If, in set one, the first article bore the name John T. McKay, in set two the same article would appear under the name Joan T. McKay. Each booklet contained three articles by "men" and three articles by "women."

The girls, seated together in a large lecture hall, were told to read the articles in their booklets and given these instructions:

> "In this booklet you will find excerpts of six articles, written by six different authors in six different professional fields. At the end of each article you will find several questions.... You are

>not presumed to be sophisticated or knowledgeable in all the
>fields. We are interested in the ability of college students to
>make critical evaluations. . . ."

Note that no mention at all was made of the author's sexes. That information was contained—apparently only by coincidence—in the authors' names. The girls could not know, therefore, what we were really looking for.

At the end of each article were nine questions asking the girls to rate the articles for value, persuasiveness, and profundity—and to rate the authors for writing style, professional competence, professional status, and ability to sway the reader. On each item, the girls gave a rating of from 1 (highly favorable) to 5 (highly unfavorable).

Generally, the results were in line with our expectations—but not completely. In analyzing these results, we used three different methods: We compared the amount of anti-female bias in the different occupational fields (would men be rated as better city planners, but women as better dieticians?); we compared the amount of bias shown on the nine questions that followed each article (would men be rated more competent, but women as more persuasive?); and we ran an overall comparison, including both fields and rating questions.

Starting with the analysis of bias by occupational field, we immediately ran into a major surprise. (See the table below.) That there is a general bias by women against women, and that it is strongest in traditionally masculine fields, was clearly borne out. But in other fields the situation seemed rather confused. We had expected the anti-female trend to be reversed in traditionally feminine fields. But it appears that, even here, women consider themselves inferior to men. Women seem to think that men are better at *everything*—including elementary-school teaching and dietetics!

Scrutiny of the nine rating questions yielded similar results. On all nine questions, regardless of the author's occupational field, the girls consistently found an article more valuable—and its author more competent—when the article bore a male name. Though the articles themselves were exactly the same, the girls felt that those written by the John T. McKays were definitely more impressive, and reflected more glory on their authors, than did the mediocre offerings of the Joan T. McKays. Perhaps because the world has accepted female authors for a long time, the girls were willing to concede that the female professionals' writing styles were not *far* inferior to those of men. But such a concession to female competence was rare indeed.

Statistical analysis confirms these impressions and makes them more definite. With a total of six articles, and with nine questions after each one, there were 54 points at which comparisons could be drawn between the male authors and the female authors. Out of these 54 comparisons, three were tied, seven favored the female authors—and the number favoring the male authors was 44!

Law: A Strong Masculine Preserve

	Mean	
Field of Article	*Male*	*Female*
Art History	23.35	23.10
Dietetics	22.05	23.45
Education	20.20	21.75
City Planning	23.10	27.30
Linguistics	26.95	30.70
Law	21.20	25.60

These are the total scores the college girls gave to the six pairs of articles they read. The lowest possible score—9—would be the most favorable: the highest possible score—54—the most critical. While male authors received more favorable ratings on all occupational fields, the differences were statistically significant only in city planning, linguistics, and—especially—law.

Clearly, there is a tendency among women to downgrade the work of professionals of their own sex. But the hypothesis that this tendency would decrease as the "femaleness" of the professional field increased was not supported. Even in traditionally female fields, anti-feminism holds sway.

Since the articles supposedly written by men were exactly the same as those supposedly written by women, the perception that the men's articles were superior was obviously a distortion. For reasons of their own, the female subjects were sensitive to the sex of the author, and this apparently irrelevant information biased their judgments. Both the distortion and the sensitivity that precedes it are characteristic of prejudice. Women—at least these young college women—are prejudiced against female professionals and, regardless of the actual accomplishments of these professionals, will firmly refuse to recognize them as the equals of their male colleagues.

Is the intellectual double-standard really dead? Not at all—and if the college girls in this study are typical of the educated and presumably progressive segments of the population, it may not even be dying. Whatever lip service these girls pay to modern ideas of equality between men and women, their beliefs are staunchly traditional. Their real coach in the battle of the sexes is not Simone de Beauvoir or Betty Friedan. Their coach is Aristotle.

REFLECTING ON MEANING

1. According to Goldberg, what is prejudice? How does it influence perception? What does he mean when he says that it "consistently twists the 'evidence' of experience"?

2. Goldberg makes a distinction between believing that women and men are different and believing that their differences necessarily make one gender inferior to the other. What does he mean? How do people come to believe that differences are deficiencies?

3. What were the goals of the study Goldberg conducted? What questions was he trying to answer? How was the study carried out? What were the results? What was the "major surprise" that Goldberg discovered in the data? Do you agree with his overall conclusions? Why or why not?

EXPLORING RHETORICAL STRATEGIES

1. In his introduction and conclusion, Goldberg makes allusions to Aristotle, Simone de Beauvoir, and Betty Friedan. What do these allusions tell you about his intended audience? How do they help him advance his thesis?

2. Goldberg occasionally takes a tone of astonishment and surprise. How does he convey these emotions? How do they affect his tone in other sections of the essay? Given his conclusions, in what ways is this tone appropriate or inappropriate?

3. The format of Goldberg's essay conforms largely to the conventions of reports in the social sciences. On the basis of this essay, can you determine what those conventions are?

Women: Invisible Cages

BRIGID BROPHY

Despite a seeming consensus that women are no longer bound by gender-based social hierarchies, argues activist and author Brigid Brophy, they are not really free; rather, they simply "look free." They are "like the animals in a modern zoo," imprisoned behind bars even more pernicious because they are invisible.

All right, nobody's disputing it. Women are free. At least, they *look* free. They even feel free. But in reality women in the western, industrialised world today are like the animals in a modern zoo. There are no bars. It appears that cages have been abolished. Yet in practice women are still kept in their place just as firmly as the animals are kept in their enclosures. The barriers which keep them in now are invisible.

It is about forty years since the pioneer feminists, several of whom were men, raised such a rumpus by rattling the cage bars— or created such a conspicuous nuisance by chaining themselves to them—that society was at last obliged to pay attention. The result was that the bars were uprooted, the cage thrown open: whereupon the majority of the women who had been held captive decided they would rather stay inside anyway.

To be more precise, they *thought* they decided; and society, which can with perfect truth point out "Look, no bars," *thought* it was giving them the choice. There are no laws and very little discrimination to prevent western, industrialised women from voting, being voted for or entering the professions. If there are still comparatively few women lawyers and engineers, let alone women presidents of the United States, what are women to conclude except that this is the result either of their own free choice or of something inherent in female nature?

Many of them do draw just this conclusion. They have come back to the old argument of the anti-feminists, many of whom were women, that women are unfit by nature for life outside the cage. And in letting this old wheel come full cycle women have fallen victim to one of the most insidious and ingenious confidence tricks ever perpetrated.

In point of fact, neither female nature nor women's individual free choice has been put to the test. As American Negroes have discovered, to be officially free is by no means the same as being actually and psychologically free. A society as adept as ours has become at propaganda—whether political or commercial—should know that "persuasion," which means the art of launching myths and artificially inducing inhibitions, is every bit as effective as force of law. No doubt the reason society eventually agreed to abolish its anti-woman laws was that it had become confident of commanding a battery of hidden dissuaders which would do the job just as well. Cage bars are clumsy methods of control, which excite the more rebellious personalities inside to rattle them. Modern society, like the modern zoo, has contrived to get rid of the bars without altering the fact of imprisonment. All the zoo architect needs to do is run a zone of hot or cold air, whichever the animal concerned cannot tolerate, round the cage where the bars used to be. Human animals are not less sensitive to social climate.

The ingenious point about the new-model zoo is that it deceives both sides of the invisible barrier. Not only can the animal not see how it is imprisoned; the visitor's conscience is relieved of the unkindness of keeping animals shut up. He can say "Look, no bars round the animals," just as society can say "Look, no laws restricting women" even while it keeps women rigidly in place by zones of fierce social pressure.

There is, however, one great difference. A woman, being a thinking animal, may actually be more distressed because the bars of her cage cannot be seen. What relieves society's conscience may afflict hers. Unable to perceive what is holding her back, she may accuse herself and her whole sex of craven timidity because women have not jumped at what has the appearance of an offer of freedom. Evidently quite a lot of women have succumbed to guilt of this sort, since in recent years quite an industry has arisen to assuage it. Comforting voices make the air as thick and reassuring as cotton wool while they explain that there is nothing shameful in not wanting a career, that to be intellectually unadventurous is no sin, that taking care of home and family may be personally "fulfilling" and socially valuable.

This is an argument without a flaw: except that it is addressed exclusively to women. Address it to both sexes and instantly it becomes progressive and humane. As it stands, it is merely anti-woman prejudice revamped.

That many women would be happier not pursuing careers or intellectual adventures is only part of the truth. The whole truth is that many *people* would be. If society had the clear sight to assure men as well as women that there is no shame in preferring to stay non-competitively and non-aggressively at home, many masculine neuroses and ulcers would be avoided, and many children would enjoy the benefit of being brought up by a father with a talent for the job instead of by a mother with no talent for it but a sense of guilt about the lack.

But society does nothing so sensible. Blindly it goes on insisting on the tradition that men are the ones who go out to work and adventure—an arrangement which simply throws talent away. All the home-making talent which happens to be born inside male bodies is wasted; and our businesses and governments are staffed quite largely by people whose aptitude for the work consists solely of their being what is, by tradition, the right sex for it.

The pressures society exerts to drive men out of the house are very nearly as irrational and unjust as those by which it keeps women in. The mistake of the early reformers was to assume that men were emancipated already and that therefore reform need ask only for the emancipation of women. What we ought to do now is go right back to scratch and demand the emancipation of both sexes. It is only because men are not free themselves that they have found it necessary to cheat women by the deception which makes them appear free when they are not.

The zones of hot and cold air which society uses to perpetuate its uneconomic and unreasonable state of affairs are the simplest and most effective conceivable. Society is playing on our sexual vanity. Just as the sexual regions are the most vulnerable part of the body, sexuality is the most vulnerable part of the Ego. Tell a man that he is not a real man, or a woman that she is not one hundred percent woman and you are threatening both with not being attractive to the opposite sex. No one can bear not to be attractive to the opposite sex. That is the climate which the human animal cannot tolerate.

So society has us all at its mercy. It has only to murmur to the man that staying at home is a feminine characteristic, and he will be out of the house like a bullet. It has only to suggest to the woman that logic and reason are the province of the masculine mind, whereas "intuition" and "feeling" are the female *forte,* and she will throw her physics textbooks out of the window, barricade herself into the house and give herself up to having wishy-washy poetical feelings while she arranges the flowers.

She will, incidentally, take care that her feelings *are* wishy-washy. She has been persuaded that to have cogent feelings, of the kind which really go into great poems (most of which are by men), would make her an unfeminine woman, a woman who imitates men. In point of fact, she would not be imitating men as such, most

of whom have never written a line of great poetry, but poets, most
of whom so far happen to be men. But the bad logic passes muster
with her because part of the mythology she has swallowed inge-
niously informs her that logic is not her *forte*.

Should a woman's talent or intelligence be so irrepressible
that she insists on producing cogent works of art or watertight
meshes of argument, she will be said to have "a mind like a man's."
This is simply current idiom; translated, it means "a good mind."
The use of the idiom contributes to an apparently watertight proof
that all good minds are masculine, since whenever they occur in
women they are described as "like a man's."

What is more, this habit of thought actually contributes to
perpetuating a state of affairs where most good minds really do belong to men. It is difficult for a woman to *want* to be intelligent
when she has been told that to be so will make her like a man. She
inclines to think an intelligence would be as unbecoming to her as
a moustache; and many women have tried in furtive privacy to disembarrass themselves of intellect as though it were facial hair.

Discouraged from growing "a mind like a man's," women are
encouraged to have thoughts and feelings of a specifically feminine
tone. For society is cunning enough not to place its whole reliance on
threatening women with blasts of icy air. It also flatters them with a
zone of hot air. The most deceptive and cynical of its blandishments
is the notion that women have some specifically feminine contribution to make to culture. Unfortunately, as culture had already been
shaped and largely built up by men before the invitation was issued,
this leaves women little to do. Culture consists of reasoned thought
and works of art composed of cogent feeling and imagination. There
is only one way to be reasonable, and that is to reason correctly; and
the only kind of art which is any good is good art. If women are to es-
chew reason and artistic imagination in favour of "intuition" and
"feeling," it is pretty clear what is meant. "Intuition" is just a polite
name for bad reasoning, and "feeling" for bad art.

In reality, the whole idea of a specifically feminine—or, for the
matter of that, masculine—contribution to culture is a contradiction
of culture. A contribution to culture is not something which could
not have been made by the other sex—it is something which could
not have been made by any other *person*. Equally, the notion that
anyone, of either sex, can create good art out of simple feeling, un-
tempered by discipline, is a philistine one. The arts are a sphere
where women seem to have done well; but really they have done
too well—too well for the good of the arts. Instead of women sharing
the esteem which ought to belong to artists, art is becoming
smeared with femininity. We are approaching a philistine state of

affairs where the arts are something which it is nice for women to take up in their spare time—men having slammed out of the house to get on with society's "serious" business, like making money, administering the country and running the professions.

In that "serious" sphere it is still rare to encounter a woman. A man sentenced to prison would probably feel his punishment was redoubled by indignity if he were to be sentenced by a woman judge under a law drafted by a woman legislator—and if, on admission, he were to be examined by a woman prison doctor. If such a thing happened every day, it would be no indignity but the natural course of events. It has never been given the chance to become the natural course of events and never will be so long as women remain persuaded it would be unnatural of them to want it.

So brilliantly has society contrived to terrorise women with this threat that certain behavior is unnatural and unwomanly that it has left them no time to consider—or even sheerly observe—what womanly nature really is. For centuries arrant superstitions were accepted as natural law. The physiological fact that only women can secrete milk for feeding babies was extended into the pure myth that it was women's business to cook for and wait on the entire family. The kitchen became woman's "natural" place because, for the first few months of her baby's life, the nursery really was. To this day a woman may suspect that she is unfeminine if she can discover in herself no aptitude or liking for cooking. Fright has thrown her into such a muddle that she confuses having no taste for cookery with having no breasts, and conversely assumes that nature has endowed the human female with a special handiness with frying pans.

Even psycho-analysis, which in general has been the greatest benefactor of civilisation since the wheel, has unwittingly reinforced the terrorisation campaign. The trouble was that it brought with it from its origin in medical therapy a criterion of normality instead of rationality. On sheer statistics every pioneer, genius and social reformer, including the first woman who demanded to be let out of the kitchen and into the polling booth, is abnormal, along with every lunatic and eccentric. What distinguishes the genius from the lunatic is that the genius's abnormality is justifiable by reason or aesthetics. If a woman who is irked by confinement to the kitchen merely looks round to see what other women are doing and finds they are accepting their kitchens, she may well conclude that she is abnormal and had better enlist her psycho-analyst's help towards "living with" her kitchen. What she ought to ask is whether it is rational for women to be kept to the kitchen, and whether nature really does insist on that in the way it insists women have breasts. And in a far-reaching sense to ask that question is much more normal and natural than learning to "live with" the handicap of women's inferior social status. The normal and natural thing for human beings is not to tolerate handicaps but to reform society and to circumvent or supplement nature. We don't learn to live minus a leg: we devise an artificial limb.

That, indeed, is the crux of the matter. Not only are the distinctions we draw between male nature and female nature largely arbitrary and often pure superstition: they are completely beside the point. They ignore the essence of *human* nature. The important question is not whether women are or are not less logical by nature than men, but whether education, effort and the abolition of our illogical social pressures can improve on nature and make them (and, incidentally, men as well) *more* logical. What distinguishes human from any other animal nature is its ability to be unnatural. Logic and art are not natural or instinctive activities: but our nature includes a propensity to acquire them. It is not natural for the human body to orbit the earth; but the human mind has a natural adventurousness which enables it to invent machines whereby the body can do so. There is, in sober fact, no such creature as a natural man. Go as far back as they will, the archaeologists cannot come on a wild man in his natural habitat. At his most primitive, he has already constructed himself an artificial habitat, and decorated it not by a standardised instinctual method, as birds build nests, but by individualised—that is, abnormal—works of art or magic. And in doing so he is not limited by the fingers nature gave him; he has extended their versatility by making tools.

Civilisation consists not necessarily in defying nature but in making it possible for us to do so if we judge it desirable. The higher we can lift our noses from the grindstone of nature, the wider the area we have of choice; and the more choices we have freely made, the more individualised we are. We are at our most civilised when nature does not dictate to us, as it does to animals and peasants, but when we can opt to fall in with it or better it. If modern civilisation has invented methods of education which make it possible for men to feed babies and for women to think logically, we are betraying civilisation itself if we do not set both sexes free to make a free choice.

REFLECTING ON MEANING

1. The author's contention that women are not free hinges on a crucial distinction: "to be officially free," Brophy states, "is by no

means the same as being actually and psychologically free." What does she mean? Do you agree that women are free only in an "official" sense? Why or why not?

2. According to Brophy, what is the effect of this hidden imprisonment on women? In what ways does it alter their conceptions of themselves? What kind of emotional toll does it take on them? How does society reinforce the gender roles that create this situation? In what ways are men, too, subject to gender-role pressures that "are very nearly as irrational and unjust"? Why does Brophy qualify this comparison?

3. Brophy claims that society holds women powerless by encouraging them to be "feminine" and by propagating "the notion that women have some specifically feminine contribution to make to culture." In what ways are women urged to be feminine? How does society advance the notion that women's contributions are different from men's?

4. "Not only are the distinctions we draw between male nature and female nature largely arbitrary and often pure superstition: they are completely beside the point. They ignore the essence of *human* nature." What does Brophy mean by this assertion? Do you agree or disagree? Why?

EXPLORING RHETORICAL STRATEGIES

1. The analogy of the caged animal is a powerful device at work throughout the essay. How does Brophy expand on this analogy in the course of the selection? Is it an appropriate analogy? Why or why not?

2. Brophy opens her essay in this way: "All right, nobody's disputing it. Women are free. At least, they *look* free. They even feel free." What does this opening suggest about the attitude she expects her audience to have on women's freedom? How does she seem to think her audience will react to her views?

3. "She inclines to think an intelligence would be as unbecoming to her as a moustache; and many women have tried in furtive privacy to disembarrass themselves of intellect as though it were facial hair." What is particularly appropriate about this analogy? What concrete image does it create? How does the word *furtive* add to the image?

Being a Secretary Can Be Hazardous to Your Health

ELLEN GOODMAN

The columnist Ellen Goodman looks at the effect of pow-
erlessness on the health of women in clerical positions. "It is
powerlessness and not power that corrupts women's hearts,"
she asserts. "And clerical workers are the number one victims."

They used to say it with flowers or celebrate it with a somewhat liquid lunch. National Secretaries Week was always
good for at least a token of appreciation. But the way the
figures add up now, the best thing a boss can do for a secretary this
week is cough up for her cardiogram.

"Stress and the Secretary" has become the hottest new syndrome on the heart circuit.

It seems that it isn't those Daring Young Women in their
Dress-for-Success Suits who are following men down the cardiovascular trail to ruin. Nor is it the female professionals who are
winning their equal place in intensive care units.

It is powerlessness and not power that corrupts women's
hearts. And clerical workers are the number one victims.

In the prestigious Framingham study, Dr. Suzanne Haynes,
an epidemiologist with the National Heart, Lung, and Blood Institute, found that working women as a whole have no higher rate of
heart disease than housewives. But women employed in clerical
and sales occupations do. Their coronary disease rates are twice
that of other women.

"This is not something to ignore," says Dr. Haynes, "since
such a high percent of women work at clerical jobs." In fact, 35
percent of all working women, or 18 million of us, hold these
jobs.

When Dr. Haynes looked into their private lives, she found
the women at greatest risk—with a one in five chance of heart
disease—were clerical workers with blue-collar husbands, and three
or more children. When she then looked at their work lives, she
discovered that the ones who actually developed heart disease

were those with nonsupportive bosses who hadn't changed jobs very often and who had trouble letting their anger out.

In short, being frustrated, dead-ended, without a feeling of control over your life is bad for your health.

The irony in all the various and sundry heart statistics is that we now have a weird portrait of the Cardiovascular Fun Couple of the Office: The Type A Boss and his secretary. The male heart disease stereotype is, after all, the Type A aggressive man who always needs to be in control, who lives with a great sense of time urgency . . . and is likely to be a white-collar boss.

"The Type A man is trying to be in control. But given the way most businesses are organized there are, in fact, few ways for them to be in control of their jobs," says Dr. Haynes. The only thing the Type A boss can be in control of is his secretary who in turn feels . . . well, you get the picture. He's not only getting heart disease, he's giving it.

As if all this weren't enough to send you out for the annual three martini lunch, clerical workers are increasingly working for a new Type A boss: the computer.

These days fewer women are sitting in front of bosses with notepads and more are sitting in front of Visual Display Terminals. Word processors, data processors, microprocessors . . . these are the demanding, time-conscious new automatons of automation.

There is nothing intrinsically evil about computers. I am writing this on a VDT and if you try to take it away from me, I will break your arm. But as Working Women, the national association of office workers, puts it in their release this week, automation is increasingly producing clerical jobs that are de-skilled, downgraded, dead-ended and dissatisfying.

As Karen Nussbaum of the Cleveland office described it, the office of the future may well be the factory of the past. Work on computers is often reduced to simple, repetitive, monotonous tasks. Workers are often expected to produce more for no more pay, and there are also reports of a disturbing trend to processing speed-ups and piece-rate pay, and a feeling among clerical workers that their jobs are computer controlled.

"It's not the machine, but the way it's used by employers," says Working Women's research director, Judith Gregory. Too often, automation's most important product is stress.

Groups, like Working Women, are trying to get clerical workers to organize in what they call "a race against time" so that computers will become their tools instead of their supervisors.

But in the meantime, if you are 1) a female clerical worker, 2) with a blue-collar husband, 3) with three or more children, 4) in a dead-end job, 5) without any way to express anger, 6) with a Type A boss, 7) or a Type A computer controlling your work day... *You better start jogging.*

REFLECTING ON MEANING

1. In what ways are clerical workers, including secretaries, power-less? Why aren't women in management equally powerless? What surprising health statistics about these different groups of women does Goodman provide?

2. What does a clerical worker's boss have to do with the level of stress she experiences? How does her home situation also con-tribute?

3. According to Goodman, how are computers contributing to the dilemma of clerical workers? How do computers reinforce rather than alleviate the lack of control that clerical workers have?

EXPLORING RHETORICAL STRATEGIES

1. What tone does Goodman adopt in this selection? What devices does she use to achieve it? How does such diction as "cough up for her cardiogram" reinforce her tone?

2. What is the effect of Goodman's concluding paragraph? What is she parodying with her inventory of "symptoms"? How does her conclusion extend the parody of her title?

3. What is the occasion for which Goodman composed this essay? What kind of essay might you normally expect to find in com-memoration of such an occasion? How has Goodman seized the occasion for more thought-provoking purposes?

Rape

DIANE JOHNSON

"No other subject," asserts author Diane Johnson, "is re-
garded so differently by men and women as rape." Examining
several recent book-length studies of rape, Johnson explores social
myths about rape and society's complicity in perpetuating it.

No other subject, it seems, is regarded so differently by men
and women as rape. Women deeply dread and resent it to
an extent that men apparently cannot recognize; it is perhaps the ultimate and essential complaint that women have to make
against men. Of course men may recognize that it is wrong to use
physical force against another person, and that rape laws are not
prosecuted fairly, and so on, but at a certain point they are apt to
say, "But what was she doing there at that hour anyway?" or "Luck-
ily he didn't really hurt her," and serious discussion ceases.

Women sense—indeed, are carefully taught to feel—that the institution of rape is mysteriously protected by an armor of folklore,
Bible tales, legal precedents, specious psychological theories. Most
of all it seems protected by a rooted and implacable male belief that
women want to be raped—which most women, conscientiously examining their motives, maintain they do not—or deserve to be
raped, for violation of certain customs governing dress or behavior,
a strange proposition to which women are more likely to accede.

While women can all imagine themselves as rape victims,
most men know they are not rapists. So incidents that would be resented on personal grounds if happening to their "own" women do
not have even the intrinsic interest for them of arguments on principle against military intervention in the political destiny of foreign
nations, as in Vietnam, where the "rape" of that country was referred to in the peace movement and meant defoliation of crops.
But unlike the interest in the political destiny of Vietnam, which
greatly diminished when the danger to American males, via the
draft, was eliminated, rape is an abiding concern to women.

Even if they don't think about it very much, most have incorporated into their lives routine precautions along lines prescribed
by the general culture. From a woman's earliest days she is attended

by injunctions about strangers, and warnings about dark streets, locks, escorts, and provocative behavior. She internalizes the lessons contained therein, that to break certain rules is to invite or deserve rape. Her fears, if not entirely conscious, are at least readily accessible, and are continually activated by a vast body of exemplary literature, both traditional and in the daily paper. To test this, ask yourself, if you are a woman, or ask any woman what she knows about Richard Speck, the Boston Strangler, and "that thing that happened over on ——— Street last week," and you will find that she has considerable rape literature by heart.

It seems important, in attempting to assess the value or seriousness of Susan Brownmiller's polemic on rape (*Against Our Will*), to understand that there are really two audiences for it, one that will know much of what she has to say already, and another that is ill equipped by training or sympathy to understand it at all. This likely accounts for a certain unevenness of tone, veering from indignation to the composed deployment of statistics in the manner of a public debater. It is not surprising that women began in the past few years by addressing their complaints about rape to one another, not to men, and one infers that the subject is still thought to be of concern only to women. It remains to be seen what if any rhetorical strategies will prove to be of value in enlisting the concern of men.

That rape is aggressive, hostile, and intended to exact female submission, and that it is the extreme expression of underlying shared masculine attitudes, is, I think, most women's intuition of the subject, even women who have not been raped but who have tacitly accepted that this is how men are. Women who have in fact been raped (more than 255,000 each year) are certain of it after the indifference, disbelief, and brutality of police, doctors, judges, jurors, and their own families. That the actual rapists, making examples of a few women, in effect frighten and control all women seems obvious, even inarguable.

What is left to be explained, though neither Brownmiller nor Jean MacKeltar, in another recent book on rape (*Rape: The Bait and the Trap*), can satisfactorily explain it, is what this primal drama of domination and punishment is about, exactly. Both books communicate an impression of an escalating conflict, with the increasing collective force of female anger and indignation about rape not only effecting some changes in judiciary and police procedures and even, perhaps, in popular attitudes, but also effecting an increase in anxiety about the subject, exemplified by the obligatory rape scenes in current movies and best sellers. Perhaps it is even female anger that is effecting an increase in rape itself, as if, whatever is at stake in this ancient hostility, it is now the rapist who has his back to the wall.

It is not too extreme to say that Brownmiller's book is exceedingly distressing, partly because it is exceedingly discouraging; it is a history of the failure of legal schemes and social sciences to improve society, at least society as viewed from a female perspective; it is the history of the failure of the social sciences even to address themselves to the peculiar mystery of male aggression toward those weaker than themselves. This failure seems in turn to demonstrate the powerlessness of human institutions before the force of patently untrue and sinister myths, whose ability to reflect, but also to determine, human behavior seems invincible. The disobedient Eve, the compliant Leda, the lying wife of Potiphar are still the keys to popular assumptions about women.

But Brownmiller's book is also distressing in another way that wicked myths and scary stories are distressing, that is, because they are meant to be. Here in one handy volume is every admonitory rape story you were ever told, horrifying in the way that propaganda is horrifying and also titillating just in the way that publishers hope a book will be titillating. Brownmiller is trapped in the fallacy of imitative form, and by the duplicitous powers of literature itself to contain within it its own contradictions, so that the exemplary anecdotes from Red Riding Hood to Kitty Genovese to the Tralala scene in *Last Exit to Brooklyn* must appeal at some level to the instincts they illustrate and deprecate. The book may be criticized for an emotional tone that is apparently impossible to exclude from an effective work on a subject so inaccessible to rational analysis. Because rape is an important topic of a potentially sensational and prurient nature, it is too bad that the book is not a model of surpassing tact and delicacy, unassailable learning and scientific methodology. Instead it is probably the book that was needed on this subject at this time, and may in fact succeed where reticence has failed to legitimate the fundamental grievance of women against men.

Much of the book is devoted to an attempt to locate in history the reasons for rape, but inquiry here is fruitless because though history turns up evidence, it offers little explanation. One learns merely that rape has been with us from earliest times, that it is associated variously with military policy, with ideas of property and possession (to rape someone's wife was interpreted as the theft of something from him), with interracial struggles and complicated tribal and class polarities of all kinds (masters and slaves, cowboys and Indians), with intrasexual power struggles, as in the rape of young or weak men in prison by gangs of stronger ones, and within families, by male relatives of young girls or children.

None of these patterns is, except in one respect, wholly consistent with the others, but viewed together they induce a kind of dispirited resignation to natural law, from which are derived the supposed constants of human nature, maybe including rape. The respect in which violations of conquered women in Bangladesh and of Indian (or white) women in pioneer America, or of men in prison, are alike is that they all dramatize some authority conflict. In war between groups of males, women are incidental victims and prizes, but in the back of the car the dispute arises between a man and a woman on her own behalf. The point at issue seems to be "maistrye," as the Wife of Bath knew; and the deepest lessons of our culture have inculcated in both sexes the idea that he is going to prevail. This in turn ensures that he usually does, but the central question of why it is necessary to have male mastery remains unanswered, and perhaps unasked. Meantime, the lesson of history seems to elevate the right of the male to exact obedience and inflict punishment to the status of immutable law.

Anthropology seems to support this, too, despite Brownmiller's attempts to find a primitive tribe (the obligingly rape-free Arapesh) to prove otherwise. Rather inconsistently, she conjectures that the origin of monogamy lies in the female's primordial fear of rape and consequent willingness to attach herself to some male as his exclusive property. If this is so, it would be the only instance in which the female will has succeeded in dictating social arrangements. In any case, alternate and better hypotheses exist for the origin of the family, generally that it developed for the protection of the young. The insouciance of Brownmiller's generalizations invites cavil and risks discrediting her book, and with it her subject. Granting that a primitive tribe can be found to illustrate any social model whatever, one would like to know just what all the anthropological evidence about rape is. If rape is the primordial norm; if, as Lévi-Strauss says, women were the first currency; if male humans in a state of nature run mad raping, unlike chimpanzees, who we are told do not, is rape in fact aberrant? Perhaps it is only abhorrent.

It seems evident that whatever the facts of our nature, it is our culture that leads women in some degree to collaborate in their own rape, an aspect of the matter that men seem determined to claim absolves *them* from responsibility. Perhaps this is implicit in the assumptions about male power they are heir to. But every woman also inherits assumptions about female submission. In even the simplest fairy tale, the vaguely sexual content of the punishment needs no elaboration: every woman darkly knows what really happened to Red Riding Hood in the woods—and to Grandmother, too, for that matter. Most women do not go into the woods alone, but the main point is that the form of the prohibition as it is expressed in most stories is not "Do not go into the woods lest you be raped," but "Obey me by not going into the woods or you *will* be raped."

Thus the idea of sexual punishment for disobedience is learned very early, and is accepted. Who has done this to you, Desdemona? "Nobody; I myself, farewell," says Desdemona meekly as she dies. Everyone feels that Carmen, that prick-tease, is "getting what she deserves," poor Lucrece's suicide is felt to be both noble and tactful, maybe Anna Karenina's too. So if a woman is raped, she feels, besides outrage, deep guilt and a need to find out what she has done "wrong" to account for it, even if her sin is only one of omission; for example, concerned citizens in Palo Alto were told a few days ago that "Sometimes women are raped because of carelessness."

To the extent that a woman can convince a jury that she was neither careless nor seductive, her attacker may be found guilty and she may be absolved from guilt, but more often in rape trials something is found in her behavior to "account" for her fate. The point is that whatever the circumstances of a rape, social attitudes and legal processes at the present time make the victim guilty of her own rape. Even the most innocent victim is likely to be told by her mother, "I told you never to walk home alone," and this is sometimes the attitude of an entire population, as in Bangladesh, where thousands of raped wives were repudiated by their husbands.

The unfortunate rape victim is in some ways worse off the more "feminine," the better socialized, she is, for she will have accepted normal social strictures: do not play rough, do not make noise or hit. Then she will be judged at the trial of her attacker on the extent to which she has struggled, hit, bitten (though she would not be expected to resist an armed robber). Not to struggle is to appear to want to be raped. In the courtroom men pretend not to understand the extent to which cultural inhibitions prevent women from resisting male force, even moral force, though in the parking lot they seem to understand it very well.

In the practical world, who are the rapists, who are the raped, what is to be done? It is here that Brownmiller's account is most interesting and most disturbing. Both Brownmiller and MacKellar agree on the statistical particulars: the rape victim is most likely a teen-aged black girl but she may be a woman of any age, and she will know her attacker to some extent in about half of the cases. The rapist is the same sort of person as other violent offenders: young, uneducated, unemployed, likely black or from another deprived subculture; the rapist is *not* the shy, hard-up loner living with his mother, victim of odd obsessions; a quarter of all rapes are done in gangs or pairs.

The sociology of rapists has some difficult political implications, as Brownmiller, to judge from the care with which she approaches it, is well aware. She traces the complicated history of American liberalism and Southern racism which has led to the present pass, in which people who have traditionally fought for human freedom seem committed to obstructing freedom for women. Historically, she reminds us, the old left, and the Communist Party in particular,

> understood rape as a political act of subjugation only when the victim was black and the offender was white. White-on-white rape was merely "criminal" and had no part in their Marxist canon. Black-on-black rape was ignored. And black-on-white rape, about which the rest of the country was phobic, was discussed in the oddly reversed world of the Jefferson School as if it never existed except as a spurious charge that "the state" employed to persecute black men.

Meantime, circumstances have changed; folk bigotry, like folk wisdom, turns out to contain a half-truth, or grain of prescience; and the black man has taken to raping. Now

> the incidence of actual rape combined with the looming spectre of the black man as rapist to which the black man in the name of his manhood now contributes, must be understood as a control mechanism against the freedom, mobility, and aspirations of all women, white and black. The crossroads of racism and sexism had to be a violent meeting place. There is no use pretending it doesn't exist.

It is at this crossroad that the problem appears most complex and most insoluble. Not only rapists, but also people more suavely disguised as right-thinking, like the ACLU and others associated with the civil-rights movement, still feel that protection of black men's rights is more important than injustice to women, whether white or black. Black men and white women are in effect pitted against one another in such a way as to impede the progress of both groups, and in particular to conceal and perpetuate the specific victimization of black women. Various studies report that blacks do up to 90 percent of rapes, and their victims are 80 to 90 percent black women, who now must endure from men of their own race what they historically had to endure from whites. A black girl from the ages of ten to fifteen is twelve times more likely than others to be a victim of this crime.

In this situation, which will win in the long run, sexism or racism? Who are the natural antagonists? It seems likely, on the evidence, that sexism, being older, will prevail.

The MacKellar/Amir book, a short, practical manual about rape, something to be used perhaps by jurors or counselors, gives a picture of the crime and of the rapist which is essentially the same as Brownmiller's. But MacKellar's advice, when compared with Brownmiller's, is seen to be overlaid by a kind of naive social optimism. What can women do? They can avoid hitchhiking; they can be better in bed: "if women were less inhibited with their men the sense of depravity that their prudishness inspires might be reduced," as if it were frustrated middle-class husbands who were out raping; authorities can search out those "many youngsters warped by a brutish home life [who] can still be recuperated for a reasonably good adult life if given therapy in time"; "Education. Education helps to reduce rape."

Maybe. But does any evidence exist to suggest that any of this would really help? Brownmiller has found none, but I suppose she would agree with MacKellar that for America's violent subcultures we must employ "the classical remedies of assimilating the people in these subcultures, economically and socially, in opportunities for education, jobs, and decent housing," and change the fundamental values of American society. "As long as aggressive, exploitive behavior remains the norm, it can be expected that individuals will make these errors and that the weaker members of society will be the victim."

Until aggressive, exploitive behavior is not the norm, a few practical measures are being suggested. The LEAA study, MacKellar, and Brownmiller are all in favor of prosecuting rape cases and of punishing rapists. Brownmiller feels the punishment should suit the crime, that it should be made similar to penalties for aggravated assault, which it resembles. MacKellar feels that the penalty should fit the criminal: "a nineteen-year-old unemployed black with a fourth-grade education and no father, whose uptight, superreligious mother has, after a quarrel, kicked him out of the home, should not be judged by the same standard nor receive the same kind of sentence as a white middle-aged used-car salesman, twice divorced, who rapes a girl he picks up at a newsstand during an out-of-town convention." She does not, by the way, say who should get the stiffer sentence, and I can think of arguments either way.

Both agree that corroboration requirements and courtroom questions about a victim's prior sexual history should be eliminated, and in this the government-sponsored study for the Law

Enforcement Assistance Administration (*Rape and Its Victims*) also agrees. At present the established view holds that whether or not a raped girl is a virgin or is promiscuous is germane to the issue of whether a forced act of sexual intercourse has occurred in a given case. This reflects the ancient idea that by violating male standards of female chastity, a woman forfeits her right to say no.

The LEAA study found that prosecutors' offices in general were doing little to urge the revision of outdated legal codes, and that the legal system is in fact impeding reform. It observes (in a nice trenchant style that makes better reading than most government reports) that

> since rapists have no lobby, the major opposition to reform measures can be expected from public defenders, the defense bar in general, and groups, such as the American Civil Liberties Union, that are vigilant with respect to the rights of criminal defendants.

The conclusion one cannot help coming to is that whatever is to be done about rape will have to be done by women primarily. Brownmiller feels that law enforcement must include 50 percent women. She finds it significant that whereas male law-enforcement authorities report 15 to 20 percent of rape complaints to be "unfounded," among the ones they actually bother to write down, women investigators find only 2 percent of such reports to be unfounded, exactly the number of unfounded reports of other violent crimes. Apparently the goal of male-female law enforcement is not without its difficulties; women police officers in Washington, D.C., recently have complained that their male patrol-car partners are attempting to force them to have sexual intercourse. Since these women are armed with service revolvers, we may soon see an escalation of what appears to be the Oldest Conflict.

MacKellar and the LEAA report both favor some sort of rape sentencing by degree, as in murder, with rape by a stranger constituting first-degree rape, and third degree taking cognizance of situations in which the victim may be judged to have shared responsibility for initiating the situation that led to the rape—for instance, hitchhiking. This is a compromise that would be unacceptable to feminist groups who feel that a woman is no more responsible for a rape under those circumstances than a man would be thought to be who was assaulted in the same situation.

It is likely that the concept of penalty by degree, with its concession to history, will prevail here, but one sees the objection on principle. While men continue to believe that men have a right to assert their authority over women by sexual and other means, rape will continue, and this in turn suggests two more measures. One is control of pornography, which Brownmiller argues is the means by which the rape ethic is promulgated. In spite of objections about censorship and about the lack of evidence that pornography and violence are related, Brownmiller's argument here is a serious one. She also feels that women should learn self-defense, if only to give them increased self-confidence and awareness of their bodies. But it is easy to see that this is yet another way in which the female might be made to take responsibility for being raped. If a women learns karate and is raped anyway, the question will become, why hadn't she learned it better?

Surely the definition of civilization is a state of things where the strong refrain from exercising their advantages over the weak. If men can be made to see that the abolition of sexual force is necessary in the long-term interest of making a civilization, then they may cooperate in implementing whatever measures turn out to be of any use. For the short term, one imagines, the general effect of female activism about rape will be to polarize men and women even more than nature has required. The cooperation of state authorities, if any, may ensue from their perception of rape, especially black-on-white rape, as a challenge to white male authority (as in the South). This in turn may produce an unlikely and ominous coalition of cops and feminists, and the generally severer prosecution and sentencing which we see as the current response to other forms of violent crime. But do we know that rapists will emerge from the prisons—themselves centers of homosexual rape—any less inclined to do it again?

Meantime, one feels a certain distaste for the congratulatory mood surrounding proposed law-enforcement reforms devoted entirely to making the crime less miserable for the victim while denying or concealing the complicity of so many men in its perpetuation. This implies a state of things worthy of a society described by Swift.

REFLECTING ON MEANING

1. What are the social myths about rape that Johnson identifies? What is the "rooted and implacable male belief" that she describes? What is the "strange proposition" that women as well as men seem to subscribe to? According to Johnson, why is rape an "abiding concern to women" but not to men? Why is it an emotional issue for women but not for men?

2. Johnson maintains that women learn early the "lessons" of rape—
"that to break certain rules is to invite or deserve rape." What
does she mean? What lessons do women learn? Johnson also asserts that "every woman also inherits assumptions about female
submission." How do these assumptions about submission reinforce the lessons society conveys about the "rules" of rape? How
do women come to accept the "idea of sexual punishment for
disobedience"?

3. What is rape, according to Johnson? Where does she supply this
definition? Why does she cast it in terms of "domination and
punishment"? In what ways is it punishment? For what? What
are the social and cultural attitudes that the act of rape makes
concrete?

EXPLORING RHETORICAL STRATEGIES

1. Johnson suggests that Brownmiller's book might be criticized
"for an emotional tone that is apparently impossible to exclude
from an effective work on a subject so inaccessible to rational
analysis." To what degree does her own essay transcend such an
emotional tone? Is an emotional tone necessarily a negative
thing? Why or why not?

2. Throughout her essay, Johnson alludes to women in myth and
literature: Eve, Leda, Potiphar, the wife of Bath, Desdemona,
Carmen, Anna Karenina—even Little Red Riding Hood. Why
does she do this? What do these allusions tell you about the kind
of knowledge she expects her audience to have? What kind of
audience did she have in mind as she composed this essay?

3. This essay is an example of a genre known as the review essay, an
essay that not only summarizes and evaluates several books on a
specific topic but that expresses the review writer's own views on
the topic. What views does Johnson hold on rape? How does she
distinguish them from her views on the books she is reviewing?

Chapter 13 —————————

GLOBAL PERSPECTIVES

Life Behind the Veil

CHERRY LINDHOLM AND
CHARLES LINDHOLM

*Harvard professors Cherry Lindholm and Charles Lind-
holm metaphorically remove the veil from Moslem women in
Pakistan, who are of a strict* purdah *society, to reveal how this
"institution of female seclusion" influences all Pakhtun societal
practices and institutions.*

The bazaar teems with activity. Pedestrians throng the narrow
streets, wending past donkey carts, cyclists, and overloaded
vehicles. Vendors haggle in the dark doorways of their
shops. Pitiful beggars shuffle among the crowds, while bearded religious mendicants wander about, their eyes fixed on a distant world.

Drifting among the mobs of men are, here and there, anonymous figures hidden beneath voluminous folds of material, who
float along like ships in full sail, graceful, mysterious, faceless, instilling in the observer a sense both of awe and of curiosity. These are
the Moslem women of the Middle East. Their dress is the customary
chador, which they wear when obliged to leave the privacy of their
homes. The *chador* is but one means by which women maintain their
purdah, the institution of female seclusion, which requires that
women should remain unseen by men who are not close relatives
and strikes Westerners as so totally foreign and incomprehensible.

Sometimes the alien aspect is tempered with a touch of Western familiarity. A pair of plastic sunglasses may gleam from behind
the lace that covers the eyes, or a platform shoe might peep forth

from beneath the hem of the flowing *chador*. Nevertheless, the over-all presence remains one of inscrutability and is perhaps the most striking image of Middle Eastern societies. .

We spent nine months in one of the most strict of all the *purdah* societies, the Yusufzai Pakhtun of the Swat Valley in the North-West Frontier Province of Pakistan. ("Pakhtun" is the designation preferred by the tribesmen, who were generally called Pathans in the days of the British *raj*.)

We had come to the Swat Valley after a hair-raising ride on a rickety bus from Peshawar over the 10,280-foot Malakand Pass. Winston Churchill came this way as a young war correspondent at-tached to the Malakand Field Force in 1897. As we came into the val-ley, about half the size of Connecticut, we passed a sign that said WELCOME TO SWAT. We were fortunate to have entrée into the com-munity through a Swati friend we had made eight years before. In Swat, women are secluded inside the domestic compound except for family rituals, such as marriage, circumcision, and funerals, or visits to saint's tombs. A woman must always be in the protective com-pany of other women and is never allowed out alone. It tells a great deal about the community that the word for husband in Pakhto, the language of the Pakhtun, is *kwawund,* which also means God.

However, as everywhere, rules are sometimes broken or, more frequently, cleverly manipulated. Our Pakhtun host's step-mother, Bibi, an intelligent and forceful woman, was renowned for her tactics. Once, when all the females of the household had been forbidden to leave the compound to receive cholera inoculations at the temporary clinic next door, Bibi respectfully bowed her head and assured the men they could visit the mosque with easy minds. Once the men had gone, she promptly climbed the ladder to the flat room and summoned the doctor to the door of her compound. One by one, the women extended their bare arms through the doorway and received their shots. Later, Bibi could honestly swear that no woman had set foot outside the compound walls.

Despite such circumventions, *purdah* is of paramount impor-tance in Swat. As one Pakhtun proverb succinctly states: "The woman's place is in the home or the grave." Years ago in Swat, if a woman broke her *purdah,* her husband might kill her or cut off her nose as punishment and as a means of cleansing his honor. If a woman is caught alone with an unrelated man, it will always be as-sumed that the liaison is sexual, and public opinion will oblige her husband to shoot her, even if he does not desire her death; to go unavenged is to be known henceforth as *begherata,* or man without honor. As such, he would no longer have the right to call himself Pakhtun.

A shameless woman is a threat to the whole society. Our host remembered witnessing, thirty years ago when he was a child, the entire village stoning an adulteress. This punishment is prescribed by Islamic law, though the law requires there be four witnesses to the sexual act itself to establish guilt. Nowadays, punishments for wifely misdemeanors have become less harsh, though adulterous wives are still killed.

In the rural areas, poorer families generally cannot maintain *purdah* as rigorously as their wealthier neighbors, for often a wife must help her husband in the fields or become a servant. Nevertheless, she is required to keep her hair covered at all times and to interact with men to a minimum. Here again, the rules are sometimes flouted, and a poor woman might entice a man with her eyes, or even, according to village men who claimed personal experiences, become more aggressive in her seductive attempts and actually seize a man in a deserted alleyway and lure him into her house. Often, the man is persuaded. Such a woman will accept money from her lover, who is usually a man from a wealthy family. Her husband is then a *begherata,* but some men acquiesce to the situation because of the money the wife is earning or because of fear of the wife's socially superior and more powerful lover. But most poor men, and certainly all the elite, keep their women under strict control.

In the Islamic Middle East, women are viewed as powerful and dangerous beings, highly sexual and lacking in personal discipline and discrimination. In Middle Eastern thought, sexual intercourse itself, though polluting, lacks the same negative connotations it has in the West. It has always been believed that women have sexual climaxes, and there is no notion of female frigidity. Male impotence, however, is well-documented, and some middle-aged and even young men admitted to us that they had lost their interest in women. Sometimes, though rarely, a young bridegroom will find himself incapable of consummating his marriage, either because he finds his bride unattractive or because he has been previously enchanted by a male lover and has become impotent in a heterosexual relationship. Homosexuality has never been seen as aberrant in the Middle East. As a famous Afghan saying humorously declares: "A woman is for bearing children, a boy is for pleasure, but ecstasy is a ripe watermelon!" However, with Western influence, homosexuality in the Middle East is now less overt. But even when it was common and open, the man was still expected to marry and produce children.

Men must marry, though women are regarded as a chaotic and anarchic force. They are believed to possess many times the sexual desire of men and constitute a potential threat to the family and the family's honor, which is based in large measure on the possession and control of women and their excessive and dangerous sexuality.

Among the Pakhtun of Swat, where the male-female relation is one of the most hostile in the Middle East, the man avoids showing affection to his wife, for fear she will become too self-confident and will begin to assert herself in ways that insult his position and honor. She may start by leaving the compound without his permission and, if unchecked, may end by bringing outside men into the house for sexual encounters, secure in the knowledge that her husband, weakened by his affection for her, will not take action. This course of events is considered inevitable by men and women alike and was illustrated by a few actual cases in the village where we lived.

Women are therefore much feared, despite the pronouncements of male supremacy. They must be controlled, in order to prevent their alarming basic natures from coming to the fore and causing dishonor to their own lineages. *Purdah* is generally described as a system that serves to protect the woman, but implicitly it protects the men and society in general from the potentially disruptive actions of the powerful female sex.

Changes are occurring, however, particularly in the modern urban centers. The educated urban woman often dispenses with the *chador,* replacing it with a simple length of veiling draped over the head or across the shoulders; she may even decide to adopt modest Western dress. The extent of this transformation will depend partly upon the attitude of the community in which she lives.

In the urban centers of the stricter *purdah* regions the public display of *purdah* is scrupulous, sometimes even more striking than that of the tribal village. Behind the scenes, though, the city-dwelling woman does have more freedom than she would have in the village. She will be able to visit not only relatives but friends without specific permission from her husband, who is out at work all day. She may, suitably veiled, go shopping in the bazaar, a chore her husband would have undertaken in the village. On the whole, the city woman will have a great deal more independence, and city men sometimes lament this weakening of traditional male domination.

The urbanized male may speak of the custom-bound tribesmen (such as the Swat Pakhtun, the Bedouin nomads of Saudi Arabia or Qashqai herdsmen of Iran) as country bumpkins, yet he still considers their central values, their sense of personal pride, honor, and autonomy, as cultural ideals and views the tribesmen, in a very real way, as exemplars of the proper mode of life. Elite families in the cities proudly emphasize their tribal heritage and sometimes send their sons to live for a year or so with distant tribal cousins, in order to expose them to the tribesman's integrity and moral code. The tribesman, on the other hand, views his urbanized relatives as weak and womanly, especially with reference to the slackening of *purdah* in the cities. Though the *purdah* female, both in the cities and in the tribal areas, rarely personifies the ideal virtues of silence, submission, and obedience, the concept of *purdah* and male supremacy remains central to the male identity and to the ideology of the culture as a whole.

The dynamic beneath the notion of male supremacy, the institution of *purdah,* and the ideology of women's sexual power becomes apparent when one takes an overall view of the social structure. The family in the Middle East, particularly in the tribal regions, is not an isolate element; kinship and marriage are the underlying principles that structure action and thought. Individuals interact not so much according to personal preference as according to kinship.

The Middle Eastern kinship system is known to anthropologists as a segmentary-lineage organization; the basic idea is that kinship is traced through one line only. In the Middle East, the system is patrilineal, which means that the male line is followed, and all the links through women are ignored. An individual can therefore trace his relationship to any other individual in the society and know the exact genealogical distance between them; i.e., the distance that must be traced to reach a common male ancestor. The system obliges men to defend their patrilineal relatives if they are attacked, but if there is no external force threatening the lineage, then men struggle against one another according to the principle of genealogical distance. This principle is nicely stated in a famous Middle Eastern proverb: "I against my brothers, my brothers and I against my cousins; my cousins, my brothers, and I against the world." The cousins in question are of course patrilineal.

Within this system, women appear to have no role, though they are the units of reproduction, the mothers of the sons who will carry on the patriline. Strange as it may seem, this is the core contradiction of the society: The "pure" patriline itself is actually descended from a woman. This helps explain the exaggerated fear of women's promiscuity and supposedly voracious sexuality. In order to protect the patriline, women must be isolated and guarded. Their sexuality, which threatens the integrity of the patriline, must be made the exclusive property of their husbands. Women, while being absolutely necessary for the perpetuation of the social order, are simultaneously the greatest threat to it.

The persistent denigration of women is explained by this core contradiction. Moslem society considers women naturally inferior in intelligence and ability—childlike, incapable of discernment, incompetent to testify in court, prey to whims and fancies. In tribal areas, women are prohibited from inheritance, despite a Koranic injunction, and in marriage they are purchased from their fathers like a commodity. Were woman not feared, these denials of her personhood would be unnecessary.

Another unique element of Middle Eastern culture is the prevalence of marriage with the father's brother's daughter. In many areas, in fact, this marriage is so favored that a boy must give explicit permission to allow his patrilineal female cousin to marry elsewhere. This peculiar marriage form, which is found nowhere else in the world, also serves to negate the woman by merging her lineage with that of her husband, since both are members of the same patriline (indeed, are the offspring of brothers). No new blood enters, and the sanctity of the patriline is steadily maintained.

However, this ploy gives rise to other problems. Cousin marriage often divides the brothers rather than uniting them. Although the bride-price is usually reduced in such marriages, it is always demanded, thus turning the brothers into opponents in a business negotiation. Furthermore, giving a woman in Swat carries an implication of inferiority; historically, victors in war took women from the vanquished. Cousin marriage thus renders the brothers' equality questionable. Finally, the young couple's fights will further alienate the brothers, especially since such marriages are notoriously contentious. This is because patrilineal male cousins are rivals for the common grandfather's inheritance (in fact, the Swati term for father's brother's son is *tarbur,* which also means enemy), and a man who marries his patrilineal cousin is marrying the sister of his lifelong opponent. Her loyalty is with her brother, and this is bound to cause frequent disputes.

Though the girl is treated like goods, she does not see herself as such. The fundamental premise of tribal life is the equality of the various landed families. There are very few hierarchies in these societies, and even the leaders are often no more than first among equals. Within this system, which as been described as a nearly perfect democracy, each *khan* (which means landowner and literally translates as king) family sees itself as superior to all others. The girls of the household feel the same pride in their lineage as their brothers and cannot help but regard their husband's families through jaundiced eyes. The new bride is prepared to defend the honor of her family, even though they have partially repudiated her by negotiating the marriage. Her identity, like that of a man, rests on her lineage pride, which she will fight to uphold. The husband, meanwhile, is determined to demonstrate his domination and mastery, since control of women is the nexus of a man's sense of self-respect.

Hostility is thus built into marriage by the very structure of the society, which pits every lineage against every other in a never-ending contest to maintain an equilibrium of power within this markedly egalitarian culture. The hostility of the marriage bond is evident from its beginnings. The reluctant bride is torn from her cot in her family's house and ensconced on a palanquin that strongly resembles a bier. The war drums that announce the marriage procession indicate the nature of the tie, as does the stoning of the palanquin by the small boys of the village as it is carried through the dusty streets. When the bride arrives at her new husband's house, his family triumphantly fires their rifles into the air. They have taken a woman! The young wife cowers in her veils as she is prodded and poked curiously by the females of the husband's house who try to persuade her to show her face. The groom himself is nowhere to be seen, having retreated to the men's house in shame. In three days, he will creep to her room and consummate the marriage. Taking the virginity of the bride is a highly charged symbolic act, and in some areas of the Middle East the display of the bloody nuptial sheet to the public is a vital part of the wedding rite. Breaking the hymen demonstrates the husband's possession of his wife's sexuality. She then becomes the junior adult in the household, subordinate to everyone, but, most especially, under the heavy thumb of her mother-in-law.

The household the bride enters will be that of her husband's father, since the system, as well as being patrilineal, is also patrilocal. She will be surrounded by his relatives and will be alone with her husband only at night. During the day he will pay no attention to her, for it is considered shameful for a man to take note of his wife in front of others, particularly his father and mother. Within the compound walls, which shield the household from the rest of the world, she is at the mercy of her new family.

Life within the compound is hardly peaceful. Wives squabble among themselves, and wives who have built a power base by having sons even quarrel with the old matriarch, their mother-in-law. This is usually a prelude to a couple moving out of the house into their own compound, and husbands always blame their wives for the breakup of the extended family, even though they, too, will be glad to become the masters of their own homes and households.

But the worst fights among women are the fights between women married to the same man. Islam permits polygamous marriage, and legally a man may have four wives. Not all men are financially able to take more than one wife, but most men dream of marrying again, despite the Swati proverb that says "I may be a fool, but not so much of a fool as the man with two wives." Men who can afford it often do take a second wife. The reason is not sexual desire, for wives do not mind if their husbands have liaisons with prostitutes or promiscuous poor women. Rather, the second wife is brought in to humiliate an overly assertive first wife. Bringing in a second wife is a terrible insult; it is an expression of contempt for the first wife and her entire lineage. The insult is especially cutting in Swat, where divorce is prohibited (though it is permitted in the Koran) and where a disliked wife must either endure her lot or retreat to her family's household and a life of celibacy. Small wonder then that households with two wives are pits of intrigue, vituperation, and magical incantation, as each wife seeks to expel the other. The Koran says a man should only practice polygamy if he is sure he can treat each wife equally; the only man we met who was able to approximate this ideal was a man who never went home. He spent his time in the men's house, talking with his cronies and having his meals sent to him.

The men's house is the best-built structure in any village, along with the mosque, which is also prohibited to women. It is a meeting place for the clan, the center for hospitality and refuge, and the arena for political manipulation. This is where the visitors will be received, surrounded by men who gossip, doze, or clean their rifles. Here, the guest might well imagine that women do not even exist. Only the tea and food that is sent over from the compound nearby tell him of the women working behind the walls.

Formerly, in Swat, most men slept in the men's house, visiting their wives secretly late at night and returning before daybreak. But now only a few elders and some ne'er-do-well youths live permanently in the elegant, aging buildings. Sometimes, however, a man may be obliged to move to the men's house for a few days if his wife makes his home too uncomfortable, for women have their own weapons in the household battles. Arguments may flare up over almost anything: the husband buying a rotten piece of meat or forgetting to bring home a length of material, the wife ruining some curd or gossiping too much with a neighbor. The wife may then angrily refuse to cook, obliging the husband to retreat to the men's house for food. The man's weapon in fights is violence, while the woman can withdraw domestic services at will.

In the early days of a marriage, when the bride is new to the household and surrounded by her husband's people, she may be fairly meek. But when her status has improved as a result of producing sons, she will become more aggressive. Her lacerating tongue is renowned, and she will also begin to fight back physically as well as verbally. Finally, her exasperated husband may silence her with a blow from a heavy stick he keeps for that purpose. No shame is attached to beating one's wife, and men laugh about beatings they have administered. The women themselves, though they decry their men's brutality, proudly display their scars and bruises, characterizing a neighbor who is relatively gentle to his wife as "a man with no penis."

The older a woman gets, the more powerful and fearless she becomes. She is aided by her sons who, though respecting their father, regard him as an obstacle to their gaining rights in land. The old man, who gains his stature from his landholding, is always reluctant to allot shares to his grown sons. Furthermore, the sons' ties of affection are much stronger with the mother. The elderly father, who is generally ten or fifteen years older than his wife, is thus surrounded by animosity in his own house. The situation of the earlier years has reversed itself, and the wife, who began alone and friendless, gains allies in her old age, while the husband becomes isolated. Ghani Khan, a modern Pakhtun writer, had described the situation well: "The Pakhtun thinks he is as good as anyone else and his father rolled into one and is fool enough to try this even with his wife. She pays for it in her youth, and he in his old age."

But many women do not live to see their triumph. In northern Swat, for every 100 women over the age of sixty there are 149 men, compared to the more equal 100 to 108 ratio below sixty. The women are worn out by continual childbearing, breast feeding, and a lack of protein. Though fertile in places, the Swat valley is heavily overpopulated with an estimated 1 million people, and survival is always difficult. The diet consists chiefly of bread, rice, seasonal vegetables, and some dairy products. Meat is a rarity and goes to the men and boys as a matter of course. They perpetuate the patrilineal clan and must survive, while women can always be replaced. The lives of men are hard, but the lives of women are harder, as witnessed by their early deaths.

In this environment, people must learn to be tough, just as they must learn to fit the structure of the patrilineal system. Child rearing serves both functions.

The birth of a boy in Swat is greeted by rejoicing, while the birth of a girl is an occasion for gloom. But the first few years for both sexes are virtually identical. Like most Middle Easterners, the Swatis practice swaddling, binding the baby tightly so that it is immobilized. Ostensibly, this is to help the baby sleep and prevent it from blinding itself with its flailing hands, but anthropologists have hypothesized that swaddling actually serves to develop a certain character type: a type which can withstand great restraint but which also tends to uncontrolled bursts of temper. This hypothesis fits Swat, where privation and the exigencies of the social structure demand stoicism, but where violent temper is also useful. We often saw Swati children of all ages lose themselves in tantrums to coerce their parents, and such coercion was usually successful. Grown men and women as well are prone to fits of temper, and this dangerous aspect makes their enemies leery of pressing them too hard.

Both sexes are indoctrinated in the virtues of their family and its lineage. In marital fights this training is obvious, as both partners heatedly assert, "Your ancestor was nothing, and mine was great!" At a man's death his sister, not his wife, is his chief mourner. And if a woman is killed it is her brother, not her husband, who avenges her.

Child training in Swat produces strong characters. When they give affection, they give it wholeheartedly, and when they hate, they hate bitterly. The conditions under which they live are cruel and cramped, and they respond with cruelty and rigidity in order to survive. But at the same time, the people are able to bear their hard lives with pride and dignity.

REFLECTING ON MEANING

1. Define the following terms: *chador, purdah, khawund, begherata,* and *khan.* How does each of these terms illuminate the Lindholms' discussion of the treatment of Swati women in Pakhtun society? In the Islamic Middle East, women are "viewed as powerful and dangerous beings, highly sexual and lacking in personal discipline and discrimination." What is the connection between fear of female sexuality and the Swati's patrilineal kinship? How do Swati marriage practices maintain the sanctity of the patriline? What is their society's view on heterosexual and homosexual sex? What is the difference between the treatment of adulteresses and adulterers?

2. In Pakhtun society, the concept of "*purdah* and male supremacy remains central to the male identity and to the ideology of the culture as a whole." How does this ideology translate into the husbands' treatment of their wives? Husbands who treat their wives gently are referred to as what? While the husband's weapon is violence, the wife's weapon is withdrawal of domestic service. What other power do females gain as they get older?

   Polygamous marriages are permitted by Islam. Why do some husbands choose to take a second wife?

3. The Lindholms report that the Swatis "practice swaddling, binding the baby tightly so that it is immobilized." What connection do these authors make between this practice and the Swati personality? How might this practice also refer to the binding restraints that this society places on its women?

EXPLORING RHETORICAL STRATEGIES

1. The Lindholms begin their essay with a description of a Swati bazaar and women attired in *chadors*. The women are described as "anonymous figures hidden beneath voluminous folds of material, who float along like ships in full sail, graceful, mysterious, faceless, instilling in the observer a sense of both awe and curiosity." How effective is this visual introduction to Swati women and this society? How does this metaphorically relate to the title of this essay?

2. This essay first appeared in *Science Digest* in 1980. While scientists and researchers attempt to report "objectively" on their objects of study, many contemporary thinkers question the notion of "pure" objectivity by arguing that all data interpretations are "subjective" to varying degrees. What researchers choose to study, how they organize and interpret their data, and the conclusions they reach are all influenced by "subjective" experience. Analyze the Lindholms' essay for degrees of objectivity and subjectivity. Where does their discussion appear more objective? Where does it appear more subjective? How might another researcher have reported on Swati society? (For example, a radical feminist like Mary Daly, in Part II of this book and in the essay that follows.)

3. How useful is the Lindholms' inclusion of specialized vocabulary to your understanding of Swati practices?

African Genital Mutilation: The Unspeakable Atrocities

MARY DALY

In this chapter from her radical feminist book Gyn/ Ecology, *Mary Daly graphically describes female genital mutilation and how it is but one manifestation of "planetary patriarchy." She seeks to break the "conspiracy of silence" about this practice, so that women will stop "murdering their own divinity."*

There are some manifestations of the Sado-Ritual Syndrome that are unspeakable—incapable of being expressed in words because inexpressibly horrible.* Such are the ritual genital mutilation—excision and infibulation—still inflicted upon women throughout Africa today, and practiced in many parts of the world in the past.† These ritualized atrocities are unspeakable also in a sec-

---

*I have chosen to name these practices for what they are: barbaric rituals/atrocities. Critics from Western countries are constantly being intimidated by accusations of "racism," to the point of misnaming, nonnaming, and not seeing these sado-rituals. The accusations of "racism" may come from ignorance, but they serve only the interests of males, not of women. This kind of accusation and intimidation constitutes an astounding and damaging reversal, for it is clearly in the interest of Black women that feminists of all races should speak out. Moreover, it is in the interest of women of all races to see African genital mutilation in the context of planetary patriarchy, of which it is but one manifestation. As I am demonstrating, it is of the same pattern as the other atrocities I discuss.

†Lest Westerners feel smugly distant from these rituals, it would be well to recall some facts of "our" culture. In a later chapter I will discuss the implications of the fact that clitoridectomies and other mutilations have been inflicted by American gynecologists. It should be noted also that slashing and mutilation of genitals are common features of contemporary gang rape, which is "as American as apple pie." Moreover, there has been a time-honored christian European tradition of infibulation and of the chastity belt. According to some, this was done in the same way as the infibulation of mares practiced in the veterinary profession, consisting of fastening together the labia by means of a ring, a buckle, or a padlock, According to Davis, the upper classes resorted less frequently to infibulation, but used instead the chastity belt, which was supposedly less painful. When one considers that some women were locked up in these for months or even years while their lords were away, the torture of accumulated excrement and of infection is beyond imagination. Such items are of course still on display in European museums, objects of merriment for guides and visitors, including female visitors who often do not comprehend their implications. See Elizabeth Gould Davis, *The First Sex* (New York: G. P. Putnam, 1971), pp. 163–67.

ond sense; that is, there are strong taboos against saying/writing the truth about them, against *naming* them. These taboos are operative both within the segments of phallocracy in which such rituals are practiced and in other parts of the Fatherland, whose leaders cooperate in the conspiracy of silence. Hags see that the demonic rituals in the so-called underdeveloped regions of the planet are deeply connected with atrocities perpetrated against women in "advanced" societies. To allow ourselves to see the connections is to begin to understand that androcracy is the State of Atrocity, where atrocities are normal, ritualized, repeated.[1] It is the City of Atrophy in which the archetypal trophies are massacred women.

Those who have endured the unspeakable atrocities of genital mutilation have in most cases been effectively silenced. Indeed this profound silencing of the mind's imaginative and critical powers is one basic function of the sado-ritual, which teaches women never to forget to murder their own divinity. Those who physically survive these atrocities "live" their entire lifetimes, from early childhood or from puberty, preoccupied by pain. Those women who inhabit other parts of the planet cannot really wish to imagine the condition of their mutilated sisters, for the burden of knowing is heavy. It is heavy not merely because of differences in conditions, but especially because of similarities which, as I will show later in this Passage, increase with the march of progress of phallotechnology.

The maze of lies and silences surrounding the genital mutilation still forced upon millions of young girls in many African countries continues to be effective. Yet it is becoming the subject of increasingly widespread attention.[2] Fran P. Hosken presents the following important definitions of the practices usually lumped under the vague and misleading expression, "female circumcision":

1. Sunna Circumcision: removal of the prepuce and/or tip of the clitoris.
2. Excision or Clitoridectomy: excision of the entire clitoris with the labia minora and some or most of the external genitalia.
3. Excision and Infibulation (Pharaonic Circumcision): This means excision of the entire clitoris, labia minora and parts of the labia majora. The two sides of the vulva are then fastened together in some way either by thorns...or sewing with catgut. Alternatively the vulva are scraped raw and the child's limbs are tied together for several weeks until the wound heals (or she dies). The purpose is to close the vaginal orifice. Only a small opening is left (usually by inserting a slither of wood) so the urine or later the menstrual blood can be passed.[3]

It should not be imagined that the horror of the life of an infibulated child/woman ends with this operation. Her legs are tied together, immobilizing her for weeks, during which time excrement remains within the bandage. Sometimes accidents occur during the operation: the bladder may be pierced or the rectum cut open. Sometimes in a spasm of agony the child bites off her tongue. Infections are, needless to say, common. Scholars such as Lantier claim that death is not a very common immediate effect of the operation, but often there are complications which leave the women debilitated for the rest of their lives.[4] No statistics are available on this point. What is certain is that the infibulated girl is mutilated and that she can look forward to a life of repeated encounters with "the little knife"—the instrument of her perpetual torture. For women who are infibulated have to be cut open—either by the husband or by another woman—to permit intercourse. They have to be cut open further for delivery of a child. Often they are sewn up again after delivery, depending upon the decision of the husband. The cutting (defibulation) and re-sewing goes on throughout a woman's living death of reproductive "life."[5] Immediate medical results of excision and infibulation include "hemorrhage, infections, shock, retention of urine, damage to adjacent tissues, dermoid cysts, abcesses, keloid scarring, coital difficulties, and infertility caused by chronic pelvic infections."*[6] In addition, we should consider the psychological maiming caused by this torture.

Yet this is an "unmentionable" manifestation of the atrocity which is phallocracy. The World Health Organization has refused for many years to concern itself with the problem. When it was asked in 1958 to study this problem it took the position that such operations were based on "social and cultural backgrounds" and were outside its competence. This basic attitude has not changed.[7] There has been a conspiracy of silence:

> International agencies, the U.N. and U.N. agencies, especially WHO and UNICEF (both devoted to health care), development agencies (such as U.S. Agency for International Development), non-governmental organizations working in Africa, missionaries and church groups concerned with health care, also women's organizations including World Association of Girl Guides and Girl Scouts, Y.W.C.A., and the Associated Country Women of the World, and others working in Africa, all know what is going on. Or they have people in Africa who know. This quite aside from the Health Departments and hos-

---

*Linda Barufaldi observed that the circumcision of the male requires only the removal of the foreskin, which not only leaves his organ of sexual pleasure intact but also makes him *less* susceptible to infection (conversation, Boston, January 1978).

pitals in African countries and the M.D.s, especially gynecologists, who get the most desperate cases. . . . The doctors know
all. But they don't speak.*[8]

It is important to ask why such a variety of organizations and
professions have other priorities. Why do "educated" persons bab-
ble about the importance of "tribal coherence" and "tradition"
while closing their eyes to the physical reality of mutilation? We
might well ask why "female circumcision" was reinforced in Kenya
after "liberation" and described by President Kenyatta, in his book
Facing Mount Kenya, as an important "custom" for the benefit of
"the people."[9] Hosken maintains that in the socialist countries in
Africa clitoridectomy and infibulation are practiced on a vast scale
without comment from the governments or health departments.
Again, one must ask why. Why do anthropologists ignore or minimize this horror? Why is it that the catholic church has not taken a
clear position against this genital mutilation (which is practiced
upon some of its own members in Africa)? Why do some African
leaders educated in the West continue to insist upon the maiming
of their own daughters?

These questions are profoundly interconnected. The appearance of disparateness among these groups and of their responses
(or nonresponses) masks their essential sameness. Even the above-
named organizations whose membership is largely female are androcratic since they are willing to participate in the conspiracy of
silence. Socialists, Catholics, liberal reformers, population planners, politicos of all persuasions—all have purposes which have
nothing to do with women's specific well-being unless this happens
to fit into the "wider" aims.

I

The components of the Sado-Ritual Syndrome are present in
African excision and infibulation. The obsession with purity is evident. The clitoris is "impure" because it does not serve male purposes. It has no necessary function in reproduction. As Benoite
Groult points out, hatred of the clitoris is almost universal, for this
organ is strictly female, for women's pleasure.[10] Thus it is by nature
"impure," and the logical conclusion, acted out by the tribes that
practice excision and infibulation, is purification of women by its

---

*As Hosken shows, a few doctors have spoken out in recent years. The evidence is to be
found in a few medical journal articles, some of which are cited in this chapter. Particularly useful are the articles of J. A. Verzin, A. A. Shandall, and G. Pieters.

removal. Furthermore, it is believed that excision encourages fidelity, that is, moral "purity," for there is a "decrease in sensitivity from the operation."[11] The term *decrease,* here, is a euphemism for *loss.* These women have been de-sensitized, "purified" of the capacity for sexual pleasure. The ideology among some African tribes which explains and justifies this brutal robbing from women of their clitoris—the purely female organ—displays the total irony of the concept of purity. There is a widespread belief among the Bambaras and the Dogons from Mali that all persons are hermaphroditic and that this condition is cured by circumcision and excision. Since they believe the boy is female by virtue of his foreskin and the girl is male by her clitoris, the sexes are purified (that is, officially distinguished) by the rites of puberty. Thus the removal of the purely female clitoris is seen as making a woman purely female. In fact, its purpose is to make her purely feminine, a purely abject object.

Infibulation goes even further, displaying yet other dimensions of the androcratic obsession with purity. For the "sewn women" are not only deprived of the organ of pleasure. Their masters have them genitally "sewn up," in order to preserve and redesign them strictly for their own pleasure and reproductive purposes. These women are 100 percent pure because 100 percent enslaved. Their perpetual pain (or the imminent threat of this) is an important condition for their perpetual purity, for pain preoccupies minds, emotions, imaginations, sensations, prohibiting presence of the Self.

II

The second component of the syndrome, erasure of male responsibility, is present by virtue of male absence at the execution of the mutilation. In most cases, it is not males who perform the brutal operations, although male nurses and surgeons now do it in some modern hospitals.[12] Moreover, there are comforting myths, ideologies, and clichés which assure political leaders and other males that they are blame-free. Together with the hermaphroditic myth, described above, there is the justification that "this is a way of teaching women to endure pain." There is also the belief among the Bambaras that a man who sleeps with a nonexcised woman risks death from her "sting" (clitoris). The Mossis believe that the clitoris kills children at birth and that it can be a source of impotence among men. A basic belief that justifies all, erasing all responsibility, is of course that these rites keep women faithful.[13] What is erased is the fact that these "faithful" wives have been

physically reconstructed for male purposes. They have been deprived of their own sexuality and "tightened up" for their masters'
pleasure—tightened through devices like wounding and sewing and
through the tension of excruciating pain.* Erasure of all this on the
global level occurs when leaders of "advanced" countries and of international organizations overlook these horrors in the name of
"avoiding cultural judgment." They are free of responsibility and
blame, for the "custom" must be respected as part of a "different
tradition." By so naming the tradition as "different" they hide the
cross-cultural hatred of women.

III

The massive spread of female genital mutilation throughout
Africa has been noted by responsible Searchers. Accurate statistics
are impossible to obtain, since the operation is usually performed
in secret. Nevertheless the ritual, which is of ancient origin, is
known to be widespread from Algeria in the north to the Central
African Republic in the south, and from Senegal and Mauritania in
the west to Somalia in the east.[14] Doctors working in Africa are in
a position to know what is going on, since women suffering from
complications connected with the operations are sometimes
brought to them. Two physicians have given lists of countries in
which female genital mutilation, in one form or another, is still
practiced.[15] Fran Hosken, using these and other sources, and relying also upon her own personal investigations, concludes that
some form of female circumcision is probably practiced in all
countries of Africa today in at least some tribal groups.[16] Hosken
believes that the practice started historically in Africa and was
taken on by Arab conquerors and later islam.[17] Ashley Montagu
maintains that infibulation and the successive operation—defibulation—are practiced among some Indian tribes in Peru and possibly
elsewhere in South and Central America.[18] Montagu also holds
that genital mutilation is still practiced in Australia.[19] It will require

*When reading this passage, Emily Culpepper pointed out the possibility that these
genitally reconstructed women are designed to offer their masters a kind of sexual experience comparable to that obtained by anal intercourse with other men. These "tight"
women are never allowed to become too loose, for this would decrease the strong
stimulation of the penis which men experience in anal coitus. For the women's genital
structure has been reduced and simplified to the dimension of a small hole. In a meta-
phorical sense, too, these women can never be "loose." This fact may give rise to the
thought that in Western society both "tight" women ("dried-up old maids") and "loose"
women ("dirty whores") are sexually wrong by male standards. For in fact female
sexuality—as an expression of female be-ing—is essentially wrong by androcratic, heterosexist standards.

a massive effort to obtain detailed and accurate information. One point is certain: this ritual spread rapidly over a large geographical area, involving the torture and maiming of millions of women, condemning them to a living death, deadening the divine spark of be-ing, the Goddess within.*

In discussing the phenomenon of the spread of sado-rituals, in the "cases" of Indian *suttee* and Chinese footbinding, I have shown that there is a pattern of proliferation from an elite to the upwardly aspiring lower echelons of society. The case can be argued that this pattern has also existed in female genital mutilation. According to Strabo's *Geography,* Pharaonic Egypt was characterized by clitoral excision, meaning the cutting off of sections of the clitoris and of the labia minora.[20] Inspection of royal female mummies has led some authorities to conclude that these high-caste women of Egypt had been excised. Huelsman claims that in ancient Egypt, female genital surgery was performed between the ages of fourteen and fifteen years. He remarks brightly that "it seems probable that even the amorous adventures of Cleopatra may have been conducted *sans* clitoris."[21] Shandall suggests that genital surgery on ancient Egyptian women was limited to the female relatives of rulers and priests. He speculates that women from these social and economic classes may not have been able to inherit property unless they had first undergone some form of genital surgery.

Indeed, a large number of Pharaonically circumcised mummies have been discovered.[22] Since the privileged classes were mummified, it would appear that excision was a feature of female life among the royalty. Benoîte Groult claims that the mummies of both Cleopatra and Nefertiti lack clitorises.[23] Although Ashley Montagu seems to think that all girls in ancient Egypt were excised, there really is not much evidence to back this up.[24] The evidence points to the existence of rites of passage involving genital mutilation of upper-class girls. Since we know that at the present time it is practiced upon girls at all levels of society among many African tribes (and most likely in other parts of the globe)[25] it is logical to think that it did spread from royalty to lower strata of society, as well as expanding outward geographically. The spread of this atrocity was

---

*According to Hosken, female genital mutilation takes place in some tribes in the following countries: Kenya, Tanzania, Ethiopia, southern Egypt, Sudan, Uganda, northern Zaire, Chad, northern Cameroon, Nigeria, Dahomey, Togo, northern Ghana, Upper Volta, Mali, northern Ivory Coast, Liberia, Sierra Leone, Guinea, Guinea Bissau, the Gambia, Senegal, Mauritania. See Hosken, *WIN News,* Vol. 11, No. 3 (Summer 1976), p. 22. Benoîte Groult states that excision in small girls still takes place in Yemen, Saudi Arabia, Iraq, Jordan, and Syria (*Ainsi soit-elle* [Paris: Grasset, 1975], pp. 93–118).

condoned, legitimated, demanded by the World Religion which is patriarchy. Although such sects as islam and christianity did not invent it, neither did they effectively stop it. More ancient than islam, it was practiced by pre-islamic Arabs. The "custom" was prevalent in widespread areas of the globe, in Aboriginal Australia, South America, India, Pakistan. Today it still massacres the bodies and spirits of millions of women in Africa, mostly women living in poverty, far removed from the palatial splendors that surrounded Cleopatra and other royal victims of sado-ritual.

IV

The use of women as token torturers is horribly illustrated in this ritual. At the International Tribunal on Crimes Against Women the testimony of a woman from Guinea was brought by a group of French women. The witness described seeing "the savage mutilation called excision that is inflicted on the women of my country between the ages of 10 and 12." In the instance she describes, which she saw with her own eyes, six women were holding down the victim, intoning prayers to drown her screams:

> The operation was done without any anesthetic, with no regard for hygiene or precautions of any sort. With the broken neck of a bottle, the old woman banged hard down, cutting into the upper part of my friend's genitals so as to make as wide a cut as possible, since "an incomplete excision does not constitute a sufficient guarantee against profligacy in girls."
>
> The blunt glass of the bottle did not cut deeply enough into my friend's genitals and the exciseuse had to do it several more times. . . . When the clitoris had been ripped out, the women howled with joy, and forced my friend to get up despite a streaming hemorrhage, to parade her through the town.[26]

The witness goes on to describe the "parade," in which the mutilated girl, dressed in a loin-cloth, her breasts bare, is followed by a dozen or so women singing:

> They were informing the village that my friend was ready for marriage. In Guinea, in fact, no man marries a woman who has not been excised and who is not a virgin, with rare exceptions.

This last sentence unmasks the male-centeredness of the entire ritual. It is men who demand this female castration, and possession in marriage is required in *their* society for survival. The apparently "active" role of the women, themselves mutilated, is in fact a passive, instrumental role. It hides the real castrators of women. Mentally castrated,* these women participate in the destruction of their own kind—of womankind—and in the destruction of strength and bonding among women. The screaming token torturers are silencing not only the victim, but their own victimized Selves. Their screams are the "sounds of silence" imposed upon women in sado-ritual.

The extent to which female token torturers have been used to mask the male master-minds of female genital mutilation is suggested in an account given by Montagu of female infibulation as practiced among tribes immediately south of the First Cataract of the Nile. Part of the procedure involves a visit to the bridegroom before the marriage by one of the women who performs the infibulation. The purpose of the visit is to obtain exact measurements of his "member." The following activity ensues:

> She then makes to measurement, a sort of phallus of clay or wood and by its aid she incises the scar for a certain distance and leaves the instrument wrapped round with a rag—in the wound in order to keep the edges from adhering again.[27]

Thus the master has his bride made to order to suit his "member." Montagu gives a similar account of a ceremony that was practiced among the Conibos of the Rio Ucalayi of Peru. He first describes the incision. Then:

> The old sorcerers rubbed some medical herbs into the bleeding parts, and after a while introduced an artificial penis, made of clay, into the vagina of the maiden, the thing being exactly the same size as the penis of the man betrothed to her. Thereafter she was considered properly prepared to marry, and was given over to her future husband.[28]

Again, the master is assured of a snug and pleasurable fit. The fact that "women did it—and still do it—to women" must be seen in this context. The idea that such procedures, or any part of them, could be woman-originated is only thinkable in the mind-set of phallocracy, for it is, in fact, unthinkable.[29] The use of women to do the dirty work can make it appear thinkable only to those who

---

*In its origin, the term *castrate* is akin to the Sanskrit *śasati,* meaning, "he cuts to pieces." This describes precisely what is done to women's bodies/minds/spirits under patriarchy: they are divided and fragmented into disconnected pieces.

do not wish to see. Yet this use of women does effectively blunt the power of sisterhood, having first blocked the power of the Self.

Most horrifying is the fact that mothers insist that this mutilation be done to their own daughters. Frequently it is the mother who performs the brutal operation. Among the Somalis, for example, the mother does the excising, slicing, and final infibulation according to the time-honored rules. She does this in such a way as to leave the tiniest opening possible. Her "honor" depends upon making this as small as possible, because the smaller this artificial aperture is, the higher the value of the girl.[30]

An indication of the strength of the stranglehold which tradition has upon the mother-daughter relationship is the fact that some women who by academic and professional standards would be considered educated also insist upon excision. The case is cited of a young Egyptian woman physician who was expecting a baby and was asked by a Danish scholar, Henny Harald Hansen, about the reasons for these mutilations. She informed him that "if the child she was expecting should be a girl she would circumcise her herself." The young woman gave several reasons. The first was religious: she was a muslim. The second was cosmetic: she wanted "to remove something disfiguring, ugly and repulsive." Third, the girl should be protected from sexual stimulation through the clitoris. The fourth reason was tradition. "The young doctor argued in support of her intention to respect tradition that the majority of husbands preferred their wives to be circumcised."[31] The fact that this woman was a physician might at first seem startling. Yet further reflection suggests that there is not such inconsistency as one might suppose, particularly in view of the facts of gynecological mutilation in present-day America, which will be discussed later in this Passage.

V

The fifth component of the syndrome, compulsive orderliness which misfocuses attention away from the fact of evil, is manifested even in the most primitive environment. Although the "surgical instrument" may be as crude as broken glass or a kitchen knife, the performance is itself highly ritualized. The "ceremony" in the Sudan is described by Montagu as "preceded with food and merriment."[32] Certain women are chosen to perform the rite. Often it is a relative who does the excising. The procedures differ among different tribes, but they always follow certain rules that have been handed down, which constitute "the way it has always been done." Thus, among the Nandi in Africa, there is a two-part horror show. The first day, stinging nettles are applied to the clitoris, so that it swells and becomes unimaginably large. The second day, an old woman chars it off with glowing coals. The mutilated girl is then sent to a convalescent hut, having been converted into property for her husband.[33] Another manifestation of the ritualized orderliness is the age of the victim: The mutilating rite takes place at different ages in different tribes, but the point is that each has its prescribed age, which often does not correspond to the individual girl's onset of puberty. It is claimed that some Arabs do it several weeks after birth, that the Somalis fix the age of mutilation at 3–4 years, that in southern Egypt it is done at 9–10 years, that in Abyssinia it is at 8 years or else 80 days after birth. Among the Malinkes and Bambaras the age is 12–15 years.[34] All of this indicates that the order imposed is the contrived order of ritual, having nothing to do with the physiological stage of development.

There are various ritual prescriptions in various places, but the obsessive repetitiveness and fixation upon minute details are clearly present. Thus, van Gennep describes some details of the ritual among the Masai of Tanganyika:

> The rites for the girls differ [from the boys'] in the following respects: several are excised at a time; their heads are shaved; they remain at home until scar tissue forms on the wound; they adorn their heads with grasses, among which they place an ostrich feather, and smear their faces with white clay; all of the women of the kraal eat a communal meal; and the marriage takes place as soon as the fiancé is able to pay what he owes on the dowry.[35]

Other tribes have other versions of this sado-ritual.[36] There are rules for the stages in the mutilation process, rules about festivity, about timing, about dress and "cosmetics," about seclusion, about relation of the maiming to marriage. These distract the attention of the participants (and of foreign specialists such as anthropologists) from the victimized women's physical agony, mutilation, life-long deprivation, deformity, pain, and premature death from complications.

VI

The sado-ritual of excision and infibulation bestows acceptability upon gynocidal behavior—even to the extent of making it normative. This is illustrated in the precept of the president of Kenya, Jomo Kenyatta, that "no proper Gikuyu would dream of marrying a girl who has not been circumcised," since this operation "is regarded as the *conditio sine qua non* for the whole teaching of tribal law, religion, and morality."[37] With these words, one chief in the Higher Order of phallocratic morality dictates its chief lesson: that women should suffer. Typically, the justification for the atrocious ritual under the reign of phallic morality involves a reversal in which the unnatural becomes normative. Only a mutilated woman is considered 100 percent feminine.* By removal of her specifically *female*-identified organ, which is not necessary for the male's pleasure or for reproductive servitude, she "becomes a woman." At first the reversal might seem astonishing, if one hears the term *woman* as representing a state of natural integrity. But if we understand this term to refer to an embodiment of the feminine, which is a construct of phallocracy, then the meaning of the expression becomes clear.†

In *La Cité magique,* Jacques Lantier reports a conversation about clitoridectomy with a tribal chief and magician. The latter illustrates the way in which atrocious, sadistic behavior has come to be regarded as normative. According to this sage:

> [God] has given the clitoris to the woman so that she can use it before marriage in order to experience the pleasure of love while still remaining pure. . . .
>
> The clitoris of very little girls is not cut off because they use it for masturbating. The clitoris of girls is sliced off when they are judged ready for procreation and marriage. When it has been removed, they no longer masturbate. This is a great hardship to them. Then all desire is transferred to the interior. Thus they then attempt to get married promptly. Once married, instead of experiencing dispersed and feeble sensations, they concentrate all [desire] in one place, and the couples experience much happiness, which is normal.[38]

---

*It is interesting to compare these attempts to feminize women with the feminization of male-to-constructed-female transsexuals. The latter, who consider themselves to be "women" (referring to "other" women as "native women") undergo operations which remove the testicles and penis and give them artificial vaginas, but no clitoris. Both of these mutilating attempts at feminization receive a large amount of legitimation by phallocracy. See Janice Raymond, *The Transsexual Empire: The Making of the She-Male* (Boston: Beacon Press, 1979).

†It may be helpful in this connection to recall Simone de Beauvoir's famous axiom: "One is not born, but rather becomes a woman." (*The Second Sex,* trans. and ed. by H. M. Parshley [New York: Vintage, 1974, p. 301). In this book of course, I use the term *women* to refer to females generally and reserve the term *feminine* to connote the male-created construct/stereotype. However, *woman* is often used by others to refer to the androcratically constructed (destroyed) female, who is, of course, considered "natural." There is, for example, the "total woman" of Marabel Morgan, and the "true woman" of Pope Pius XII and Pope Paul VI.

So much for brutish and monodimensional male wisdom and romance, the purpose of which is to negate the complexity of female experience. It is perfectly obvious who "god" is in this delightful tale (which has a number of variants). The legitimating myth not only erases pain and mutilation, but turns it all into the right, good, and fit. It is god's (man's) plan. Even the fact that "they feel deprived" is made to seem a marvelous prelude for the "great happiness" to come. By now we are in a position to guess the nature of this "happiness."

But it is not necessary to guess. Dr. G. Pieters, a gynecologist who worked in a hospital in Somalia (1966–1968) explains that defibulation–the opening of the scar of the infibulated girl–is performed with a knife when she is married. The same author says that intercourse takes place immediately and it must be frequent during the first weeks of marriage, because otherwise the wound might close again.[39] The deception inherent in the magician's tale of female sexuality and marital bliss boggles the mind. Yet we should not fall into the trap of allowing ourselves to think that such religious/ mythic legitimation is entirely foreign to "our" Western society. As Fran Hosken points out, the medical profession and especially Freud in the West "are enthralled by the same male-created misconception: that of vaginal orgasm."[40] This is the universal test of the "normal" woman. Moreover, the logical acting out of this misconception, brutal and unnecessary gynecological surgery, including clitoridectomies, is not unknown in nineteenth- and twentieth-century American medicine (a point to be discussed in Chapter Seven).

As I have shown in analyzing other ritual atrocities, the acceptability and normative character of the monstrous rite becomes so ingrained that it continues even after the circumstances of its original performance appear to have changed drastically. Thus "practical *suttee*," as we have seen, has continued to take place in India for more than a century after it was legally abolished. In the case of African female genital mutilation, in some countries the practice has moved from the arena of old women with broken bottles and kitchen knives in the forest to the sterile rooms of modern hospitals. This is the case in the Sudan, in Egypt, and throughout Somalia–but only, of course, for a small number of girls. According to Dr. Pieters, the wealthy do not use the hospitals, but have private surgeons. It does not require great imagination to realize that the medical profession, rather than rejecting these horrors, has even made a specialization out of them, to its own economic benefit.

Dr. Pieters, whose article I have cited above, observed these operations in a hospital of the European Common Market in Mogadishu, the capital of Somalia. It is clear that no religious rituals (in the commonly accepted sense of the term *religious*) are involved in the hospitals, although moslem leaders and parents oppose stopping the atrocity. What has happened is that the barbarous rites of religion have been replaced (for these "privileged" few) by the barbarous rites of modern medicine. In the latter, male nurses wear surgical gloves and gowns, and use disinfectants, (insufficient) local anesthetic, surgical scissors (for cutting off the labia minora and excising the clitoris), catgut (for suturing), silk (for sewing), and sometimes penicillin.[41] As in other parts of the world, refined, "white" destruction by the practice of "medicine" perpetuates and "purifies" the religious rituals of gynocide.

VII

Finally, we find the legitimation of the sado-ritual by the last rites of "objective" scholarship. Thus, for example, Felix Bryk, in a book entitled *Dark Rapture: The Sex Life of the African Negro,* introduces his telling description of female genital mutilation with a maze of deceptive expressions and manifestations of crass indifference. Alluding to the "gallant fight" being put up by missionaries to stop this "custom," he writes:

> It is hoped that the barbaric custom, *which is no less cruel than that of circumcision of the male*[!] may be gradually abolished through education and punishment. Personally I do not believe that punishment and education will do any real good in this instance because the custom is primarily practiced for erotic reasons [emphasis mine].[42]

Hags may well ask: "*Whose* erotic reasons?" The author's use of the expression "no less cruel" can be recognized as totally mendacious, when one compares excision and infibulation to the relatively minor operation of male circumcision. Had he written that male circumcision is "no less cruel" than female mutilation, this simply would have been a blatant lie. Instead, he performs a semantic trick, giving an illusion of justice or even of generosity toward the female sex in his assessment of the situation. Given the fact that this author himself presents a horrifying description of excision among the Nandi, it might seem astonishing that he can erase its reality in the same book. However, we have encountered this sort of gross contradiction in works of re-search concerning *suttee* and footbinding. The use of sensational materials, combined with erasure/denial of their significance, is a familiar pattern in patriarchal scholarship.

Bryk, who at the end of his foreword irrelevantly informs us that he is writing on Mount Elgon, "2,350 meters above sea level," is so high above the subject of his book, apparently, that he can give the detached opinion that "punishment and education" will not "do any real good"–a perspective which the physically and mentally mutilated women are in no position to refute. It is from this lofty perspective that he is able to interpret the Nandi bride's wedding night plea, "Let me be!" This comes, Bryk explains, "more out of passion than dread."[43] A few lines down we read a description of the scene to which she protests "more out of passion than dread":

> During the first night, among the Nandi, some of his friends wait to hold her down in case she refuses to obey her husband. If the hymen happens to be too tough for ordinary defloration, the husband pierces it with a knife *without letting her know* [emphasis mine].

Despite his bird-like perspective when writing the book on Mount Elgon, this scholar, in doing his re-search, was not above endangering the life of one of these young victims, whom he describes as "the poor, mutilated child." He writes:

> I recall how once, *driven by curiosity,* I crossed the door of the sacred sanctuary [where the recently circumcised girl was confined], in spite of all restrictions, at a time when no woman was around [emphasis mine].[44]

In that society, his seeing the child was a violation of taboo, and could have resulted in the girl's death–a fact of which he was aware.

It is important to note Bryk's views on sex differences and on race. One can imagine him looking down upon the earth from Mount Elgon with his telescope as he utters the following bit of wisdom about "woman" and "man":

> Woman is forever woman, and man everywhere man; independently of race or color of skin–white, black, yellow, or copper-red; whether ugly or beautiful; despite youth or age; beyond good and evil.[45]

The universality of the patriarchal role-defined society is thus described and legitimized. It is "beyond good and evil." On the next page we read about racial differences:

> They [Blacks] like to lie–particularly to the whites–just as children do, because, like children, they cannot comprehend the moral necessity for truthfulness.[46]

It is obvious, then, that Blacks are different from the author, who is a paragon of truthfulness. Women are also "forever" different from him, but all women of all colors are alike. It would be helpful if women of all races could hear this message of patriarchy with the deep understanding/hearing of the labyrinthine inner ear, for it describes succinctly the sexual caste system, pointing to its fundamentally same view of all women.

There is a danger presented by such unabashedly racist books that the underlying, universal misogyny will go unnoticed. Haggard criticism should enable women who have been intimidated by labels of "racism" to become sisters to these women of Africa— naming the crimes against them and speaking on their behalf— seeing through the reversal that is meant to entrap us all. It is truly *racist* to keep silent in the face of these atrocities, merely "studying" them, speaking and writing deceptively about them, applying different (male-created) standards to them, failing to see and name the connections among them, Beyond racism is sisterhood, *naming* the crimes against women without paying mindless respect to the "social fabric" of the various androcratic societies, including the one in which we find our Selves imprisoned.

Among the most mystifying practitioners of sado-ritual scholarship legitimating female genital mutilation are "noted" anthropologists, for example Arnold van Gennep. First of all, the subject is erased in the index, having been lumped together with male circumcision under the single entry, *circumcision*. If one looks up this topic, one finds excision of the clitoris discussed incidentally. The following statement sums up the author's views:

> The length of the clitoris varies with individuals and races. In certain cases, the object of the excision may be to remove the appendage by which *the female resembles the male* (a view which is *correct* from an anatomical point of view), and the operation is nothing more than a rite of sexual differentiation on the *same order* as the first (ritual) assigning of *dress, instruments, or tools* proper to each sex [emphases mine].[47]

It might seem to require a special talent to assemble this much misinformation/deception in one brief footnote. In what sense is the idea that the clitoris is an "appendage" by which the female "resembles" the male "correct"? According to Merriam-Webster, the term *resemble* means: to be like or similar to. Leaving aside the fact that many women would consider this not only absurd but insulting, one might ask what the author could possibly have in mind in this "anatomical point of view." Would he agree that cutting off the penis is "nothing more" than a rite on the same order as "assigning of dress," et cetera? One can safely assume that he would not, and this throws some light on the implications of his use of the term *resembles* in this context. Van Gennep apparently sees the clitoris precisely *not* from an "anatomical" perspective, but for what it symbolizes/signifies: the potential in females for the independence, power, and prerogatives which are preserved exclusively for males by all the phallocratic "rites of sexual differentiation." For this reason he can minimize and erase the physical reality of female pain and mutilation.

We should not be surprised to read on the very next page not only the familiar remark that excision will "*diminish* sexual excitability," but also his inclusion of the clitoris among the organs which "because of their histological constitution, undergo all sorts of treatment without harming an individual's *life* or *activity* [emphases mine]."[48] The other organs which van Gennep compares to the clitoris are the ear and nose, but of course the "treatment" is not at all comparable. Our scholar has in mind such operations as "cutting off the ear lobe" or perforating it. He is of course not discussing the total removal of both ears or slicing off the nose, which would be comparable to total removal of the clitoris. Finally, the author fails to mention infibulation, which is the most horrifying part of female genital mutilation. This erasure completes his contribution to the vast body of ignorance about his subject, "the rites of passage."

The freudian psychoanalyst, Marie Bonaparte, also muddies matters in her famous "Notes on Excision" in her book, *Female Sexuality*. In this academic treatise she takes issue with Bryk's theory that "the Nandi males, in this way, seek to maximally feminize their females by doing away with this penile vestige, the clitoris, which, he adds, must result in encouraging the transfer of orgastic sensitivity from the girl's infantile erotogenic zone, the clitoris, to the adult erotogenic zone of the woman, which must necessarily be the vagina at puberty."[49] Bonaparte concludes that the Nandi men may have had such a wish, but that even such cruel excision would not achieve this aim. To support her response she cites cases of excised women who continued to refuse to "internalize [their] sexuality." Although she recognizes the cruelty of excision, Bonaparte's attitude toward these women is detached; she "studies" them.

Her analysis, moreover, is couched in the falsifying jargon and framework of freudian/fraudian theory, which assumes the reality of the "vaginal orgasm." Her language contains absurd phrases, such as "physical *intimidation* of the girl's sexuality by this cruel excision... [emphasis mine]."[50] The term *intimidation* is hardly accurate in this context. More freudian than Freud, Bonaparte lacks not only social perspective but the sensitivity and imagination to even begin to relate to the situation of these women outside the doctrinaire freudian framework. Thus she declares in passing that the "mutilations are delegated to the old women who doubtless enjoy thus revenging their age on the young."[51] Such terms as *doubtless, enjoy,* and *revenging* reflect the male-identified ignorance/arrogance of father Freud's acolyte and disciple. To say the least, they are not based upon evidence. Bonaparte's poverty of imagination about the feelings of other women is damning evidence of the mind mutilation of women in phallocracy.

Mircea Eliade also contributes generously to the body of ignorance in his book, *Rites and Symbols of Initiation,* which has a section entitled "Initiation of Girls." He is perfectly silent about genital mutilation, making no reference either to excision or to infibulation. He does note that "female initiatory rites—at least so far as they are known to us—are less dramatic than the rites for boys."[52] If we take the term *dramatic* to mean "showy," this is probably true. There is generally more ceremony surrounding the circumcision of a boy—more sound and fury. In the case of millions of mutilated girls, there is less "show" and far more reality in the initiation rites— horrible reality. This Eliade chooses to ignore (genuine ignorance in this case would seem to be impossible). He mentions that girls are "isolated" at menstruation and refers to dietary taboos. Focusing upon some Australian tribes, he points out signs which mark the *end* of female initiation, such as tattooing and blackening of the teeth. He writes: "The essential rite, then, is the solemn exhibition of the girl to the entire community."[53] Since this is written as a general statement, giving the impression that it applies generally to the initiation of girls in "ancient" stages of culture, it is essentially deceptive (skipping over excision and infibulation), erasing by its deceptiveness the essential patriarchal rite: dismemberment of female be-ing.

Just as Eliade fails to convey the physical/psychological mutilation which is the sado-ritual of "initiation of girls" into androcracy, so also he fails to see/name the ecstatic reality which is initiation and process in gynocentric be-ing. Yet, oddly and obtusely, he points to some clues. Thus on the symbolic level he gives information whose Background meaning must be lost on most of his readers, as it is on himself. He writes of the periods of seclusion which are part of girls' puberty rites, and remarks that they often learn such skills as spinning and weaving. Discussing the symbolism of these crafts, he says:

> The moon "spins" Time and "weaves" human lives. The Goddesses of Destiny are spinners. We detect an occult connection

between the conception of the periodical creations of the world (a conception derived from a lunar mythology) and the ideas of Time and Destiny, on the one hand, and on the other, nocturnal work, women's work, which has to be performed far from the light of the sun and almost in secret. In some cultures, after the seclusion of the girls is ended they continue to meet in some old woman's house to spin together.[54]

Spinsters reading such works of re-search can search and find lost threads of connectedness. Thus when Eliade goes on to say that "spinning is a perilous craft," which can be carried on only in special houses during particular periods and until certain hours, we hear the meaning of this peril in the deep recesses of the labyrinthine inner ear. And when he says that "in some parts of the world spinning has been given up, and even completely forgotten, because of its magical peril," we recognize the peril as our own, and know that we have neither given up nor forgotten. Indeed, in the face of the atrocities associated with phallocratic female initiation into femininity, we must respond not only with exposé. Nor is feminist analysis enough. Most importantly, we must live through the genuine initiation, which is not into femininity but into Self-centering female integrity. This means exorcising the atrocities not only by seeing/naming/acting against them, but also by refusing to remain fixated upon them, and by exercising our new and ancient craft of spinning. This is the initiation of Spinsters, our heritage and new beginning.

The words of Eliade convey something of this woman-centered quality of spinning:

In some places—Japan, for example—we still find the mythological memory of a permanent tension, and even conflict, between the groups of young spinning girls and the men's secret societies. At night the men and their Gods attack the spinning girls and destroy not only their work, but also their shuttles and weaving apparatus.[55]

The members of "the men's secret societies" throughout patriarchy have never ceased to fear and envy the gynaesthetic gift for Spinning.*...

*In the summer of 1976 I saw a living confirmation of this "mythological memory of a permanent tension" at a folklore festival in Heraklion, Crete. The theme of one of the folk dances was the theft of spindles from a group of young girls by some invasive "playful" males after which the latter danced around with these stolen spindles/sticks held between their legs in the position of erect penises.

NOTES

1. Theologians such as Paul Tillich have noted that while there may in some sense be "sins," in a more original sense there is Sin, which is a state. However, Tillich and other theologians of patriarchy are not in a position to name this State accurately. This is demonstrated in Paul Tillich's *Systematic Theology,* 3 vols. (Chicago: University of Chicago Press, 1951–63), Vol. II, pp. 44–47.

2. See *Women's International Network News,* ed. by Fran P. Hosken (187 Grant Street, Lexington, Mass. 02173), Vol. 1, No. 3 (June 1975), Vol. 1, No. 4 (October 1975), Vol. 2, No. 1 (January 1976), Vol. 2, No. 2 (spring 1976), Vol. 2, No. 3 (summer 1976). In the last-mentioned issue, Hosken gives an extensive bibliography. The reader is advised to consult *WIN News* for up-to-date information.

3. See Hosken, *WIN News,* Vol. 2, No. 1 (January 1976), p. 30. See also J. A. Verzin, M.D., "Sequelae of Female Circumcision," *Tropical Doctor,* October 1975, p. 163. I have cited only the first three of the types of circumcision described by Verzin. He lists a fourth type, which he believes is practiced only among the Ditta Pitta tribes in Australia: "*Type IV: Introcision.* This is the cutting into the vagina or splitting of the perineum, either digitally or by means of a sharp instrument, and is the severest form of female circumcision." Verzin maintains that Type III (Pharaonic circumcision) is practiced throughout the Sudan, Ethiopia, and Somaliland.

4. Jacques Lantier, *La Cité magique et magie en afrique noire* (Paris: Librairie Arthème Fayard, 1972), p. 279.

5. Ibid., pp. 279–80. Lantier describes marriage among the Somali. When the bride goes to her husband's house he takes off her clothes and beats her until the blood flows. Since he cannot "deflower" her (that is, break the scar) with his penis, he uses a knife. Before using the knife, he forces a piece of wood, "specially tailored," into the vaginal orifice—a precaution designed to protect the perineum, in order not to cause a fistula on the rectum. Then he plunges in the knife before having intercourse with her. There is more:

    "Selon la tradition, le mari doit avoir durant huit jours des rapports réiterés et prolongés. Ce 'travail' a pour objet de 'fabriquer' un vestibule en empèchant la cicatrice de se refermer. Pendant ces huit jours, la femme reste étendue et bouge le moins possible afin de tenir la plaie béante. Au lendemain de la nuit des noces, le mari fixe sur son épaule son poignard ensanglanté; il va faire des visites afin de recueillir l'admiration générale. Cette 'formalité' remplie, il rentre aussitôt chez lui reprendre son ouvrage."

    Another source on infibulation and defibulation is Eugenio Lenzi, "Damage Caused by Infibulation and Infertility," *Acta Europaea Fertilitatis,* Vol. 2, No. 47 (1970), pp. 47–58. Asim Zaki Mustafa, in his article, "Female Circumcision and Infibulation in the Sudan," *Journal of Obstetrics and Gynaecology of the British Commonwealth,* Vol. 73, pp. 302–6, discusses infibulation in the Sudan, with an emphasis upon resultant complications. He imparts the interesting information that an individual named Tiggani, who was the only psychiatrist in the Sudan for several years, in a personal communication in 1965 conveyed his opinion that circumcision provides a "happy social occasion" for Sudanese women who normally enjoy little in the way of entertainment. This psychiatrist maintains that "had it been unpleasant or unacceptable it would have perished long ago." Mustafa also informs us: "Rectal intercourse not infrequently takes place in error because the vaginal introitus has been obliterated" (p. 305). See also M. F. Ashley Montagu, "Infibulation and Defibulation in the Old and New Worlds," *American Anthropologist,* n.s. 47 (1945), pp. 464–67: Allan Worsley, "Infibulation and Female Circumcision: A Study of a Little-Known Custom," *Journal of Obstetrics and Gynaecology of the British Empire,* Vol. 45 (1938) pp. 686–91.

6. See Hosken, *WIN News,* Vol. 2, No. 1 (January 1976), p. 36. See also Verzin, "Sequelae of Female Circumcision"; Mustafa, "Female Circumcision"; Lenzi, "Damage Caused by Infibulation." See also the article (unsigned), "Excision in Africa," *ISIS International Bulletin,* No. 2 (October 1976), pp. 12–15. ISIS is a collective of women providing an information and communication service for the women's movement internationally. The address in Switzerland is Case Postale 301, 1227, Carouge, Switzerland. Money orders can be sent to this address. Subscriptions for individual women and women's groups are $10.00; for libraries and other institutions, $20.00.

7. See Hosken, *WIN News,* Vol. 1, No. 3 (June 1975), p. 41.

8. Hosken, *WIN News,* Vol. 2, No. 1 (January 1976), p. 30.

9. Jomo Kenyatta, *Facing Mount Kenya: The Tribal Life of the Gikuyu,* with an introduction by B. Malinowski (New York: Vintage, 1965), p. 125 ff. In his introduction, the prestigious scholar Malinowski writes: "As a first-hand account of a representative African culture, as an invaluable document in the principles underlying culture-contact and change; last, not least, as a personal statement of the new outlook of a progressive African, this book will rank as a pioneering achievement of outstanding merit."

10. Benoîte Groult, *Ainsi soit-elle* (Paris: Bernard Grasset, 1975), p. 96. The entire fourth chapter of this book, entitled "La Haine du C.," pp. 93–118, is worth reading. Since the author does not document her work, however, the Searcher will want to consult also more primary sources, such as those indicated in these notes.

11. "Excision in Africa," *ISIS,* p. 14. See Lenzi, "Damage Caused by Infibulation," p. 55; Worsley, "Infibulation and Female Circumcision," p. 688. Hosken in "Genital Mutilation of Females in Africa: Summary/Facts," a fact sheet available from *WIN News,* points out that in the Sudan, where most of the women, including city-dwellers, are infibulated, the ceremony is called *tahur,* which means "cleansing."

12. G. Pieters, "Gynécologie au pays des femmes cousues," *Acta Chirurgica Belgica,* No. 3 (May 1972), p. 180. This article, on gynecology "in the country of the sewn women," is extremely valuable.

13. "Excision in Africa," *ISIS,* pp. 12–14.

14. Ibid., p. 12.

15. See Verzin, "Sequelae of Female Circumcision," in which he maintains that "circumcision" is done not only throughout Africa, but in Brazil,

Eastern Mexico, Peru, several Asian countries, Australia, and, in Europe, among the Skopsi, a christian Russian sect, to ensure "perpetual virginity." Another strong argument for wide geographical distribution is given by Dr. Ahmed Abu-El-Futuh Shandall, in his article "Circumcision and Infibulation of Females," in *Sudan Medical Journal,* Vol. 5, No. 4 (1967), pp. 180–81. See also Ben R. Huelsman, "An Anthropological View of Clitoral and Other Female Genital Mutilations," in *The Clitoris,* ed. by Thomas P. Lowry, M.D., and Thea Snyder Lowry, M.A. (St. Louis, Mo.: Warren H. Green, 1976), p. 121.

16. Hosken, *WIN News,* Vol. 2, No. 1 (January 1976), p. 30.

17. Ibid., p. 32.

18. Montagu, "Infibulation and Defibulation," pp. 464–67.

19. M. F. Ashley Montagu, "Ritual Mutilation among Primitive Peoples," *Ciba Symposia,* Vol. 8, No. 7 (October 1946) pp. 421–36.

20. Huelsman, "An Anthropological View," p. 123.

21. Ibid., p. 124.

22. Shandall. "Circumcision and Infibulation," pp. 178–79.

23. Groult, *Ainsi soit-elle,* p. 94.

24. Montagu, "Ritual Mutilation," p. 434.

25. See Huelsman, "An Anthropological View," p. 121.

26. Diana E. H. Russell and Nicole Van de Ven, eds., *The Proceedings of the International Tribunal on Crimes Against Women* (Millbrae, Calif.: Les Femmes, 1976), p. 151.

27. Montagu. "Infibulation and Defibulation," pp. 465–66.

28. Ibid., p. 466.

29. There are other details of the infibulated woman's life that support the evidence concerning who is behind the scenes controlling the gynocidal set-up. Thus Pieters points to the fact that in some parts of Arabia salt is stuffed into the vagina after childbirth in order to shrink the orifice so that intercourse will be more pleasurable for the husband. A common result of this is vaginal stenosis. See Pieters, "Gynécologie au pays," p. 189. Pieters refers to B. M. L. Underhill, "Salt Induced Vaginal Stenosis in Arabia," *Journal of Obstetrics and Gynaecology of the British Commonwealth,* 1963, Vol. 71, No. 293.

30. Lantier, *La Cité magique,* p. 278: "La mère achève son intervention en veillant à ménager un orifice très étroit, destiné a ne laisser passer que les urines el les menstrues. Il y va de son honneur que le trou soit le plus petit possible, car, chez les Somali, plus le passage artificiel est étroit et plus la femme est considerée."

31. Henny Harald Hansen, "Clitoridectomy: Female Circumcision in Egypt," *Folk,* Vol. 14–15 (1972/73), p. 18.

32. Montagu, "Infibulation and Defibulation," p. 465.

33. Felix Bryk, *Dark Rapture: The Sex-Life of the African Negro,* English version by Dr. Arthur J. Norton (New York: Walden Publications, 1939), pp. 89–90.

34. Arnold van Gennep, *The Rites of Passage,* trans. by Monika B. Vizedom and Gabrielle L. Caffee (Chicago: University of Chicago Press, 1960), p. 71.

35. Ibid., p. 86.
36. Ibid., p. 87.
37. Kenyatta, *Facing Mount Kenya,* pp. 127–28. On page 130, Kenyatta expounds upon his thesis as follows: "For years there has been much criticism and agitation against *irua* [genital mutilation] of girls by certain misinformed missionary societies in East Africa, who see only the surgical side of the *irua,* and, without investigating the psychological importance attached to this custom by the Gikuyu, these missionaries draw their conclusion that the *irua* of girls is nothing but a barbarous practice and, as such, should be abolished by law.

"On the other hand, the Gikuyu look upon these religious fanatics with great suspicion.... The abolition of *irua* will destroy the tribal symbol which identifies the age-groups, and prevent the Gikuyu from perpetuating that spirit of collectivism and national solidarity which they have been able to maintain from time immemorial."
38. Lantier, *La Cité magique,* pp. 271–72: "(Dieu) a donné le clitoris à la femme pour qu'èlle puisse l'utiliser avant le mariage afin d'éprouver le plaisir de l'amour tout en restant pure....

"On ne tranche pas le clitoris des toutes petites filles puisqu'il leur sert à se masturber. On tranche celui des jeunes filles que l'on juge disposées à la procréation et au mariage. Quand on leur a enlevé le clitoris, elles ne se masturbent plus. Cela les prive beaucoup. Alors tout le désir se porte vers l'intérieur. Elles cherchent donc à se marier promptement. Une fois mariées, au lieu d'éprouver des sensations dispersées persées et faibles, elles concentrent tout au même endroit et les couples connaissent beaucoup de bonheur, ce qui est normal."
39. Pieters, "Gynécologie au pays," pp. 182–83.
40. Hosken, *WIN News,* Vol. 2. No. 1 (January 1976), p. 35.
41. Pieters, "Gynécologie au pays." pp. 180–81.
42. Bryk, *Dark Rapture,* pp. 87–88.
43. Ibid., p. 100.
44. Ibid., p. 90.
45. Ibid., p. 27.
46. Ibid., p. 28.
47. Van Gennep, *The Rites of Passage,* p. 72, note 2.
48. Ibid., p. 73.
49. Marie Bonaparte, *Female Sexuality* (New York: International Universities Press, 1953), p. 191.
50. Ibid., p. 204.
51. Ibid., p. 207.
52. Mircea Eliade, *Rites and Symbols of Initiation: The Mysteries of Birth and Rebirth,* trans. by Willard R. Trask (New York: Harper Torchbooks, 1965), p. 42.
53. Ibid., p. 43.
54. Ibid., pp. 45–46.
55. Ibid., p. 46.

REFLECTING ON MEANING

1. This chapter from Mary Daly's *Gyn/Ecology* describes ritual female genital mutilation as one manifestation of the "Sado-Ritual Syndrome" which "teaches women never to forget to murder their own divinity." What does she mean by this? Why has there been a worldwide "conspiracy of silence" about this practice?

2. Daly discusses several components of the "Sado-Ritual Syndrome": the notion of purity, the erasure of male responsibility, its widespread practice, and the "active" role of women. How does her discussion of these components in reference to female genital mutilation support her argument that it is also "deeply connected with atrocities perpetrated against women in 'advanced' societies"? Do you accept this argument? To what atrocities against women in advanced societies might she be referring?

3. Daly proposes that this ritual is legitimated by religion and myth. What arguments does she use to support this assertion? Also, she suggests that both "*objective* scholarship" and an "underlying, universal misogyny" reinforce the acceptance of this practice. What evidence does Daly use to support these statements?

4. Daly has been accused of racism and imperialism for her critiques of Indian *suttee* (widow burning), Chinese footbinding, African genital mutilation, European witchburnings, and American gynecology. What evidence does she offer to counter these accusations? Does she present a compelling argument? What right does an American feminist have to critique another culture's ritualized practice?

EXPLORING RHETORICAL STRATEGIES

1. Daly asks a number of questions throughout this piece and then seeks to answer them. How effectively does she answer her own questions?

2. Daly utilizes a rhetorical strategy of reappropriating negative terms such as *Hags* and *Spinsters* to make her argument. Why does she use these terms? What effect does her use of these words have on your understanding of her essay?

3. This essay is divided into a number of sections, each explaining how female genital mutilation reveals components of the Sado-Ritual Syndrome. How does this organization contribute to the essay's overall effectiveness? Do the graphic descriptions of the prac-

tice of female genital mutilation and its aftereffects enhance Daly's argument? What is your emotional response to this essay?

Here Come the Brides

JOHN KRICH

The following excerpts are from a longer essay originally printed in Mother Jones *in 1986. Here, John Krich discusses the mail-order bride business and includes interviews with American husbands and their Asian wives.*

The condominiums come in mirror images, but not the occupants. On the front door of one stucco chalet hangs a Chinese character made of brass. Call it cross-cultural mistletoe for the couple living inside, another product of a growing American phenomenon. The husband turns out to be a small-town white kid come to the big city, prematurely middle-aged, middlebrow in his conspicuous collections of carvings and trophies, middle management, though never quite as managerial as he'd like, flashing a salesman's charm that readily gives way to anger. The wife is young, comely, and Asian: wearing house sandals but groomed for a party, a good listener whose skills have been severely taxed, uncomfortable with her new language but comforted by her new surroundings, covering her suspicion with drowsiness, a bit sunken along with the living room. As she offers tea and the homemade egg rolls called *lumpia,* nurses her newborn, and beams at the wedding album, it is hard to imagine that she was plucked from a row of snapshots in a mail-order catalog. Or that this marriage wasn't arranged in heaven, but in Hawaii—by an introduction service called Cherry Blossoms.

Then come the corrections in one another's version of events, made most gingerly; the nervous jokes about age difference; the curious blanks drawn when trying to remember the names of close in-laws; the references to unspecified conflicts and secret diaries where "he write that he travel looking for other girls to marry after me"; the questions that the wife pretends she can't grasp until she retreats into the "no comment" of a nap, causing the whispered confessions—which come whenever she "lets me out of her sight"—about how "it's been no picnic," about the bitching, the sulking, the misunderstandings.

And there's that troublesome word *love,* which is either ac-tively disdained—in favor of talk about "trade-offs" or "liabilities and assets"—or flashed continually, like an expensive Javanese mask. Love is blind, as they say—especially in this context, where there's so much to be blind about. The longer they tell their story, the more this couple reveals the forces rending them apart, and the fears that made them cleave together. Cozy as it all seems, the world beyond keeps swirling through this condo. Settled on their white ottoman, they remain a man and woman in flight—like so many who have chosen the path of these postal courtships.

The men: *"The woman I yearn to spend my life with does not seem to reside in North America."*

The women: *"I believe the god will let us to be together one day. Is that a dream? I love only American music."*

That world is not only getting smaller; it's getting lonelier. Never has it been easier for nations to mingle, and never have ex-pectations been greater for one culture to provide what the other lacks. Economic interdependencies give way to psychic ones: those with power seek those with beauty, those with money seek those with heart. It's not surprising then that the delivery of Asian brides to mostly white American grooms has, within the last five years, become a multimillion-dollar-a-year industry. Since there's a perceived shortage of U.S. homemakers willing to shoulder tradi-tional matrimonial tasks, some entrepreneurs are going abroad—where the labor can be bought cheaper and the quality control kept more rigid. Imperialists of the heart, these men strike out for poorer lands in search of the raw materials necessary to the manu-facture of their fantasies. If emotional fulfillment is as vital to U.S. national security as South African chrome, then it must be secured in regular shipments. Love itself has become the ultimate con-sumer good, and, as with so many others, an increasing number of shoppers are no longer buying American.

The catalogs: *"Congratulations! You have taken the first step to-wards discovering an eternal treasure! For many discerning men, there can be no other choice than a Lady of the Orient. These women possess wit, charm and grace unmatched anywhere in the world. [They] are faithful and devoted to their husbands.... When it comes to sex, they are not de-monstrative; however, they are uninhibited [and] believe sex is healthy. She wakes up in the morning with a smile on her face and she does wake up in the morning! You have heard the phrase 'A Woman of the 80s.' We rec-ommend a Woman for all time.* An Asian Woman!"

Although no one has kept exact figures, it's a safe bet that 10,000 marriages have resulted from these air-mail relationships over the past 12 years. Most of the pen pal businesses are crude cop-ies of the formula established by Cherry Blossoms, which, under the direction of Harvard Ph.D. and ex-hippie John Broussard, has become the highest-volume matchmaking shop. Begun at the whimsical request of a single male in 1974, Cherry Blossoms has now expanded to publishing three separate, bimonthly directories, running up to 48 pages, featuring Philippine "Island Blossoms," Asian women in general, and miscellaneous hopefuls from Peru to Yugoslavia. The services' fees run from $5 to $10 dollars for an introductory batch of a few sample addresses to $300 for all current and back issues—depending upon a variety of plans in which the subscriber may be offered "first crack" at a designated number of women. The clients also get their predilections listed in the services' register and their names placed in newspaper ads throughout the Far East.

Cherry Blossoms sends along a chatty newsletter describing women deemed less photogenic, offered at discount rates. This mimeographed sheet also alerts the men to "rotten apples": women who use their letters to solicit "samples of foreign currency" for their private collection or ask for donations for "typhoon relief."

The men: *"American girls left me really disappointed. They look like tubs of lard stuffed into Levi's. They're pushy, spoiled rotten, and they talk like sailors. They're not cooperative, but combative—and they never appreciate what you do for them. In the morning, you wonder how many guys before me? Was it the football team? Maybe it's our fault, the fault of men for repressing them for so long. But they're not psychologically together. They just don't seem to know what they want."*

Haven't we heard this somewhere before? In a curious role reversal, these last of the supermachos offer the classic complaints women have long made about men: they're confused, immature, promiscuous; they're also opinionated and materialistic. They fear commitments and neglect personal satisfactions in favor of careers. They let themselves go to seed: one disgruntled husband even suggested that all women want is "to watch TV and booze it up." Worst of all, they tend to be smarter or more successful than the men, who are left exhausted by the jostling for position entailed by the recent redefining of sexual roles.

The men: *"It's not easy when everything is up for discussion. Why don't you do this? Why don't you do that? Even my mother gives me a hard time. She wants to know why I don't cook once in a while. Now I just smile and tell her, 'I'm retired from all that.' My wife smiles too."*

Few of these men are trailer park misfits or the sort of gents who paper their bedrooms in aluminum foil. In one of the many surveys that the introduction services trot out as proof of their mainstream appeal, the statistics indicate that those who seek Asian brides are above average in education, income, and status.

These same samplings tell us that the average age at marriage for the husbands is 52; for the wives, 32. The Asian bride trade is tailor-made for those men driven to sustain youth beyond its normal bounds. For divorced men and elderly widowers with more modest goals, it can simply be a quick means of re-acquiring a sock-sorter or a live-in nurse.

But the surveys cannot test the would-be husbands for insecurity. The more the men rail against the women's movement, the more they show themselves to be its unwanted offspring. They want a refuge from chaos: all of them speak of wanting someone "who'll be there every night," as one put it, "who won't cheat, and who I can trust to do right by me—even down to how she takes care of the dog." Responding to the lure of far-off places, these men seek the girl-next-door. Through no fault of their own, she's become the girl-next-continent.

The men: *"It's very safe. There are no messy endings. And it's slow enough that you really get to know someone—not like dating here, when suddenly you get in way over your head."*

Once they get to know someone, the men venture out to meet their pen pal—or pals. For some of them, their travels in search of Miss Right constitute their sole and fleeting opportunity to feel like swashbucklers. They recount their "shopping trips," as they call them, in a tone usually reserved for discoverers of the North Pole: "We didn't know each other. We're from two different cultures; and here, in the middle of Taipei, we were gonna meet up for a blind date, which was, when you think about it, unbelievable." Lo and behold, the sales clerks from Peoria cross the international date line to become the emperors of Quezon City! Their pen pals serve as a parade of willing tour guides, and the two-week vacation takes on the power of a hallucination. In such heady moments, they may forget that they came for a mate and instead use a variety of appetites—especially since, as one pointed out, "a lot of the girls, even if they're virgins, will spend the night with you if they think that will do the trick." Others concentrate dutifully on their chosen lady—presuming her charms match up to her penmanship—savoring a courtship whose Victorian pace is enforced by watchful relatives.

The men: *"I couldn't believe it once I got over there. The choices were mindboggling. All the girls called me 'Superman.' It was like I was a white god. You walk around here, you're just another schmuck. In Cebu City, the heads were turning. You'd think Robert Redford or Paul Newman hit town."*

The women: *"I tell him, if you make love to me, you must marry me. I thought him sincere because he travel to see my mother. Thirty hours* *to Mindanao. Even after he propose, he keeps looking. He go to Hong Kong, Malaysia, traveling around for long time to see pen pals there. He had other girlfriend in Philippines. I go up to his hotel room instead of waiting in the lobby. I find them together. Then the game was up.*

The men: *"I don't think the transition was too rough on her. She cried every day for two years."*

The women: *"I don't cry anymore. I used to write every day. Now I write only at Christmas. A neighbor teach me to play bingo. Now I have bingo; I don't miss my family so much."*

For the mail-order bride, commitment is the easy part. Once married and ensconced in the United States, the women find that persistent homesickness is only the first hurdle. The standard refugee traumas are bad enough, but these imported brides have to grapple in isolation with two equally challenging adjustments. They must learn the customs of a new country and a new husband all at once. Often, they become acquainted with the hindrances of the latter before they've been exposed to the opportunities of the former. If becoming an American is their main aim, they are at the complete mercy of their spouse for the three years until citizenship is granted—and the husband holds the power to deport her if she doesn't play by his rules. It is in this sense that every mail-order bride, no matter how willing, is a captive.

The women: *"That first year, I cannot go out by myself. I would get lost. I know how to drive. I got my license. I just don't know the area too well, and I'm afraid to talk to other people. . . . I rather stay in Taiwan. Speak my own language. I feel more useful there."*

The men: *"Most girls think they know what to expect, but they don't. Most of the guys lie and bullshit to them. They make them think this is the land of milk and honey. They assume that as soon as you get off the boat, there's a job waiting for you."*

A surprising number of these "traditionalist" couples want, or need, the women to seek employment. But lacking the language skills, or finding that their education counts for little, those who expect to work for a living quickly learn that those vaunted opportunities are not quite open at all.

And strangely enough, the common complaint that the husbands seem to voice is that they have gotten too much "loyal wife" for the money. These men who claim to abhor the assertiveness of their own countrywomen report that they can't communicate with their new partners until they've become a bit more like themselves. To a man, they speak of having to teach their wives to express their feelings, even anger. Americanization begins at home.

The women: *"It's true. I don't want to write check without his permission. I take a long time to learn to say it is not his money, but* our *money."*

The men: *"She won't go anywhere without me or do anything without me—not even go to sleep. She practically asks for permission to go to the toilet. She always says it's the Filipino way. And finally, sometimes, I have to just say, honey, this is not the god-damn Philippines. And this is my way."*

"My way" can be enforced with fists, although actual instances of wife battering among mail-order couples are difficult to trace. Many of the women are not aware of shelters and social services or are reluctant to use them for fear of deportation. For every rare one who does come forward, there are surely many more who must cope by themselves with some gradient of coercion. Challenged with evidence of abuse cases, the mail-order husbands like to cite the rumors they've heard of brides who take their American men for all the money they're worth, then disappear once they've got their citizenship papers. To the husband, one crime is no more justifiable than the other. In this bargain, the terror cuts both ways—and the keeper is often as fearful and watchful as the captive.

The men: *"My wife keeps saying she's going to walk out one of these days—I can't tell if she's kidding or not."*

The women: *"Here, I got more freedom. But mostly I don't look out windows. My husband not like me talking. He's not bad man, just a nasty guy, with temper."*

Just as the situation breeds betrayal, sudden or gradual, so it provides incentives for success. It will take many years before we know whether these marriages prove any more durable than those of American marriages in general—although, statistically speaking, that wouldn't take much. Yet unlike their American counterparts, these newlyweds show an uncommon determination to bridge their differences. Few of the wives are going to casually give up on their effort: most have been schooled in making the best of it on the home front and do not accept divorce as an alternative. These women have cast too much aside—and the men have invested an equal amount in effort, cash, and the idealization of their quest.

The men: *"The first year was very tough. With the conflicts we had, if we hadn't already been married, we probably never would have gotten married."*

The women: *"Your mate is picked by God. You have only to be patient and get along."*

If Asian women seem more willing than their American sisters to make compromises, that is because some bring with them a different model of what marriage is supposed to provide. Where wedlock is seen primarily as a pragmatic partnership, it ceases to carry the burden as an emotional cure-all. This view of marriage, based in its most idealized form on mutual aid and on the slow unearthing of feeling, has certainly proven useful to the continuation of the species throughout the centuries—and it is one these 20th-century husbands strain to emulate.

The men: *"When I married her, I didn't love her. I admired her and I respected her, and I decided to take a chance. In the Asian tradition, one learns to love someone. And I feel it's growing every day. It's not the same thing as in the States. It comes slowly; it's healthier this way."*

The replacement of American homemakers with Asian stand-ins confirms the old axiom that "none are free until all are free." Still, taken as a whole, the phenomenon hardly represents a serious inroad into the gains made by women. These are gains that appear irreversible worldwide, and it will take a great deal more than a few thousand rather fragile "old-fashioned" marriages to reverse the tide. The march toward a workable equality of the sexes is not what's threatened by the growing attraction of white American males to Asian women and the ideal they are imagined to embody; the only thing threatened is the relatively new concept of marrying for passion and separating for lack of same. It is one more joust—this time from the male side—over our contemporary prescriptions for happiness.

The men: *"We believe in traditional roles—like the man washes the car, the woman sweeps. It's so easy to get along that way, where everything's clear."*

The women: *"It's not true that Asian men and American men different. Men are men everywhere—some help the women out, and some don't."*

Some American feminists and Asian-American organizations have condemned the mail-order trade as legalized prostitution and pen pal marriage as inherently abusive, but such rhetoric serves to obscure reality rather than transform it. If the Asian trade leads to a kind of slavery, then it is a volunteered servitude that is but a single link of chain apart from the unwritten contract that binds any man to any woman. Judging these brides by Western standards often means trying to convince the oppressed of just how unhappy they would feel if they could only see their true condition. Unfortunately, the path of human want is rarely politically correct, and history does not move by morally approved acts. Listening to the voices rising from these catalogs of need, what emerges is that those needs are not there to be labeled false or backward. They are there to be met.

The women: *"I am here in this stranger place, with no one can share my loneliness." "Do you think you can maybe like me, love me? Need someone for loving. Isn't a joke."*

There are bound to be more and more stories of intercultural courtship—where happy endings are unlikely, but surprise endings can do the same job. For often as not, the reprieve that's granted is that neither party ends up getting anything that resembles the order they've placed. "If it was really mail order," one husband joked, "I'd have made my wife a bit younger. And a lot richer!" Where a human heart is the cargo, the customer can never be sure of exactly what he's ordering or whether he ever gets it delivered intact. The no-fault bride turns out to know very well how to point a finger. The bullying husband ends up in an arm wrestle with his own stereotypes.

The men: *"Asian women are not the subservient types that the media make us believe" "They can be very strong willed. I'll tell you, my wife won't take no shit off nobody."*

The women: *"In America, it's not easy like I think. You can't pick money off the streets. It's hard work, enjoying my life."*

In the Posturepedic nuptial bed, over morning bowls of Raisin Bran, on proverbial weekend outings, it turns out that, most of the time, there's no Suzy Wong present, no Simon Legree. He is no John Wayne and she is no geisha. Instead of "inborn submissiveness," she demonstrates, with exposure to new possibilities, a pesky tendency toward human enlargement. Confronted with the silence that comes with slavish assent, reinforcing his solitude, he discovers rather enlightened cravings for a loud and living mate. Behind the triple locks of matrimony, the sprinkler systems and the electric eyes, they are not master and servant, but two people grappling with the long odds against durable understanding. Trapped in the most daunting circumstances, impelled by the most muddled intentions, all they can do is carry on the grim work of making the world one—with an ancient talisman hung outside for good luck.

REFLECTING ON MEANING

1. According to Krich, why is it not surprising that arranged marriages between Asian mail-order brides and white American men became a "multimillion-dollar-a-year industry" in the early 1980s? Why do so many men seek this type of marriages? What is the relationship between the women's movement and the number of men seeking foreign wives? After reading the interviewees' comments, do you think that either the American men or the Asian women are completely satisfied with their arranged marriages?

2. According to Krich, statistics reveal that the men who "seek Asian brides are above average in education, income, and status." Why might successful men prefer an arranged marriage? One of the interviewees says that "American girls left me really disappointed. They look like tubs of lard stuffed into Levi's [sic]. They're pushy, spoiled rotten, and they talk like sailors. . . . In the morning, you wonder how many guys were before me." What do these comments reveal about the male speaker's insecurities? What do they reveal about the type of wife that he would prefer? What is your emotional response to these comments?

3. The "average age at marriage for the husbands is 52; for the wives, 32." What potential problems might a twenty-year age difference combined with an enormous cultural difference have on these arranged marriages? How might this age difference reinforce male security and female insecurity?

EXPLORING RHETORICAL STRATEGIES

1. This essay begins with a description of a brass Chinese character that decorates the front door of a home. Next, Krich symbolically enters the house and interviews various mail-order bride participants: American husbands and their Asian wives. Finally, the essay ends with another reference to the "ancient talisman hung outside for good luck." Is this framing device effective or ineffective? Why might the notion of "good luck" be appropriate to a discussion of arranged marriages?

2. What rhetorical effect does Krich's use of quotations from American men and Asian women have on his essay? What is your opinion of the excerpt from the mail-order bride catalog? Krich problematizes his discussion by explaining both the pros and cons of the mail-order bride business. Do you accept all of his arguments? Are some more effective than others? What was your opinion on arranged marriages prior to reading this essay? Has your opinion been changed by Krich's essay? Why or why not?

3. Cherry Blossoms, the highest-volume matchmaking shop, distributes what different types of publications? Consider the specific quotations that Krich cites from these publications: "featuring Phillipine 'Island Blossoms' . . . the subscriber may be offered 'first crack' at a designated number of women . . . mimeographed sheet also alerts the men to 'rotten apples.'" How do these quotations foreground this publication's objectification of women?

TAKING A STAND
QUESTIONS FOR CONSIDERATION

1. This part highlights two public issues that have become feminist causes: psychological and physical violence against women. What makes these issues of special concern to feminists? To what extent are they gender issues? Select one of these issues, summarize the views of the appropriate authors on these questions, and explain your own point of view. Is the issue a gender issue by definition and, thus, of special concern to feminists? Or, perhaps, does the issue transcend gender politics?

2. Many authors in Part V argue that women remain powerless despite recent advances in civil rights and changing social attitudes. What are the concrete manifestations of powerlessness that they see? Taken together, do their essays provide a convincing case that women are indeed powerless? Is their collective assessment of women's status valid? In exploring this issue, consider especially the essays by Brophy, Johnson, the Lindholms, and Daly.

3. Several authors claim that women themselves actually reinforce their own powerlessness because society teaches them to do so. What are the various means by which society encourages women to internalize their sense of powerlessness? To what extent is such social propaganda a vital force at work on both women and men? Consider Brophy's definitions of persuasion; Johnson's views on myth and the lesson of sexual punishment for disobedience; Goldberg's allusions to Aristotle; Daly's account of how mothers participate in the genital mutilation of their daughters; and the Lindholms' discussion of Moslem female society.

4. What is *prejudice? Discrimination?* Are the two terms synonymous? Using the essays of at least two of the authors in this section, analyze the meanings of these terms and construct your own definitions. Consider Goldberg's examination of prejudice and Johnson's examination of rape to supplement your discussion. You might also consider hook's essay in Part II.

5. What are the roles of home and family in reinforcing women's powerlessness? What insights into this question do the Lindholms, Daly, and Krich provide? What implications does Goodman suggest? In shaping your response to this question, you may also wish to consider the historical perspectives of Mill and Gilman in Part II, and the social perspectives of Syfers and Mainardi in Part IV.

6. What kind of treatment do women receive in the various systems and institutions that make up our society? How are they rendered powerless by, for example, the corporate world, organized religion, and the economic, welfare, and justice systems? You may find the essays by Goodman, Johnson, the Lindholms, and Daly helpful. For a historical perspective, review the selections by Daly, Pope Pius XI, and Gilman in Part II.

7. A recurrent analogy in this and other parts of the text is the comparison between women's powerlessness and imprisonment or slavery. Why do authors who write about gender issues make extensive use of such analogies? How do these analogies allow them to explore connections between gender and race? Do their analogies differ in significant ways? In this part consider Brophy's "invisible cages" and the Lindholms' discussion of *purdah*. You also might want to look at the essays by Mill and Sanger in Part II and the essay by Syfers in Part IV.

8. Several articles in Part V discuss physical violence against women: Daly's account of female genital mutilation, the Lindholms' revelations about the treatment of Moslem adulteresses, and Johnson's discussion of rape. The Chinese practice of footbinding occurred for almost one thousand years, while *suttee* (widow burning) is still practiced in some cultures. Why do these violent practices continue to occur in spite of decades of feminists' attempts to gain equality for women? Is violence against women indicative of specific cultures' attitudes toward women, or does it reflect worldwide misogyny? Construct your argument by combining these authors' analyses of violence against women with your own opinion.

Credits *(continued from page ii)*